Henry Thomas Buckle

The miscellaneous and posthumous works of Henry Thomas Buckle

In two volumes, volume two

Henry Thomas Buckle

The miscellaneous and posthumous works of Henry Thomas Buckle
In two volumes, volume two

ISBN/EAN: 9783742806208

Manufactured in Europe, USA, Canada, Australia, Japa

Cover: Foto ©Andreas Hilbeck / pixelio.de

Manufactured and distributed by brebook publishing software
(www.brebook.com)

Henry Thomas Buckle

The miscellaneous and posthumous works of Henry Thomas Buckle

THE

MISCELLANEOUS AND POSTHUMOUS WORKS

OF

HENRY THOMAS BUCKLE

A NEW AND ABRIDGED EDITION

IN TWO VOLUMES.——VOL. II.

CONTENTS

OF

THE SECOND VOLUME.

—————

POSTHUMOUS WORKS.

FRAGMENTS.

EXTRACTS FROM COMMON PLACE BOOK.

FRAGMENTS.

———⋄———

TENDENCY OF THE LAWS RESPECTING APPRENTICES.

SEE Smith's Wealth of Nations, pp. 50-53. Apprenticeships were entirely unknown to the ancients.[1] He says[2] that the effect of the laws respecting them was to increase the wealth of towns at the expense of the wealth of the country, which they did by raising the price of manufactures. Of course, by increasing the profits of manufactures they diverted a good deal of capital from agriculture to manufactures. Smith has given[3] a slight history of the laws respecting apprentices. Seven years was originally the term of its duration in Europe for incorporated trades, all of which incorporations were called universities. By the 5th of Elizabeth, called the Statute of Apprenticeship, it was enacted that no person should exercise any trade unless he had served to it an apprenticeship of seven years, and thus what had been only the by-law of particular corporations became statute and general law. The words of the statute plainly mean the whole kingdom, but have been interpreted to mean only market towns, and only those trades which were established in England before 5th Elizabeth. In Paris five years is a very common term of apprenticeship ; in Scotland (where corporation laws are less oppressive than in any other European country), only three years.

It is worthy of remark that this absurd statute of apprenticeship (5 Eliz.) was not repealed till 1814, and even then a reservation was made of 'the existing rights, privileges, or by-laws of the different corporations.'[4] How long will this contemptible spirit

[1] P. 51.　　　　　[2] Pp. 52, 53.　　　　　[3] Pp. 50, 51.
[4] M'Culloch's Principles of Political Economy, Edinburgh, 8vo, 1843, p. 372.

of corporation and of caste be allowed to predominate in our national councils? 'Rights and privileges'! As if any body of men ought to have rights and privileges which are injurious to the country at large.[1]

Jacob observes that the effect of these laws was to prevent the increasing manufactures from absorbing the surplus agricultural population.[2] In that remarkable work, The Brief Conceipt of English Policy, published in 1581, the author, who was at least half a century before his age, protests with unusual freedom against the statute of apprenticeship.[3] See, in the Journal of the Statistical Society,[4] evidence of 'the extent to which the mischievous system of compulsory apprenticeship had been adopted in the incorporations of the counties of Norfolk and Suffolk' from 1820 to 1835.

Early in the seventeenth century, if not before, receiving apprentices was an ordinary source of profit to great actors. The services of such apprentices were regularly bought and sold. This appears from Henslowe's Diary.[5]

The effects of guilds and corporations is to check population.[6] Storch looks on the custom of apprenticeship as an unmitigated evil; but he has fallen into the error of supposing that its effect is to raise wages, and therefore raise price.[7] In 1643 the apprentices assisted in fortifying London against the king, and were so important a body that Charles attempted to gain them over; and at Oxford, which has always been a steady friend to despotism, there was published an 'Exhortation,' the object of which was to aid the royal efforts. It has been printed by Mr. Mackay.[8] The old holidays being laid aside as superstitious, the apprentices in 1647 had a grand meeting in Covent Garden to oblige their masters to grant some other times of recreation. It is hardly necessary to say that they succeeded in their object. Mr. Wright has printed one of the notices of meeting which the apprentices affixed

---

[1] See also M'Culloch's Commercial Dictionary, 8vo, 1849, p. 45.

[2] Inquiry into the Precious Metals, vol. ii. p. 111.

[3] See the passage in Harleian Miscellany, vol. ix. pp. 187, 188.

[4] Vol. i. p. 19.

[5] See Collier's History of Dramatic Poetry, vol. iii. pp. 433, 444.

[6] See Mill's Political Economy, 8vo, 1849, vol. i. pp. 431, 433.

[7] Économie Politique, St. Pétersbourg, 8vo, 1815, tome i. pp. 360-362; tome ii. p. 183.

[8] Songs of the London Prentices, pp. 67-69, edit. Percy Society, 8vo, 1841.

to the walls of London.[1] In 1659 they are accused of having
frequently run away with their masters' daughters.[2] On Sundays
they were expected to accompany their masters to church; but
they not unfrequently left them at the church doors and went to
the tavern.[3] An intelligent observer, who was in England in the
year 1500, says that it was usual in London for widows to marry
the apprentices of their late husbands.[4]

OBSERVATIONS UPON FREEMASONRY.

ABOUT 1820 (?) 'one Morgan, a freemason, living in the western
part of the State of New York, wrote a book in exposure of masonry,
its facts and tendencies.' The consequence was that he was
arrested and carried over into Canada; 'shut up in the fort at
Niagara village, where the Niagara river flows into Lake Ontario,
. . . put into a boat, carried out into the middle of the river, and
thrown in with a stone tied to his neck. For four years there
were attempts to bring the conspirators to justice, but little was
done. The lodges subscribed funds to carry the actual murderers
out of the country. Sheriffs, jurymen, constables, all omitted
their duty with regard to the arrest.' The upshot was that the
spirit of the Americans was roused. Anti-masonic societies were
formed; in some States the law prevents the lodges taking in new
members, and masonry is almost overthrown.[5]

THE CONDITION AND INFLUENCE OF WOMEN.

MISS MARTINEAU[6] says, 'Forty years ago the women of New
Jersey went to the polls and voted at State elections. The general
term "inhabitants" stood unqualified; as it will again when the
true democratic principle comes to be fully understood. A
motion was made to correct the inadvertence, and it was done
as a matter of course without any appeal, as far as I can learn,

---

[1] Political Ballads, pp. 18, 19. Percy Society, vol. iii.
[2] Wright's Political Ballads, p. 172.
[3] See The Pleasant Conceites of Old Hobson, 1607, p. 9. Percy Society, vol. ix.
[4] Italian Relation of England, Camden Society, vol. xxxvii. p. 26.
[5] Miss Martineau's Society in America, Paris, 8vo, 1842, vol. i. pp. 19, 20, part
i. chap. i.
[6] Ibid. pp. 104, 105, part i. chap. iii. section vii.

from the persons about to be injured. Such acquiescence proves nothing but the degradation of the injured party.' As to the present state of women in the United States, see Miss Martineau's 'Society in America,' vol. ii. pp. 156-178, part iii. chap. ii. Even this partial writer says,[1] 'The Americans have in the treatment of women fallen below, not only their own democratic principles, but the practice of some parts of the Old World.'

She says,[2] 'Divorce is more easily obtained in the United States than in England.' This delights her, and she adds,[3] 'In Massachusetts divorces are obtainable with peculiar ease. The natural consequence follows; such a thing is never heard of. A long-established and very eminent lawyer of Boston told me that he had known of only one in all his experience.' . . . At Zurich 'the parties are married by a form, and have liberty to divorce themselves, without any appeal to law, on showing that they have legally provided for the children of the marriage. . . . There was some levity at first, chiefly on the part of those who were suffering under the old system, but the morals of the society soon became, and have since remained, peculiarly pure.'

Miss Martineau tells us,[4] 'It is no secret on the spot that the habit of intemperance is not unfrequent among women of station and education in the most enlightened parts of the country.'

Adam Smith says,[5] 'The fair sex, who have commonly much more tenderness than ours, have seldom so much generosity. That women rarely make considerable donations is an observation of the civil law. *Raro mulieres donare solent.*'

The reason that the wages of women are generally lower than those of men is that, owing to custom opening so few employments, their field of employment is overcrowded.[6] Hence, I suppose, the more agricultural a nation is, the higher will be the wages of women as compared to those of men. This is the case in France. Perhaps we may in this way discover one cause of the declining influence of women. They are less *valuable* than formerly. The advance of civilization diminishes the proportion

[1] Society in America, vol. i. p. 156.   [2] P. 165.   [3] P. 166.
[4] Ibid. vol. ii. p. 184.
[5] Theory of Moral Sentiments, part iv. chap. ii. vol. ii. p. 19, London, 1822, 12mo.
[6] Mill's Political Economy, 8vo, 1849, vol. i. pp. 487, 488.

of those who are employed on the soil, and thus lowers their wages.

In London we have cases of women working at shirt-making, and similar occupations, eighteen hours a day, and earning four shillings a week.[1]

For another reason why the influence of women has declined, see art. PURITANS.

Camden says of Lady Burleigh, the daughter of Sir Anthony Cook, 'She was a woman very well versed in the Latin and Greek tongues.'[2] His mentioning it shows that such learning was not common.

Dr. Combe thinks that any eccentricity on the mother's side is more likely to be prevalent among the children than if it had been on the father's side.[3]

Gifford has noticed how little attention is paid by Ben Jonson to drawing female characters. This, I should suppose, was because the parts of women were played by boys.[4] But the character of the Lady Would-Be, in the Fox, shows the growing influence of the female mind. Women must have been gaining ground when it was worth Jonson's while to ridicule them by so comprehensive a satire. See also his attack on the Lady Collegiates in the Silent Woman ;[5] and he allowed women of reputation to attend the meetings of his club—I suppose at the Mermaid.[6]

Early in the seventeenth century Gifford says, 'Daggers, or, as they were more commonly called, knives, were worn at all times by every woman in England.'[7]

At the very beginning of the seventeenth century a lady says it is unnatural to see 'books in women's hands.'[8]

Chevenix[9] takes for granted the mental inferiority of women. Vico[10] observes that the wife bringing a dowry is evidence of her freedom.

[1] See Thornton on Over-Population, 8vo, 1846, p. 60.
[2] Annals of Elizabeth, in Kennet, vol. ii. p. 609.
[3] Principles of Physiology applied to Health, and edit., Edinburgh, 8vo, 1835, p. 273.
[4] Jonson's Works, vol. i. p. 161, and iv. p. 460 ; but see vi. 409, and vii. 151.
[5] Ibid. vol. iii. pp. 346, 347.   [6] Ibid. vol. v. p. 254.
[7] Note in Ben Jonson, vol. v. pp. 220, 221.
[8] See Middleton's Works, 8vo, 1840, vol. i. p. 163.
[9] Essay on National Character, 8vo, 1832, vol. ii. p. 316.
[10] Philosophie de l'Histoire, p. 218.

Chevenix,[1] who has attempted to trace the history of women, particularly notices the effect of arts and manufactures in increasing their power.

I doubt if the attention paid to women is of northern origin. The ancient Finns treated them very badly.[2]

A writer of great observation says, 'There is perhaps no instance of a man of distinguished vigour and activity of mind whose mother did not display a considerable amount of the same qualities.'[3]

Lawrence well says,[4] 'A nervous and hysterical fine lady and her lapdog are the extreme points of degeneracy and imbecility of which each race is susceptible.'

The first work on the education of women was Fénélon's 'Education des Filles,' in 1688; but 'he discourages too much the acquisition of knowledge by women.'[5] Sir John Reresby, who was in Germany in 1656, gives a curious account of the depressed state of the women.[6] Charles XII. of Sweden did not care for women.[7]

Montaigne is unfavourable to their education, and says they are incapable of friendship.[8] He adds[9] that he had known women swallow sand and ashes in order to get pale complexions. He says[10] that a fashion had recently grown up among women, of pulling hair out of their foreheads. In the Indian Archipelago women are better treated than generally in the East.[11] Coleridge says,[12] 'The Greeks, except perhaps in Homer, seem to have had no way of making their women interesting but by unsexing them, as in the instances of the tragic Medea, Electra, &c.' At vol. i. pp. 199, 200, Coleridge says, 'Women are good novelists, but

[1] Essay on National Character, vol. II. p. 333.

[2] See Prichard's Physical History of Mankind, vol. III. pp. 287, 288.

[3] Combe, The Constitution of Man in Relation to External Objects, Edinb. 1847, 8vo, p. 192; and see Combe's Moral Philosophy, p. 121, 8vo, 1840.

[4] Lectures on Man, 8vo, 1844, p. 163.

[5] See Hallam's Literature of Europe, vol. III. pp. 417, 418.

[6] Reresby's Travels and Memoirs, 8vo, 1831, pp. 139, 140.

[7] Œuvres de Voltaire, tome xxii. p. 54.

[8] Essais de Montaigne, Paris, 8vo, 1843, Livre I. chap. xxiv., xxvii., pp. 73, 102, 469, 520, 521.

[9] Ibid. Livre I., chap. xl. p. 156.

[10] Ibid Livre I. chap. xlix. p. 186.

[11] See Crawford's History of the Indian Archipelago, Edinb. 8vo, 1820, vol. I. pp. 73, 75, 78.   [12] Literary Remains, vol. I. p. 95.

indifferent poets ; and this because they rarely or never thoroughly distinguish between fact and fiction.' Perhaps polygamy is the first stage in the improvement of women. In Borneo women are well treated, because polygamy makes them *dear*.' In England at the end of the seventeenth century women still learned Latin and Greek.' Mr. Marshall ' thinks the sexual passions stronger among Europeans than among Asiatics. Catlin, who speaks so highly of the North American Indians, allows that the women are the 'slaves of their husbands.' ' They neither worship nor eat with the men.' They marry from eleven to fifteen, and some have even had children at twelve.' It is ' very rare' for a woman to have more than four or five children.' Parturition is very easy ;' polygamy universal.' Schlegel '' mentions 'that high reverence for females which is everywhere inculcated in the laws and exemplified in the poems of the Hindoos.' Herbert Mayo '' says, 'Girls as children are healthier than boys,' because they are *nearer* to women than boys are to men, i.e. the voice and skin have less to alter. But, says Mayo,'' their one disease is education, which is so absurd that they nearly all have diseased spines.'' At Embomma, on the Congo, 'the men will not eat the flesh of a fowl until the woman has tasted of it, to take off the fetish, as they express it ;'' but at the same place 'the cultivation of the ground is entirely the business of slaves and women.' ''

Napoleon said everything depends on the mother,'' and yet he cared so little about women *socially* that he was in favour of the Eastern way of shutting them up,'' but *physically* he was very fond of women.'' Mr. F. Newman '' denies that Christianity has improved the position of women ; and he observes '' that 'with

I See Low's Sarawak, 8vo, 1848, p. 148.
3 See Southey's Life of Wesley, 8vo, 1846, vol. L p. 30.
3 Transactions of Literary Society of Bombay, vol. iii. p. 352.
4 Catlin's North American Indians, 8vo, vol. i. p. 57.
5 Ibid. vol. ii. pp. 232, 233.   6 Ibid. vol. l. pp. 121, 214, 215.
7 Ibid. vol. ii. p. 228.   8 Ibid. p. 229.   9 Ibid. vol. l. p. 118.
10 Lectures on Literature, Edinb. 8vo, 1818, vol. l. p. 210.
11 Philosophy of Living, 8vo, 1838, pp. 114, 115.
12 Ibid. p. 115.   13 Ibid. pp. 118, 123.
14 Tuckey's Expedition to the Zaire, 1818, 4to, p. 124.   15 Ibid. p. 120.
14 Alison's Hist. of Europe, vol. iv. p. 2. See also vol. vii. p. 1, and vol. xiii,
p. 200.
17 Ibid. vol. vi. p. 51   18 See vol. xi. pp. 587, 606 ; vol. xiii. p. 209.
19 Phases of Faith, 8vo, 1850, pp. 162-169.   20 Ibid. p. 163.

Paul the *sole* reason for marriage is that a man may, without sin, vent his sensual desires. He teaches that, *but* for this object, it would be better not to marry ;' and he takes no notice of the *social* pleasures of marriage. Newman says,[1] 'In short, only in countries where Germanic sentiment has taken root do we see marks of any elevation of the female sex superior to that of pagan antiquity ;' and [2] 'the real elevators of the female sex are the poets of German culture, who have vindicated the spirituality of love, and its attraction to character.' In 1717 Lady Montagu[3] says: 'Some of our ladies who set up for such extraordinary geniuses upon the credit of some superficial knowledge of French and Italian.' In 1752, Lady Montagu writes,[4] 'To say truth, there is no part of the world where our sex is treated with so much contempt as in England.' Mackay[5] says, 'The ancients laid it down as incontrovertible that women are the source of all evil ; an unmitigated hindrance to mankind inflicted on them by the wrath of the gods.' Kemble[6] ascribes to the German element the modern respect for women. In Great Britain and Ireland there are more females than males ; and in France the excess of women is still greater ; but in Spain nearly equal, and in the United States an excess of males.[7] There are rather more male than female servants.[8] Of the depositors in the Savings Banks, nearly seven in eight are women.[9] The proportionate number of female compared with male criminals is diminishing,[10] but in Scotland the female criminals are more numerous.[11] Tocqueville[12] says that in Protestant countries young girls always have more liberty than in Catholic ones ; and that, when this is combined with a democratic state of society, the liberty becomes very great, as is the case in America. The American girls are chaste in manners rather than in mind ;[13] and though when unmarried they have great liberty, as soon as they are married they have scarcely any.[14] For industrious and religious nations naturally

[1] Phases of Faith, p. 163.
[2] Ibid. p. 165.   [3] Works, 8vo, 1803, vol. II. p. 243.
[4] Ibid. vol. iv. p. 149.   [5] Progress of the Intellect, 8vo, 1850, vol. I. p. 419.
[6] Saxons in England, vol. I. pp. 232, 233.
[7] Porter's Progress of the Nation, vol. I. pp. 15, 16.
[8] Ibid. pp. 67, 68 ; vol. III. p. 18.   [9] Ibid. vol. III. p. 147.
[10] Ibid. p. 179.   [11] Ibid. p. 215.
[12] Démocratie en Amérique, tome v. p. 57.   [13] Ibid. p. 58.
[14] Ibid. p. 61.

consider marriage a very grave affair.[1]   On this account early
marriages are very rare in America ; and the American women do
not marry till their reason is ripened.[2] Göthe says of Germany
about 1772, that the influence of Richardson's novels and Lessing's
Sara Sampson had raised the standard of female morals.[3] Feudality treated women badly ; chivalry well.[4] English women remained Catholics longer than men did.[5] In 1839 it is said that
the effects of Sunday [schools] were principally shown on women,
there being twice as many female as male scholars.[6] In spite of
the decrease of crime, the number of female offenders is on the
increase.[7] It has been attempted to be shown [8] that the number
of illegitimate children is the measure of morals. Barry, who
had the best means of knowing, says of the women in the Orkney
Islands, 'Though their education, as in other places, is inferior
to that of the men, their understandings are in general superior.'[9]
Until Peter I., the Russian women were kept as secluded as those
of Asia.[10] The Indians everywhere treat their women with contempt,[11] and so do the Burmese.[12] Kohl says,[13] 'Female voices
are never heard in the Russian churches; their place is supplied
by boys : women do not yet stand high enough in the estimation
of the churches or of the people to be permitted to sing the
praises of God in the presence of men.' Christianity diminished
the influence of women.[14] In 1645 women used to preach in
London.[15] There is said to be a good article on the state of
women in Greece in No. 43 of the Quarterly Review. According
to Thirlwall,[16] 'the freedom of women was not peculiar to Sparta.
It prevailed in all Dorian states, though not perhaps equally, and
is thought to have been once universal in Greece. It is observed
that in Homer there is no trace of the seclusion of women after
marriage ; nor do they appear to have been insignificant or much

[1] Démocratie en Amérique, pp. 61, 62.   [2] Ibid. p. 63.
[3] Wahrheit und Dichtung, in Werke, Band ii. Theil ii. p. 179.
[4] See Mill's History of Chivalry, vol. i. pp. 235, 256.
[5] Hallam, Constitutional History of England, vol. i. p. 399.
[6] Journal of Statistical Society, vol. ii. p. 67.   [7] Ibid. vol. ix. p. 182.
[8] Ibid. vol. xiv. p. 8.   [9] Barry's History of the Orkney Islands, p. 333.
[10] See Comte, Traité de Législation, vol. iii. p. 172.
[11] See Heber's Journey through India, vol. ii. p. 71.
[12] See Symes's Embassy to Ava, vol. ii. pp. 219, 385.
[13] Russia, 8vo, 1844, p. 255.
[14] See Neander's History of the Church, vol. i. p. 252.
[15] Parliamentary History, vol. iii. p. 422.   [16] History of Greece.

depressed.' Mrs. Napier [1] refers to Middleton's Cicero for the
fact that the Romans paid great attention to having nurses who
spoke pure Latin, so as not to corrupt the language of their children. At p. 163 Mrs. Napier says, 'In France, where from the
time of Catherine de Medicis the corruption of morals had been
proverbial, it is well known that women reigned in every transaction of the empire;' but I may say the French never cared for
domestic life—too vain. Mrs. Napier [2] well says, 'It is only in
arduous pursuits the superiority of men invariably appears. In
low stages of civilization it occasionally happens that the advantage is observed to be on the side of women; for any circumstance
in their habits that imposes on them the necessity of greater exercise of observation and judgment turns the balance in their favour.
But in the complicated and laborious offices of civilized societies,
no education would give general superiority or even equality to the
female sex; the demand for laborious investigations and the
highest power of combination and invention is too constant, both
in professions and sciences.' Among barbarians, *all* have the
same sort of education. Intellect is more valued than ever, and
knowledge more available, and yet women worse educated than
ever. See Carie's Comparative Anatomy, vol. i. pp. 274, 290,
357; vol. ii. p. 133. Society becomes more complex, and men
less impulsive; hence *natural* divergences increase, and *hence* increased difference between men and women, and loss of female
influence. Combe [3] says, 'In all countries which I have visited
I have remarked that the female head, though less in size, is more
fully developed in the region of the moral sentiments in proportion to the other regions than that of the male.' Hallam [4]
denies that respect for women is due to Christianity, and says that
it first arose in the south of France about the end of the tenth
century. He observes of Beaumont and Fletcher, [5] 'The best of
Fletcher's characters are female; he wanted that large sweep of
reflection and experience which is required for the greater diver
sity of the other sex.' He says [6] of Massinger, 'He has more
variety in his women than in the other sex, and they are less

[1] Rights and Duties of Women, vol. i. p. 99.
[2] Ibid. vol. i. p. 282.
[3] North America, Edinb. 1841, vol. i. p. 130.
[4] Literature, vol. i. pp. 126, 127.
[5] Ibid. vol. iii. p. 113.   [6] Ibid. p. 115.

mannered than the heroines of Fletcher.' Bourgoing [1] says that
Pæderasty 'est absolument inconnue en Espagne.' Townsend [2]
says in regard to Spanish women having lovers or *cortejos*, that it
was owing ' to the introduction of Italian manners, on the arrival
of Charles III. from Naples, with the previous want of reasonable
freedom in the commerce of the sexes.' Mary Carpenter says, [3]
' All persons who have come much into actual intercourse with
boys and girls of " the perishing and dangerous classes " have fully
agreed with my own experience, that the girls are far the most
hardened and difficult to manage. A strong concurrent testimony
of this was presented to me yesterday by one of the Commissioners
of Lunacy, who had been himself for a long course of years the
manager of a large institution. The females he found infinitely
more outrageous than the males ; and, when excited, they used
language indicating a depth and intensity of wickedness which he
would not have thought the heart of a man, still less, as he said,
that of a woman, could have conceived.' Baretti, who was in
Spain in 1760, says with surprise, that Spaniards are *not* jealous. [4]
See also on the cortejos, who are said to be quite innocent, vol. iii.
pp. 102–111.   Baretti says, [5] ' In Calderon's days it was not permitted to men to act upon the stage, so that men's characters
were then acted by women ; and it is but of late years that the
Spaniards have obtained this permission, I cannot tell whether by
the Government or the Inquisition. See the whims of nations !
In England, about a century ago, no women were allowed to act ;
and this has been during many years past, and is still the practice
in the Pope's capital and in Portugal.' In 1806, Blanco White
writes, [6] ' The ancient Spanish jealousy is still observable among
the lower classes ; and while not a sword is drawn in Spain upon
a love quarrel, the knife often decides the claim of more humble
lovers.' In 1776, in Valencia, the farmers would not let their
wives sit with them at table. [7] In Spain husbands are never
jealous, but their wives are notoriously profligate. [8]   In 1766,
' in no part of the world are women more caressed and attended

[1] Tableau de l'Espagne, Paris, 1808, tome ii. p. 345.
[2] Journey through Spain, vol. iii. p. 145.
[3] Transactions of Association for Social Science, 1858, p. 239.
[4] Journey through Portugal and Spain, Lond. 1790, vol. ii. p. 292.
[5] Ibid. vol. iii. p. 23.   [6] Doblado's Letters, p. 268.
[7] Swinburne's Spain, vol. i. p. 149.
[8] Townsend's Spain, vol. ii. pp. 142, 144, 147, 149-151.

to than in Spain ;' but very unchaste, owing partly to the Fandango dance.[1]

Knox and Buchanan were great enemies of women ; and in 1567 the Scotch Parliament declared that no woman should hold any authority.[2] Even Aylmer, in 'The Harborow,' though *defending* women against Knox, holds the coarsest language about them.[3] Hume[4] says coiners 'are more mildly dealt with if they are males, being drawn to the gallows and hanged till they be dead. But, by a strange distinction, a woman coiner has judgment to be burned alive.' In 1685, 'the first trace in Scotland of systematic education of young ladies in elegant accomplishments,' *i.e.* in boarding schools.[5] Clarendon[6] contemptuously says that many lawyers practise ' the *womanish* art of inveighing against persons.' Mill[7] well says that even the physical and mental inferiority of women may be partly owing to *hereditary* effect of the evil position and subordination in which they have been held. John Lysenes, 'a Lutheran divine of the seventeenth century,' wrote in favour of polygamy.[8] In 1641 the learned Anna Maria Schuman published a Latin dissertation, ' Whether the study of literature is suitable to a Christian woman.'[9] Cardan was born in 1501, and in his advice to his son he says, 'A woman is a foolish animal, and, therefore, full of fraud; if you bestow overmuch endearment on her you cannot be happy ; she will drag you into mischief.'[10] Lord John Russell[11] says, 'Every one must have observed the new influence which is not being asserted or sought, but is falling to the lot of women in swaying the destinies of the world.' Of *male* criminals three-fifths are under thirty years of age ; but in *female* crime, age produces less effect : ' the criminal tendency seems to be distributed more equally over the earlier period of active life ; and when we look to the recommittals, we are tempted to infer that the comparatively small number of instances in which criminals appear as female offenders is largely balanced by the inveteracy of the

[1] Thicknesse's Journey through France and Spain, Lond. 1777, vol. L. p. 236.
[2] Irving's Life of Buchanan, p. 295, Edinb. 1817.
[3] M'Crie's Life of Knox, p. 131.
[4] Commentaries on the Law of Scotland, Edinb. 1797, vol. II. p. 470.
[5] Chambers's Domestic Annals of Scotland, vol. II. p. 482.
[6] Hist. of the Rebellion, p. 123.   [7] Logic, 1846, vol. II. pp. 444, 445.
[8] Rose, Biog. Dict. vol. ix. p. 369.   [9] Ibid. vol. xi. p. 492.
[10] Jerome's Life of Cardan, 1854, vol. II. p. 197.
[11] Association for Social Science, 1859, p. 17.

criminal tendency in that sex when once developed.'[1]   At p. 557,
'The number of males who emigrate is, in consequence of the
demand for their labour in all new colonies, much greater than
females.' After the middle of the seventeenth century, the
Quakers set up 'women's meetings,' to the disgust of many and
in the teeth of St. Paul's opinion.[2] In 1616 the General Assembly at Aberdeen complained that 'women take upon them to
teach schools.'[3] Sir David Lyndsay 'everywhere speaks with a
sort of Turkish contempt of women.'[4] Lyndsay was born about
1490.[5] In 1655 'a reference from the Session of Falkland to
the Presbytery (of Cupar) was presented, craving their advice :
"What should be done with a man that strikes his wife and will
not forbear it?"'[6] They referred it to other presbyteries ; but I
do not find that anything came of it, though sessions and presbyteries were ready enough to punish.[6] An appellation 'as from a
superior to an inferior, or as from an husband to a wife.'[7] 'Do
not likewise the Papists and Lutherans err, who maintain that it
is lawful for laics or women to administer the sacrament of baptism in case of necessity? Yes.'[8] 'No vow can take away that
obligation which is upon wives to obey their husbands.'[9] Hunter [10]
takes for granted that 'women and children' cannot bear pain so
well as men. 'The blood of males is richer in nutritive parts by
nearly one and a half per cent. than that of females.'[11] Hunter
says [12] that men and women recover equally well from 'local
disease.' He says,[13] 'Men will bear bleeding better than women.'
The editor of Hunter's Works [14] says, 'Probably Haller's estimate
of the actual quantity of blood in the body approaches as nearly
to the truth as any ; viz. one-fifth of its weight, of which three-
fourths or more were supposed to be in the veins, and one-fourth

1 Transactions of Social Science, 1859, p. 365.
2 Fox's Journal, Reprint, Lond. 1827, vol. II. pp. 212, 213, 318.
3 Calderwood's History of the Kirk, vol. vII. p. 225.
4 Lyndsay's Works, by Chalmers, Lond. 1806, vol. I. p. 16.
5 Ibid. p. 3.
6 Selections from Presbyteries of St. Andrew's and Cupar. Edinb. 1837,
4to, p. 171.
7 Durham on Solomon, p. 108.
8 Dickson's Truth's Victory over Error, p. 246.
9 Cockburn's Jacob's Vow, Edinb. 1696, p. 19.
10 Works, by Palmer, vol. I. p. 606.
11 Note in John Hunter's Works, vol. III. p. 44, edit. Palmer, 1837.
12 Ibid. p. 274.   13 Ibid. p. 381.   14 Ibid. p. 98.

or less in the arteries.—El. Phys. v. i. 3.' Hunter says,[1] 'Too
little action arises from a disposition to act within the necessary
bounds of health, which produces real weakness and a bad state
of health with debility, without any visible state of disease, as we
often see in fine ladies. . . . Even the habit of indolence in the
mind, joined with inactivity of the voluntary actions (which is
generally produced from an indolent state of the mind), produces
the same effects, especially as we see in women.' Compare 360
on connection between this and the superstition of women.
Thomson[2] says, 'The quantity of blood in a moderate-sized man
is about twenty-six pounds avoirdupois.' Lithgow, about 1620,
contemptuously says, 'Crocodilean sex' of the tears of women.[3]
Sir Richard Fanshaw, English ambassador at Madrid, writes to
Secretary Bennet in 1663-4, from Cadiz, that the governor of
Cadiz was very civil ; and 'at supper, he and his lady would bear
me and my wife company, which I, accepting as a great favour,
told him my wife should eat with her ladyship, retired from the
men after the Spanish fashion, it being more than sufficient they
would not think strange we used the innocent freedom of our own
when we were among ourselves. But by no means, that he would
not suffer : and, to keep us the more in countenance, alledged
this manner of eating to be now the custom of many of the greatest families of Spain ; and had been from all antiquity to this day,
of the majestical house of Alva, the generosity whereof, particularly in the person of the present duke, he took this occasion to
celebrate very highly. So, in fine, he had his will of me in this
particular.'[4] 'Polygamy was permitted among the Mexicans,
though chiefly confined, probably, to the wealthy classes.'[5] In
Peru it was practised by the king and 'great nobles.'[6] In Peru
no male could marry under twenty-four, and no female under
eighteen or twenty.[7] Mr. Ward, who was well acquainted with the
Mexican Indians, says, 'I do not know anything in nature more
hideous than an old Indian woman.'[8] M'Culloch[9] says polygamy
was allowed to *all* Peruvians. The Mexican girls married at

[1] Works, vol. i. p. 512.   [2] Animal Chemistry, Edinb. 1843. p. 349.
[3] Nineteen Years' Travel, p. 451, 11th edition. Edinb. 1770.
[4] Fanshaw's Original Letters, Lond. 1702, 8vo. p. 33.
[5] Prescott, vol. i. p. 128.
[6] Prescott's Conquest of Peru, vol. i. pp. 107, 304.   [7] Ibid. p. 107.
[8] Ward's Mexico, vol. ii. p. 74.   [9] Researches concerning America, p. 364.

twelve.[1] At Leghorn, about 1660, Italian husbands were very
jealous, and would scarcely let their wives go out.[2] Until the
middle of the seventeenth century it was the universal custom in
Spain for women (even ladies) to take their meals separate from
their husbands, or to sit on the floor.[3]

In the sixteenth century ladies of the highest rank, incited by
the example of Elizabeth, used to kill game with the cross-bow.[4]
Christian[5] says, 'Ann, Countess of Pembroke, had the office of
hereditary sheriff of Westmoreland, and exercised it in person.
At the assizes of Appleby she sat with the judges on the Bench.
—Harg. Co. Litt. 326.' The rise of modern literature diverted
the attention of studious women from the classical authors. This,
by drawing a distinction between the two sexes, made women more
feminine, and enabled them to refine the coarser instincts of man.
The civil law allowed husbands to beat their wives ; and so did
the common law, until 'in the politer reign of Charles II. this
power of correction began to be doubted.'[6] Christian has a long
and pathetic note in Blackstone, iii. 143, on the little protection
which our law has given to a woman against the arts of a seducer.
But I doubt if there should be any such protection at all, except
in the case of a promise of marriage. The truth is that the seduc-
tion is often on the other side ; and men are as much exposed to
the arts of women as women to those of men. On this, as on
many other subjects, sentiment has been allowed to usurp the
place of reason in our jurisprudence. M. Cousin expresses very
strong opinions against female authors.[7] Muller denies that there
is any evidence of gallantry towards women in the Northern
Sagas ;[8] but it appears[9] that this respect was paid to women by
the Goths before they were acquainted with Christianity. See
also some very ingenious remarks in Mallet's Northern Antiquities.[10]
He says that the ancient northern nations greatly respected women ;
and that this was because they valued highly every appearance of

---

1 Ixtlilxochitl. Histoire des Chichimegues, tome i. p. 342.
2 Lives of the Norths, vol. ii. pp. 328, 329.
3 See Dunlop's Memoirs of Spain, Edinb. 1834. vol. ii. p. 396.
4 See Drake's Shakespeare and his Times, 1817, 4to. vol. ii. p. 182.
5 Note in Blackstone's Commentaries. 8vo. 1809, vol. i. p. 339.
6 Blackstone's Comment. vol. i. p. 445, who cites I. Lld. 113, iii. Keb. 433.
7 See Cousin's Littérature, Paris, 1849, tome ii. pp. 3–7.
8 Price's Preface to Weston's History of English Poetry, vol. I. pp. 94, 95.
9 Ibid. pp. lii, liii.   10 Lond. 1847. pp. 199–201.

nature; and because women are more *natural*, more spontaneous than men. Besides this, piracy being common, women were in want of defenders and deliverers. There were even female poetesses.[1] Some of the Anglo-Saxon ladies were learned.[2] On the extent to which the increased influence of women has softened our manners, it is to be observed that the increase of towns increases the proportion of female births. On the natural mildness of woman, see Roussel, Système de la Femme, p. 45, though I cannot agree with this able writer that this mildness is entirely due to her organisation.

Roussel well says that the Greeks, Jews, and Germans did not cause oracles to be pronounced by women because they respected the female sex, but because their ignorance induced them to consider as sacred those convulsive diseases to which women are peculiarly subject.[3] To this I may add that women are more subject to insanity than men, and that many barbarous nations respect the insane. The pedantic notion that women should be scientific, or even learned, is refuted with ability and eloquence in Roussel, Système de la Femme, Paris, 1845, pp. 94-100.

In Madagascar, women pay homage to their husbands by licking their feet.[4] However, Ellis says[5] that women have more liberty than in most Eastern countries, and that young people see each other before marriage. He adds[6] that no woman ventures to marry within twelve months of her husband's death; and a husband, on divorcing his wife, may prevent her from remarrying.

In 1812, Niebuhr, who had been reading Klopstock's Correspondence, writes respecting it: 'The character of the women, too, is a remarkable feature of the times of Klopstock's youth. The cultivation of the mind was carried incomparably further with them than with nearly all the young women of our days; and this we should scarcely have expected to find in the contemporaries of our grandmothers. It was not, therefore, the work of our native literature; for that first rose into being along with and under the influence of the love inspired by these charming maidens. For some time after the Thirty Years' War the ladies

---

[1] See Wheaton's History of the Northmen, 1831, p. 52. He quotes Münter, Kirchengeschichte, Band i. Seite 197.

[2] See Wright's Biographia Britannica Literaria, 8vo, 1842, vol. i. pp. 32, 33.

[3] Roussel, Système de la Femme, Paris, 1845, pp. 53. 54.

[4] See Drury's Madagascar, 8vo, 1743, pp. 64-95, and p. 222.

[5] History of Madagascar, 1838, vol. i. p. 163.   [6] Ibid. p. 174.

of Germany, particularly those of the middle classes, were excessively coarse and uneducated, as is proved beyond a doubt by a curious Book of Manners which I have bought this winter. This wonderful alteration must have taken place, therefore, during the eighty years from 1660 to 1740, though we are quite ignorant how and when it began.'[1]

Comte makes no doubt of the necessary inferiority of women,[2] but he says[3] that though inferior to men in reason and intelligence, they are superior in sympathy and sociability. See also tome v. pp. 221-223, where he remarks that under polytheism they are first allowed to enter the priesthood, a right which monotheism abrogates. See also pp. 440-444, where he says that Catholicism has done women great service by diminishing their political and priestly powers, and concentrating them on domestic life. He remarks[4] that the essential differences between men and women are, like all other differences, increased by civilization.

In 1797 the celebrated Dr. Currie writes: 'Women speak more distinctly than men at the same period of life. . . . When a labouring man and his wife come to consult me, the female is always the orator.'[5]

Lord Campbell[6] says of Bacon, 'Like several extraordinary men, he is supposed to have inherited his genius from his mother.' So did Wilberforce.[7]

In the middle of the seventeenth century the ladies of the ancient house of Savelli, at Rome, still retained their old custom of never leaving their palace, or if they did so, only appearing in closely shut-up carriages.[8]

The Mongols and Tartars 'marry very young ;' and as they openly buy their wives, the women of course have no portion or dowry. Polygamy is allowed, but 'the women lead an independent life enough.'[9]

---

[1] The Life and Letters of B. G. Niebuhr, Lond. 8vo, 1852, vol. i. p. 337.
[2] Philosophie Positive, tome iv. pp. 509-574.   [3] Ibid. p. 573.
[4] Ibid. pp. 443, 444.
[5] Life and Correspondence of Dr. Currie. By W. W. Currie, 8vo. 1831. vol. i. p. 216.
[6] Lives of the Chancellors, vol. ii. p. 285.
[7] See Life of Wilberforce, 8vo, 1838, vol. i. p. 5.
[8] Ranke, Die Römischen Päpste, Band iii. pp. 60, 61.
[9] Hue's Travels in Tartary and Thibet vol. i. pp. 184-187.

In Siberia many of the shamans, or priests, are women.[1]

There is more water in the blood of females than in that of males.[2]

The fluid which lubricates the brain and spinal marrow is more abundant in women than in men, and in old men it is twice as plentiful as in adults, and it is very abundant in idiots.[3] In women blood contains more water than in men; and in lymphatic temperaments there is more water than in the blood of sanguineous ones.[4] The reviving reputation of the humourist pathology gives increased importance to these facts.

The increased courtesy is shown even in the way of declaring war, in which countries now never abuse each other, but display 'la plus noble décence.'[5]

In the manufacturing towns males marry early, therefore they are near the same age as their wives; hence the proportion of females born is increased.[6]

It is not considered so respectable for a woman to keep a school as for a man; hence education is worse, and particularly in France and Germany, where the State interferes.

From 1836 to 1846 'the yearly average number of persons who were charged with offences in England and Wales was 25,812, viz. 20,969 males, 4,843 females; but comparatively *no* educated woman commits a crime.'[7]

On the age at which in different climates menstruation occurs see Rep. of British Association for 1850; Transact. of Sections, p. 135.

We take shame to ourselves for not having sooner noticed this very interesting, and in some respects very important work; the author unknown; and yet the book gone through two editions, though written on a subject ignorantly supposed to be going on well. That women can be satisfied with their state shows their deterioration. That they can be satisfied with knowing nothing, &c.

---

[1] Bell's Travels through Asia, Edinb. 1788, 8vo, vol. I. p. 248.

[2] See Fourth Report of British Association, p. 125.

[3] Cuvier, Progrès des Sciences Naturelles, tome II. p. 397.

[4] Clark's Report on Animal Physiology, in Fourth Report of British Association, p. 126.

[5] Vattel, Le Droit des Gens, tome II. p. 170.

[6] Saddler's Law of Population, vol. II. p. 316.

[7] See Reports of British Association for 1847; Transactions of Sections, p. 105.

The mother of Cuvier was a very able woman.[1]

Flourens[2] says that the increased desire of observing gave rise everywhere in the seventeenth century to academies of science where such facts could be registered.

In the progress of society since the sixteenth century, women have not kept their ground. Civilization increases divergence; hence, if allowed to run its course, women must naturally decline in power. Sydney Smith, the first writer on women, erroneously says there is no original difference. In agricultural countries, as in France, women are better treated and have more wages. Compare Sparta with Athens. Women being more deductive have more sympathy with art than with science; hence their influence in the sixteenth century, the great age of art. There is now a higher intellectual standard and a diminished regard for *manners*, once the source of women's power as giving scope to *tact*. Their excellence consists in *moral* superiority; but morals have *not* progressed; intellect *has*. The age of imagination has passed, and that of intellect has come. Girls are more precocious than boys; hence coming in contact with nature, when *unripe*, they are rather imaginative than critical. Philippa, wife of Edward II., Jeanne de Montfort, Countess of Bretagne. Under Charles II., as physical science rose, the influence of women decreased. The progress of knowledge, by developing differences, has increased divergences. They have learnt to despise the arts of compounding a pleasant pudding or combining a tasty pie. They no longer wear their keys at their girdles; nor do they carry receipts in their pockets. They have ceased to be useful, and they have not learnt to be agreeable. It is in consequence of these things that we hail with great pleasure the appearance of the present work, which is not a manifesto of rights, but a guide and a clue. Writers like Miss Martineau and Mary Wolstoncraft have done much harm. There are no such things as natural rights; and if women are ignorant and superstitious, the less influence they have the better. Is a woman to have influence because she lisps broken Italian at the piano? Late in the eighteenth century there rose clubs which followed up the blow of scientific societies, and still further increased the divergence of the sexes. The great increase of nervous diseases

1 See Flourens, Histoire des Travaux de Cuvier, Paris, 1845, p. 65.
2 Ibid. pp. 146, 147.

caused by increasing excitement makes men more irritable ; hence
the weaker goes to the wall ; and this we see among the lower
orders, where *manners* having progressed little, women are worse
treated than ever.   Hence, among the higher classes, the increasing
influence of women is only *apparent*; they are no longer beaten
or kicked, because kicking is not polite.   Looking at the increase
of courtesy and general kindness, the respect paid to women has
not increased so fast as it ought to have done.   We are more
courteous to everything.   We no longer horsewhip our servants,
nor flog our children into fits.   Hospitals and charities have no
other idea beyond that of protecting the weak.   The encouragement given to intellect by Government is happily passing away,
and women ought to confer on intellect social fame, and by this
alliance they would recover their old power.   The increasing loss
of wealth, which is partly cause and partly effect of diminished
aristocracy, lessens the sympathy between the sexes, and gives a
new standard of merit; and this took place in the seventeenth
century, when nobles began to marry city heiresses.   The laws,
too, respecting women have improved ; but not so fast as they
have improved on other matters.   The nearest approach to
perfect equality is among savages who are *all* stupid and ignorant.
The truth seems to be that while civil and political equality are
increasing, moral and intellectual equalities are diminishing.
Men are *thinkers*, women *observers*; but formerly there was no
thinking, and observation of trifles carried the day.   In Mrs. Grey's
works are no crude notions about women having a right to vote
or sit in Parliament.   In the sixteenth century began the great
movement when, says Shakespeare, the heel of the courtier, &c.
That the democratic, sceptical, and inductive movement works
even now more good than harm, and eventually will work unmitigated good, is certain, but in the meantime it causes individual pain, and of this women are the natural correctives;
hence it were to be wished their influence should increase, and
women could correct the too rapid democracy and scepticism.
Classical literature is no longer studied by both sexes.   Women
are physically too excitable, too prone to come into contact with
external nature, and this evil nurses painting and music and
Italian—the most enervating of all literatures, the only great
thinkers being Macchiavelli, Beccaria, and Vico.   If these remarks are well founded, we should expect to find an increased

divergence between the sexes in the seventeenth and eighteenth
centuries. And such we find to be actually the case in learned
societies and clubs; and in the seventeenth century the beginning of this was coffee-houses. Among the lower orders, the
diminution of agriculture caused by chemical manures and increased skill in ploughing, &c., has increased the manufacturing
population, and therefore has increased the number of pursuits
in which women are unable to participate. Comparing barbarism
with imperfect civilization, the influence of women increases;
hence the hasty inference that it goes on increasing, an inference
fortified by the fact that women receive an increased *external*
respect. In France, twice as many agriculturists as in England;
hence women have more influence, and their wages are higher.
While the pursuits of men have become more great, the pursuits
of women have become more little.

' Both in England and France the proportion of male to female
criminals is about four to one, and that result varies but slightly
during several years.' [1]

Turgot [2] erroneously says, ' L'asservissement des femmes aux
hommes est fondé par toute la terre sur l'inégalité des forces
corporelles.' But women have *two* sorts of inferiority—*physical*
and *mental*.

In Ireland the number of females that cannot write is slightly
greater than the number of males. [3]

Napoleon said, ' My opinion is that the future good or bad
conduct of a child entirely depends upon the mother.' [4] Moore [5]
says that women endure pain better than men, because they have
' less physical sensibility. This theory I offered to put to the test by
bringing in a hot teapot, which I would answer for the ladies of
the party being able to hold for a much longer time than the men.'

In 1593, in Italy, ' only men and the masters of the family go
into the market and buy victuals; for servants are never sent for
that purpose, much less women, which if they be chaste, rather
are locked up at home, as it were in prison.' [6] But, says Moryson, [7] in Bergamo ' the very women give and receive salutations

[1] Report of British Association for 1839; Transactions of Sections, p. 117.
[2] Œuvres, tome ii. p. 247, Disc. sur l'Histoire.
[3] See Report of British Association for 1843; Transactions of Sections, p. 91.
[4] O'Meara's Napoleon in Exile, vol. ii. p. 100, 3rd edition, Lond. 1822.
[5] Memoirs, by Lord J. Russell, vol. vii. pp. 53, 54, 1st edit.
[6] Fynes Moryson's Itinerary, part i. p. 70, Lond. 1617, folio.   [7] Ibid. p. 177.

and converse with the French liberty, without any offence to their husbands, which other Italians would never endure.' In Holland women had most freedom ; they managed the shops and looked after the accounts, while the men were idle.' See also p. 288, where Moryson says that Dutch married women not only had the right of bequest, but possessed in their lifetime the control of their husbands' common every-day actions. On the other hand, the Germans treated their wives very ill, and would not let them eat at the same table.' On the influence of women, see J. S. Mill's Essays, vol. ii. p. 165, and p. 449 of Mrs. Mill's Essay in the same work ; also pp. 262, 425, 435. Saint-Simon, who was in Spain in 1721 and 1722, observes' that greater favour is shown to bastards in Spain than in any other Christian country. This he ascribes to the influence of the Mahommedans. 'The natural sterility of Spanish women, who, though they may have children by good luck, leave off child-bearing much sooner than the women of other nations.' 'The great and main duty which a wife, as a wife, ought to learn, and so learn as to practise it, is to be subject to her own husband . . . There is not any husband to whom this honour of submission is not due ; no personal infirmity, frowardness of nature, no, not even on the point of religion, doth deprive him of it.' 'The sum of a wife's duty unto her husband is subjection.' Abernethy' is opposed to beauty in women ; for he says, 'Seldom is it found that beauty and shamefastness do agree.' At p. 445 this wise man praises persons who castrate themselves. 'Humanity is the virtue of a woman ; generosity, of a man. The fair sex, who have commonly much more tenderness than ours, have seldom so much generosity.' Hutchison' says that for husbands to inflict on their wives 'any corporal punishment must be tyrannical and unmanly.' 'Dr. Marshall Hall found that, from patients with congestive apoplexy, from forty to fifty ounces of blood might be drawn without producing syncope ; whilst in acute inflammations

1 Fynes Moryson's Itinerary, part iii. p. 97.   3 Ibid. p. 220.
2 Mémoires, Paris, 1840-1842, tome xxxv. pp. 240-246.
4 History of Cardinal Alberoni, Lond. 1719, p. 250.
5 Fergusson on the Epistles, 1656, p. 242. See also p. 356.
6 Physick for the Soul, p. 437.
7 Smith's Theory of Moral Sentiments, vol. ii. p. 19.
8 System of Moral Philosophy, vol. ii. p. 165.

the *tolerance* is usually less by about ten ounces.'[1] Williams says,[2] 'Nervous diseases are most common and obstinate in the female sex ; but they are more serious in the male sex.' About nine times as many men have aneurisms as women.[3] Males are more subject to pericarditis ;[4] to pneumonia 'in the proportion of ten to one.'[5] Females 'appear to be more prone' to 'tuberculosis of the lung.'[6] But 'cancer of the lung is incomparably more frequent in males than in females.'[7] On diseases of women compared with men, see Rokitansky's Pathological Anatomy, vol. iii. p. 177 ; vol. iv. pp. 271, 303.

THE CAUSES AND EFFECTS OF DUELLING.

OF all the vices natural to a modern republic, duelling is the most brutal and the most constant. It is the last resource of a baffled coward. It was entirely unknown to the generous spirit of antiquity, but is most frequent in the United States of America, that wretched burlesque of an ancient republic which possesses the forms of democracy without the spirit of liberty. Miss Martineau[8] says, ' I was amazed to hear a gentleman of New England declare, while complaining of the insolence of the Southern members of Congress to the Northern under shelter of the Northern men not being duellists, that, if he went to Congress, he would give out that he would fight.' In the single city of New Orleans 'there were fought, in 1834, more duels than there were days in the year ; fifteen on one Sunday morning. In 1835 there were 102 duels fought in that city between the 1st of January and the end of April ; and no notice is taken of shooting in a quarrel.'[9]

It seems probable that the tendency of civilization is to increase timidity. If this be the case, duelling may be defended on the ground taken up by Adam Smith, that it renders the restraint of anger by fear still more contemptible than it otherwise would be.[10]

---

[1] Williams's Principles of Medicine, 1848, pp. 177, 333.   [2] Ibid. p. 449

[3] Hasse's Patholog. Anatomy, by Sydenham Society, pp. 94, 142.

[4] Ibid. p. 119.   [5] Ibid. p. 215.

[6] Ibid. p. 316.   [7] Ibid. p. 370.

[8] Society in America, Paris, 8vo, 1842, vol. ii. p. 108, part iii. chap. i.

[9] Ibid. vol. ii. pp. 130, 131.

[10] Theory of Moral Sentiments, part vi. section 3. vol. ii. p. 94.

In 1589, 'Sir William Drury was killed in a duel by Sir John Boroughs.'[1]

By the end of the sixteenth century duelling had become a regular system, and books were written in England to teach a gentleman how to give the lie in a satisfactory manner.[2] The famous Dr. A. Clarke thought that in many cases duelling is more criminal than suicide.[3]

The object of duelling was to punish injuries which the law left unpunished. This could only be done by putting the weak and unskilful on a level with the strong and skilful ; thus the introduction of pistols instead of swords was a great improvement, and, I doubt not, has led the way to that better state of things when the combined authority of laws and manners will be sufficient to repress such offences.

Henry IV. of France issued edicts against duels.[4] Towards the end of the sixteenth century Ben Jonson killed a man in a duel.[5] In 1629 he attacks duelling in 'The New Inn ; but the satire, though very moral, is also very tedious.[6]

Chevenix has well said that duelling 'is more prevalent in vain than in proud nations.'[7] This remark may be applied to individuals, and I believe that nothing but an ungovernable burst of passion would induce a really proud man either to send or accept a challenge.

In 1592 gentlemen seem not to have worn their rapiers, but to have made their servants carry them.[8]

In Porter's Two Angrie Women of Abington,[9] Coomes complains that the ' poking fight of rapier and dagger' was becoming common, and the sword and buckler falling into disuse. Mr. Rimbault[10] says that rapiers 'were introduced in England during Elizabeth's reign by a desperado named Rowland Yorke ; and

---

[1] Camden's Elizabeth, in Kennet, vol. ii. p. 557.

[2] See Drake's Shakespeare and his Times, 1817, 4to, vol. ii. pp. 158, 159, and Ben Jonson, 1816, vol. iv. p. 107.

[3] See his Letter, dated 1732, in Mrs. Thomson's Memoirs of Viscountess Sundon 2nd edition, 8vo, 1848, vol. ii. p. 120.

[4] See Capefigue, Histoire de la Réforme, tome viii. p. 98.

[5] See his Life, by Gifford, p. xix in vol. i. of Jonson's Works.

[6] Ben Jonson's Works, vol. v. pp. 416-418.

[7] Essay on National Character, 8vo, 1832, vol. i. p. 159.

[8] See Park's edition of Harleian Miscellany, vol. v. p. 420.

[9] 1599 ; Percy Soc. vol. v. p. 61.

[10] Note to Rowland's Four Knaves, Percy Society, vol. ix. p. 132.

their lightness and convenience soon gave them a permanent footing in the place of the heavy swords previously worn.'

I suspect that as the trial by battle became disused, the people, clinging to their old customs, became more addicted to duelling. Blackstone says [1] that the last trial by battle waged in the Common Pleas was in 1571. I must therefore consider duelling as the *result of the decline of chivalry.* While the trial by battle was allowed, it was natural to punish those who went about armed. Thus the 2 Edward III. forbids any one to carry dangerous arms.—Blackstone, iv. 149. Christian says,[2] 'The last time that the trial by battle was awarded in this country was in the case of Lord Rae and Mr. Ramsay in 7th Car. I.' But it was ordered as late as 1819, for I have read an account of the trial in Rush's Residence at the Court of London. It was afterwards got rid of by some flaw on that occasion, and at once put an end to by Act of Parliament. In 1560, Cecil was so displeased with some remarks thrown out by the Bishop of Ross, in a diplomatic negotiation, that he challenged him to fight. 'I offered in that quarrel to spend my blood upon any of them that would deny it.'[3] Margaret of Austria, aunt to Charles V., mentions in 1529 the duel which was to have been fought between the Emperor and Francis I.[4] Lord Brougham can only find a parallel for our wager of battle in the barbarism of a Persian law.[5] Allen says, 'Private war has disappeared, and the only vestige of it that remains is the practice of duelling.'[6] He adds [7] that Britton did not mention private war: 'the practice was going into disuse; and in less than half a century it was adjudged to be illegal.' This, as he says, was partly owing to 'the regular distribution of justice in the courts of eyre and assize.' Montesquieu observes that the licence given to single combat was a consequence and a remedy of the laws which permit negative proofs. If the defendant could swear himself innocent, it seemed natural that the plaintiff should have some subsequent appeal.[8] If this is well founded, duelling may be connected with the use of

---

[1] Commentaries, vol. III. p. 338.   [2] Note in Blackstone, vol. iv. p. 348.
[3] Haynes's State Papers, p. 337.
[4] See Correspondence of Charles V., edited by Mr. Bradford, Lond. 8vo. 1850, p. 224.
[5] Brougham's Political Philosophy, 2nd edit. 8vo. 1849, vol. I. p. 123.
[6] Allen on the Prerogative, 8vo. 1849, p. 118.   [7] Ibid. p. 121.
[8] Esprit des Lois, livre xxviii. chap. xiv. and xviii. Œuvres. Paris, 1835, pp. 446, 449.

Courts of *Conscience*, such as Chancery, or even the Court of Requests. See also respecting the trial by combat p. 448, and read the whole of livre xxviii. In 1565, Count Egmont was reproached by Philip II. for being in a company where some foolish joke was passed against Granvella. Egmont replied that no disrespect was intended to the king, and that, if he had thought any of the jokers had such intention, he would have instantly challenged him: 'so würde er selbst ihn vor seinen Degen fordern.'[1] In 1576 foreigners in London wore rapiers;[2] and Fleetwood says,[3] 'His garments were a cloke and a rapier after the Italian fashion.' 'Bludgeons and bucklers' were in 1586 the ordinary weapons.[4] In 1580 the French Ambassador, whilst passing the bars at Smithfield, was stopped because his rapier was longer than the statute allowed,[5] by which we learn that there were officers sitting at Smithfield Bars whose business it was to *cut* swords that were too lengthy. In 1562 a proclamation forbade any one to carry a sword having a blade more than a yard and a quarter long.[6] Cranmer, when archbishop, challenged the Duke of Northumberland.[7] Madame de Crequy says that the firmness of Louis XIV. had, during the last seventeen years of his reign, put an end to duels. 'On n'avait pas ouï parler d'un seul duel depuis dix-sept ans.'[8] But she adds[9] that after his death they became frequent on account of the weakness of the regent; 'La fureur des duels était si fort encouragée par la faiblesse et l'incurie du Duc d'Orléans, qu'on n'entendait parler que de jeunes gens tués et blessés.' Duels were practised by the ancient Persians.[10] In 1600 the first instance in Scotland of a duellist 'suffering death when nothing unfair was proved.'[11] Lithgow, who was in Spain in 1620, says the Spaniards never fight duels.[12] Respecting duels fought by women, see COMMON PLACE BOOK, art. 1093.

[1] Abfall der Niederlande, in Schiller's Werke, Band viii. Seite 179, Stuttgart, 1838.

[2] See Fleetwood's Letter in Wright's Elizabeth, vol. ii. p. 38.

[3] Ibid. p. 40.   [4] See Leycester Correspondence, Camden Society, p. 228.

[5] See Lord Talbot's Letter in Lodge's Illustrations of British History, vol. ii. p. 168.   [6] Machyn's Diary, p. 281, Camden Soc. vol. xiii.

[7] Todd's Life of Cranmer, vol. ii. p. 353.

[8] Souvenirs de la Marquise de Crequy, Paris, 8vo, 1834, tome i. p. 255.

[9] Ibid. p. 348.

[10] See Malcolm's History of Persia, 8vo, 1829, vol. i. pp. 26, 38, 39, 41.

[11] Pitcairn's Criminal Tales, vol. ii. p. 112. See for this, vol. iii. p. 502.

[12] Lithgow's Nineteen Years' Travels, 11th edit. Edinb. 1770, p. 243.

NOTES ON THE TENDENCY OF EDUCATION.

Miss Martineau [1] says, 'The provision of schools is so adequate [in the United States] that any citizen, who sees a child at play during school hours, may ask, "Why are you not at school?" and, unless good reason be given, may take him to the school-house of the district.' Mr. Mill says, 'It is not allowable exercise of the powers of Government to impose on parents the legal obligation of giving elementary instruction to children.' [2]

Adam Smith [3] says, probably with truth, that education at boarding schools and colleges has seriously injured the morals of France and England. Southey, in a letter written in 1823, has some good remarks on the comparative advantages of public and private education. He expresses the strongest horror of boarding schools, and greatly prefers, I think with reason, day schools. [4]

By educating a nation you increase its wealth in two different ways; for you increase the desire of accumulation, and at the same time, by making the labourer more intelligent, you make his labour more productive. [5] It also prevents over-increase of population. [6]

The advantages of education to the lower orders merely in an economical point of view are well stated by Mr. Thornton, who, I think, prefers oral instruction to any other. [7]

Of the real benefits of education, Hannah More, though she did so much to impart them, had no competent idea. In 1801 she wrote a long and formal defence of her conduct to the Bishop of Bath and Wells. She says, 'To teach the poor to read without providing them with *safe* books has always appeared to me an improper measure; and this consideration induced me to enter upon the laborious undertaking of the Cheap Repository Tracts.' [8]

---

[1] Society in America, Paris, 8vo, 1842, vol. II. p. 185, part III. chap. III.

[2] Principles of Political Economy, vol. II, p. 524. See also Mill's Essays, vol. I. p. 89.

[3] Theory of Moral Sentiments, part vI. sect. 2, chap. I. vol. II. pp. 65, 66. Lond. 1822, 12mo.

[4] The Life and Correspondence of R. Southey, edited by the Rev. C. C. Southey, 8vo, 1849, 1850, vol. I. pp. 79, 80. See also vol. v. p. 218.

[5] Mill's Principles of Political Economy, Lond. 1849, 8vo, 2nd edit. vol. I. pp. 131-136, 202, 203, 227.   [6] Ibid. pp. 464, 465.

[7] See Thornton on Over-Population, 8vo, 1846, pp. 327-377.

[8] Roberts's Memoirs of Mrs. Hannah More, 2nd edit. 8vo, 1834, vol. III. p. 135.

Those who have read Hannah More's works will easily understand
this sentence. By *safe* books she meant books which, under pretence of imparting spiritual knowledge, neglected intellectual
knowledge and made men pious and useless. Roberts says that
Hannah More, 'adverting to the multitude of improving and
entertaining books which were daily issuing from the press for the
use of children and young persons, added, "In my early youth
there was scarcely anything between Cinderella and the Spectator."'[1] This was said about 1820. Hannah More, in her Strictures on Female Education (the Preface to which is dated 1799),
repeats her mischievous opinion that it is of no use to educate
the poor, unless we tell them what to read, and 'furnish them with
such books as shall strengthen and confirm their principles.'[2]

There is yet another point of view in which education of the
poor becomes so important. It is well known to physiologists
that a deficiency of nutriment affects the brain.[3] It, therefore,
follows that the lower the real reward of the labourer, the greater
is the necessity of education, in order in some degree to obviate
the evils arising from the deficiency of his food.[4]

In and after 1557 the Quakers set up private schools both for
boys and girls.[5]

The mischievous effects on the health of young girls caused by
the absurd regulations of modern boarding schools are scarcely
to be believed ; but they are well attested.[6] Boys have suffered
less.[7] I suppose, then, that the average life of men has increased
more than that of women.

The school books commonly used in England in the middle
of the sixteenth century are enumerated by Mr. Drake.[8]

The way in which an increased spirit of providence among
the lower orders increases the wealth of the country to which
they belong is very clearly explained by Mr. Rae,[9] who indeed

[1] Roberts's Memoirs of Mrs. Hannah More, 2nd edit. 8vo, 1834, vol. iv. p. 132.
[2] Works, 8vo, 1830, vol. v. p. 140.
[3] Combe's Physiology of Digestion, 2nd edit. Edinb. 8vo, 1836, pp. 247-250.
[4] See also Combe's Physiology applied to Health, 3rd edit. Edinb. 8vo, 1835, p. 276.
[5] See Fox's Journal, reprint, 1817, vol. ii. pp. 84. 278, 279, 357.
[6] See some evidence in Combe's Principles of Physiology applied to the Preservation of Health, Edinb. 1835, 8vo, 3rd edit. pp. 130-133.
[7] Ibid. pp. 135, 157.
[8] Shakespeare and his Times, 1817, 4to, vol. i. pp. 25-27, 57.
[9] New Principles of Political Economy, Boston, 8vo, 1834, pp. 200-204.

has discussed all the causes of accumulation with remarkable ability.

In that very remarkable work, The Brief Conceipt of English Policy, published in 1581, the doctor notices and reprobates the increasing disregard shown to the universities. He observes that it had become customary to remove young men from them at an earlier age than formerly, 'whereby the universities be in manner emptied.'[1] In 1559, Elizabeth ordered that 'the parson or curate of the parish shall instruct the children of his parish for half an hour before evening prayer on every holyday and second Sunday in the year in the Catechism, and shall teach them the Lord's Prayer, Creed, and Ten Commandments.'[2] In 1562 the Speaker of the House of Commons stated, in his place in Parliament, that 'the schools in England are fewer than formerly by a hundred.'[3]

The North American Indians never punish their children.[4]

The stimulus which Protestantism has given to great schools is ably, but perhaps a little too strongly, put by M. Villers.[5]

Blackstone was in favour of compulsory education, but this, I fear, not from any enlightened reason, but from an over-love of Government interference.[6]

In 1551, Dr. Wotton promised the 'searchor' at Dover (I suppose of the Custom House) that he would appoint his son to 'a Roome yn our Gramer school,' and expresses a wish that he should be first examined by the schoolmasters.[7]

Kant proposed that in education *no* opinions should be concealed from the student. In this noble liberality he was not only in advance of his own, but of the present age. Even M. Cousin says, 'Ce serait beaucoup hasarder.'[8]

Cousin speaks strongly in favour of *public* education, which he prefers to *private*; because, by placing every one under the same rule, it gives them the idea of *duty*.[9] Cousin seems to think[10] that the State is bound to *enforce* education.[11]

[1] Harleian Miscellany, edit. Park, vol. iv. p. 150.

[2] Neal's History of the Puritans, edit. Toulmin, 8vo, 1882, vol. I, p. 129.

[3] Collier's Ecclesiastical History, 8vo, 1840, vol. vi. p. 336.   See also D'Ewes' Journals of Parliament, 1682, p. 65.

[4] See Buchanan's Sketches of the North American Indians, 8vo, 1824, p. 70.

[5] Essai sur la Réformation, Paris, 1820, pp. 280-286.

[6] Commentaries, edit. Christian, 8vo, 1809, vol. I, p. 451.

[7] Haynes's State Papers, p. 113.

[8] Histoire de la Philosophie, Paris, 1846, part i. tome v. pp. 245, 255.

[9] Ibid. part I. tome I. pp. 350, 351.   [10] Ibid. part i. tome iii. p. 215.

[11] See also tome iv. pp. 300, 301.

The tendency of Calvinism is to extend education.[1]

Mere education, popularly so called, that is, reading and writing does a nation little good. The Chinese are a remarkable instance; for of this sort of education they have more than any people in the world, but yet are unable to emerge from their present ignorance. See some good remarks in Brougham's Political Philosophy.[2] This he ascribes to the 'manifest intention which the sovereigns have always had to limit the literary acquisitions of their subjects,'[3] and to the efforts of the rulers to make education a political engine.[4] The influence of education in checking population is noticed by M. Quetelet;[5] but he adds[6] that merely teaching to read and write does not lessen crime so much as is supposed. Mr. Alison notices the tendency of education to 're-strain the operation of the principle of increase.'[7] He adds[8] that in Ireland 'the proportion attending the primary schools is greater than in Scotland.' See[9] his ill-written and ill-argued attacks upon the secular education of the lower orders.[10] Reed, in a spirit far beyond his age, says, 'Notwithstanding the innumerable errors committed in human education, there is hardly any education so bad as to be worse than none.'[11] Ranke observes that it was a peculiarity of the early German literature that its best works were written for the purpose of education.[12] The struggles between Protestants and Catholics must have favoured education. Each party wished to strengthen itself in every way, and there was none so effective as education.

Glanvill says,[13] 'Thus a French top, the common recreation of schoolboys, thrown from a cord which was wound about it, will stand, as it were, fixed on the floor it lighted.' And in Plus Ultra, 1668, p. 117, he says, 'Every one that hath outgrown his cherry-stones and rattles.'[14] Until early in the seventeenth century, or

[1] See my notes on Calvinism.
[2] and edit. 8vo, 1849, vol. i. pp. 162, 167, 184.   [3] Ibid. p. 171.
[4] Ibid. p. 185.   [5] Sur l'Homme, Paris, 8vo, 1835, tome i. pp. 108-110.
[6] Ibid. tome ii. p. 245.
[7] Alison's Principles of Population, 8vo, 1840, vol. i. p. 93.
[8] Ibid. p. 511.   [9] Vol. ii. pp. 292-346.
[10] See also my remarks on Crime.
[11] Reed's Inquiry into the Human Mind, Edinb. 8vo, 1814, p. 441.
[12] Die Romischen Päpste, Berlin, 1838, Band i. Seiten 76, 77.
[13] Vanity of Dogmatising, 1661, p. 80.
[14] See also his Vanity of Dogmatising, p. 243.

even later, children wore 'long coats' at seven years of age.[1] Evelyn's son went to Oxford in 1666, aged thirteen, and 'was newly out of long coates.'[2] In 1682, Evelyn[3] mentions the vast expense 'the nation is at yearly by sending children into France to be taught military exercises.' It used to be common for parents to punish their children so severely as to lame them.[4] Montaigne had the most liberal ideas about education.[5] Charron[6] has some sensible remarks on education, which he seems to have taken from Montaigne. In the Polynesian Islands the children used 'to resist all parental restraint.'[7] An Indian expressed his surprise that the white people were so cruel as to whip their children.[8] Grammar schools resulted from the dissolution of monasteries.[9] 'Like one of our schoolboys' satchels, made of wrought stuff, and lined with leather.'[10] Locke, who was himself at Oxford, used to express his contempt for the system of education pursued there.[11] As to the proportion of persons educated in different countries, see Alison, History of Europe, vol. ix. p. 271. At the Madras School, late in the eighteenth century, one of the masters was dismissed because he punished children by biting their fingers.[12] In Tartary the discipline of the boys brought up by the priests is very severe.[13] Porter[14] says, 'In the whole of England and Wales, among 367,894 couples married during three years (1839, 1840, 1841), it appeared that there were 122,458 men and 181,378 women who either could not write at all, or who had attained so little proficiency in penmanship that they were averse to the exposure of their deficiency.' Colleges, properly so called, were not established in France till the end of the fifteenth century.[15] Monteil says[16] that

1 See Wordsworth's Ecclesiastical Biography, 3rd edit. 8vo, 1839, vol. iv. p. 317.

2 Evelyn's Diary, 8vo, 1827, vol. II. p. 281, and see p. 282.

3 Ibid. vol. III. p. 70.

4 Essais de Montaigne, livre II. chap. xxxi., Paris, 8vo, 1843, pp. 448, 449.

5 See Montaigne's Works, edit. Hazlitt, pp. 54-76, 63, 69, 177.

6 De la Sagesse, Amsterdam, 1783, 8vo, tome II. p. 177.

7 Ellis, Polynesian Researches, 8vo, 1831, vol. III. p. 205.

8 See Catlin's North American Indians, 8vo, 1841, vol. II. p. 241.

9 Nichols, Literary Illustrations of the Eighteenth Century, vol. v. p. 99.

10 Calamy's Own Life, 8vo, 1829, vol. I. p. 190.

11 King's Life of Locke, 8vo, 1830, vol. I. p. 5.

12 Southey's Life of Dr. Bell, vol. i. pp. 184, 186.

13 See Huc's Travels in Tartary and Thibet, vol. I. pp. 58, 59, 177, 178.

14 Progress of the Nation, vol. III. p. 278.

15 See Monteil, Histoire des Divers États, tome I. p. 162.

16 Ibid. tome II. p. 8.

in 1380 there were at Paris only forty schoolmasters and
twenty schoolmistresses. Laing says that State interference in education has done much harm abroad.[1] In Prussia education is
compulsory to a cruel extent,[2] and the Prussians are lower in
morals than any other nation.[3] In Journal of Statistical Society for
1838, vol. i. p. 47, it is said, 'The endowments for purposes of
education in this country possess an immense annual income,
amounting, it is probable, to not less than [£]1,500,000. On the
origin of day schools, &c., see p. 459. Fletcher says[4] of 'the
labouring classes' that 'the day-schooling of the same classes is of
yet more recent origin ; for it cannot be dated earlier than 1798,
when Dr. Bell published his Experiments on Education made at
the male asylum at Madras, and Joseph Lancaster began practically to develop the same principles in the schools now designated
British Schools. Nor was it until 1808 that the British School
Society was founded on its present basis, nor until 1811 that the
National Society was established. The next great step was the
establishment of the first infant school in England in 1818.' In
England and Wales, where there are most domestic servants, there
is most education. This shows the utility of luxury by increasing
contact.[5] Education increases with property.[6] On the opinion
of Guerry see vol. xii. 219. Giving the children at national schools
a *costume* has done great harm by irritating the pride of the
parents.[7] Vast numbers of the poor who attend schools afterward
forget even how to read.[8] For a comparative list of the proportion which, in the different countries of Europe, the educated bear
to the uneducated, see Journal of Statistical Soc., vol. ii. p. 386 ;
and at p. 396 it is observed that education has diminished in
Holland since the Dutch in 1830 ceased to make it compulsory.[9]

After all, I think, the simplest argument against Government
interfering in education is that, hitherto, whatever they have
touched they have injured. They have increased crime, usury,
irreligion, smuggling.

The inferior schools in Birmingham teach nothing worth learn-

[1] Observations on Denmark, p. 31.
[2] Laing, Notes of a Traveller, 1st series, p. 165.   [3] Ibid. pp. 167, 168.
[4] Journal of Statistical Society, vol. x. p. 196.   [5] Ibid. p. 207.
[6] Ibid. vol. xii. p. 235.   [7] Ibid. vol. i. p. 455. See also vol. vi. p. 213.
[8] Ibid. vol. ii. pp. 61, 73.   [9] See also vol. iii. pp. 341, 342.

ing.[1]   Parents prefer sending their boys even to schools kept by women ; and such schools are infinitely more numerous than those kept by men.[2]   By the Visigothic Code, 'If a master shall chastise his pupil so that death ensue, if he can prove that the chastisement was more severe than he intended, he shall not be punished or defamed.'[3]   Hallam[4] says that Hughes' Life of Barrow 'contains a sketch of studies pursued in the University of Cambridge from the twelfth to the seventeenth century.'   He adds[5] that even Milton, notwithstanding his expression, 'complete and generous education,' had narrow views, and confines his course of education to 'ancient writers.'   Locke is too rigid, and recommends that 'children should be taught to expect nothing because it will give them pleasure.'[6]   However, he rather prefers private to public education.[7]   Hallam says :[8] 'No one had condescended to spare any thoughts for female education till Fénelon in 1688 published his earliest work, Sur l'Éducation des filles. . . . His theory is uniformly indulgent; his method of education is a labour of love.'[9]   The foundation and free grammar schools are nearly all founded by clergymen of the Church of England, and taught by them, and for the most part arose in consequence of the monasteries being broken up.   Out of 436 foundation schools, 115 date from the reign of Elizabeth; but, after this, the rate of increase gradually lessens, and, 'in the long reign of George III., only twelve were founded,' owing to 'the religious indifference of the eighteenth century.'[10]   At p. 226 it is said that the first 'ragged schools' in London were in 1844; but that 'an isolated effort had been made in the country some thirty years before.'   On the history &c. of public schools, see M'Culloch's British Empire, 1847, vol. ii. p. 318, et seq.   On legalised cruelty in education, see Hume's Commentaries on the Laws of Scotland, i. pp. 13, 45, 358, 389; vol. ii. p. 40.   'Uneducated persons are utterly unable to separate any two ideas which have once become firmly associated in their minds; but the cultivated being more accustomed to exercise their imagination, have experienced sensations and thoughts in more varied combinations, and not formed inseparable

[1] Journal of Statistical Society, vol. iii. p. 35.   [2] Ibid. vol. vi. p. 214.
[3] Dunham's Hist. of Spain, in Lardner's Cyclop. vol. iv. p. 86, Lond. 1832.
[4] Literature, vol. iii. p. 249.   [5] Ibid. p. 410.
[6] Ibid. p. 413.   [7] Ibid. p. 414.   [8] Ibid. p. 417.   [9] Ibid. p. 417.
[10] Transactions of Association for Promotion of Social Science, 1858. pp. 124-127.

combinations.'[1] 'The children of the labouring classes see very
little of school after the age of ten.   Their habits are so migratory
that only thirty-four per cent. are found in the same school more
than two years; and of 2,262,000 children between the ages of
three and fifteen who are not at school, 1,500,000 are absent
without any necessity or justification.   Some learn nothing; and
more forget entirely what they have learned.'[2]   At p. 63, 'Among
the causes to which the absence of 1,800,000 children from school
is attributable, that to which the greatest prominence is given,
is the indifference of parents, arising not so much from a disregard of the welfare of their children as from a doubt whether
school teaching will be of use in the daily struggles of life.'   At
p. 212, 'During the last twenty or thirty years' great improvement has been effected in the education of the lower classes, and
perhaps in that of the higher; but not in that of the middle
classes.   It was to remedy this last deficiency that in 1857 or
1858 'the Statute of Examination was passed by the University
of Oxford.'[3]   The amiable Hutcheson[4] allows the infliction on
children of 'moderate chastisements, such as are not dangerous to
life.'   Pain sours the temper.   It has been lessened in surgery
from ether to chloroform; also from improvement in operations,
and from medicine *encroaching* on surgery by curing diseases
without the knife.   Sprengel[5] says that in operations for the
stone, 'la plupart des auteurs qui ont écrit sur la chirurgie au
seizième siècle, se plurent à compliquer le grand appareil.'   The
famous Baulot at Paris, at the end of the seventeenth century,
operated for the stone on forty-two persons, of whom twenty-five
died.[6]   See also[7] the complicated way mentioned by Celsus of so
simple an operation as the extraction of a tooth.   Even Avicenna
would not take out a tooth that was solid in the jaw;[8] and 'till
Arculanus, no one thought of stopping teeth with gold.'[9]   Until
the sixteenth century, castration was a common remedy for
hernia,[10] and even later it was believed to be the only remedy for
sarcoceles.[11]   As civilization advances, violent accidents are less

[1] Mill's Logic, 1856, vol. I. p. 268.
[2] Transactions of Association for Social Science. 1859. p. 59.
[3] Ibid. pp. 211-213.   [4] Moral Philosophy, vol. II. p. 191.
[5] Hist. de la Médecine, tome vii. p. 221.   [6] Sprengel, tome vii. p. 226.
[7] Ibid, tome viii. p. 215.   [8] Ibid. p. 244.
[9] Ibid. p. 251.   [10] Ibid. p. 229.   [11] Ibid. p. 232.

common, and tetanus diminishes. Less superstition diminishes
nervous diseases. The horrible and useless operation of amputating the bosom in cancer, Sprengel, viii. 413. Children used to
be flogged after being taken to executions.[1] On diminution of
pain in surgical operations, see Kemble's Saxons in England,
vol. ii. p. 433.

DEMOCRACY.

HUME has observed that republics are more favourable to science,
monarchies to art. The United States seem unkind to the latter.
Miss Martineau says,[2] 'I did not meet with a good artist among
all the ladies in the States. I never had the pleasure of seeing a
good drawing, except in one instance; or except in two, of hearing
good music.' She says:[3] 'If the American nation be judged by
its literature, it may be pronounced to have no mind at all.' At
p. 212, 'The periodical literature of the United States is of a
very low order. I know of no review, where anything like enlightened impartial criticism is to be found.' As a specimen of
their taste, Miss Martineau tells us:[4] 'I heard no name so often
as Mrs. Hannah More's. She is much better known in the country
than Shakspeare. . . . Byron is scarcely heard of.' Roberts says[5]
of 'Cœlebs,' 'Thirty editions of 1,000 copies each were printed
in that country during the lifetime of Mrs. Hannah More.' In
a letter written in 1820, Hannah More communicates to Sir W.
Pepys the great success of her works in America. This seems to
have opened her eyes to Transatlantic virtues, for she adds: 'I
am glad to have my prejudices against that vast republic softened.
They are imitating all our religious and charitable institutions.
They are fast acquiring *taste*, which, I think, is the last quality
that republicans do acquire.[6] . . . They seem to be improving in
religion, morals, and literature. . . . They treat me better than
I deserve. They have sent me an edition of my own works
elegantly bound.'[7] Finally,[8] 'The Americans have little dramatic
taste.'

---

[1] Grosley's Tour to London, vol. i. p. 173.
[2] Society in America, Paris, 8vo, 1842, vol. ii. p. 177.
[3] Ibid. p. 207.   [4] Ibid. p. 214.
[5] Memoirs of Mrs. Hannah More, 2nd edit. 8vo, 1834, vol. iii. p. 273.
[6] Ibid. vol. iv. p. 159. See in the same strain, vol. iv. p. 217.
[7] Ibid. vol. iv. p. 278.
[8] Society in America, Paris, 8vo, 1842, vol. ii. p. 237.

Adam Smith[1] has a very acute remark on the importance of the distinction of ranks.

Mr. Mill finely says that it is more important in a democracy than in any other form of government to restrain the power of public opinion, because its tendency is to destroy originality and independence of thought.[2] The comparative advantages of democracy and monarchy are stated by Blackstone with more fairness than one could have expected.[3] Lord Brougham seems to deny the common idea that republics are warlike.[4] Alison finds fault with the Americans that they have 'no sort of attachment, either to the land which they have cultivated, or which they have inherited from their fathers.'[5] In the fourteenth century in France, the butchers were the recognised leaders of the mob.[6]

MEDICINE.

THE rapidly increasing knowledge of medicine in England in the seventeenth century must have produced remarkable effects. The diminution of pain is, looking at things in a large point of view, the least of the benefits derived from the soothing hand of the accomplished physician. His influence on the progress of civilization consists in being enabled to lengthen life. During fifty years in England the expectation of life was doubled. By this means men were enabled to perfect their discoveries with only one half the risk, before incurred, of being interrupted by death. It may be safely laid down that, supposing all other things equal, the greatest discoveries will be made by the most long-lived people. In pure science, the results which a mighty genius has achieved, may indeed be embodied by him in a material form and handed down to posterity as a foundation on which future philosophers may build. But the experience, the fine and subtle sagacity, the delicate perception of analogies and differences, these are the work of time as well as of genius, and these are the qualities which cannot be embodied, which cannot be bequeathed.

---

[1] Theory of Moral Sentiments, part vi. section 2, chap. I. vol. ii. p. 72.
[2] Principles of Political Economy, 2nd edit. 8vo. 1849, vol. ii. pp. 511, 512.
[3] Commentaries, edit. Christian, 8vo. 1809. vol. I. pp. 49, 50.
[4] Political Philosophy, 2nd edit. 8vo. 1849, vol. I. pp. 358, 359.
[5] Principles of Population, 1840, vol. i. p. 551, and see pp. 552, 553.
[6] See Monteil, Hist. des Français des Divers États, tome ii. p. 154.

It is in this point of view that medicine, by lengthening the average duration of life, increases the general fund of national wisdom.

Dr. Combe notices that the principle of division of labour has operated injuriously upon medicine ;[1] and see to the same effect the sensible evidence of Dr. Farre, given before a Committee of the House of Commons.[2] The College of Physicians, it was stated by one of the Committee (No. 3446), are so absurd as to 'endeavour to discourage the union of medicine with surgery.' Mr. Lawrence also gave his opinion that in the same course of lectures anatomy, pathology, and physiology should be combined.[3]

In 1563, the government pay to surgeons was 1s. 6d. a day, exactly three times the amount received by common soldiers See Haynes's State Papers, p. 398. In 1588, it was also 1s. 6d.[4] The ague was very common formerly.[5] In 1568, there was no physician at Berwick, or even in the neighbouring country.[6] The increasing cultivation of medicine encouraged the rising school of metaphysics. Mr. Morell[7] well says of physicians that, 'from the habit of outward observation, the general tone of their philosophy flows most readily in the sensational channel'—i.e., adapts itself to the philosophy of Locke, who had studied medicine. It is curious to observe that Reed, and, I think, most of the Scotch idealists, were *clergymen*. Wolsey's physician was a Venetian.[8] See the admirable remarks in Quetelet, Sur l'Homme.[9] He notices that the great use of medicine is to increase the average duration of life. The celebrated Gilbert, who, in some things, was in advance of Bacon, was physician to Queen Elizabeth and to James I.[10] His great point was insisting upon experiment. Whewell mentions him in the highest terms.[11] Alison says :

[1] Principles of Physiology applied to the Preservation of Health, 3rd edit. Edinb. 1835, 8vo, pp. 34, 35.

[2] Report from the Select Committee on Medical Education, 1834, folio, part I. p. 223, Nos. 3443-3445.

[3] Report on Medical Education, part II. p. 160.

[4] See Murdin's State Papers, p. 614.

[5] Haynes's State Papers, pp. 509, 527, 602. Murdin's State Papers, p. 138.

[6] See Lord Hunsdon's Letter to Cecil, in Haynes's State Papers, p. 509.

[7] View of the Speculative Philosophy of Europe, 8vo, 1846, vol. I. pp. 409, 410.

[8] See Correspondence of Charles V., edited by Mr. Bradford, Lond. 8vo, 1850, pp. 306, 307.

[9] Paris, 8vo, 1835, tome I. pp. 325, 326.

[10] Whewell's Philosophy of the Inductive Sciences, 8vo, 1847, vol. II. p. 213.

[11] Ibid. pp. 212, 213.

'Perhaps the best test of public happiness is to be found in the average duration of human life.'[1] If I rightly understand Mr. Green, he says that Sydenham was the first in England who united science and experience in medicine.[2] He adds[3] that Hunter's Fundamental Principles of Inflammation is 'one of the most masterly performances of inductive investigation, and unprecedented in the science to which it is a contribution.' Among the arts, medicine, on account of its eminent utility, must always hold the highest place. In England, an immense impulse was now given to its study, which, occupied as it is with the observation of phenomena, produced most important effects on the age. Cousin says[4] that Hartley's Observations on Man is 'la première tentative pour rattacher l'étude de l'homme intellectuel à celle de l'homme physique.' Until the beginning of the eighteenth century there were no means in Scotland of studying medicine.[5]

In 1811, Sir James Mackintosh, who had received a medical education, writes, 'Those who frequently contemplate the entire subjection of every part of the animal frame to the laws of chemistry, and the numerous processes through which all the organs of the human body must pass after death, acquire habits of imagination unfavourable to a hope of an independent existence of the thinking principle, or of a renewed existence of the whole man. These facts have a more certain influence than any reasonings on the habitual convictions of men. Hence arises in part the prevalent incredulity of physicians. The doctrine of the resurrection could scarcely have arisen among a people who burned their dead.'[6] In 1784, Gibbon writes that Tissot assured him that, for gouty persons, the moisture of England and Holland is most pernicious ; the dry pure air of Switzerland most favourable to a gouty constitution ; that experience justifies the theory, and that 'there are fewer martyrs of that disorder in this than any other country in Europe.'[7] Coleridge[8] throws out a sweeping and arrogant reproach upon 'the humoural pathologists in

[1] Principles of Population, 8vo, 1840, vol. I. p. 221.
[2] Green's Vital Dynamics, 8vo, 1840, vol. I. pp. 79, 8a.   [3] Ibid. p. 87.
[4] Hist. de la Philosophie, 2nde série, tome iii. p. 25.
[5] See Bower's History of the University of Edinburgh, vol. II. pp. 128, 161.
[6] Memoirs of the Life of Sir James Mackintosh, edited by his Son, 8vo, 1835 vol. II. p. 118.
[7] Gibbon's Miscellaneous Works, 8vo, 1837, p. 353.
[8] Biographia Literaria, 8vo, 1847, vol. I. p. 100.

general.' Not one of the so-called specifics has been discovered deductively or even been justified *à priori*. Medicine is still theological. A modern writer, who is in possession of some of Locke's MSS. says, 'For medicine, his original profession, he had very little respect.'[1] 'Hiérophile fut le premier qui soupçonna l'existence du système lymphatique.'[2] The invention of microscopes in 1620 facilitated induction in medicine,[3] and by increasing materials, checked deductive flights. Fludd anticipated Toricelli in the barometer.[4] In 1626, Sanctorius first used the thermometer in medical observations.[5]

It is said[6] that, in 1635, Fournier discovered the lacteals. An eminent surgeon has shown statistically, that the danger of surgical operations is much greater than is commonly supposed.[7] After operations, there are fewer deaths in England than in any other country, and *most* in the United States of America. Persons who return from India alive are generally very healthy.[8] In West Indies, venereal disease very rare.[9] Among adults, there are more cases of diseased heart than of phthisis, and the prevalence of consumption in England has been enormously exaggerated.[10] On consumption in India, see Journal of Statistical Society, vol. iii. p. 133. It is *not* true that phthisis *pulmonalis* is more fatal or more frequent in cold countries than in hot ones.[11] 'Typhus fevers cannot be caused by animal or vegetable decomposition.'[12] The great measure of the spread of disease is not any particular condition of the air, but the dew point.[13] Influence of age on disease, vi. 162. On the influence of employments on health, see an interesting essay in Journal of Statistical Society, vol. vi. pp. 283-304 ; 'the tendency to consumption varies inversely as the amount of exertion.'[14] There is no connection between sickness and mortality. Bakers are less subject to sickness than butchers, but seem not to live longer. See Statist. Soc., viii. 329, where it is also said that, in Scotland, the mortality is greater than in Eng-

---

[1] Foster's Original Letters of Locke, Sidney, &c., 8vo, 1830. p. cxlii.

[2] Sprengel, Histoire de la Médecine, tome iv. p. 44.   [3] Ibid. pp. 337, 339.

[4] Ibid. tome v. p. 9.   [5] Ibid. p. 390.   [6] Ibid. tome iv. p. 205.

[7] See Essay, by B. Phillips, in Journal of Statistical Society, vol. i. pp. 104, 105.

[8] Journal of Statistical Society, vol. i. p. 282.   [9] Ibid. p. 142.

[10] See Dr. Clendinning's Paper, in Journal of Statistical Society, vol. i. pp. 143, 145, 146, 147.

[11] Journal of Statistical Society, vol. ii. p. 37.   [12] Ibid. vol. iii. p. 234.

[13] Ibid. vol. vi. pp. 135, 136.   [14] Ibid. vol. vii. p. 239, see also p. 239.

land, the illness less. As men get older, they are more liable to
illness, but can *bear* it better.[1] All diseases, even lockjaw, which
is apparently the capricious result of accident, are guided by law.[2]
So far is scrofula from being a particularly English disease, that
no country is so free from it, and scrofula is generally 'much less
prevalent than it was in the seventeenth and eighteenth centuries.'[3] Blindness has greatly diminished since the decrease of
small-pox; but even now half the cases of blindness are caused
by it.[4] Owing to the police, hydrophobia is becoming extinct in
London.[5] Bishop Heber[6] says that in Ceylon, 'Most of the
workmen employed by government here are Caffres. The first
generation appears to stand the climate well, but their children
are very liable to pulmonary affections.' Turner says that in
Tibet, dropsy is the most obstinate and fatal disease to be met
with in the country.[7] At p. 415, he says, 'Gravelish complaints
and the stone in the bladder are, I believe, diseases unknown
here.' In the state of Salvador in Central America, goître is very
common.[8] On disease caused by wind, see Journal of Geographical Society, vol. xi. p. 63; and on relation between disease
and state of atmosphere, see 3rd Report of British Association,
Transactions of Sections, p. 461. Contagion never spreads more
than a few feet.[9]

CONNECTION BETWEEN MEDICINE AND HISTORY.

ABOUT one-fifth of the deaths result from specific causes—i.e.
from morbid poisons, such as small-pox, typhus fever, &c.[10] Note
this when I say all great plagues from the East. See No. xviii.

    Chorea or St Vitus's Dance was not known till about the four-
teenth century. It is more common in girls than in boys; and
'is rarely seen after twenty.'[11]

[1] Journal of Statistical Society, vol. viii. p. 341.
[2] See Phillips on Scrofula, in Statistical Society, vol. ix. p. 154.
[3] Journal of Statist. Soc. vol. ix. pp. 153, 155, 157, Essay by Benjamin Phillips.
[4] Statistical Soc. vol. xiv. p. 64.   [5] Ibid. vol. xv. p. 90
[6] Journey through India, vol. iii. p. 182.
[7] Turner's Embassy to Tibet, 4to, 1830, p. 412.
[8] Stephens's Central America, vol. ii. p. 58.
[9] See Fourth Report of Brit. Association, pp. 76, 99.
[10] Williams's Elementary Principles of Medicine in Encyclop. of the Medical
Sciences, p. 527.   [11] Ibid. p. 543.

Pyrosis, or water-brash, is common in Scotland, Ireland, and Sweden, and 'seldom occurs except in those who live on a low and insufficient diet.'[1] But see Cullen's Works, 8vo, 1827, vol. ii. p. 412.

'The largest class of ascites arises from diseases in the kidney.'[2]

Dr. Williams[3] says that insanity 'has, though perhaps erroneously, been supposed to be extended in proportion to the degree of civilization.' In 1839, the deaths from it in England and Wales were 424—i.e. 226 males and 198 females. According to Esquirol, insanity attacks males and females in the same proportion. In about ten per cent of the insane 'there is not a trace of disease, either of the brain or its membranes,' so that 'insanity is merely a functional disease of the brain.'[4] Above the age of fifty, it is rarely cured.[5] It used to be often treated by bleeding; but this is now allowed to be bad, because it rather excites than calms.[6] Music produces an injurious effect.[7]

The sedentary habits of civilization must diminish tetanus, which is common in armies on active service, being often the result of wounds. In civil life, it is chiefly caused by straining or contusions. It is most common in adults, and among men to women as about five to one. Larrey says that 'this disease, if left to nature, is quickly fatal.'[8]

Pyrosis is caused by insufficient diet; and therefore has, I suppose, diminished. It is still common in Scotland, in Ireland, and according to Linnæus, in Sweden.[9]

Scurvy, which in the middle ages was a fatal epidemic, has now given way in consequence of the advance of agriculture enabling the farmers to kill the best meat in winter; and, in consequence, also of a more general use of vegetables.[10]

A form of worm, called *Tricocephalus dispar*, is 'common in Germany, much less so in France, and still more rarely in this country.' See Williams's Elementary Principles of Medicine[11]

---

[1] William's Elementary Principles of Medicine in Encyclop. of the Medical Sciences, pp. 552, 553. But see Cullen's Works, 8vo, 1827, vol. ii. p. 412.
[2] Williams's Elementary Principles of Medicine in Encyclop. of the Medical Sciences, p. 608.
[3] Ibid. p. 570.   [4] Ibid. p. 531.   [5] Ibid. p. 535.
[6] Ibid. p. 535.   [7] Ibid. p. 536.   [8] Ibid. pp. 544, 545.
[9] Ibid. pp. 552, 553.   [10] Ibid. p. 562.   [11] Ibid. p. 558.

He adds [1] that worms are caused by an excess of vegetable food, 'that diet favouring the secretion of mucus which is the nidus of these animals.' The Hindoos live on rice, and nine out of ten of them suffer from worms. At p. 560, Dr. Williams says, 'Three fourths of the inhabitants of Cairo are said to be infected with tænia.'

I suppose diseases of the liver have increased. Dr. Williams says [2] the liver 'receives nerves from the eighth pair, thus putting it under the influence of the passions. . . . Jaundice is most common in the heyday of the passions, or between twenty and forty. Women are supposed to be more liable to this affection than men.'

Dr. Williams says [3] : 'The kidneys are the organs by which ten-elevenths of all the azote introduced into the system as aliment is discharged.' He adds,[4] 'The ultimate issue of every case of diabetes is probably fatal.' He says [5] that the more animals are fed with animal diet, the more loaded their urine is with lithic acid. A lady cured herself of gravel by eating more than a pound of sugar every day for six weeks. Therefore French wines and port are injurious.

Excitability by causing amenorrhœa produces insanity.[6]

Apoplexy, I suppose, has increased, being chiefly caused by excessive use of fermented liquors. In England and Wales in 1839 the deaths from apoplexy were one in thirty-three.[7] It is also the result of moral causes, as is known from the increase in France. It is likewise caused by sudden changes in the weather, which exhaust the nervous power. This is probably 'the cause of apoplexy prevailing to such an extent at Edinburgh and Rome as to be almost endemic.' [8]

Splenitis or 'inflammation of the substance of the spleen' is 'extremely rare' in England, and is only found for the most part in 'paludal counties,' as Cambridge or Essex. Common in the East Indies, and particularly in Bengal.[9]

Inflammation of the lungs is caused by many morbid poisons. It is probably owing to the paludal poison 'that although, as a

[1] Williams's Elementary Principles of Medicine in Encyclop. of the Medical Sciences, p. 559.

[2] Ibid. p. 566.   [?] Ibid. p. 576.   [?] Ibid. p. 580
[3] Ibid. p. 583.   [?] Ibid. p. 587.   [7] Ibid. p. 589.
[?] Ibid. p. 590.   [9] Ibid. p. 650.

general principle, diseases of the chest diminish in frequency as we approach the equator, yet that in the West Indies the inflammatory pulmonary affections greatly exceed those of this country.'[1]

An animal, when domesticated, becomes more liable to tubercular disease than he was when wild. Hence, we find that the inhabitants of towns, though they have more of the comforts of life than agriculturists, are much more subject to phthisis.[2] 'The returns of the army have shown to the astonishment of everybody that phthisis is more frequent in the West Indies than even in this country.' Dr. Williams adds :[3] 'Race has an influence in the production of phthisis. In this country, the tendency of the creole and negro to phthisis is notorious.' Religious melancholy, as seen in nunneries, will cause first suppression of menses and then phthisis.[4]

Typhus fever is limited to the space between 60° and 40° N. latitude. There is no evidence that it is caused by the putrefaction of dead animal matter, though such putrefaction by *depressing* will predispose to the disease.[5] It prevails equally in all seasons ; but, being unknown in the tropics, it seems that the poison must be volatilised or *destroyed* at a high temperature ;[6] but[7] Dr. Williams says it is more frequent in summer and autumn than in winter and spring. 'In a large ventilated ward, a space of three feet around the patient's person so dilutes the poison that the disease rarely spreads.'[8] 'The most remarkable symptom of the typhoid poison is the extreme degree of prostration, both of the physical and intellectual powers of life which it produces.'[9] In France, the deaths are to the attacks from 1 in 3 to 1 in 4½. 'Women are supposed to have more chance of recovery than males.'[10] Bleeding is most pernicious ; for, when an animal is poisoned, the result is more rapid and fatal in proportion as the animal has been bled.[11]

The scarlet fever, measles, and smallpox are 'supposed to have first originated in Arabia, about the middle of the sixth century.'[12]

Scarlet fever is most fatal among the poor, and is 'twice as fatal

[1] Williams's Elementary Principles of Medicine in Encyclop. of the Medical Sciences, p. 663.

[2] Ibid. p. 689.   [3] Ibid. p. 691.   [4] See a curious case at p. 691.
[5] Ibid. p. 721.   [6] Ibid. p. 722.   [7] Ibid. p. 723.
[8] Ibid. p. 723.   [9] Ibid. p. 725.   [10] Ibid. p. 726.
[11] Ibid. p. 727.   [12] Ibid. p. 728.

in towns as in the country.' 'Both sexes are attacked in nearly equal proportions.' The infecting distance is 'much greater than in typhus.'[1] It is contagious, and communicated by fomites; and the susceptibility to the disease is nearly always exhausted by a first attack.[3] Formerly bleeding was always used; but it is very in-injurious.[3] In measles 'the influence of season is exceedingly trifling.'[4] Measles, as well as scarlet fever and typhus, are propagated by fomites,[5] more fatal in towns than in the country.[6] The smallpox is infectious for many yards round the person; and, as we know from inoculation, it is contagious by fomites.[7] The most amazing law relating to it is that the introduction of the variolous poison by the cutaneous tissue should produce an infinitely milder disease than when the same poison is absorbed by a mucous tissue. Perhaps one person in a hundred is attacked a second time with the smallpox.[8]

Dr. Williams says:[9] 'If, however, the doctrine of a spontaneous generation of a poison by the human body be tenable, it is more probably true of erysipelas than of any other disease;' for it is often produced by the bite of a leech, or even the slightest puncture. It is infectious, contagious, and spreads by fomites.[10]

Hooping-cough is not traced earlier than A.D. 1510; now it has spread all over the world. It is very rare for a person to have it a second time. It is certainly infectious, and communicated by fomites; and probably it is contagious.[11] Out of ten fatal cases, nine belong to the poorer classes.[12]

Syphilis is entirely propagated by human contagion, and is peculiar to man; 'for, in no instance, has matter taken from the primary sore produced any similiar affection in animals.'[13] It is milder in tropical than in northern climates; its matter will not produce gonorrhœa; nor will the matter of gonorrhœa produce syphilis.[14] No prior attack, however severe, will exempt the constitution from a second.[15] There was, for a long time, no satisfactory treatment for syphilitic affections of the bones and the periosteum; but the iodide of potassium is a specific remedy.[16]

[1] Williams's Elementary Principles of Medicine in Encyclop. of the Medical Sciences, p. 728.

[3] Ibid. p. 728.	[5] Ibid. p. 732.	[4] Ibid. p. 733.
[5] Ibid. p. 734.	[6] Ibid. p. 736.	[7] Ibid. p. 738.
[6] Ibid. p. 738.	[9] Ibid. p. 745.	[10] Ibid. p. 746.
[11] Ibid. p. 749.	[12] Ibid. p. 751.	[13] Ibid. p. 755.
[14] Ibid. p. 756.	[15] Ibid. p. 756.	[16] Ibid. p. 767.

Gonorrhœa, like syphilis, seems to be peculiar to man.   It is uncommon in hot countries ; but this is probably the result of cleanliness.   It is of course contagious, and we know *can* be transmitted by fomites   Susceptibility to its poison is probably never exhausted ; but each succeeding attack is less violent, 'till, in some cases, the danger of infection almost vanishes.'[1]   'The matter of gleet is supposed to be non-contagious ; but this doctrine is dangerous, and is probably the cause of frequent infections immediately after marriage.'[2]   Copaiba was first used in 1702 ; latterly cubebs has been employed, but with still inferior success ;[3] and in women is 'entirely inert,' unless the urethra is affected.[4]

A disease, I suppose, peculiar to civilization, is cellulitis venenata, which 'occasionally affects the anatomist from punctures received in dissection,' and also butchers, farriers, and cooks, when the animals are in a morbid state.[5]

The paludal poison, which is very destructive, must have diminished.[6]   Dr. Williams adds,[7] 'It appears that *race* greatly affects the liability to this class of disease ;' and, while in the West Indies the white troops lose $4\frac{1}{2}$ in 1,000, the black troops lose 37.

Dr. Clarke observes that negroes and Malays are more subject than other classes to tubercular phthisis ; but this, says Prichard, does not show an essential difference of race, but merely arises from that change in the organic structure caused by successive generations living in a warm climate.[8]

In the Indian Archipelago the inhabitants are little liable to inflammable disease.   Gout and scrofula are unknown ; stone and dropsy rare ; but in Java there is 'a disease analogous to the venereal,' and the same as the yaws.[9]

In the South Sea Islands, the smallpox, measles, hooping-cough, &c., are 'unknown ;' but 'inflammatory tumours are prevalent,' and a peculiar disease of the spine is common.[10]

In Borneo, ague, diarrhœa, ophthalmia, and skin diseases are common ; and 'madness is said to be not uncommon' among the

---

[1] Williams's Elementary Principles of Medicine in Encyclop. of the Medical Sciences, p. 770.

[2] Ibid. p. 772.   [3] Ibid. p. 773.   [4] Ibid. p. 775.

[5] Ibid. p. 788.   [6] Ibid. p. 793.   [7] Ibid. p. 798.

[8] Prichard's Physical History of Mankind, vol. i. p. 158.

[9] Crawford's History of the Indian Archipelago, Edinb. 8vo. 1820, vol. i. pp. 33, 34.

[10] Ellis, Polynesian Researches, 1831, iii. 38, 39.

Dyaks.[1] Low[2] says of the Dyaks : 'European medicines have great effect upon their constitutions ; so that in all cases smaller doses than usual must be prescribed for them.'

Tetanus is very common in the Friendly Islands.[3] The inhabitants of the Friendly Islands 'are very subject to induration of the liver and certain forms of scrofula.'[4]

In 1700, Locke, who had studied medicine, writes: 'A diabetes is a disease so little frequent that you will not think it strange if I should ask whether you in your great practice ever met with it.'[5]

Apoplexy is caused by failure in the cerebral powers.[6]

On temperament, read the Introduction to Herbert Mayo's Philosophy of Living.

'Although here, as well as abroad, they keep to the system of leaving the public in the dark respecting the pestilence, things come to light from time to time, from which the danger seems to grow more and more decided. The plague does not simply slay its victims and depopulate countries ; it eats away the moral energies as well, and often quite destroys them ; thus, as I have shown in my last public lecture before the Academy, the sudden and complete degeneracy of the Roman world, from the time of Marcus Antoninus onward, may be referred to the oriental plague which then entered Europe for the first time ; just as six hundred years earlier the plague, which was, strictly speaking, a yellow fever, coincides too exactly with the termination of the ideal period of antiquity not to be regarded as a cause of it. In such epidemics the best individuals always die, and the rest degenerate morally. Times of pestilence are always those in which the animal and the devilish in human nature assume prominence. Neither need we be superstitious, or even pious, to regard great pestilences as something more than a conflict of the physical with the human history of the earth. I fear my conviction that it indicates the victory of the negative and destructive of the two contending principles, would be thought terribly Manichæan and impious.'[7]

---

[1] See Low's Sarawak, 8vo, 1848, pp. 304, 305. [2] Ibid. p. 309.
[3] See Mariner's Tonga Islands, 2nd edit. 8vo, 1818, L. 189 ; IL 242, 243.
[4] Ibid. vol. L. p. 434. Also, to diseased testicles, &c. ; see vol. II. pp. 246-260.
[5] Foster's Letters of Locke, Sidney, &c., 8vo, 1830, p. 71.
[6] See Mayo's Philosophy of Living, 1838, pp. 147-151.
[7] Letter from Niebuhr, dated Berlin, 1816, in the Life and Letters of Niebuhr, London, 8vo, 1852, vol. II. p. 97.

Leigh Hunt, who was a good deal in Italy, says : [1] 'The consumption, by the way, of olive oil is immense. It is probably no mean exasperator of Italian bile. The author of an Italian Art of Health approves a moderate use of it both in diet and medicine, but says that, as soon as it is cooked, fried, or otherwise abused, it inflames the blood, disturbs the humours, irritates the fibres, and produces other effects very superfluous in a stimulating climate.'

In 1796, Professor Cleghorn writes from Cairo that the English consul at Alexandria has advised him, as a protection against plague, 'to anoint my body with oil as a certain antidote,' &c. [2]

Cullen [3] says : 'A permanent grief and anxiety also, which so often excites hypochondriac disorders, will frequently cure hysterics. Thus, in the year 1745, whilst the people laboured under constant anxiety about the rebellion, nervous patients were observed in Scotland to remain remarkably free from their usual complaints.'

Between 1670 and 1673, Sir W. Temple [4] says of Holland : 'The diseases of the climate seem to be chiefly the gout and the scurvy.'

Sir W. Temple [5] notices the great increase of gout in England within twenty years, which he ascribes to the larger consumption of wine.

Sir W. Temple [6] says : 'The stone is said to have first come among us after hops were introduced here.'

Sir T. Browne [7] says of rickets : 'The disease is scarce so old as to afford good observation.'

For some absurd notions respecting medicine in the middle ages, see Sprengel, Histoire de la Médecine, tome ii. p. 401.

No specific has been deductively proved. Indeed mercury was first employed in syphilis on account of its supposed similarity to leprosy, and its use was long confined to charlatans. [8]

Sprengel [9] says that rickets are first mentioned *not* by Glisson, but by Reusner, in 1582.

[1] Autobiography, 8vo, 1850, vol. iii. p. 145.
[2] Southey's Life of Dr. Bell, 8vo, 1844. vol. i. p. 520.
[3] Works, Edinb. 8vo, 1827, vol. ii. 505.
[4] Works, 8vo, 1814. vol. i. p. 149.   [5] Ibid. vol. iii. p. 248, 272.
[6] Ibid. vol. iii. p. 303.   [7] Works by Wilkin, vol. iv. p. 44.
[8] See Sprengel, Histoire de la Médecine, tome iii. p. 72.
[9] Ibid. tome v. pp. 598, 599.

Huc[1] says : ' The Chinese report marvels of the jin-seng, and, no doubt, it is for Chinese organisation a tonic of very great effect for old and weak persons ; but its nature is too heating, the Chinese physicians admit, for the European temperament, already in their opinion too hot.'[2]

In the fourteenth and fifteenth centuries, in France, bleeding was universal.[3]

The body of Charles IX. of France was opened.[4]

TENDENCY, ETC., OF THE PURITANS.

THE bigotry of Puritanism has left a living sting which still corrodes the very heart of the nation. See some good remarks on the intolerant spirit of the English character in Mill's Principles of Political Economy, 8vo, 1849, vol. ii. p. 506.

Perhaps it is to the spirit of Puritanism that we owe the little influence of women and the consequent inferiority of their education. Mr. Mill truly says[5] that, in the fifteenth and sixteenth centuries women were relatively more intellectual than they are at present. This is the more to be regretted, for the civilizing effect of women is, perhaps, more felt when the division of labour is fully established. Women reap the benefit of that division without incurring its disadvantages.[6] Just before the accession of Elizabeth, Knox and his friend Goodman wrote against women.[7] This perhaps rose from the accident of the throne being occupied by Mary.

The Puritans held pleasure to be sinful ; and this belief remained long after their political overthrow. At the Restoration the aristocracy were once more predominant, and their tastes mingled with the old taste of the Puritans. The result is still seen in our national character, which presents a combination of love of expense and indifference to pleasure. There, perhaps, never was a country in which was to be found so much splendour and so little gaiety as in England. This, which makes us so

[1] Travels in Tartary, vol. i. p. 106.
[2] See also Bell's Travels in Asia, Edinb. 8vo, 1788, vol. ii. pp. 142, 143.
[3] See Monteil, Histoire des Français des Divers États, tome ii. pp. 78, 223 ; tome iv. p. 123.
[4] See Capefigue, Histoire de la Réforme et la Ligue, tome iii. p. 340.
[5] Political Economy, 1849, vol. ii. p. 532.   [6] Ibid. vol. i. p. 157.
[7] Lingard, vol. v. p. 356.

unamiable as a people, tends in a most extraordinary degree to increase our wealth. The indifference to pleasure makes accumulation more easy, while the love of display renders it more necessary. This has been admirably touched on by Mr. Mill,[1] who, however, seems to consider our love of display unfavourable to the increase of wealth. But this I greatly doubt. There can be no question that the unproductive expenditure of the upper classes is unfavourable to accumulation ; but when united as in England with an indifference to pleasure, it gives an object and a stimulus to labour, which, I believe, no other combination could possibly supply. The remarks which Dr. Shebbeare made a century ago are perfectly applicable at the present day. ' You see more people on the roads of England than in all Europe, and more uneasy countenances than are to be found in the world besides.'[2] And [3] ' money is all that is zealously pursued in this nation.' Again,[4] 'The idea of luxury in England is ill understood ; it does not deserve that name ; it is profusion only, another species of self.'

About and after 1570 the Catholics pretended to be Puritans, in order to weaken the Church by encouraging disputes.[5] Mr. Hallam [6] says, ' The first instance of actual punishment inflicted on Protestant Dissenters was in June 1567.' For this he quotes Strype's Parker, 242 ; Grindall, 114. Mr. Hallam says,[7] ' It was a kind of maxim among the Puritans that Scripture was so much the exclusive rule of human action, that whatever in matters, at least concerning religion, could not be found to have its authority was unlawful.' The monition doctrine, adds Hallam, is refuted in 'the whole second book' of Hooker. In a long list of official 'instructions,' very early in the reign of Mary, the commissioners are charged by the queen to punish all persons who live in adultery.[8] In 1561, Knox complains, in a letter to Cecil, that 'whoremongers' and 'adulterers' are not punished.[9]

Leigh Hunt says,[10] ' When I came to England, after a residence of four years abroad, I was grieved at the succession of fair

[1] Political Economy, 1849. vo . i. p. 213.
[2] Angeloni's Letters on the English Nation, 8vo, 1755. vol. i. pp. 37, 38.
[3] Ibid. p. 45.   [4] Ibid. p. 90.
[5] See the Note in Hallam's Constitutional History, 8vo, 1842, vol. i. p. 119.
[6] Ibid. p. 178.   [7] Ibid. p. 212.
[8] Haynes's State Papers, p. 198.   [9] Ibid. p. 372.   See art. Jansenism.
[10] Autobiography. 8vo, 1850, vol. iii. p. 179.

sulky faces which I met in the streets of London. They all appeared to come out of unhappy homes. In truth, our virtues or our climate, or whatever it is, sit so uneasily upon us, that it is surely worth while for our philosophy to inquire whether, in some points of moral or political economy, we are not a little mistaken. Gypsies will hardly allow us to lay it to the climate.'

Mr. Morell [1] has very well stated the 'fundamental distinction between the principles of legislation and those of private morality.' The Puritans, even in the reign of Elizabeth, were considered by the Catholics as the most zealous among their English persecutors.[2]

Soames says that they did not bear the name of Puritan until 1564.[3] Soames[4] mentions two instances of Catholics pretending to be Puritans, viz., Heath, brother of the ex-Archbishop of York, and a Dominican called Faithful Cummin. The Bishop of St. Asaph says, 'The declaration of open war between the High and Low Church parties may be considered to have taken place in 1566, when the proclamation of the queen gave, as it were, the sanction of law to the advertisements which the bishops had previously put forth.'[5] The good effects caused by increasing luxury are well stated in Esprit des Lois, livre vii. chap. 4, Œuvres de Montesquieu, Paris, 1835, p. 239. He supposes that proud nations are always idle : ' La paresse est l'effet de l'orgueil ; le travail est une suite de la vanité.'[5]

In 1628 it was proposed by Bayer and Schiller to establish a new astronomical nomenclature. The planets were to be called Adam, Moses, and the patriarchs. The twelve signs were to be the twelve apostles ; the constellations were to be called after places mentioned in the Bible.[7]

The Puritans of the sixteenth century encouraged horse-racing, ' as a substitute for cards and dice.'[6] Perhaps we owe to this some of our fine breeds of horses.

[1] View of the Speculative Philosophy of Europe, 8vo, 1846, vol. I. pp. 360, 361.
[2] See an extract from Gerard's MS. in Mr. Tierney's note to Dodd's Church History, vol. III. p. 86.
[3] Elizabethan Religious History, p. 52.   [4] Ibid. pp. 78, 79.
[5] Short's History of the Church of England, 8vo, 1847. p. 267.
Esprit des Lois, xix. chap. ix. p. 339 ; and see livre xiv. chap. ix. p. 303.
Whewell's Philosophy of the Inductive Sciences, 8vo, 1847, vol. II. p. 515.
[6] Drake's Shakespeare and his Times, 1817, 4to, vol. I. p. 297 ; and COMMON PLACE BOOK, art. 423.

Perhaps the greatest and most beneficial work of Puritanism was the destruction of the remains of chivalry. The fire of the ancient chivalry had indeed begun to dim since the end of the thirteenth century, but its forms still lingered on, and were ready, should circumstances allow, to be imbued with their early energy. These forms, with the exception of the law of primogeniture, which, to the disgrace of an enlightened age, still defaces the statute-book, all perished in that great storm which overwhelmed the Crown, the law, and the altar. When Charles II. returned from exile, he could not restore feudality.

Did not blue coats for servants go out of use? COMMON PLACE BOOK, art. 917. This was the last remains of the dress of retainers.

It was usual to wear linen shirts with ornaments finely worked by the needle. In place of these ornaments the Puritans used to embroider the shirt with texts from the Bible.[1]

Ben Jonson's dedication to Sejanus, which is dated 1607, shows the bitterness of feeling between the Puritans and the stage.[2] It appears they particularly objected to starch in their linen.[3] In 1610 the Puritans lived in great numbers at Black-friars, where they were the chief dealers in feathers, &c.[4] Banbury was particularly famous for them ; and in Bartholomew Fair, acted in 1614, a Puritan is called ' a Banbury-man.'[5] The Puritans would not say *mass* even when the profane word was mitigated by being compounded. Thus they called Christmas *Christide*.[6] Ben Jonson was never weary of attacking the Puritans.[7] In Bartholo-mew Fair, acted in 1614, Jonson ridicules the long graces with which the Puritans used to preface their meals.[8] It would seem that they were very fond of pork.[9] In the Magnetick Lady, acted in 1632, Jonson ridicules the divisions into *doctrine* and *use* which

---

[1] See Gifford's note in Ben Jonson's Works, vol. II. p. 155 ; and see COMMON PLACE BOOK, art. 1078.

[2] Jonson's Works, 8vo. 1816, vol. III. pp. 161-165 ; and for other indications of the quarrel see vol. IV. pp. 81, 191, and the amusing but bitter attack in The Alchemist, vol. IV. pp. 91-100.

[3] Ibid. vol. iv. p. 96.   [4] Ibid. vol. iv. p. 20, and vol. ii. p. 466.

[6] Ibid. vol. iv. p. 360.   [5] Ibid. vol. iii. p. 178, and vol. iv. p. 95.

[7] Ibid. vol. III. pp. 67, 369 ; vol. iv. pp. 383-385, 399, 436-438 ; and indeed the whole of Bartholomew Fair. See also vol. vi. pp. 259-262, 342 ; vol. vii. p. 410 ; viii. pp. 163, 192 ; and vol. ix. p. 153.

[8] Ibid. vol. iv. pp. 383, 384.   [9] Ibid. vol. iv. pp. 400, 438, 462.

the Puritans used to make in their sermons.[1] In the same play he has a most ungenerous allusion to the punishment inflicted on Prynne.[2] They would not say *godfathers* or *godmothers*, but witnesses.[3]

At the very beginning of the seventeenth century their hostility to the theatre is mentioned.[4]

Tocqueville[5] says, 'l'Angleterre, le pays de l'Europe où l'on a vu pendant un siècle la liberté la plus grande de penser, et les préjugés les plus invincibles.'

Early in the seventeenth century numbers of the Puritans fled to Amsterdam. This is alluded to in Middleton's Works, i. 205; iii. 255; iv. 45, 437.

The Puritans hated organs.[6] They encouraged witchcraft, I think.

'There were only three Protestant preachers in the University of Oxford in the year 1563, and they were all Puritans.'[7] In Cambridge they were as strong, if not stronger. The University had a right to license twelve ministers every year to preach anywhere in England without episcopal licence. This privilege was exercised in favour of the Puritans, and Parker in vain attempted to have it rescinded.[8] Neal says[9] that, in 1566, 'in Trinity College all except three declared against the surplice, and many in other colleges were ready to follow their example.' He adds[10] that, in 1571, 'the University of Cambridge was a nest of Puritans.'

But the Puritans at once began to advocate principles which struck at the very root of all legislative authority. Their own historian tells us that, even in 1559, they 'insisted that those things which Christ had left indifferent ought not to be made necessary by any human laws.'[11] They forgot that, when a Government pays a sect, it has a right to stipulate in return what that sect shall do. Elizabeth bore herself high. The very year after her accession, Sandys, Bishop of Worcester, complained

---

[1] Jonson's Works, vol. vi. p. 55.   [2] Ibid. vol. vi. p. 73.
[3] Ibid. vol. vi. p. 93. and vol. viii. p. 180.
[4] See Middleton's Works, 8vo, 1840, vol. i. p. 206.
[5] Démocratie en Amérique, vol. ii. p. 111.
[6] COMMON PLACE BOOK, art. 2213.
[7] Neal's History of the Puritans, edit. Toulmin, 1822, vol. i. p. 145.
[8] Ibid. vol. i. pp. 178, 179.
[9] Ibid. vol. i. p. 180.   [10] Ibid. vol. i. p. 320.   [11] Ibid. vol. i. p. 126.

that she had a crucifix in her chapel. To this complaint the queen replied by a threat of deprivation.[1]

In 1560 the Puritans published at Geneva a translation of the Bible with marginal notes. One of these notes laid down that disobedience to kings was allowable, and another note, on 2 Chron. xv. 16, censured Asa for not having executed his mother as well as deposed her.[2] In 1562 the Puritans were so strong in Convocation that their proposals to simplify the Church of England were only rejected by a majority of one.[3] This decision Neal calls 'very unkind,' but if the queen had been forced to change her policy, the Catholics, then very powerful, would certainly have flown to arms, and a civil and religious war would have ensued.

It is remarkable that the chief leaders of the great separation of 1566 were 'all beneficed within the diocese of London.'[4]

In 1556 they 'excepted to the use of godfathers and godmothers to the exclusion of parents from being sureties for the education of their own children.'[5] And in 1585 they petitioned Whitgift that 'in baptism the godfathers may answer in their own names and not in the child's.'[6]

In 1571 the Puritans seem to have made their first great effort in Parliament.[7]

At the beginning of Elizabeth's reign, if not before her accession, Goodman, an English Puritan, wrote a work against the government of women; and it was with great difficulty that, in 1571, he was induced to recant his sentiments.[8] The rise of the Brownists was an important epoch. I think the Mar-Prelate Controversy did not begin till *after* 1588. It was apparently in 1591 that Parliament passed their most cruel Act against the Puritans.[9]

In 1592 appeared Hooker's work. His principle, that all who are born within the confines of an established church and baptised into it are bound to submit to its laws, is, as Neal says,[10] inconsistent with the principles of the Reformation. This was a slavish dogma, and it seems to me that Hooker was to the Church what Hobbes was to the State.

Fenner, a contemporary, says that, in 1586, a third of the

1 Neal's History of the Puritans, edit. Toulmin, 1822, vol. I. p. 132.
2 Ibid. vol. I. p. 136.   3 Ibid. vol. I. p. 151.   4 Ibid. vol. I. p. 197.
3 Ibid. vol. I. p. 194.   6 Ibid. vol. I. p. 368.   7 Ibid. vol. I. p. 215.
4 Ibid. vol. I. p. 227.   9 Ibid. vol. I. p. 426.   10 Ibid. vol. I. p. 449.

clergy were suspended.[1] Neal says[2] that, in 1602, 'the noncon-
forming clergy were about fifteen hundred.' Hitherto the dispute
had been merely about ceremonies and discipline ; but, in 1595
and 1596, the spread of Arminianism in the Church gave rise to a
controversy about doctrine, for the Puritans had always remained
Calvinists.[3] At length the violence of the Puritans fairly roused
the civil power. Towards the end of the sixteenth century they
were prosecuted, not in the spiritual but in the temporal courts ;
and Anderson, one of the judges, declared in his charge that he
would hunt all the Puritans out of his circuit.[4]

The very tradespeople had Bibles lying on their shopboards,
which, if we may believe contemporary evidence, did not prevent
them from cheating their customers.[5] The lowest and most infamous of mankind did not escape the moral epidemic.

In the city the clergy were nearly all Puritans ; and, in 1566,
Archbishop Parker summoned before him 'all the London curates
and rectors.'[6] Collier has given some extracts from the attacks
made by John Knox on female sovereigns.[7]

The Puritans now began rapidly to organise themselves. In
1583 the Brownists first arose.[8] Such was the horror the Puritans
had of oaths that they thought swearing as bad as, if not worse than,
murder.[9] In 1570, Grindal, Archbishop of York, wrote to Cecil
that, at Cambridge, Cartwright, who was by far the most able
opponent of the bishop, was so popular that 'the youth of the
university, which is at this time very toward in learning, doth
frequent his lectures in great numbers.'[10] In 1572 the first
Presbyterian church in England arose at Wandsworth.[11] In 1583,
in six counties alone, there were suspended no less than 233
clergymen.[12] In 1578 or 1579 appeared Stubbs' Gaping Gulph, an
insulting Puritanical work.[13] Collier [14] says, 'It is somewhat re-

[1] Neal's History of the Puritans, edit. Toulmin, 1822, vol. i. p. 382.
[2] Ibid. vol. i. p. 463.   [3] Ibid. vol. i. pp. 451, 453.
[4] Ibid. vol. i. pp. 460, 461.
[5] See Maroccus Extaticus, 1595, p. 11, Percy Soc. vol. ii.
[6] Collier's Eccles. Hist. vol. vi. p. 429.
[7] Ibid. pp. 274-276 ; and see at p. 278 his insulting letter to Elizabeth.
[8] Ibid. vol. vii. p. 3.
[9] See a curious passage in Rich's Honestie of this Age, 1614, p. 56 ; Percy Soc.
vol. xi.   [10] Collier's Ecclesiast. Hist. vol. vi. 483.
[11] Neal's Puritans, vol. i. pp. 243, 244.   [12] Ibid. vol. i. p. 323.
[13] Collier, vol. vi. pp. 607, 608.   [14] Ibid. vol. vii. p. 74.

markable that the Puritans were most active in setting up their discipline and scattering their scandalous pamphlets, when the Spanish Armada was sweeping the seas, and menacing the kingdom with a conquest.[1] For this he cites Bancroft's Dangerous Positions. In 1592 a most illiberal Act was passed, forcing, under severe penalties, every one under sixteen to go to church. See the account given by Collier,[1] who allows that the Act was directed against the Puritans. Deering, a celebrated Puritanical clergyman, in a sermon before the queen, flatly told her that her motto might be ' As an untamed heifer.'[2]

The characteristic of Puritanical legislation was, I think, the confusion of public morals with private morals.[3]

Scarcely had the fears caused by the massacre of Bartholomew passed away, when the Puritans began to assume the aspect of an organised party. The French ambassador, whose voluminous despatches record every great movement in England, mentions them for the first time in October 1573, when he writes to his court that for several days the council had been considering their demands for toleration.[4] A month later he says that the Puritans were becoming as troublesome in England as the Huguenots in France, or the Gueux in Flanders.[5] In December 1573 he writes that 'plus de mille cinq cent personnes de qualité sont de ceste secte.'[6] He again mentions them at tome vi. p. 279. It is a very curious fact that 'Gorbuduc,' the first tragedy in the English language, was partly written by Thomas Norton, a Puritan.[7] In 1565, Harding, a Catholic, taunts Bishop Jewel : 'May we not remember the times when, at first beginning of your sects, you rejected all doctors' authorities as writings of men, and admitted only your lyvely Word of the Lord?'[8]

Early in the reign of Elizabeth the clergy were so diminished that the bishops did not dare to enforce the law for fear of denuding the Church. Sandys, afterwards Archbishop of York, objected to the episcopal garments ;[9] and so did Pilkington, Bishop of

---

[1] Collier, vol. vii. pp. 163-165.   [2] Neal, vol. l. p. 283, but he gives no date.
[3] See art. Metaphysics.
[4] Correspondance de Fénélon, Paris, 1840, tome v. p. 435.
[5] Ibid. p. 456 ; see also p. 462.   [6] Ibid. p. 470.
[7] See Collier's History of Dramatic Poetry, vol. ii. pp. 481, 482 ; and Warton's Hist. of English Poetry, 8vo, 1840, iii. 289.
[8] Strype's Annals, vol. l. part ii. p. 524.
[9] Sandys' Sermons, edit. Parker Society, p. xvii.

Durham.[1] In 1588 or 1589 the Puritans began to express a confident opinion that they could overthrow the episcopacy.[2] Maskell says,[3] 'The University of Oxford, during the first twenty or thirty years of the reign of Queen Elizabeth, had been remarkable for the strong leaning which it displayed towards the Puritan view of the religious questions of the day.' The Puritan onslaught began directly after the Armada.[4] The Puritans appear to have had a great contempt for the civil law.[5] The Bishop of Winchester declared that 'men might find fault, if they were disposed to quarrel, as well with the Scripture as with the Book of Common Prayer.'[6] In the same work, p. 69, the bishops are blamed for favouring the 'Papists.' This shows the intolerance of the Puritans. In 1586, Leycester seems to deny that he was a Puritan.[7] In 1590 the queen wrote a remarkable letter to James, warning him of the rising spirit of Puritanism.[8] As early as 1550 the Puritans began to sneer at the 'Christians of the Court.' See a very curious letter from Turner to Cecil, in Tytler's Edward VI. and Mary I. 333–337. Lord Fountainhall died in 1722; and his sitting-room in his house at Edinburgh contained a cabinet 'ornamented with a death's head at the top.'[9] Hallam[10] says the Puritans under Elizabeth formed a majority of the Protestants.

John Halle, an English surgeon, in the middle of the sixteenth century, has published a prayer which surgeons should use before undertaking a difficult operation.[11]

Mr. Lewis acutely says, 'It may generally be observed that the tendency of the Roman Catholics is to slide into superstition, that of the Protestants into fanaticism.'[12]

It was with difficulty that Elizabeth could hold in the bishops. They did everything to insult and irritate the Puritans. All this was a serious error.

[1] See Collier's Ecclesiastical History, 8vo, 1840, vol. vi. p. 396.
[2] See the evidence for this in Maskell's History of the Martin Mar-Prelate Controversy, 1849, pp. 51–54. [3] Ibid. p. 120.
[4] See Bishop Cooper's Admonition, 1589, p. 25, 8vo, 1847.
[5] See Hay and Work for Cooper, 1589, pp. 45, 46, 8vo, 1845.
[6] See An Epistle to the Terrible Priests, 1589, p. 42, 8vo, 1843.
[7] Leycester Correspondence, edit. Camden Soc. p. 311.
[8] See it in Letters of Elizabeth and James VI., Camden Soc., 1849, p. 63.
[9] Chambers's Traditions of Edinburgh, 8vo, 1847, p. 62.
[10] Constitutional History, vol. I. p. 186, note.
[11] Historiall Expostulation, 1565, p. 49; and see p. 47, Percy Soc. vol. xi.
[12] Lewis on Irish Disturbances, 8vo, 1836, p. 401.

It has been often said, that by persecuting a sect you increase its power and its numbers ; and the history of Christianity in the first three centuries is triumphantly appealed to as an instance. But nothing can be more shallow than such an allegation. If we did not know the clumsy eagerness with which nearly all ecclesiastical writers seize every circumstance that can be supposed to exalt the merit of their own church and blacken the reputation of their adversaries, we should be at a loss to understand how it is that the researches of Pearson, Dodwell, and Lardner have not more generally diffused a knowledge of the fact that the persecutions of the early church were slight and insignificant. The truth is, if they had been so severe as some would have us believe, it would have been hardly possible for Christianity to have survived the shock. There can be no doubt that a resolute and powerful Government, by a course of consistent unflinching severity, can utterly destroy any sect which forms only a small part of its subjects ; and if Augustus had possessed the spirit of Galenus (?) and Maximian (?), Christianity would in all probability be but a relic of history. London might now be studded with the gilded minarets of mosques from which the faithful would be summoned to their daily prayers, and British subjects might be at this moment bowing the knee before the shrines of a pagan temple. But, happily for Christianity and happily for the best interests of man, the spirit of persecution is rarely aroused until the sufferers are too numerous to be entirely destroyed. The conduct of the pagan emperors in the third century was an exact counterpart of the conduct of the Christian bishops in the sixteenth century. The bishops neglected the Puritans until the Puritans grew so strong that they did not dare to drive them to desperation. They would not pass by their conduct with impunity ; they dared not punish it capitally. They therefore pursued a middle course, which has always irresistible charms for weak-minded men. They irritated, but, with few exceptions, they did not strike. The treatment to which the Puritans were subject was oftener insulting than injurious. In 1573 one of them was brought before the Commission. His name was White. The opportunity of a brutal joke was too tempting to be lost. The chief justice asked, ' Who is this ?' 'White, an't please your honour,' answered the prisoner. ' White as black as the devil,' was the reply.[1] In 1585 another unfortunate Puritan

[1] Neal's Hist. of the Puritans, L 256.

was brought up before Aylmer, Bishop of London, who said to him, 'Thou art a very ass; thou art mad. Thou courageous! Nay, thou art impudent. By my troth, I think he is mad; he careth for nobody.' 'Though I fear not you, I fear the Lord,' was the sturdy reply. 'He hath an arrogant spirit; he can scarce construe Cato, I think,' rejoined the amiable successor of the apostles.[1]

The truth is, the bishops acted rather from irritability at the opposition than from conscientious motives. In their hearts they cared little about those points for which they professed such reverence. Even Sandys, Archbishop of Canterbury, who was an active persecutor of the Puritans, and did not die till 1588, says that many of the rites and ceremonies of the Church of England should be reformed; and, even of those which he approves, he does not dare to say that they are necessary.[2]

The bishops drove the Puritans from the Church, but they left them in the country. They sent them forth beggars, but still they left them at liberty. The consequences might have been easily foreseen. The discarded clergy were received into the houses of their lay patrons, who employed them as chaplains to their households and tutors to their children.[3] With minds burning with hatred against episcopacy, and not particularly in love with a Government which protected it, they availed themselves of their position to instil into their pupils their own sentiments.

We cannot wonder that in this they succeeded. The natural docility of children renders them, for the most part, ready to believe all that they are told; and to youth, just bursting into manhood and ignorant of the wiles of the world, there is something singularly captivating in the idea that they are espousing the weaker side. The result was that, by the end of the sixteenth century, there arose a new generation, who, because they hated bishops, easily learnt to hate kings who protected bishops. The almost omniscient sagacity of Elizabeth enabled her to discern the signs of the coming storm, and to prepare against it.

But the moment James mounted on the throne all was changed. The early Puritans were men of the most contracted and ascetic ideas. The reasons that induced them to separate from the Church were of the most frivolous nature; and it was not until their union with the patriots towards the end of the sixteenth

[1] Neal's Hist. of the Puritans, vol. I. p. 352.   [2] Ibid. p. 400.
[3] Ibid. p. 306.

century had lent importance to their objects, that they acquired
either dignity or interest.   The first overt act by which the Puritans abandoned the Church was in 1566 ; [1] and their own historian
tells us that after this, and until Cartwright began to preach, the
dispute 'had hitherto been chiefly confined to the habits, to the
cross in baptism, and kneeling at the Lord's Supper.' [2]   Nothing
but a knowledge of the pettiness of theological disputes could
allow us to believe that such a schism could have arisen about
such insignificant trifles.   Elizabeth has been often censured for
not yielding on such unimportant points to the conscientious
scruples of honest men.   But it is singular that those who advance
the argument do not see that it cuts both ways.   It is true that,
the more trivial the points at issue, the more absurd it was in the
Puritans to insist on their being given up.   Since, then, one party
must yield, surely it was most proper that that deference should be
paid to the majority and to the executive Government.

After the Armada the Brownists rapidly increased.   The
danger, as it diminished from without, increased from within.   In
1593 Penry drew up a most offensive address to Elizabeth. [3]   This,
I think, is the first instance in which the Puritans insulted the
queen.   Another of them, Darrowe, told Whitgift to his face that
he 'was a monster, a persecutor, a compound of he knew not
what, neither ecclesiastical nor civil, like the second beast spoken
of in the Revelations.' [4]

It was not till 1595 that the dispute between the Puritans and
the Church launched into doctrines. [5]   This was the result of the
spread of Arminianism in the Church of England. [6]   Collier says [7]
that it was not till 1570 that the Puritans 'attacked the government
of the Church ;' before that time 'the habit of the clergy and the
sign of the cross were formerly the only things they stuck at.'

HISTORY OF WITCHCRAFT, ETC.

CAMDEN, speaking of Elizabeth's affection for Dudley, suggests that
it may have been caused by 'something in his birth, or planets
that ruled it.' [8]

[1] Neal's Hist. of the Puritans, vol. I. pp. 187, 191.
[2] Ibid. pp. 210, 211.   [3] Ibid. pp. 438, 439.
[4] Ibid. p. 435.   [5] Ibid. p. 451.
[6] Ibid. p. 453.   [7] Eccleslast. Hist. vol. vi. p. 481.
[8] Annals of Elizabeth, in Kennett. vol. ii. p. 383.   See also p. 549.

For Elizabeth's own superstitions, see MSS. Elizabeth, No. 9.

Camden[1] gravely relates that Beza, in consequence of the appearance of an extraordinary star, foretold the death of Charles IX.

Southey, who was perhaps better acquainted with what may be called occult literature than any writer of his time, says, 'The books of palmistry have been so worn by perusal that one in decent preservation is now among the rarities of literature.'[2]

Drake says[3] that James's Demonology 'rendered a profession of the belief in sorcery and witchcraft a matter of fashion, and even of interest.' Perhaps from this time the court was more superstitious than the people.

There were days on which it was lucky, and others on which it was unlucky, to buy or sell. These days were carefully noted in the almanacks, and distinguished by characteristic marks.[4] The price of these almanacks was 1d. apiece.[5]

Directly after the Restoration the Royal Society was established; in 1666, the French Academy; and in 1667 and 1675, the Observatories of Paris and Greenwich.[6]

The admirable play of The Devil is an Ass was brought on the stage in 1616. One of its main objects is to ridicule witchfinders;[7] and in Volpone, which was acted in 1605, he ridicules witchcraft.[8] In the notes to the Masque of Queens in 1609, Ben Jonson shows great reading among books on witchcraft,[9] though, as Gifford observes,[10] this no more shows that he believed in witchcraft than that he believed in the pagan deities.

The custom of consulting conjurors is ridiculed in an amusing scene in The Family of Love, which was acted in 1607.[11]

'The disposition of ascribing all our knowledge to experience appears in Newton and the Newtonians by other indications,' &c. &c.[12]

[1] Kennet, vol. II. p. 446.   [2] The Doctor, edit. Warter, 8vo, 1848, p. 528.
[3] Shakespeare and his Times, 1817, 4to, vol. I. p. 314.
[4] See Ben Jonson's Works, 8vo, 1816, vol. iv. p. 43; and Sordido at vol. ii. p. 7.
[5] See Gifford's note in Ben Jonson, vol. ii. p. 42.
[6] Whewell's Philosophy of the Inductive Sciences, 8vo, 1847, vol. ii. p. 270.
[7] See Ben Jonson's Works, 8vo, 1816, vol. v. pp. 8, 157; and in particular the clever scene at pp. 148-154.
[8] Ibid. vol. iii. p. 321; and for other instances in which he laughs at witchcraft, see vol. iv. p. 502.
[9] Ibid. vol. vii.   [10] P. 14.
[11] Middleton's Works, 8vo, 1840, vol. ii. pp. 137-142.
[12] Whewell's Philosophy of the Inductive Sciences, 8vo, 1847, vol. ii. p. 292.

It is idle to attribute the destruction of superstition to the Reformation. Protestants were as superstitious as Catholics.

.   .   .   .

But Protestantism is more favourable to civilization than Catholicism; the Protestant believes less than the Catholic; he has fewer saints, fewer martyrs, fewer miracles,—in other words, fewer ultimate facts.

On the want of harmony existing at present between science and theology, see some good remarks in Combe's Constitution of Man, pp. 13-16. It will hardly be believed that, when sulphuric acid was first used to lessen the pains of childbirth, it was objected to as 'a profane attempt to abrogate the primeval curse pronounced upon woman.'[1] Scepticism is shown by works on natural theology, which attempted to *prove* what men formerly fancied they *instinctively* believed. The injury which the theological principle has done to the world is immense. It has prevented them from studying the laws of nature.

The superstitions respecting good and bad days were by no means confined to the lower classes. See some clever ridicule in 1619 in Middleton's Works.[2] In 1652 there was actually published a popular ballad to ridicule the 'belief in prophecies and prognostications.' It may be found in Mr. Wright's Political Ballads.[3] Whenever anything was lost, the sufferer had recourse to one of the wise men who were to be found in every town and nearly in every village. But their power was fast waning. An amusing description of one of their tricks is given in Chettle's Kind Hart's Dream.[4] The almanacks sold at 1*d.* each were a great source of popular knowledge. If there was a storm, every one looked to see if the almanack had predicted it.[5] In 1603 a 'Minister of God's Word,' called George Giffard, published a very remarkable work called A Dialogue concerning Witches and Witchcraft.[6] The author takes an important step in advance, for he denies the power of witches, though, by a strange confusion of language, he recognises their existence. Thus, to give a single

[1] Combe, p. 138.   [2] 8vo, 1840, vol. v. pp. 149, 150.
[3] Pp. 123-126, Percy Society, vol. III.
[4] 1592. pp. 52-53. Percy Society, vol. v.
[5] See Dekker's Knights Conjuring, 1607, p. 9, Percy Soc. vol. v.
[6] It has been reprinted by the Percy Society, vol. III.

instance, he denies[1] that witches can raise a storm; but says that the devil, being aware that a storm is approaching, incites them to predict it. Here we see the first dawn of that enlightened scepticism which eventually put an end to the belief in witchcraft. Giffard strongly censures juries for condemning persons because witnesses were found who declared them to be witches, and, in a spirit before his age, asks,[2] 'If others take their oath that in their conscience they think so [i.e. think them to be witches], is that sufficient to warrant me upon mine oath to say it is so?'[3] In 1582 the whole country was convulsed with fear. Richard Harvey, brother to the great Cambridge astrologer, discovered that in the very next year there would be a conjunction of Jupiter and Saturn. What was to be done? How was the impending calamity to be averted? People were wild with horror. But Nash, in his Pierce Pennilesse, and even Elderton the ballad-maker, and Tarleton the buffoon, ridiculed the popular apprehensions.[4] Neal[5] denies that the Puritan clergy claimed a power of exorcising the devil. If they believed in witchcraft, we can understand why Charles II. laughed at it.

Fortune-tellers are ridiculed in the Pleasante Conceites of Old Hobson, 1607, p. 11, Percy Soc. vol. ix.

Astronomy meant what we now call astrology. Thus, in Halle's Historiall Expostulation[6] we have—'I knowe, quoth he, by astronomy the influence of the stars, and thereby perceive when and how long any place should be unto me fortunate.'

In a draught of Discipline, bearing the name of the Bishop of Exeter, and presented to Convocation in 1563, it is proposed 'that witchcraft may be capitally punished,'[7] Parliament having, in 1562, made it capital to use witchcraft 'whereby any one happens to be killed or destroyed.'[8]

Glanville on Witchcraft was a favourite book with Mrs. Lewis, the fashionable and lovely mother of the author of The Monk.[9] Southey allowed the advantages of knowing mineralogy and botany,

[1] A Dialogue concerning Witches and Witchcraft. Percy Soc. vol. III. p. 94.
[2] Ibid. p. 106.
[3] At all events, the *evidence* of witches seems not to be denied; see pp. 13, 18, 30, 71.
[4] See Mr. Rimbault's Notes to Rowland's Four Knaves, Percy Soc. ix. 104.
[5] Hist. of the Puritans, vol. I. p. 458.   [6] 1565. Percy Soc. vol. xi. p. 9.
[7] Collier's Ecclesiastical History, 8vo, 1840, vol. I. pp. 386, 387.
[8] Ibid. vol. vi. p. 366.
[9] See the Life and Correspondence of M. G. Lewis, 8vo, 1839, vol. I. p. 28.

but only because they 'add to our outdoor enjoyments, and have
no injurious effects. Chemical and physical studies seem, on the
contrary, to draw on very prejudicial consequences. Their utility
is not to be doubted; but it appears as if man could not devote
himself to these pursuits without blunting his finer faculties.'
This was written in 1816.[1] Those who *observe* more than they
reflect become superstitious. They *see* phenomena which they
cannot *explain*. Even Blackstone, who in several things was
before his age, is evidently half inclined to believe in witchcraft.
See his amusingly cautious and, as it were, reverential remarks
towards this wretched superstition in his Commentaries.[2] He says[3]
that it was not till 9 Geo: II. c. 5 that it was forbidden to prosecute any one for witchcraft; and that though, according to Voltaire,
Louis XIV. issued an edict forbidding the tribunals to receive
informations of witchcraft, 'yet Voughlans[4] still reckons up
sorcery and witchcraft among the crimes punishable in France.'
After the captivity of Mary the Second, the jealousy of Government
was excited by the astronomical and magical researches which
were instituted in order to determine her fate. See the questions
put in 1571 to Robert Higforth in Murdin's State Papers.[5] Mr.
Morell[6] well says that sensualism, or, as he calls it, sensationalism,
is the natural result of a too exclusive study of physical science.
Hence I may connect the decline of superstition and rise of
Locke. Indeed, I may trace this back to Bacon, who analysed
nature, while Descartes analysed *thought*.

Lady Southwell, one of the maids of honour to Elizabeth,
mentions that at her death there was 'discovered in the bottom
of her chair the queen of hearts, with a nail of iron knocked
through the forehead of it.'[7] In the system of ecclesiastical law
which Cranmer drew up in 1552, one of the articles 'imposes
punishment at the ordinary's discretion upon persons admitting
the practice of idolatry, witchcraft, and the like.'[8]

The tendency of increasing civilization to lessen the habit of
accounting for phenomena on supernatural grounds is slightly

[1] Life and Correspondence of Robert Southey, 8vo, 1849, 1850, vol. iv. p. 191.
[2] Edit. Christian, 8vo, 1809, vol. iv. pp. 60, 61. [3] Ibid. p. 62.
[4] Du Droit Criminel, pp. 353, 459. [5] Pp. 70, 71, 97, 98.
[6] View of the Speculative Philosophy of Europe, 8vo, 1846, vol. i. pp. 64, 65.
[7] See her relation in Dodd's Church History, edit. Tierney, vol. iii. p. 72.
[8] Soames's History of the Reformation of the Church of England, vol. iii. p. 711.

but firmly touched by M. Quetelet, who notices the analogy it bears to the progress of an individual from infancy to manhood.[1]

Whewell says of the schoolmen, 'Though, like the Greeks, they thus talked of experiment, like the Greeks, they showed little disposition to discover the laws of nature by observation of facts.'[2] It has been well observed that such words as ill-starred, disastrous, exorbitant, a *sphere* of action, &c., show how much our language has been affected by astrological opinions.[3] As one religion is succeeded by another, the ritual of the old religion supplies the form in which the witch mumbles her spells, and the magician invokes his spirits. See this remarked by a very learned writer, Mr. Price, in his Preface to Warton's History of English Poetry.[4] In 1562 the Bishop of Exeter presented a paper to the ecclesiastical synod, in which he desired 'that there be some sharp, penal, yea, capital pains for witches, charmers, sorcerers, enchanters, and such like.'[5] As early as 1574 the Puritans used to pretend to cast out evil spirits.[6]

When it was proposed to connect two rivers in Portugal by means of a canal, the Inquisition refused to allow it, on the ground that, if God had wished them to be united, He would have united them Himself.[7]

For a good history of laws, &c., respecting witchcraft, see pp. i-xx of Mr. Wright's Introduction to the Proceedings against Alice Kyteler, Camden Soc., vol. xxiv.

The Scotch and idealistic philosophy must have been favourable to the superstitions of Puseyism. M. Cousin well says that Christianity particularly relies upon *à priori* argument.[8] Cousin says that all the Scotch school, from Hutcheson downwards, denied the *à priori* proof in favour of a God.[9] Bower says that Robert Monson, who was born at Aberdeen in 1620, was 'the first person who ever made the attempt to reduce botany to a science.'[10] At the end of the seventeenth century Thomasius first

[1] Quetelet, Sur l'Homme, Paris, 1835, tome ii. pp. 273, 274.
[2] Philosophy of the Inductive Sciences, 8vo, 1847, vol. ii. p. 145.
[3] Ibid. vol. ii. pp. 490, 491.   [4] Vol. i. pp. 44, 45.
[5] Strype's Annals of the Reformation, vol. i. part i. p. 521, Oxford, 8vo, 1824.
[6] Ibid. vol. ii. part i. pp. 483, 484.
[7] Storch, Économie Politique, St. Pétersbourg, 1815, tome v. p. 361.
[8] Cousin, Histoire de la Philosophie, 2nde série, tome iii. pp. 372, 373.
[9] Ibid. première série, tome iv. p. 33.
[10] History of the University of Edinburgh, vol. ii. p. 326.

ventured to attack the prosecutions for witchcraft, and to oppose himself to the use of torture, though in spite of this there are instances of such prosecutions as late as the end of the eighteenth century.[1]

Drury, in a religious dispute with the natives of Madagascar, gravely insisted that 'a man had one rib less on one side than the other.'[2]

Selden upset the theological notion of tithes, which even Hooker advocated.

Rabelais[3] ridicules judicial astrology. Since the Mahommedan dominion, the fear of witchcraft has ceased in the Indian archipelago.[4] Coleridge[5] says, 'Fanaticism, the universal origin of which is in the contemplation of phenomena without investigation into their causes.' Coleridge[6] makes it an argument in favour of the inspiration of the Bible, that there is nothing in it in favour of witchcraft. The Methodists, I suspect, by encouraging the notion of witchcraft, prevented it from dying out so soon as it would otherwise have done.[7] Indeed, in his Journal,[8] Wesley says that men who disbelieve witchcraft are deists. Besides this, his journals are full of monstrous stories.

The first known instance of witches burnt in England is in the reign of Henry II.[9] Wright says[10] that among us, during the fourteenth and fifteenth centuries, sorcery was used *politically*; after which began 'what may be termed *par excellence* the age of witches.' Our darkest witch-period was under James I.[11] He says[12] that credulity about witches 'seems to have risen to its greatest height at the time of the Reformation.' During the fifteenth and sixteenth centuries it was less in England than in any country,[13] and our first statute against it was in 1541.[14] Wright says,[15] 'The great witch persecution in England arose under the Commonwealth.' He says,[16] 'In general, the countries

---

1 Schlosser's History of the Eighteenth Century, vol. L pp. 191, 192.
2 Drury's Madagascar, 8vo, 1743. p. 181.
3 Œuvres, Amsterdam, 8vo, 1725. tome ii. p. 93, livre II. chap. viii.
4 See Crawford's History of the Indian Archipelago, 8vo, 1820, vol. III. p. 137.
5 Literary Remains, vol. L p. 241.   6 Ibid. vol. iv. pp. 54, 55.
7 See Southey's Life of Wesley, 8vo, 1846, vol. II. pp. 89, 277–279.
8 8vo, 1851, pp. 602, 713.
9 See Wright's Sorcery and Magic, 8vo, 1851, vol. L p. 15.
10 Ibid. p. 24.   11 Ibid. p. 179.   12 Ibid. p. 226.
13 Ibid. p. 227.   14 Ibid. p. 279.   15 Ibid. vol. ii. p. 145.
16 Ibid. p. 244.

of Northern Europe appear to have been less subject to these
extensive witch prosecutions than the South ; although there the
ancient popular superstitions reigned in great force.' Wright
says[1] that the case of Jane Wenham (in 1712) 'is the last
instance of a witch being condemned by the verdict of an English
jury;' and the context shows how many of the clergy exerted
themselves to procure her condemnation. Locke, at Montpelier
in 1676, mentions a man who 'about four years ago sacrificed a
child to the devil.'[2] Even in 1699, in London, people were
terrified by an eclipse of the sun.[3] In Scotland the belief in
witchcraft survived the belief in England, and to deny it was
atheism.[4] In 1691 witchcraft was punished in France.[5] Morley[6]
says that 'Andreas Alciatus, the great jurist of his age,' 'born
near Como, about 1493,' was an opposer of torturing witches, and
apparently disbelieved in witchcraft. He also opposed astrology,
and wished that astrologers should be punished (p. 22).

Witchcraft. Charles II.—But even in point of morals, the
Restoration was by no means an unmixed evil. The overthrow
of Puritanism by the Independents had gone far to check the
alarming progress of superstition. The magnanimous intellect of
Cromwell was not to be imposed on by the miserable jargon of
priests ; and there is little doubt that, if his life had not been
prematurely shortened, superstition would have been checked.
But this result was hastened by the Restoration. It will be con-
venient to consider these results under the two heads of decline
of particular superstitions and the general decline of priestly
influence.

There are few superstitions which have been so universal as
a belief in witchcraft. The serene theology of Paganism despised
the wretched superstition, which has been greedily believed by
millions of Christians. Even the early Church, encumbered with
the most uncouth superstition, did not hold it so long as the
Roman influence predominated in her councils. But when the
Western Empire obtained her independence in the fifth century

[1] Wright's Sorcery and Magic, 8vo, 1851, vol. i. p. 326.
[2] King's Life of Locke, 8vo, 1830, vol. i. p. 119.
[3] See Evelyn's Diary, vol. iii. p. 372.
[4] See Burt's Letters from the North of Scotland, 8vo, 1815, vol. i. pp. 220, 221, 268, 269.
[5] See Monteil, Hist. des Français des Divers États, vol. viii. p. 41.
[6] Life of Cardan, 1854, vol. ii. p. 21.

we find the first faint indication.   In our own country it was
eagerly adopted.   It was reserved for the reign of Elizabeth to
enter the first protest.   In 1594 (?) Reginald Scott (?) boldly
attacked the prevalent belief.   But he made few converts.

Under the Puritans the eagerness against witches became an
awful mania.   During the years of their rule more persons were
burnt as witches than in the preceding years.

But when Cromwell had gained the ascendency all this was
changed.   The Puritans were religious bigots.   The Independents
were political bigots.   So long as they retained the name of a
republic, so long as they preserved the democratic element, they
cared little about anything else.   The course which Cromwell
had pursued from knowledge, Charles II. pursued from laziness.
Charles II. was thoroughly an idle man.   This indifference spread
rapidly from the throne to the court, and slowly from the court
to the people.   At length Shadwell, one of the most wretched
scribblers even of that age, but a man of considerable literary
influence, boldly undertook to ridicule witchcraft on the public
stage.   But the caution with which he found it necessary to
proceed is instructive.   Supported by the court, he says in his
preface, 'For my part, I am, as it is said of Surly in the
Alchymist, somewhat costive of belief.'[1]   But he adds that he
felt himself bound to represent actual witches ; otherwise 'it
would have been called atheistical by a prevailing party, who take
it ill that the power of the devil should be lessened.'   The whole
of the play is on the same strain.   The meanest and most foolish
characters are represented as believers in witchcraft, the more
enlightened ones as ridiculing it.   Sir Edward Hartford treats
the prevailing opinion with supreme contempt.[2]

Boyle wrote The Sceptical Chemist and the Sceptical Naturalist.
The establishment of the Royal Society lessened superstition.   It
called the attention of men from theology, just as politics had
done before the Restoration.   The *power* of men was increased,
and they despised theology.   Besides this, *new* topics were
introduced.   The Ne Plus Ultra contains an able defence of the
Royal Society, and supplies evidence of the hatred felt of it by
some of the clergy.

Rogers[3] says that Bishop Parker and his patron, Archbishop

1 Shadwell's Works, vol. iii. p. 218.   2 Ibid. p. 233.
3 Essays, 8vo, 1850, vol. i. pp. 69, 70.

Sheldon, though, like the Puseyites, dogmatic as to rites, were really very sceptical. Rogers quotes Burnet for this ; and as to Parker's love of Rome, he refers to the testimony of Father Petre in Dove's Life of Marvell.

HISTORY OF THE ENGLISH NAVY.

On the 28th of April 1560, Sir Nicolas Throckmorton writes to Cecil, ' Bend your force, credit, and device to maintain and increase your navy by all the means you can possible ; for in this time, considering all circumstances, it is the flower of England's garland.'[1] In November 1562 the Duke of Norfolk, the Earl of Pembroke, and the admiral order ' that 1,000 of masters and maryners be prest upon the coast of England next to Newhaven, to be transported thither for the setting away of the principal ships first that are at this present there.'[2] In April 1563 the Earl of Warwick writes from Newhaven to the Council respecting a ' galley' which it is ' necessary' to have, and which ' will occupy nine score and twelve rowars (having forty-eight oars and four men to every owar), and thirty mariners,' &c.[3] On the 10th of May 1563, Elizabeth orders the Lord Admiral ' to cause 300 mariners to be prested and taken up on the sea-coast next towards Newhaven, and sent thither with all spede possible.'[4]

Jacob[5] says that the 14 Henry VII. cap. 10 ' gave encouragement to the construction of ships, and caused the education of a considerable number of seamen.'

In 1761 ' copper plates were first used as sheathing on the "Alarm" frigate,' and, by the year 1780, ' the whole British navy was coppered—an event which may be considered as forming an important era in the naval annals of the country.'[6] It was reserved for Davy to discover the mode of arresting the corrosion of the copper by voltaic action[7].—a discovery which, as connected with others, was of the greatest importance, but which, owing to some disturbing causes, was eventually relinquished as impracti-

[1] Forbes's Elizabeth, vol. i. p. 416.
[2] Ibid. vol. ii. p. 172.   [3] Ibid. 382.   [4] Ibid. p. 415.
[5] History of the Precious Metals, 8vo, 1831, vol. II. p. 17.
[6] Paris, Life of Sir Humphrey Davy, 8vo, 1831, vol. ii. pp. 224, 225.
[7] Ibid. pp. 255-256.

cable.[1] Among the many fabulous advantages which M. Villers ascribes to the Reformation, one is that it gave rise to the English navy.[2]

The French ambassador at London, in a despatch to his own Government in August 1570, gives an account of the rapidity with which Elizabeth had made her navy ready for sea. She fitted out 'vingt-neuf de ses grands navires bien artillez, et bien garnys de toutes munitions de guerre,' having 5,500 men on board.[3] A month later he mentions ten of her ships with 3,500 men on board, 'dont les huict centz sont harquebouziers.'[4] As to the determination of Elizabeth to have a navy, Soames[5] cites Bishop Carleton's Thankful Remembrance of God's Mercy, London, 1625, p. 4.

The extension of popular liberty gave rise to a national navy The people soon perceived that their prince could only oppress them by calling in the aid of the military power. Of this power they therefore became jealous, and resisted all the attempts of the sovereign to increase it. But of the naval power they could have no such apprehensions; and the energies natural to a free people were dedicated to increasing that power which alone they could increase without danger to themselves. The English were the first who built frigates.[6]

On the 10th of January 1559 the Duke of Norfolk, in a letter to Cecil, mentions 'her Majestie's navie;'[7] and on the 8th of February 1559 the Duke of Norfolk writes that there were in the Frith (of Forth, I suppose) 'her Majestie's seed navie to the number of thirteen men-of-war.'[8] However, on the 11th of February 1559, Lord Montague and Sir Thomas Chamberlain wrote to the Council that even at Plymouth there was 'no shipp above sixty tonnes, and these neyther furnished with ordinance, victuall, nor other munition, as is requisitt for this voyage.'[9] In July 1560, Portsmouth was the great place of assemblage for 'the Queene's Majestie's ships.'[10]

---

[1] Paris, Life of Sir Humphrey Davy, 8vo, 1831, vol. ii. p. 270.

[2] See Villers, Sur la Réformation, Paris, 1820, p. 170. On Impressment, see COMMON PLACE BOOK, art. 2226.

[3] Correspondance de Fénélon, Paris, 1840, tome iii. p. 269.   [4] Ibid. p. 306.

[5] Elizabethan Religious History, p. 91.

[6] See Evelyn's Diary, vol. iii. p. 292.

[7] Haynes's State Papers, pp. 221, 224.   [8] Ibid. p. 237.

[9] Ibid. p. 239.   [10] Ibid. pp. 357, 358.

Hume quotes 'Monson, p. 196,' to the effect that Elizabeth's
navy at her death consisted of 42 vessels, but that 'none of these
ships carried above 40 guns; that 4 only came up to that
number; that there were but 2 ships of 1,000 tons, and 23 below
500, some of 50, and some even of 20 tons; and that the whole
number of guns belonging to the fleet was 774.' See in Murdin's
State Papers[1] a list of the queen's navy in 1588, where it is said[2]
that she had 34 ships, bearing 6,225 men, and of 12,190 tons.
This was exclusive of vessels with Sir F. Drake, and also of those
sent by the city of London; but the entire total of the naval
force opposed by England to the Spaniards was, ships 191, tonnage
31,985, men 15,272. In 1592, Elizabeth had 38 vessels; the
amount of their tonnage is not added up.[3] In 1572 even the
French ambassador confessed that she had 'le plus beau et
magnifique équippage de navyres que prince ni princesse de
l'Europe.'[4] In January 1573 the French ambassador writes to
his own court that Elizabeth 'a faict presant d'un navyre de 600
tonneaulx, et de deux aultres de 150 tonneaulx, chacun à son
admiral,' and that the admiral had given the large one to his
son and the other two to his relations.[5] In 1543 the Bishop of
Winchester and the Lord St. John write to the Earl of Hertford
that, although they cannot give 'the peculiar declaration of the
furniture of every ship in every port,' yet they are 'assured that
there be departed from hence and ready to depart from other
ports the number of 160 sail of ships.'[6]

In 1544 the Earl of Hertford writes to the Lords of the Council
that there was not enough money in hand to pay 'the month's
wages now expired of the captains, soldiers, and mariners of the
fleet, being about 5,000 in number.' He says that 30,000l. was
put aside for that purpose.[7]

It seems that in 1573 it was usual for ships, before engaging,
to hoist a red cross. See Correspondance de Fénélon, tome v.
p. 317; but compare p. 319, where it is said that this was done
by merchant vessels in suspicious times.

Had Elizabeth in 1573 a sort of body-guard of 'neuf cent
harquebousiers'?[8]

[1] Pp. 615-618.   [2] P. 618.
[3] See Murdin, p. 619. For the expense of the navy, see p. 620, &c.
[4] Correspondance de Fénélon, tome v. p. 146.   [5] Ibid. p. 243.
[6] Haynes's State Papers, p. 20.   [7] Ibid. p. 30.
[8] See Correspondance de Fénélon, tome v. p. 329.

In 1574 the French ambassador writes to his court that Elizabeth had ordered all her great ships, except four, to put to sea; and that 3,000 mariners were already prepared to go on board; but that to pay them she had only appropriated 35,000 'éscus,' although 80,000 would be required, besides the expenses of the gunpowder.[1] Sixteen days later he writes[2] that, in four days, six vessels with 2,500 men would sail. Two months afterwards he again writes[3] that Elizabeth was about 'mettre ses grands navyres dehors, en nombre de vingt-cinq, aultant bien équippés qu'il y en ait en ceste mer, avec les barques et aultres vayssaulx qui suivront, oultre les particuliers qui seront bien aultant.' In August 1574, Elizabeth's 'grands navires' were at Rochester.[4]

In June 1552 the French ambassador writes that the English were fitting out 'ung grand équipage de mer, lequel je pense n'estre moindre de vingt bons navires.'[5] In March 1554 he writes that all the queen's navy except five vessels were ordered to join the emperor's forces.[6] In March 1554, Mary had in all thirty ships of war.[7] In May 1554 the queen's ships, which were sent to Spain, put into Plymouth to be victualled.[8] In May 1554 she had so neglected her ships that many of them were not even seaworthy.[9] In August 1554 she completely stripped and unvictualled many of her ships, in order to supply those of Spain.[10] Indeed, Noailles was informed that she sent several of her sailors and captains to enter into the imperial service.[11]

ADMINISTRATION OF JUSTICE AND INFLUENCE OF LAWYERS.

A REMARKABLE evidence of the absence of justice is supplied by a letter in Forbes's State Papers,[12] dated London, May 1560, in which Mr. Peyto, writing to Sir Nicolas Throckmorton, the English ambassador in France, gives an account of a scuffle between Sir Thomas Sheldon and another. He says, ' The matter is here afore the counsell, neither of them wantyng friendes, but *whose*

---

[1] Correspondance de Fénélon, tome vii. p. 96.   [2] Ibid. p. 111.
[3] Ibid. p. 179.   [4] Ibid. tome vi. p. 489.
[5] Ambassades de Noailles, Leyde, 1763, tome ii. p. 42 ; and see p. 48.
[6] Ibid. tome iii. p. 140.   [7] Ibid. p. 144.
[8] Ibid. p. 204.   [9] Ibid. p. 220 ; and see tome iv. pp. 219, 220.
[10] Ibid. tome iii. pp. 295, 296.   [11] Ibid. tome iv. pp. 80, 81.
[12] Vol. i. pp. 443, 444.

*friendes most hable to stonde in stede, th' ende of the judgment will
declare.*[1] On January 17, 1569, the Earl of Sussex writes to Cecil
respecting a gentleman concerned in the rebellion. He says,
'He is my wife's cousin, and therefore, if any seek to *beg* him, I
beseech you to procure his stay in the queen's majesty's hands.'[1]

In Ormerod's History of Cheshire[2] there is a curious letter
from Sir Ralph Egerton, sheriff of Cheshire, to John Talbot, in
which he promises to summon a jury of his own appointment,
provided Talbot does not name any of his relations on it, as in
that case they might be challenged. The jury had to try a lawsuit
respecting property, to which Talbot was one of the chief parties.
The letter is dated 3rd March 1579. There were men who made
a trade of serving on juries and selling their verdicts. These, in
the sixteenth century, were so well known a body as to have a distinct name, and were called 'Ringleaders of Inquests.'[3]

In 1601, Ben Jonson attacked the lawyers in The Poetaster.[4]
Livery of seisin was rarely effected except by open force ; and
each party used to have their friends well armed. This is alluded
to in 1609 in Ben Jonson's Works.[5] In The Magnetick Lady,
written in 1632, Ben Jonson attacks the partiality of a 'London
jury.'[6] Indeed, false swearing was so common that a particular
word was invented for those wretches who systematically perjured
themselves for money. Such hirelings were called Knights of the
Post.[7]

In 1627 we find a complaint 'that if one have ten shillings
owing him, nay, five or less, he cannot have it but by suit in law
in some petty court, where it will cost thirty or forty shillings
charge of suit.'[8] Even the satiric Nash pays a high compliment
to the legal eloquence of his time.[9] Rich,[10] after speaking favour-
ably of the law, adds, 'Our Inns of Court now, for the greater
part, are stuffed with the offspring of farmers, and with all other
sorts of tradesmen ; and these, when they have gotten some few
scrapings of the law, they do sow the seeds of suits.'

    [1] Sharpe's Memorials of 1569, 8vo, 1840, pp. 157, 158. In a note is another
curious begging letter.
    [2] 1819, vol. ii. pp. 241, 242.
    [3] See Stow's London, edit. Thoms, 8vo, 1842, p. 72.
    [4] See Ben Jonson's Works, 8vo, 1816, vol. ii. p. 404.   [5] Ibid. vol. iii. p. 451.
    [6] Ibid. vol. vi. pp. 60, 61.   [7] Middleton's Works, vol. v. p. 512.
    [8] Harleian Miscellany, edit. Park, vol. iii. p. 211.   [9] Ibid. vol. vi. p. 1
    [10] Honestie of this Age, 1614, Percy Soc. vol. xi.

It is supposed that Calixtus, in 1630, was the first who raised religious ethics to a science ; but M. Villers says [1] 'qu'en 1577 avait déjà paru à Genève celui de Lambert Daneau ou Danæus intitulé Ethices Christianæ libri tres, et où la morale religieuse est traitée méthodiquement.'

On horrible judicial cruelties, see Spottiswoode's History of the Church of Scotland, i. p. 217 ; Chambers's Domestic Annals of Scotland, vol. i. p. 471 ; vol. ii. p. 383 ; Buchanan's History of Scotland, vol. i. p. 911.

Mr. Trollope says that formerly in France women were always put to death by drowning ; and that 'the first time a woman was hung in France was in the reign of Charles VII.' [2]

The corruption of jurymen was so notorious that it enriched our language with a new word ; and to attempt to influence a jury by gifts or by promises was known as the crime of Embracery. [3]

Blackstone says 'frequenting houses of ill fame is an indictable offence.' [4] For this he cites 'Poph. 208.' The forcible entries, so common in the reign of Elizabeth, were illegal ; for, by the 5 Ric. II. Stat. I. c. 8, it was ordered that the remedy by entry should be peaceable and easy ; [5] and the 20 Hen. III. c. 2 ordered that, if in case of illegal disscisin, on which the party disseised recovered legal seisin, the disseisor shall proceed to a redisseisin, he shall be imprisoned, and by a later statute, 52 Hen. III. c. 8, shall be fined. To which penalties the 13 Edw. I. c. 26 added double damages to the party injured. [6] In 1548 the most eminent lawyers used to leave London between the terms. [7] In October 1553, Mary caused 110l. 'to be distributed among the judges and learned counsell that took pains in the indictment of the late duke of Northumberland.' [8] 'Embraceries' are mentioned in 1553. [9] Cecil, in a paper drawn up in 1579, recommends 'that penal laws be not dispensed withall for private men's profits.' [10] A very sagacious writer says, 'Little reliance is in general to be placed on the

[1] Essai sur la Réformation, Paris, 1820, p. 265.
[2] Trollope's Brittany, 8vo, London, 1840, vol. I. p. 172.
[3] Blackstone, vol. iv. p. 140.   [4] Comment. vol. iv. p. 64.
[5] Blackstone, 8vo, 1809, vol. iii. p. 179.   [6] Ibid. vol. iii. p. 188.
[7] See Haynes's State Papers, p. 73.   [8] Ibid. p. 189.
[9] Ibid. p. 195.   [10] Murdin's State Papers, p. 325.

dying declarations of criminals, although they are sought after with great eagerness.'[1]

M. Cousin says of Domat, 'Il est incomparablement le plus grand jurisconsulte du dix-septième siècle ; il a inspiré et presque formé D'Aguesseau ; il a quelquefois prévenu Montesquieu, et frayé la route à cette réforme générale des lois entreprise par la révolution et réalisée par l'empire.'[2] We owe to him also the Calvinistic spirit of Jansenism. Frederick Schlegel regrets that, in consequence of the influence of classical association, the laws of the German nations should have been so much modified by the civil law, which, he says, was too *severely just*, and did not make allowances enough.[3] In the same part [4] he well points out the real difference which is and *ought to be* between law and justice. St. Basil orders for murder a penance of twenty years ; for apostasy a penance of 'a whole life.' This is quoted by Collier, who considers it a model of wisdom.[5]

Bucer wished to have 'those crimes capitally punished in all commonwealths which were death by the law of Moses ;' and he particularly mentions among such crimes those who recommended a false religion, or who broke the Sabbath.[6] As to the oath *ex officio*, see the contemporary authorities in Soames's Elizabethan Religious History, pp. 403-405. At the end of Elizabeth's reign grew up the custom of stopping the ecclesiastical courts by *prohibitions* from Westminster Hall.[7]

The Bishop of St. Asaph has collected some instances of the *venality* of justice in the reign of Elizabeth.[8] On the absurd theory of an original compact, see Lord Brougham's Political Philosophy.[9] He says [10] Hobbes 'was the first writer who put forth a philosophical statement of the doctrine of the original or social compact.' He observes [11] that even in 1314 we find the doctrine of Resistance supposed to be originated in A.D. 1688.

Lord Brougham looks on expediency as the basis of all law

[1] Lewis on Disturbances in Ireland, 8vo, 1836, p. 223.
[2] Cousin's Littérature, Paris, 1849, tome iii. p. 151.
[3] Philosophy of History, 8vo, 1846, pp. 265, 266.   [4] Ibid. pp. 265, 966.
[5] Ecclesiastical History, vol. v. p. 260, 8vo, 1840.   [6] Ibid. p. 417.
[7] Soames's Elir. Relig. History, p. 516.
[8] History of the Church of England, 8vo, 1817, p. 283 ; and as to the oath *ex officio*, see p. 301.
[9] 2nd edit. 8vo, 1849, vol. i. pp. 34-38.   [10] Ibid. p. 39.
[11] Ibid. pp. 59, 60.

and government. (Political Philosophy, 2nd edit. 8vo, 1849, vol. i.
pp. 46, 50, 494. See p. 69, where he seems to consider the judicial forces more important than the legislative power.) Lord
Brougham has observed that the introduction of so beautiful and
scientific a system as the civil law tended in Europe to raise the
reputation of the men who studied it, and thus increase the dignity
of lawyers.[1] Lord Brougham asserts most positively that members
of Parliament should *not* be paid ; and he notices that in other
professions men do not mind confessing that all their property is
derived from it, while no man would make such a confession as
regards politics.[2] It seems likely that the notion of an original
compact had its rise in the Saxon engagements between a man and
his hlaford.[3] When the judges were made for life, I suppose their
power lessened. Montesquieu well says, ' Dans toute magistra-
ture, il faut compenser la grandeur de la puissance par la brièveté
de sa durée.'[4] With the increase of liberty penal laws always
become less severe.[5] Montesquieu adds,[6] ' C'est donc de la
bonté des lois criminelles que dépend principalement la liberté du
citoyen ;' and,[7] ' C'est le triomphe de la liberté lorsque les lois
criminelles tirent chaque peine de la nature particulière du crime.'
Written libels will be tolerated in monarchies, punished in aristocracies.[8] He seems to think attainders not indefensible.[9] As
to taxes, he anticipates Bentham. He says,[10] ' Dans l'impôt de
la personne, la proportion injuste serait celle qui suivrait exactement la proportion des biens ;' and he adds that every one has a
certain sum *necessary* to him, and that this should not be taxed.
The freer the government, the more complicated the laws.[11]
Montesquieu thinks *one* witness too little, but *two* sufficient to
take away a man's life.[12] He well says that laws have nothing to
do with repentance.[13] I quite agree with Alison[14] that Malthus has
underrated the influence of laws. Mr. Alison, who has had considerable experience in such matters, denies the common assertion

[1] Political Philosophy, vol. i. p. 342.   [2] Ibid. vol. ii. pp. 30, 32.
[3] See Allen on the Royal Prerogative, 8vo, 1849, pp. 66-68.
[4] Esprit des Lois, livre ii. chap. iii. Œuvres, p. 196, Paris, 1835.
[5] Ibid. livre vi. chap. ix. p. 231.   [6] Ibid. livre xii. chap. ii. p. 280.
[7] Ibid. chap. iii. p. 281.   [8] Ibid. chap. xiii. p. 286.
[9] Ibid. chap. xix. p. 289.   [10] Ibid. livre xiii. chap. vii. p. 294.
[11] Montesquieu, pp. 226-228.   [12] Ibid. p. 281.
[13] Esprit des Lois, livre xxvi. chap. xii. pp. 426, 427.
[14] Principles of Population, 8vo, 1840, vol. i. p. 329.

that transportation is not feared by criminals.[1] Mr. Alison gravely adds,[2] 'Nothing can be more obvious than the fundamental principles of criminal jurisprudence;' but I cannot say he has thrown much light on them. He opposes an unpaid magistracy.[3] He dislikes imprisonment, and recommends that 'for the second offence transportation should be invariably inflicted.'[4] Adam Smith complains of the neglect of 'natural jurisprudence, of all sciences by far the most important, but hitherto perhaps the least cultivated.'[5]

In 1585, Fleetwood, recorder of London, writes to Burghley, 'It is growen for a trade now in the courte to make meanes for reprieves; twenty pounds for a reprieve is nothing, although it be but for bare ten daies.'[6] In 1586 we find a letter from Walsingham, from which it would appear that the custom of sending felons to the galleys was then very recent. See Egerton Papers, p. 116, Camden Soc. For proof of the arbitrary interference with the course of law at the end of the sixteenth century, see Lodge's Illustrations of British History, 1838, vol. ii. p. 386. Read Twysden on the Government of England, Camden Society, vol. xlv.

It was usual in the sixteenth century to hang pirates at the lower water-mark at Wapping.[7] In 1562 the lord keeper advises Parliament 'to make your laws as few and as plain as may be.'[8] In 1584 the Archbishop of York seems to taunt the House of Commons with having many young members.[9] Cousin says that the object of penal laws should be to punish crime in proportion to its viciousness, not in proportion to its effects on society.[10] Before 1710 neither the Roman law nor the municipal law of Scotland was taught in any of the Scotch universities.[11]

By the system of ecclesiastical laws drawn up by Cranmer,

---

[1] Principles of Population, 8vo, 1840, vol. ii. pp. 137, 138.
[2] Ibid. p. 139. [3] Ibid. p. 139. [4] Ibid. pp. 140, 143.
[5] Theory of Moral Sentiments, 1822, vol. ii. p. 60.
[6] Wright's Elizabeth, 8vo, 1838, vol. ii. p. 247.
[7] See p. 351 of Mr. Nichol's Notes to Machyn's Diary, London, 1848. p. 351.
[8] D'Ewes' Journal of Parliament. 1682, p. 66.
[9] D'Ewes' Journal of Elizabeth, p. 360.
[10] Histoire de la Philosophie, 2nde série, tome iii. pp. 189, 190.
[11] Tytler's Life of Kames, Edinburgh, 1814, vol. i. p. 15.

adultery, either in man or woman, was punished by 'banishment or perpetual imprisonment.'[1]

According to the Malagasy laws, a man who breaks maliciously one of his neighbour's limbs, is 'fined fifteen heads of cattle, which are delivered to the party injured;' and whoever robs his neighbour of an ox or cow 'is obliged to restore it tenfold.'[2] Hooker[3] anticipates the argument of Coleridge against universal suffrage. In the thirteenth century we find something like the social compact laid down by a Persian moralist.[4] In 1678, Locke seems to hold it.[5] Schlegel[6] says that during the 180 years between the consulate of Cicero and the death of Trajan was developed the science of jurisprudence, 'the only original intellectual possession of great value to which the Romans can lay undisputed claim.' Alison[7] ascribes to Mackintosh the great principle that punishment should be *certain*, ignorant that Beccaria first laid it down. Lord Campbell says,[8] 'In the reign of Henry VIII. there were 72,000 executions.'

On the opening of the Legislative Assembly, in October 1791, 'l'extrême jeunesse s'y faisait remarquer en foule.'[9] Charles Butler[10] says that 'the Jus Ecclesiasticum of Van Erpen, the only work perhaps which the Continent has produced that can be compared with Mr. Justice Blackstone's Commentaries.'

In Holstein or Schleswick 'the succession by gavelkind prevails—the youngest son, and not the eldest, succeeds to the father's land.'[11] Laing says that this has been ascribed to the feudal *jus primæ noctis*, but the real fact is that holding the land was formerly a sort of bondage, and the elder son preferred being a man-at-arms in the baron's castle. Alison[12] says positively that the 'Mercheta mulierum' existed in France.

On the absurdity of making laws *logically* complete, quote Tocqueville, Démocratie en Amérique, i. 209, 210. Tocqueville

[1] Todd's Life of Cranmer, vol. ii. p. 29.
[2] Drury's Madagascar. 8vo, 1743, p. 240.
[3] Ecclesiastical Polity, Book I. sect. 7, Works, vol. I. p. 90.
[4] See Transactions of the Literary Society of Bombay, vol. i. pp. 29, 30.
[5] See King's Life of Locke, 8vo, 1830, vol. I. p. 217.
[6] Lectures on the History of Literature, I. 159.
[7] Hist. of Europe, vol. ix. p. 621.
[8] Lives of the Chancellors, vol. II. p. 231.
[9] Lamartine, Histoire des Girondins, Bruxelles, 8vo, 1847, tome I. p. 252.
[10] Reminiscences, vol. i. p. 116.   [11] Laing's Denmark, pp. 139, 140.
[12] History of Europe, vol. i. p. 199.

says,[1] 'L'Angleterre n'ayant point de constitution écrite, qui peut dire qu'on change sa constitution?' The absurdity of introducing free institutions among a people not ripe for them appears from what has taken place in Mexico.[2] Tocqueville[3] is in favour of universal suffrage, in which the people elect electors as in the American Senate. He says[4] that despotism is more injurious in *preventing* production than in taking away its fruits. He well says[5] that a trial by jury is useful, not because it secures justice, but because it accustoms men themselves to be *responsible*, and to show 'the sovereignty of the people.' Ranke says,[6] 'Louis XI. was the first monarch who decidedly recognised the fundamental doctrine that the officers of justice were not removable at pleasure.' Bracton, in the middle of the thirteenth century, uses the civil law 'by way of illustration, not as authority,' though Lord Campbell[7] regrets that 'the prejudices of English lawyers' have always prevented them making more use of the civil law. Sir William de Thorpe, in the middle of the fourteenth century, was chief justice. He, says Lord Campbell,[8] 'from an obscure origin rose to power and wealth, without being a Churchman—a very unusual occurrence in those days; but the law was becoming what it has since continued, one of the ties by which the middling and lower ranks in England are bound up with the aristocracy, preventing the separation of the community into the two castes of noble and roturier, which has been so injurious in the Continental states.' From the fifteenth century until the reign of Charles II., judges of the highest rank used to settle 'differences privately by arbitration, on the voluntary submission of the parties.'[9] Lord Campbell says,[10] 'Till Lord Coke arose in the next generation, England can scarcely be said to have seen a magistrate of constancy, who was willing to surrender his place rather than his integrity.' And on the merit of Coke, see p. 239. Since 1628 'torture has never been inflicted in England.'[11] For lawyers, 'the full-bottom wig and the three-cornered cocked hat were introduced from France after the Restoration.'[12] Hale was a great student of Roman law.[13] The coif, 'to conceal the want of clerical

---

[1] Démocratie en Amérique, vol. i. p. 311.
[2] Ibid. p. 138.
[3] Ibid. p. 152.
[4] Civil Wars in France, 8vo, 1852, vol. i. p. 101.
[5] Lives of the Chief Justices, vol. i. p. 63.
[6] Ibid. p. 135.
[7] Ibid. p. 392.
[8] Ibid. p. 482.
[9] Ibid. vol. ii. p. 20.
[10] Ibid. vol. iii. p. 23.
[11] Ibid. p. 89.
[12] Ibid. p. 207.
[13] Ibid. p. 518.

tonsure.'[1] Commercial law began under Chief Justice Holt.[2] Holt put an end to receiving evidence respecting the *antecedents* of a prisoner. He also procured an Act to allow witnesses for the prisoner to be examined on oath;[3] but he always employed 'the French system' of interrogating the prisoner.[4] Lord Mansfield was appointed chief justice in 1756. 'His first bold step was to rescue the bar from the monopoly of the leaders.'[5] 'He formed,' says Campbell,[6] 'a very low, and, I am afraid, a very just estimate of the common law of England which he was to administer.' He almost created the law of insurance.[7] 'He likewise did much for the improvement of commercial law in this country by rearing a body of special jurymen at Guildhall, who were generally returned on all commercial causes to be tried there.'[8] Lord Campbell says,[9] 'After Bacon, Mr. Justice Blackstone was the first practising lawyer at the English bar who, in writing, paid the slightest attention to the selection or collocation of words.' Descartes[10] says laws should be few, but *well kept*. Liebig[11] well says, 'In times in which the means of detecting poisons with the greatest certainty were not yet known, the rack was used to make the discovery.' Tocqueville[12] well says that the institution of trial by jury is more beneficial *politically* than *judicially*: it makes men feel responsible, and gives them a sense of power. 'Je ne sais si le jury est utile à ceux qui ont des procès; mais je suis sûr qu'il est très utile à ceux qui les jugent.' Comte[13] opposes the abolition of punishment of death. Mr. Mill observes that, according to the laws of association, ideas spring up synchronically or successively according as the sensations have been synchronous or successive; and he adds, 'Of witnesses in courts of justice, it has been remarked that eye-witnesses and ear-witnesses always tell their story in the chronological order; in other words, the ideas occur to them in the order in which the sensations occurred; on the other hand, that witnesses who are inventing rarely adhere to the chronological order.'[14]

[1] Campbell's Chief Justices, vol. i. p. 72.
[2] Ibid. vol. ii. p. 137.
[3] Ibid. pp. 140, 141.
[4] Ibid. p. 174.
[5] Ibid. p. 398.
[6] Ibid. p. 402.
[7] Ibid. p. 405.
[8] Ibid. p. 407.
[9] Ibid. p. 566.
[10] De la Méthode, in Œuvres, vol. i. p. 141.
[11] Letters on Chemistry, 8vo. 1851. p. 293.
[12] Démocratie en Amérique, tome iii. pp. 23–26, 28, 29.
[13] Philosophie Positive, vol. iv. p. 123.
[14] Mill's Analysis of the Phenomena of the Mind, 8vo. 1829. vol. i. p. 58.

Miss Wood has printed a letter from Lady Blount to Cromwell, written in 1535, which, as she says, 'affords a curious specimen of an early electioneering squabble.'[1] At vol. iii. p. 315 there is an order issued by Mary, in 1557, to the sheriffs, ordering them to take care that there were returned to Parliament 'men given to good order, Catholic and discreet.'

In 1614 it was usual to fine drunkards five shillings.[2] Early in the seventeenth century it was a standing joke to call a jury 'godfathers-in-law.'[3]

Before the reign of Charles II. our dramatists constantly allude to the shameless practice of selling the guardianship of wards.

In 1608 we find 'I had rather give you a counsellor's double fee to hold your peace.' (Middleton's Works, 8vo, 1840, ii. 364; iv. 459.)

'Begging for a fool' occurs in Middleton's Works, 8vo, 1840, vol. iii. p. 16; vol. iv. p. 134.

The severity of the law against sheep-stealing is indignantly noticed in Middleton's Works, iv. 460. Before the doors of the sheriffs were large posts, on which proclamations were put.[4]

Blackstone says,[5] 'Experience will abundantly show that above a hundred of our lawsuits arise from disputed facts, for one where the law is doubted of.' At the accession of Mary I. it was necessary again to accredit the French ambassador at her court.[6]

NOTES FOR HISTORY OF MONEY AND PRECIOUS METALS.

In France, in 1563, a crown was worth 6s. 8d. English money.[7] Ormerod says,[8] 'According to Stow[9] and a MS. chronicler,[10] Richard the Second selected Beeston for the custody of his treasure and jewels, to the immense amount of 200,000 marks.'

Storch says[11] that in the time of Charlemagne the purchasing

---

[1] Letters of Royal and Illustrious Ladies, 8vo, 1846, vol. ii. pp. 167, 168.
[2] Ben Jonson's Works, vol. v. p. 139.   [3] Ibid. vol. iv. p. 489.
[4] Middleton, iii. 58.
[5] Commentaries, edit. Christian, 1809, vol. iii. p. 330.
[6] Ambassades de Noailles, Leyde, 1763, tome ii. p. 96.
[7] Forbes's Elizabeth, vol. ii. p. 470.
[8] History of Cheshire, 1819, vol. ii. p. 147.   [9] Annals, p. 321.
[10] Harl. MSS. 2111, 98.
[11] Economie Politique, St. Petersbourg, 8vo, 1815, tome ii. pp. 199, 200.

power of silver was four times as great as in the beginning of the
nineteenth century. He adds:[1] 'La découverte des mines
d'Amérique a répandu dans le monde environ dix fois plus
d'argent qu'il n'y en avait auparavant; cependant il n'a fait
baisser sa valeur en Europe que dans les proportions de quatre à
un.' Jacob, who was not acquainted with the researches of
Storch, says that during the sixteenth century the effect on price
was as three to one.[2] Storch supposes[3] that the depreciation
of the value of the precious metals reached its lowest point
between 1650 and 1700. See also[4] Storch's estimate of the production and consumption of the precious metals since the discovery
of America, where he seems chiefly to have followed Humboldt.
See also[5] an estimate of the circulating capital of Europe.   In
valuing Roman money, Storch follows Garnier,[6] and he evidently
thinks the price of corn is a decisive evidence of the value of money,
a mistake into which he fell in common with all the earlier political
economists.[7]   He says,[8] that just before the discovery of America,
the proportionate value of gold to silver was as one to ten, or one
to twelve. And he adds[9] that until 1545 Europe received more
gold than silver. He says[10] that Denmark and France are the
only two countries which do not add some seignorage, besides
reimbursing themselves for the cost of coining. In September,
1553, '7,000 livres sterlings' were '21,000 or 22,000 escuz sol;'[11]
and a few months later, Noailles writes from London, '20,000
livres de ceste monnoye est de la notre environ 65,000 escus sol;'[12]
and again,[13] '12,000 livres esterlins sont environ 40,000 escus sol.'
The Venetian ambassador in 1557 says that there were 'many of
the staplers—those to whom the exportation of wool is committed—possessed of from 50,000 to 60,000 sterling; all or the
greater part is ready.'[14]   In 1585, Sir Francis Drake *had* brought
into the Tower 23,411 lbs. in weight of silver, and 101 lbs. of

---

[1] Ibid. tome III. p. 60.
[2] History of the Precious Metals.
[3] Économie Politique, St. Pétersbourg, 8vo, 1815, tome iii. p. 64.
[4] Ibid. tome vi. pp. 57–70, note 1.   [5] Ibid. pp. 76–83, note all.
[6] Ibid. tome II. p. 288.   [7] Ibid. tome iii. pp. 60, 64.
[8] Ibid. p. 66.   [9] Ibid. p. 67.
[10] Ibid. p. 93.
[11] Ambassades de Noailles, Leyde, 1762, tome II. p. 137.
[12] Ambassades de Noailles, Leyde, 1762, tome iii. p. 120.   [13] Ibid. p. 205.
[14] Michele's Report in Ellis's Original Letters, 2nd series, vol. II. p. 220.

gold.[1] In 1571, 7,000 crowns Flemish were equal to 2,000*l.*
sterling.[2] In 1572, 'ryalls' were worth 6*d.* each.[3] In 1572,
florins were worth three shillings and fourpence.[4] In 1573, the
price of silver in England was 4*l. es.* 10½*d.* an ounce.[5] In
1583, seven French 'souse' were two groats English.[6] In 1569,
60,000*l.* sterling were 200,000 'escuz.'[7] It is evident that one
'livre' sterling was equal to 3½ crowns.[8]

In 1571, 2,000 marks were equal to 4,000 crowns.[9] In 1575,
10*l.* sterling were 'cent livres tournoys.'[10] In September 1574,
Fénelon writes that some Germans, Dutch, and French in England
had forged 1,000,000 crowns of the coin of France, Spain, and
Flanders, and that they had done this with the secret permission
of some of Elizabeth's Council.[11] These forgeries were so admirably executed that they could not be distinguished from the
originals,[12] and when some of the coiners were arrested, Elizabeth's
Council had them discharged.[13] In the Egerton Papers,[14] there
is an account of the money coined between 1586 and 1590. See[15]
Collier's assertion that, in 1602, 'money was of about five times
the value it bears at present.' Monteil, on no good authority,
says[16] that the specie in France in the fourteenth century was ten
millions, at six livres the silver mark. And he adds[17] that at the
end of the seventeenth century it was 500,000,000. On the
amount of gold and silver Europe has received from America, see
an essay by Danson in Journal of Statistical Society, vol. xiv.
pp. 11-44. On the value of silver since 1350, see Smith's Wealth
of Nations, pp. 75-88.

HISTORY AND INFLUENCE OF THE ARISTOCRACY.

ELIZABETH, at her accession, finding all the old nobility Catholics,
was obliged to seek her ministers among men of a lower rank.

[1] See Murdin's State Papers. pp. 539, 540.   [2] Ibid. p. 189.
[3] Ibid. p. 217.   [4] Ibid. p. 241.
[5] Ibid. p. 244.   [6] Ibid. p. 388.
[7] Correspondance Diplomatique de Fénelon, Paris, 1840, tome ii. p. 141.
[8] Fénelon, tome ii. pp. 361, 371; tome iii. pp. 112, 271; tome v. p. 313;
tome vii. pp. 449, 456, 497.   [9] Ibid. tome iv. p. 215.
[10] Ibid. tome vi. p. 490, and see p. 540.   [11] Ibid. pp. 241, 242.
[12] Ibid. p. 260.   [13] Ibid. pp. 245, 246.
[14] I'p. 182-185. Camden Society.   [15] Ibid. p. 347.
[16] Histoire des Français des Divers Etats, tome ii. p. 256.
[17] Ibid. tome vii. p. 163.

This paved the way for the decline of the aristocracy, and the wretched insurrection of 1569 naturally induced the queen to throw all her weight into the scale opposed to those haughty nobles who had dared to dictate to her. The duke of Norfolk was a Protestant. Elizabeth put Essex to death. Leicester sprung from the very dregs of the people. His grandfather was Dudley, the wretched and base-born confidant of Henry VII. (?)

. . . .

There was yet another circumstance which knit together the English aristocracy, and gave them the character of a caste. I allude to the universal custom of younger brothers of rank going to serve as pages in families of the nobility. This multiplied their points of contact, and made them more personally acquainted with each other than they otherwise would have been. See a re-markable conversation in The New Inn, acted in 1629.[1]

Dr. Paris, whose prejudices, if he has any, are certainly not democratic, says : 'In England, we may in vain search amongst the aristocracy for one who feels a dignified respect for the sciences.'[2] And a century has just elapsed since Dr. Shebbeare wrote: 'No man of letters is acceptable to the great ; they look on him as a kind of satire on their actions, and feeling within their own vacuity, are by no means pleased with beholding in another what they want themselves.'[3]

Dekker[4] says: 'You mistake if you imagine that Pluto's porter is like one of those big fellows that stand like giants at lords' gates, having bellies bumbailed with ale, in lamb's wool, and with sacks, and cheeks strutting out like two footballs, being blown up with powder beef and brewis.'

As the monarchical power declined, the aristocratic power rose, and the Church was not strong enough to keep it down. It remained for Elizabeth to destroy their *moral* power. Though other great sovereigns had diminished their wealth and abridged their privileges, Elizabeth was the first who systematically ex-cluded them from her counsels. Mr. Hallam[5] says that the Haynes' and Murdin's State Papers show that in 1569 the duke

---

[1] Ben Jonson's Works, 8vo, 1816, vol. v. pp. 332, 333.
[2] Life of Sir Humphrey Davy, 8vo, 1831, vol. ii. p. 181.
[3] Angeloni's Letters on the English Nation, 8vo, 1755. vol. ii. p. 14.
[4] Knights Conjuring, 1607, 44. Percy Soc. vol. v.
[5] Constitutional History, vol. i. p. 131.

of Norfolk actually invited Alva to invade England, and that it is probable from p. 10 of Murdin that Norfolk, on this occasion, pretended to be a Catholic. In 1557, the Venetian ambassador says that the English nobility 'all live in the country, remote from the city.'[1] He adds that all the nobility kept stores of arms for their retainers, and that some of the most powerful could bring thousands of men into the field. Aristocracy fell with chivalry. Frederick Schlegel says: 'The heroic spirit of chivalry and the whole moral character of the middle age were long paramount in England ; and hence in the poetry of no country, if we except the Spanish, is that spirit so conspicuous.'[2] Northumberland was incited to the rebellion of 1569 by the queen having granted away a copper-mine found on his estate.[3] In 1572 the duke of Norfolk was executed, and soon afterwards his eldest son, the earl of Arundel, was arrested, and in 1595 died in confinement. The earl of Northumberland was thrown into the Tower, and in 1585 executed.[4] Forman speaks twice of ' the Duke of Arligrove ;' who was he ?[5] Lord Brougham has pointed out how it is that as the monarchy declines, the aristocracy rises in power.[6] Lord Brougham, after giving a striking description of the savages who devastated Europe, says,[7] 'The present distribution of rank and power and influence in Europe may be mainly traced to the character and habits of those savage tribes.' Brougham says,[8] 'The first patent of peerage was granted in Richard the Second's reign, in the year 1387.' This was, I suppose, a blow to the aristocracy. At vol. i. pp. 344-354, Brougham has estimated with considerable ability the tendencies of an hereditary aristocracy. And he adds [9] that as the people rise in importance, the prince finds it necessary to court the nobility. Lord Brougham says: [10] 'The period in a nation's progress at which the aristocratic power is naturally established, must always be while the body of the people are in a low state of refinement.'

Henry I. 'employed all the energies of the law and the ser-

---

[1] Michele's Report in Ellis's Original Letters, 2nd series, vol. II. pp. 220-222.
[2] Philosophy of History, Lond. 1846, p. 430.
[3] Soames' Elizabethan Religious History, p. 143.   [4] Ibid. pp. 346, 347.
[5] Autobiography of Dr. Simon Forman, from 1552 to 1602, edit. Halliwell, 1849, 4to. p. 54.
[6] Political Philosophy, 2nd edit. 8vo, 1849, vol. I. p. 78.
[7] Ibid. p. 306.   [8] Ibid. p. 315.   [9] Ibid. p. 354.
[10] Ibid. vol. II. p. 19.

vices of corrupt judges to entrap and convict great landowners, whose forfeited estates on their attainder he bestowed on men of the basest and most abandoned lives.'[1] He adds:[2] 'The power of the barons and of all landed proprietors was exceedingly increased by the famous statute De Donis, which allowed them to entail their real property, and thus to sustain the landed aristocracy.' During the Wars of the Roses, the old nobility was almost extinguished, and a further increase was given to the royal power by the state of its finances. Almost all the concessions made by the Crown had been the result of its pecuniary difficulties ; but Henry VII. was not thus embarrassed, for he was avaricious, and 'was the first king since Henry III. who ever lived within his income.'[3]

Mr. Alison seems to think it of Divine origin, for he gravely says of the 'gradation of ranks' that 'it may safely be concluded that it is intended to answer some important purpose in the economy of nature ;'[4] and yet this same celebrated Tory writer confesses the low tastes of many of our aristocracy ;[5] but he takes for granted[6] that it is the 'hereditary aristocracy which forms the great political distinction between the eastern dynasties and the European monarchies,' and hence he infers[7] the necessity of primogeniture ; but he opposes entails.[8]

Schiller ascribes to Charles V. the policy of impoverishing the aristocracy of the Low Countries by sending them on expensive embassies: 'Unter dem scheinbaren Vorwande von Ehrenbezeugungen.'[9] In 1585, Leicester was charged with improperly assuming the title of 'excellency,' but to this he replied that strangers had always so called him ever since he had been made an earl.[10] In 1500, an intelligent observer remarked of the English that 'every one, however rich he may be, sends away his children into the houses of others, whilst he in return receives those of strangers into his own.'[11] Ranke *seems* to say that in Italy in the sixteenth century, the aristocratic spirit was stronger in the

---

[1] Political Philosophy, 2nd ed. 8vo, 1849, vol iii. p. 217.   [2] Ibid. p. 232.
[3] Brougham's Political Philosophy, vol. iii. p. 251.
[4] Principles of Population, 8vo, 1840, vol. i. p. 89.   [5] Ibid. vol. ii. p. 65.
[6] Ibid. p. 50.   [7] Ibid. pp. 50, 51.   [8] Ibid. pp. 57, 58.
[9] Abfall der Niederlande in Schiller's Werke, Band viii. Seite 66, Stuttgart, 1838.
[10] See Leycester Correspondence, p. 94.
[11] Italian Relation of England, Camden Soc. vol. xxvii. p. 25.

north than in the south.[1]   See also[2] some interesting remarks on
the rise of the aristocratic principle in Italy early in the sixteenth
century, shown by the general introduction of titles, &c.   In
1669, Pepys met 'a country gentleman,' who spoke 'about the
decay of gentlemen's families in the country, telling us that the old
rule was, that a family might remain fifty miles from London one
hundred years, one hundred miles from London two hundred
years, and so farther or nearer London more or less years.   He
also told us that he hath heard his father say, that in his time it
was so rare for a country gentleman to come to London, that
when he did come, he used to make his will before he set out.'[3]
The porter's lodge was used in 1669 for whipping.[4]

Weld[5] says that two of the secretaries of state in the reign of
Charles II., Sir Leoline Jenkins and Sir Joseph Williamson, 'had
both been tutors.'

Combe[6] says that the sons of young parents are generally
born with feeble brains ; and the eldest son of a noble family has
generally less intellect than his brothers.   This, of course, is an
argument against primogeniture.   It cannot be concealed that
the aristocracy, though, like every other class, improving, have
not maintained their relative superiority to the great body of the
people.   Adam Smith defended aristocracy on the ground that it
is necessary for men to be led by *external* marks ; but now the
progress of education enables men to perceive *internal* merit.[7]
In 1695, Evelyn[8] says : 'Never were so many private bills for
unsettling estates, showing the wonderful prodigality and decay of
families.'

Alison[9] says that a great misfortune in France was the title
going to *all* the children, which prevented a *fusion* between the
nobles and people.

Sir William Temple,[10] about the middle of the reign of
Charles II., says, 'I think I remember within less than fifty
years the first noble families that married into the city for down-
right money.'   The spirit of their miserable etiquette has reached

[1] Die Römischen Päpste, Berlin, 1838, Band I. Seite 394.   [2] Ibid. p. 489.
[3] Pepys's Diary, 8vo, 1828, vol. iv. pp. 319, 320.   [4] Ibid. p. 328.
[5] History of the Royal Society, 8vo, 1848, vol. I. p. 263.
[6] Lectures on Moral Philosophy, 8vo, 1840, p. 115.   [7] Ibid. p. 379.
[8] Diary, vol. iii. p. 341.   [9] History of Europe, vol. I. p. 100.
[10] Works, 8vo, 1814, vol. iii. p. 59.

its height in China. Early in the seventeenth century, when the aristocratic power began to revive in Rome, the custom was introduced of a person stopping his carriage on meeting one of superior rank.[1] In Sweden, there is a great passion for titles and personal decorations among the middle classes; and this has lowered their moral standard.[2] Tocqueville[3] says that no nation ever *created within itself* an aristocracy; but that all aristocracies are the result of conquest. The power of the French nobles was so great that Richelieu was accused of a 'monstrous abuse of authority' in declaring war against their consent.[4]

Aristocracy, I think, passes through the different stages of *strength, age, birth, wealth,* and *intellect.* Of strength, when men have no knowledge; of age, when, there being no science, all knowledge is *empirical,* and experience everything; of birth, when the accumulation of wealth or conquest raise a few families above the others.

There are hardly any really old aristocratic families in Europe.[5]

It has been shown from decisive evidence that the shortest-lived classes are kings, then nobles, then 'gentry,' then 'professional persons'—particularly 'clergy'; while the longest lives of all are agriculturists.[6] The marriages of the aristocracy are very unfruitful.[7] The North American Indians have a remarkable respect for old people.[8] As the division of labour arose, there sprung up professions, and it was soon seen that *they* were not hereditary, and that men are not born great lawyers or good physicians. In Letters from the Baltic, 8vo, 1841, vol. ii. p. 134, it is said of the Estonians, that they pay attention solely to *birth,* and 'that none of that undue preference is given to wealth, as in countries more advanced,' ii. p. 134; and at p. 139 the authoress says : 'In Russia, no one may advance in the military service, in Estonia, no one may purchase an estate, and in Weimar, no one may enter the theatre by a particular door, who has not a *de*

---

[1] Ranke, Die Römischen Päpste, Band III. Seiten 63, 64.
[2] See Laing's Sweden, pp. 64, 65, 117–121.
[3] Démocratie en Amérique, tome III, p. 960.
[4] St. Aulaire, Histoire de la Fronde, tome I. p. 10.
[5] Journal of the Statistical Society, vol. ii. p. 463.
[6] Ibid. vol. viii. pp. 73, 74, 76, 77, 306; vol. ix. pp. 41–43, 45, 47, 49 ; vol. x. p. 65; vol. xiii. pp. 313, 314, 315, 320 ; vol. xiv. p. 295.
[7] Ibid. vol. xiv. p. 79.
[8] See Buchanan's North American Indians, 8vo, 1824, pp. 71, 72.

prefixed to his name.' Forbes says : [1] 'I can with pleasure and with truth record that the generality of Indians, of whatever religious profession, whether Hindoos, Mahomedans, or Parsees, pay a great respect and deference to age ; the hoary head is by them considered a "crown of glory."' 'Marriages under the age of twenty' have bad physical results.[2] Intermarriage between relatives causes congenital deafness.[3]

In the agreement between the Scotch and the duke of Norfolk in 1559, the duke has himself entitled 'the noble and mighty *prince*, Thomas, duke of Norfolk.' [4] The duke of Norfolk *before* his arrest assumed a high and almost independent [style]. See his Letters in Haynes's State Papers, pp. 299, 442. In January 1562, the queen's treatment of the earl and countess of Hertford seems to have caused great discontent in London.[5] In 1570, the duke of Norfolk was in debt.[6]

Elizabeth, immediately after her accession, appointed eight new councillors, of whom two only were men of rank, the Marquis of Northampton and the Earl of Bedford ; the others were Sir Thomas Parry, Sir Edward Rogers, Sir Ambrose Cave, Sir Francis Knowles, Sir Nicholas Bacon, and Sir W. Cecil. In 1561, she threw the earl of Hertford into the Tower because he married without her consent. Another means by which the queen weakened the aristocracy was by her expensive visits. Hume [7] quotes Life of Burghley, published by Collins, p. 40, to the effect that each visit she made to Burghley 'cost him two or three thousand pounds.'

Mary's desire to gratify the nobility was so great that it even conquered her superstition, and induced her to consent that they should not be disturbed in their possession of the Church property they had acquired during the reign of Henry VIII. That this was her reason we know from Ambassades de Noailles, iv. 36.

In September, 1571, the duke of Norfolk was thrown into the Tower 'without any trouble save a number of idal rascal people, women, men, boys, and girls, running about him, as the manner is, gazing at him ;' [8] but what I suppose was his first arrest in 1569

[1] Oriental Memoirs, vol. i. p. 132.
[2] Transactions of Association for Social Science, 1859, pp. 506, 507.
[3] Ibid. pp. 544, 545.   [4] Haynes's State Papers, p. 254.
[5] Ibid. p. 396.   [6] Ibid. p. 597.
[7] Appendix to Elizabeth, No. III.   [8] Murdin, p. 149.

very much displeased the Londoners;[1] and in 1571, he writes[2] that even the Londoners, *though they disliked him*, ran from all parts to salute him as he was going to the Tower, and censured government for arresting him. The consequence was that the greatest precautions were used in the capital by reinforcing the watch, &c.[3] In January, 1572, the French ambassador writes from London to his court that when the duke of Norfolk was tried, the guards were doubled at the palace, the streets lined with troops, and the prisoner himself taken to Westminster by water on account of 'grande crainte de sédition par la ville.'[4]

The queen several times countermanded the execution of the duke of Norfolk.[5] This was perhaps from a fear of a rising among his dependants.

In 1585, Morgan writes to Mary of Scotland to the effect that the great families in the north of England had received 'a great check' by the appointment of Sir A. Paulet as her keeper.[6]

The aristocracy, by the coolness of Elizabeth, were driven back to the bosom of the church, which, in the hope of securing her favour, some of them had quitted. In March, 1586, Morgan writes to Mary of Scotland: 'The earl of Arundel is now a sound Catholic, and his affliction which followed in short time after his reconciliation to the Catholic church had without doubt done him infinite good.'[7]

In 1588, a colonel in the army, if 'a nobleman,' received 20s. a day; if he were only 'a knight, or nobleman's son,' he received 13s. 4d.[8]

In 1548, Sharington said that the admiral (brother to the Protector) had stated that 'he could make or bring those which be within his rules, and of his own tenants and servants, if he should be commanded to serve, ten thousand men.'[9] This must be an exaggeration. In a list of instructions drawn up just after the accession of Mary we find : 'To remember the lords at London, to send away the greater part of their train.'[10]

In January, 1575, the French ambassador writes to his court that the earl of Oxford was very much suspected by Elizabeth.[11]

[1] Correspondance de Fénelon, tome ii. p. 278.   [2] Ibid. tome iv. p. 235.
[3] Ibid. p. 262.   [4] Ibid. p. 348.
[5] See Murdin's State Papers, p. 177.   [6] Ibid. p. 445.
[7] Ibid. p. 489.   [8] Ibid. p. 615.
[9] Haynes's State Papers, p. 106.   [10] Ibid. p. 192.
[11] See Correspondance Diplomatique de Fénelon, tome vi. p. 361.

Mary, unlike Elizabeth, discouraged the aristocracy from
coming to London. This part of her policy is noticed by the
French ambassador.[1] She even, on the apprehension of an insurrection, ordered them to assemble their retainers in the country.[2]

Mary courted the aristocracy in order to induce them to consent
to her marriage with Philip. This is noticed as her object in
Ambassades de Noailles, Leyde, 1762, tome ii. p. 272. See also
p. 287, and tome iii. p. 147.

Even before the rebellion of 1659 broke out, the Catholic
nobility assured the French ambassador of their favourable inclination towards France.[3] This is the more observable, because
at this juncture the French cabinet assumed a very hostile
attitude, and made Elizabeth apprehensive of a combination of
France and Spain against her.[4] The French government had
just gained a victory over the Huguenots. This encouraged the
English Catholics to persevere. A month before the northern
rebellion broke out, the French ambassador at London writes to
his court : ' Les protestans de ce royaulme ont faict tenir quelques
jours la nouvelle de vostre victoire si secrecte, ou bien l'ont faicte
aller si deguysée, que n'en poulvant les Catholiques avoir quasi
aulcune notice, ilz ont envoyé devers moi bien fort secrectement,
mais non sans ardeur et affection, pour sçavoir ce qui en estoit.'[5]
The whole of Fénelon's sixty-eighth dispatch affords too many
proofs of the unpatriotic feelings of the English Catholics.[6] But
the reader must not fall into the vulgar error of ascribing this to
their religion. If the Catholics had been in possession of the
government, the Protestants would have acted the same disgraceful
part.

In 1536, when Henry VIII. was at the very height of his
power, the duke of Norfolk wrote to him that it was necessary
that the northern borders of England should be governed by
' some man of great nobility ;' and his council not only confirmed
this, but added that 'his majesty could not be served upon his
marches but by noblemen.'[7]

[1] See Ambassades de Noailles, Leyde, 1763, tome ii. p. 110 ; tome iii. p. 30.
[2] Ibid. tome v. p. 321.
[3] Correspondance Diplomatique de Fénelon, Paris, 1840, tome i. pp. 231, 333.
[4] Ibid. pp. 117, 118, 209, 217.
[5] Ibid. tome ii. p. 296.
[6] See also for further evidence ibid. tome iii. pp. 18, 76.
[7] See the two very curious letters in the Hardwicke State Papers, vol. i. pp. 39-43.

While matters were thus tending to the consolidation of a system (Primogeniture) which, if it had been fully established, would have thrown all power into the hands of a few families, and converted England into an oligarchy, there was fortunately an influence at work which saved the nation. This was the clerical power. It is obvious that such a system was entirely opposed to its genius. The Catholics, with a wisdom which we cannot sufficiently admire, had at an early period established the celibacy of the clergy. This, indeed, was consistent with the whole course of their policy. The church, being essentially a moral power, could only hope to maintain itself by precluding the possibility of its functions becoming hereditary, which, by making their exercise the result of the accident of birth, would have degraded the hierarchy to the level of that stupid aristocracy by which it was surrounded. It was therefore with great alarm that the ecclesiastical power now saw the rise of a principle so antagonistic to their own policy.

The earl of Arundel had been one of the negotiators of the peace of Château Cambresis ; but he, in 1564, was confined to his own house.[1] In 1569, there was a quarrel between Cecil and the duke of Norfolk.[2]

The aristocracy, repressed by Henry VII. and Henry VIII., rose in arms against Edward VI. and his uncle. In October, 1549, Lord Russell and Sir William Herbert write to the Protector Somerset respecting ' the civil dissension which has happened between your grace and the nobility.'

In 1553–54, Renard, in a letter to Charles V., speaking of the English, mentions ' the intestine hatred between the nobility and the people.'[4]

LAWS OF PRIMOGENITURE.

AMONG the various circumstances by which the great landed proprietors had endeavoured to secure their power, and perpetuate it in their own families, the laws of primogeniture and entail occupy a conspicuous place. The economical evil of these laws will be hereafter considered ; at present, I shall merely give a view of

[1] See Wright's Elizabeth, vol. I. p. 180.
[2] See Lodge's Illustrations of British History, 1838, vol. I. pp. 475–477.
[3] Tyler's Edward VI. and Mary, vol. I, p. 217.
[4] Ibid. 1839, vol. ii. p. 136.

their history, and particularly of the attempts which have been made to evade their operation.

When the whole fabric of European society was broken up by the dissolution of the Western Empire, there was introduced into Europe a system which was regardless, and indeed ignorant, of the refined wisdom of the civil code, and was only adapted to the barbarians who enacted it. In such a state of society as then existed, money being almost unknown, and trade, manufactures, and commerce being entirely unknown, land was not merely the sole wealth, but it was the sole source of power, and even of security. Those who found themselves possessed of it immediately (?) endeavoured to strike out some mode by which at their death the whole of it should be retained intact. Hence the law of primogeniture. And as it was found advisable to check the extravagance of the heir, a contrivance was hit upon to prevent him from alienating the estate which had descended to him. This contrivance was the law of entail. How much of these laws was known to our Saxon ancestors it is difficult from the fewness of existing documents satisfactorily to determine; but it is certain that the statute known as *De Donis* was the first formal recognition of them in England.

See Blackstone, 8vo, 1809, ii. 116-119. He says that the statute De Donis, though an admitted nuisance, was allowed to be unchecked for nearly 200 years till 12 Edw. IV., when it was first determined by the court in Taltarune's case 'that a common recovery suffered by tenant in tail should be an effectual destruction thereof. Year Book, 12 Edw. IV. 14, 19.' The next step was the 32 Henry VIII. c. 36, 'which declares a fine duly levied by tenant in tail to be a complete bar to him and his heirs, and all other persons claiming under such entail.'

In England, the declining power of the sovereign enabled the aristocracy to introduce primogeniture. By the laws of Henry I. the eldest son had only the best of his father's feuds;[1] and even in the reign of Henry II. Glanville says that 'soccage estates frequently descended to all the sons equally;' but under Henry III. 'we find by Bracton that soccage land, in imitation of land in chivalry, had almost entirely fallen into the right of succession by primogeniture.'[2] But see vol. ii. pp. 287-290, where it is said

---

[1] Blackstone, vol. ii. p. 214.   [2] Ibid. pp. 215, 216.

that before a law of Henry I., no man could sell lands he had himself purchased ; and even by that law he could not alienate those that had descended to him. But by *Quia Emptores*, 18 Edw. I., 'all persons except the king's tenant in capite, were allowed to alienate *all* or any part of their lands; and by 1 Edw. III. even these tenants could aliene by paying a fine to the king.'

As to the *Statute of Fines*—4 Hen. VII.—about which so much has been said, it is merely a copy from a statute of Richard III. So much for the policy of Henry VII.1 See Hallam's Const. History, 1842, i. 11. Mr. Hallam adds, pp. 12, 13 (on the authority of Reeves' English Law, iv. 133), that the object of this statute was not to give tenant-in-tail a greater power over his estate, but rather to check suits for the recovery of lands by establishing a short term of prescription. Indeed, 'in 2 Henry VII. the judges held that the donors of an estate tail might restrain the tenant from suffering a recovery.'

The mischiefs of such a law were not likely to be generally perceived ; but, when men began to inquire as well as to observe, means were adopted to evade it. These means were taken from the civil law. Fines and recoveries. The operation of fines had gradually become very cumbersome and expensive. The proclamations upon them are so numerous that no less than sixteen days in every term were occupied in making them ; 1 but the 31 Eliz. c. 2 ordered that the fines should only be proclaimed four times.2 In the system of ecclesiastical laws which Cranmer drew up in 1552, a father is not allowed to disinherit his son unless he has received some serious injury from him.3

'Before the Conquest, lands in England passed by will, that having been the custom of the Anglo-Saxons and Danes, as of the Romans, though not of the Germans.'4 He adds,5 'the custom of gavelkind existed in Ireland till it was put down by a decision of the judges, 3 Jac. I. ; and in North Wales till the Stat. 34 Hen. VIII.' On the mischievous effect of primogeniture, see vol. i. p. 320. At vol. i. p. 360, Brougham ascribes its origin to

1 This is stated in 31 Eliz. c. 2, in Reeves' English Law, vol. v. p. 94.   2 Ibid.
3 Soames' History of the Reformation of the Church of England, vol. iii. pp. 718, 719.
4 Brougham's Political Philosophy, 2nd. edit. 8vo, 1849, vol. i. p. 285.
5 Ibid. p. 286.

'the influence of the monarchical principle, especially when combined with aristocracy.' He adds [1] that entails were introduced
under the empire, but 'Justinian confined them early in the sixth
century to four descents.' In England 'the law of entail dates
from 1285 ;' and the introduction of entails seems to have followed the establishment of the power of alienation.

Examine the history of Borough English. Montesquieu says [2]
that in Tartary, in Brittany, and the Duchy of Rohan, the
youngest son inherited ; and that this is a law incidental to the
pastoral state ; for the elders had already left their father and
taken cattle with them, the youngest son only remaining at home.
In 1721, Montesquieu enters his protest against 'l'injuste droit
d'aînesse.' [3] In France the division of lands, so far from *increasing*, has actually diminished relatively to the population. [4]

It was to improve the security of these important portions of
the law that Elizabeth now directed her attention. In the twenty-
third year of her reign a law was passed ordering that no recovery
nor fine should be reversed on account of any rasure, or incon-
gruous Latin, or indeed for any want of form or words. It was
also ordered that every writ upon which common recoveries
should be suffered might at the desire of any person be enrolled
in Parliament, and kept in an office called the Office of Inrol-
ment. [5]

The judges, mostly consisting of men who had an interest in
depressing the aristocracy (?), vigorously seconded the policy of
Elizabeth, and baffled all the attempts made by the great landed
proprietors to break down the principles which had been established.

In the same way when attempts were made to limit estates by
a proviso in a deed, the courts again interposed, and refused to
allow the limitation. In 42 Elizabeth it was decided in Corbet's
case that 'a proviso to cease an estate tail, as if the tenant-in-tail
were dead, was repugnant, impossible, and against law ; for the
death of tenant-in-tail was no *cesser*, but only his death without
issue.' Reeves says that the object of the courts was to prevent

[1] Brougham's Political Philosophy, 2nd. edit. 8vo, 1849, vol. i. p. 361.
[2] Esprit des Lois. livre xviii. chap. 21, Œuvres, Paris, 1835. p. 331.
[3] Lettres Persanes, No. cxx. Œuvres des Montesquieu, p. 81.
[4] Journal of Statistical Society, vol. vi. pp. 192, 193, 196.
[5] Reeves, History of English Law, vol. v. pp. 52, 53.
[6] Ibid, vol. v. pp. 75, 77, 78.

perpetuities. This is perhaps the same case as that given by Dyer, 351, and 1 Rep. 83,[1] where it was decided that, 'To make an estate limited to one and the heirs male of his body to cease, as if he was naturally dead on his attempting any act by which the limitation of the land or the estate in tail should be barred, is not good.' It was also determined, I. Vent 21, in Tomlin, *in voce* Proviso (but *when*?), that in the case of a testator who devised lands to a man and the heirs male of his body, such devise to cease if he attempted to alien, the proviso was void. But in Elizabeth's reign provisos were *not* illegal in wills.[2]

The interpretation of the Statute of User was equally unfavourable to the landed proprietors. The scholastic refinements on the construction of that statute had been so numerous as to involve the doctrine of uses in an almost endless labyrinth of complications.

. . . .

The Judges expressed in the strongest language their dislike to the principle of perpetuity involved in the attempt to preserve contingent uses. They did not hesitate to say from their place on the judgment bench, that, sooner than give their sanction to such perpetuities, they would, if there had been any doubt as to the law of this case, have grounded their decision upon the broad ground of public expediency.[3] Bacon put forth all his powers on this occasion against the contingent use.[4] This was a decision of the greatest importance, and Reeves says : 'This case became afterwards a leading decision, not only in uses, but on all contingent limitations.'[5]

In the 4 Hen. VII. it had been declared by statute that a fine should be a bar against all claimants, unless they made claim by way of action or lawful entry within five years ; and in the 32nd of Henry VIII. this provision was extended so as to bar estates tail.[6] The great landed proprietors, unable to evade the law, endeavoured to lighten its pressure ; and laid down that if the five years had commenced, and on the death of the ancestor the right descended to the infant, such infant should, within five years after

---

[1] Quoted in Tomlin's Law Dict. in v. Proviso.
[2] See Reeves, English Law, vol. v. p. 78.
[3] See the remarkable passage in Reeves, vol. v. pp. 167, 168. See also p. 194.
[4] P. 195   [5] History of English Law, vol. v. p. 202.
[6] Tomlin's Law Dictionary, vol. l. 3 t.

he came of age, be allowed to claim the estate.[1] Only three years after the accession of Elizabeth this point was mooted in the great case of Stowell and Zouch, when it was decided that the infant should be barred. This case was reported by Plowden, and a very lucid abstract may be found in Reeves' English Law, v. 53–62.

The last great stronghold of the defenders of perpetuities was the provisos allowed to be inserted in 'executory devises' (?). Our law had always paid a great respect to bequests ; and under their shelter attempts were made to secure perpetuities. Indeed, in the 13th of Elizabeth, it was settled in the Common Pleas 'that a tenant-in-tail might be restrained from alienation by the original donation.'[2] But when, twenty-four years later, a similar case was brought up before the same court, a conference was held with the other judges, and it was unanimously determined that such proviso was void.[3] About the same time, the same decision was given in a similar case in the Court of Common Pleas.[4] However, in the case of Brett *v.* Rigden, which was a case of devise of land in 10 Eliz, it was decided that it was absolutely necessary that there should be a donee in esse capable to take the thing the moment it verted.[5]

REMARKS ON THE POOR LAWS.

*   *   *   *   *   *   *   *

MARRIAGES were made very early. In 1599, the celebrated Dr. Forman married a girl of sixteen.[6] In a lawless age, marriages are naturally early to avoid the risks of abduction. The feudal system too encouraged early marriages by making the hand of a rich ward a *property.* Even Montesquieu[7] says : ' De tout ceci, il faut conclure que l'Europe est encore aujourd'hui dans le cas d'avoir besoin de lois qui favorisent la propagation de l'espèce humaine.' But while population was thus outstripping capital there grew up a strange idea that a precisely opposite process was going on, and that it was necessary to encourage marriages. I

[1] Reeves, English Law, vol. v. p. 53.
[2] Reeves, vol. v. p. 168, who quotes Plowden, p. 408.
[3] Moore, p. 364, in Reeves, English Law, vol. v. p. 171.
[4] Ibid. p. 592, in Reeves, vol. v. p. 172.
[5] Plowden, p. 341, in Reeves, vol. v. pp. 73, 74.
[6] See Autobiography of Dr. Forman, edit. Halliwell, 1849, p. 30.
[7] Esprit des Lois, livre xxiii. chap. vi., Œuvres, Paris, 1835, p. 404.

believe this notion lingered till the time of Malthus. Montesquieu adopts it in his youthful work,[1] and also in his great work, the Esprit des Lois. Montesquieu notices the stimulus given to population by doing away with the celibacy of the clergy.[2]

I have thus stated a few of the most obvious circumstances which paved the way to the depression of the people and the increase of the poor. But there is yet another cause, which, though less obvious, is more important than any I have stated, which is in full operation at the present moment, and which, as it seems likely to become more efficient, is almost the only real inconvenience which man has sustained in passing from barbarism to civilization.

The feelings and passions of the mind, which are so complicated in their first appearance, are still more complicated in their ultimate effects. Thus, the advance of general benevolence, which is perhaps one of the most unerring tests of civilization, has produced one serious mischief,—I allude to the establishment of foundling hospitals. To provide for those who are left destitute by no fault of their own, and who are utterly unable to provide for themselves, is a labour so soothing to our sympathies that it may appear a refined political paradox to point out its inconveniences. And yet those inconveniences are great and permanent. The love of a mother for her offspring is one of those feelings which not only ennoble our common nature, but which form one of the most certain protections to the whole of an organised society. The establishment of foundling hospitals, by removing the apprehensions of a mother as to the fate of her child, is a direct incentive to bastardy and to concubinage. This is evident on a mere view of the nature of things, and is supported by the most decisive statistical evidence.

M. Quetelet suggests[3] that the religious ceremonies performed in Catholic countries at the bedside of a patient may often accelerate or even cause his death. If this is true, the mortality must be greater in Catholic than in Protestant countries.

In Alison's Principles of Population, 8vo, 1840, there are some singularly superficial remarks upon the poor laws and population. See, for instance, vol. i. p. 36, where he quite forgets the neces-

---

[1] Lettres Persanes, No. cxlii. pp. 75, 76.
[2] Ibid. No. cxviii. Œuvres, Paris, 1835. p. 60.
[3] Sur l'Homme, tome i. p. 229.

sity of cultivating inferior soils. He says [1] with truth that artisans
and men engaged in commerce must be fed by the labours of
agriculturists ; hence he supposes that the increase of trade and
commerce in England, is a proof that productiveness is gaining
ground upon population ; and he adds [2] that the same thing is
shown by the low interest of money. He charitably says [3] that the
attacks made on the poor laws proceed from the vexation of the
selfish at being *obliged* to contribute towards the support of the
poor. Alison, who has had good opportunities of observing,
says that the poorer the labouring classes are, the greater the
number of their marriages. [4] Amid all this nonsense, Alison has
one good remark. He says that, while slavery existed, the landlords were obliged to feed their slaves ; but when that was done
away with, it was necessary for government to feed them, *hence*
poor laws ; and, while in Russia, Poland, Hungary, and Moravia
there are no poor laws (because the poor, being the *property* of
their masters, have a claim on them), yet we find them in every
civilized country, in England, Scotland, France, Flanders, Austria,
Prussia, Switzerland, and Norway. [5]

HISTORY OF PRICES.

In 1569, military horsemen paid 'one penny a meale, and one
penny night and day for haye.' [6] At pp. 333, 334, of Sharp's
Memorials of the Rebellion, is a list of the expenses incurred in
1571 and 1572 for the Earl of Northumberland. Among them is,
'for iij post-horses from Alnwick to Morpeth, 3s. 4d.,' and the
same from Morpeth to Newcastle, and from Newcastle to Durham.
Mention is made in 1560 of 'the ordynarye bordes heare at vid.
the meale.' [7] This seems to have been at one of the towns of the
north of England ; but Sir C. Sharp does not say which.

Jacob [8] has published the contract prices at the Royal Hospital
at Chelsea for 1730 to 1732, and 1791 to 1793, both inclusive, by
which it appears 'that, in the sixty years, the advance on bread,
beef, mutton, cheese, and butter had been at the rate of 20 per

[1] Principles of Population, vol. I. pp. 58, 59.
[2] P. 63.   [3] Vol. ii. p. 192.
[4] Alison's Principles of Population, 8vo, 1840, vol. ii. pp. 206-214.
[5] Ibid. pp. 170-175.
[6] Sharp's Memorials of the Rebellion, 8vo, 1840, p. 24.   [7] Ibid. p. 378.
[8] History of the Precious Metals, vol. III. p. 303.

cent. ; that on pease and oatmeal more, and that on coals still more.'[1]

In Woodchurch church, Cheshire, there is 'suspended a large table, containing a list of the benefactors to the parish,' in which 'appears the name of James Goodier, of Barnstow, who gave 20 marks in 1525 to buy 20 yoke of bullocks for the poor of the parish, afterwards set apart for the purchase of cows, to be hired out to the poor at 2s. 8d. per annum.'[2]

Early in the sixteenth century, Goodman's Fields had a farm, at which Stow, when a young man, used to buy milk, 'three ale pints for a halfpenny in the summer, nor less than one ale quart for a halfpenny in the winter.'[3] In 1533, it was ordered in London that beef should be sold for a halfpenny, and mutton for a halfpenny farthing a pound, very much to the displeasure of Stow, who says that before that time the price of beef was 1d. for 3 lbs. ; a fat ox, 26s. 8d. ; a fat wether, 3s. 4d. ; a fat calf, the same; and a fat lamb, 12d.[4] In 1547, the price of Malmsey wine was one penny halfpenny the pint.[5] At the beginning of the sixteenth century, the price of soap varied in London from ½d. to 1½d. the pound.[6] In 1531, Stow gives a list of prices in London : a 'great beef,' 26s. 8d. ; 'carcass of an ox,' 24s. ; and a 'fat mutton,' 2s. 10d. ; a 'great veal,' 4s. 8d. ; pigeons, 10d. a dozen.[7] The rise of prices is noticed in a proclamation by Elizabeth in 1560,[8] but is solely ascribed to the depreciation of the currency. In Stafford's Brief Conceipt of English Policy, published in 1581, the rise of prices is frequently mentioned. Of labourers, we are told : 'All things are so dear that by their day wages they are not able to live ' ;[10] and[11] 'such of us as do abide in the country still cannot with 200l. a year keep that house that we might have done with 200 marks but sixteen years past.' Again : 'I have seen a cap for 13d. as good as I can get now for 2s. 6d. ; of cloth, ye have heard how the price is risen. Now a pair of shoes cost 12d., yet in my time I have bought a better for 6d. Now I can never get a horse shooed under 10d. or 12d.,

[1] Jacob, vol. ii. p. 219.
[2] Ormerod's History of Cheshire. 1819, vol. ii. p. 288.
[3] Stow's London. edit. Thoms. 8vo. 1842, p. 48.
[4] Survey of London, 8vo, 1842, p. 71.   [5] Ibid. p. 90.
[6] Ibid. p. 94.   [7] Ibid. p. 145.
[8] See it in Harleian Miscellany, edit. Park, vol. viii. pp. 68-71.
[9] See it in vol. ix. of Harleian Miscellany.   [10] P. 147.   [11] P. 149.

where I have also seen the common price was 6d.'[1] He says[2] that within thirty years the price of 'the best pig or goose that I could lay my hand on' had risen from 4d. to 12d. ; that a good capon, which could then have been purchased for 3d. to 4d., had doubled or trebled in price ; and that the same proportional rise had taken place in hens, which had been 2d. each, and chickens, which had been 1d. each. He adds[3] that a man with 300l. a year could scarcely live so well as his father would have done on 200l. a year. Dekker notices the rise in prices, but ascribes it to the increase of population.[4] In Giffard's Dialogue concerning Witches,[5] one of the speakers says of a friend of his : 'He lost six hogs, he would not have took fifteen shillings a hog for them'; and[6] we hear of a 'gelding worth ten pounds.' Croke, in his will dated 1554, says : 'I bequeath to every of my servants, men and women, a black livery at 7s. or 8s. the yard, the men to have coats, the women gowns.' See documents relating to the Croke Family, p. 63 in Percy Soc., vol. xi. At p. 64, we hear of black gowns, at 10s. the yard. In 1573, 'the hire of two hacknies from Sittingbourne to Canterbury' was 4s. ; from Rochester to Sittingbourne, the same ; and, from Canterbury to Gravesend, also for two hacknies, 10s.[7] In 1576, the hire of a horse was from 18d. to 20d. a day ;[8] but in 1582 it had advanced to 2s. See at p. 183, four entries for that amount. In 1573 flannel was 9d. a yard.[9] In 1578 'cotten candles' were 4d. a pound, and 'cearing candle' 12d. ;[10] and in 1580 'cotten candles' were 4d. a pound.[11] In 1574 coals were 8d. 'the sack,'[12] and in 1576 they were 9d.,[13] and the same price in 1578.[14] In 1580 they had risen to 10½d.,[15] and in 1580 they were 1s.,[16] and also in 1581 they were 1s.[17] In 1573 they were 22s. a load ;[18] in 1580 they were 26s. ;[19] but in 1581 they were only 18s.[20] In 1586 Charles Paget writes from Paris to Mary of Scotland that 'every-

[1] Stafford's Brief Conceipt of English Policy, 1581, p. 154.
[2] P. 156.   [3] P. 173.
[4] A Knight's Conjuring, 1607, p. 39, Percy Society, vol. v.
[5] 1603, Percy Society, vol. viii. p. 9.   [6] At p. 19.
[7] See p. 45 of Mr. Cunningham's very valuable Extracts from the Accounts of the Revels at Court, Shakesp. Soc. 8vo, 1842.
[8] See several entries at pp. 111, 112 of Cunningham's Revels.
[9] See Cunningham's Revels, p. 54.   [10] Pp. 131, 132, 144.
[11] P. 157.   [12] P. 87.   [13] P. 119.   [14] P. 124.   [15] P. 166.
[16] P. 164.   [17] P. 174.   [18] See two entries at pp. 63, 70.
[19] Pp. 157, 158, 72.   [20] P. 180, and another entry at p. 181.

thing is excessive dear.' See Murdin's State Papers, p. 507, and again at p. 510, 'all things being unreasonable dear.'

The French Ambassador, in a letter to his own court written at London in May 1574, complains bitterly of the dearness of everything; and that in one year the price of all provisions had risen 50 per cent, and some 100 per cent;[1] but the context shows that the French Ambassador was afraid that the French court would cut down his salary. Early in Elizabeth's reign the usual allowance to ambassadors for their diet was 3*l*. 6*s*. 8*d*. a day.[2] In 1586, provisions at 'Margat in Kent,' were much dearer than in London.[3] In 1469 the price of the best sheep in Nottinghamshire was something above 13*d*. each.[4] In 1481, 'fat oxen' cost 18*s*. each.[5] In the Rutland Papers[6] there is a curious list of articles with their prices in 1521. 'Bieffes' are 40*s*., 'muttons' 5*s*., 'veales' 5*s*., 'hogges' 8*s*. In 1516, the price of lead was from 4*l*. to 4*l*. 6*s*. a fother; the fother was 2,000 pounds.[7] In 1575, at Rouen, diaper cost 8*s*. 2*d*. the ell; and 'whited canvass' 3*s*. 5*d*. the ell.[8] In 1575, Ralph Barber, who seems to have been a commissioner or merchant, enters in his accounts, 'Two shirts for my man at 3*s*. 4*d*. a piece.'[9] In the same year, he puts down 16*d*. per week for three weeks 'for my horse grass at Rye.'[10] In 1548, candles cost 2*d*. a pound.[11] In 1548 (?) 'muttons' cost 5*s*. a piece.[12] In 1593, the provisions necessary for the Royal Household were contracted for at fixed prices.[13] 'Fat and great veals of the age of six weeks and upwards 6*s*. 8*d*. a piece; fat and good lambs 12*d*. each; capons 4*s*. a dozen; hens 2*s*. a dozen; pullets 18*d*. a dozen; geese 4*s*. a dozen; and chickens 1*s*. the dozen.'[13] See also at pp. 276, 277, a letter in which Elizabeth's fishmonger proposes to Sir William More to buy some of More's carp for which he offers 12*d*. to 18*d*. each. In 1556, coals cost 16*s*. the load.[14] In 1552, a proclamation was issued commanding all butchers in London to sell 'beef, mutton, and veal,

[1] Correspondance de Fénelon, Paris, 1840, tome vi. p. 119.
[2] See Wright's Elizabeth, 8vo, 1838, vol. i. p. 449.
[3] See Leycester Correspondence, Camden Society, p. 51.
[4] See Plumpton Correspondence, Camden Society, p. 21.
[5] Ibid. p. 41.   [6] Camden Society, p. 41.
[7] See Lodge's Illustrations of British History, 1838, vol. i. pp. 20, 29.
[8] Ibid. vol. ii. p. 69.   [9] Ibid. p. 72.
[10] P. 71.   [11] Loseley's Manuscripts, edited by Kempe, p. 81.
[12] Ibid. p. 179.   [13] Ibid. p. 273.   [14] Ibid. p. 12.

the best, $1\frac{1}{2}d.$ the pound, and necks and legs, at $\frac{3}{4}d.$ the pound, and the best lamb the quarter $8d.$'[1]   In 1553, three tons of beer cost together $3l.$ $1s.$ $8d.$; a quarter of beef, weighing 110 pounds, cost $9s.$ $2d.$; a side of beef, weighing 145 pounds, cost $12s.$ $1d.$; ' a veal, $4s.$; half a veal, $2s.$ $4d.$; two muttons, $9s.$ $4d.$'[2]   In 1621, the price of everything was low, except corn.[3]   The rise of prices is noticed in a letter from Hooper to Cecil in 1551.[4]   He says[5] that ' the body of a calf is in the market, $14s.$; the carcass of a sheep at $10s.$'   See also[6] a paper on the ' Causes of the Universal Dearth in England,' dated 1551, in which it is said,[7] ' The purveyor alloweth for a lamb worth $2s.$, but $12d.$; for a capon worth $12d.$, $6d.$; and so after that rate.'   In 1775, Captain Topham writes from Edinburgh, ' The necessaries of life are almost as dear as in London.'[8]   In 1550, Sir John Mason writes from Paris to the English Council : ' It is a marvellous thing to see the dearth of this country.   I assure your lordship that all kinds of victuals bear double the price of what they do in England.'[9]   See also[10] the complaint in 1551 of Bishop Hooper, that in consequence of enclosures, prices even of meat had greatly risen.   On the rise of prices in consequence of the discovery of America, see Blanqui, Histoire de l'Économie politique, tome i. pp. 329, 330. For lists of prices see Monteil, Histoire des Français des Divers États, tome i. pp. 145, 146, 156 ; tome iii. p. 41 ; tome iv. p. 43 ; tome v. p. 216 ; tome vi. p. 240 ; tome viii. pp. 100-117.   In Journal of Statistical Society, vol. ii. pp. 214-216, there is a curious list of prices at Penzance, in Cornwall, from 1746 to 1813. In Journal of Statistical Society, vol. xiii. p. 213, is stated the interesting fact that the lower classes, both in food and dress, ask for things of a certain price, as $3d.$ of cheese, &c., so that a rise in price affects not their *pockets*, but their *comforts*.   In 1741, the ordinary price of cherries at Birmingham was ' a halfpenny a pound.'[11]   Keith's Church and State in Scotland, vol. ii. p. 387.

.   .   .   .

[1] Machyn's Diary, Camden Society, vol. xlii. p. 24.
[2] Chronicle of Queen Jane and Mary, Camden Society, 1850, p. 112.
[3] Yonge's Diary, Camden Society, vol. xli. p. 52.
[4] Tytler's Edward VI. and Mary, vol. i. pp. 364-367.   [5] P. 365.
[6] At pp. 367-371.   [7] P. 369.
[8] Letters from Edinburgh, 8vo, 1776, p. 111.
[9] Tytler's Edward VI. and Mary, 8vo, 1839, vol. i. p. 298.   [10] P. 365.
[11]. Hutton's Life of Himself, 8vo, 1816, p. 48.

HISTORY AND INFLUENCE OF THE COLONIES.

It was not till 1607 that the English first formed a permanent colony. This small beginning of so great an empire was at Jamestown, in Virginia.[1] In 1611 Moll says, 'Take deliberation, sir; never choose a wife as if you were going to Virginia.'[2] Lord Brougham agrees with the general opinion that democracies treat their colonies worse than monarchies treat theirs.[3] He truly adds [4] that the mother country should willingly give up the colonies, and thus part with them in a kindly spirit. Dawson Turner says, that the sailors of Dieppe 'established a colony for the promotion of free trade in Canada, if indeed they were not the original discoverers of that country.'[5] Twiss [6] observes that colonies, by creating a demand for labour, stimulate population in the mother country.

While the domestic administration of Elizabeth had secured internal tranquillity, her foreign administration had excited public spirit. The nation burned with energy. The great Queen well knew how to employ the spirit of her people. Spain groaned under the devastation of the English cruisers. In the Atlantic, in the Baltic, in the Mediterranean, in the Pacific, foreign flags lowered their pennons to the English flag (?). Drake, Gilbert, and Raleigh extended the boundaries of geographical knowledge, and the whole nation was rife with hope. But the great Queen was gathered to her fathers, and was succeeded by a whining pedant. James I. loved peace, not from policy, but from fear. It was not so much that he cherished tranquillity as that he hated enterprise. The national vigour which he would not direct against the spoliators of his daughter he was equally afraid of encouraging at home. But it was too late to repress the spirit of the nation, and the reign of James I. is the epoch of colonisation. The advantages were incalculable. On the one hand wages were kept up,

---

[1] McCulloch's Dictionary of Commerce, 8vo, 1849, p. 335.
[2] Middleton's Works, 8vo, 1840, vol. ii. p. 472.
[3] Brougham's Political Philosophy, 8vo, 1849, vol. i. pp. 510, 511 : and vol. iii. p. 135.
[4] Ibid. vol. ii. p. 20.
[5] Turner's Tour in Normandy, in 2 vols. Lond., 8vo, 1830, vol. i. p. 20.
[6] Progress of Political Economy, 8vo, 1847, p. 220.

which an unprecedented increase of population had seriously lowered. Besides this, we owe to the colonists the first sound principles of legislation.

*　　*　　*　　*　　*　　*　　*

HISTORY ETC. OF WAGES.

THE wardrobe book of Margaret of Anjou, wife to Henry VI., extends from 1452 to 1453. By it we learn that 'her herbman, or gardener, received 100s. a year; her valet of the washing house (called *scalding* house), 40s.; her twenty seven armour-bearers or esquires, 143l. 4s. 4d. in all; and her twenty-seven valets, 93l. 15s. 6d.'[1]

In 1533, the wages of English soldiers in Calais were 8d. a day,[2] or sometimes 6d.[3] In 1541 'the board wages of a woman attending upon the late Countess of Sarum within the Tower' were paid for eighty-three weeks at 18d. a week.[4] In 1537 the maids-of-honour at the court of Anne Boleign received 10l. a year, out of which they had to provide a wardrobe and keep a maid.[5]

In 1379, the wages, in London, of labourers to clear out ditches seem to have been 5d. a day. But this was, perhaps, unusually high; and in 1519 they were also only 5d., while every 'vagabond' (by which, I suppose, is meant the lowest sort of casual labourers) received 'one penny the day, meat and drink.'[6] In 12th of Edward II. the keeper of the king's leopards in the Tower received 'three halfpence a day for diet.'[7] In 14th Edward II. the allowance fixed for prisoners in the Tower, was 'a knight 2d. a day, an esquire 1d. a day, to serve for their diet.'[8] In 1532, West, bishop of Ely, had a hundred servants 'continually in his house.' Half of them received for wages, 53s. 4d., the other half 40s. each yearly, besides a winter and summer dress.[9] In 38th Henry VIII. it was arranged between the king and the city that 'the vicar of Christ's Church was to have 26l. 13s. 4d. the year; the vicar of Bartholomew 13l. 6s. 8d.; the visitor of Newgate

---

[1] Miss Wood's Letters of Royal and Illustrious Ladies, 8vo, 1846, vol. i. p. 98.
[2] Ibid. vol. ii. p. 87.　　　　　[3] Pp. 227, 228, 307.
[4] Ibid. vol. iii. p. 94.　　　　　[5] Ibid. vol. ii. p. 314.
[6] Stow's London, edit. Thoms, 8vo, 1842, p. 8.　[7] Ibid. p. 19.
[8] Ibid. p. 20.　　　　[9] Ibid. p. 34.

(being a priest), 10*l.* ; and five priests who aided in administering the sacrament, &c., each 8*l.*; two clerks, each 6*l.*; and a sexton, 4*l.*'[1] In The Devil is an Ass, which was acted in 1616, Pug offers himself as a servant without wages ; an offer which Fitzdottrel, 'a squire of Norfolk,' accepts, and he says he will turn away his other man 'and save four pounds a year by that.'[2] This makes it evident that wages of servants were 4*l.* a year, and as the scene is laid in London, this probably applies to the metropolis.

In a curious tract in 1538, directed against the monks, it is said : 'Who is she that will set her hands to work to get three pence a day, and may have at least twenty pence a day to sleep an hour with a friar, a monk, or a priest? What is he that would labour for a groat a day, and may have at least twelve pence a day to be a bawd to a priest, a monk, or a friar?'[3] In the time of Tusser it was estimated that one-tenth of the produce of a farm went for rent, and another tenth for wages.[4] It is stated in a proclamation of Elizabeth, in 1560, that just before the reformation of the coinage, wages of soldiers and serving men were from 20*s.* to 20 nobles 'and so upward by the yere.'[5] Money wages did not advance in the same proportion that the value of money fell. In 1581, Stafford writes of labourers, 'All things are so dear that by their day wages they are not able to live,'[6] and we are told[7] that the chief sufferers in the rise of prices were those who had 'their livings and stipends rated at a certainty, as common labourers at 8*d.* a day, . . . serving men to forty shillings a year'; and again[8] 'where 40*s.* a year was honest wages for a yeoman afore this time, and 20 pence a week board wages was sufficient, now double as much will skant bear their charge.'

In a song, published in 1609, we have :—

> 'The serving man waiteth fro' street to street,
> With blowing his nails and beateth his feete,
> And serveth for forty shillings a yeare.'[9]

[1] Stow's London, edit. Thoms, 8vo, 1842, p. 119.
[2] Ben Jonson's Works, 8vo, 1816, vol. v. pp. 21, 22.
[3] Harleian's Miscellany, edited by Park, vol. ii. p. 542.
[4] See Five Hundred Points of Husbandry, edited by Mavor, 1816, pp. 195. 196.   [5] Harleian Miscellany, vol. viii. p. 70.
[6] Brief Conceipt of English Policy in Harleian Miscellany, vol. ix. p. 147.
[7] Ibid. p. 154.   [8] Ibid. p. 174.
[9] Songs of the London 'Prentices, edited by Mr. Mackay for the Percy Society, 8vo, 1841, p. 150.

In 1571 the wages of porters were 12d. a day;[1] and in 1580 we find an entry,[2] under the year 1580, 'the porter at 12d. the daye, and as moche the night.' In 1584, plumbers received 16d. a day.[3] In 1580, 'wyerdrawers' from 16d. to 20d.[4] In 1573, painters had from 20d. to 12d.;[5] and in 1574 they are all put down at 20d.[6] In 1572, common carpenters 12d. a day;[7] in 1573, 16d.[8] and 14d.;[9] in 1580, 16d.;[10] in 1582, also 16d.;[11] and the same in 1584.[12]

In 1573-74, the wages of tailors were 20d., 16d., and 12d. a day.[13] In 1576, 12d. and 20d.;[14] in 1577 the same;[15] and they remained the same in 1582 and 1584.[16]

In Haynes's State Papers[17] there is an account of the expense in 1563 of the East, West, and Middle Marches, by which we learn that the soldiers and the gunners received each 6d. a day. The wages of household servants are put down at 6l. 8s. 4d. a year,[18] and 'one surgeon' at 1s. 6d. a day.[19] In 1588, the surgeon still had only 1s. 6d.[20] In 1588, the wages of seamen in the queen's navy was 14s. a month.[21] In the 20th of Richard II., the following daily wages were paid to those who had the custody of the castle and city of Porchester. The door-keeper and one lad under him 4½d.; the artilleryman, 6d.; the guard, 3d.[22] In 1580, Dr. Dee paid a female servant, Jane, 6s. 8d. a quarter, and a nurse 10s. a quarter;[23] but another woman, who perhaps was a wet nurse, received 6s. a month.[24] However, in 1595, he engaged a 'dry nurse,' who is to have '3l.,' her yere's wagis, and a gown cloth of russet.'[25] In 1592, he writes: 'Richard cam to my service, 40s. yearly and a livery.'[26] In 1602, workmen received 18d. a day; labourers, 12d.; and diggers of gravel, 10d.; also 'cutters of berche,' 10d. Bricklayers received 18d. a day.[27] In 1585, soldiers

[1] See the Revels at Court, edited by Mr. Cunningham, Shakespeare Society, 8vo, 1842, p. 2.　　[2] P. 156.　　[3] P. 190.　　[4] P. 156.

[5] P. 69.　　[6] P. 81.　　[7] P. 40.　　[8] P. 52.

[9] P. 69.　　[10] Pp. 156, 169.　　[11] P. 178.　　[12] P. 190.

[13] Pp. 62, 77, 81.　　[14] Pp. 102, 115.　　[15] Pp. 143, 151.　　[16] Pp. 178, 189.

[17] Pp. 397-401.　　[18] P. 402.　　[19] P. 398.

[20] Murdin's State Papers, p. 614.　　[21] Ibid. p. 620.

[22] Rot. Parl. 20, Richard II. p. 2; 1st February quoted by Mr. Williams in the note at p. 184 of his edition of Chronicque de Richart Deux d'Angleterre, Lond. 8vo, 1846.

[23] Dee's Diary, Camden Society, vol. xix. p. 8.

[24] Pp. 15, 34, 36.　　　　[25] P. 54.　　　　[26] P. 40.

[27] See Sle's account in the Egerton Papers, Camden Society, p. 348.

received 8d. a day.[1] In 1521, the hire of labourers was 6d. a day.[2] In 1557, the English soldiers received 6d. a day for the infantry, and 9d. for the cavalry; but the council in the north proposed that, on account of the 'dearth of things,' they should be raised, 'the footmen to 8d. and the horsemen to 12d.'[3] In 1589, it was ordered that 'every soldier, at all musters and trainings, shall have, over and besides 8d. a day for his wages, a penny a mile for the wearing and carriage of his armour and weapon, and other furniture, so that it exceed not six miles.'[4] In 1540, the wages of painters for the king's revels were '12d. per diem.'[5] In 1551, we find carpenters receiving 1d. per hour; bricklayers the same; labourers, ½d. an hour; plasterers 11d. a day; painters, 7s. 6d. a day.[6] In 1548 (?), Sir Thomas Cawarden paid his servants 40s. a year.[7] In 1621, the labour market was in England so overstocked that many persons offered 'to work for meat and drink only.'[8] In 1512, Sir Edward Howard received as admiral 10s. a day, and the captains 18d.; the men 5s. every lunar month for wages, and another 5s. for victuals.[9] In 1541, workmen at Calais received 8d. a day and the commonest labourers 6d.[10] In 1841, Bishop Copleston writes to Archbishop Whately that he wishes more notice to be taken 'of my speculations on the origin and occasion of the first poor laws in this country. The depreciation of money, I am persuaded, was the main cause, wages not rising with the price of provisions and other necessaries.'[11] In 1686, there was such jobbing in Ireland that, though the king allowed 6d. a day, the soldiers had only 2d. to live upon.[12] In 1705, the common wages of a labourer were 9s. a week; those of a tile-maker 16s. to 20s.[13] In 1676, at Montpellier, 'wages for men 12 sous, for women 5 sous at this

[1] See Leycester Correspondence, Camden Society, p. 27.
[2] Rutland Papers, edit. Camden Society, p. 42.
[3] Lodge's Illustrations of British History, 1838, vol. I. p. 323. See also p. 330.
[4] Ibid. vol. II. p. 403. [5] Loseley Manuscripts, by Kempe, 1835, p. 70.
[6] Ibid. p. 96. [7] Ibid. p. 179.
[8] Yonge's Diary, Camden Society, vol. xli. p. 52.
[9] Chronicle of Calais, Camden Society, vol. xxxv. p. 67.
[10] Ibid. pp. 198, 199.
[11] Memoirs of Edward Copleston, Bishop of Llandaff, by W. J. Copleston, Lond. 8vo, 1851, p. 85.
[12] See Clarendon Correspondence, 1828, 4to, vol. I. pp. 340, 341. See also the details at pp. 379, 380.
[13] See Wilson's Life of De Foe, vol. II. pp. 311, 313.

time' (in January); 'in summer, about harvest, 18 for men and 7 for women;'[1] and in the Grave country, in 1678, peasants received 7 sous a day.[2] In 1680, the English silkweavers received 1s. a day.[3] Comte[4] says Hallam has shown that the real reward of labour has diminished since the fourteenth century. For a list of wages from 1800 to 1836, see Porter's Progress of the Nation, vol. ii. pp. 251-254; Monteil, Histoire des Français des Divers États, tome i. pp. 117, 119, 147; tome v. pp. 217, 284; tome vi. p. 124. In Cornwall, early in the reign of Elizabeth, the wages of the labourers in the tin mines were 4d. a day, out of which the labourer had to spend more than 2d. to find himself 'meate and drinke.' In 1601, Raleigh said that, since 'the granting of my patent' in 1585, wages had risen in Cornwall from 2s. to 4s. a week.[5] On the wages at Penzance, from 1565 to 1770, see Journal of Statistical Society, vol. ii. pp. 217, 218. In 1787, Jefferson travelled through the south of France and north of Italy. He says, at Beaujolois, 'The wages of a labouring man here are five louis; of a woman, one half.'[6] Near Montelimart, in Dauphiné, 'Day labourers receive sixteen or eighteen sous a day, and feed themselves.'[7] At St. Remis, 'a labouring man's wages here are one hundred and fifty livres; a woman's half, and fed.'[8] At Aix, near Marseilles, 'the wages of a labouring man are one hundred and fifty livres the year; a woman, sixty to sixty-six livres, and fed.'[9] At Bordeaux 'they never hire labourers by the year; the day wages for a man are thirty sous, a woman fifteen sous, feeding themselves.'[10] On wages and prices, see Tytler's History of Scotland, Edinburgh, 1845, vol. i. p. 63; vol. ii. pp. 216-221.

CHIVALRY.

Miss Wood has printed a letter from a Mrs. Creke to Cromwell, about 1536, which, as she says, affords 'a curious illustration of

[1] King's Life of Locke, 8vo, 1830, vol. i. p. 102.
[2] Ibid. pp. 146, 147.
[3] See Twiss's Progress of Political Economy, 8vo, 1847. p. 58.
[4] Philosophie Positive, tome vi. p. 336.
[5] See Journal of Statistical Society, vol. i. pp. 71, 72, and Parliamentary History, vol. i. p. 908.
[6] Correspondence of Jefferson, by Randolph, vol. ii. p. 119   [7] Ibid. p. 122.
[8] Ibid. p. 195.   [9] Ibid. p. 127.   [10] Ibid. p. 153.

the system of wardship which was prevalent even in the middle and lower classes of society.'[1]

Puritanism destroyed chivalry.

Chevenix truly says that the progress of military arts alone was enough to destroy chivalry.[2]

Among the various circumstances which resulted from the decline of chivalry, one of the most important was the rise of duelling, which, though unnecessary, and even barbarous in a refined age, has contributed not a little to refining the manners of Europeans.

At the end of the sixteenth century the minstrels declined so much in fame that, by the 39th of Elizabeth, they were classed among 'rogues, vagabonds, and sturdy beggars.' 'This Act,' says Percy, 'seems to have put an end to the profession,'[3] though the *name* is sometimes used.[4] Percy has published[5] a curious poem, 'The Turnament of Tottenham,' in which chivalry is ridiculed. He does not mention the date, but from the language I should assign it to the fourteenth century. There is another ballad, called 'The Dragon of Wantley,' which is a satire on works and romances of chivalry, and was written early in the seventeenth century.[6] Even in the reign of Elizabeth the minstrels were exceedingly well paid.[7]

William Schlegel says : 'From a union of the rough but honest heroism of the northern conquerors and the sentiments of Christianity, chivalry had its origin, of which the object was, by holy and respected vows, to guard those who bore arms from every rude and ungenerous abuse of strength, into which it was so easy to deviate.'[8] Schlegel adds :[9] 'The spirit of chivalry has nowhere outlived its political existence so long as in Spain.'

Warton says[10] that in 1237 we have 'the most early notice of a professed book of chivalry in England.' It has been supposed that Milton was a great reader of the romances of chivalry, but this is doubted by Mr. Keightley, a very competent authority.[11] Ever since the foundation of the Order of the Garter by Edward

---

[1] Letters of Royal and Illustrious Ladies. 8vo, 1846, vol. II. pp. 267, 268.
[2] Essay on National Character, 8vo, 1832, vol. II. pp. 387, 388.
[3] Percy's Reliques, 8vo, 1845, pp. xxi, xxii.   [4] See p. xxxviii.
[5] Pp. 92, 95.   [6] Pp. 268-271.   [7] P. 132.
[8] Lectures on Dramatic Art. Lond. 1840, vol. I. p. 14.   [9] Vol. II. p. 355.
[10] History of English Poetry, 8vo. 1840, vol. I. p. 118.
[11] See Keightley's Tales and Popular Fictions, Lond. 1834. p. 25.

III., there had been held on St. George's Day a grand feast, which lasted for three days. But in 1567, Elizabeth, with the view apparently of doing away with the custom, ordered that for the future it should be kept wherever the sovereign might happen to be.[1] In A.D. 1600, a gentleman in Shropshire died, and his widow actually offered the Secretary of State 1,000l. to be permitted to have the wardship of her own son.[2] Early in the sixteenth century the Spanish aristocracy was, I suppose, the only one then existing which could have produced a Loyola.[3]

·   ·   ·   ·   ·   ·   ·

TOWNS AND CITIES.

In a curious Discourse, written in 1578 by a friend of Stow's, it is said : 'Navigation, I must confess, is apparently decayed in many port towns, and flourisheth only or chiefly at London';[4] and early in the seventeenth century it had become so usual to sell the paternal acres and live in London, that the practice is noticed in Every Man out of his Humour.[5] In a tract called The Present State of England, published in 1627, complaint is made of the eagerness with which people flocked to London from the country.[6] In Stafford's Brief Conceipt of English Policy, 1581, it is said that 'the most part of all the towns of England, London only excepted,' is 'fallen to great poverty and desolation.'[7] This rush to London is ascribed[8] to the great rise in prices which compelled several country proprietors to break up their establishments 'and get their chambers in London or about the court, and there spend their time.'[9] Early in the seventeenth century, Rich notices that 'those whose ancestors lived in stately palaces like princes in their country, bravely attended by a number of proper men, now come and live in the cittie.'[10] Bertie, in a letter to

---

[1] Lodge's Illustrations of British History, 1838, vol. L p. 443.
[2] Sydney Letters, edit. Collins, folio, 1746, vol. ii. p. 197.
[3] See the admirable remarks in Ranke, Die Römischen Päpste, Berlin, 1838. Band i. pp. 179, 180.
[4] Stow's London, edit. Thoms, 8vo, 1842, p. 205.
[5] Ben Jonson, Works, edit. Gifford, 8vo, 1816, vol. ii. pp. 30, 31.
[6] Harleian Miscellany, edit. Park, vol. iii. p. 210.
[7] Ibid. vol. ix. p. 147.   [8] P. 173.   [9] See also pp. 179, 186.
[10] Mr. Cunningham's Introduction to Rich's Honestie of this Age, Percy Society vol. xl. p. xviii.

Cecil in 1569, contrasts the opulence of husbandmen with the poverty of artificers.

Mr. Alison is very severe upon cities, and says that the increase of crime in England is the result of their increasing population.[2] Animal decomposition is not dangerous, and the salubrity of the country has been overrated.[3]

Comte[4] points out the beneficial effects arising from the condensation of population.[6] The Anglo-Saxons had no idea of citizenship like that of the Athenians and Romans, but made the possession of land and not birth the full qualification.[6] Kemble[7] observes that situation is the most powerful element of the prosperity of cities, as we see in Munich and Madrid. He says[8] at first those who assembled in cities were under the authority of the castellan; and 'in truth *burgh* does originally denote a castle, not a town.' In France, in the fourteenth century, none but artisans and tradesmen lived in towns; the clergy and nobles remained on their estates.[9] Monteil[10] says that about the time of the crusades, at the very end of the eleventh century, citizens began to free themselves. It seems to be doubtful[11] whether Laon or Noyon is the first commune; that of Noyon dates from the beginning of the reign of Louis le Gros. Alison[12] says with great simplicity that cities are always democratical. Tocqueville[13] thinks that for the future, cities will increase according to the increase of political rights. In the battles of Crecy and Poitiers, the French nobles were almost annihilated, and this aided the civic communities, which were also favoured by the kings of France.[14] Louis XI. did immense things for the towns.[15] This shows the unimportance *nationally* of morals; for a bad prince like Louis XI. did great good. Henry III. was the first king

[1] See Haynes's State Papers. p. 519.
[2] Alison's Principles of Population. 8vo. 1840. vol. L pp. 4, 46, 47, 140, 141, 517, 518, 568.
[3] Mayo's Philosophy of Living. 2nd edit. 8vo, 1838, p. 214.
[4] Philosophie Positive, vol. iv. pp. 642–644.   [5] See also tome vi. p. 96.
[6] Kemble's Saxons in England, vol. L pp. 88, 89.   [7] Ibid. vol. II. p. 367.
[8] P. 323.
[9] Monteil, Histoire des Français des Divers Etats, tome L pp. 18, 19.
[10] Vol. iii. pp. 122, 123.   [11] Pp. 123, 125.
[12] History of Europe, vol. L p. 224.
[13] Démocratie en Amérique, vol. II. p. 206.
[14] See Ranke's Civil Wars of France, 8vo, 1852, vol. I. pp. 60, 61. Also p. 63.
[15] Ibid. vol. I. p. 101.

who regularly lived in Paris, and under him the city wonderfully increased.[1] In 1588, the population of Paris was half a million.[2] In the middle of the fifteenth century the 'bourgeoisie' of Paris were becoming important enough to be courted by kings.[3] Cities are not in themselves unhealthy; but the mortality is great because in them many persons follow unhealthy occupations.[4] In London bricklayers are more subject to fever than persons who clean the sewers and collect the night soil ! ! ! [5]

BEGGARS IN ENGLAND.

EVEN as late as the end of the sixteenth century Gifford supposes beggars who were diseased or infected used to go about with a *clap dish*, a wooden vessel with a movable cover by clapping which they gave notice of their state.[6] And in 1607, see Middleton's Works, 8vo, vol. ii. p. 169.

In Every Man in his Humour, acted in 1598, Brainworm, wishing not to be known, takes as the most natural disguise the character of a mendicant soldier ; [7] and in Every Man out of his Humour, acted in 1599, there is a character who goes about begging, pretending to be a soldier.   Indeed, it was so common for soldiers to beg, that there was a particular word invented for those who solicited charity under the pretence of having been in the army.   Such begging was called *skeldring*, and is repeatedly mentioned by Ben Jonson.[8]   These disbanded soldiers, when pleading for charity, used to say 'God pays.'   This seems to have become almost proverbial.[9]

In The Roaring Girl, in 1611, when Trapdoor begs, he disguises himself as a poor soldier.[10]   Those who were sent to Bridewell in 1608 were obliged to 'beat chalk, make linen,' &c.[11]

---

[1] Ranke's Civil Wars of France, 8vo, 1852, vol. ii. p. 108.
[2] Ibid. p. 191.   [3] See Montell, Divers États, vol. iv. p. 307.
[4] Journal of the Statistical Society, vol. viii. p. 312.
[5] Ibid. vol. xi. pp. 73, 75, 76, 77, 80.
[6] Note in Ben Jonson's Works, 8vo, 1816, vol. i. p. 44.
[7] Jonson's Works, vol. i. p. 54.
[8] Ibid. 8vo, 1816, vol. ii. pp. 8, 396, 397, 401, 453, 514.
[9] See Ben Jonson's Epigram, Works, vol. viii. p. 158.
[10] Middleton's Works, 1840, vol. ii. pp. 534, 535.
[11] Ibid. vol. iii. pp. 221-236.

In 1669, the pillars of the Temple were 'hung with poor men's petitions.'[1] Were there many mendicant Irish in London? Dekker[2] has, 'more bare than Irish beggars.' In 1578, Googe writes : 'Sir William Drury, a paragon of arms at this day, was wont, I remember, to say that the soldiers of England had always one of those three ends to look for : to be slaine, to begge, or to be hanged.'[3] Rich has preserved the formula of complaint used by the London beggars early in the seventeenth century.[4] By the common law apparently (*but query*) it was felony for soldiers and sailors to wander about the realm, or for persons to pretend to be such.[5] In 1575, Sir Thomas Smith mentions 'the common rowtes nowadays of roging beggars by the highway side, naming themselves soldiers of Ireland lately discharged.'[6] In 1641, Evelyn[7] was struck by the admirable arrangements made in Holland for the poor.

On the poor laws in France, see Monteil, Histoire des Français des Divers États, tome vi. pp. 88-92. A sort of one seems to have been known in A.D. 1530.[8] Foundling hospitals increase illegitimate births.[9] 'The Foundling Hospital of Palermo receives all children deposited in the wheel, without inquiry, and without distinction of sex. About half of the foundlings die within the second year.'[10] The poorer people are, the more they marry.[11] In Frankfort, persons are not allowed to marry unless they have a certain income ; hence, says Colonel Sykes,[12] an immense increase of illegitimate children. The bad influence of foundling hospitals is noticed by Comte.[13] In 1592 the House of Lords made 'a contribution for the relief of such poor soldiers as went begging about the streets of London.'[14]

---

[1] Rowley's Search for Money, Percy Society, vol. II. pp. 27, 47.
[2] Knights Conjuring, 1607, Percy Society, vol. v. p. 40.
[3] Mr. Cunningham's Introduction to Rich's Honestie of this Age, in Percy Society, vol. xi. p. viii.
[4] The Honestie of this Age, 1614, Percy Society, vol. xi, p. 18.
[5] Blackstone's Commentaries, vol. iv. 165. He quotes 3 Inst. 85.
[6] Smith's Letters to Burleigh in Wright's Elizabeth, vol. II. p. 29.
[7] Diary, 8vo, 1827, vol. I. pp. 28, 29.   [8] Monteil, vol. vi. p. 91.
[9] See Journal of the Statistical Society, vol. ii. p. 109.
[10] Ibid. vol. v. p. 200.   [11] Ibid. vol. vi. pp. 152, 153, and vol. I. p. 170.
[12] Ibid. vol. vii. p. 344.   [13] Traité de Législation, tome I. p. 506.
[14] Parl. History, vol. I. p. 864.

HISTORY OF RENTS.

IN a 'supplication' to Henry VIIL, printed in 1544, it is said that 'scarce a worshipfull man's lands, which in times past was wont to feed and maintain twenty or thirty tall yeomen, a good plentiful household for the relief and comfort of many poor and needy, and the same now is not sufficient and able to maintain the heir of the same lands, his wife, her gentlewomen, a maid, two yeomen or lackeys.'[1]   So that the rise of rents did not meet the rise of prices.

In a very curious pamphlet published in 1627, it is stated that within sixty years rents had quintupled.[2]   The rise of rents is mentioned by Greene in 1592.[3]   But there is no doubt that the rise was not equal to the rise in prices.   In Stafford's Brief Conceipt of English Policy, 1581, the knight says that he is compelled to raise the rents of those lands which fall in, but that he has comparatively little opportunity of doing so.   'I do either receive a better price than of old was used, or enhance the rent thereof, being forced thereto for the charge of my household, that it is so increased over that it was ; yet in all my lifetime I look not that the third part of my land shall come to my disposition, that I may enhaunce the rent of the same ; but it shall be in men's holding either by lease or by copy granted before my time and still continuing, and yet like to continue in the same state for the most part during my life and percase my sonnes.'[4]

Dr. Lingard strangely supposes that the rise of rents in the middle of the sixteenth century was caused by a rise in the value of produce, which in its turn was caused by a depreciation of the currency.[5]   In 1746, Mr. Pilkington took 'a pretty decent room at 3l. a year in Great White Lion Street, at the sign of the Dove, near the Seven Dials.'[6]

ROYAL REVENUE AND TAXES.

SIR ROBERT NAUNTON says that during the war with Spain and Ireland, the military expenses of Elizabeth ' 300,000l. per annum

---

[1] Harleian Miscellany, edit. Park, vol. ix. p. 464.
[2] Ibid. vol. iii. p. 207.   [3] Ibid. vol. v. p. 400.
[4] Ibid. vol. ix. pp. 148, 149. See also p. 173.
[5] History of England, Paris, 1840, vol. iv. p. 250.
[6] Richardson's Correspondence, 8vo, 1804, vol. ii. p. 147.

at least, which was not the moiety of her other disbursements and expenses.'[1] He mentions[2] an instance of the care with which she superintended the finances of the country. In the Brief Conceipt of English Policy, 1581, Stafford says of taxes, 'And yet that way of gathering treasure is not always most safe for the prince's surety ; and we see many times the profits of such subsidies spent in the appeasing of the people that are moved to sedition partly by occasion of the same.'[3] There is no doubt that the 'loans' demanded by Elizabeth were in reality compulsory. There is proof of this in a letter written in 1597 copied from the Harleian Manuscripts by Mr. Hallam ;[4] but Hallam adds[5] that the queen always faithfully repaid them, and 'incurred no debt till near the conclusion of her reign.' Lingard[6] says, 'From the report of the Senator Barbaro in the senate of Venice (communicated by H. Howard of Corby, Esq.) it appears that the king's (i.e. Edward VI.) income greatly exceeded his ordinary expenditure in time of peace ; the former being about 350,000l., and the latter about 225,000l. ;' but a year's war in Scotland, adds Lingard, 'had plunged him deeply in debt,' and forced him to borrow money from Antwerp at very high interest. In September 1553, Mary *borrowed* of the Londoners ' 24,000 ou 25,000 escuz sol.'[7] In the same letter Noailles says[8] that 7,000l. sterling are 21,000 or 22,000 escuz sol. But five months later we find her so poor that she could scarcely pay the purveyors of her own palace ;[9] and yet in the very same month she lent money to the Emperor to enable him to fit out his fleet with greater rapidity.[10] Philip was himself surprised at her poverty,[11] to remedy which she adopted the ruinous expedient of borrowing money at high interest.[12] In October 1555 Parliament granted her 16 deniers in the pound, which Noailles estimates[13] would amount to 'environ un million d'or.' Butler[14] quotes Andrews, History of Great Britain, vol. ii. p. 35, to the effect that Elizabeth received yearly 20,000l. from the rich Catholics as the price of dispensations permitting them to abstain from

---

[1] Harleian Miscellany, edit. Park, vol. ii. p. 85.   [2] P. 86.
[3] Ibid. vol. ix. p. 155.
[4] Constitutional History, 8vo, 1842, vol. i. p. 239.   [5] P. 240.
[6] Paris, 1840, vol. iv. p. 260.
[7] Ambassades de Noailles, Leyde, 1763, tome ii. p. 136.   [8] P. 137.
[9] Ibid. tome iii. pp. 96, 97.   [10] Tome iii. p. 120.
[11] Tome iv. p. 80.   [12] Tome v. p. 171.   [13] Tome v. p. 187.
[14] Historical Memoirs of the Catholics, 8vo, 1822, vol. i. p. 292.

church. Montesquieu, from whom so many political writers have stolen without acknowledgment, says : ' Règle générale : on peut lever des tributs plus forts à proportion de la liberté des sujets.'[1] See Wright's Elizabeth, 8vo, 1838, vol. i. p. 143, and vol. ii. p. 361. In the Egerton Papers[2] there are printed the instructions issued in 1600 respecting the sale of Crown lands. For an account of the revenue of Henry VII. in the year 1500, see Italian Relation of England, Camden Soc. vol. xxxvii. p. 47 *et seq.* Alison[3] says Cromwell raised nearly 5,000,000*l.* a year, 'or more than five times as much ' as that raised by Charles I.

In Haynes's State Papers[4] there is one of the queen's privy seals for a loan of money, dated 1569. In it the amount is guaranteed to be repaid within twelve months after it is received. For the expense of the army and navy in 1587 and 1588, see Murdin's State Papers, p. 620, &c., and p. 619, where the yearly expense of victualling the ships and of the wages is 113,438*l.* This, of course, is exclusive of the cost of repair and the chance of loss. The accounts which follow are very confused.

In 1571 the queen could not pay the loans borrowed under the seal when they became due ; and she therefore thought it necessary to apologise, and to request that her creditors would ' be content to forbear payment for such a time as seven months is.'[5] In 1579 [it was] proposed that there should be regular loans made and kept for the Government in banks, whereof there should be one in each shire.[6]

In 1580 the expenses of the queen in Ireland alone were 'above 10,000*l.* a month.'[7] See also p. 664, where Raleigh writes to Sir Robert Cecil in 1593, 'Her Majesty hath good cause to remember that a million hath been spent in Ireland not many years since.'

In Haynes's State Papers[8] there is a minute made by Secretary Paget, from which it appears that in 1545 the military and naval expenses were for six months 104,000*l.*, and that an intended ' benevolence ' was expected to produce 50,000*l.* to 60,000*l.* He

[1] Esprit des Lois, livre xii. chap. xii. Œuvres, p. 296.
[2] Camden Society, pp. 285-287.
[3] History of Europe, vol. vii. pp. 3, 4. [4] P. 518.
[5] Murdin's State Papers, p. 181.
[6] Ibid. p. 327. [7] Ibid. p. 346.
[8] Pp. 54-56.

suggests that ' lands ' should be sold for 40,000*l.* In Haynes's State Papers [1] there is presented a minute by Secretary Cecil, from which it appears that in 1552 the king owed nearly 220,000*l.* The embarrassed Secretary suggests all sorts of expedients for meeting the deficiency.

In April 1575, Elizabeth borrowed by privy seal 60,000 ' livres esterlin (qui sont 200,000 escus) ; ' of this London paid half, the clergy one-sixth, and the other two-sixths, ' le commun du royaulme.' [2]   In 1570 the queen found great difficulty in raising ' l'émprunt de trois mil privés scelz qu'elle a naguières imposez,' and would not use force, fearing another insurrection. [3]

PROGRESS AND TENDENCY OF ENCLOSURES.

GREENE says, [4] ' And first I alledge against the grasier that he forestalleth pasture and medow grounds for the feeding of his cattall, and wringeth leases of them out of poor men's hands.' [5] But the fullest view I have seen of the tendency of enclosures is in Stafford's Brief Conceipt of English Policy, published in 1581, and reprinted in the Harleian Miscellany. [6]   The author says : ' I have known of late a dozen ploughs within less compass than six miles about me, laid down within these seven years, and where three score persons or upwards had their livings, now one man with his cattell hath all.' [7]   The great increase of enclosures is said to have been within thirty years, and chiefly in Essex, Kent, and Northamptonshire. [8]   The reason is clearly stated : [9] ' So long as they find more profit by pasture than by tillage, they will enclose and turn arable land to pasture ; ' and it is proposed [10] to reduce the profits on pasture lands by putting a duty on the export of wool, and at the same time [11] allow the free exportation of corn. Mr. Lewis [12] seems to consider that the enclosures in the sixteenth century were beneficial by destroying the cottier system, and thus relieving the peasants from a ' state of quasi-villenage.'

---

[1] Murdin's State Papers, pp. 126-128.
[2] Correspondance Diplomatique de Fénélon, Paris, 1840, tome vi. pp. 413, 414.
[3] Ibid. vol. iii. p. 160.   [4] Quip for an Upstart Courtier, 1592.
[5] Harleian Miscellany, edit. Park, vol. v. p. 418.
[6] Vol. ix. pp. 139-192.   [7] P. 147.
[8] Brief Conceipt of English Policy, Harl. Misc. vol. ix. p. 160.
[9] P. 161.   [10] P. 162.   [11] P. 163.
[12] Irish Disturbances, 8vo, 1836, pp. 314, 315.

In Tytler's Edward VI. and Mary [1] there is a letter from John
Hales, one of the commissioners appointed to investigate the
causes of the conversion of arable into pasture land. It is dated
July 1548, and addressed to the protector; but contains nothing
of moment. See also [2] a letter in 1551 from Hooper to Cecil, in
which the bishop complains that the price of meat had become
immense because cattle were no longer bred, but only sheep; and
'they be not kept to be brought to market, but to bear wool,
and profit only to their master.' In 1551 it was estimated that
there were in the realm 'thirty hundred thousand sheep,' of
which 1,500,000 were 'kept on the commons, and rated at 1d.
the piece.' [3]

PROGRESS OF TOLERATION.

NEAL says: [4] 'In the first eleven years of her reign (Queen
Elizabeth) not one Roman Catholic was prosecuted capitally for
religion,' and that during the next ten years there were only
twelve priests executed. In 1591 (?) a law was passed which
Neal calls the most cruel that had yet been enacted against the
Puritans.[5] In 1584, Whitgift, archbishop of Canterbury, drew
up twenty-four articles for the use of the Court of High Commission.[6] These articles were so violent that Burleigh wrote to him
stigmatising them in the strongest terms. He says: [7] 'I find
them so curiously penned, so full of branches and circumstances,
that I think the Inquisition of Spain used not so many questions
to comprehend and trap their priests.' Two months later—September 1584—the lords of the council remonstrated with the
archbishop; [8] and a treatise to the same effect was written by
Beale, clerk of the queen's council.[9] He would certainly not have
ventured on this course without feeling certain of Elizabeth's
approbation. In 1584, Aylmer, bishop of London, wrote an
angry letter to the council, but the only notice they took of it
was to remonstrate with that violent prelate.[10] Punishments
gradually became milder. It is stated by Barrington [11] that

---

[1] Tytler's Edward VI. and Mary, 8vo, 1839, vol. i. pp. 113-117.
[2] Ibid. p. 365.   [3] Ibid. p. 370.
[4] History of the Puritans, vol. i. p. 444.   [5] Ibid. vol. i. p. 426.
[6] Ibid. vol. i. p. 337.   [7] P. 339.   [8] P. 341.
[9] Ibid. vol. i. p. 342.   [10] Ibid. pp. 346, 350, 351.
[11] Ancient Stat. p. 269, quoted by Christian, note to Blackstone's Commentaries,
vol. i. p. 137.

'exile was first introduced as a punishment by the legislature in the 39th of Elizabeth.' Parliament has created 160 felonies ![1] An Act of Parliament [2] ordered prisoners to be boiled to death, and Coke[3] mentions several persons who suffered this frightful punishment.[4] In the seventeenth century—(but *when ?*)—a boy eight years old was hung for setting fire to two barns. See Blackstone,[5] who quotes Emlyn on 1 Hal. P. C. 25. He adds, on the authority of Foster, 72, that 'in very modern times' a boy of ten was hung for murdering his bedfellow. Lingard accuses Elizabeth of introducing the Inquisition into England.[6] It is a remarkable proof of the effect of intolerant laws that ' the ratio of Catholics to Protestants in Ireland has, therefore, gone on regularly increasing from the period of the Revolution.'[7] Mr. Lewis well adds [8] that religious persecution fails because it is not sufficiently energetic. Lewis[9] quotes Kohlrausch, Deutsche Geschichte, p. 470, to the effect that Gustavus Adolphus treated just in the same way both Catholics and Protestants.

In a paper addressed in 1597 by an English Catholic to Philip II., it is stated that there are 'four hundred secular priests in the kingdom.'[10] Hunter, a Jesuit, states that under Elizabeth there were not more than five or six Jesuits at any one time in England.[11] In 1550 it was Cranmer who at length succeeded in inducing Edward to sign the warrant ordering Joan Butcher (or Joan of Kent) to be burned for heresy in Smithfield.[12]

Even the Puritans, whom Elizabeth hated, she would not allow Parker to persecute.[13] In 1576, Elizabeth made Grindal archbishop of Canterbury, which, as Soames says, was a very conciliatory measure towards the Puritans.[14] In 1579, Hammond was burned at Norwich for denying the Trinity, &c.[15] In 1581, Campion was executed—but the usual butchery was prevented by Charles Howard, the Lord Admiral, who would not allow him to

---

[1] Blackstone, vol. iv. p. 18.   [2] 22 Henry VIII. c. li.   [3] 3 Inst. 48.
[4] Blackstone, vol. iv. p. 196.   [5] Vol. iv. p. 24.
[6] History of England, Paris, 1840, vol. iv. p. 351.
[7] Lewis on Irish Disturbances, 8vo, 1836, p. 346.
[8] Pp. 374. 375.   [9] C. 379.
[10] Dodd's Church History, Appendix, vol. iii. p. lxviii.
[11] Ibid. edit. Tierney, vol. iii, Appendix, p. clxii.
[12] Collier's Ecclesiastical History, vol. v. p. 385.
[13] Soames's Elizabethan Religious History, 8vo. 1839. p. 42.
[14] Ibid. p. 220.   [15] Ibid. p. 234.

be cut down till he was dead.[1] In 1588, Francis Kett, 'a master of arts, and probably a clergyman,' was burnt at Norwich for his opinions on Christ; but, says Soames, 'his case was the last in which Elizabeth's government answered reflections upon its catholicity by fire and fagot.'[2] In the reign of Elizabeth five persons were burned as Unitarians (two in London and three in Norwich), and five Protestants, Nonconformists, were hung.[3] Soames says[4] that only five persons in the reign of Elizabeth were 'actually condemned as religious offenders.'

It was in an age of dissoluteness that toleration grew up. The dissoluteness passed away; the toleration remains. The Regency which, as Mr. Macaulay has observed, presents a strong analogy to the court of our Charles II., seems to have given rise in France to toleration.[5]

A strong argument against severe laws is their needless cruelty; but a still stronger one is the impossibility of administering them. M. Quetelet, who has made a curious calculation from the criminal statistics of France, shows that if an individual is accused of crime against persons, the chances are 477 to 1000 that he will be condemned; but in an accusation for crime against *property*, the chances of condemnation rise from 655 to 1000.[6] I may add that this inequality, which can only arise from a reluctance to inflict severe penalties, is in reality more than 655 to 477, because we naturally look with more severity on murder than on robbery, so that *à priori* the chances of punishing a murderer would be greater than of punishing a robber. The influence of sympathy on the executive is shown by the fact that women have a much better chance of acquittal than men.[7]

In 1585 the archbishop of Canterbury ordered inquiries to be made if the minister 'once every Sabbath day put the churchwardens in mind of their duty to note who absented themselves from divine service, and upon the goods and chattels of such to levy 12d. a piece.'[8] Strype says that in 1560 the queen, at the

---

[1] Bartoli, p. 214, quoted in Soames' Elizabethan Relig. Hist. p. 306.
[2] Elizabethan Religious History, p. 354.
[3] Ibid. p. 595.   [4] Ibid. p. 598.
[5] See a remarkable passage in No. 12. of Lettres Persanes, published in 1721; Œuvres de Montesquieu, Paris, 1835, p. 41.
[6] Quetelet, Sur l'Homme, 1835, tome ii. p. 297 et seq.
[7] Ibid. pp. 299, 602.
[8] Strype's Whitgift, vol. i. p. 462; vol. iii. p. 179.

prayers of the bishops, first ordered images to be removed from the churches.[1]

At the merciful and politic proceedings of Elizabeth the bishops and clergy were seriously displeased. With the bigotry which, unhappily for the interests of religion, seems almost characteristic of their profession, they endeavoured to goad the queen into a general persecution of the Catholics.

In 1565 the Prince of Orange, himself a Catholic, laid down in the clearest language the principles of religious toleration. See his remarkable speech in Schiller's Abfall der Niederlande.[2] He says :[3] 'Eine so lange Erfahrung sollte uns endlich über-wiesen haben, dass gegen Ketzerei kein Mittel weniger fruchtvoll is als Scheiterhaufen und Schwert.' I suspect that the *impolicy* of persecution was perceived before its wickedness. The first great consequence of the decline of priestly influence was the rise of toleration.

In 1595, Robert Southwell, a Catholic priest, was executed at London, and the hangman wished to cut the rope before he was dead, in order as usual to butcher him alive ; but this the people would not allow.[4] An unfeeling expression was current : 'Make this letter a heretic,' *i.e.* burn it.[5] Sir Henry Wotton, who wrote at the end of the sixteenth century, expresses himself in favour of toleration.[6] 'Le dernier auto-da-fé célébré à Madrid est de 1680 ;'[7] but in Portugal the last was in 1755 ; and that this was the last is perhaps owing to the eloquent chapter of Montesquieu.[8] Cheke's letter to Mary in 1556, declaring his readiness to change his religion, is in Ellis's Original Letters of Literary Men.[9] M. Cousin, who on the whole takes a very unfavourable view of Locke, still admits that he has the great merit of always appealing to *reason*.[10] See the remarkable sophistry with which Todd[11] has attempted to clear the archbishop of the stain of intolerance.

[1] Annals, vol. I. part I. pp. 330-332.
[2] Werke, Band viii. pp. 217-220.   [3] P. 218.
[4] See Challoner's Missionary Priests, Manchester, 8vo, 1803, vol. I. p. 177.
[5] See Leycester Correspondence, ed/t. Camden Society, p. 342.
[6] See Wotton's State of Christendom, Lond. folio, 1657, p. 129.
[7] Villemain, Littérature au xviiie Siècle, tome iii. p. 165, Paris, 1846.
[8] Ibid. p. 170.   [9] P. 19, Camden Society, 1843.
[10] Histoire de la Philosophie, 2nde série, tome iii. p. 67.
[11] Life of Cranmer, vol. II. pp. 331, 332.

The duke of Northumberland died a Catholic in 1553, and yet little more than twelve months before his execution he writes to Cecil declaring that he had been a Protestant more than twenty years.[1] This I may add to the case of Sir John Cheke, who also became a Catholic at the accession of Mary.

Drury, who was fifteen years in Madagascar, says that religious persecution is unknown, and this he ascribes to the absence of any separate order of priesthood.[2] Ellis observes that the king of Madagascar is the high priest.[3] Mr. Newman[4] observes that, with the exception of the Persians and Jews, all the ancient nations were to a certain degree tolerant—*i.e.* they had none of the proselytizing spirit : but ' this kind of toleration by no means gave scope for inquiry or progressive amendment. It was a toleration of public religions or sects, not of individuals ;'[5] and[6] he says that the toleration known to paganism was not ' conducive to the advance of truth.' Charron[7] opposes toleration on religious grounds. In Bohemia, in 1508, it was first publicly laid down that a Christian ought not to compel any one to embrace the true faith.[8] Even Fuller thought the magistrate ought not to punish error.[9] Coleridge truly says that Whitgift and Bancroft were more criminal than Bonner and Gardner.[10] The murder of Servetus was approved by Melanchthon and the Protestants generally.[11] Coleridge[12] makes the curious admission that ' toleration then first becomes practicable when indifference has deprived it of all merit.' Even Locke in his first work, written in 1660, is inclined to deny the right of complete toleration, but in 1667 he had very liberal sentiments.[13] Mr. F. Newman, who looks on toleration as the result of *intellectual progress*, says,[14] ' Nevertheless, not only does the Old Testament justify bloody

---

[1] Tytler's Edward VI. and Mary, vol. II. p. 148.
[2] See Drury's Madagascar, 8vo, 1743, pp. 188, 231.
[3] History of Madagascar, 1838, vol. I. p. 359.
[4] Lectures on the Contrasts of Ancient and Modern History, 8vo, 1847, pp. 37-42.   [5] P. 39.   [6] P. 40.
[7] De la Sagesse, Amsterdam, 1782, 8vo, tome II. p. 13.
[8] See Talvi's Languages and Literature of the Slavic Nations, New York, 1850, p. 190.
[9] See Coleridge's Literary Remains, vol. II. p. 384.
[10] Ibid. vol. II. pp. 388, 389.
[11] Ibid. vol. III. p. 74, and vol. iv. p. 379.   [12] Ibid. vol. III. p. 189.
[13] See King's Life of Locke, 8vo, 1830, vol. I. pp. 11-15, 289, 290.
[14] Phases of Faith, 8vo, 1850, p. 168.

persecution, but the New teaches that God will visit men with fiery vengeance *for holding an erroneous creed.*' The Popes were the first who attempted to secure toleration for the Jews.[1] Read Zeuss, Die Deutschen und die Nachbarstämme, Munich, 1837, praised very highly in Kemble's Saxons in England, vol. i. p. 4. Parr, in a letter to Charles Butler,[2] says, 'I pay great deference to Thuanus, and I think his preface a most admirable defence of toleration.' Capefigue[3] says, 'La grande transaction de Passau, l'acte le plus important dans l'histoire du droit public, parce que, proclamant pour la première fois la liberté de conscience, il fit passer l'Allemagne sous l'empire d'un principe tout politique.' Calvin had predetermined to put Servetus to death.[4] In 1607 it was laid down that the king, if he conquer an infidel country, 'may massacre all the inhabitants.'[5] Bishop Tomline[6] says, 'The reigns of James II. and of George III. are the only reigns since the time of Queen Mary, in which some additional severity was not enacted against Roman Catholics.' Orme[7] says that Owen, in his treatise Of Toleration, 'has the honour of being the first man in England who advocated, *when his party was uppermost,* the rights of conscience, and who continued to the last to maintain and defend them.'

The principle of toleration, so far as the Catholics were concerned, is clearly laid down in what appears to be a proclamation of Elizabeth in 1569;[8] but in 1571 the queen writes to the archbishop of Canterbury, declaring that she will have 'a perfect reformation of all abuses attempted to deform the uniformity prescribed by our laws and injunctions, and that none should be suffered to decline either on the left or on the right hand from the direct line limited by authority of our said laws and injunctions.'[9] In 1579, Lord Burghley proposes as a remedy against the 'comfort of obstinate Papists,' that there should be 'penalties increased upon recusants.'[10] In a letter from Thomas Morgan to Curle, dated the 25th of January 1586, that arch-conspirator

[1] Kemble's Saxons in England, vol. ii. pp. 89, 90.
[2] Butler's Reminiscences, vol. ii. p. 235.
[3] Histoire de la Réforme et la Ligue, tome i. p. 348.
[4] Ibid. tome ii. p. 72.
[5] Campbell's Lives of the Chief Justices, vol. i. p. 236.
[6] Life of Pitt, vol. ii. p. 400. note.   [7] Life of Owen, pp. 102, 103.
[8] Haynes's State Papers, pp. 591, 592.   [9] Murdin's State Papers, p. 183.
[10] Ibid. p. 331.

says that Elizabeth 'hath banished within these twelve months a hundred priests, or thereabouts, whereof some of them have lived many years close prisoners in England, and some of them be grown lame and impotent.'[1]

In August 1575 the French ambassador writes to his court, without expressing any surprise, that some Dutchmen had been burned in London for heresy.[2] After the failure of Wyatt's rebellion, the French ambassador at London writes to his court, 'Il n'y a par toute la ville triomphe que de gibets et testes de justiciez par-dessus les portes.'[3] In February 1554 he writes to his court that the burning the heretics gave great delight to the people, and even to the very children;[4] but in May 1556 he says that the executions had reached such a height as to disgust the people.[5] In October 1573 the French ambassador writes from London, 'Ces libelles que les angloys qui sont à Louvein en avaient envoyé semer ung nombre, ont mis du trouble beaucoup en ceste court.'[6]

An able but eccentric writer says: 'Genuine belief ended with persecution. As soon as it was felt that to punish a man for maintaining an independent opinion was shocking and unjust, so soon a doubt had entered whether the faith established was unquestionably true. The theory of persecution is complete. If it be necessary for the existence of society to put a man to death who has a monomania for murdering bodies, or to exile him for stealing what supports them, infinitely more necessary is it to put to death, or send into exile, or to imprison, those whom we know to be destroying weak men's souls, or stealing from them the dearest of all treasures. It is because—whatever we choose to say—it is because *we do not know, we are not sure,* they are doing all this mischief; and we shrink from the responsibility of acting upon a doubt.'[7]

A writer greatly attached to Christianity says: 'It is a fact not to be disputed that some of the most enlightened minds of the day have nurtured a secret opposition to the doctrines of

---

[1] Murdin's State Papers, p. 481.
[2] Correspondance de Fénelon, vol. vi. p. 490.
[3] Ambassades de Noailles, Leyde, 1762, tome iii. p. 83.
[4] Ibid. tome iv. p. 173.   [5] Tome v. p. 370.
[6] Correspondance Diplomatique de Fénelon, tome v. p. 424.
[7] Froude, Nemesis of Faith, 8vo, 1849, pp. 84, 85.

Christianity, owing to the intellectual intolerance of its abettors.'[1] And [2] he adds, 'We cannot conceal our fear that should the theological odium pursue the spirit of philosophy with the rancour which has too often been experienced, the result must in time be fatal to the best interests of morality and of religion itself.' Again,[3] Morell says : 'In England a distrust and contempt for reason prevails amongst religious circles to a wide extent ; many Christians think it almost a matter of duty to decry the human faculties as poor, mean, and almost worthless ; and thus seek to exalt piety at the expense of intelligence. Delusive hope ! Is not Christianity itself a matter of intelligence ? Must not its claim to authority be weighed by the human reason ?'

Mr. Butler, who from his religious bias had a natural tendency to exaggerate the persecutions of the Catholics by Elizabeth, says that the 35 Eliz. c. 2 'was the first penal statute made against Popish recusants by that name, and as distinguished from other recusants.'[4] He adds [5] this 'closed the penal code of Elizabeth against her English Catholic subjects.' In 1581 and 1582 fifteen priests were sentenced to die. Twelve of them, who refused to deny the right of the Pope to depose Elizabeth, were executed ; the remaining three, who consented explicitly to deny such right, were pardoned.[6] Butler says,[7] 'Between the Armada and the death of Elizabeth more than one hundred Catholics were hanged and embowelled, merely, we must repeat, for the exercise of their religion.' Between 1558 and 1563, Butler can only find three Acts against the Catholics.[8] But of these the first, which protected the queen's supremacy, only affected persons who held ecclesiastical or civil offices ; the second 'affected only the Protestant clergy, and persons in general who should speak against the Common Prayer-Book.' The third Act was passed in the fifth of Elizabeth, and extended the penalties for not taking the oath of supremacy to all who had said or heard mass. But even this was evidently a mere vindication of the civil power against the Church, and at the same time Butler confesses [9] that 'it was far from being generally carried into execution.' In Dodd's Church

[1] Morell's History of Speculative Philosophy, 8vo, 1846, vol. II. p. 225.
[2] Ibid. p. 227.   [3] Ibid. p. 505.
[4] Butler's Historical Memoirs of the Catholics, 8vo, 1822, vol. I. p. 293.
[5] Ibid. vol. II. pp. 42-44.   [6] Ibid. vol. I. p. 424-431.
[7] Ibid. vol. II. p. 11.   [8] Ibid. vol. I. pp. 345-347.   [9] P. 347.

History[1] there is an elaborate list of those Catholics who suffered capitally in the reign of Elizabeth ; but in it I [do not find that any one was executed before 1573, and then only one, Thomas Woodhouse.[2] But I think there is an earlier instance.

In the system of ecclesiastical laws drawn up by Cranmer, in 1552, the punishment of death is pronounced against heretics. For this Lingard quotes the Reformatio Legum Ecclesiasticarum. This Soames cannot deny, but he asserts that by heretics were meant those who rejected Christianity.[3] Indeed, he adds[4] that it was not intended to punish capitally opinions which in the Reformatio Legum are called heresies. It is certain[5] that those who reject 'the Christian religion' are to be 'put to death and forfeit all their property.' Soames himself expresses on this subject[6] the most illiberal opinions.

Broughton, one of the most learned men of the age, held some opinions respecting the word *gehenna*, which did not please Archbishop Whitgift, who therefore sent officers to apprehend him, to avoid whom Broughton fled the realm. Eventually the archbishop adopted that very opinion for maintaining which he had persecuted Broughton, but refused in any way to further the ecclesiastical promotion of the man he had so cruelly injured. For the particulars of this disgraceful affair see Strype's Life of Whitgift.[7] The reputation of Broughton was so great that the Turks offered him the use of the temple of Sophia if he would go to Constantinople and read in Hebrew or Greek.[8]

Grindal, in 1559, asked the celebrated Peter Martyr to write to Elizabeth not to continue the crucifix in her chapel. But Peter knew better, and politely refused.[9]

In consequence partly of the general increase of knowledge, and partly of the diminished influence of the clergy, there had been gradually growing up in the minds of men an indifference to mere rites and dogmas of religion. Sir John Cheke, the learned tutor of Edward VI., in order to save his life, publicly recanted his religion during the reign of Mary.[10] Men became less superstitious and more moral.

[1] Edit. Tierney, vol. III, pp. 159-170.   [2] See p. 165.
[3] History of the Reformation of the Church of England, vol. iv. pp. 314-316, note.
[4] Ibid. p. 318.   [5] Ibid. p. 317.   [6] Ibid. vol. iii. p. 722.
[7] Vol. II. pp. 220-222, 320, 355, 389.   [8] Vol. ii. p. 407.
[9] Strype's Life of Grindal, p. 48.   [10] Strype's Life of Cheke, pp. 111-127.

Strype, whom no one will accuse of loving the Catholics, fully exonerates Elizabeth from the charge of having an undue regard for their religion.[1] In 1558 and 1559 Elizabeth deprived in all 192 spiritual persons, of whom fourteen were bishops.[2]

Bonner, ex-bishop of London, was kept in prison for his own safety. Indeed, he was so hated by the people, that when he died, it was found advisable to bury him in the middle of the night, 'to prevent any disturbances that might have been made by the citizens.'[3]

In 1587 some justices of the peace were Catholics.[4]

In Strype's Annals[5] there is a list copied from a book, printed at Antwerp, of the Catholics executed in London from 1570 to 1587. For evidence of the intolerant spirit of the bishops, see Strype's Parker, vol. ii. p. 120.

Alphonso de Castro, confessor to Philip II., preached in England in favour of tolerance.[6]

In order to check violent recriminations, Elizabeth, in 1558, forbade any one to preach without a licence. Lingard represents this as directed against the Catholics, but he ought to have known that she punished Protestant clergy who presumed to disobey it.[7] In 1578 the bishop of Ely said 'that he much rejoiced that her majesty was somewhat severe against her enemies the Papists. Would God that all her magistrates, high and low, would follow diligently her godly view ! I trust, hereafter, her highness and her magistrates will prosecute severely the same trade.'[8] In 1580 the archbishop of York wrote to the treasurer, requesting him 'to deal roundly with all the obstinate, of what calling soever, noble as well as mean.'[9]

These, and similar acts, have been often assigned to a partiality which Elizabeth is supposed to have for the Catholic worship. But after a long and careful study of her reign, I think myself authorised to say that this supposition is entirely gratuitous. No historian has advanced any evidence to support what has now

[1] Strype's Annals, vol. i. part i. p. xi.   [2] Ibid. p. 106.
[3] Ibid. part ii. p. 298.
[4] Ibid. vol. iii. part ii. pp. 462, 463. See also vol. iv. p. 402, and Strype's Life of Whitgift, vol. i. p. 514.
[5] Ibid. vol. iii. part ii. pp. 494- 495.
[6] See White's Evidence against Catholicism, p. 250.
[7] Strype's Annals, vol. i. part i. p. 63.
[8] Ibid. vol. ii. part ii. p. 196.   [9] Ibid. p. 341.

become a traditional hypothesis; and, so far as my reading extends, it is not warranted by any contemporary document which has come down to us. The truth seems to be that in religious matters she was naturally tolerant. Her mind, bent on great objects, cared little for polemical dispute; and it was not until a later period, when her temper was soured by opposition, that she descended to the level of such men as Bonner and Cranmer. Protestant historians, who, with two or three brilliant exceptions, have always been intolerant, choose to represent this as the Popish inclination of Elizabeth.

HISTORY ETC. OF THE THEATRE.

THE Puritans, who had been employed twenty years in maturing their power, now first began to make head against the theatre. In 1577 appeared the first attack on the stage, Northbrooke's Treatise against Dancing, Dicing, Plays. In 1579, Gosson's School of Abuse; in 1581 or 1582, his ' Plays confuted in Five Actions;' in 1583, Stubbe's Anatomy of Abuses; in 1587, Rankin's Mirror of Monsters; in 1599, Dr. Rainold's Overthrow of Stage Plays; in 1610, Histriomastix; in 1615, the ' Refutation of the Apology for Actors.' [1] In spite of these attacks dramatic literature advanced with a rapidity of development for which it would be difficult to find any parallel. It would seem as if even the imagination of the Puritans was captivated by that splendid array of genius which toward the end of the reign of Elizabeth adorned the theatre. At all events, it is remarkable that after the work of Rainold's in 1599 there was, with the exception of the two anonymous tracts I have just alluded to, no formal attack on the stage for thirty-four years, when Prynne's Histriomastix was published.[2] But in the meantime a still more formidable opponent appeared. It is remarkable that the Lord Mayor and Aldermen of London had from the beginning so steadily opposed the stage that neither the players nor their patrons could ever succeed in obtaining a fixed place of exhibition

[1] See some account of these works in Preface, pp. v-x, to the Shakespeare Society's reprint of Gosson's School of Abuse.
[2] See Introduction to Shakespeare Society's reprint of Heywood's Apology for Actors, p. l.

within the limits of the city.[1] They were therefore driven to
the liberties and suburbs, from which they not unnaturally made
war upon their persecutors, and covered them with ridicule. The
friends of the city magistrates were not slow to retaliate, and a
bitter and long-continued enmity grew up between the two parties,
and the citizens were ready to aid the Puritans in overthrowing
the theatre.

Heywood observes with regret that it had become usual in
plays to satirise great persons.[2]

In 1805, Southey writes, 'Fifteen years ago, the more melancholy a tale was, the better it pleased me; just as we all like
tragedy better than comedy when we are young.'[3]

Mr. Cunningham, whose valuable works upon our early literature are so well known, says that James I. 'saw five times as
many plays in a year as Queen Elizabeth was accustomed to see.'[4]

In the middle of the sixteenth century, the Dutch Protestants
availed themselves of the stage to ridicule their opponents.[5]
Hooft at the beginning of the seventeenth century created the
Dutch drama, which has, however, always been poor in comedy.[6]
Like the Greek, its chorus was very important.[7] Just before
the breaking out of that great Protestant rebellion which secured
the independence of Holland, the Dutch ridiculed the clergy on
the stage.[8]

Mr. Collier thinks Northbrooke hardly a Puritan.[9] His is
the first regular attack on the stage.[10] This attack on it is at
pp. 84-403. Sir Walter Scott notices that the French, who are so
lively, have made their stage very declamatory: 'while the
Spaniard, grave, solemn, and stately, was the first to introduce in

---

[1] See some evidence in Mr. Collier's Introduction to Northbrooke, pp. xi. and
xii.

[2] Apology for Actors, edit. Shakesp. Soc. p. 61, and see note at p. 66.

[3] Life and Correspondence of Robert Southey, edited by the Rev. C. C. Southey.
8vo, 1849, 1850, vol. ii. p. 322.

[4] Revels at Court in the Reigns of Elizabeth and James, edit. Shakespeare
Society, 8vo, 1842, p. xxxiv.

[5] See Van Kempen, Geschiedenis der Letteren in de Nederlanden, Gravenhage, 8vo, 1821, deel i. blad 70, and Schiller's Werke, Band viii. p. 54, Stuttgart,
1838.

[6] Ibid. vol. i. pp. 128, 129.   [7] Ibid. p. 131.

[8] Abfall der Niederlande in Schiller's Werke, Band viii. p. 186.

[9] Introduction to Shakesp. Soc. reprint, p. xvi.   [10] Ibid. p. v.

the theatre all the bustle of lively and complicated intrigue,—the flight, and the escape, and the mask, and the ladder of ropes,' &c.'[1] Of this peculiarity in the French drama Scott attempts no explanation ; and as to the Spanish, he merely ascribes it to the unceasing wars either between the Spaniards and Moors, or between the Castilians and Arragonese.

The immediate consequence of the outburst of dramatic talent was the rise of a body of profound and original thinkers.[2] We know from the experience of history that in every country the dramatists have preceded the metaphysicians. It is thus that the taste is first cultivated, and is soon developed into original thought. M. Cousin has well observed that genius is only taste in action.[3] He finely adds,[4] ' L'art est la reproduction libre de la beauté, et le pouvoir en nous capable de la reproduire s'appelle le génie.' Cousin[5] refutes the common notion that the business of art is to copy nature ; and he finely says that art is superior to nature because it gives a greater development to moral beauty. ' La nature peut plaire davantage, l'art touche plus, parce qu'il s'adresse plus directement à la source des émotions profondes. L'art peut être plus pathétique que la nature, c'est le signe et la mesure de la grande beauté.'[6] Cousin rejects the idea that the great object of art is illusion, and that the drama, for instance, to be perfect, should make the spectator believe that it is real. In fact, as he says, its business is to raise the dignity of man by transporting him above the realities of existence.[7] The theatre refined manners. It was to the people in the sixteenth century what chivalry was to the nobles in the thirteenth century, and the pomp and *forms* of chivalry, which were in full force till Puritanism, must have favoured it. M. Quetelet[8] has made a very curious statistical comparison between the dramatists of France and England. The English authors have been rather more precocious than the French,[9] but in both countries the dramatic power has gone on increasing until the age of fifty or

---

[1] Life of Le Sage, in Scott's Miscellaneous Prose Works, 8vo, Paris, 1837, vol. III. p. 210.   [2] Note this under James I.
[3] Histoire de la Philosophie, part I. tome II. p. 150.   [4] Ibid. p. 172.
[5] Ibid. pp. 174–179.   [6] Ibid. pp. 175, 176.
[7] Quote a fine passage, pp. 179, 180 ; see also p. 186.
[8] Sur l'Homme et le Développement de ses Facultés, Paris, 1835, tome II. pp. 112–120.
[9] Ibid. p. 115.

fifty-five, when it has diminished, both in regard to the value and the number of the works produced.[1] Quetelet makes the important remark[2] that the tragic talents (in France, at least) develop themselves more rapidly than the comic—that is to say, that the greatest French tragedies have been written by younger men than the greatest French comedies.

In 1563 the Bishop of London wrote to Cecil, expressing a wish to put an end to the performances of plays in London.[3] In 1584, Fleetwood, recorder of London, was violently opposed to theatres.[4] In France there have been more great actresses than great actors. This is ascribed to the greater sensibility of women, to their greater flexibility of voice and movement, and to their general superiority in tact and address.[5] On the slavish manner in which the dramatic writers of Italy early in the sixteenth century copied the ancients, see Ranke.[6] This, I think, only applies to Italy.[7] Menzel[8] says the Germans have never had a great theatrical literature, because they have no great metropolis.

It is said by the author of the well-known Commentary on Voltaire, that his Merope in 1743 was 'la première pièce profane qui réussit sans le secours d'une passion amoureuse.'[9] In 1760 appeared Voltaire's Tancred, which, says the Biographie Universelle,[10] reminds us of Zaïre ; but *after* this his tragic genius degenerated. Voltaire says,[11] 'La coutume d'introduire de l'amour à tort et à travers dans les ouvrages dramatiques, passa de Paris à Londres vers l'an 1660 avec nos rubans et nos perruques.' Coleridge says,[12] 'The talent for mimicry seems strongest where the human race are most degraded.' 'With all theatrical representations, not only are the Persians, but the Moslems of every country, perfectly unacquainted.'[13] In 1576, Henry III. introduced the Italian theatre.[14] In Germany the

[1] Sur l'Homme et le Développement de ses Facultés, Paris, 1835, tome ii. p. 115.
[2] Ibid. p. 118.
[3] Wright's Elizabeth, 1838, vol. i. p. 167.   [4] Ibid. vol. ii. pp. 227, 229.
[5] Roussel's Système de la Femme, Paris, 1845, p. 39.
[6] Die Römischen Päpste, Berlin, 1838, Band i. pp. 65, 66.   [7] Ibid. p. 68.
[8] German Literature, vol. iii. p. 161.
[9] Œuvres de Voltaire, Paris, 1820, tome i. p. 399.
[10] Biographie Universelle, tome xlix. p. 486.
[11] Sur les Anglais, lettre xviii., Œuvres, tome xxvi. p. 112.
[12] Biographia Literaria, 8vo, 1847, vol. i. p. 74.
[13] Transactions of Literary Society of Bombay, vol. ii. p. 101.
[14] See Sismondi, Histoire des Français, tome xix. p. 386.

theatre has no influence, and the people do not care for it.[1]   At
Petersburg it is everything, and the authoress of Letters from the
Baltic [2] says, 'From the national enjoyment which Russians of all
classes take in every description of scenic diversion, the theatre is
particularly a popular amusement.'

It has been supposed that the introduction of scenery was a
cause of the decline of dramatic poetry ; but I rather believe it to
be an *effect* ; for, when the mind was less stimulated, the eye must
be more pleased.

In the next volume, in which I shall relate the decline, and, I
fear, the final fall of the English drama, I shall examine the causes
which regulate the fluctuations of dramatic genius ; at present I
shall give merely a hasty view of its rise and the influence which
it exercised on our national civilisation.

Under Charles II. all our great masters were forgotten.
Shakespeare was neglected ; for how could his merits be appre-
ciated by a corrupt and ignorant court ?   Ben Jonson was
neglected, for his powers chiefly consisted in depicting national
manners which had already become obsolete.[3]   Schlegel says [4]
that the Germans have not had a theatrical literature because they
are too *speculative*, and that for the drama a *practical* spirit is
necessary.   He adds,[5] ' In Italy and Germany, where there are
only capitals of separate states, but no general metropolis, great
difficulties are opposed to the improvement of the theatre.'   He
forcibly states the influence of the stage on the *mind* of a
people.[6]   Schlegel says that tragedy is more moral than comedy :[7]
in tragedy the powers are more concentrated ; in comedy, more
dispersed,[8] and it has a much lower ideal.[9]   Tragedy delights in
unity, comedy in exuberance.[10]   See also [11] where he says that
tragedy deals with *fate*, comedy with *accident*, and comedy
'connects together, like tragedy, events as causes and effects ;
but it connects them by the law of experience, without any
reference, as in tragedy, to one idea.'   He says [12] that as soon as
we sympathise with the characters, comedy is at an end ; for its

[1] Laing's Notes of a Traveller, 1st series, pp. 269-271.
[2] Letters from the Baltic, 8vo, 1841, vol. ii. pp. 249, 250.
[3] Schlegel's Dramatic Literature, 8vo, 1840, vol. ii. p. 298.
[4] Ibid. vol. i. p. 29.   [5] Ibid. p. 324.   [6] Ibid. pp. 31-39.
[7] Ibid. pp. 42-45, 78.   [8] Ibid. pp. 196, 197.   [9] Ibid. pp. 198, 199, 224.
[10] Ibid. p. 200.   [11] Ibid. pp. 242, 243.   [12] Ibid. p. 256.

business is not moral instruction, but to increase our experimental knowledge.[1]

The first regular tragedy is the Sophonisba of Trissino; but the author was a 'spiritless pedant,' and in the middle of the sixteenth century the pastoral drama of Tasso and Guarini forms a new epoch.[2]

Perhaps the patronage of James I. corrupted the taste of the drama; and I should not be surprised if this explains the retirement of Shakespeare. Schlegel well says that the taste of a court is nearly always bad.[3] The first French tragedies are those of Jodelle.[4] I have already observed that the decline of the clergy was fatal to architecture; and, by an analogous process, the decline of the aristocracy was fatal to the drama. As the nobility sank, and the spirit of caste fell before the levelling hand of democracy, the theatre necessarily fell. Schlegel well says of the time of Shakespeare, 'The distinction of rank was yet strongly marked; and this is what is most to be wished for by the dramatic poet.'[5] But our democracy was *religious* as well as *political*; this was another motive that the Puritans had in attacking the drama. There are yet other reasons. The Catholic religion favoured the drama. The stage also will naturally decline as history advances and becomes more philosophic and less picturesque; also, when a sense of the ridiculous increases, and audiences become more fastidious. Schlegel[6] notices the advantage of chronicles. And[7] Schlegel says, 'If the effeminacy of the present day is to serve as a general standard of what tragical composition may exhibit to human nature, we shall be forced to set very narrow limits to art, and everything like a powerful effect must at once be renounced.' Schlegel adds," 'It is deserving of remark that Shakespeare, amidst the rancour of religious parties, takes a delight in painting the condition of a monk, and always represents his influence as beneficial.'

As to the rise of the drama, Schlegel is very superficial. Indeed, he does not examine the cause, but gets over the difficulty by *stating* it. See vol. ii. p. 273, where he says, 'There are periods in the human mind,' &c.; but *why* are there?

---

[1] Schlegel's Dramatic Literature, vol. I. pp. 257, 258.
[2] Ibid. pp. 306, 307.
[3] Ibid. vol. ii. p. 113.   [4] Ibid. p. 121.
[5] Ibid. p. 174.
[6] Ibid. p. 298.
[7] Ibid. p. 377.
[7] Ibid. p. 142.

Schlegel says [1] that Elizabeth desired Shakespeare to represent Falstaff in love, hence the Merry Wives of Windsor; but for this I believe there is no good authority.

Schlegel says [2] that the Greeks always played with masks. Sophocles was almost the only Greek dramatist who was not an actor. [3] Schlegel accounts for the decline of dramatic art by a metaphor. [4] With Euripides the Greek drama declined, [5] and this was because he copied human nature too exactly. [6] He ridicules women. [7] Aristophanes alone saw his real faults. [8] 'The history of ancient tragedy ends with Euripides,' [9] who became too *utilitarian*, for tragedy should not give *practical* instruction. [10] In Greece tragedy was 'exhausted;' it died a natural death; but comedy was cut short by the hand of power, [11] which silenced Aristophanes and killed Socrates. [12] The Greek women were certainly present at tragedies, but *probably* not at the old comedy. [13] The plays of Aristophanes suppose prodigious knowledge in the audience. [14] The middle comedy has no personal satire nor chorus, [15] but it is in fact only a transition to the new comedy, [16] which last is the old 'tamed.' [17] It imitates Euripides, but studies what is *natural*, and ridicules objects themselves. [18] The old comedy is 'a pleasant dream;' the new comedy is 'serious in form,' [19] and represented the manners of the day, [20] and is nearer to tragedy than the old comedy was. [21] Our clowns are like the old comedy. [22] Perhaps Ben Jonson, by representing *manners*, laid the foundation of the corruption of our stage.

Plautus and Terence are not original. [23] The Greeks respected authors: the early Romans despised them. [24] The Romans sometimes played without masks: the Greeks never. [25] In tragedy, the Romans (less mild than the Greeks) show their own contempt of pain and death. [26] The only specimens left are those of Seneca. [27] As to the unities, see vol. i. pp. 331-356. Of the unities, the

[1] Schlegel's Dramatic Literature, vol. II. p. 237.   [2] Ibid. vol. I. p. 66.
[3] Ibid. p. 122.   [4] Ibid. p. 142.   [5] Ibid. pp. 144, 145.
[6] Ibid. p. 147.   [7] Ibid. p. 152.   [8] Ibid. pp. 157-222.
[9] Ibid. p. 191.   [10] Ibid. p. 240.   [11] Ibid. p. 205.
[12] Ibid. p. 206.   [13] Ibid. p. 208.   [14] Ibid. p. 212.
[15] Ibid. pp. 237, 238.   [16] Ibid. p. 239.   [17] Ibid. p. 240.
[18] Ibid. p. 241.   [19] Ibid. p. 242.   [20] Ibid. p. 244.
[21] Ibid. p. 252.   [22] Ibid. pp. 253, 254.   [23] Ibid. p. 261.
[24] Ibid. pp. 261, 262.   [25] Ibid. p. 287.   [26] Ibid. pp. 291, 292.
[27] Ibid. p. 293.

only one of which Aristotle 'speaks with any degree of fulness'
is the unity of action : of the unity of place he says nothing,[1] and
Aristotle himself knew little of the theory of the fine arts.[2] There
is as much *real* unity in Shakespeare's tragedies as in Æschylus
and Sophocles.[3] The French are right in preferring a comedy in
verse to one in prose.[4] The English and Spanish theatres are
essentially similar.[5] The romantic drama, like painting, unites
what is dissimilar, and mixes together seriousness and mirth.[6]
Schlegel, who speaks of Seneca's tragedies with well-deserved
severity, says that both Corneille and Racine have borrowed a
great deal from him.[7] He says that the French have taken more
from the Spaniards than from the Italians,[8] and adds [9] that of the
French, 'Racine is perhaps the oldest poet who seems to have
been altogether unacquainted with the Spaniards, or at least who
was in no manner influenced by them.' He says [10] that the
Italians were much indebted to the Spanish theatre. It is to the
influence of Seneca that we must attribute many of the most
serious faults of Corneille.[11] Schlegel says [12] that comedy is
'morality in action, the art of life.' He says [13] that neither the
Spanish nor English dramatists have borrowed from each other.
' The formation of these two stages is equally independent of
each other ; the Spanish poets were altogether unacquainted
with the English ; and in the older and most important period of
the English theatre I could discover no trace of any knowledge
of Spanish plays (though their novels and romances were certainly known) ; and it was not till the time of Charles II. that
translations from Calderon made their appearance.' He adds,[14]
' Calderon had many predecessors ; he is at once the summit and
almost the conclusion of the dramatic art among the Spaniards.'
As masks were disused, perhaps the theatre naturally became
more moral ; for masks hide the blushes of women. Schlegel is
very unsatisfactory as to the causes of the change which took
place in our drama after the Restoration.[15] He adds, however,
I think with truth,[16] 'Pope, who, however, passes for a perfect

1 Schlegel's Dramatic Literature, vol. I. p. 333.
2 Ibid. pp. 334, 335.   3 Ibid. p. 345.   4 Ibid. vol. II. p. 40.
5 Ibid. pp. 100, 101.   6 Ibid. pp. 102-104.   7 Ibid. vol. I. p. 296.
8 Ibid. pp. 297-328.   9 Ibid. p. 392.   10 Ibid. p. 316.
11 Ibid. p. 396.   12 Ibid. vol. II. p. 47.
13 Ibid. p. 95.   14 Ibid. p. 105.
15 Ibid. p. 272.   16 Ibid. p. 285.

judge of poetry, had not even an idea of the first elements of the dramatic art.[1] Schlege supposes[1] that Beaumont and Fletcher 'entertained no very extravagant admiration' of Shakespeare. He speaks in the highest terms of Calderon,[2] and adds[3] that after him nothing of the least value appeared ; but ' I recollect having read a Spanish play, the object of which was to recommend the abolition of the torture.' Lessing was the first in Germany who praised Shakespeare.[4] Perhaps the æsthetic investigations of the Germans prevent their having a great dramatic literature.[5] In the seventeenth century Shakespeare was hardly known out of England.[6] The best comedies in England have been written by young men ; but there is hardly an instance of an inexperienced writer writing a good tragedy.[7] The Count of Lauraguais, afterwards Duke de Brancas, introduced the custom of making actors dress on the stage according to their characters.[8]

Cibber states that the Maid's Tragedy of Beaumont and Fletcher was forbidden to be acted in the reign of Charles II.[9] Beaumont and Fletcher seem to have enjoyed a great popularity in the beginning of the eighteenth century ;[10] and respecting their reputation in the first half of the seventeenth century, see the Shakespeare Society's Papers, vol. iii. p. 94. In the same volume is an interesting article[11] headed 'Salmacis and Hermaphroditus not by Francis Beaumont.'

I have already noticed the rise of the English drama ; I have now to consider its decline—perhaps its final fall. It will be found a universal rule that as a nation advances, its taste for theatrical amusement declines. With the progress of civilisation there arise new tastes and new resources. Books are multiplied, and the diffusion of education increases the desire of reading them. The advance of liberty throws open to all the arena of speculative politics which before had been confined to a few. The facilities of travelling create an excitement before unknown, and instead of journeys being made only for business, they are

---

[1] Schlegel's Dramatic Literature, vol. ii. p. 303.
[2] Ibid. pp. 348, 349.
[3] Ibid. p. 363.
[4] Ibid. p. 374.
[5] Ibid. p. 400.
[6] Ibid. p. 368.
[7] See Prior's Life of Goldsmith, 8vo, 1837, vol. I. p. 214.
[8] Mémoires de Segur, tome i. pp. 134. 135.
[9] See Cibber's Apology for his Life, 8vo, 1756, vol. i. p. 250.
[10] See The Postman Robbed of his Mail, Lond. 12mo, 1719. p. 149.
[11] No. xiii.

also made for pleasure. All these things drive from the theatre
the active, the voluptuous, and the gay.

Such was the state of things at the Restoration. Under
Elizabeth and James I. immense sums had been paid for entertainments. The profits of actors were enormous. Men of character paid for having their pieces acted, and Sir Walter Scott
notices the character of the pieces, which can only be accounted for
on the ground of a superior class of audience. Under Charles II.
the dissolute and the ignorant crowded the theatres, where amid
thunders of applause was performed the miserable ribaldry of
Shadwell and Killigrew. As a proof that the decay of taste was
only in the court and at the theatre, though Shakespeare and Ben
Jonson were neglected on the stage for the wretched plays of
Dryden, the Paradise Lost of Milton was received with raptures
by the people.

Perhaps in our own times Hannah More did something to
lower the reputation of the theatre. Her bigoted attack on the
stage is reprinted by Mr. Roberts.[1] Her main argument is that
it gives too high notions of honour—false honour, as she calls it.[2]
It is hardly necessary for me to say that this, which she considers
a decisive objection to the theatre, is precisely the means by
which it has aided in civilising and unbrutalising man. The
drama has done in modern times what chivalry did in the
twelfth and thirteenth centuries. Under Charles II., for the first,
and, as I trust, for the last time in England, the theatre became
a professed engine of vice. Contrary to the ordinary principles of
mankind, the more degrading were the sentiments and the more
indecent the language, the more tumultuous was the applause.

'It is unfair to take the stage as a proof, and to ask why we
have not Molières and Shakespeares starting up at every period.
The preceding age has gleaned all the twenty or thirty characters
of strong and extravagant humour which lie upon the surface of
society, not because it had greater talents for humour, but merely
because it was the preceding age. The blustering captain, the
inebriated and witty rake, the obese alderman, the squire in
London, slaving poets, homicide physicians, chambermaids, valets,
and duennas, are all gone; employed by dramatic writers who
had the first of the market. These characters cannot be re-intro-
duced on the stage; they are worn out there; but they exist in

[1] Memoirs of Hannah More, 8vo, 1834. vol. iv. pp. 381-393.   [2] Ibid. p. 386.

real life, and of course *must* exist while men are what they have been.'[1]

There were two causes of its decline : 1st, the increase of other amusements, such as travelling, &c. ; 2nd, political excitement. An attempt was made early in the seventeenth century to introduce political characters on the stage. If the same licence had been allowed that was allowed to the early Greek dramatists, it is likely that our theatre would have continued to flourish just as Menander followed Aristophanes. But the combined authority of the court and the master of the revels was too strong. The consequence was that a large amount of ability was carried from the stage to the senate, where it soon shook the throne. The folly of James in all this is inconceivable. He should have allowed the *safety-valve* of the theatre. A Government is never so secure as when it allows to its opponents the liberty, and even the abuses of the press. The more people talk, the less they will do.

BALLADS.

Mr. Wright, who is a very high authority on such matters, has observed that after the Restoration even the very ballads became more indecent.[1] Indeed, some verses are so coarse that Mr. Wright has felt himself obliged to omit them.[3] Mr. Chappell[4] says, 'From very early times down to the end of the seventeenth century the common people knew history chiefly from ballads. Aubrey mentions that his nurse could repeat the history of England from the Conquest down to the times of Charles I. in ballads.' In the reign of Edward VI. Protestant ballads began to be written. (Percy's Reliques, 8vo, 1835, p. 117.) As to the *duration* of tradition, see Common Place Book, arts. 1191 and 1198. In our own country, I believe, none of the ballads sung by the Saxons before they were acquainted with letters are extant ; but we know that, in what I have called the second stage

---

[1] Elementary Sketches of Moral Philosophy, delivered at the Royal Institution, in the years 1804, 1805, and 1806, by the late Rev. Sydney Smith, M.A., 8vo, 1850. p. 148.

[2] Political Ballads, published by the Percy Society, vol. iii, p. xiii.

[3] Ibid. p. 250.

[4] Introduction to the Crown Garland of Golden Roses, Percy Society, vol. vi. pp. vii, viii.

of ballads, they became in England, as elsewhere, quite unfit for
historic purposes. Thus we are told that the minstrels 'made no
scruples of changing the names of the personages they introduced
to humour their hearers.'[1]   Percy, in an ingenious, but in point
of learning, superficial dissertation on the Ancient Metrical Romances, says, 'It was not probably till after the historian and
the bard had long been disunited that the latter ventured at pure
fiction.'[2]   The Finns were ignorant of the art of writing until
they were conquered by the Swedes in the twelfth and thirteenth
centuries,[3] but hardly anything was written in it before the
sixteenth century.[4]   The question as to whether the early Germans were acquainted with letters seems to depend on the meaning we assign to a sentence of Tacitus : 'Literarum secreta viri
pariter ac feminæ ignorant.'[5]   Blackwell[6] says that the Scandinavians were acquainted with Runic letters in or before the sixth
century, but few are remaining before the eleventh century.   The
Anglo-Saxons, before their conversion, had a Runic alphabet,
which indeed they used in MSS. as late as the twelfth century,
but 'their form rendered them inconvenient for writing extensively.'[7]   Clarke says that the Latin poets drew many of their
details from specimens of ancient art, as sculpture, &c.[8]   Is it
possible that European poetical history has been corrupted by an
unfaithful sculpture and painting?   Clarke says that the Laplanders 'have no national poetry, not even so much as a song ;'[9]
neither have they the least knowledge of music.[10]   Mr. Keightley
has noticed the great deficiency of fairy tales, &c., in Spain.[11]
M. Van Kempen positively says that the Germans were ignorant
of the art of writing : 'Dat de oude Deutschers in den Heideu-
schen tijd in de schrijfkunst onbedreven waren schijnt voldongen te
zijn ; slechts in het Noorden vindt men zekere schrijfteckenen
Runen genaamd.'[12]   The first Dutch historian seems to have been

[1] Percy's Reliques, p. 30.   [2] Ibid. p. 168.
[3] See Prichard's Physical History of Mankind, vol. iii. p. 284.
[4] Ibid. p. 289.
[5] Mallet's Northern Antiquities, 8vo, 1847, pp. 222, 223.
[6] Additions to Mallet, pp. 228-231.
[7] Wright's Biographia Britannica Literaria, 8vo, 1842. vol. i. p. 105.
[8] Clarke's Travels, 8vo, 1817, vol. iii. p. 101.
[9] Travels, 8vo, 1824, vol. ix. p. 386.   [10] Ibid. pp. 440, 547. 548.
[11] Keightley's Fairy Mythology, Lond. 1850, p. 456.
[12] Van Kempen, Geschiedenis der Letteren in de Niederlande. Gravenhage,
1821, 8vo, deel i, blad 2.

Miles Stoke, at the very end of the thirteenth century ; [1] but there was one who wrote in Latin (Sigebert) as early as the twelfth century.[2] His work is 'vol fabelen in de oude tijden.'[3] The widely spread story of the Seven Sleepers is an evidence of the want of invention.[4] Aubrey says, 'My nurse had the history from the Conquest down to Charles I. in ballad.'[5] Read Thornton Romances, Camden Society, vol. xxx. In the middle of the eighteenth century the police in Paris used 'to take up ballad singers who presume to sing any songs that have not been licensed.'[6] It is curious to observe how little use our early historians have made of the Anglo-Saxon ballads. This, I suspect, arose from our being a conquered and despised people. The same cause would make our forefathers cling more to their traditions; and I doubt if in any civilised country ballads lingered so long among the people as in England.

The Russians have traditions similar to those of Charlemagne and his Twelve Peers.[7] Talvi says [8] that in Teutonic ballads there are few instances of talking animals, but that in the Slavic songs they are very common ; while in the Spanish they are unknown. The ballads of the Servians have been only recently printed, but are very old.[9] The present Dalecarlians are better acquainted with the history of the appearance of Gustavus Vasa among them than is Geyer himself.[10]

HISTORY OF THE PRESS ETC.

IN 1585, Whitgift obtained an order from the queen that there should be no printing press except in London and in the two universities; and that even there no book should be printed that had not been read by the Archbishop or Bishop of London, or by their chaplain.[11] And in 1586 he allowed Ascanio, an Italian merchant, to import certain Roman Catholic books.[12]

[1] Van Kempen, Geschiedenis der Letteren in de Niederlande, Gravenhage. 1821, 8vo, deel i. blad 2, p. 14.
[2] Ibid. blad 28.   [3] Ibid. blad 29.
[4] See Gibbon's Decline and Fall, pp. 552, 553. end of chap. xxxiii.
[6] Thoms's Anecdotes and Traditions, p. 102, Camden Society, 1839, vol. v. p. 102.   [6] The Police of France, London, 4to, 1763, p. 51.
[7] See Talvi's Slavic Nations, New York, 8vo, 1850, p. 64.
[8] Ibid. p. 327.   [9] Ibid. p. 379.
[10] Laing's Sweden, p. 215.
[11] Neal's History of the Puritans, 8vo, 1822, vol. i. 369, 370.   [12] Ibid. p. 285.

In 1534, the 25th Henry VIII. c. 15 says that there are
Englishmen who can print as well as any foreigners, and, on this
account, 'forbids the sale of bound books imported from the
Continent.'[1] Even M. Cousin is in favour of limitations on the
freedom of the press.[2] The influence of a free press has been
estimated by one of the most original inquirers of our time.[3]
M. Quetelet observes that its tendency is to deprive revolutions
of their violence by hastening the period of reaction. I do not
know if every reader will immediately understand this; but it
is impossible to give an abridgment of his weighty but very com-
pressed remarks.

In 1572, Day, the printer, wished to set up a shop against the
walls of St. Paul's; but the mayor and aldermen would not allow
him to have it in the churchyard.[4] On the power of the press, see
some original remarks in Tocqueville, Démocratie en Amérique.[5]
In 1563 there was in France a rigid censorship of the press.[6]

Essai historique sur la Liberté d'Écrire chez les Anciens et du
Moyen-Âge; sur la Liberté de la Presse depuis le quinzième
Siècle, par Gabriel Peignot, Paris, 1832, 8vo. In this work,
consisting of 218 pages, Peignot has given scarcely anything
beyond bibliographical anecdotes. The following facts I note as
being exceptions.

By a statute in 1323, confirmed in 1342, and in 1405, it was
ordered 'que les *escrivains* de livres n'en pouvaient communiquer
aucun soit par vente, soit par louage, qu'il n'ait été préalablement
examiné, corrigé et approuvé par l'une des facultés de l'Université.'[7]
Peignot says of printing,[8] 'Ce bel art dont le berceau est dé-
finitivement fixé à Mayence malgré les prétentions de Haarlem
et de Strasbourg'!!! He does not offer the slightest argument to
support his positive assertion respecting a subject which has been,
and still is, warmly disputed. Peignot states,[9] 'En 1543 on
publia à Venise le premier *Index* des livres défendus qui soit
connu; il a pour titre: Index generalis Scriptorum interdictorum,

[1] Hallam's Constitutional History of England, vol. I. p. 81.
[2] Histoire de la Philosophie, Paris, 1846, part I. tome iii. pp. 340, 341.
[3] Quetelet, Sur l'Homme, Paris, 1835, tome II. pp. 289, 290.
[4] See Wright's Elizabeth, 1838, vol. I. p. 447.
[5] Tome II. pp. 98-110, and tome iv. pp. 177-182.
[6] See Journal of Statistical Society, vol. III. p. 376.
[7] Peignot, p. 20, and Dubreuil, Antiquités de Paris, p. 118.   [8] Ibid. p. 31.
[9] Ibid. p. 55.

Venetiis, 1543.' He says that the first index was published in
Spain in 1559.[1]

In p. 58, Peignot says, 'Voici l'un des premiers actes de
l'autorité qui exige une sorte de garantie relativement à la
publication des ouvrages. C'est une déclaration de Henri II, du
11 Décembre 1547, "qui ordonne que le nom et surnom de celui
qui a fait un livre soit exprimé et exposé au commencement
du livre, et aussi celui de l'imprimeur avec l'enseigne de son
domicile."'

In p. 76, Peignot says, ' Il nous semble que c'est de l'ordonnance de 1629 qu'on peut dater la véritable origine des censeurs
nommés par le chancelier, et pris parmi les hommes de lettres et
les savants.' This order is given in pp. 74, 75, in which, after
expressing the great inconvenience arising from the extreme
liberty of the press, it proceeds to forbid any book being printed
before it has been seen in manuscript and approved by such
persons as the chancellor or guard of the seals may appoint for
that purpose. Respecting this order Peignot, however, remarks,[2]
'Ce n'est pas que la censure proprement dite ait commencé à
l'ordonnance de 1629 dont nous parlons ; elle était exercée,
comme nous l'avons vu, par l'université, dès le treizième siècle ; et
pendant très-longtemps ce corps, qui s'était rendu si formidable,
a fait valoir ses droits exclusifs à la censure universelle, comme
les tenant du pape. Mais depuis Charles IX et les troubles qui
ont signalé le règne de Henri III, et surtout la Ligue, l'université
ayant un peu perdu de son crédit et de sa puissance, fut insensible-
ment réduite à la censure des écrits sur la religion.'

Peignot says[3] that the first statute respecting the liberty of
writing is in A.D. 1275. In pp. 104, 105 Peignot says that
it is a very difficult, *not to say impossible* thing to remedy the
licentious evils of the press without trespassing on the rights
'd'une sage liberté.' Monsieur Peignot then proceeds to observe
that ' this difficulty has been perfectly felt and very well expressed
by a celebrated Englishman, Samuel Johnson, in his reflections
upon the Areopagiticus of Milton ; ' a work, adds Peignot,
'où ce *fougueux républicain*, cité déjà dans la note précédente,
soutient la liberté indéfinie de la presse.' Thus he speaks of
Milton ! ! ! in p. 107. After quoting Johnson's remarks, he

<hr>

[1] Peignot, p. 61.   [2] Ibid. p. 77.   [3] Ibid. p. 14.

observes,[1] 'Ces réflexions sont fort judicieuses. Elles doivent d'autant plus nous frapper, qu'elles partent d'un écrivain, *très-attaché à tous les genres de liberté dont son pays est si renommé pour offrir le modèle*.' Milton then is nothing but a 'fiery republican ;' and Johnson, the Tory bigot, is a man 'attached to every sort of liberty for which his country is celebrated' ! ! !

Peignot[2] says that in 1547 a proclamation issued by Henry II. was one of the first acts of authority directed against the liberty of the press.   However, Leber, in pp. 8, 9 of his De l'État Réel de la Presse et des Pamphlets, 8vo, 1834, Paris, has given some earlier instances.

In Le Clerc, Bibl. Choisie, xxvi. 246 *et seq.*, are some interesting remarks on the laws of the ancient Romans respecting usury.

Leber, De l'État de la Presse.   Great restrictions on the liberty of the press in the sixteenth century.[3]

It was the Reformation which induced Francis I. to destroy the liberty of the press.[4]   The preachers in the sixteenth century were directed as to the manner in which they should handle the topics of the day.[5]

ORIGIN OF THE MIDDLE AND MONEYED CLASSES.

RICH[6] says, 'In former ages he that was rich in knowledge was called a wise man ; but now there is no man wise but he that hath wit to gather wealth.'   In the preceding chapter I have traced the history of the decline of aristocratic power : and in the ordinary course of events the decline would have been accompanied by a corresponding increase in the authority of the Crown ; but, happily, there arose in England during the sixteenth century another body which was more than able to balance the power of the prince, and which twice during the seventeenth century saved England from a despotic sovereign, and once saved it from the still gloomier horrors of a military tyranny.   All this was effected by the middle class ; a class of which the slightest vestige is not to be found in the records of antiquity, nor, indeed, has ever been known to exist except in a few of the most favoured countries of Europe, and in that mighty republic of America.   Elizabeth

[1] Peignot, p. 108.   [2] Ibid. p. 58.   [3] Leber, p. 4.
[4] P. 7.   [5] P. 12.
[6] The Honestie of this Age, 1614, p. 14, Percy Society, vol. xi.

destroyed villenage ; at all events, at the accession of James I. there was hardly a trace of it.[1]

Montesquieu finely says, 'Règle générale : dans une nation qui est dans la servitude, on travaille plus à conserver qu'à acquérir ; dans une nation libre on travaille plus à acquérir qu'à conserver.'[2] Mr. Alison has well observed that it is the middle classes which prevent the increase of wealth being fatal to a country.[3]

ARMINIANISM.

THE first four books of Hooker's Ecclesiastical Polity appeared in 1594, and in 1597 the fifth.[4] In 1595 the disputes between the Puritans and the Church *first* became doctrinal—the former maintaining the Divine origin of the Sabbath and predestination.[5] In 1595, to appease this, the Lambeth Articles were drawn up and consented to by Whitgift, by the Archbishop of York, and by Fletcher, Bishop of London, &c.[6] In them it was laid down that the number of the predestined was *fixed*. Neal says[7] that before this dispute 'the Articles of the Church of England were thought by all men hitherto to favour the explication of Calvin.' Even Collier confesses that when in 1594 Arminianism arose, ' the Puritans held the Calvinistic side, and here it must be confessed they were abetted by no small number of the conforming clergy.'[8] He makes no doubt[9] that Whitgift believed the Lambeth Articles, but he undertakes to show[10] 'that these Lambeth Articles were not the general doctrine of the English Reformation.' But Collier promises more than he performs. His first quotation is from Jewel's Apology, and is not decisive. Dr. Baroe, indeed, professor in Cambridge in 1574, attacks the Calvinian doctrine of predestination ; and Harsnet, in a sermon at Paul's Cross in 1584, 'takes occasion to break out with some warmth against the Calvinian doctrine of reprobation.' Collier observes[11] that in 1595 the University of Cambridge 'began to make a stand upon the pre-

[1] Brougham's Political Philosophy, 8vo, 1849, vol. i. p. 292.
[2] Esprit des Lois, xx. chap. iv. Œuvres, Paris, 1835. p. 351.
[3] Principles of Population, 8vo, 1840, vol. i. pp. 118, 119.
[4] Neal's History of the Puritans, 8vo, 1822, vol. i. p. 446.
[5] Ibid. pp. 451-453. [6] Ibid. pp. 451. 455. [7] Ibid. p. 453.
[6] Ecclesiastical History, 1840, vol. vii. p. 184. [9] Ibid. p. 186.
[10] Ibid. pp. 188-191. [11] Ibid. p. 195.

destinarian novelties, to throw off the impositions of Calvinism, and recover the old doctrine of the Reformation.' See also the account of this quarrel in Soames' Elizabethan Religious History, pp. 463-478, and Short's History of the Church of England, 8vo, 1847, p. 308.

Cheney, Bishop of Gloucester, died in 1578. He was 'a Lutheran and a free-willer.'[1] The ignorance of the clergy caused many, such as Campion, to join the Church of Rome ; and by the end of the sixteenth century the Church of England was in imminent danger of dissolution. At this moment the rising fame of Arminius suggested the formation of a party which might stand midway between Calvinism and Popery. To this party James I. inclined, for he was disgusted with the Scotch Calvinists, and the bishops found many things in the writings of Arminius favourable to their order. The presence of many Dutch in London also favoured this. I suspect that much of the Arminianism was brought from Scotland. At the end of the sixteenth century there was constant communication between Holland and Scotland, and the Scotch were often educated in Holland.[2]

OBSERVATIONS UPON SUICIDE.

DE la Manie du Suicide et de l'Esprit de Révolte. Par. J. Tissot, Professeur de Philosophie à la Faculté des Lettres de Dijon. Paris, 8vo, 1840.

M. Tissot thinks that suicide is scarcely known to barbarous nations, and that the more a people reflect, the more likely they are to commit it.[3] He well explains[4] why suicides are uncommon among barbarians : 'C'est tout simplement parce que leurs passions féroces se portent au dehors, qu'ils réfléchissent peu sur eux-mêmes,' &c. He supposes[5] that if there were more convents suicides would be less frequent ; and he remarks[6] 'que le suicide est dû plus souvent à des causes morales qu'à des causes physiques.' At all events, there seems no doubt from the statistical evidence brought forward by M. Tissot that in the present century the number of suicides has greatly increased.[7] Indeed, he says,[8] 'S'il faut en

---

[1] Strype's Annals, vol. II. part II. p. 52.
[2] See Bower's History of the University of Edinburgh. vol. I. pp. 259, 260.
[3] Tissot, pp. 2, 34, 151.   [4] Ibid. p. 47.   [a] Ibid. p. 132.
[6] Ibid. p. 77.   [7] Ibid. pp. 31, 43, 150.   [8] Ibid. p. 32.

croire M. Schoen,[1] on a fait en France et en Prusse à l'époque des
guerres de la république et du consulat l'horrible découverte des
sociétés de suicides dont les statuts obligeaient les membres à se
donner la mort.   En Prusse, le dernier membre de cette affreuse
tontine a, dit-on, terminé ses jours en 1819.[2]   It is probable, but
not certain, that as civilisation advances, suicides increase.[2]

Tissot says[3] that animals never intentionally kill themselves.
Comte says that suicide *is* known to animals ; but this is denied
by Lewis.[4]

At p. 15, M. Tissot quotes Schoen, Statistique de la Civilisation,
p. 156, to the effect that suicide is more common among Protestants
than among those of the Greek and Romish Churches.

Tissot says[5] that suicide is much more common in towns than
in the country.   Indeed, it is said that, when other things are
equal, the proportion is 14 to 4.[6]

It has been supposed that climate has much to do with suicides,
and that they are most common in cold, damp countries ; but this
Tissot denies,[7] because there are fewer at St. Petersburg than at
Paris, and more in summer than in winter.   See also the evidence,[8]
from which it is evident that they are more common in summer
than in spring, and in spring than in winter.   See also evidence to
the same effect in Quetelet, Sur l'Homme, Paris, 1835, tome ii.
pp. 152, 158.

Tissot says[9] that the greatest number of suicides are between
the age of 20 and 30, and, according to Esquirol, particularly
from 20 to 25.[10]   Tissot[11] quotes M. Broussais to the effect that
' les deux tiers de suicides sont des hommes.'   In Berlin, the
suicides committed are in the proportion of five men to one woman ;
in Geneva, four to one.[12]   Most of the women who commit suicide
are married ; most of the men are single.[13]   Tissot[14] says that
according to Falset, quoted by Broussais, ' les deux tiers des
suicides sont célibataires ; ' but M. Prevost ' n'en trouve que sept
contre six.'

---

[1] Statistique générale et raisonnée de la Civilisation Européenne, p. 151.
[2] Quetelet, Sur l'Homme, vol. ii. p. 151.
[3] Tissot, p. 20.
[4] Observation in Politics, 8vo, 1852, vol. i. p. 25.
[5] Tissot, p. 21.
[6] Quetelet, Sur l'Homme, tome ii. pp. 147, 152.
[7] Tissot, p. 50.
[8] Ibid. pp. 149, 150.
[9] Ibid. p. 60.
[10] Ibid. p. 161.
[11] Ibid. p. 140.
[12] Quetelet, tome ii. pp. 152, 153.
[13] Ibid. p. 154.
[14] Tissot, pp. 147, 148.

Tissot says,[1] 'Nous devons signaler ce qu'il est convenu d'appeler l'onanisme comme une des causes éloignées les moins équivoques des suicides. Les médecins sont unanimes à ce sujet.'

In the above work Tissot has attempted an exhaustive analysis of the causes of suicide. Blackstone says, 'The attempting it seems to be countenanced by the civil law,' and quotes Ff 49, 16, 6.[2] Christian adds,[3] 'The instances of females attempting or committing suicide are now very numerous.'

Montesquieu, who had been in England, says, 'Les Anglais se tuent sans qu'on puisse imaginer aucune raison qui les y détermine ; ils se tuent dans le sein même du bonheur.'[4]

In France, from 1827 to 1831 inclusive, the proportion of suicides to the entire population was 1 to 18,000.[5] In 1835 the proportion was 1 to 20,000.[6]

Men commit most suicides between 35 and 45 ; women between 25 and 35.[7]

Napoleon, after abdicating in 1814, tried to poison himself.[8] Rousseau is suspected to have killed himself.[9]

Comte[10] says the ancients admired it ; but Catholicism has the great merit of discouraging it.

Tocqueville[11] says that in America suicide is rare ; insanity common.

Tallemant des Réaux,[12] who wrote in the middle of the seventeenth century, says the English are melancholy and very prone to it.

Lerminier[13] takes for granted that suicide is unknown to animals. There are more suicides in summer than in winter.[14]

In 1836 the population of New York was nearly 300,000, and the yearly suicides 42.[15]

[1] Tissot, p. 142.
[2] Commentaries, edit. Christian, 1809, vol. iv. p. 189.   [3] Ibid. note, p. 190.
[4] Esprit des Lois, livre xiv. chap. xii., Œuvres de Montesquieu, Paris, 1835, p. 305.   [5] Quetelet, Sur l'Homme, tome li. p. 148.   [6] Ibid. p. 158.
[7] Ibid. vol. ii. p. 159, but see p. 155.
[8] Alison's History of Europe, vol. xlii. pp. 207, 208.
[9] Villemain, Littérature au xviiie Siècle, tome ii. p. 301.
[10] Philosophie Positive, tome v. p. 438.
[11] Démocratie en Amérique, Bruxelles, 1840, tome iv. p. 217.
[12] Historiettes, vol. ii. p. 122.   [13] Philosophie du Droit, tome i. p. 185.
[14] See Journal of Statistical Society, vol. i. pp. 102-108.
[15] Ibid. vol. ii. pp. 5, 25.

There are more suicides among military men than among civilians.[1] It is said that sailors, being more lively and cheerful than soldiers, are less prone to commit suicide.

In Prussia, in 1838, out of 100,000 deaths, 370 were by suicide.[2]

Among convicts of Norfolk Island suicide is very rare.[3] Buchanan, who appears to have seen a good deal of the North American Indians, says of them, 'Suicide is not considered by the Indians either as an act of heroism or of cowardice ; nor is it with them a subject of praise or blame. They view this desperate act as the consequence of mental derangement ; and the person who destroys himself is to them an object of pity. Such cases do not frequently occur.'[4] At and near Benares, suicide (independently of the suttees) is very common. The usual way is by drowning, and this is done sometimes with religious views, sometimes after a quarrel, that their blood may lie at their enemy's door.[5] In Kamtschatka and in the Kurile Islands, suicide is very common, and this is not on religious grounds, but simply because 'they think it more eligible to die than to lead a life that is disagreeable to them.'[6] Kohl[7] says, 'There are fewer suicides in St. Petersburg than in any capital in Europe. On an average, not fifty occur in a year ; for every 10,000 inhabitants, therefore, not more than one yearly lays violent hands upon himself.' Among the earlier monks there were several cases of suicide ;[8] but in the sixth century the Church exerted itself against suicide.[9] Ford[10] says that in Spain 'suicide is almost unknown.' Suicide was rare among 'the lively Greeks,' but common among 'the proud Romans.'[11]

IMPROVEMENT OF MORALS.

THE lord had the right of *selling* his female tenant until wardship was abolished. It is remarkable that her lord lost the benefit if the marriage was delayed till she was sixteen ; and that the

---

[1] See Journal of Statistical Society, vol. II. p. 253 ; see also vol. IV. 12, 13.
[2] Ibid. pp. 366, 367.   [3] Ibid. viii. 33.
[4] Buchanan's North American Indians, 8vo, 1824, p. 184.
[5] Heber's Journey through India, vol. I. pp. 353, 389.
[6] Grieve's History of Kamtschatka, pp. 176, 200, 238.
[7] Russia, 8vo, 1844, p. 194.
[8] See Neander's History of the Church, vol. III. p. 337.   [9] Ibid. vol. v. p. 142.
[10] Handbook for Spain, 1847, p. 337.
[11] Smith's Theory of Moral Sentiments, vol. II. pp. 157, 159.

18 Eliz. c. 7, which makes it a capital crime to abuse a consenting child under ten, 'seems to leave an exception for these marriages by declaring only the *carnal* and *unlawful* knowledge of such woman-child to be a felony. Hence the abolition of the feudal wardship and marriage at the Restoration may, perhaps, have contributed not less to the improvement of the morals than of the liberty of the subject.'[1] What distinguishes Ireland from all other civilised countries is that crimes intended to produce a *general* effect, such as threatening notices, murders to intimidate *others*, &c., are more numerous than crimes committed with a view to benefit the criminal, such as robbery, or murder as an act of *personal* revenge.[2] For horrible cruelty in punishment, see Tytler's Hist. of Scotland, Edinburgh, 1845, vol. i. pp. 201, 227, 229, 230 ; vol. iii. p. 150.

HORSES.

FROM an early period great attention had been paid in England to encouraging the breed of horses. Indeed, I believe there was no personal chattel so protected.[3] In 1555 the French ambassador in London writes to the King of Navarre that he had endeavoured to procure for him 'des juments blanches de ce pays pour mettre en son parc de Pau ;' but after inquiring in all the English fairs, he had not been able to meet with any ; but he was given to hope that they might be procured in the north.[4] In 1559 there were no horses 'for the draught of grete ordynaunce' to be found north of Yorkshire and Nottinghamshire.[5] The Venetian ambassador, who was a very intelligent observer, writes in 1557 that England 'produces a greater number of horses than any other country of Europe. But the horses being weak and of bad wind, fed merely on grass, being like other cattle and animals kept in field or pasture which the temperature of the climate admits of, they are not capable of any great exertion, and are held in no estimation. . . . The horses which we commonly see in the cavalry are all foreign, imported from Flanders.'[6] Alison says,[7] 'Each horse requires

[1] Christian's note in Blackstone's Commentaries, 8vo, 1809, vol. II. p. 131.
[2] See Lewis on Local Disturbances in Ireland, Lond. 8vo, 1836, pp. 94-97.
[3] See Blackstone's Commentaries, 8vo, 1809, vol. II. p. 451.
[4] Ambassades de Noailles, Leyde, 1763, tome v. pp. 63, 64.
[5] See Haynes's State Papers, pp. 230-242.
[6] Michele's Report in Ellis's Original Letters, 2nd series, vol. II. p. 224.
[7] Principles of Population, 8vo, 1840, vol. i. p. 198.

as much food as eight persons. . . . In the expedition to Russia
it is calculated that Napoleon lost 200,000 horses, and France
contains 2,500,000.' Egwin of Worcester, who died about 718,
'before leaving Mercia ordered a smith to make for him heavy
fetters of iron closed with locks "such as they fixed about the feet
of horses."'[1] In 1578, Gilbert Talbot writes to his father, the
Earl of Shrewsbury, from Charing Cross, 'There are two Friesland horses, of a reasonable price for their goodness. I have
promised the fellow for them 33*l.* I think them especial good
for my ladyship's coach.'[2] In 1687 the Bishop of Chester
'bought two horses, one for eleven guineas, and the other
5*l.* 1*s.* 0*d.*'[3] In 1747 'Yorkshire is esteemed the best county in
England for horses.'[4] In Great Britain, more than 600,000
horses.[5]

HEREDITARY AND DIVINE RIGHTS OF KINGS.

IT is very curious that to assert that the king and parliament
cannot limit the crown was 'a high misdemeanour, punishable
with the forfeiture of goods and chattels,' during the *whole* of the
seventeenth century. Indeed, the 13 Elizabeth, c. 1, made it high
treason during the life of that queen.[6] In 1593 was published
'A Conference about the Next Succession, by R. Doleman.' In
this work, which is attributed to the famous Parsons, it is distinctly
laid down that the right of succession to any government does *not*
depend on natural and divine laws, but merely on human and
positive laws.[7] On the accession of Edward VI., Cranmer, Archbishop of Canterbury, in the coronation sermon, said that the
king's 'crown, being given him by God Almighty, could not, by a
failure in the administration, be forfeited either to church or
state.'[8] In 1549 the king's council ordered Dr. Hopkins, chaplain to Mary, to tell her that Edward 'is king by the ordinance of
God.'[9] Calvin at different times expressed different opinions

[1] Wright's Biographia Britannica Literaria, 8vo. 1842, vol. I. p. 224.
[2] Lodge's Illustrations of British History, 8vo. 1838, vol. II. p. 99.
[3] Cartwright's Diary, Camden Society, 1843, p. 68.
[4] Nichols's Literary Illustrations of the Eighteenth Century, vol. III. p. 356.
[5] Alison's History of Europe, vol. x. p. 247.
[6] Blackstone's Commentaries, edit. Christian, 1809, vol. iv. p. 92.
[7] Butler's Memoirs of the Catholics, 8vo. 1822, vol. II. p. 22.
[8] Collier's Ecclesiastical History, 8vo. 1840, vol. v. p. 184.   [9] Ibid. p. 343

respecting passive obedience.[1]   At vol. i. pp. 99-101 of his Political Philosophy,[2] Lord Brougham has given a good though popular account of the tendency of civilisation to convert an elective into an hereditary monarchy.   The comparative advantages of hereditary and elective monarchies are very temperately discussed by Lord Brougham.[3]   He, like most able political writers, prefers the hereditary form.   The great increase of the royal authority under the Tudors is shown by the number of parliaments they summoned as compared with the Plantagenets.[4] Allen says, 'Under the Saxons the crown was elective.'[5]   He adds[6] that Richard III. 'is the first king of England who can be said to have ascended the throne without the form at least of an election, and without any interval having elapsed between the death of his predecessor and his own accession.   There are public acts in his name dated in the first year of his reign, before his coronation had taken place.'   Hemingford says that Henry III. was regularly elected, and the nine days that elapsed between his father's death and his own coronation are 'considered as an interregnum during which the throne was vacant';[7] and even the accession of Edward I. was dated, not from his father's death, but from his own recognition.[8]   However, 'since the accession of Edward I. there has been no interregnum unless when the line of succession has been broken,' and, at the accession of James I., 'it was declared to be the law of England "that there can be no interregnum within the same."'[9]   Allen says,[10] 'There is no trace among the Anglo-Saxons, as among the Franks, of a general oath of fealty to the king from all his subjects,' and the oath taken by an Anglo-Saxon to his hlaford 'contains no reservation of fealty or obedience to the king.'[11]   But William I. procured a law which 'obliges every freeman in his dominions to take an oath of fealty to his person without reserve or qualification.'[12]   Allen follows Lye in saying that the etymology of king is *not* the same as *can*, but 'cyning is derived from *cyn*, which means kindred, family, tribe, nation,' and in Anglo-Saxon 'is manifestly a patronymic.'[13]   On

---

[1] See the note in Soames' Elizabethan Religious History, 8vo, 1839, p. 36.
[2] 2nd edit. 8vo, 1849.   [3] Ibid. vol. i. pp. 363, 364.
[4] See the list in Brougham's Political Philosophy, vol. iii. p. 252.
[5] Rise of the Royal Prerogative, 8vo, 1849, p. 44.   [6] Ibid. p. 45.
[7] Ibid. p. 46.   [8] Ibid. pp. 46, 47.
[9] Ibid. p. 47.   [10] Ibid. p. 64.   [11] Ibid. p. 69.   [12] Ibid. p. 70.
[13] Ibid. pp. 175, 176.

hereditary bishops, &c., see COMMON PLACE BOOK, art. 991. Sir
Henry Wotton, who wrote at the end of the sixteenth century,
clearly, though cautiously, affirms the right of resisting bad princes.
The resistance, he says, must be made by parliament ; but if the
sovereign refuse to summon a parliament, the nation has a right
of compelling him to do so.[1]

Early in the sixteenth century a design seems to have been
seriously entertained of making the Papacy hereditary.[2] Voltaire[3] says the Visigothic Vamba 'est le premier roi qui ait cru
ajouter à ses droits en se fesant sacrer, et il fut le premier que les
prêtres chassèrent du trône.' Hooker's view seems to be the right
one, though on shallow grounds.[4] Even Chillingworth held the
monstrous doctrine of passive obedience.[5] Lord Dartmouth[6]
says it was not heard of before James I. The language of Montaigne is most unfavourable to divine right.[7] In Java there is no
hereditary nobility, and the sovereign is supreme.[8] Charron distinctly says the kingly power is limited.[9] At the end of the sixteenth century the Jesuits denied the divine right, and said that
all power proceeded from the people.[10] The Protestants, on the
other hand, affirmed the divine right.[11] Ranke[12] says that in the
works of Hotmann, a Frenchman, in the reign of Henry III.,
'the idea of the sovereignty of the people makes its appearance in
French literature.' See also Capefigue.[13] Calvin distinctly upholds
the doctrine of passive obedience ;[14] and the divine right is
supported by the French Protestants early in the seventeenth

---

[1] Wotton's State of Christendom, Lond. folio, 1657, pp. 201–207.

[2] See Ranke, Die Römischen Päpste, Berlin, 1838, Band I. pp. 45–59.

[3] Essai sur les Mœurs, chap. xxvii. note in Œuvres de Voltaire, tome xv.
p. 483.

[4] Ecclesiastical Polity, book i. sect. 10. Works, vol. , p. 109.

[5] Religion of Protestants, 8vo, 1846, p. 372, and Des Maizeaux, Life of Chillingworth, 8vo, 1795, p. 298.

[6] Note in Burnet's History of his own Time, vol. iii. p. 382.

[7] See Essais de Montaigne, Paris, 8vo, 1843, livre iii. chap. vi. p. 573.

[8] Crawfurd's History of the Indian Archipelago, Edinburgh, 8vo, 1820, vol. iii.
p. 15 ; see also Ellis's Polynesian Researches, 2nd edit. vol. iii. p. 94.

[9] De la Sagesse, Amsterdam, 8vo, 1782, tome ii. pp. 13, 38.

[10] Ranke, Päpste, vol. ii. pp. 186–190.

[11] Ibid. pp. 193, 194.

[12] Civil Wars in France, 8vo, 1852, vol. ii. p. 62.

[13] Histoire de la Réforme et la Ligue, tome iii. p. 311.

[14] Medley's History of the Reformed Religion in France, 1832, vol. i. p. 110.

century.[1] Indeed, Amyrant wrote a work expressly to advocate
passive obedience.[2]

OBSERVATIONS ON METAPHYSICS.

THE increase of Puritanism was increased (?) by that school of
Jansenists and Mystics which asserted that things were only just
because God willed them to be just.   This dangerous error in
morals is well refuted by M. Cousin.[3]

Hobbes, who first (?) laid down the idea of government being
founded on an original compact, added that if the government
broke the compact the governed were nevertheless bound by it.[4]
Subsequent writers, such as Locke, recognised the original compact, but denied the right of infraction.   The idea of an original
compact which was the foundation of government now began to
be generally advocated.   This idea, though utterly false, was, like
many other errors, of signal advantage.

The less beautiful the climate, the more likely are thinkers to
arise.   See COMMON PLACE BOOK, art. 1854.

See, in Cousin's Histoire de la Philosophie,[5] a magnificent
and, as I think, decisive vindication against Kant of the capacity
of metaphysics for affording proofs as certain as those of mathematics.

Perhaps Hutcheson was the first who clearly saw that government was *not* founded on a contract.[6]

Morell, an enthusiastic student of German philosophy,[7] says,
'The great peculiarity which distinguishes the modern philosophy of Germany from that of every other country is the use
of the ontological instead of the psychological method.'   Contrary, he says, to Bacon, Descartes, and Locke, they 'begin by
laying down the most primitive and abstract *notion* we have of
existence, as though it were a reality, and proceed onward until
step by step they have constructed the whole universe.'   Morell

---

[1] See Quick's Synodicon in Gallia, Lond. folio, 1692, vol. I. p. 412, and vol. II,
p. 397.

[2] Biographie Universelle, tome li. p. 81.

[3] Histoire de la Philosophie, Paris, 1846, part i. tome ii. p. 278, &c.

[4] See Cousin's Histoire de la Philosophie, Paris, 1846, part i. tome iii. p. 282.

[5] Paris, 1846, part i. tome v. pp. 240-244.

[6] See Cousin's Histoire de la Philosophie, 1846, part i. tome iv. pp. 186, 187.

[7] History of Speculative Philosophy, 8vo, 1846, vol. II. p. 180.

says of the Germans, 'They have not been willing to tolerate anything whatever that is merely experimental, or even that includes an inductive process.'[1] See also vol. ii. p. 378, where Morell says that the Germans always prefer the ancient deductive synthetical method to the Baconian inductive, analytical method.

Frederick Schlegel says, 'The second corruption of Christianity was from Arianism, which corresponds to what in modern times is called rationalism,' &c.[2]

Morell says, 'By the tendencies of a metaphysical system we mean the whole mass of ultimate consequences which can be fairly and logically drawn from its acknowledged principles.'[3] This shows his ignorance of the application of metaphysics to history. The real tendency of a system is not what *can* be *logically* inferred from it, but what is likely to be inferred.

Whewell well refutes the popular notion that discoveries are accidental.[4]

Lord Brougham says that in metaphysics 'we must be content with evidence of an inferior kind to that which the mathematical sciences employ.'[5]

Whewell[6] says, 'In the inductive sciences a definition does not form the basis of reasoning, but points out the course of investigation.' There appears to be no doubt that Schelling *à priori* anticipated the discovery that electricity was producible from common magnetism.[7] It has been observed, and I think with great truth, that there are more false facts than false theories in the world.[8] A very competent authority, Mr. Green, says that Schelling's speculations 'cannot but be admitted to have had an invigorating influence on the progress of natural science.'[9] Even in physical science it is allowable as it were to *feel one's way*, and to draw inferences from analogies.[10] Metaphysics, as it must be

[1] History of Speculative Philosophy, 8vo. 1846, vol. ii. p. 494.
[2] Philosophy of History, Lond. 8vo. 1846, p. 313.
[3] History of Speculative Philosophy, 8vo. 1846, vol. ii. p. 442.
[4] Philosophy of the Inductive Sciences, 8vo, 1847, vol. ii. pp. 23–26.
[5] Political Philosophy, 2nd edit. 1849, vol. i. p. 2.
[6] Philosophy of the Inductive Sciences, vol. i. p. 575.
[7] Whewell, vol. i. pp. 371, 372.
[8] Mayo's Outlines of Medical Proof, 1850, p. 13.
[9] Green's Vital Dynamics, 8vo, 1840, p. 38.
[10] See the rules for ascertaining causes laid down in Herschel's Discourse on Natural Philosophy, 8vo, 1830, pp. 152, 164, 165.

the end of all knowledge, so it was the beginning of all knowledge. Coleridge well says, 'Thus in the thirteenth century the first science which roused the intellects of men from the torpor of barbarism was, as in all countries ever has been and ever must be the case, the science of metaphysic and ontology.'[1] Lord Brougham is certainly mistaken in supposing that Hume was the first who asserted 'that we only know the connection between events by their succession one to another in point of time ; and that what we term causation, the relation of cause and effect, is really only the constant precedence of one event, act, or thing to another.'[2] Brougham talks[3] of 'the necessarily imperfect nature of inductive evidence.' On the nature of axioms and on logic, read Cousin, Histoire de la Philosophie, 2nd series, tome iii. pp. 272–340. Cousin says that Locke's system leads to scepticism and materialism.[4] Baxter, who lived in Scotland, appears to have directed Lord Kames's attention to metaphysics.[5] In 1751, Kames published Essays to show that the laws of morality are certain and unchangeable.[6] Bower says,[7] 'The University of Edinburgh possesses the high honour of having been the first public seminary in Europe in which the Newtonian philosophy was publicly taught.' This was by David Gregory, about 1690.[8] Hooker[9] anticipates Locke in denying the existence of innate ideas. Glanville very clearly saw that the senses do *not* deceive us.[10] Mr. Lawrence speaks in the highest terms of the applicability of Brown's 'Cause and Effect' to the physical sciences.[11] For some curious cases of 'double consciousness,' see Mayo on the Truth in Popular Superstitions.[12] Coleridge[13] erroneously supposes that the senses sometimes deceive us. He thinks, but doubtfully, that Jeremy Taylor is the first good English writer

---

[1] Hints towards the Formation of a more Comprehensive Theory of Life, by S. T. Coleridge, edited by Dr. Watson, Lond. 8vo, 1848, p. 28.
[2] Brougham's Lives of Men of Letters and Sciences, 8vo, 1845, vol. i. p. 200.
[3] Ibid. p. 391.
[4] Histoire de la Philosophie, 2de série, tome iii. pp. 243–253.
[5] See Tytler's Memoirs of Kames, Edinburgh, 1814, vol. i. pp. 31–37.
[6] Ibid. p. 183.
[7] History of the University of Edinburgh, vol. ii. p. 81.   [8] Ibid. p. 82.
[9] Ecclesiastical Polity, book i. sect. 6, in Works, vol. i. pp. 85, 86.
[10] The Vanity of Dogmatising, 8vo, 1661. pp. 91–94.
[11] Lawrence's Lectures on Man, 8vo, 1844, p. 56.
[12] Combe's Elements of Phrenology, Edinburgh, 6th edit. 1845. p. 149.
[13] Literary Remains, vol. iii. p. 350.

before 1688 who uses the word *idea* as a mental image.[1] Coleridge says [2] that what is *objectively* a law is *subjectively* an idea. He insists on the great importance of distinguishing between the reason and the understanding, and between ideas and conceptions.[3] De Foe has some acute remarks on 'never inquiring after God in those works of nature which, depending upon the course of things, are plain and demonstrative.'[4] In 1679, Locke mentions contemptuously 'an Hobbist.'[4] In a letter written in 1734, Voltaire[6] clearly states the absurdity of thinking that a materialist must be an atheist. Dr. Whewell has attempted, I think unsuccessfully, but certainly with great ability, to confirm the truth of the idea of substance by the history of physical knowledge.[7] The Romans as thinkers were infinitely inferior to the Greeks.[8] Tocqueville says,[9] 'Une idée fausse mais claire et précise aura toujours plus de puissance dans le monde qu'une vraie idée mais complexe.' Herbert Mayo well says that a great truth always goes through three stages. Napoleon says, 'A man, before doing anything of consequence, ought to digest his dinner and sleep a night upon it ; and then, if he is of the same opinion the following day, it is the real determination of his mind ; if not, it is only a caprice or whim.' [10]

SUBSTANCE.

JAMES MILL says, 'But what is the rose, besides the colour, the form, and so on ? Not knowing what it is, but supposing it to be something, we invent a name to stand for it. We call it a *substratum*. This substratum, when closely examined, is not distinguishable from cause. It is the cause of the qualities ; that is, the cause of the causes of our sensations. The association then is this. To each of the sensations we have from a particular object we annex in our imagination a cause ; and to these several

---

[1] Literary Remains, vol. iii. p. 380.
[2] Church and State, 2nd edit. 1830, p. 7.   [3] Ibid. p. 71.
[4] Wilson's Life of De Foe, vol. ii. p. 269.
[5] See King's Life of Locke, 8vo, 1830, vol. i. p. 191.
[6] Œuvres, tome lvi. p. 392.
[7] Philosophy of the Inductive Sciences, vol. i. pp. 404-419, and 407, 408.
[8] See Whewell's Philosophy of the Inductive Sciences, vol. ii. p. 137.
[9] Démocratie en Amérique, vol. ii. p. 18.
[10] Forsyth's Captivity of Napoleon, Lond. 1853, vol. ii. p. 277.

causes we annex a cause common to all, and mark it with the name substratum.'[1] Again,[2] he says, 'The term "quality," or "qualities of an object," seems to imply that the qualities are one thing, the object another. And this in some indistinct way is no doubt the opinion of the great majority of mankind. Yet the absurdity of it strikes the understanding the moment it is mentioned. The qualities of an object are the whole of the object. What is there beside the qualities? In fact, they are convertible terms: the qualities are the object, and the object is the qualities.' Reid's mode of proving a subject is whimsical enough. He says that because we *call* a phenomenon a quality, and because qualities must have a subject, *therefore* substance exists.[3] Locke, in his Essay, seemed to doubt the existence of *substance*; 'but in his first letter to the Bishop of Worcester he removes this doubt, and quotes many passages of his Essay to show that he neither denied nor doubted of the existence of substances both thinking and material.'[4] Reid, with singular presumption, says that a man who denies the existence of substance 'is not fit to be reasoned with.'[5] Mr. Newman[6] truly says that 'we should not attain greater accuracy by expunging the two words' (substance and matter) 'from our vocabulary.' But I do not know of any metaphysician who has proposed to expunge them. The real question, I apprehend, is not whether *substance* is a useless word; but whether it is expressive of that which has an objective existence, or whether it is a mere verbal generalisation.

LEASES.

THE Statute of User, 27 Hen. VIII. c. 10, turned user into possession by making cestui qui use terre tenant. The courts in interpreting this laid down that as the statute only spoke of those who were *seised* to use, it did not extend to term of year or any other chattel interest of which the termor cannot be *seised*, but only *possessed*; 'and therefore if a term of 1,000 years be limited to A, to the use of or in trust for B, the statute does not execute

---

[1] Analysis of the Mind, vol. I. p. 263.   [2] Ibid. vol. II. p. 53.
[3] Essays on the Powers of the Mind, Edinburgh, 1808, vol. I. p. 276.
[4] Reid's Essays, Edinburgh, 1808, vol. II. p. 278.   [5] Ibid. vol. I. p. 38.
[6] Natural History of the Soul, 8vo. 1849, p. 92.

this use, but leases it at common law.'[1]   This, I suppose, would
encourage long leases.

CHANCERY AND ITS EQUITABLE JURISDICTION.

FOR this, I suppose, the way was paved by the Courts of Requests.
They were established by an act of the Common Council in the
reign of Henry VIII., but were not legal till 3 Jac. I.[2]   The
Bishop of St. Asaph says that Sir T. More is the first instance of
a layman being made Lord Chancellor.[3]

ÆSTHETICS AND HISTORY OF THE ARTS.

MARY employed a painter named Nicolas, who, though born in
France, had been thirty-two years in England, and was patronised
by Henry VIII. and Edward VI. ;[4] but his business seems merely
to have been to paint the standards, &c., of the army.[5]   In 1568,
in a conversation between Mr. White and Mary of Scotland, a
question was raised as to whether carving, painting, or 'working
with the needle' was 'the most commendable quality.' Mary
inclined towards painting, but Mr. White seemed to lean the
other way.[6]   On the difference between the *real* and the *true*,
see Cousin, Histoire de la Philosophie, Paris, 1846, part i.
pp. 385, 386.   Cousin says that Hutcheson was the first who revived
the Platonic theory that all beauty was referrible to moral beauty.[7]
He adds[8] that Hutcheson first placed sentiment above sensation ;
and Reed first placed reason above sentiment.   He says,[9] 'Fille
de la scholastique, la philosophie moderne est demeurée longtemps étrangère aux grâces, et les Recherches d'Hutcheson pré-
sentent, je crois, le premier traité spécial sur le beau, écrit par
un moderne.   Elles ont paru en 1725 (je ne vois avant la Re-
cherche que l'ouvrage fort ennuyeux de Crouzas, "Traité du

[1] Blackstone, vol. ii. p. 336, who quotes Bacon, Law of Uses, p. 315. Jenk.
p. 244, Poph. 76, Dyer, 369.
[2] Ibid. 8vo, 1809, vol. iii. p. 82.
[3] Short's History of the Church of England, 8vo, 1847, p. 95.
[4] Ambassades de Noailles, Leyde, 1762, tome ii. p. 255; see also tome iv.
p. 61.
[5] Ibid. tome iv. pp. 155, 156.
[6] See White's Letter to Cecil in Hayner's State Papers, pp. 509-511.
[7] Histoire de la Philosophie, Paris, 1846, part i. tome iv. p. 527.
[8] Ibid. p. 540.   [9] Ibid. tome iv. p. 84.

Beau," Amsterdam, 1712). Cette date est presque celle de
l'avènement de l'esthétique dans la philosophie européenne.
L'ouvrage du père André en France est de 1741, celui de Baumgarten en Allemagne est de 1750.' He adds[1] that in æsthetics
Hutcheson's great merit is having distinguished the faculty
which perceives pure beauty from the two which were generally
supposed to comprise the entire soul, viz. understanding and
physical sensibility. He says[2] that the theory that beauty is the
agreement of beauty and variety was borrowed by Hutcheson
from Plotinus. Cousin[3] says, 'Le dix-huitième siècle d'un bout
de l'Europe à l'autre n'a pas produit un artiste de génie, et il a
manqué la grande poésie parce qu'il a ignoré la vraie morale et
la grande métaphysique.' But I believe that when metaphysics
began art would decline, because men became hypercritical. The
influence of chivalry upon the arts is noticed in Schlegel's Philosophy of History.[4] Lord Brougham says of despotism, 'The
arts of poetry, painting, and sculpture may well flourish under its
influence.'[5] He adds that it is not tyranny, but want of cultivation, which has prevented them flourishing in the East ;[6] but
surely many parts of Asia were more cultivated than England at
the time of Chaucer. I rather ascribe it to a want of imagination
in the Asiatic mind. Brougham says[7] that under *free* govern-
ments the fine arts 'have at all times flourished the most steadily
and abundantly.' M. Quetelet thinks that among the moderns
art has suffered from a too servile imitation of the ancients.[8]
Dr. Whewell has an ingenious idea that the middle ages owed
their feebleness in science to the indistinctness of their ideas ;
and that it was the arts, peculiarly the fine arts, which first re-
medied this evil. On their indistinctness of ideas, see his History
of the Inductive Sciences.[9] He well says[10] that one of the proofs
of this is 'the fact that mere collections of the opinions of physical philosophers came to hold a prominent place in literature.'[11]
He then observes[12] that 'in all cases the arts are prior to the

[1] Histoire de la Philosophie, Paris, 1846, part I. tome iv. p. 99.
[2] Ibid. p. 98.   [3] Ibid. p. 101.
[4] Lond. 8vo, 1846, pp. 371-374.
[5] Political Philosophy, 8vo, 1849, vol. I. p. 155.
[6] Ibid. p. 155.   [7] Ibid. p. 156.
[8] Quetelet, Sur l'Homme, Paris, 1835, tome II. pp. 256, 257.
[9] 8vo, 1847, vol. I. pp. 253-279.   [10] Ibid. p. 255.   [11] Ibid. p. 280.
[12] Ibid. p. 351.

related sciences ;[1] and[1] he gives a view of the architecture of
the middle ages ; and says[2] that the 'indistinctness of ideas
which attended the decline of the Roman Empire appears in the
forms of their architecture ;' but by the twelfth century 'everything showed that, practically at least, men possessed and applied
with steadiness and pleasure the idea of mechanical pressure and
support.'[3] He denies[4] the Arabic origin of Gothic architecture.
Whewell says,[5] 'And thus the natural process of vision is the
habit of seeing that which cannot be seen ; and the difficulty of
the art of drawing consists in learning not to see more than is
visible. But again, even in the simplest drawing, we exhibit
something which we do not see. However slight is our representation of objects, it contains something which we create for ourselves. For we draw an *outline*. Now an outline has no existence in nature.' He says,[6] 'It appears probable that neither
poetry nor painting, nor the other arts which require for their
perfection a lofty and spiritualised imagination, would have appeared in the noble and beautiful forms which they assumed in
the fourteenth and fifteenth centuries, if men of genius had at the
beginning of that period made it their main business to discover
the laws of nature, and to reduce them to a rigorous scientific
form.' He adds[7] that some of the earliest attempts to found in
the sixteenth century a rational philosophy were made not by
men of science but by men of art, such as Leonardo da Vinci. I
suspect civilisation is generally unfavourable to the fine arts.
Reed says, 'They are nothing else but the language of nature,
which we brought into the world with us, and have unlearned by
disuse, and so find the greatest difficulty in recovering it. Abolish
the use of articulate sounds and writing among mankind for a
century, and every man would be a painter, an actor, and an
orator.'[8] He adds[9] that the fine arts are all founded upon the
connection between signs and the things signified by them.[10] At
p. 165 he remarks that painting is the only profession in which it
is necessary to distinguish 'the appearance of objects to the eye

[1] History of the Inductive Sciences, 8vo, 1847, tome I. pp. 360-369.
[2] Ibid. p. 361.   [3] Ibid. p. 263.   [4] Ibid. p. 364.
[5] Philosophy of the Inductive Sciences, 8vo, 1847, vol. I. pp. 114, 115.
[6] Ibid. vol. ii. p. 176.   [7] Ibid. pp. 205, 206.
[8] Reed's Inquiry into the Human Mind, Edinburgh, 8vo, 1814, pp. 97, 98.
[9] Ibid. p. 111.   [10] Ibid.; see also p. 310.

from the judgment we form by sight of their colour, distance, magnitude, and figure.' William Schlegel says of Winkelmann, 'No man has so deeply penetrated into the innermost spirit of Grecian art.'[1] Mr. Green observes that the motions of our different parts 'all tend to the circular and curvilineal in their movements, a circumstance which mainly tends to confer on human motion the character of beauty.'[2] But may not the fact that they *do* tend to the circular have given rise to the notion that the circular has the character of beauty? In his Mental Dynamics[3] he says that, although the ancients invested the *Finite* with beauty, yet we have the merit in the fine arts, poetry, and the drama of the expression of the Infinite. Schiller says, I think truly, 'Mit kurzen Worten: die katholische Religion wird im Ganzen mehr für ein Künstlervolk, die protestantische mehr für ein Kaufmannsvolk taugen.'[4] Ranke ascribes the decline of art in Italy, in the latter half of the sixteenth century, to the decline of religious enthusiasm.[5] He adds[6] that when, at the end of the sixteenth century, the Church of Rome recovered its power, the fine arts began to revive, and there arose in poetry Tasso, in painting Caracci. Adam Smith[7] observes that in painting we may, but in sculpture we may not, imitate mean and disagreeable objects. Sir J. Reynolds (Works, vol. ii. p. 24) could not understand the reason. The reason is[8] that in statuary there is not a sufficient disparity between the imitated and the imitating object; for, he observes,[9] the exact resemblance of two objects of art always lessens the merit of both. Thus colouring is unpleasant in sculpture, because it still further lessens the disparity.'[10] Hence we often grow tired of looking at the most beautiful artificial flowers, but never of looking at a beautiful painting of flowers. This is because the first are too like.'[11] Thus the pleasure we receive from painting and sculpture, so far from being connected with deception, is incompatible with it, and is altogether founded upon wonder at seeing how well art has sur-

[1] Lectures on the Dramatic Art, Lond. 1840, vol. i. p. 47.
[2] Green's Vital Dynamics, 8vo, 1840, p. 77.
[3] 8vo, 1847, pp. 24, 25.
[4] Abfall der Niederlande in Schiller's Werke, Stuttgart, 1838, Band viii. p. 53.
[5] Die Römischen Päpste, Berlin, 1838, Band i. pp. 491, 492.
[6] Ibid. pp. 496–498.
[7] Essays on Philosophical Subjects, Lond. 4to. p. 138.   [8] Ibid. p. 140.
[9] Ibid. p. 136.   [10] Ibid. p. 140.   [11] Ibid. p. 141.

mounted the disparity nature has put between the two things.[1]
In painting the disparity is greater than in sculpture ; hence we
are pleased at many subjects when represented in a painting
which would afford no pleasure in sculpture.[2]   Schlosser says that
Baumgarten ' is the well-known inventor of a new philosophical
science, æsthetics, which was afterwards transplanted to Berlin by
his disciple Schulze.'[3]   Grimm observes that the more is *written*
on the fine arts the less they flourish.[4]   Morellet supposes that the
more men *reason* the less they are alive to mere artistic beauty ;
and he gives himself as an instance.[5]   Cousin thinks that modern
sculpture is impossible.[6]   Gibbon says,[7]   'All superfluous ornament is rejected by the cold frugality of the Protestants ; but the
Catholic superstition, which is always the enemy of reason, is
often the parent of the arts.'   Archdeacon Hare says,[8] 'In
Coleridge's Remains [9] this fondness for fantastic and verbal analogies, which was so prevalent in a large portion of our Jacobite
and Caroline divines, is ascribed to their study of the fathers.
There may be some truth in this remark ; at least, a large part of
the fathers are tainted with the same fault ; but it is much the
same thing as we find in so many poets of Charles the First's time,
who in like manner substitute fanciful images and fantastical
combinations for imaginative impersonation and harmonies.   Nor
is this practice confined to the poets.   Indeed, this is an ordinary
characteristic of the state of transition between an imaginative or
spiritual age, and one under the predominance of the reflective
critical understanding.'   The Aztecs have so odd a notion of
beauty that they flatten the heads of their children at birth.[10]
Lieber, whose admiration for Niebuhr was unbounded, says of
him, 'Though he loved the fine arts and was delighted by
master-works, still I believe he had no acute eye for them.'[11]   See
some ingenious remarks in Hare's Guesses at Truth, first series,

[1] Essays on Philosophical Subjects, Lond. 4to, pp. 145, 146.   [2] Ibid. p. 147.
[3] History of the Eighteenth Century, vol. ii. p. 173.
[4] Correspondance Littéraire, tome iii. pp. 98, 99.
[5] Mémoires de Morellet, Paris, 8vo, 1821, tome i. pp. 56, 57.
[6] Histoire de la Philosophie, part ii. tome ii. pp. 13, 14.
[7] Life of himself in Miscellaneous Works, 8vo, 1837, p. 72.
[8] The Mission of the Comforter, 8vo, 1850, p. 221.
[9] Vol. iii. pp. 104, 117, 175.
[10] See Lawrence's Lectures on Man, 8vo, 1844, p. 251.
[11] Reminiscences of B. G. Niebuhr, Lond. 8vo, 1835, p. 60.

pp. 48-70, 3rd edit. Lond. 8vo, 1847. Archdeacon Hare says [1] that 'a taste for the picturesque' must always arise late in a country, because it is the result of 'looking at pictures.' On the fine arts, and on wit, humour, &c., see Coleridge's Literary Remains, vol. i. pp. 100, 131-138, 155, 174, 216-230, 266-273; vol. ii. pp. 7-83. Townley, who by his collections, &c., did so much for the arts, was a Catholic; [2] and so, I suppose, was Lord Arundel, his ancestor. [3] It is remarkable that Swiss scenery has never been represented by any great poet or painter. [4]   Laing [5] says, 'All Swedes are performers on some musical instrument, and understand music;' and he adds [6] 'that the taste of the Swedish people for the beauty of form in the fine arts is far more advanced and developed than ours.' Protestantism unfavourable to the arts. [7] Sir J. Reynolds, 'at a very early period of his life,' showed taste for the arts; [8] but to the end of his life never knew anatomy. [9] Reynolds says [10] that taste is acquired, and some good judges do not at first admire Raphael. Reynolds first came into note in 1752, when he was twenty-nine. [11] From Henry VIII. to George I. all the painters in England were foreigners; and even under George I. and George II. there were, with the exception of Hogarth, no better ones than Richardson, Thornhill, and Hudson. [12] But in 1760 the first public exhibition was opened, [13] though in 1711 an attempt had been made to establish an academy. [14] It was in consequence of the exertions of Boydell that we first exported instead of importing engravings. [15] Sir J. Reynolds always says 'artists must *not* imitate nature;' [16] for he says, [17] 'The end of art' is not to imitate nature, but 'to produce a pleasing effect upon the mind;' and 'the great end of art is to strike the ima-

---

[1] Hare's Guesses at Truth, p. 48.

[2] See Nichols's Literary Illustrations of the Eighteenth Century, vol. iii. p. 721 *et seq.*

[3] Ibid. p. 735.

[4] See Alison's History of Europe, vol. iv. pp. 432, 433.

[5] Tour in Sweden, 1839, p. 68.

[6] Ibid. p. 73.

[7] See the remarks of Beechey in Sir J. Reynolds's Works, vol. i. pp. 7-12; see also Reynolds's own Observations, vol. ii. 189, 190.

[8] Ibid. vol. i. p. 37.   [9] Ibid. pp. 6, 48.   [10] Ibid. pp. 62, 63, 67.

[11] Ibid. pp. 115, 118.   [12] Ibid. pp. 25, 26.   [13] Ibid. p. 143.

[14] Ibid. p. 147.   [15] Ibid. pp. 183, 184.

[16] Works, vol. i. pp. 329, 336, 394; vol. ii. pp. 68, 127.

[17] Ibid. vol. ii. p. 74.

gination.'[1] A painter 'must compensate the natural deficiencies of his art ;' and as 'he cannot make his hero talk like a great man, he must make him look like one.'[2] And I may say that in the drama where they *do* talk, we are hurried for *time*. In painting we have *time*, but no *voice*. Reynolds observes that *all* accessories should be sacrificed ; but that *we* do not esteem art sufficiently to make 'the sacrifice the ancients made, especially the Grecians, who suffered themselves to be represented naked, whether they were generals, lawyers, or kings.'[3] Sculpture, having only 'one style,' can only correspond to 'one style' in painting ; and the sole object of sculpture is *beauty*.[4] Reynolds's remarks[5] on architecture are unsatisfactory. From Angelo to Maratti the Italian painters constantly declined.[6] The Dutch painters only address the eye ;[7] and for a list of the great Dutch painters see p. 206, and see vol. i. pp. 358, 359 ; vol. ii. p. 128. See also at the end of Reynolds's works[8] a chronological and alphabetical list of painters. Neither Scotland nor modern Germany has produced great painters. Why ? Metastasio said that the Improvisatori had done much harm to poetry.[9] In 1793 the French, merely from hostility to Christianity, waged war against the fine arts.[10] Vico[11] says that in an early state of civilisation poetry is sublime, because reason is weak.[12] Vico says[13] that the art of engraving metals must precede the art of painting, because the latter is most abstract. In the fourteenth century the ode was still hardly known in France.[14] In the fourteenth century it was laid down[15] that in sculpture all personages must be clothed *except angels*, who were allowed to be naked. In the fourteenth century great opposition was made in France to the 'new taste' for painting.[16] Monteil thinks[17] that oil-painting did not become general till the beginninng of the fifteenth century. Lamartine[18] says : 'La musique, le moins intellectuel et le plus sensuel de

[1] Reynolds's Works, vol. i. p. 347.
[2] Ibid. pp. 348, 349, 439.   [3] Ibid. p. 420.
[4] Ibid. vol. ii. pp. 6, 7, 12.   [5] Ibid. p. 75.
[6] Ibid. p. 129.   [7] Ibid. 205.
[8] Ibid. p. 428 *et seq.*   [9] Ibid. p. 46.
[10] See Georgel, Mémoires, vol. iv. p. 387.
[11] Philosophie de l'Histoire, p. 117.   [12] Ibid. p. 268.   [13] Ibid. p. 260.
[14] See Monteil, Histoire des Divers États, vol. i. p. 223.
[15] Monteil, Histoire des Français, tome i. p. 240.
[16] Ibid. tome ii. pp. 311, 315.   [17] Ibid. vol. iv. p. 161.
[18] Histoire des Girondins, vol. vii. p. 81.

tous les arts.' See some ingenious remarks in Comte, Traité de Législation, tome ii. pp. 34, 38.   He says that every race thinks perfect beauty consists in an *exaggeration* of its own peculiarities. 'Mr. Hamilton used to observe that Burke knew every subject of human knowledge except two, gaming and music.'[1]   Between the city of Guatemala and the Pacific there are some beautiful waterfalls, very accessible, but 'nobody ever visits them.'[2]   He adds[3] that near Leon, in Nicaragua, is a fine volcano which nobody ever goes to see.   The Biographie Universelle[4] says that Beaumarchais's Eugénie has 'une espèce d'intérêt dont Diderot avait donné l'exemple dans son Père de Famille.'   See a most striking article on music in Fraser's Magazine, October 1857 (containing review of my book).   The writer observes that music, among other things, increases sympathy and diminishes cruelty. The Spaniards have no landscape painters, and none of their writers on America describe scenery.[5]   Inglis[6] says 'the state of modern sculpture in Spain is more promising than that of painting.' Ford[7] says, 'In Spain, as among the classical ancients, *land-skip* was only an accessory or conventional, and seldom treated as a principal, either in art or literature.'   At p. 432, 'the pen and pencil were sculpturesque rather than picturesque.'   Tom Moore was born and died a Catholic ; and his mother, who had great influence over him, was 'a sincere and warm Catholic.'[8]   Sir Walter Scott 'confessed that he hardly knew high from low in music,' and 'Lord Byron knew nothing of music.'[9]

The essential difference between ancient and modern art is that the first is *plastic*, the other *picturesque* ; and, as Hemsterhuys says, the 'ancient painters were probably too much sculptors.'[10]   Schlegel applies the remark to poetry.   Greek art is the perfection of beauty, but too sensual,[11] and 'among the Greeks human nature was in itself

[1] Bisset's Life of Burke, and edit. 1800, vol. i. p. 108.
[2] Stephen's Central America, vol. i. p. 292.
[3] Ibid. vol. ii. p. 14.   [4] Tome iii. p. 636.
[5] Ticknor's History of Spanish Literature, vol. ii. p. 436 ; vol. iii. p. 22 ; and Hoskin's Spain, 1851, vol. ii. pp. 174-176.
[6] Spain, vol. i. p. 249.   [7] Handbook for Spain, 1847, p. 341.
[8] Moore's Memoirs by Lord J. Russell, vol. i. pp. xxii. 29 ; vol. iv. p. 305 ; vol. vii. p. 61.
[9] Ibid. vol. iv. p. 342, Lond. 1853.
[10] Lectures on Dramatic Art and Literature, by A. W. Schlegel, Lond. 1840, vol. i. pp. 9-70.   [11] Ibid. p. 12.

all-sufficient.'[1] The poetry of the ancients was the poetry of enjoyment, ours is that of desire.'[2] 'The moderns have never had a
sculpture of their own.'[3] This, as Schlegel well says,[4] accounts
for the ancients having so great a love for the 'unities.' Sculpture
fixes our attention on a group regardless of external accompaniments,
whereas painting delights in secondary objects. Thus the *plastic*
spirit of antiquity is different from the *picturesque* spirit of romantic
poetry. Schlegel well says[5] that 'genius is the almost unconscious
choice of the highest degree of excellence, and consequently it is
taste in its greatest perfection.'

In 1814, Campbell writes from Paris, 'Any little *taste* in painting I know full well I have not got ; but the pleasure of the
paintings grows upon me ; though still far, far inferior to that of
the *statues*.'[6] Dr. Beattie, the intimate friend of Campbell, says
of him, ' He was always fond of music ; particularly those airs
with which he had been familiar in early life.'[7] In 1838, Campbell writes that Burney has not done justice to the early English
musicians : 'Handel studied Purcell, and looked up to him as a
master. . . . The fact is that England, until fifty years ago, was
fertile in great musical poets. Witness her Purcell, her Bull, her
Locke, her Lawes, and Arne.'[8]

Crawford[9] says that the Javanese, 'in common with all semi-
barbarians, are good imitators ; but in this respect they fall short
of the Hindus.' See also respecting the Javanese theatre, vol. i.
pp. 127-132.

In 1811, Sir James Mackintosh writes, 'It is, you know, a
favourite notion of mine, that the sensibility to the beauties of
natural scenery is a late acquirement of civilised taste. Mr.
Twining, in his translation of Aristotle's Poetics, observes that there
is no single term, either in Greek or Latin, for "prospect."'[10]

Leigh Hunt[11] observes that poetry flourishes best in an in-
clement climate ; painting in a beautiful one. Hence, while we
have such fine poets, our painters are indifferent. I may shortly

---

[1] Lectures on Dramatic Art and Literature, by A. W. Schlegel, Lond. 1840,
vol. i. p. 15.   [2] Ibid. p. 16.
  [3] Ibid. p. 18.   [4] Ibid. p. 357.   [5] Ibid. pp. 7, 8.
  [6] Beattie's Life and Letters of Campbell, 8vo, 1849, vol. ii. p. 268.
  [7] Ibid. vol. iii. p. 362.   [8] Ibid. p. 265.
  [9] History of the Indian Archipelago, Edinburgh, 8vo, 1820, vol. i. pp. 47, 203.
  [10] Memoirs of Sir J. Mackintosh, vol. ii. p. 125.
  [11] Autobiography, 8vo, 1850, vol. ii. p. 297.

express Hunt's idea by saying that poetry derives its materials from *within* ; painting from without. He says, ' It is observable that the greatest poets of Italy came from Tuscany, where there is a great deal of inclemency in the seasons. The painters were from Venice, Rome, and other quarters ; some of which, though more northern, are more genially situated. The hills about Florence made Petrarch and Dante well acquainted with winter ; and they were also travellers and unfortunate.'

Alison, in his ' Beauty,' follows the sensual school of æsthetics, and resolves beauty into association. His views, and many of his illustrations, are adopted by Mr. James Mill, who, however, points out an error of his in relation to form.[1] Wilkie ' has been heard when his fame was high to declare that he could draw before he could read, and paint before he could spell.'[2] Wilkie, as a child, disliked arithmetic,[3] but was very mechanical, and loved to construct mills, carriages, &c., and even the arts of shoemaking and weaving.[4] Wilkie was born in Fifeshire in 1785 ; therefore he was only twenty-one when, in 1806, the appearance of the Village Politicians raised him to the height of fame.[5] We find Wilkie constantly insisting upon the superiority of painting from nature to imagination.[6] In 1805, when nineteen, he writes, ' I am convinced now that no picture can possess real merit unless it is a just representation of nature ;'[7] and for similar expressions see p. 185. But in 1836, when he was fifty-one, he writes, ' If art were but an exact representation of nature, it could be practised with absolute certainty and assurance of success ; but the duty of art is of a higher kind. . . . Art is only art when it adds mind to form.'[8] In 1825, at the age of forty, he complains that after Michael Angelo paintings seem to have been made ' more for the artists and connoisseur than for the untutored apprehension of ordinary men.'[9] In 1827 and 1828, when he was in Spain, he notices the striking similarity between Velasquez and the best English paintings.[10] But he observes[11] that, among all classes in Spain, Murillo was the favourite. Wilkie was never fond of paint-

<hr>

[1] Analysis of the Phenomena of the Mind, 8vo, 1829, vol. ii. pp. 203, 204.
[2] The Life of Sir David Wilkie, by Allan Cunningham, 8vo, 1843, vol. i. p. 11.
[3] Ibid. p. 13.   [4] Ibid. p. 15.
[5] Ibid. p. 115.   [6] Ibid. p. 58.
[7] Ibid. p. 76.   [8] Ibid. vol. iii. p. 131.
[9] Ibid. vol. ii. 197.   [10] Ibid. pp. 486, 519.
[11] Ibid. p. 516.

ing portraits.[1] Allan Cunningham says[2] that Wilkie did not care
for the 'picturesque' in scenery, but preferred men. Wilkie is
said *once* to have been in love ; but that is doubtful.[3] Early in
1825, Wilkie, then aged forty, was seized with a 'nervous debility'
which prevented him from painting, or, indeed, attending to anything more than five minutes at a time, and yet otherwise he
remained in perfect health.[4] At length, in April 1827, he writes,
'I have again begun to paint.'[5] He afterwards recovered, but
died apparently rather suddenly in 1841, aged fifty-six.[6] Allan
Cunningham says[7] that Wilkie's first style was copying nature; the
second style, which he did not live to work, was grander and more
historic. Wilkie thought colour one of the very first things.[8]
Wilkie says that the Catholic religion is more favourable to art
than the Protestant.[9] He thinks[10] that the Greek sculptors began
by learning painting. In 1840 he writes from Constantinople
that the Turkish religion was so unfavourable to art that he found
no one there who took any interest in it.[11] Wilkie observes that
none of the great Christian painters had taken the trouble to go
to the Holy Land.[12] Dr. Burney, who was a friend of Herschel,
mentions that that great astronomer told him in 1797 'that he had
almost always had an aversion to poetry,' unless 'truth and science
were united to fine words.'[13] Dr. Burney, who knew Pitt, writes
in 1799 that he was indifferent to music. 'Mr. Pitt neither knows
nor cares one farthing for flutes and fiddles.'[14]

M. Comte[15] has admirably shown that the love of imaginative
expression is the result of personification, characteristic of the early
forms of superstition. On the rise of the æsthetic principle see
also tome v. pp. 104-161, where are some ingenious remarks on
the influence of religion on the fine arts. At tome vi. p. 158 he
says that the abstract character of monotheism is unfavourable to
the fine arts.[16]

[1] Cunningham's Life of Wilkie, vol. iii. p. 62.
[2] Ibid. pp. 477, 478.   [3] Ibid. vol. II. pp. 54, 55
[4] See the interesting details in vol. ii. pp. 219, 251, 252, 286, 287, 303, 323, 343, 345, 349.
[5] Ibid. p. 414.   [6] Ibid. vol. iii. pp. 472, 473.
[7] Ibid. pp. 494, 495.   [8] Ibid. vol. ii. p. 443.   [9] Ibid. pp. 223, 437.
[10] Ibid. p. 269.   [11] Ibid. vol. iii. p. 354.   [12] Ibid. pp. 415, 438.
[13] Madame D'Arblay's Memoirs of Dr. Burney, 8vo, 1832, vol. iii. pp. 253, 254.
[14] Ibid. pp. 274, 275.   [15] Philosophie Positive, vol. v. pp. 47-49.
[16] Ibid. vol. vi. pp. 170, 171, 196-208, 231, 232, 251-259.

Mozart was born in January 1756. 'At four years of age, or earlier, he composed little pieces which his father wrote down for him.'[1] At the age of six 'Mozart knew the effect of sounds as represented by notes, and had overcome the difficulty of composing unaided by an instrument.'[2] In April 1764, when Mozart was eight years old, there used to be placed before him difficult pieces by Bach, Handel, Paradies, &c., 'which he played off not only at sight and with perfect neatness, but in their exact time and style.'[3] His organisation was so delicate that in 1763 not only the sound of a trumpet, but even the sight of one, caused him great alarm.[4] Holmes says[5] of Mozart that, 'when travelling with his wife through a beautiful country, he would at first gaze attentively and in silence on the view before him; by degrees, as the ordinary serious and even melancholy expression of his countenance became enlivened and cheerful, he would begin to sing, or rather to hum, and at last exclaim, "Oh, if I had but the thema on paper!" . . . Mozart always composed in the open air when he could.' Mozart, though often exhilarated by wine, is said by his sister-in-law never to have been drunk.[6] A short time before Mozart died he had an idea, amounting to monomania, that he had been poisoned.[7] He died in 1791, 'at the age of thirty-five years and ten months.'[8] Holmes adds,[9] 'Mozart's notion that he had been poisoned was always treated by those about him as a fantastic idea; and, in fact, the post-mortem examination discovered nothing extraordinary beyond inflammation of the brain.' From the account given by Holmes, Mozart, so far from having the irritability generally ascribed to artists, was a man of the most remarkable mildness, and of a very forgiving temper. His generosity was almost criminal profusion.

Keats greatly preferred *association* to *scenery*. He says, 'Scenery is fine, but human nature is finer.'[10] Wordsworth says, 'Poetic excitement, when accompanied by protracted labour in composition, has throughout my life brought on more or less bodily derangement;' and he mentions that when he wounded

[1] The Life of Mozart, by Edward Holmes, Lond. 8vo. 1845, p. 9.
[2] Ibid. p. 18.   [3] Ibid. p. 32.   [4] Ibid. p. 20.
[5] Ibid. p. 231.   [6] Ibid. p. 300.
[7] Ibid. 8vo. 1845, pp. 344, 345.   [8] Ibid. p. 349.   [9] Ibid. p. 349.
[10] See his letter from Teignmouth in 1818, in Life, Letters, and Literary Remains of John Keats, by R. M. Milnes, 8vo. 1848, vol. I. p. 218.

his foot, a cure could not be effected until he left off composing.[1]
He adds,[2] 'Nevertheless, I am, at the close of my seventy-third
year, in what may be called excellent health ; so that intellectual
labour is not necessarily unfavourable to longevity. But, perhaps,
I ought here to add that mine has been generally carried on out
of doors.' In 1822, Wordsworth had an accident, from the effects
of which he rapidly recovered, which, says his nephew Dr. Wordsworth, 'was owing, humanly speaking, to his very temperate habits.
To the same cause it may be ascribed that during his long life
he was scarcely ever confined to the house by so much as a day's
illness.'[3]

'Sculpture had always languished in England, even while
painting had flourished under Vandyke and his successors.'[4]   In
1773, Dr. Brown published his Dissertation on Poetry and Music,
'to show that music, dance, and poetry were united in the savage
state of man, have been separated by civilisation, and ought to be
reunited.'[5]

Comte says[6] that the real cause of the decline of the æsthetic
principle is that, owing to a diminution in the theological spirit, we
cease to sympathise with its *objects*.

Lord Campbell[7] says, 'Few poets deal in finer imagery than
is to be found in the writings of Bacon ; but if his prose is sometimes poetical, his poetry is always prosaic.'

Huc[8] says of the Tartars, west of China, 'The Lamas are far
better sculptors than painters.' In 1780 an intelligent German
says of the Bohemians, 'Their fondness for music is astonishing.'[9]
Laing[10] well says that we overrate the fine arts because we associate them with great persons, *i.e.* we see them favoured by kings,
nobles, &c. Laing says,[11] 'The Swiss appear to be a people very
destitute of imagination and its influences ; remarkably blind to
the glorious scenery in which they live. Rousseau, the only
imaginative writer Switzerland has ever produced, observes "that

[1] Memoirs of William Wordsworth, by Christopher Wordsworth, 8vo, 1851,
vol. ii. p. 55.
[2] Ibid. pp. 55, 56.   [3] Ibid. p. 211.
[4] Pictorial History of England, vol. iv. p. 757.   [5] Ibid. vol. v. p. 637.
[6] Philosophie Positive, vol. vi. p. 284.
[7] Lives of the Chancellors, vol. ii. p. 430.
[8] Travels in Tartary, Thibet, and China, vol. i. p. 90.
[9] Riesbeck's Travels through Germany, vol. ii. p. 140.
[10] Notes of a Traveller, 1st series, 8vo, 1842, p. 13.   [11] Ibid. p. 320.

the people and their country do not seem made for each other." [1] This Laing ascribes [1] to the fact that they have always been hirelings, as warriors or as domestic servants. Laing [2] is very severe on music as a civilising medium. Mr. Martineau finely says that ideas of pleasure or of pain being more strongly associated than other ideas, and all associations being either synchronous or successive, and pain and pleasure being more strongly felt in the synchronous than in the successive, it follows that 'in minds of strong organic sensibility synchronous impressions will predominate, producing a tendency to conceive things in pictures :' hence *artists* ; ' while persons of more moderate susceptibility to pleasure and pain will have a tendency to associate facts chiefly in order of their succession,' and become men of science.—Mill's Logic, 1856, vol. i. pp. 525, 526. See also vol. ii. p. 433, where it is observed that this is the difference between observing *objects* and events. On æsthetics see J. S. Mill's Essays [Dissertations], vol. i. pp. 63 to 94.

HISTORY ETC. OF LITERATURE.

IN 1553 the French ambassador, writing from London, mentions 'ung libraire François qui se tient içy de longtemps.' [3] In 1571, London booksellers sold so few books that they were obliged to lend their services in writing letters for other people. This was the case with Henry Cockayne, a bookseller in Fleet Street. [4] Dr. Whewell says that when Bacon wrote ' scarce any branch of physics existed as a science except astronomy.' [5] Schlegel observes that in France the sense of the ridiculous, which is the result of high social cultivation, has been fatal to poetry. [6] He adds [7] that in the northern literature there is little intrigue ; for that life is there founded on mutual confidence ; while the southerns, though they have stronger passions, also possess greater powers of dissimulation. Schlegel adds, [8] 'The Spanish poets were not, as was usual in other European countries, courtiers, scholars, or engaged in some

---

[1] Notes of a Traveller, 1st series, 8vo, 1842, pp. 320, 321.
[2] Ibid. 2nd series, pp. 348-358.
[3] Ambassades de Noailles, Leyde, 1763, tome ii. p. 274, and see p. 292.
[4] Murdin's State Papers, pp. 121, 122.
[5] Whewell's Philosophy of the Inductive Sciences, 8vo, 1847, vol. i. p. 11.
[6] Lectures on Dramatic Art, 8vo, 1840, vol. i. pp. 381, 382.
[7] Ibid. vol. ii. p. 325.   [8] Ibid. p. 356.

civil employment ; of noble birth for the most part, they led a warlike life.' On the influence of literature on the progressiveness of man, see some able remarks in Greene's Mental Dynamics.[1] The celebrated Clarke observed that the north of Europe has produced great naturalists and chemists, ' because natural history is almost the only study to which the visible objects of such a region can be referred ; and almost all its men of letters are still natural historians or chemists.'[2] And[3] 'since the days of Aristotle and of Theophrastus, the light of natural history had become dim until it beamed like a star from the north.' At p. 462 he says of a Swedish clergyman, 'Like almost all the literary men of Sweden, he had attended more to natural history than to anything else.' At vol. x. p. 32 he says of the natural history of Sweden, 'This branch of science is more particularly studied than any other. There is hardly an apothecary or a physician who has not either a collection of stuffed birds, or of insects,' &c. A writer, very learned in European mythology, says, respecting the different tales of dwarfs, ' Like the face of nature, these personifications of natural powers seem to become more gentle and mild as they approach the sun and the south.'[4] Of the Celtic race he says,[5] ' Its character seems to have been massive, simple, and sublime, and less given to personification than those of the more eastern nations. The wild and the plastic powers of nature never seem in it to have assumed the semblance of huge giants and ingenious dwarfs.' Lord Burghley never patronised literature ; and, in a letter written in 1575 to the Earl of Shrewsbury, sneers at 'human learning.'[6] Paper and printing were so dear in London that, in 1538, Coverdale and Grafton went to Paris to print their Bible there. See the accounts from manuscripts in the Chapter House at Westminster in Todd's Life of Cranmer, vol. i. pp. 228–234. In 1675, Evelyn[7] says of Sir W. Petty's Map of Ireland, ' I am told it has cost him near 1,000l. to have it engraved at Amsterdam.' In 1686, Evelyn mentions[8] ' that Milton wrote for the regicides ' ! ! ! Kemble[9] says, ' The genius of the Anglo-Saxons does

[1] 8vo, 1847. pp. 22, 23.
[2] Clarke's Travels, vol. ix, pp. 108, 109.   [3] Ibid. p. 212.
[4] Keightley's Fairy Mythology, Lond. 1850, p. 264.   [5] Ibid. p. 361.
[6] Lodge's Illustration of British History, 1838, vol. ii. p. 56.
[7] Diary, 8vo, 1827, vol. ii. p. 403.   [8] Ibid. vol. iii. p. 210.
[9] Saxons in England, vol. i. p. 405.

not indeed seem to have led them to the adoption of those energetic and truly imaginative forms of thought which the Scandinavians probably derived from the sterner natural features that surrounded them.' On the state of public libraries in 1848, and the ratio which, in the different countries of Europe, the number of volumes bears to the number of inhabitants, see Journal of Statistical Society, vol. xi. pp. 251, 252.

TRAVELLING.

In 1593 the Lords of the Council wrote to the Lord Lieutenants of Sussex, directing them to make inquiry as to what persons had gone abroad. Those who were Protestants were not to be molested, but the friends of those who were Catholics were to be called on to give security for their appearance on a certain day.[1] This letter seems to have been a circular; for a copy of it addressed to Burghley is in Murdin's State Papers, pp. 667, 668.

A very able statistical inquirer says of Europe, 'On pourrait dire qu'on trouve le plus de lumières là où il existe le plus de communications, et où coulent de grands fleuves comme le Rhin, la Seine, la Meuse, &c.'[2] As travelling increased, political economy arose.

Perhaps the immediate effect of the Acts passed by Mary were bad. A very intelligent traveller, who was struck with the excellent state of the roads in Sweden and Denmark, ascribes it 'to the emulation and rivalship excited among the inhabitants to excel each other in their respective shares of the work.' There, as formerly in England, each peasant has to repair some particular part of the road, a plan, Clarke thinks, which 'might be imitated advantageously in Great Britain.'[3] In 1557 all the waggons between York and Newcastle, and all the sacks within twenty miles of Newcastle, were insufficient to convey about five hundred quarters of wheat from Newcastle to Berwick.[4] The Swedes mend their own roads; but the moral inconveniences of this are considerable.[5] For some very curious information respecting the wretched travelling 150 years ago, see Clarendon Correspondence, edited by

[1] Ellis's Original Letters, 2nd series, vol. III. pp. 171–174.
[2] Quetelet, Sur l'Homme, Paris, 1835, tome ii. p. 185.
[3] Clarke's Travels, vol. ix. p. 268; vol. x. pp. 134, 478, 479, 8vo, 1824.
[4] Lodge's Illustrations of British History, 1838, vol. i. pp. 346, 347.
[5] See Dillon's Winter in Lapland and Iceland, 8vo. 1840, vol. ii. pp. 13–15.

Singer, 4to, 1828, vol. i. pp. 193, 198, 202, 203. See also p. 269, where we find that in 1686 there was no packet-boat between Scotland and Ireland, but correspondence had to go through London. At vol. i. p. 197, the Earl of Clarendon writes in 1685, from St. Asaph, 'There is in the city, as it is called, two very pretty inns who have room for fifty horses.' In Italy, in 1655, it was 'extraordinary to get clean sheets.'[1] For the mode of travelling in France, and expenses in 1677, 1678, see King's Life of Locke, i. 149. For the cost of travelling in France in the sixteenth century, see Monteil, Histoire des Divers États, tome v. pp. 30–33. In 1625 Parliament requested, and the king promised, that no one should be allowed to have his children educated abroad.[2] The formation of roads in the Highlands has lessened crime.[3]

Even in our own times the importance of travelling is obvious, and we rarely find an untravelled man who is not full of prejudice and bigotry. But in the sixteenth century its importance was much greater ; for, as there were no authentic accounts of foreign countries, it was impossible to know them except by *seeing* them.

A writer early in this century, quoted by Mr. Lewis,[4] says that in Ireland 'to horsewhip or beat a servant or labourer is a frequent mode of correction. But the evil is not so great among the gentlemen of large property, whose manners have generally been softened by education, *travelling*,' &c.

FRENCH IN ENGLAND IN THE SIXTEENTH CENTURY.

Such great numbers of French Protestants fled to England that in 1568 Cecil was obliged to apologise to the French ambassador for allowing them to settle in London ;[5] and immediately after the massacre of St. Bartholomew a great number of French came to London.[6] This caused continued remonstrances from the French Cabinet ; but Elizabeth positively refused to send them from England.[7] However, they soon began to return to France. In October 1573 more than five hundred of them left London for

---

[1] Reresby's Travels. 8vo, 1831, p. 103.
[2] Parliamentary History, vol. ii. p. 23.
[3] See Porter's Progress of the Nation, vol. ii. p. 10.
[4] Local Disturbances in Ireland, 8vo, 1836, p. 53.
[5] Correspondance diplomatique de La Mothe Fénelon, Paris, 1840, tome i. p. 74 ; see also tome iii. p. 311.
[6] Ibid. tome v. pp. 136, 162, 177, 202, 362, 410 ; tome vi. pp. 9, 59.
[7] Ibid. p. 231.

that purpose,[1] and in November 1574 they were followed by 'la pluspart de toutz ces françoys qui restoient icy.'[2] And yet in 1575 they were so numerous that the French ambassador complained of the rejoicing they publicly made in London for a defeat sustained by the French king.[3] Indeed, there were four ministers settled in London as 'conseil d'estat de ceulx de la nouvelle religion de France et de Flandres.'[4] In 1563 a sermon was preached by the Bishop of Winchester, at which 45l. was collected for the French refugees in England.[5] Prescott[6] says, 'On the 12th of March, 1558, the diet having accepted the renunciation of Charles, finally elected Ferdinand as his successor. It is another proof of the tardy pace at which news travelled at that day, that the tidings of an event of so much interest did not reach Yuste till the 29th of April One might have thought that this intelligence would have passed from mouth to mouth in less than half the time that it is stated to have taken to send it by courier. That this was not so can only be explained by the low state of commercial intercourse in that day, and by the ignorance of the great mass of the people, which prevented them from taking interest in public affairs.'

PUBLIC AND INTERNATIONAL LAW.

On the death of Charles IX., Elizabeth told the French ambassador that his powers had expired, and that he must have fresh ones from the new king ;[7] and in spite of his protestations she persevered in this view.[8] Lord Brougham says that the law of nations arose out of the federal union of Germany.[9]

THE SPIRIT ETC. OF JANSENISM.

Cousin observes[10] that Hutcheson's Manual of Logic was only an abridgment of the Port Royal Logic ; and he says[11] that Hutche-

---

[1] Correspondance diplomatique de La Mothe Fénelon, Paris, 1840, tome vi. p. 426.
[2] Ibid. p. 280.   [3] Ibid. p. 394.   [4] Ibid. p. 380.
[5] See Machyn's Diary, Camden Society, vol. xlii. p. 305.
[6] Additions to Robertson's Charles V. p. 568.
[7] Correspondance diplomatique de Fénelon, tome iv. p. 153.
[8] Ibid. pp. 156, 170, 185.
[9] Political Philosophy, 2nd edit. 8vo, 1849, vol. i. pp. 490-492.
[10] Histoire de la Philosophie, Paris, 1846, tome iv. p. 45.   [11] Ibid. p. 156.

son, like Fénelon, made *love* the basis of all religion, and [1] that his theory inclined to mysticism. Indeed, Cousin says [2] that Hutcheson borrowed from the Logic of the Port Royal his celebrated division of the faculties of the understanding. Mr. Morell strangely says, 'Pascal's scepticism is all aimed against the *abuses* of philosophy.' [3]

Cousin well says that mysticism is 'le coup de désespoir de la raison humaine, qui, après avoir cru naturellement à elle-même, et débutée par le dogmatisme, effrayée et découragée par le scepticisme, se réfugie dans le sentiment, dans la pure contemplation et l'intuition immédiate.' [4] It is therefore, as Cousin well says, [5] that mysticism naturally came *after* sensualism, idealism, and scepticism.

STATISTICS.

COUSIN has a foolish note on statistics, in which he depreciates what he does not understand. [6] The metaphysician despises the statistician, the statistician laughs at the metaphysician ; and to these petty quarrels are sacrificed the interests of knowledge. In France 100 marriages produce 408 births. [7] Quetelet [8] agrees with Malthus that if there were no checks, population would increase geometrically. In 1835 the homicides in France were estimated to be annually to the whole population as 1 to 48,000. [9] In consequence of the general advance of civilisation during the seventeenth century, there sprang up those habits of prudence which so eminently distinguish civilised men from savages. This gave rise to the desire to equal the vicissitudes of life, and hence the origin of insurances, which can only exist in a people far advanced in the scale of society. Young rams perhaps have most female offspring. See some experiments recorded in Combe's Constitution of Man in relation to External Objects, Edinburgh, 1847, pp. 483, 484. When old men marry young women, the offspring are generally daughters ; hence the reason why in the East, where polygamy is practised, more females are born than

---

[1] Histoire de la Philosophie, Paris, 1846, tome iv. p. 158. [2] Ibid. p. 414.
[3] Morell's View of Speculative Philosophy, 8vo, 1846, vol. i. p. 252.
[4] Ibid. p. 17.
[5] Cousin, Histoire de la Philosophie, 2nde série, tome III. p. 13.
[6] Histoire de la Philosophie, Paris, 1846, part i. tome iv. p. 173.
[7] Quetelet, Sur l'Homme, tome i. p. 80. [8] Ibid. p. 273.
[9] Ibid. tome ii. p. 158.

males.[1] In 1757, Voltaire[2] writes : 'C'est à Breslau, à Londres et à Dordrecht, qu'on commença il y a environ trente ans à supputer le nombre des habitants par celui des baptêmes. On multiplie dans Londres le nombre des baptêmes par 35, à Breslau par 33.' In 1686 there were great disputes about the population of London and Paris.[3] Comte[4] peremptorily rejects the application to sociology of the doctrine of chances. Porter says[5] that the diminution of births and marriages is *not* owing to increased prudence, but to 'the increased duration of life,' which increases the number of those who *cannot* become parents. The average inhabitants to a house in England are 5·6 ; in Middlesex, 7·4.[6]

Alison[7] says that in Paris the illegitimate births are to the legitimate as 10 to 19, but there is nothing more absurd than to make this a test of morals, for prostitutes and men given to venery have few children.

Capefigue[8] gives an account of the very important statistical labours undertaken by Louis XIV. from 1695 to 1700, which he says[9] remain in manuscript, and have never been consulted. The statisticians think that political economy is inductive, and is based on figures.[10]

'The greatest numbers of births are found in the first months of the year.'[11] Among the poor who nurse their own children there is generally an interval of two years before the birth of the next child.[12]

In 1783 the native king of Burmah 'took a census of the population of the Burmese Empire.'[13]

The French suppose that in illegitimate births the proportion of females is greater than in legitimate ones ; but, according to the Report of the Registrar-General for 1843, the reverse of this is the case in England ; 'the legitimate boys being as 105·4 to 100 girls, while the illegitimate are 108 to 100.'[14] But Colonel Sykes

---

[1] See Combe's Lectures on Moral Philosophy, 8vo, 1840, pp. 134, 135.
[2] Œuvres, tome lx. p. 326.
[3] See Ray's Correspondence, edited by Dr. Lankester, 8vo, 1841, p. 189.
[4] Philosophie Positive, vol. iv. pp. 512–516.
[5] Progress of the Nation, vol. i. p. 33.
[6] Porter, vol. iii. p. 8.   [7] History of Europe, vol. i. p. 215.
[8] Louis XIV. tome ll. pp. 85–88.   [9] Ibid. p. 86.
[10] See Journal of Statistical Society, vol. i. p. 317 : vol. ii. 104 : vol. vi. 322.
[11] Ibid. vol. ii. p. 110.   [12] Ibid. vol. iii. p. 320.   [13] Ibid. vol. iv. p. 335.
[14] Sykes, On Statistics of Frankfort, in Statistical Society, vol. vii. p. 345.

adds,[1] 'The Frankfort returns support the French view, and so
do the Prussian.'[2] It is *possible* that the climate of India influences the proportion of sexes born.[3] Read Works of Casper and
Villermé, and Quetelet, Statistique Morale, 1846, in tome xxi. of
Mémoires de l'Académie Royale de la Belgique, Statist. Soc. xii.
231. Bishop Heber[4] says, 'The population of Lucknow is
guessed at 300,000. But Mussulmans consider every attempt to
number the people as a mark of great impiety, and a sure presage
of famine or pestilence ; so that nothing can be known with
accuracy.' Comte[5] says, 'Dans les pays orientaux on ne tient
aucun registre des décès ni des naissances.' For a curious instance even of the present imperfect state of statistics see Talvi's
Slavic Nations, New York, 8vo, 1850, p. 226.

POLITICAL ECONOMY.

THE foundation of this great science, without which it could not
for a moment exist, is the supposition that men are the best judges
of their own material interest. Mr. Morell strangely says, ' The
axiom, that men follow their interest whenever they know it, cannot, we contend, be sustained with any approach to plausibility ;'
and this he makes out by adding that many men have desires
contrary to their own interest.[6] But who ever said that *all* men
follow their own interest? It is a *general*, not a universal rule,
and no mixed sciences have universal rules for their base.

In 1721, Montesquieu distinctly says that an increase of money
would not be an increase of wealth.[7] Alison actually supposes
' that prices inevitably rise in the old and wealthy community from
the great quantity of the precious metals in the existing currency
which their opulence enables them, and their numerous mercantile
transactions compel them, to keep in circulation ; and consequently,' &c. &c. ! ! !" In 1829, Southey writes to Dr. Gooch,
' As for the political economists, no words can express the thorough
contempt which I feel for them. They discard all moral con-

[1] Sykes, On Statistics of Frankfort, in Statistical Society, vol. vii. p. 345.
[2] Ibid. see vol. ix. p. 82, and vol. x, p. 161.
[3] Ibid. vol. viii. pp. 50, 51. On the proportion of illegitimate births in different countries see vol. x. p. 162.
[4] Journey through India, vol. II. p. 90.
[5] Traité de Législation, vol. iii. p. 105.
[6] History of Speculative Philosophy, 8vo, 1846, vol. II. pp. 464, 465.
[7] Lettres Persanes, No. cvi, Paris, 8vo, 1835, p. 71.
[8] Alison's Principles of Population, 8vo, 1840, vol. II. p. 409.

sideration from their philosophy, and in their practice they have
no compassion for flesh and blood.'[1]   As to Southey's knowledge
of political economy, see [2] his remarks on Malthus. A living philosopher, whose extraordinary abilities have even ennobled the name
of Herschel, speaks in a very different way of political economy.[3]

Foreign travels, by showing a greater number of political
phenomena, made men *think*, and gave rise to political economy.
It is thus, for instance, at a later period, that Malthus collected
the materials for his great work on population when travelling
in the north of Europe with the celebrated Clarke.[4]

Mr. Keightley has an ill-suppressed sneer at political economy.[5]   Ferguson gravely says, 'To increase the number of mankind may be admitted as a great and important object.'[6]

The *first* great work on commercial legislation is the Discorso
Economico of Antonio Bandini, addressed in 1737 to the Grand
Duke of Tuscany, but not published till 1775.[7]   In 1769, ' Pietro
Verri, a Milanese, in his work "Sulle Leggi Vincolanti," maintained the doctrine of absolute and universal freedom of commerce.'[8]   Brougham [9] refers to the learned article on political
economy in Penny Cyclopædia, vol. xviii. p. 339. In 1758 appeared the Tableau Économique de Quesnai ; and in 1768, his
Physiocratie.[10]   At p. 138, Lord Brougham has some very superficial remarks on wages. Lord Brougham seems not to be aware
that Anderson was the first who put forward the doctrine of
rent.[11]   I suspect Adam Smith was well acquainted with the Italian
economists. At all events, in 1755 he was very familiar with
foreign literature.[12]   The study of political economy in France
must greatly have favoured free discussion. Madame du Hausset
who was a friend of Quesnai, says, ' Il recevait chez lui des personnes de tous les partis, mais en petit nombre, et qui toutes

[1] Life and Correspondence of R. Southey. 8vo, 1850, vol. vi. p. 58.

[2] Ibid. p. 100.

[3] See Herschel's Discourse on Natural Philosophy, 8vo, 1831, p. 73.

[4] See Clarke's Travels, 8vo, 1824, vol. ix. p. 43. and compare on Malthus,
Otter's Life of Clarke, vol. i. pp. 442, 476.

[5] See Keightley's Tales and Fictions, Lond. 1834, p. 8.

[6] Ferguson on the History of Civil Society, Lond. 8vo, 1786, p. 96.

[7] Brougham's Men of Letters, vol. ii. p. 91.   [8] Ibid. p. 91.

[9] Ibid. p. 92.   [10] Ibid. p. 95.

[11] Brougham's Historical Sketches of Statesmen, 16mo, 1846, vol. iv. p. 21.

[12] See Stewart's Life of Adam Smith. p. xi, prefixed to Smith's Philosophical
Essays, 4to, 1795.

avaient une grande confiance en lui.   On y parlait très hardiment
de tout.'[1]   She adds[2] that Quesnai considered De la Rivière
to be the only man fit to conduct the French finances. Schlosser
well says that the real authors of the destruction of the provincial
divisions of France were the economists.[3]

In 1757, Grimm[4] writes from Paris that the Ami des Hommes,
by Mirabeau, which had just appeared, had made a great sensation.
In 1759, Grimm writes from Paris:[5] 'Autrefois nos mauvais
auteurs faisaient des romans et des vers détestables ; aujourd'hui
tout le monde veut écrire sur l'agriculture, sur le commerce, sur la
population.'   In 1763 he writes, 'On a vu ériger par tout le
royaume des sociétés d'agriculture.'[6]   In 1550, Sir John Masone, in
a letter to Cecil, strongly states the impossibility of fixing prices
by laws.[7] Coleridge was so ignorant of political economy as to
suppose that if tithes were done away with rents would rise.[8]   He
evidently despised it,[9] and Southey makes the same error.[10]   De
Foe's economy is sometimes sound and sometimes the contrary.[11]
Combe[12] ignorantly supposes that when profits fall, wages will fall.
He adds[13] that 'the leading aim of the economists has been to
demonstrate the most effectual means of increasing wealth.'
Alison[14] says of Paul of Russia, 'His prodigalities even contributed
to the circulation of wealth.'   Fox 'had never read the Wealth
of Nations.'[15]   Comte speaks of political economy with the greatest contempt.[16]   Sir W. Temple[17] shows a complete ignorance of
political economy.   Manufactures, &c., carried on by the Danish
Government, were a pure loss, but falling into private hands they

[1] Mémoires de Madame du Hausset, Paris, 8vo, 1824, pp. 57, 58.
[2] Ibid. p. 123.   [3] History of the Eighteenth Century, vol. ii. p. 159.
[4] Correspondance Littéraire, tome ii. p. 213.   [5] Ibid. pp. 404, 405.
[6] Ibid. tome iii. p. 385 ; see also p. 534.
[7] See his letters in Tytler's Edward VI. and Mary, vol. i. p. 341.
[8] Biographia Literaria, 8vo, 1847, vol. i. p. 235 ; and Church and State, p. 91.
[9] Literary Remains, vol. i. pp. 348, 349.
[10] Life of Wesley, 8vo, 1846, vol. i. p. 264.
[11] Wilson's Life of De Foe, vol. ii. pp. 309, 310.
[12] Lectures on Moral Philosophy, 8vo, 1840, p. 225.   [13] Ibid. p. 254.
[14] History of Europe, vol. v. p. 547.
[15] See Alison's History of Europe, vol. vii. p. 172, and for another piece of
ignorance see vol. xiii. p. 204.
[16] Philosophie Positive, tome iv. pp. 261-260, 645 ; tome v. pp. 447, 736 ; tome
vi. pp. 332, 334, 440.
[17] Works, vol. i. p. 176 ; vol. ii. pp. 117, 118 ; vol. iii. pp. 2-58.

became profitable.[1] Whewell[2] calls political economy an *inductive*
science.   Ricardo objects that a legacy duty is bad, because it
falls on the capital ; but to this Porter replies that *because* it falls
on the capital it is not felt, and is therefore so far good because it
does not engender irritation.[3] Laing[4] shows a complete misap-
prehension of one important point in political economy. Our
political economists, by showing that each man was the best judge
of his own affairs, thus extended the suffrage. Tocqueville thinks[6]
that the Americans construct instruments—such, for instance, as
ships—very slightly because they are constantly expecting new improvements.   But I believe the real cause is a high rate of profits.
In the middle of the seventeenth century, Tonti, an Italian,
proposed what are now called tontines.[7] For a curious instance
of the way in which great crimes were caused by an economical
blunder of the Sicilian Government, see Journal of the Statistical
Society, vol. ii. p. 454.   The first chair of political economy in
Europe was founded at Naples, and occupied by Genovese.[8]   On
the influence of the price of food on revolutions, see a remarkable
essay in Journal of Statistical Society, xiii. 152-167, and quote
Porter, xiii. 216, who says that when all the earnings of the
labourer are employed in procuring food, there can be no society
or moral progress.   In 1799, Malthus travelled with Clarke to
gather materials for his work on Population, of which, however,
says Otter, he had already published a first edition.[9]

At the end of the sixteenth century, Sully restored the French
finances.[10] He was a great friend to agriculture,[11] and repealed
those taxes which pressed on the cultivation of the soil, but he
forbade the exportation of specie and coin,[12] and violently opposed
manufactures and commerce.[13] England set the example of allowing the exportation of the precious metals.[14] This was chiefly
effected by Thomas Mun and Sir Dudly Diggs.[15] This gave rise

---

[1] Laing's Sweden, pp. 15, 16.
[2] Philosophy of the Inductive Sciences, vol. I. p. vii.
[3] Porter's Progress of the Nation, vol. II. pp. 312, 313.
[4] Denmark, 8vo, 1852, p. 189.   [5] Ibid. p. 307.
[6] Démocratie en Amérique, vol. iv. pp. 53, 54.
[7] Monteil, Histoire des Français des divers États, tome vii. p. 103.
[8] See Mr. Goodwin's valuable papers on the Two Sicilies, in Journal of Statistical Society, vol. v. p. 57.
[9] Otter's Life of Clarke, vol. i. pp. 442 and 476.
[10] Twiss, Progress of Political Economy, 8vo, 1847, p. 38.   [11] Ibid. p. 39.
[12] Ibid. p. 40.   [13] Ibid. pp. 42, 44.   [14] Ibid. p. 46.   [15] Ibid. pp. 47, 48.

to the commercial system ;[1] but it was not till 1663 that full permission was given by Parliament to export the precious metals.[2] Twiss thinks that the mercantile system introduced a spirit of commercial jealousy, and a disposition to interference on the part of the statesmen.[3]

After the death of Henry IV., France was in confusion till 1661, when Mazarin died, having recommended to Louis XIV. Colbert, who was entirely opposed to the economical views of Sully, and who looked upon agriculture as subordinate to manufactures and commerce.[4] He forbade the exportation of coin,[5] and the result was that its price fell one-half, and half the land was put out of cultivation.[6] In his tariff of 1664 he encouraged the exportation of French raw materials, and discouraged the importation of foreign manufactured goods.[7] In 1667 he raised the import duties still higher, but lowered them by the peace of Nimeguen in 1678.[8] He encouraged commerce, and allowed the exportation of the precious metals.[9]

In 1667, Sir William Petty laid down that labour was the foundation of value ;[10] and in 1697, Sir Dudley North ' made an able statement of the true principles of commerce.'[11] Locke distinguishes between *natural* value or utility, and *actual* value, and ascribed the difference to the amount of labour required to produce them. But by the *value* he meant ' the capacity of satisfying the wants of men,' and ' greater value with him was identical with greater usefulness.'[12] He *seems* to have known the difference between value in use and value in exchange ; but he wanted the clearness of Petty ;[13] and Law, in 1705, was the first who broadly laid down the difference between value and utility.[14] His fundamental error was confounding money with capital.[15] On account of the fluctuations in the precious metals he proposed to substitute land, and at the same time save expense by making paper supply the place of coin.[16] Owing to the different methods of taxation, the economists of England paid more attention to the production, those of France to the distribution, of wealth.[17]

[1] Twiss, Progress of Political Economy, 8vo, 1847, pp. 48, 53. [2] Ibid. p. 49.
[3] Ibid. p. 56.   [4] Ibid. pp. 67, 68.   [5] Ibid. p. 68.
[6] Ibid. p. 70.   [7] Ibid. p. 71.   [8] Ibid. p. 71.
[9] Ibid. p. 74.   [10] Ibid. pp. 81, 82.   [11] Ibid. p. 83.
[12] Ibid. pp. 86, 87.   [13] Ibid. pp. 88, 89.   [14] Ibid. p. 93.
[15] Ibid. p. 98.   [16] Ibid. 96, 99-101.   [17] Ibid. p. 130.

The failure of Law weakened Colbertism, and paved the way for Quesnai's system.[1] Quesnai proposed only one tax, levied at once on the real produce of the land.[2] De Gournay, too, aided Quesnai in attacking the mercantile system.[3] Turgot was the greatest of the economists or physiocrats ; their great opponent was Necker.[4] In 1768, Beccaria, and, in 1771, Vein also opposed them, but did not fall into the errors of the mercantile system.[5] The establishment of the mercantile system was an event of the greatest importance. According to its expounders, labour employed in manufacture was more productive than labour employed in agriculture.[6] This was an error, but an error productive of the best effects ; for by weakening the influence of agriculturists, it accelerated the march of civilisation. I have no doubt that the influence of Quesnai's school has retarded the progress of general knowledge in France as compared with England ; for though the French want some natural advantages we possess, the deficiency is not enough to account for the prodigious excess of their agricultural population. The first stimulus was given by Sully, who laboured to destroy the French manufactures. Respecting Malthus, see Twiss, Progress of Political Economy, pp. 203–225, and 213, 222. On the economical policy of Sully, see Blanqui, Histoire de l'Économie Politique, tome i. pp. 347–361. He despised manufactures,[7] but freed France from debt.[8] On the system of Colbert, see Blanqui, tome i. pp. 362–378, and, in particular, pp. 363, 366, 368, 372. He exempted from all taxes a father of ten children.[9] M. Blanqui[10] is not afraid to say that without smuggling commerce would have been destroyed. ' C'est à la contrebande que le commerce doit de n'avoir pas péri sous l'influence du régime prohibitif.' M. Blanqui[11] says that our navigation laws have not been beneficial, even in a political point of view ; and of course economically there is no doubt as to their evil results. On origin of banks see Blanqui, tome ii. pp. 38–41. Blanqui[12] observes that Quesnai was a natural reaction after the failure of Law ; and for a view of his school see pp. 75–95. I think I may say Law was for the state, Quesnai for the people ; Law for *accumulation*, Quesnai for *distribution*.

[1] Twiss, Progress of Political Economy. p. 141.
[2] Ibid. p. 148.
[3] Ibid. p. 152.
[4] Ibid. p. 153.
[5] Ibid. pp. 153, 155.
[6] Ibid. p. 182.
[7] Blanqui, *op. cit.* tome i. p. 349.
[8] Ibid. p. 361.
[9] Ibid. p. 374.
[10] Ibid. tome ii. p. 25.
[11] Ibid. tome ii. pp. 33–35.
[12] Ibid. pp. 75, 76.

Blanqui [1] has some good remarks on the importance of *distribution*. For account of Malthus, see Blanqui, tome ii. pp. 131–142. Lord Brougham, at the beginning of his Life of Adam Smith, gives a pretty good account of the history of political economy, and observes that in the eighteenth century the French began to study it, *not knowing* that the Italians were working at it at the same time. This shows how its study depended on general causes.

ETHICS.

MORELL [2] says that the best ethical inquiries in modern times are those of Jouffroy in his Mélanges Philosophiques.

The sensual school of metaphysics fail in æsthetics ; but, I think, they fail still more in ethics. James Mill, for instance, resolves friendship and kindness into association ; and says, 'We never feel any pains and pleasures but our own.' [3] His analysis of the origin of parental affections, though inducted in the same manner, is perhaps more satisfactory, [4] but still I strongly suspect that something has been overlooked. [5] At pp. 244, 245, Mill observes that we know that our own virtue is the reason why men are virtuous to us ; and, therefore, with the idea of our own acts of virtue are associated the ideas of the great advantage we derive from the virtuous acts of our fellow-creatures. 'When this association is formed in due strength, which it is the main business of a good education to effect, the motive of virtue becomes paramount in the human breast.' 'In the same way he accounts for the desire of posthumous fame ; [6] and see in particular [7] his ingenious attempts to explain why we often prefer praiseworthiness to praise.

Jeremy Taylor took great pains with the Ductor Dubitantium, which he looked on as his capital work, and which he published in 1660. [8] At p. cclxxii Heber ignorantly says of Taylor's Ductor Dubitantium, 'He has preceded in the same track the labours

---

[1] Blanqui, Histoire de l'Economie Politique, tome II. p. 127.
[2] History of Speculative Philosophy, 8vo, 1846, vol. II. p. 414.
[3] Analysis of the Mind, 8vo, 1829, vol. II. pp. 174, 175.
[4] Ibid. pp. 177, 183.   [5] See what he says at p. 212.
[6] Ibid. pp. 246, 247.   [7] Ibid. p. 249.
[8] See Heber's Life of Taylor, in vol. I. of Taylor's Works, 8vo, 1828 pp. lxxvi. and xcvi.

of Tucker and of Paley.'[1] 'Sous le règne même de Louis XIV. tromper au jeu n'était pas une action déshonorante dans la bonne société.'[2] Neander[3] says Ambrose of Milan was the first who applied ancient ethics to Christian morals. 'Fortune favours fools' is a proverb 'in all the languages of Europe.'[4] Melmoth published notes on Cicero's De Amicitiâ in which 'he refuted Lord Shaftesbury, who had imputed it as a defect to Christianity that it gave no precepts in favour of friendship, and Soame Jenyns, who had represented that very omission as a proof of its divine origin.'[5] The New Testament overlooks the importance of *pride* and *individuality*, and takes a gross view of women.

CHURCHES.

IN 1594, London churches were used as prisons.[6] We know, from a sermon preached in 1561 by the Bishop of Durham, that it was common in St. Paul's church for persons to be 'talking, buying and selling, fighting and brawling.'[7] In 1561 the queen was obliged to issue a proclamation forbidding persons to 'shoot any handgun or dag within the cathedral church of St. Paul.'[8] In 1571 the Archbishop of York was obliged to order throughout his diocese that no minstrels or morrice-dancers should be allowed to perform in the churches during 'the time of divine service or of any sermon.'[9] In 1562 the Bishop of Exeter presented a paper to the ecclesiastical synod in which he requested 'that there be some order taken for the punishment of them that do walk and talk in the church at time of common prayer and preaching, to the disturbance of the ministers, and offence to the congregation.'[10]

---

[1] See King's Life of Locke, 8vo, 1830, vol. ii. pp. 122, 123.
[2] Comte, Traité de Législation, vol. i. p. 64.
[3] History of the Church, vol. iv. p. 365.
[4] Mill's Logic, 1856, vol. ii. p. 335.
[5] Rose's Biog. Dict. London, 1848, vol. x. p. 85.
[6] Stonyhurst MS. in Mr. Tierney's edit. of Dodd's Church History, vol. iii. p. 115.
[7] Pilkington's Sermon in Strype's Parker, Oxford, 1824, vol. i. p. 187, and Strype's Grindal, p. 81.
[8] Strype's Grindal, p. 84.   [9] Ibid. p. 250.
[10] Strype's Annals, vol. i. part i. p. 522

CALVINISM.

IT is often said that speculative principles do not influence the conduct ; and this is undoubtedly true of many subjects, particularly of morals. However, we know that a belief in predestination does influence the conduct of the Turks.[1] Those infamous assassins the Thugs are fatalists. 'Fatalism is a prominent dogma of the creed of the Thugs.'[2] On the democratic tendency of Calvinism, see Esprit des Lois, livre xxiv. chap. v., Œuvres de Montesquieu, Paris, 1835, p. 408.

The doctrine of justification by grace, and a contempt of good works, made immense progress in the sixteenth century, even among those who had no regard for Luther and who venerated the Pope.[3]

The Calvinists reciprocated the hatred of the Catholics.

At the end of the sixteenth century Rollock was very active in spreading Calvinism in Edinburgh.[4]

Todd boldly says that the tenets of the Church of England, as settled by Cranmer, have been but little altered, and are essentially anti-Calvinistic (Life of Cranmer, vol. ii. p. 268). See also pp. 301–318, where, on the authority of Waterland, he denies the Calvinism of the seventeenth Article,[5] and he quotes[6] Archdeacon Tottie, who says that the Liturgy is the best comment upon the Articles ! In 1543, Cranmer says, 'Men are to themselves the authors of sin and damnation ;'[7] and it is supposed[8] that Cranmer required the pre-existence of good works as necessary to salvation.

In 1636, Knott, an English Catholic, says that Calvinism, 'once a darling in England, is at last accounted heresy ; yea, and little less than treason.'[9]

Coleridge says,[10] 'And this, I fancy, is the true distinction between Arminianism and Calvinism in their moral effects.

---

[1] Brougham's Political Philosophy, 2nd edit. 8vo. 1849, vol. I. p. 404.
[2] Illustrations of the History and Practices of the Thugs, 8vo, 1851, p. 113.
[3] See Ranke, Die Römischen Päpste, Berlin, 1839, Band I. pp. 138–146.
[4] See Bower's History of the University of Edinburgh, vol. I. p. 104.
[5] Life of Cranmer, p. 303.   [6] Ibid. p. 308.
[7] Ibid. p. 309.   [8] Ibid. p. 316.
[9] Des Maizeaux, Life of Chillingworth, 8vo, 1725, p. 112.
[10] Literary Remains, vol. III. p. 303.

Arminianism is cruel to individuals, for fear of damaging the race by false hopes and improper confidences; while Calvinism is horrible for the race, but full of consolation to the suffering individual.' Southey[1] has a most violent remark on Calvinism.

The Church of England till 1620 was Calvinistic.[2]

On the bad effects of the doctrine of election, see King's Life of Locke, 8vo. 1830, vol. ii. pp. 98, 99. In the sixteenth century the Protestants became more Calvinistic; the Catholics more Arminian.[3] Arminianism was chiefly held by the Jesuits, who by their support of free will injured their influence in Spain when they were attacked by the Inquisition and Dominicans.[4] The Dominican doctrine was favoured by Clement VIII.,[5] who, however, did not venture to give any decision.[6] It was also favoured by Paul V.[7]

On Calvin's miserable bigotry see Ranke, Civil Wars of France, 8vo, 1852, vol. i. pp. 216, 218. Orme says,[8] 'Previous to the Synod of Dort, though individuals might have believed and taught differently, Calvinism was the prevailing theological system of this country. The complexion of the Thirty-nine Articles is evidently Calvinistic.'

Mr. Morell[9] says that ' Hartley and Priestley drew the doctrine of philosophical necessity from their peculiar psychological principles.' This was followed up by Goodwin, Belsham, and Bray.[10] According to Morell, this school holds that man is born without moral principles, and that what produces pleasure is good, what produces pain is evil;[11] that pleasure in contemplation is *desire* or *will*, which is therefore never free.[12] Morell adds[13] that the Calvinistic metaphysician would consider crime almost entirely as the result of bad government. From this, I suppose, would follow sympathy with the criminal, and perhaps mildness in laws which punished *civil* offences; *severity* in those which punished *state* offences. Hence the Calvinistic school would value highly education as well as laws; for they are the most effective modi-

---

[1] Life of Wesley, 8vo, 1846, vol. i. p. 321.
[2] See Nichols, Literary Illustrations of the Eighteenth Century, vol. iv. p. 326.
[3] Ranke, Päpste, vol. ii. pp. 296, 257.   [4] Ibid. p. 301.
[5] Ibid. p. 306.   [6] Ibid. p. 307.   [7] Ibid. p. 355.
[8] Life of Owen, p. 32.
[9] View of the Speculative Philosophy of Europe, 8vo, 1846, vol. i. p. 367.
[10] Ibid. pp. 367, 368.   [11] Ibid. p. 369.   [12] Ibid. p. 370.
[13] Ibid. p. 383.

fications of the *will*. Indeed, Morell [1] says that Socialism 'is the fullest development of philosophical necessity which the present age has known ;' and adds [2] that the great error of Socialism is to deny the freedom of the will, and exaggerate the advantages of education. Mr. Morell, I regret to say, has made very improper remarks on Mr. Owen.

Dr. Jackson, who had seen and thought a great deal of the military profession, accounts for the courage of the Scotch by their religion : 'The Scotch are Calvinists in religious belief; and Calvinists believe that everything which happens in life is preordained by Providence to happen ; consequently that individual life is as secure in the rage of battle as in the shades of peace. Such opinion influenced the conduct of the Lowland Scot, fortified his mind in the dangers of war,' &c. [3]

'Jansenism is a sort of Catholic Calvinism. It affords a new instance of the more pure and severe moralists naturally adopting a doctrine of self-debasement, and, in Pascal's language, of self-hatred, and of their referring every action, enjoyment, and hope, exclusively to the all-perfect Being. The Calvinistic people of Scotland, of Switzerland, of Holland, and of New England have been more moral than the same classes among other nations. Those who preached faith, or in other words a pure mind, have always produced more popular virtue than those who preached good works, or the mere regulation of outward acts. The latter mode of considering Ethics naturally gives rise to casuistry, especially when auricular confession makes it necessary for every confessor to have a system, according to which he can give opinion and advice to his penitent. The tendency of casuistry is to discover ingenious pretexts for eluding that rigorous morality and burdensome superstition which in the first ardour of religion are apt to be established, and to discover rules of conduct more practicable by ordinary men in the common state of the world.' These admirable remarks were made by Sir J. Mackintosh in 1808, and are in Memoirs of Mackintosh, edited by his Son, 8vo, 1835, vol. i. p. 411.

In Scotland the Episcopalians liked ornaments in their churches ; the Presbyterians hated them. [4]

---

[1] View of the Speculative Philosophy of Europe, 8vo, 1846, vol. i, p. 386.
[2] Ibid. pp. 386, 396.
[3] Jackson's View of the Formation, Discipline, and Economy of Armies, 8vo, 1845, p. 199.   [4] Burton's History of Scotland, 1853, vol. ii. p. 547.

MANUFACTURES.

THE influence of the Civil Law, I suppose, increased the disrespect
with which an ignorant age naturally treated manufactures. I
have already pointed out the effect of the feudal system was
to create a powerful nobility; and it is evident that the same
cause must have given a factitious dignity to agriculturists.
Because property in land was the original source of nobility, men,
by the influence of association, continued to respect the possession
of it, even when its possession ceased to confer rank.[1] At the
same time the dread of novelty made men look with contempt on
the innovations of manufactures and commerce. The influence
of feudal association in making men respect landowners still exists
among the unreflecting part of modern politicians. It is seen in
the language that is held by some men respecting the supposed
importance of the agricultural interest; and it is seen in the
insane laws of primogeniture and entails which are still permitted to deform our statute-book.

In 1568, Sir Francis Knollys writes to Cecil, 'I am glad of
your bettered news of the matters of Count Lodowyke. I must
needs commend the artificial usage of your copper mines.'[2] In
1549 it was proposed that a law should be passed compelling
every possessor of a certain number of acres of ground to sow
some of them with flax and hemp. It was also proposed that the
families of all farmers should not be allowed to wear any shirts
except those spun within their own houses, or at least in the
country.[3] In the same paper[4] it is proposed that whoever fells
a tree shall be obliged to sow and maintain another for it. At
p. 284 there is a letter dated 1598 from Sir John Popham to the
queen respecting tin, in which he says that for five years together
'there was yearly brought to the coinage xii^c thousand pounds weight
of tin,' of which about a fourth was spent in England; and about
'ix^c thousand pounds' exported. The usual price was 48s. the
hundred. On the extraordinary adaptability of iron to the wants
of man, see a good passage in Prout's Bridgewater Treatise, 8vo,
1845, p. 127. In 1562 a petition from Kingston-upon-Thames

---

[1] Brougham's Political Philosophy, vol. I. p. 319.
[2] Wright's Elizabeth, 8vo, 1838, vol. I. pp. 293, 294.
[3] Egerton Papers, Camden Society, 1840, p. 12.   [4] Ibid. p. 13.

complains that an iron mill in the neighbourhood has consumed so much wood that the price of it has been raised from 3*s*. to 4*s*. a load, and that of charcoal from 10*s*. to 20*s*. The petitioners request that the mill may be put down by Act of Parliament.[1] In 1575 the council orders that no more iron ordnance shall be made in Surrey, because it had been exported to foreigners, and because iron mills and forges had 'greatly consumed the woods.'[2] In 1586 the inhabitants of the neighbourhood of Guildford complained ' of an Italian having erected a glasshouse in those parts, whereby the woods are likely to be consumed to the prejudice of the whole country.' In consequence of this petition the council order that the Italian should appear before them, and that in the meantime the working of the glasshouse should be stayed.[3] Several bills were passed against iron mills, because it was feared that the working of them would destroy our woods.[4] The general use of coal by doing away with this fear must have given a great stimulus to our iron manufactures. In 1686 a manufacture of velvet was set up in Ireland.[5] In 1675, Locke saw at Pont St. Esprit, in France, 'the way of winding silk by an engine that turns at once 134 bobbins.'[6] Copper was not found in Great Britain to any extent till about 1700.[7] It is doubtful if manufactures are prejudicial to health, and it is certain that those who work at them are *not* particularly liable to consumption.[8] Bishop Heber[9] gives a very clear account of the way they make attar of roses near Benares.

THE REFORMATION AND PROTESTANTISM.

IT has been calculated that in France the loss in the productiveness of industry caused by the celebration of Catholic holidays amounted in the last century every year to nearly 2,500,000*l*. sterling.[10] The Reformation gave an air of ferocity even to litera-

[1] Loseley Manuscripts, by Kempe. p. 488. [2] Ibid. p. 490.

[3] Ibid. p. 493.

[4] See D'Ewe's Journals of Parliament, folio, 1682, pp. 30, 31, 55, 269, 305.

[5] See Clarendon Correspondence, edit. Singer, 1828, 4to, vol. i. p. 321.

[6] King's Life of Locke, 8vo, 1830, vol. i. p. 96.

[7] See Journal of Statistical Society, vol. i. p. 65.

[8] Ibid. vol. v. pp. 277, 278, 279, 280; see also vol. vi. p. 200.

[9] Journey through India, vol. i. p. 250.

[10] Dupin's Note in Œuvres de Montesquieu, Paris, 1835, pp. 413, 414.

ture. This is confessed by a great Protestant (?) writer.[1] 'La Suisse fut le premier pays hors de l'Allemagne où s'étendit la nouvelle secte qu'on appelait la *primitive église*.'[2] This, Voltaire says, was the work of Zwinglius. On the vulgar idea that the Reformation secured the liberty of conscience, see some good remarks by Lord King.[3] The Reformation lowered wages by doing away with holidays, and this gave rise to the poor laws.[4] Comte[5] says that Luther did nothing, but that everything was already prepared ; and respecting the injury done to morals by the Reformation allowing divorce, see pp. 686, 688. Even Ranke does not venture to explain the success of the Reformation in some countries, and its failure in others. He merely says[6] 'es verdiente wohl,' &c. Ranke[7] seems to ascribe the failure of the Reformation in France to the alliance between the Crown and the Church. The Emperor Maximilian acknowledged that he had no power over his own subjects.[8] Connect this into the success of the Reformation in Germany. Ranke[9] candidly confesses that 'many had adopted the reformed system in the expectation that it would allow them greater freedom in their personal habits.'[10] He says, 'The rise of German Protestantism was possible only because a number of the princes and cities had been permitted by resolutions of the imperial diet to refuse the aid of the secular arm to ecclesiastical laws.' This remark had already been made by Capefigue.[11] Ranke[12] thinks that the traditions of the Waldenses *did* favour the Reformation in Southern France ; but, he adds, this is a point not yet proved. In the sixteenth century the great vassals used to sign their letters in France with all the pomp of the king.[13] Capefigue truly says that the Reformation, under the pretence of freedom, compelled men to adopt its opinions.[14] Reformation connected

---

[1] Abfall der Niederlande in Schiller's Werke, Stuttgart, 1838. Band viii. p. 194.

[2] Essai sur les Mœurs, chap. cxxix. Œuvres de Voltaire, xvii. p. 217.

[3] Life of Locke, 8vo, 1830, vol. ii. pp. 68, 69.

[4] See on this Blanqui, Histoire de l'Économie Politique, Paris, 1845, tome i. p. 288 *et seq.*

[5] Philosophie Positive, tome v. pp. 643, 644.

[6] Päpste, vol. ii. p. 23.

[7] Civil Wars of France, 8vo, 1852, vol. i. p. 188.

[8] Ibid. p. 150.   [9] Ibid. p. 214.   [10] Ibid. p. 228.

[11] Histoire de la Réforme, tome i. p. 62.

[12] Civil Wars of France, vol. i. p. 234.

[13] Monteil, Histoire des divers États, tome v. p. 162.

[14] Histoire de la Réforme, tome i. p. 164 ; tome viii. p. 336.

with the Albigenses.[1]   On the coarseness of Luther, see Capefigue,
i. 337, 338 ; and on his enormous influence in Germany, p. 340.
Capefigue [2] says that the Interim of Charles V. having a *political*
view was attacked by both parties.   He says [3] that the Act of
Passaw is the first proclamation of liberty of conscience.   On the
encouragement to political inquiry see iv. p. 160.   Capefigue [4]
says that probably Lutheranism, so far from emancipating the
multitudes, merely took property from the clerks to give it to the
barons, and thus *reconstructed* feudality.   Capefigue [5] says that in
1615 the Diet of Ratisbon cared nothing for *material* interests, but
only for religion.   'At the beginning of the sixteenth century the
principal booksellers came from Basle in Switzerland.' [6]   The
objection of English Roman Catholics to marry during Lent is
gradually diminishing. [7]

CIVILISATION COMPARED WITH BARBARISM.

'ON a remarqué cependant que l'homme civilisé est généralement
plus fort que l'homme pris dans l'état sauvage.' [8]   And the same
thing is said still more positively by Archbishop Whately. [9]   Even
Reid, who was far too acute a thinker to fall into the paradox of
Rousseau, supposes that barbarians are stronger than civilised men. [10]
The error of supposing that old times are better than the present
ones is amongst uninformed men almost universal.   Mr. Price, who
has ably examined its causes, observes that it is precisely in the
same way that a belief has arisen that men were formerly giants
and long-lived. [11]   Ranke allows that there is an essential difference
between ancient and modern civilisation. [12]   He says [13] that the
ancient civilisation is in a great measure owing to a union of Church

---

[1] Histoire de la Réforme, tome I. pp. 192, 193.
[2] Ibid. pp. 345, 347.   [3] Ibid. p. 348.
[4] Ibid. tome viii. p. 330.
[6] Richelieu, Mazarin et La Fronde, tome I. pp. 142, 143.
[8] Journal of Statistical Society, vol. III. p. 165.
[7] Ibid. vol. iv. p. 41.
[8] Quetelet, Sur l'Homme, Paris, 1835, tome ii. p. 272, and see p. 67.
[9] Lectures on Political Economy, Lond. 8vo, 1831, p. 59.
[10] See Reid's Inquiry into the Human Mind, Edinburgh, 1814, pp. 439, 440.
[11] Price's Preface to Warton's History of English Poetry, 8vo, 1840, vol. I. pp.
23, 24.
[17] Die Römischen Päpste, Berlin, 1838, Band i. p. 34.   [13] Band I. pp. 3, 4.

and State. Lawrence [1] observes that civilised men are more powerful than savages. Ritter has noted the connection between the
extent of sea-coast and civilisation.[2] Archdeacon Hare oracu-
larly tells us, without a word of explanation, that 'the ultimate tendency of civilisation is towards barbarism.'[3] Ellis [4] observed that
English sailors were stronger than South Sea Islanders. We need
not be afraid of retrograding. There are many things which distinguish us from the ancient form of civilisation. We have public
opinion, and printing to disseminate it. Political economy first
taught us that nations gain by each other's gain.[5] While Europe
is secure against internal decay, the chances of an inroad of barbarians is still less. The invention of gunpowder and the successive improvements in the manufacture of weapons, and chemical
art being concentrated on gunpowder, makes war, barbarous as it
is, depend upon acts too delicate in their origin and scientific in
their application for barbarous nations. In every instance where
Europeans have come into contact with barbarians they have fled
before us, and great empires have been founded by a handful of
men. Besides, the barbarians are decreasing. Finally, our
experience is greater, and we have no slavery.

Democracy is no longer dangerous. The influence of mind
increases in three distinct ways : 1st. Those classes who oppose it
are losing their power. 2nd. Civilisation, as Comte says, increases
the difference of men. 3rd. Education increases the ease with
which that difference is perceived. Even Alison [6] confesses that
after Napoleon's expedition to Egypt, our decisive superiority over
barbarians is no longer a disputable point. Alison [7] thinks nations
must decay. Porter says,[8] 'Of 5,812,276 males twenty years of
age and upwards, living at the time of the census of 1831, there
were said to be engaged in some calling or profession 5,466,182,'
&c. Laing [9] thinks Europe is tending towards federalism. Tocqueville [10] denies the existence of a stationary state. The *regular*

[1] Lectures on Man, 8vo, 1844, pp. 274-276.
[2] Prichard's Physical History of Mankind, Lond. 8vo, 1837. vol. II. pp. 354. 355.
[3] Guesses at Truth, second series, 2nd edit. 8vo, 1848, p. 234.
[4] Polynesian Researches, 8vo, 1831, vol. I. p. 98.
[5] See Johnson's absurd remark.
[6] History of Europe, vol. iv. pp. 652, 653.   [7] Ibid. vol. vi. p. 120.
[8] Progress of the Nation, vol. III. p. 2.
[9] Notes of a Traveller, first series, pp. 26-28.
[10] Démocratie en Amérique, tome II. pp. 87, 88.

labour of a policeman is immense, certainly greater than any exercise savages can go through.[1] The only peculiarity I have found common to *all* barbarous nations is improvidence—indifference to the future. The assertion of Whately, &c., that civilised men are stronger than barbarians must not be put too generally.[2]

Polygamy has been succeeded by adultery.[3] Insanity is, like crime, more often cured than formerly, because treated more mildly. The *wants* of men have increased faster than their *resources*, so that countries have not *spare strength* enough to go to war.[4] Lord Mahon [5] says, 'Drunkenness, a vice which seems to strike deeper roots than any other in uneducated minds.' One of the most intelligent of modern missionaries very frankly says that the introduction by the Christians of vaccination into Thibet would probably overthrow Lamanism.[6]

CRIMES, THEIR STATISTICS ETC.

In France, for every 4,463 inhabitants, one is yearly accused of crime,[7] and out of 100 accused 61 are condemned.[8] In the Low Countries the proportionate number accused is nearly the same,[9] but there are fewer crimes against persons.[10] In France, during 1828 and 1829, the more intellectual the classes, the greater was the proportion which crimes against persons bore to crimes against property ;[11] but from this no general conclusion can be drawn against education.[12] In winter we have the *minimum* of crimes against persons, and the *maximum* of crimes against property : in summer, precisely the reverse.[13] For every 100 men accused in France there are 23 women accused ;[14] but for crimes against property the proportion is 26 to 100, for those against persons only 16 to 100.[15] This perhaps is the result of *weakness*, for in cases of poisoning the numbers are equal for the two sexes,[16] so that the difference in morality is not so great as is generally sup-

[1] See Journal of Statistical Society, vol. ii. p. 194.
[2] See Comte, Traité de Législation, tome iii. p. 327 *et seq*.   [3] Ibid. p. 432.
[4] See Laing's Sweden, p. 417.   [5] History of England, vol. ii. p. 187.
[6] Hue's Travels in Tartary and Thibet, vol. ii. p. 199.
[7] Quetelet, Sur l'Homme, Paris, 1835, tome ii. p. 165.
[8] Ibid. pp. 165, 166.   [9] Ibid. p. 171.   [10] Ibid. p. 172.
[11] Ibid. pp. 176, 177.   [12] Ibid. pp. 176–179.   [13] Ibid. p. 211.
[14] Ibid. p. 213.   [15] Ibid. p. 214.   [16] Ibid. p. 217.

posed.[1] In men at the age of twenty-five, in women at thirty, the
tendency to crime is at its height,[2] but the tendency to theft *always*
remains.[3] Of all the circumstances which control the tendencies
to crime, age is the most active.[4]   Alison speaks of 'the prodigious increase of crimes in England.'[5]   He adds[6] that in Lanark-
shire 'crime is increasing six times as fast as the number of people ; '
and he quotes Moreau to the effect that 'the number of individuals
charged with serious offences is in England five times greater than
it was thirty years ago ; in Ireland, six times ; but in Scotland,
twenty-nine times.'[7]   He adds[8] that 'since 1820, commitments
for felonies and other serious crimes have increased about 185 per
cent. in England ; ' in Ireland, 200 ; in Scotland, 250 per cent. ;
and as population has not advanced more than 50 per cent., 'over
the whole empire serious crime is augmenting four times, in Scotland five times, as fast as the number of the people.' See the
table at p. 326, where I find that the commitments are nearly *equal*
in England and Ireland ; in 1820 they were in each country every
year from 12,000 to 13,000 ; in 1838, 23,000 to 25,000.   In Sweden
and Norway the crime is even greater.[9]

Alison notices[10] that in America education does *not* prevent
crime ; in France it increases it. In Iceland, suicide is scarcely
known ;[11] indeed, almost the only crimes known are offences
against property, 'and even these are both rare and trivial.'[12]   In
Sweden highway robberies are hardly known.[13]   In 1553, Renard
seems to say that the English committed more violent crimes in
summer than in winter.[14]   Combe says,[15] 'Thus a public execution, from the violent stimulus which it communicates to the
lower faculties of the spectators, may within twenty-four hours of
its exhibition be the direct cause of a new crop of victims for the
gallows.' At pp. 372-374 he has some clever remarks on the
bad working of the jury system. Mr. Wright[16] says positively

[1] Quetelet, Sur l'Homme, Paris, 1835, tome II. p. 219.
[2] Ibid. pp. 230, 231.   [3] Ibid. p. 235.   [4] Ibid. p. 242.
[5] Principles of Population, 8vo, 1840, vol. i. p. 156.
[6] Ibid. vol. ii. pp. 97, 98.   [7] Ibid. p. 317.   [8] Ibid. pp. 325, 326.
[9] Ibid. p. 327.   [10] Ibid. p. 320.
[11] Dillon's Winter in Lapland and Iceland, 8vo, 1840, vol. I. p. 142.
[12] Ibid. p. 139, and see p. 296.
[13] Ibid. pp. 154, 155.
[14] Tytler's Edward VI. and Mary, 8vo, 1839, vol. II. p. 334.
[15] Constitution of Man, 8vo, 1847, p. 353.
[16] St. Patrick's Purgatory, 8vo, 1844, p. vi.

that crime diminished from the Reformation to the end of Elizabeth, increased under James I. and Charles I., and since then has
been constantly diminishing. Combe [1] thinks punishment should
be *entirely* addressed to reforming the criminals, and not as an
example. Plint [2] says, 'The absolute ratio of crime for all England in 1801 is shown in the table to have been 54 in 100,000,
and in 1845, 156 in 100,000—nearly threefold.' He says [3] that
many people, owing to ignorance of the method of calculation,
believe that the increase has been greater. When food is dear,
crime is increased and marriages diminished.[4] However,[5] Plint
quotes, and apparently believes, some evidence to show that crime
is now decreasing.[6] Increased longevity must, I suppose, lessen
crime ; for, says Plint,[7] 'Mr. Neison has shown in an elaborate
paper in the Statistical Magazine for October 1846, that about
64 per cent. of all criminal offences in England and Wales is committed by persons from fifteen to thirty years of age.' Alison [8]
actually supposes that the increasing crimes in England are the
result of diminished punishment. Laing [9] says that Sweden is
'in a more demoralised state than any nation in Europe.' But
Laing's coarse and slovenly estimate [10] of 'persons convicted of
some criminal offence' is worth nothing until we know what the
laws punish as criminal. The only precise statements of Laing
are that in 1836 the rural population of Sweden was 2,735,487,
which supplied '28 cases of murder, 10 of child murder, and 4 of
poisoning ; 13 of bestiality, 9 of robbery with violence.' [11] From
1 in 140 to 1 in 134 are yearly convicted of 'criminal offence ;' [12]
while in England and Wales, in 1831, 1 in 707 were accused, and
1 in 1,005 convicted.[13] In 1836, the rural population of Sweden,
2,735,000, committed 3,328 crimes, of which 1,176 were thefts,
2,080 assaults, and 7 perjury.[14] This only makes 1 in 822, and
yet Laing [15] says that 'in 1837, of the country population of
2,735,487, 1 in 460 has been punished for criminal offence.' This

[1] Moral Philosophy, 8vo, 1840, p. 301.
[2] Crime in England, 8vo, 1851, p. 11.   [3] Ibid. p. 12.   [4] Ibid. p. 46.
[5] Ibid. p. 27.   [6] Ibid. p. 138.   [7] Ibid. p. 86.
[8] History of Europe, vol. ix. pp. 623, 624.
[9] Tour in Sweden, 8vo, 1839, pp. 108, 109.   [10] Ibid. p. 109.
[11] Ibid. p. 110.   [12] Ibid. pp. 109, 110.   [13] Ibid. p. 111.
[14] Ibid. p. 106.   [15] Ibid. pp. 134, 135.

shows the absurdity of the expression 'criminal offence.' Female criminals 'are in the proportion of about 1 in 3.'[1]

In the province of Gifle, 120 miles from Stockholm, the country population is 95,822, of whom '1 in 595 has been condemned in 1837 for moral offences, not including as such the police transgressions or offences against conventional laws ;' and of these, five were murders.[2] The illegitimate births in Stockholm are 1 to $2\frac{3}{10}$,[3] while in Paris they are 1 in 5, and in the other towns of France 1 in 7¼ ; in London and Middlesex 1 in 38 ! ! ! No women who can afford it ever nurse their children.[4] And yet, with the exception of Denmark, no country is so educated as Sweden.[5] Laing[6] ascribes this to 'their low civil condition, their state of restriction and pupilage in all that relates to the free use and enjoyment of their industry and property, which works out a low moral condition which even religious knowledge and education cannot elevate ;' and masters may beat their servants.[7]

But the influence of the clergy is immense. We find[8] 'one in every 126 of the whole population living by teaching the Swedish people their religious and moral duties.' In Gothland there is 'one minister of religion to every 435 individuals ;'[9] and crime there is immense.[10] And the Swedish clergy are powerful as well as numerous. Laing[11] mentions a case of one of them flogging a woman for having an illegitimate child. 'In no country in Europe is the church establishment so powerful and perfect.'[12]

Porter[13] has vainly attempted to make out that education lessens crime. He says[14] that Guerry[15] has shown that 'in the departments where the greatest amount of instruction had been imparted, there the greatest amount of crime was found to exist ;' but Porter pertinently observes that the crimes were *committed* by the uninstructed ; and this was natural, because, where many persons were instructed, they would monopolise employment, and poverty would drive the ignorant to crime ; besides, in an *instructed* community offences would not be so readily overlooked as in an

---

[1] Tour in Sweden, 8vo, 1839, p. 140.
[2] Ibid. p. 213 ; and as to Gothland, see pp. 322, 323.
[3] Ibid. p. 113.   [4] Ibid. p. 116.   [5] Ibid. pp. 186, 242, 243, 275, 425.
[6] Ibid. p. 276.   [7] Ibid. p. 276, and see p. 432.   [8] Ibid. p. 245.
[9] Ibid. p. 321.   [10] Ibid. pp. 322, 323.   [11] Ibid. p. 278.
[12] Ibid. pp. 425, 426 ; see also for its intolerance p. 324.
[13] Progress of the Nation, vol. iii. pp. 200-221.   [14] Ibid. pp. 211, 212.
[15] Statistique Morale de la France.

ignorant one. But [1] Porter seems to say that education will *not* diminish crime. 'The great end of all punishment, the deterring of offenders.'[2] *More* than ⅓ of persons in gaol have previously been in prison.[3] During 1834 nearly 100,000 persons were in prison in England and Wales. This includes *all* the most trivial offences.[4] Porter says,[5] 'In England and Wales the number of persons now committed for trial is five times as great as it was in the beginning of the century.' 'The number of convictions in proportion to committals is now much greater than formerly.'[6]

In the fifteenth century, in France, all criminal prisoners were kept on bread and water alone, unless the judge made an order to the contrary.[7] In 1785 the Solicitor-General, in bringing forward a new police bill, said 'it was a certain truth that, of the whole number hanged in the metropolis, 18 out of every 20 were under the age of 21.'[8] In 1785, Alderman Townshend,[9] insisting on the necessity of certainty in punishment, said, 'So it was with thieves; their calculation was that, for every offender convicted, one out of thirty-three only was executed.' Comte [10] positively says crime is constantly decreasing. Comte [11] observes that drunkenness is promoted by an ignorance of the results; but Liebig [12] says that it is the *effect* of poverty, deficient nutriment requiring the *compensation* of alcohol. Laing [13] says that no men are so moral as Londoners; for none have to struggle so much with temptation; and what is virtue but temptation conquered? Should we praise a savage for not committing burglary where there are no houses, or not picking a pocket where there are no clothes? Crime is increased—1st. By increased ability in the thief; 2nd. By greater number of things to steal; 3rd. By more artificial wants. 'It is ascertained that three-fourths of the criminals under seventeen years of age are the children of bad parents.'[14] At p. 86 it is said that crime is caused by drunkenness, and that 'by foul air and the depressing influence of bad localities, bringing with it a

---

[1] Progress of the Nation, vol. I. pp. 220, 221. [2] Ibid. p. 133.
[3] Ibid. p. 140. [4] Ibid. pp. 140, 141. [5] Ibid. vol. III. p. 172.
[6] Ibid. p. 179.
[7] Montell, Histoire des Français des Divers États, tome IV. p. 58.
[8] Parliamentary History, vol. xxv. p. 889. [9] Ibid. p. 907.
[10] Traité de Législation, tome I. pp. 53, 54. [11] Ibid. pp. 58, 59.
[12] Letters on Chemistry, p. 255.
[13] Notes of a Traveller, first series. pp. 281, 282.
[14] Transactions of Association for promoting Social Science, Lond. 1859, p. 15.

fierce desire for stimulants ; and by bad and deficient water.'[1]
' Bad water and bad air ' the two causes of crime.[2]

At Liverpool the Recorder ' disallows the expenses of prose-
cutors who have been robbed through their own carelessness in
exposing goods at the doors of their shops ; but the only effect is
to render the shopkeepers indifferent about prosecutions in any
subsequent loss.'[3] In England and Wales one-fourth of the
criminals are between 20 and 25 years old, and ' nearly three-fifths
between 15 and 30.'[4] At p. 389, 'Upwards of 30 per cent of
our criminal population range between the ages of 16 and 45.'
At p. 396, ' With regard to the causes of crime in Baden and
Bavaria, each of the governors *assured* me that it was *wine* in one
country and *beer* in the other which filled the gaols.' A reform-
atory where ' music and singing are cultivated as much as possible,
and have much tended to eradicate the low and vulgar propensi-
ties of the lads.'[5] At p. 643, ' Very rarely do you find a man who
is fond of flowers taken up for misdemeanour of any kind.'

PHILOLOGY.

' LANGUAGE is often called an instrument of thought, but it is also
the nutriment of thought ; or rather, it is the atmosphere in
which thought lives,' &c. &c.[6] Reinier Prodinius, who died in
1559, was a celebrated Dutch philologist. ' Hij was een van
de voornaamste beoefenaars der spraakafleiding (*etymology*) der
Latijnsche tale, op wiens gronden Vossius naderhand bouwde.'[7]
Contrary to the general opinion, Cousin says disputes are generally
not about words, but about things.[8] Lord Brougham supposes
that Tooke's Diversions of Purley contains original discoveries.[9]
Coleridge[10] has some admirable remarks on the tendency of words
to *desynonymise*. To *resent*, which now only means to *take ill*,

---

1 Transactions of Association for Social Science, 1859, pp. 88, 89.
2 Ibid. p. 91.   3 Ibid. p. 355.
4 Ibid. p. 365.   5 Ibid. p. 408.
6 Whewell's Philosophy of the Inductive Sciences, 8vo, 1847, vol. L pp. 270, 271.
7 Van Kampen, Geschiedenis der Letteren in de Niederlanden, Gravenhage,
8vo, 1821, deel L blad 75.
8 Histoire de la Philosophie, 2nde série, tome III. p. 218.
9 Brougham's Historical Sketches of Statesmen, Lond. 1845, vol. III p. 142
et seq.   10 Biographia Literaria, 8vo, 1847, vol. L p. 80.

formerly also meant to *take well*.   See an instance in Pepys's
Diary, 8vo, 1828, vol. iv. p. 247.   Prichard [1] says of Mount Altai,
'The Turkish name of *Alta-in-oole* means the Golden Mountains.'
In the Australian and Polynesian languages there is a singular,
dual, and plural.[2]   Prichard says,[3] 'In a barbarous state of
society, and principally in one of early and imperfect but growing
refinement of mind, the imagination has more influence in the
formation of language than in a more advanced stage.'   Lemontey,
in his 'Louis XIV.,' says that first in this reign *honnête* changed
its meaning, and 'that, till the latter half of the reign of Louis an
"honnête homme" was the name for an upright, not for an inoffen-
sive man.'[4]   Father Nobili, early in the seventeenth century,
was the first European who well understood Sanscrit.[5]   Burton [6]
says that the inhabitants of Scinde 'have no proper name for the
Indus in general and vulgar use; the Mitho Daryan or "Sweet Water
Sea" is the vague expression commonly employed.'   It used to be
thought that lunacy was caused by the moon ; hence the word ; and
now the word is used to justify the opinion.[7]   Georgel [8] says that
in 1790 the crime 'lèse nation' was a 'mot nouveau.'   See some
very ingenious remarks on the Latin language in Vico, Philosophie
de l'Histoire, pp. 125-131, and 140-143, and 222-226.   He says
(p. 244) that as the Romans did not know what luxury was until
they saw a native of Tarentum, they called a perfumed man 'un
Tarentin,' &c.   Compare this with Adam Smith.   At the end of the
fourteenth century in France 'le nom de serf commence à devenir
une insulte.'[9]   Monteil says,[10] 'Le mot de financier, qui vient de
finer, payer, est d'origine moderne.   Je doute qu'il ait été en usage
avant le treizième ou douzième siècle : mais il l'était au quator-
zième, ainsi qu'on le voit dans les ordonnances de ce temps.'
Kiel, the Tekelia of Ptolemy, is said to be still called by the Platt
Deutsch peasantry Tokiel or Tomkiel.[11]   Laing says,[12] 'Mediatise is a

[1] Physical History of Mankind, vol. iv. p. 281.
[2] See ibid. vol. v. p. 276.
[3] Ibid. p. 319.
[4] Stephen's Lectures on the History of France, 8vo, 1851, vol. ii. p. 442 ; and
see note in Des Réaux, Historiettes, vol. v. p. 213.
[5] Ranke, Die Päpste, Band ii. p. 494, note.
[6] Sindh and the Races in Indus, 8vo, 1851, p. 380.
[7] See Georgel, De la Folie, p. 440.   [8] Mémoires, tome iii. p. 94.
[9] Monteil, Hist. des Français des Divers États, tome ii. p. 178.
[10] Ibid. p. 180.   [11] Laing's Denmark, 8vo, 1852, p. 22.
[12] Notes of a Traveller, first series, p. 122.

word which came into use at the Congress of Vienna of 1814-15.'
Tocqueville[1] says, 'Le seul Milton a introduit dans la langue
anglaise plus de six cents mots, presque tous tirés du latin, du grec
et de l'hébreu.' He says[2] that as nations become democratic,
their love of generalisation is shown even in their language. Thus
the Americans carry the abstraction so far as to talk of 'the capaci-
ties' for capable men, or of 'eventualities' for everything that can
happen. For two curious instances in which the Greeks were led
into error by foreign language, see History of Maritime and Inland
Discovery (by Cooley), 8vo, 1830, vol. i. p. 67. In 1797 'circulating medium' was a new expression.[3] 'Cowper Law' is said
to be derived from 'Cupar, a town where little mercy was shown
to the Highland rovers.'[4] Lord Mahon[5] wishes 'Fatherland,' a
'Teutonic' word, to be used in English. The word *riotte* is lost
in French, but from it we have *riot*.[6] In 1798 'uncandid' is
spoken of as a new word, or at all events 'a word in fashion.'[7] In
1689 it is said[8] that 'by the employment' of a man, was not good
English ; but that it should be 'by the *employ*.' In 1738 '*socking*,
which is a cant term for pilfering and stealing tobacco from ships
in the river.'[9] The Danish language is still understood in part of
Westmoreland.[10] Comte[11] well says that one reason why conquerors adopt the manner and language of the conquered is that
they marry their women, and that the next generation prefers the
language, &c., of their mothers (with whom they are constantly) to
that of their fathers. In 1764, Dr. Grieve, in translating the
valuable Russian account of Kamtschatka, says at chapter xx.,
'This chapter in the original contains an account of three different
dialects of the Kamtschatdales, which, as they are very unintelligible to an English reader, we think proper to omit.'[12] This is the
whole of the chapter ! ! ! Lake Peten is in Yucatan. 'In this
lake are numerous islands, one of which is called Peten Grande,

[1] Démocratie en Amérique, tome iv. p. 103.   [2] Ibid. pp. 109-110.
[3] See Parliamentary History. vol. xxxiii. pp. 340, 343, 548.
[4] Mahon's Hist. of England, 1853, vol. i. p. 198, and vol. ii. p. 44.
[5] Ibid. p. 213.
[6] Notes in Lettres de Madame de Sévigné, 1843, tome i. p. 120.
[7] Parliamentary History, vol. xxxiv. p. 48.
[8] Ibid. vol. v. p. 463.   [9] Ibid. vol. viii. p. 1274.
[10] Journal of Statistical Society, vol. ii. p. 334.
[11] Traité de Législation, tome iii. pp. 62, 63.
[12] Grieve's History of Kamtschatka. p. 222.

Peten itself being a Maya word, signifying an island.'[1] For a blunder caused by language, see Journal of Geographical Society, vol. xii. p. 32.

MANNERS (*for Preface*).

WILLIAM SCHLEGEL goes so far as to consider taste in dress 'a criterion of social cultivation or deformity.'[2]   Dawson Turner says that in the country about Caen the dress of the women is like that worn in England in the fifteenth and sixteenth centuries ; and 'as to the cap which the Cauchoise wears, when she appears *en grand costume*, its very prototype is to be found in Strutt's Ancient Dresses.' See Turner's Tour in Normandy, London, 8vo, 1820, vol. i. p. 8, where he also gives a representation of this high cap.

POPULATION.

'Scantly you have two miles without a town or a village in-habited.'[3]   In 1563, when the plague was in London, Cecil writes to Sir Thomas Smith, 'They dye in London above one thousand in a weke.'[4]

PHYSIOLOGY ETC. (*for facts*).

THE Icelanders are tall, fair, but 'white hair, instead of being universal, is by no means as common as in Scotland and Denmark.'[5]

In 1774, Captain Topham says that in Scotland he 'never saw either an exceedingly deformed person or an aged, toothless, paralytic highlander.'[6]   Ellis[7] says that in the South Sea Islands the chiefs are superior to the common people in height and in physical strength.   But this is explained by Williams[8] as the result of superior diet.   Catlin[9] observes the peculiarity of

[1] Stephens's Central America, vol. iv. p. 192.
[2] Lectures on Dramatic Art, Lond. 1840, vol. ii. pp. 327, 328.
[3] Cooper's Admonition, 1589. p. 92. 8vo, 1847.
[4] Wright's Elizabeth, 8vo, 1838, vol. i. p. 138.
[5] Dillon's Winter in Lapland and Iceland, 8vo, 1840, vol. i. p. 133.
[6] Letters from Edinburgh, 8vo, 1776, p. 79.
[7] Polynesian Researches, 8vo, 1831, vol. i. p. 82.
[8] Missionary Enterprise in the South Sea Islands, 8vo, 1837, pp. 512, 513.
[9] North American Indians, 8vo, 1841, vol. i. p. 193.

their heads, which, he adds,[1] 'is produced by artificial means in
infancy.'[2]   For their stature, &c., see pp. 225, 226.   High
training, &c., does *not* wear out the frame ; but, on the whole,
'looking to the human race, it is certain that the average exercise used is excessive, and more harmful than beneficial.'[3]   Alison talks very confidently about the difference of race, but con-
tradicts himself.[4]   In the retreat from Moscow the French bore
the cold better than the Russians, and the survivors 'almost all
were Italians or Frenchmen from the provinces to the *south* of
the Loire.'[5]   In 1675 it was considered remarkable that the
blood of a negro should be red instead of black.[6]   On *race*, see
Comte, Philosophie Positive, tome iii. p. 355.   Dr. Prichard[7] says,
'According to Burton, the offspring of parents advanced in years
are more subject than others to melancholy madness.'   Laing[8]
takes it for granted that 'the Gothic' care more than 'the
Celtic race' for the 'enjoyments and luxuries of civilised life.'
In Leeds the lowest classes have most children ; then the outdoor
'handcraftsmen ;' then the indoor ; then tradesmen ; and 'independent and professional people' the fewest of all.[9]   Hutchinson,
in his Paper on Vital Statistics, says,[10] 'The pugilists, without
exception, are the finest class of men I have examined.'   The
Indians are less subject to cholera than the Europeans ; but this
is said to arise from their greater temperance[11]—'a sufficient proof
that the Malay race is never likely to become assimilated to the
climate of Ceylon.'[12]   In India all the lower classes of native
women are short, but the better sort are the average European
height.   This was told Heber by Dr. Smith.[13]   Heber[14] observes
that the Brahmins are superior in intellect, and have *fairer complexions* than the other castes.

   Murray[15] says of Bruce the traveller's father, 'It may be

---

[1] North American Indians, 8vo, 1841, vol. ii. p. 41.   [2] Ibid. pp. 110-112.
[3] Mayo's Philosophy of Living, 2nd edit. 8vo, 1838, pp. 125, 126, 131.
[4] See Alison's History of Europe, vol. ii. pp. 336, 338 ; see also vol. vi. p. 136 ;
vol. viii. pp. 525, 526.   [5] Ibid. vol. xi. p. 183.
[6] Ray's Correspondence, by Dr. Lankester, 8vo, 1848, p. 120.
[7] Treatise on Insanity, 8vo, 1835, p. 159.
[8] Observations on Denmark, p. 154.
[9] Journal of Statistical Society, vol. ii. pp. 423, 424 ; see also note at vol. iii.
pp. 252, 253.   [10] Ibid. vol. vii. p. 203.
[11] Ibid. vol. x. pp. 121, 122, 123.   [12] Ibid. p. 258.
[13] See Heber's Journey through India, vol. ii. pp. 509, 510.
[14] Ibid. vol. i. p. 120.   [15] Life of Bruce, p. 24.

remarked as an instance of the transmission of bodily as well as mental qualities, through a long line of descendants, that the features and character of Robert Bruce, the firm and haughty leader of the Scottish church in the reign of James VI., were retained by his representatives at the distance of two centuries.' Kohl [1] says of St. Petersburg, 'In no other towns are there so few cripples and deformed people ; and this is not merely owing to their being less tolerated here than elsewhere, but also, it is said, to the fact that the Slavonian race is less apt than any other to produce deformed children.' Kohl, near Odessa, 'found the wife of the Bulgarian, who, as it usually happens with women, had preserved the national features more unaltered than her husband.' [2] On the absurdity of *vis vitæ*, see Liebig's Letters on Chemistry, 8vo, 1851, p. 13. The ancient Celts in England had very small hands. [3] In 1846, Sir Benjamin Brodie told Moore 'that among the many dying patients he had attended he had but rarely met with one that was afraid to die.' [4] 'The negro race is remarkably exempt 'from calculus ; but so are *all* the inhabitants of 'tropical countries.' [5] Chossat 'found that defective nourishment notably reduced the weight of all the structures of the body except only those of the nervous system, which were wonderfully little diminished by it.' [6] The pale globules of the blood were known to Hewson. [7]

TENDENCY OF CLASSICAL LITERATURE.

COMBE [8] suggests that great injury has resulted from teaching children to admire the literature and history of Greece and Rome. Even Lawrence [9] says, 'Let us never forget that the principal and richest portion of our intellectual treasure consists of the literature and history of two nations of antiquity, whose astonishing superiority seems to have arisen principally from their having enjoyed freedom.' Even Milton recommends hardly anything

---

[1] Russia, 8vo, 1844, p. 30.   [2] Kohl's Russia, p. 435.
[3] See Report of British Association for 1850 ; Transactions of Sections, p. 145.
[4] Moore's Memoirs, by Lord J. Russell, Lond. 1856, vol. viii. p. 22.
[5] Erichsen's Surgery, 1854, 2nd edit. p. 946.
[6] Williams's Principles of Medicine, p. 169.
[7] See Gulliver's edition of Hewson's Works, p. 282.
[8] Constitution of Man in Relation to External Objects, Edinburgh, 1847, 8vo, p. 264.   [9] Lectures on Man, 8vo, 1844, p. 332.

but the ancient writers[1] Sancroft, in 1663, notices the decline of ' Hebrew and Greek learning.'[2]   On the absurdity of studying so much classics, and on the low civilisation of the Greeks and Romans, see Combe's Lectures on Moral Philosophy, 8vo, 1840, pp. 74, 75, 108, 109. In 1693, Evelyn[3] mentions that his daughter 'has read most of the Greek and Roman authors and poets.' Lewis[4] has collected some evidence of the slow diffusion of *news* among the ancients. Even Sir W. Temple, the great admirer of the ancients, will not allow that they generally were wiser than we.[5] Laing[6] has some very severe remarks on the boasted civilisation of the Romans ; and Tocqueville[7] speaks contemptuously of their great works, as aqueducts, &c. The ablest writers now never make classical allusions or quote ancient authors ; therefore a great inducement to study the classics is taken away. In the sixteenth century ambassadors were obliged to harangue princes in Latin.[8] Ancients ignorant of geography.[9] Mills[10] mentions the absurdity of ascribing the progress of Europe to the revived study of classical literature. The Venetian family, Cornaro, derived their descent from the Roman Cornelia.[11] For instance of the classical pedantry of Beza, see Smedley's History of the Reformed Religion in France, vol. i. p. 213. On the vices of the ancients and absurd respect felt for them, see some striking remarks in Comte, Traité de Législation, tome i. pp. 51, 52, 402 ; tome iii. p. 470 ; and on their contempt for commerce, p. 501 *et seq.*, and tome iv. pp. 7, 15. On the absurdity of admiring ancient languages for their synthetic and inflexional state, see Report of British Association for 1852, Transactions of Sections, p. 82.

[1] Hallam's Literature of Europe, vol. iii. p. 410.
[2] D'Oyly's Life of Sancroft, 2nd edit. 8vo, 1840, p. 78.
[3] Diary, vol. iii. p. 324.
[4] Method of Observation in Politics, vol. i. p. 431.
[5] Temple's Works, 8vo, 1814, vol. i. p. 14.
[6] Notes of a Traveller, first series, pp. 386, 406.
[7] Démocratie, tome iv. p. 85.
[8] Montesi, Histoire des Français, tome iv. p. 154.
[9] See History of Maritime and Inland Discovery, by Cooley, 1830, vol. i. p. 89.
[10] History of Chivalry, vol. ii. p. 170.
[11] Lettres de l'atin. vol. iii. p. 697.

THEOLOGY AND RELIGIOUS SUPERSTITIONS.

ONLY women and eunuchs are allowed to see the king of Dahomey eat or drink.[1] The Japanese robbers think that they can cause deadly sleep by throwing into a house they intend to plunder earth from a newly opened grave.[2] Low[2] says of the Dyaks of Borneo, ' Death to their ignorant and unenlightened minds displays no terror.' The inhabitants of the Friendly Islands believe that men were formerly giants.[4] On the connection between lust and religion, see Southey's Life of Wesley, 8vo, 1846, vol. i. p. 173. Vans Kennedy thinks[5] that the 'indelicacy' of a part of the Hindoo religion ' has no effect on their morals.' A writer who has seen the religious customs of many different nations observes that the most ignorant are 'the most fixed and stubborn' in religion.[6] On the origin of superstition Locke has some ingenious but, I think, unsatisfactory remarks.[7] For an instance of the mischief caused by an established church, see Combe's Lectures on Moral Philosophy, 8vo, 1840, p. 82. Many Protestant theologians have maintained that prayer produces no effect on the Deity.[8] Alison[9] has well observed that the difficulty of Protestantism is to keep scepticism from the uneducated, the difficulty of Popery to keep it from the educated; because Popery appeals to the senses, Protestantism to the intellect. Comte observes that miracles are an evidence of the decline of the theological spirit.[10] At tome v. p. 44 he says, I think with truth, that animal worship is not so common as is generally supposed. Archbishop Whately[11] thinks that what we call the *cause* of a superstition is in reality its *effect*. Sir W. Temple[12] thinks comets may affect mind and body. Sir T. Browne[13]

[1] See Forbes's Dahomey and the Dahomans, 8vo, 1851, vol. i. p. 79.
[2] Crawford's History of the Indian Archipelago, Edinb. 8vo, 1820, vol. i. p. 56.
[3] Sarawak, 8vo, 1848, p. 263.
[4] See Mariner's Tonga Islanders, 2nd edit. 8vo, 1818, vol. i. p. 313.
[5] Transactions of Literary Society of Bombay, vol. iii. p. 155.
[6] Catlin's North American Indians, 8vo, 1841, vol. i. p. 183.
[7] See King's Life of Locke, 8vo, 1830, vol. i. p. 101.
[8] Combe's Moral Philosophy, 8vo, 1840, pp. 434-438.
[9] History of Europe, vol. x. p. 240.
[10] Philosophie Positive, tome iv. pp. 673, 674, 679, 683-685.
[11] Errors of Romanism, 8vo, 1830, p. 178.
[12] Works, 8vo, 1814, vol. iii. p. 45.   [13] Works, vol. iii. p. 329.

believes that oracles were supernatural. The diminution of superstition will take away one cause of madness.[1] Kemble[2] seems to think that the process is that myths, as they become popular, deteriorate and 'assume traits of the popular humorous spirit.' The Saxons, and even many ecclesiastics, believed that hell was cold.[3] Kemble says (vol. i. p. 47), 'It is indeed probable that all capital punishments among the Germans were originally in the nature of sacrifices to the gods.' At Marseilles, in 1646, Monconys[4] was told that seven of the 11,000 virgins were buried ; he also heard that the Queen Blanche, by entering the chapel and making a vow to the Virgin, recovered her sight.[5] In 1663 Monconys[6] was shown at Oxford a horn which the Jews said was made like those with which the walls of Jericho were blown down. In 1648 it was still the common opinion that an eclipse or comet always preceded any accidents to kings or empires.[7] Göthe says that men soon give up a superstition when they find it contrary to their interest.[8] The mortality among children is greatly increased by carrying them to church to be baptised. See Quetelet, Sur l'Homme, tome i. p. 167 ; and at p. 229 it is observed that religious ceremonies at the bedside of a patient cause death. Pilgrimages are eagerly followed by the Mahometans even now. Doctrine of a God not universal. Of the Orkney Islanders, in 1805, Barry says,[9] 'Thursdays and Fridays are the days in which they incline to marry ; and they scrupulously and anxiously avoid it at any other time than when the moon is waxing.'[10]

'Toutes les religions font des promesses ou des menaces dont il n'est pas facile de vérifier l'accomplissement.'[11] The negroes believe that the devil is white.[12] Telling fortunes by palmistry is practised by the Tibetans.[13] Symes says,[14] 'The Birmans have a superstitious abhorrence of any person's passing over them when

---

[1] See Prichard on Insanity, 8vo, 1835, pp. 19, 20, 30, 187, 198 ; and Pinel, Traité sur l'Alienation Mentale, pp. 41–45, 108, 119, 151, 164, 165, 431, 457, 479.
[2] Saxons in England. vol. i. p. 382.
[3] Ibid. pp. 394, 395.
[4] Voyages, 1695, 12mo, tome i. p. 195.
[5] Ibid. tome iv. p. 22.
[6] Ibid. tome iii. p. 95.
[7] Ibid. tome v. pp. 103, 104.
[8] Wahrheit und Dichtung, in Göthe's Werke, Band ii. Theil ii. p. 145.
[9] History of the Orkney Islands, p. 342.
[10] Ibid. p. 342.
[11] Comte, Traité de Législation, tome i. pp. 275, 276.
[12] Ibid. tome ii. p. 37.
[13] See Turner's Embassy to Thibet, p. 284.
[14] Embassy to Ava, vol. iii. p. 255.

they are asleep.' The Kamtschatkans 'are very great observers
of dreams, which they relate to one another as soon as they are
awake in the morning, and judge from thence of their future
good or bad fortune ; and some of these dreams have their interpretation fixed and settled. Besides this conjuration they pretend
to chiromancy, and to foretell a man's good or bad fortune by the
lines of his hand ; but the rules which they follow are kept a
great secret.'[1] Blanco White says,[2] 'I am inclined to believe
that the illuminated grottoes of oyster-shells, for which the
London children beg about the streets, are the representatives of
some Catholic emblem, which had its day as a substitute for a
more classical idol.' Neander looks on Christianity as a development. See his History of the Church, vol. i. pp. 4, 6, 20, 38, 60,
61, 269, 379, 465 ; vol. ii. pp. 118, 132, 157, 164 ; vol. iii. p. 488 ;
vol. vi. p. 412. At vol. i. p 100, and vol. iii. p. 71, Neander has
some unfair and uncritical remarks. In the fifth century a
number of hypocrites became Christians.[3] He says,[4] 'The
nomadic life, which prevailed over the largest portion of Arabia,
ever presented a powerful hindrance to the spread of Christianity.'
In the fourth century images were first used in churches,[5] and
'heathen melodies' introduced into 'church psalmody.'[6] Neander[7] says, 'The weavers, an occupation which from its peculiar
character has ever been a favourite resort of mystical sects.'
Formerly in France a man who died on Good Friday was deemed
a saint.[8] White meat *mortifies the flesh* by its want of iron.[9]
Laing, who is anything but sceptical, says there is no country in
Europe where there is so much morality and little religion as
Switzerland.[10] He says[11] the Swiss are remarkable 'for a sense of
property ;' and[12] that the Catholics are more religious than the
Protestants. He says[13] that now Rome is busily engaged in
educating the people and propagating knowledge.

[1] Grieve's History of Kamtschatka, Gloucester, 1764, 4to, p. 206.
[2] Doblado's Letters from Spain, p. 302.
[3] See Neander, vol. iii. pp. 139, 140.
[4] Ibid. p. 166.
[5] Ibid. p. 413.
[6] Ibid. p. 451.
[7] History of the Church, vol. vi. p. 358.
[8] Ibid. vol. vii. p. 457.
[9] Liebig's Letters on Chemistry, 8vo, 1851. p. 433.
[10] Notes of a Traveller, first series, pp. 323. 324, 333.
[11] Ibid. p. 354.
[12] Ibid. p. 430.
[13] Ibid. pp. 349, 440.

NATIONAL CHARACTER OF THE DUTCH.

BURNET, who was in Holland in 1664, says, 'There seemed to be among them too much coldness and indifference in matters of religion.'[1] Hallam[2] calls Holland 'the peculiarly learned state of Europe during the seventeenth century.' Burnet says,[3] 'I was never in any place where I thought the clergy had generally so much credit with the people as they have there.' In 1716 the Dutch were remarkable for cleanliness.[4] Sir W. Temple's Observations upon the United Provinces were written between 1669 and 1673. He mentions the great simplicity of living even among the highest ranks,[5] but luxury was creeping in.[6] The lower people fond of drink, but the highest classes more temperate;[7] but none ate much. 'Their great parsimony in diet, and eating so very little flesh, which the common people seldom do above once a week.'[8] The people are 'cold and heavy;'[9] 'so little show of parts and of wit, and so great evidence of wisdom and prudence.'[10] 'I have known some among them that personated lovers well enough, but none that I ever thought were at heart in love.'[11] He mentions[12] their remarkable cleanliness. He says[13] of rich families, 'Their youth, after the course of their studies at home, travel for some years as the sons of our gentry use to do; but their journeys are chiefly into England and France, not much into Italy, seldomer into Spain. . . . The diseases of the climate seem to be chiefly the gout and the scurvy.'[14] In Holland the clergy *never* had any jurisdiction,[15] and there was great toleration.[16] Temple mentions[17] their burning nutmegs to raise the price. As late as 1669 and 1670 'there was hardly any foreign trade among them.' After England, there is no country so badly off for pauperism as Holland; and this is owing 'to the existence of so many thousand endowed institutions for the relief of the poor.'[18] Laing[19] says that the import-

---

[1] Own Time, Oxford, 1823, vol. I. p. 357.
[2] Literature of Europe, vol. III. p. 243.   [3] Own Time, vol. III. p. 293.
[4] See Lady Mary W. Montagu's Works, 8vo, 1803, vol. I. p. 201.
[5] Works, 8vo, 1814, vol. I. pp. 113, 116.   [6] Ibid. p. 184.
[7] Ibid. pp. 142, 143.   [8] Ibid. p. 147.   [9] Ibid. p. 114.
[10] Ibid. p. 115.   [11] Ibid. p. 141.   [12] Ibid. p. 132.
[13] Ibid. p. 135.   [14] Ibid. p. 149.   [15] Ibid. p. 157.
[16] Ibid. pp. 159-162.   [17] Ibid. p. 183.
[18] Porter's Progress of the Nation, vol. I. p. 113.
[19] Notes of a Traveller, first series, pp. 7, 8.

ance of the Dutch herring fisheries has been greatly exaggerated.
He supposes[1] that the *sole* cause of the ruin of Holland was that
she was the broker and carrier of Europe ; but as the nations
advanced, they did this business themselves. After Descartes,
Holland was the great refuge of scepticism.[2] Laing says,[3] 'The
Dutch people, eminently charitable and benevolent as a public,
their country full of beneficial institutions, admirably conducted
and munificently supported, are as individuals somewhat rough,
hard, and, though it be uncharitable to say so, uncharitable and
unfeeling.'

NATIONAL CHARACTER OF THE FRENCH.

FROM phrenology it appears that the French are remarkable for
vanity, and the English for pride.[4]   All the ancient writers notice
the 'boldness, levity, fickleness,' and unchastity of the Gauls ;[5]
and Prichard adds,[6] 'Of all Pagan nations the Gauls and
Britons appear to have had the most sanguinary rites.' In 1818
Dr. Combe observed at Paris that the heads of Frenchmen
'sloped backwards from the nose' more rapidly than the heads of
Frenchwomen ; and, says George Combe, this difference in the
reflective organs not being found among the sexes in England
accounts for the greater influence women have in France.[7]   In
1753, Voltaire[8] candidly allows that the French are not inven-
tive.[9] M. de Barante[10] says the vanity of the French is chiefly
the result of men of letters being indignant at the absence of
political power. Richelieu in his Mémoires[11] mentions the particular levity of the French. Sir J. Reynolds[12] observes that in
art they are very quick *extempore* for invention, but not for
finishing their paintings. Laing[13] says that the French are more
honest than the British. He praises[14] their subdivision of property.

[1] Notes of a Traveller, first series, p. 9.
[2] See Lamartine, Histoire des Girondins, tome i. p. 221.
[3] Notes of a Traveller, first series, p. 14.
[4] See Combe's Elements of Phrenology, 6th edit. Edinburgh, 1845, pp. 87, 90.
[5] Prichard's Physical History of Mankind, vol. iii. p. 178.   [6] Ibid. p. 187.
[7] Combe's Life of Dr. Combe, Edinburgh, 8vo, 1850, p. 71.
[8] See Correspondence in Œuvres, vol. lix. pp. 313, 314.
[9] See also tome lxi. p. 41 ; lxvi. p. 466.
[10] Littérature Française au xviiie Siècle, p. 80.   [11] Tome ii. pp. 132, 133.
[12] Works, vol. ii. pp. 57, 58.
[13] Notes of a Traveller, first series, p. 54.   [14] Ibid. p. 53.

'The French, with all their centralisation, have roads infinitely inferior to ours.'[1]   Laing says,[2] 'In France, at the expulsion of Louis Philippe, the civil functionaries were stated to amount to 807,030 individuals.'   The Prince de Montbarey says,[3] 'Il faut le dire avec toute la vérité que je professe, le Français dans toutes les classes, et dans toutes les circonstances, ne sait jamais garder un juste milieu.'   Tocqueville[4] says that the Americans, notwithstanding the wildness of their lives, value women so highly as to make rape a capital offence; while in France, such is the 'mépris de la pudeur' and 'mépris de la femme' that it is difficult to get a jury to convict on such a charge.   In France there are 138,000 functionaries.[5]   He says[6] that there is no country where the social distance between master and servant is so slight as in France; nowhere is it so great as in England.   The lower order of French are more civilised than the lower order of English, while the lower order of Germans are at the bottom of the scale.   This is explained by the *language*, which in Germany is like Latin or Greek, synthetic, not calculated for the *diffusion* but for the *preservation* of knowledge.   See in Journal of Statistical Society, vol. iii. pp. 376, 377, 'a classification of new works' (i.e. books) 'in France from 1829 to 1833.'   I believe one reason why the French have so many memoirs is because they are a vain people, and dare not write on political subjects.   The French historians, long accustomed to memoirs, are now, like Thierry, Barante, and Capefigue, become too *personal* and *anecdotal*.   Comte[7] says there is nothing remarkable in the Code Napoléon, and nothing not to be found in preceding laws.   And on the retrogressive spirit of Napoleon see Comte, Traité de Législation, iv. 269.

NATIONAL CHARACTER OF THE SPANISH.

Schlegel[8] says, 'In general, ever since its first commencement, the poetry of Spain has always been more cultivated by nobles and knights than by mere *literati* and authors.'   There was no country where entails had been so general and injurious as in

---

[1] Laing's Notes, 2nd series, pp. 118, 119.   [2] Ibid. p. 185.
[3] Mémoires, vol. i. p. 162.
[4] Démocratie en Amérique, tome i. p. 82.   [5] Ibid. tome i. p. 220.
[6] Ibid. tome v. p. 23.   [7] Traité de Législation, tome i. pp. 356-357.
[8] Lectures on the History of Literature, vol. ii. p. 92.

Spain ;[1] and ecclesiastics were very numerous and influential.[2]
Charles V. arrested the development of towns.[3] Villemain[4] says
that, except Herodotus, all Greek historians were public men, and
so were Machiavelli, Guicciardini, Davila, Fra Paolo, and De Thou.
I believe this was the point where Spain stopped. There was no
division of labour.

Keightley[5] notices the great deficiency of fairy tales, &c., in
Spain. Little is known about the statistics of Spain ; but there
is an interesting paper on mortality, &c., of Cadiz in Journal of
Statistical Society, vol. iv. p. 131.

In Spain, to be a physician, it was necessary to be able to
defend the doctrine of the Immaculate Conception.[6] See also[7]
the absurd treatment of the Spanish colonies. Blanco White, in
1798, says,[8] 'The influence of religion in Spain is boundless. It
divides the whole population into two comprehensive classes,
bigots and dissemblers.' See also[9] the extraordinary loyalty of
the Spaniards, and [10] their absurd love of titles and of numerous Christian names. For their absurd etiquette see p. 51.
Men of high rank are rewarded for fighting with bulls ; and
preachers who assail the theatres never venture to preach against
bull-fights.[11] In 1801 no Spaniards travelled for amusement.[12]
In Seville twelve sermons preached every day.[13] Religious
melancholy disease.[14] Jealousy of women has left the upper
classes, but is still an active passion among the lower.[15] Blanco
White[16] speaks in the highest terms of Moratin as a dramatic
genius. He adds[17] that the Spanish language is too grand and
not flexible enough for poetry ; that since the beginning of the
sixteenth century 'our best poets have been servile imitators of
Petrarch and the writers of that school.' Respecting the 'suppression of the Jesuits in Spain,' see Doblado, Appendix, p. 445
et seq. A celebrated traveller, Mr. Kohl, says, 'The environs of

---

[1] Alison's History of Europe, vol. viii. p. 407.   [2] Ibid. p. 410.
[3] See Blanqui, Histoire de l'Économie Politique, Paris, 1845, tome i. p. 282.
[4] Littérature au xviiie Siècle, tome ii. pp. 391, 392.
[5] Fairy Mythology, 8vo, 1850, p. 456.
[6] Comte, Traité de Législation, tome iii. p. 497.   [7] Ibid. tome iv. p. 118.
[8] Letters from Spain, by Doblado, 1822. p. 8.   [9] Ibid. pp. 11, 12.
[10] Ibid. pp. 32, 44, 323.   [11] Ibid. pp. 142, 148.   [12] Ibid. p. 160.
[13] Ibid. p. 220.   [14] Ibid. p. 252 et seq.   [15] Ibid. p. 268.
[16] Ibid. p. 379.   [17] Ibid. p. 381.

St. Petersburg are more sterile and unproductive than those of any capital in Europe, Madrid excepted.'[1]

After the conquest, Guatemala 'remained in a state of profound tranquillity as a colony of Spain,' and the Indians *all* became Catholics; but early in the nineteenth century 'a few scattering rays of light penetrated to the heart of the American continent; and in 1823 the kingdom of Guatemala, as it was then called, declared its independence of Spain,' and formed a republic with San Salvador, Honduras, Nicaragua, and Costa Rica. But there were quickly formed two parties—'the aristocratic, central, or servile,' and the 'federal, liberal, or democratic;' 'the latter composed of men of intellect and energy, who threw off the yoke of the Romish Church.'[2] The clergy excited the people to murder the liberals as 'heretics;' and the most horrible excesses were committed at the capital, Guatemala.[3] Stephens went there in 1839, and he says,[4] 'From the moment of my arrival I was struck with the devout character of the city of Guatemala,' i.e. churches were filled. He says,[5] 'There was but one paper in Guatemala, and that a weekly, and a mere chronicler of decrees and political movements;' 'the priests always opposed to the liberal party.'[6] He says the brutal and ferocious Carrera had 'a strange dash of fanaticism;'[7] and '[8] 'Carrera's fanaticism bound him to the church party.' Stephens[9] gives an extraordinary account of the religious mania he witnessed at Quezaltenago, in 1840. At Palenque he met a padre who had been severely punished because 'his surplice had been soiled by the saliva of a dying man.'[10] In 1840, Stephens, being becalmed in a Spanish vessel, the sailors ascribed it to the presence of heretics on board.[11] Stephens, who had great opportunities of observing, says,[12] 'But the countries in America subject to the Spanish dominion have felt less sensibly perhaps than any other in the world the onward impulse of the last two centuries.' In Yucatan, 'forty or fifty years after the conquest, the Indians were abandoning their ancient usages and customs, adopting the rites and ceremonies of the Catholic church, and having their children baptised with Spanish

---

[1] Kohl's Russia, p. 138.
[2] Stephens's Central America, vol. i. pp. 194, 195   [3] Ibid. pp. 196, 197
[4] Ibid. p. 210.   [5] Ibid. p. 222.   [6] Ibid. p. 225.
[7] Ibid. p. 234.   [8] Ibid. p. 245.   [9] Ibid. vol. ii. pp. 214, 215.
[10] Ibid. p. 366.   [11] Ibid. pp. 464, 467.   [12] Ibid. vol. iii. p. 190

names.'[1] Stephens[2] gives a disgusting account of a bull-fight he
saw at Merida in 1841. In Yucatan most of the 'padres' have
recognised mistresses.[3] On the great mineral treasures of Spain
see Liebig's Letters on Chemistry, 8vo, 1851, p. 499.

At Salamanca, in 1806, says Bourgoing,[4] 'Quand on sait au
reste que Salamanca outre cette cathédrale a encore vingt-sept
paroisses, vingt-cinq couvents d'hommes, quatorze de filles, on
n'est plus étonné de sa pauvreté et de sa dépopulation.'

Under Philip II., Spain, with about 10,500,000 inhabitants, had
58 archbishops, 684 bishops, 59,500 convents and monasteries,
'312,000 prêtres séculiers, 200,000 ecclésiastiques de moyen ordre,
et plus de 400,000 religieux.'[5]

According to the official returns of the census of 1787, the
ecclesiastics of all descriptions, including 61,617 monks, 32,500
nuns, and 2,705 inquisitors, amounted to 188,625 individuals.[6]
And it appears from the official returns published in the Coreo
Literario of Madrid, in 1833, that notwithstanding the attacks
made upon the ecclesiastical state during the French war and
subsequently, it then comprised 175,574 individuals, of whom
61,727 were monks, and 24,007 nuns. In Laborde's Spain[7] it is
said that, in 1787–88, the population was 10,143,975, of which
125,000 were 'secular and regular clergymen.' This is *exclusive*
of 22,337 'nuns or friars.'[8] Laborde says[9] that in 1788 Spain,
with a population of 11,000,000, had 147,657 spiritual persons, i.e.
one sixty-ninth, while France actually had 460,078, which, with a
population of 25,000,000, makes one fifty-second of the whole.
According to the Government returns of 1787, the population was
10,268,150, of which those devoted to religion were 188,625, and
of them 61,617 were monks in prime of life ;[10] and even in 1833
there were 61,727 monks. Cook[11] estimates the clergy at 130,000.
In 1830, says Inglis,[12] '130,000 friars.' Avila, with 1,000 houses,
had sixteen convents and eight parish churches.[13] In Segovia
less than 2,000 families had 25 churches and 21 convents.[14]

[1] Stephens's Central America, vol. iii. p. 270.
[2] Ibid. pp. 26-38.   [3] Ibid. vol. iv. pp. 114-116.
[4] De l'Espagne, tome i. p. 62.   [5] Sempéré, tome i. p. 266.
[6] Townsend, vol. ii. p. 813.   [7] Vol. iv. pp. 25, 28, 40, 41.
[8] Ibid. p. 28.   [9] Ibid. vol. v. pp. 15, 16.
[10] M'Culloch, vol. ii. p. 711 ; and Townsend, vol. ii. pp. 213, 214.
[11] Spain, vol. i. p. 222.   [12] Spain, i. 295.
[13] Townsend, vol. ii. p. 98.   [14] Ibid. pp. 117, 118.

Income.—M'Culloch [1] says, 'According to an official statement drawn up in 1812, it appears that the clergy were in possession of about one-fourth part of the landed property of the kingdom, exclusive of tithes and other casual sources of income, producing in all a total gross revenue of about eleven millions sterling a year.' In 1749, in Castile,[2] 'L'état séculier possédait 61,196,166 mesures de terre, dont les produits s'élevaient à 817,282,098 réaux ; l'état ecclésiastique possédait 12,209,053 mesures de terre, dont les revenus étaient 161,392,700 réaux.'[3] In 1555, Alva stated 'que dans les seuls royaumes d'Espagne, les ecclésiastiques possèdent pour plus de deux millions de ducats en fonds de terre.'[4] Dunham [5] says that soon after the accession of Ferdinand VI. (which was in 1746) the returns of a commission showed that, comparing 'the relative possessions of the lay and clerical orders, the whole annual income of the former was 1,630,296,143 reals ; of the latter, 340,890,195. The absorption of one-fifth by an order which could contribute nothing to the community, but, on the contrary, derived its support from the other, was a lamentable state of things. In England, where the whole ecclesiastical revenues do not yield three millions, while the returns from land, manufacture, commerce, funded property, &c., certainly return 250 millions, we are sufficiently inclined to join in condemnation of the enormous wealth of the church ; what shall we say to the proportion of not one-eightieth, or one-fifth ?'

In 1403 the Archbishop of Toledo was 'le plus riche de toute la chrétienté.'[6] Wealth of the clergy.[7]

About 90 days are feast days.[8]

Cook estimates the clergy at 130,000.[9] San Felipe, population 12,000, and ten convents. Medina Rio Seco, population 8,000, and three parish churches and six convents. Lerida, population 18,000, and eleven convents. Tarragona possessed eleven convents, though its population was under 8,000. Valladolid, with 20,000 souls, boasted of forty-six convents and fifteen parish churches ; and we are assured that Segovia, in 1826, with a population of 10,000, had twenty-one convents and twenty-six churches.

[1] Geog. Dict. vol. ii. p. 711.
[2] Sempéré, Monarch. Espag. vol. ii. p. 162.
[3] Ibid. vol. i. p. 247.
[4] Fleury, tome xxi. p. 16.
[5] Laborde, vol. iv. pp. 42, 43.
[6] Ibid. p. 102.
[7] Vol. v. p. 282.
[8] Prescott, vol. iii. p. 435.
[9] Spain, vol. i. p. 222.

In Toledo, the population being in 1786 under 25,000, there were
twenty-six parish churches and thirty-eight convents.   In Valencia
there were, in 1786, 100,000 people and forty-four convents ; in
Granada, 80,000, and forty convents ; in Malaga, 42,000, and
twenty-five convents.   In Xeres, in 1776, the population was
40,000, of whom 2,000 were ecclesiastics.   Alicante contained
18,000 inhabitants and eight convents ; Onhuela, 21,000, and
thirteen convents.   In Guadix we find 6,000 souls, with four
churches and seven convents ; in Ecija, 28,000, with six churches,
eight chapels, and twenty convents ; and Seville, possessing a population of barely 100,000, was bounteously provided with 100 convents.   On Madrid, Laborde, tome iii. p. 93, and Barretti,
tome ii. p. 300.   In Cordova 32,000 souls and forty-four convents ; Baza, 15,000, and five convents.

These convents, churches, and chapels were for the most part
richly endowed, it being considered that the clergy having rendered vast services to Spain by keeping the faith pure, they should
be well paid.   The court was drained and bankrupt, the people
were slaves, but the church must be upheld.   The Archbishop of
Toledo, in 1786, had more than 90,000l. ; and, 'besides the archbishop, there are forty canons, fifty prebendaries, and fifty chaplains.   The whole body of ecclesiastics belonging to the cathedral
is 600, well provided for.'

As partly cause and partly consequence of this, the people retained and still retain their ignorance ; for the clergy knew that
on it was based their own power.

In 1690, in Cadiz, there were thirteen convents.[1] In 1679
the Archbishop of Compostella, in Galicia, had ' 70,000 écus de
rente,'[2] i.e. '60,000 ducats.'[3] Southey[4] says there are fewer clergy
in England than anywhere else.   Alison[5] says that, in 1787, there
were '22,480 priests and 47,710 regular clergy belonging to
monasteries or other public religious establishments.' On Toledo,
see Laborde, tome iii. p. 84.   In 1786, Barcelona, with a population of 95,000, contained thirty-seven convents.   'There were no
fewer than 12,000 Franciscan convents before the invasion of

[1] Labat, Voyages en Espagne, vol. i. p. 99.
[2] Ibid. p. 164.   [3] Ibid. p. 314.
[4] Southey, Common Place Book, vol. iii. p. 635.
[5] History of Europe, vol. viii. p. 410.

Spain by Napoleon's troops.'[1] At Alicant, in Valentia, there were, in 1694, 'six convents for men and two nunneries.'[2]

Prescott[3] says, 'The Archbishop of Toledo, by virtue of his office primate of Spain and grand chancellor of Castille, was esteemed after the Pope the highest ecclesiastical dignitary in Christendom. His revenues at the close of the fifteenth century exceeded 80,000 ducats. He could muster a greater number of vassals than any other subject in the kingdom, and held jurisdiction over fifteen large and populous towns, besides a great number of inferior places.'

NATIONAL CHARACTER OF THE IRISH.

In Clarendon Correspondence, 4to, 1828, vol. i. p. 373, there is a very curious account of the wretched state of the Irish in 1686, between Dublin and Kildare. See also p. 536, where the Earl of Clarendon writes that the old English planters were in Ireland the most important. In 1686 kitchen-gardens began to be common in Dublin.[4] The Bible was not translated into Irish 'till nearly the middle of the seventeenth century' by Bishop Bedell.[5]

In 1760 there were German colonies near Limerick.[6] Wesley mentions[7] the 'fickleness' of the Irish. In 1771 he expresses his surprise[8] at the improvements made in Ireland 'within a few years.' In 1747 he says[9] that in Ireland there were no Protestants except those 'transplanted lately from England.' Heber says[10] that, unfortunately for Ireland, 'among the English clergy who were the first heralds of Protestantism to her shores, a large proportion were favourers of the peculiar system of Calvin, a system of all others the least attractive to the feelings of a Roman Catholic.' In 1725, Lady Mary W. Montagu writes,[11] 'Wit has taken a very odd course, and is making the tour of Ireland.' On

---

[1] Quin's Ferdinand, vol. vii. p. 157.
[2] Travels through Spain, by a Gentleman, Lond. 1700, p. 66.
[3] Ferdinand and Isabella, vol. i. p. lxix.
[4] Clarendon Correspondence, vol. i. p. 407.
[5] See Southey's Life of Wesley, vol. ii. p. 149.
[6] See Wesley's Journals, 1851, 8vo, p. 464.   [7] Ibid. p. 557.
[8] Ibid. p. 649.   [9] Ibid. p. 258.
[10] Life of Jeremy Taylor, p. cxx, in Taylor's Works, 8vo, 1828, vol. i.
[11] Works, 8vo, 1803, vol. iii. p. 146.

Ireland, read works of Sir William Temple, vol. iii. pp. 1–28. Laing[1] observes that in Ireland the *division* of land goes on without the sense of ownership. In 1799 it was observed that the Irish were always superior when abroad to when at home.[2] In Limerick extremely early marriages, even at thirteen.[3] The Irish, it is well said, are idle because wages are too low.[4]

ITALIANS, THEIR NATIONAL CHARACTER ETC.

BURNET[5] mentions the indifference of the Romans to religion. In 1655, Sir John Reresby[6] says that the Italians never got drunk. In the time of Montaigne the Italians still preserved their reputation for ability.[7] In 1759, Lady M. W. Montagu writes[8] that a great change had taken place among the Italians, who were no longer jealous of their women, and that this change 'began so lately as the year 1732, when the French overran this part of Italy.' She writes in 1718[9] that the fashion of Cicisbeos, which had begun at Genoa, 'is now received all over Italy.' In 1740 'the Abbé Conti tells me often that these last twenty years have so far changed the customs of Venice that they hardly know it for the same country.'[10] And in 1752 she writes from Brescia,[11] 'The character of a learned woman is far from being ridiculous in this country.' In 1740 many Italians were 'atheists.'[12] In 1741 lotteries had become general.[13] In 1741 Italian husbands were no longer jealous.[14] In 1777, Swinburne writes,[15] 'There is no place where music seems to be in less esteem than Naples, or where so little is heard.' A writer well acquainted with Naples says, 'The Neapolitan peasants are a rough but kind-hearted set

---

[1] Notes of a Traveller, 2nd series, p. 82.
[2] Parl. History, vol. xxxiv. p. 722.
[3] Journal of the Statistical Society, vol. iii. pp. 322, 323; and for their admirable patience under the sufferings of starvation, see p. 326.
[4] Statistical Society, vol. vii. p. 24.
[5] Own Time, vol. iii. p. 163.
[6] Travels, 8vo, 1831, p. 103.
[7] Essais de Montaigne, Paris, 8vo, 1843, livre iii. chap. viii. p. 586.
[8] Works, 8vo, 1803, vol. v. p. 89.   [9] Ibid. vol. iii. p. 51.
[10] Ibid. p. 199.   [11] Ibid. vol. iv. p. 148.
[12] Correspondence between Ladies Pomfret and Hartford, 2nd edit. 8vo, 1806, vol. i. p. 234.
[13] Ibid. vol. ii. p. 330.   [14] Ibid. vol. iii. p. 259.
[15] Courts of Europe, 8vo, 1841, vol. i. p. 164.

of people, who only require to be well used and honestly treated to become good subjects and hard labourers ;[1] but even the better classes are miserably ignorant.[2] An author of the fourteenth century regrets the progress of luxury in Italy.[3]

CHARACTER OF THE SCOTCH.

MR. CHAMBERS says,[4] 'It is quite remarkable, when we consider the high character of the popular melodies, how late and how slow has been the introduction of a taste for the higher class of musical composition in Scotland. The Earl of Kelly, a man of yesterday, was the first Scotsman who ever composed music for an orchestra. This fact seems sufficient. It is to be feared that the beauty of the melodies is itself partly to be blamed for the indifference to higher music.' Wesley made little or no impression in Scotland.[5] In 1768, Wesley[6] writes, 'When I was in Scotland first, even at a nobleman's table, we had only flesh meat of one kind, but no vegetables of any kind ; but now they are as plentiful here as in England. Near Dumfries there are five very large public gardens, which furnish the town with greens and fruit in abundance.' Dr. Cullen[7] says it has long been usual in Scotland for people of all ranks to wash their children with cold water from the time of their birth. As to the supposed freedom of Scotland from crime, an eminent Scotchman suggests[8] that this arises from an indifference about the Scotch people respecting the detection of criminals. In Scotland there are more wills and bequests of property than in England.[9] Laing says,[10] 'It is a peculiar feature in the social condition of our lowest labouring class in Scotland, that none perhaps in Europe of the same class have so few physical and so many intellectual wants and gratifications.' On the management of the poor in Scotland, read Journal of the Statistical Society, vol. iv. pp. 288-319. At p. 314 it is

---

[1] Journal of the Statistical Society, vol. v. p. 177.   [2] Ibid. p. 203.
[3] See Comte, Traité de Législation, tome i. p. 462.
[4] Traditions of Edinburgh, 8vo, 1847, pp. 245, 246.
[5] See Southey's Life of Wesley, 8vo, 1846, vol. ii. pp. 138, 145, 146.
[6] Journals, 8vo, 1851, p. 866.
[7] Works, Edinburgh, 1827, vol. ii. p. 626.
[8] Laing's Sweden, p. 128.
[9] See Porter's Progress of the Nation, vol. iii. p. 130.
[10] Notes of a Traveller, first series, p. 272.

said of the Scotch, 'The great cause of pauperism is the custom of marrying young.' In 1628, Sir Benjamin Rudyard said of Scotland, 'Though that country be not so rich as ours, yet they are richer in their affection to religion.'[1] In August 1650 all Scotchmen were ordered to leave England.[2] Scotland has had a public system of 'religious instruction since 1696;' and 'England is the only civilised European country which in 1857 has no nationally organised plan of education.'[3] See also pp. 185, 186, 202, 203, where it appears that this was due to Fletcher of Saltoun. At p. 202, 'In 1696 a law was passed by the Scottish Parliament, ordaining that there should be, in all time coming, and in every one of the thousand parishes of Scotland, an endowed school for teaching the elementary branches of education. This enactment has been in force ever since;' but 'this system was the work of the 'Presbyterian clergy,' and under it 'there was little healthful exercise of the intellect.'[4] Scotland is a healthy country, and the people cautious and frugal; hence the mortality in 'country districts' is remarkably low, 'less than fifteen annual deaths per 1,000.'[5]

For the ignorance of women in Scotland, see Burton's Life and Correspondence of Hume, vol. i. pp. 196-198, and Hume's Philosophical Works, vol. ii. p. 59. George Combe[7] says of his father, 'His education extended only to reading, writing, mensuration, and book-keeping. He never learned either grammar or the art of spelling. In the middle of the last century even the gentry in Scotland were not in general better educated.' In 1786, Lord Buchan writes from Scotland, 'The middling class of people here are either too poor or too much occupied in professional engagements to prosecute any inquiry that does not promise a pecuniary reward.'[8] There was no middle class, and many gentlemen educated at the universities used to be obliged for a living to keep public-houses.[9] Much greater crime in Scotland than in England.[10] 'The total offences seems to be less than

[1] Parliamentary History, vol. II. p. 387.　　　　[2] Ibid. vol. iii. p. 1353.
[3] Transactions of Assoc. for Social Science, 1858, p. 181.
[4] Ibid. p. 203.　　　　[5] Ibid. p. 203.　　　　[6] Ibid. p. 359.
[7] Life of Dr. Andrew Combe, Edinburgh, 8vo, 1850, p. 6.
[8] Nichols's Literary Illustrations, vol. vi. p. 514.
[9] See Burt's Letters from the North of Scotland, vol. i. p. 66.
[10] Journal of Statist. Soc. vol. vi. p. 236.

in England, but murder and robbery with violence is much more common.[1] The Scotch consume twice as much spirits as the English![2] and the illegitimate births are immense.[3] On the present immigration of Scotch into England, see Statist. Soc. vol. xv. pp. 88, 89 ; Grenville Papers, vol. iv. p. 340 ; curious letters on Scotland in Forster's Life of Goldsmith, vol. i. pp. 446-448 ; Parr's Works, vol. vii. p. 558 ; Correspondence of Sir J. E. Smith, vol. i. p. 66 ; Russell's Memorials of Fox, vol. iii. pp. 344, 361 ; Bedford Correspondence, vol. iii. p. 55 ; Albemarle's Rockingham, vol. ii. p. 300. Finish the chapter by saying that, when the cholera broke out, the Scotch irreligiously, and to the disgrace of an enlightened age, petitioned Palmerston. Then was seen the difference between the two countries. The English minister, a great lover of power, and though an able man by no means a remarkable one, took a large view, and England supported. But we do not find that Scotland protested against the impiety. Conclude by saying that, happily, the Scotch, though superstitious, are not loyal, and are therefore saved from being, like Spain, exposed to both evils.

On the *present* animosity of the Scotch clergy against all innocent amusements, and on the connection between this and the drunkenness of the people (stimulus being the only amusement), see and quote a curious letter in p. 5 of the Times of Friday, September 10, 1858. In the eighteenth century the Presbyterians hated genius, and the wits and the clergy were so incessantly at war that it became an acknowledged function of literature to attack the clergy ; and, as this was unpopular, literary men became a degraded class, as in Smollett and Burns.[4] Dr. Archibald Pitcairne was at the head of these profane wits.[5] In the eighteenth century some of the best Scotchmen 'connected themselves with other countries.'[6] Burton[7] says, 'Burns, with all his strong democratic tendencies, was a sentimental Jacobite.' On the *separation* of intellectual and practical classes, see Burton, vol. ii. pp. 552-555, where it is said that in the time of Knox and in the seventeenth century 'it was felt that the Scotch tongue was becoming provincial, and those who desired to speak beyond a

---

[1] Journal of Statist. Soc. vol. x. pp. 326, 329, 330.
[2] Ibid. vol. x. p. 330; vol. xiii. pp. 359, 360.
[3] Ibid. vol. xiv. p. 68.
[4] Burton's History of Scotland, vol. ii. p. 561.
[5] Ibid. pp. 559, 560.
[6] Ibid. p. 563.
[7] Ibid. p. 418.

mere home audience wrote in Latin.' 'Those who are acquainted with the epistolary correspondence of learned Scotchmen in the seventeenth century will observe how easily they take to Latin, and how uneasy and diffident they feel in the use of English.' At the end of the seventeenth century 'Scotland had not kept an independent literary language of her own, nor was she sufficiently expert in the use of that which had been created in England. Hence the literary barrenness. The men may have existed, but they had not the tools.' 'Not till Burns came forward did the Scottish tongue claim an independent place in modern literature.' But much earlier 'one distinguished man wrote in Scotch, Allan Ramsay.'[1] Thomson shook it off, 'and became the most characteristic painter of English rural life and scenery.'[2] In 1799, Niebuhr writes from Edinburgh, 'Scotland stands far and wide in high repute for piety, and has done so from the commencement of the Reformation. The clergy in general are not good for much; that is allowed by every one who knows the country. The piety of the people is, for the most part, mere eye-service; an accustomed formality without any influence on their mode of thinking and acting.'[3]

In 1696, for, I think, the first time, the Church *consulted* with the 'State' about 'appointing fasts and thanksgivings.'[4] On the history of the Scotch Church in the eighteenth century, see Spalding Miscellany, i. 197 *et seq.* and p. 227 *et seq.* At vol. iii. p. 22, Lord Grange writes in 1733, 'Neither for our own sake nor for our country's ought the divines to be suffered to meddle beyond their own sphere.'

M'Culloch[5] says, 'Scotland, from being about the middle of the last century one of the worst cultivated countries of Europe, is now one of the best. At this moment, indeed, the agriculture of the best farmed counties of Scotland is certainly equal, and is by many deemed superior, to that of Northumberland, Lincoln, and Norfolk, the best farmed counties of England. The proximate cause of this extraordinary progress must be sought for in the rapid growth of manufactures and commerce, and consequently of large towns, and the proportionally great demand for

---

[1] Burton's History of Scotland, vol. ii. p. 554.   [2] Ibid. p. 555.
[3] Life and Letters of Niebuhr, 8vo, 1852, vol. i. pp. 440, 441.
[4] Acts of General Assembly, from 1638, p. 253.
[5] M'Culloch's Geog. Dict. vol. ii. p. 655.

agricultural produce since the peace of Paris in 1763, and especially since the close of the American war. . . . Down to the
close of the American war, the farm buildings in most parts of
Scotland were mean and inadequate in the extreme,' and filthily
dirty. 'The dunghill was universally opposite the door, and so
near it that in wet weather it was no easy matter to get into the
house with dry feet.' (Hence perhaps the custom of going about
without stockings.) 'The change that has taken place in these
respects during the last half-century has been signal and complete.
In none but the least accessible and least improved districts are
any of the old houses now to be met with.' See M'Culloch's
Geog. Dict. vol. ii. p. 655, and see his British Empire, vol. i.
pp. 428, 488. At p. 656, 'In respect of farming implements,
Scotland has very much the advantage over England.' At p. 657,
the arable land in Scotland is inferior to that of England ; but in
the former country rent is *decidedly higher*, owing to the greater
skill and economy of Scotch farmers. 'Rent has increased much
more rapidly in Scotland than in England : so rapid an increase
of rent is probably unmatched in any old settled country, and
indicates an astonishing degree of improvement. . . . We have,
indeed, no hesitation in affirming that no old settled country
of which we have any authentic accounts ever made half the
progress in civilisation and the accumulation of wealth that
Scotland has done since 1763, and especially since 1787.'[1] For
these changes since 1760 M'Culloch refers[2] to Robertson's Rural
Recollections. M'Culloch[3] says of Roxburghshire or Teviotdale,
that 'Dawson, the great improver of Scotch husbandry, occupied
a farm near Kelso, in this country, and in it, soon after 1760, he
set to work the first plough drawn by two horses, driven by the
ploughman, that was ever seen in Scotland. And if he was not
the first to set the example of raising turnips, he was the first
practical farmer by whom they were profitably cultivated on a
large scale.' At p 281, 'In 1727 a small field of eight acres
within a mile of Edinburgh, sown with wheat, was so extraordinary
a phenomenon as to attract the attention of all the neighbourhood.' M'Culloch[4] says of schools, 'While within 1837 and
1845 the number of pupils has increased upwards of a third, the

[1] M'Culloch's Geog. Dict. vol. ii. p. 657.   [2] Ibid. p. 657. note.
[3] British Empire, vol. i. p. 276.
[4] Ibid. vol. ii. p. 376.

proportion learning Gaelic has decreased a half; and the Erse of
the Highlanders is gradually giving way to the English.' On
great rise of rent, see M'Culloch's British Empire, vol. i. pp. 296,
298, and Anderson's Prize Essay on the Highlands, pp. 130-133.
He says [1] that 'the annual value of the agricultural produce' of
England is 141,606,857*l.*, and that of Scotland 27,744,286*l.* See
also good remarks in pp. 565, 567, where it is said that since the
peace of Paris in 1763, and more particularly since the American
war, 'rent down to 1815 increased more rapidly in Scotland than
in England;' but the 'rental of Scotland has not increased since
the peace nearly so fast as that of England.' This probably is
'because the system of farming having been more improved in
1814 in Scotland than in England, the former had less progress
to make.' He says of Scotland,[2] 'The entire rental of the kingdom is not supposed to have exceeded 1,000,000*l.* or 1,200,000*l.*
in 1770. In 1795 it is believed to have rather exceeded
2,000,000*l.*, and between that epoch and 1815 it increased two
millions and a half more.' In 1842 'the gross rental' was
5,586,528*l.*[3]

M'Culloch shows[4] 'that the number of students who attend the
Scotch universities is less now than it was twenty-five or thirty
years ago.' At p. 369 is an account of the successful efforts made
by the Protestant clergy in and after 1560 to establish schools in
every parish. In 1697 was passed 'the Act for the settling of
schools. By this memorable law every parish had to furnish a
commodious school-house and a stipend to a schoolmaster.'
This, says Macaulay [5] 'is the cause of the Scotch everywhere dis-
tancing their competitors.' 'The effect could not be immediately
felt. But before one generation had passed away, it began to be
evident that the common people of Scotland were superior in
intelligence to the common people of any other country in
Europe.' And yet in that very year, and indeed '*in that very
month*,' the Scotch persecuted witches and infidels, and put to
death Thomas Aikenhead, a boy of eighteen, for blasphemy.[6] In
and after 1470 we find the first 'corporations of trades.'[7]

[1] M'Culloch's British Empire, vol. I. p. 573.
[2] Ibid. p. 567.   [3] Ibid. p. 567.   [4] Ibid. vol. II. pp. 365, 366.
[3] History, vol. iv. p. 780.
[6] Ibid. pp. 781-784.
[7] Pinkerton's History, vol. ii. pp. 410, 411.

(What follows was written in September 1859.)

The land was inclosed, drained, and manured. The same spirit of industry, method, and perception of regularity and sequence which was shown in manufactures now for the first time also appeared in agriculture, though, from the greater incapacity of farmers, the improvement was slower ; but its early traces are clearly discernible. Chalmers, in his learned work but detestable style, says,[1] 'The star of agricultural melioration began to twinkle at the Union. In 1723 a Society of *Improvers in the Knowledge of Agriculture* was formed at Edinburgh, consisting of all who were either high, or opulent, or learned, or ingenious in Scotland.'[2] At vol. ii. p. 31 Chalmers says, ' In 1698 was printed at Edinburgh, Husbandry Anatomised, or several Rules for the better Improvement of the Ground. In 1706 was given to the public by Lord Belhaven, Advice to the Farmers of East Lothian how to Improve their Grounds. In 1724 the Society of Improvers at Edinburgh published A Treatise on Fallowing, Raising Grasses, &c.' And other works followed in 1729, 1733, and 1743. In Roxburghshire, ' before 1743, the practice of draining, inclosing, summer fallowing, sowing flax, hemp, rape, turnip and grass seeds, planting cabbages after and potatoes with the plough in fields of great extent, was generally introduced.'[3] At vol. ii. p. 868 Chalmers says, ' The year 1723, when the Society of Improvers was established, may perhaps be deemed the true era. From this period a sort of enterprise may be traced in every shire.' Of Galloway he says,[4] ' One of the first steps towards improvement, which was marked with insurrection, was inclosures in 1724.' At p. 286, ' The real improvement of the soil in this district began effectually in 1740, where shell marl was discovered, or at least attended to, as a useful manure.' At vol. iii. p. 796, ' Potatoes, almost the only green crop, and almost the only instance wherein drill husbandry is practised, were introduced to Paisley and Renfrew about the year 1750 from Kintyre, and were at that time first planted in the field.'

In the county of Aberdeen, in the parish of Kennellar, says Sinclair, ' grass seeds had not been seen in this parish in any considerable quantity before the year 1750 ; till about that

[1] Caledonia, vol. i. p. 673. [2] Ibid. vol. ii. pp. 311, 312, 734.
[3] Ibid. pp. 143, 869. [4] Ibid. vol. iii. p. 285.

time they were not kept for sale by the merchants in Aberdeen, and consequently could not be much known among our farmers.'[1] ' Improvements of land by inclosing, planting, and raising artificial grasses, cabbages, and turnips.'[2] At vol. iv. p. 11, 'It is only about twenty years ago that the farmers began to clean their land by sowing turnips and to sow grass seeds.' 'Turnip for twenty years past has been sown in the fields, and clover and rye-grass have become a constant part of the rotation.'[3] ' Artificial grass, as clover and rye-grass, begins to be more cultivated with more attention.'[4] 'About 1740' the proprietor of Dankeith (in the parish of Symingham, in the county of Ayr) ' was among the first who introduced rye-grass into Ayrshire.'[5] At vol. vi. p. 193, 'The people begin to see the advantage of sowing grass seeds, and adhering to a regular rotation of crops.' In counties of Haddington and Berwick 'improvements in husbandry have within these last thirty years made rapid progress, especially in fallowing their lands, clearing it of stones, regular rotations of crops with turnips and grass.'[6] In county of Aberdeen, 'potatoes, turnips, flax, and artificial grasses were introduced about fifty years ago (i.e. 1743) by the late Lord Strichen.'[7] At vol. vi. p. 439, ' Before the introduction of the turnip husbandry and the raising of clover and rye-grass, the farmers were frequently obliged in the winter season to drive their sheep into the low country and purchase hay for them. . . . The introduction of the use of lime as a manure has been of great benefit to the arable grounds. Very considerable crops of oats, barley, and pease have by means thereof been raised from land which in its natural state was of little or no value. It not only occasions a more plentiful, but also a much earlier crop.' *Finish by saying that all this let loose and made available more hands for manufactures; so that the improvements in agriculture diminish the influence of the agricultural classes.* 'Sir John Dalrymple, grandfather to the present baronet, was the first person who introduced into Scotland the sowing of turnips and the planting of cabbages in the open field.'[8] In the parish of Toryland, in the county of Kirkcudbright, it is said,[9] about 1730 John Dalywell saw 'the advantage of inclosing, subdividing,

[1] Sinclair's Statistical Account of Scotland, vol. iii. p. 497.
[2] Ibid. p. 553.   [3] Ibid. vol. iv. p. 395.   [4] Ibid. p. 444.
[5] Ibid. vol. v. p. 396.   [6] Ibid. vol. vii. p. 403.   [7] Ibid. p. 417.
[8] Ibid. vol. ix. p. 282.   [9] Ibid. p. 314.

and improving land. He was the first who discovered and made use of marl. By this manure he raised upon the poorest land the most luxuriant crops of different kinds of grain, to the astonishment of all the country around. He meliorated the soil, and raised the finest crops of natural and artificial grasses.'

In part of Ayrshire 'within thirty years' (i.e. 1764) 'all the arable and a great part of the pasture lands have been inclosed.'[1] About 1720 the Earl of Haddington 'introduced the sowing of clover and other grass seeds' into the county of Haddington in the synod of Lothian.[2] At Salton, in county of Haddington, 'so early as the beginning of this century, lime was adopted as a manure ; but was gradually discontinued and at length totally laid aside, from an opinion that it was of no advantage in the improvement of land.'[3] 'When grass was introduced as a crop, the old tenants were much offended, and said "it was a shame to see *beast's meat* growing where *men's meat* should grow."'[4] 'Grass seeds, such as rye-grass and clover.'[5] 'In 1740 shell marl was discovered in Galloway, and abundant crops produced by the use of this manure.'[6] In county of Haddington, 'the first example of fallowing ground, in the beginning of the eighteenth century.'[7] In county of Aberdeen, lime was used about 1734.[8] In 1749 'the cultivation of potatoes' in the county of Ross.[9] 'Benefit of inclosures and green crops.'[10] 'Cultivating and planting large tracts of waste moor ground, making substantial regular fences, and liming his lands.'[11] 'The grasses sown are rye-grass, red, white, and yellow clover, and narrow plantain or rib-grass.'[12] 'Little waste ground in the parish. What is wet they are draining ; what is uncultivated and arable they are bringing into tillage ; what is not arable they are planting.'[13] 'About 1750 potatoes began to be planted' at Northmaven in the county of Orkney.[14] In county of Fife, 'in the beginning of the eighteenth century Lord St. Clair began to plant and enclose.'[15] In county of Aberdeen, in 1745, 'began plantations.'[16] 'Kelp was totally unknown in the Highlands until about 1735.'[17] 'Waste land

[1] Sinclair's Statistical Account of Scotland, vol. x. p. 38.

[2] Ibid. p. 171.   [3] Ibid. p. 253.   [4] Ibid. p. 612.
[5] Ibid. p. 630.   [6] Ibid. vol. xi. p. 65.   [7] Ibid. p. 85.
[8] Ibid. p. 412.   [9] Ibid. p. 425.   [10] Ibid. p. 503.
[11] Ibid. p. 565.   [12] Ibid. p. 601.   [13] Ibid. vol. xii. p. 191.
[14] Ibid. p. 354.   [15] Ibid. p. 508.   [16] Ibid. vol. xiii. p. 181.
[17] Ibid. p. 305.

drained, levelled, and inclosed.'[1] In county of Forfar 'some years before 1750 he first of this parish (of Monifieth) began to inclose land, and between 1750 and 1752 to use lime as a manure.'[2] 'When the use of marl or lime as a manure was unknown, and that of dung was the sole one, a certain quantity of it arising from the confinement of the cattle during winter could only be obtained.'[3] 'Tracts of common and barren land brought into culture.'[4] 'Green crops—viz., potatoes, turnips, and sown grass.'[5] At vol. xiv. p. 505, 'Before the Union, Scotland had no foreign market for her sheep and black cattle; and consequently had no motive to raise more of these than her own domestic consumption demanded, which was extremely small, as little butcher's meat was used. But after the Union the price of cattle rose, and landlords perceived that it would be as profitable to cultivate land for rearing and feeding cattle as for raising grain. They therefore enclosed their grounds and united several of their small farms.'[6] Rae[7] says that at the end of the eighteenth century 'the construction of the plough in Scotland was so improved that two horses did the work of six oxen. The diminution of outlay thus produced, giving the farmer from a smaller capital an equal return, encouraged him to apply himself to materials which he would otherwise have left, as his forefathers had done, untouched. He carried off stones from his fields, built fences, dug ditches, formed drains, and constructed roads. Lime was discovered to be a profitable manure. The additional returns which the hard clay thus converted into a black loam yielded were spent in the cultivation of land, before waste. The cultivation of turnips was introduced, and instead of useless fallows, the farmer had a large supply of a nutritive food for his cattle. This reacted on the inhabitants of towns, and their industry was augmented by the increased returns yielded by the country and by the new demands made by it. Rocks were quarried, the metal left the mine, large manufacturing establishments arose, wharfs, docks, canals, and bridges were built, villages were changed into towns, and towns into cities.' In the county of Kirkcudbright 'shell marl was first discovered and used' about

---

[1] Sinclair's Statistical Account of Scotland, vol. xiii. p. 463.
[2] Ibid. p. 491.   [3] Ibid. vol. xiv. p. 9.   [4] Ibid. p. 104.
[5] Ibid. p. 156.   [6] Ibid. p. 505.
[7] New Principles of Political Economy, p. 261.

1732.[1] In Kincardine 'in so little repute was farming before the year 1712, that the proprietor of Brotherston found it necessary to give premiums in order to induce tenants to rent his farms.'[2] In 1722, the first kelp made in the Orkneys.[3] Lime in Aberdeenshire about 1750.[4] 'Enclosing, draining, and clearing the ground of stones.' 'Clear his land of weeds, either by applying proper manure, or by raising potatoes, turnips, and other green crops, or by exerting himself in summer fallowing.'[5] In Perthshire, 'the first marl-pit was partially drained and opened for public sale about the year 1734.'[6] In part of the county of East Lothian there was in 1700 little planting, 'it being supposed no trees could grow because of the sea air and north-east winds ; ' but 'in 1707 the inclosing and planting of the moor were begun.'[7] At Kelsyth, in county of Stirling, potatoes were first cultivated in the fields in 1739. They had previously been 'raised in gardens, and there was a common prejudice that they could be raised nowhere else to advantage.'[8] Even natural manure was difficult to get, though always abundant in the large cities, for 'it was not till after the year 1750 that carts came to be in general use, at least to the west of Edinburgh, though they had been long employed on the cast side ; the conveyance of all materials having been before that period in sacks, hurdles, or creels upon the backs of horses. About 1730 the offals and manure of the streets of Edinburgh sold at 2d. per cart ; at present the cart-load sells sometimes for 1s. 6d. or upwards.'[9] Adam Smith[10] says, 'It is not more than a century ago that in many parts of the Highlands of Scotland butcher's meat was as cheap or cheaper than even bread made of oatmeal. The Union opened the market of England to the Highland cattle. Their ordinary price at present is about three times greater than at the beginning of the century, and the rents of many Highland estates have been tripled or quadrupled at the same time. In almost every part of Great Britain a pound of the best butcher's meat is in present times generally worth more than two pounds of the best white bread, and in plentiful years it is sometimes worth three or four

1 Sinclair's Statistical Account of Scotland, vol. xv. p. 82.   2 Ibid. p. 220.
3 Ibid. p. 395.   4 Ibid. vol. xvi. p. 471.
5 Ibid. vol. xvii. p. 229.   6 Ibid. p. 469.
7 Ibid. p. 576.   8 Ibid. vol. xviii. pp. 282, 283.
9 Ibid. p. 363.   10 Wealth of Nations, p. 626.

pounds.'[1]   At p. 63 Adam Smith says, 'The use of the artificial grasses, turnips, carrots, cabbages, and other expedients to make a greater quantity of land feed a great number of cattle, reduces the superiority of the price of butcher's meat compared to that of bread.' See also p. 93 *a* and *b* on the low price of cattle in Scotland before the Union, owing partly to the ignorance of manure.   At p. 94 *a* Adam Smith says, 'Of all the commercial advantages, however, which Scotland has derived from the union with England, the rise in the price of cattle is perhaps the greatest. It has not only raised the value of all Highland estates, but it has perhaps been the principal cause of the improvement of the low country.'   On application of chemistry to agriculture in 1749, see Thomson's Life of Cullen, vol. i. p. 62.

.   .   .   .

In 1710 'the greatest number of the Episcopalians continue under the direction and influence of the exauctorate Bishop of Edinburgh, who is entirely in the interest of the Pretender, and will allow none of his followers to pray for the queen.'[2]

In 1693, by virtue of an Act of Parliament, no one could sit in the Assembly unless he took an oath to William. This the church furiously resisted as Erastianism, and William at the last moment was forced to give way.[3] This mollified the Assembly, and 'from this time there was a full reconciliation between the established church and King William.'[4] 'The seeds which in their ripening brought on the Church of Scotland the reproach of lukewarmness, if not of a slight degree of scepticism, were thus sown in the reaction against stern fanaticism.'[5] In 1703, Anne being queen, alarm was excited by the inclination of Government to favour episcopacy.[6] In 1706, during negotiations for the Union, Presbyterianism was secured by a clause 'specially excluding the discipline and government of the church from the deliberations of the commission,'[7] and it was understood that 'each nation must keep its own church.'[8] And by the Act of [Union] Presbyterianism was declared 'unalterable, and the only government of the church within the kingdom of Scotland.'[9] This

---

[1] See Cairns, On Butcher's Meat in Australia, in Fraser's Magazine. On Gold.

[2] Ellis's Original Letters, first series, vol. iii. p. 358.

[3] Burton, vol. i. pp. 231–233, 234.   [4] Ibid. p. 236.

[5] Ibid. p. 256.   [6] Ibid. pp. 354, 355.   [7] Ibid. pp. 394, 424.

[8] Ibid. p. 401.   [9] Ibid. pp. 466, 467.

made 'the moderate Presbyterians favour the Union;'[1] but the
zealous Covenant men and Cameronians opposed it as involving
an alliance with the idolatrous church of England.[2] In 1706-7
'the comfortable established clergy were different men from the
theocrats of Dunbar and Bothwell Brig; and the sagacious Car-
stairs, though no longer their moderator and chairman, led them
by his counsel.'[3] In 1710 Government slighted the Assembly
so much as to despise the fasts it ordered.[4] In 1712, even the
'Patronage Act,' so unfavourable to the scriptural classes, failed
to rouse the church;[5] and 'it was clear that the Assembly was
now a very different body from that which twenty years earlier
had offered dangerous defiance to King William.'[6] But in 1711-
12, MacMillan 'organised the first secession from the church of
Scotland.'[7] In 1714 the General Assembly deposed two clergymen for not praying for the king;[8] but the Episcopalians were
the great Jacobites; and 'it was from the rebellion of 1715 that
the British Government was awakened to, and acted on, the fact
that the Hanover settlement had a great friend in the Scottish
Presbyterian establishment, and a bitter enemy in Scottish episcopacy.'[9]

In 1715-17 'the church of Scotland was becoming daily more
important as an ally of the Hanover government, and a friend of
the landed gentry.'[10] But the old Covenanting spirit was active,
and at length caused dissent,[11] and claimed the power of working
miracles.[12] Burton[13] says priestly power decayed *because* the state
protected the church. I think the fact was that the clergy relaxed their zeal for the people because they ceased to need the
people. The first great proof of decay of the church was the rise
of a lay and sceptical philosophy. 'Much as has been said about
the fervent religion of the Scotch, very little of it has ever existed among the upper classes.'[14] Burton says,[15] 'The decrease
of discipline was one of the main grievances which created
dissent in the eighteenth century.' Between 1720 and 1730
disputes broke out between the General Assembly and pres-

[1] Burton, vol. i. pp. 429, 430.
[2] Ibid. pp. 431, 432; compare, respecting the Cameronians, pp. 32-55.
[3] Ibid. p. 445.   [4] Ibid. pp. 39, 40.   [5] Ibid. p. 55.
[6] Ibid. p. 56.   [7] Ibid. p. 69.   [8] Ibid. p. 90.
[9] Ibid. vol. ii. p. 220.   [10] Ibid. p. 282, and see p. 311.
[11] Ibid. pp. 290, 291.   [12] Ibid. p. 295.   [13] Ibid. p. 298.
[14] Ibid. p. 303.   [15] Ibid. p. 301.

byteries.[1] In 1732 everything was aggravated by disputes
respecting patronage, the complaint being that 'no absolute
power of rejection was given to the congregation;' and now
Ebenezer Erskine formed his body of seceders.[2] In Scotland
dissent assumed a very different and more *rampant* character
than in England.[3] The followers of Erskine reproached the
church of Scotland with its toleration, and not rebuking 'great
men' as of old.[4] The seceders, however, always refused to unite
with the Cameronians,[5] and the secession was not completed till
1740.[6] 'Their church was particularly that of the humbler
classes.'[7] They discouraged attacks upon Government,[8] and when
the Jacobites approached Edinburgh in 1745 'there was a
marked zeal among the seceders to help in the defence of the
city.'[9]

After 1715 'the Episcopalian non-jurors were not hard pressed
by the Government;'[10] but 'in the rebellion of 1745 the Scottish
episcopal church came forth again so flagrantly in support of the
Stuarts that severe restraints could no longer be avoided.'[11]
Respecting 'the secession which took place in 1732,' see Bogue
and Bennett's Hist. of Dissenters, vol. iv. p. 57 *et seq.*; Martineau's Hist. of England, vol. ii. pp. 318, 583.

McCulloch[12] says, 'At present, and since 1712, the privilege
of appointing clergymen to parishes has been vested in the Crown
or in private patrons;' but this 'right of patronage has long been
exceedingly unpopular, and its enforcement in spite of public
opinion occasioned the great secession from the church in 1741.
The General Assembly, by the *Veto Act* in 1834, gave the congregations belonging to parishes a right to reject a presentee if he
were not acceptable to them; but it was decided by the House of
Lords in 1839 that the General Assembly had no power to pass
the Veto Act, and that all proceedings under it were null and
void.' This roused the General Assembly, who met in 1843, and
protesting that 'the courts of the church are coerced by the civil
courts,' an immense number seceded and formed the Free Church
of Scotland.[13] All the seceding ministers voluntarily gave up

[1] Burton, vol. ii. pp. 314-316.   [2] Ibid. pp. 321, 322, 324, 325, 327.
[3] Ibid. see some good remarks in pp. 328, 329.   [4] Ibid. pp. 332, 333.
[5] Ibid. p. 336.   [6] Ibid. p. 337.   [7] Ibid. p. 341.
[8] Ibid. p. 344.   [9] Ibid. p. 452.   [10] Ibid. p. 357.
[11] Ibid. p. 358.   [12] Geog. Dict. vol. ii. p. 66a.
[13] See also McCulloch's British Empire, vol. ii. pp. 288-291.

'their homes and incomes,' but the greatest liberality was shown
in Scotland in building and endowing churches. In 1845, 570
new churches had been built, and 'the total numbers within the
pale of the free church may be estimated at 600,000;'[1] so that,
as McCulloch says,[2] 'the established church is no longer the
church of a decided majority of the people, and religious animosities and fanaticism have been widely diffused.'[3] It is said
that the Scotch clergy have become more bigoted since the
French Revolution.[4]

On persecution of Simson, see Index to Wodrow's Analecta,
vol. iii. p. 235; on Webster and Pitcairn, Analecta, vol. iii. p. 307.
In 1711, Wodrow writes,[5] 'At Edinburgh I hear Dr. Pitcairn
and several others do meet very regularly every Lord's day, and
read the Scripture in order to lampoon and ridicule it.'[6] Wodrow
says that this even extended among the clergy; 'young preachers
also began in the eighteenth century to insist on *reason* and
inquiry, and to oppose church judicatories.[7]

After 1688 the moderation of the Crown attempted to dissolve
the alliance between the people and the clergy, but only checked
fanaticism *for a time*, thus showing how weak *political* causes
are in the presence of *social* ones. The two great evils of the
church complained of in and after 1712 by Wodrow were 'toleration' and 'patronages.'[8] However, in 1731 the most powerful
Scotch nobles were determined to retain the patronage.[9]

Pitcairn [10] says there is a curious account of the marriage of
James IV. by John Young, Somerset Herald, in Leland's Col-
lectanea, vol. iv. p. 258. Pitcairn says [11] that in Archæologia,
vol. xxii. p. 7, are 'Observations upon a Household Book of
James V., by Henry Ellis.' The clergy mourned over the declining power of the kirk after 1688.[12] On black-mail, see Mackenzie's Criminal Laws, p. 165. A servant could not be punished
for committing a crime in obedience to his master's orders.[13]

1 Geog. Dict. p. 662.   2 Ibid. p. 663.   3 British Empire, p. 294.
4 Combe's North America, vol. iii. pp. 227-234. 424. 425.
5 Analecta, vol. i. p. 323.
6 Ibid. vol. ii. p. 255; see also on this increase of scepticism, vol. iii. pp. 129,
184; vol. iv. p. 63.   7 Ibid. vol. iii. 147, 155. 167, 169, 178, 239, 240, 412.
8 Ibid. vol. ii. pp. 39, 133.   9 Ibid. iv. p. 246.
10 Criminal Trials, vol. i. p. 118.
11 Ibid. vol. i. p. 209.   12 Howie's Biog. Scoticana, p. 579.
13 Mackenzie's Criminal Laws, p. 170.

Phrenology, being deemed too *dangerous* in England, found its boldest advocates in Scotland—Combe and Spurzheim.[1] On Scotch bigotry *within the last year*, see Fraser's Magazine for December 1859, pp. 680–683. External gaiety being repressed, incest and other crimes more hideous still grew rife, and were safely and securely practised. Insufferable dulness and taciturnity.

. . . . In Scotland, as in France before 1789, the tyranny and impudent pretensions of the clergy made educated men Deists.[2] A clergyman says,[3] ' In this part of the country it is only fashionable for the lower classes of the people to attend the church. The higher orders are above the vulgar prejudices of believing it necessary to worship the God of their fathers.'[4] How could educated men listen to their stuff? In 1696 clergy losing ground over educated classes.[5] Topham [6] says that in Scotland ' Deism is the ruling principle.' The middle class of tradespeople were ignorant and poor.

Stephen [7] says, ' The unchaste vices have been more universally practised in Scotland in all periods of her history than in any other Christian country in the world.' In the middle of the eighteenth century the Scotch clamoured for penal laws against the Catholics.[8] On hostility between theology and physical knowledge, see Wodrow's Correspondence, vol. i. pp. 95, 96 ; vol. ii. p. 361.

In 1709 it began to be noticed that the clergy were less respected.

Sir William Hamilton says that nowhere has there been so little classical learning as in Scotland.[9]

In 1706, Blair of Dundee held some remarkably sound views on the nervous system.[10]

[1] Elliotson's Physiology, p. 403.
[2] Life of Adam Smith, in Ruse's Biog. Dict. and Chalmers's Biog. Dict.
[3] Sinclair's Statist. Account, vol. x. p. 605.
[4] To the same effect see vol. xi. p. 165.
[5] Cockburn's Jacobins, pp. 348, 377.
[6] Letters from Edinburgh, 1776, p. 238.
[7] History of the Church of Scotland, vol. i. p. 41.
[8] See Russell's History of the Church in Scotland, vol. i. p. 286 ; also Stevenson's Hist. of the Church of Scotland, p. 55 ; see also Burton's Hist. of Scotland, vol. i. p. 201.
[9] Discussions in Philosophy, pp. 329, 338, 379, and see p. 341.
[10] Wagner's Physiology, p. 528.

Pitcairn tried to apply to medicine 'the rigid rules of mathematical demonstration.' [1]

. . . . From a general point of view we might expect that the works of the great northern thinkers would have exercised a favourable influence over the literature of England, written as they were in our own language, and frequently published at our own capital. But unfortunately the hatred between the English and the Scotch at this period was as great as it had been before they were finally united into one empire. The old feelings of animosity, so far from being assuaged by the Act of Union, seemed to be increased by the mutual recriminations with which the passing of that Act was accompanied. The English taunted the Scotch with their poverty ; the Scotch reproached the English with their ignorance. In 1682 the celebrated Sir Thomas Browne writes to his son in disapproval of a charter which had just been granted to the physicians of Edinburgh. His great fear was that this concession would induce too many Scotchmen to leave their own country. For, he says, 'if they sett up a colledge and breed many physitians, wee shall bee sure to have a great part of them in England.' The University of Oxford was so vexed with the union with Scotland that it refused to congratulate Anne on its completion.

In London those satires were greedily read which were directed against the inhabitants of Scotland by Johnson, Wilkes, Churchill, Junius, &c. ; and during the administration of Lord Bute, and indeed long after it, every tale against him was willingly circulated because he was a native of that abhorred country. In Edinburgh the great writers who adorned that capital could not conceal the contempt with which they regarded their southern neighbours. They derided the greatest efforts of our genius. Indeed, nothing but national prejudice could make a man of such fine taste as Adam Smith depreciate the greatest poet the world has ever seen. Hume said [2] that the Epigoniad of Wilkes was equal to Paradise Lost, and that Home's play of Douglas was superior to Macbeth. Lord Monboddo is perhaps the last man of any reputation who has attacked the Newtonian philosophy. His attacks, which were made in 1779, I only know from the notice in Whewell's Philosophy of the Inductive Sciences. [3] Wilkes was

[1] Thomson's History of Chemistry, vol. I. p. 208.
[2] See remarks on Shakespeare in History of England.
[3] Vol. I. pp. 266, 267.

burnt in effigy at Edinburgh. Lord Monboddo, who as a scholar possessed considerable reputation, said that the Douglas of Home was not only superior to any of Shakespeare's plays, but was better than anything Shakespeare could have possibly written.

Hume, whose open disposition prevented him from concealing his opinions, says in one of his letters from Paris, 'It is probable that this place will be long my home. I feel little inclination to the factious barbarians of London.' On another occasion he writes to Blair respecting England, 'The little company there that is worth conversing with are cold and unsociable; or are warmed only by faction and cabal; so that a man who plays no part in public affairs becomes altogether insignificant, and if he is not rich he becomes even contemptible. Hence that nation are relapsing fast into the deepest stupidity and ignorance.' When Gibbon's Roman Empire was published the astonishment of Hume was unbounded. In 1776 he writes to the great historian, 'I own that if I had not previously had the happiness of your personal acquaintance, such a performance from an Englishman in our age would have given me some surprise. You may smile at this sentiment; but as it seems to me that your countrymen for almost a whole generation have given themselves up to barbarous and absurd faction, and have totally neglected all polite letters, I no longer expected any valuable production ever to come from them.' Indeed, violent as were the animosities between the French and English, it seemed to be understood that every patriotic Englishman ought to hate a Scotchman even more than he hated a Frenchman. After the quarrel between Hume and Rousseau, Adam Smith wrote to Hume to dissuade him from publishing an account of it; for, said he, your opponent 'will have a great party, the Church, the Whigs, the Jacobites, the whole wise English nation, who will love to mortify a Scotchman, and applaud a man that has refused a pension from the king.'

Such sentiments as these were fully reciprocated by the English. But as our countrymen had always inflicted great injuries upon Scotland, it was natural that they should hate the Scotch even more than they were hated by them. Even in the slightest things this prejudice was allowed to appear. Horace Walpole was almost the only Englishman of any reputation who ventured to utter a word in their favour. But for doing this he

was severely attacked in the North Briton and in the Public
Ledger, the two most influential periodicals which were then
published in London.

On one occasion Home offered for performance a tragedy
which he had just written ; but it was considered so hazardous to
act in London a play written by a Scotchman, that Garrick refused
to accept it unless the author would conceal his name, and would
allow to have it attributed to an Englishman. To this Home
agreed, and during twelve nights the tragedy was received wi h
universal applause. But on the thirteenth night, the secret
having by some means transpired, the piece was not only condemned, but Garrick was threatened with having his house burnt
down for having dared to bring on the English stage the production of a Scottish author.

A few years before this occurred, Macklyn wrote a farce called
Love à la Mode, the merits of which are anything but remarkable.
But as it contained a character in which the Scotch were turned
into ridicule, it met with immense success, and not all the influence of Lord Bute could prevent it from being constantly acted.
Nor was it merely by the mob of a theatre that such feelings were
displayed. Rawlinson, who early in the eighteenth century was
an historian and antiquary of some repute, had bequeathed a
considerable property to the Society of Antiquaries. But by a
subsequent clause he revoked the whole of the gift, and one of
the reasons which he assigned for doing so was that a Scotchman
had been elected secretary to the society. Indeed, the national
prejudices were so strong that they more than once threatened to
embroil the two countries. In 1713 the disputes respecting the
extension to Scotland of the malt tax caused such mutual recriminations that a motion made in the House of Lords to bring
in a bill for repealing the Union was only lost by a majority of four
votes. In 1736, a tumult having arisen at Edinburgh, Captain
Porteous, who commanded the town guard, ordered his men to
fire on the mob. For this wanton outrage, which caused the death
of several persons, he was brought to trial, found guilty, and condemned to die. The English Government, instead of allowing the
sentence to be carried into execution, granted a reprieve ; but the
Scotch, who were determined that the murderer of their country-
men should not escape, rose in arms, seized the gates of the city,
burst open the prison in which Porteous was confined, dragged

him to the Grassmarket where criminals usually suffered, and there hanged him deliberately, and with all the formalities of a legal execution. In our own time such an act, if it could possibly occur, would be only considered as an infraction of the law, would be punished, and would soon be forgotten. But such were the feelings that a century ago existed between England and Scotland, that so slight a matter was found sufficient to threaten the most dangerous results. The Scotch took it up as a national question, and unanimously declared that they would protect the murderers of Porteous. The English were as determined to revenge his death; and the ministers of the Crown openly stated that, if resistance were offered, the punishment should extend to the whole country; and the queen, who was then acting as regent, threatened so to desolate Scotland that it should be turned into a hunting-field. Parliament, which was then sitting, displayed the greatest warmth; and it was actually moved in the peers that the lord-justice of Scotland should be brought as a criminal before the bar of the house. This monstrous proposition, which, if persisted in, would probably have caused a civil war, was by the influence of more moderate men with difficulty rejected; but, to the great offence of the Scotch, their judges were eventually compelled to come to London, and to appear as witnesses before what they considered a hostile and almost a foreign jurisdiction. At the head of English affairs there was at this time Sir Robert Walpole, a man of great abilities and of still greater moderation. He was one of the ministers of the Crown during three successive reigns, and was its chief adviser for more than twenty years. But the Scotch looked upon him as their declared enemy, and hated him with a bitterness which still further exasperated the national animosities. He indeed was driven from office in 1742; but three years afterwards broke out that great northern rebellion which he is said to have predicted, and in which the Scotch, as is well known, penetrated to the centre of England. They were afterwards entirely defeated; but the infamous cruelties of their English conquerors left a deep impression on their minds, and the names of Cumberland and Culloden long remained the by-words of national hatred. In the Highlands these feelings have lingered even to our own time; and although in the Lowlands they gradually died away, still they left a soreness which frequently embarrassed the English Government.

Towards the end of the reign of George II. the lord chancellor, in his place in Parliament, complained that the Scotch seemed absolutely determined not to pay the imperial taxes, and he submitted to the house whether some measure could not be adopted to compel them to do so. For his own part, he said that he was not acquainted with any means by which so desirable a result could be effected.

After the death of George II. the same prejudices long predominated. Sir Nathaniel Wraxall, who, although a weak man, was an attentive observer of passing events, has made the remark that the unpopularity of George III. during the first twenty years of his reign was chiefly caused by the indignation which the English felt at seeing a Scotchman placed at the head of affairs. This, if true, is a remarkable proof how inveterate the hostility must have been ; for the king dismissed Lord Bute only three years after his accession, and never ventured again to place a Scotchman at the head of his Government. Even Lord Chatham was violently attacked because he entrusted a Scotchman with the Privy Seal of Scotland. Indeed, so late as 1804, when Barrow was made one of the secretaries of the Admiralty, Lord Melville expressed his delight at finding that he was an Englishman ; for, said he, ' Mr. Pitt and myself have been so much taunted for giving away all the good things to Scotchmen, that I am very glad on the present occasion to have selected an Englishman.' And in 1805, so lenient a judge as Wilberforce, after highly praising Dundas, mentions it as a remarkable fact that, instead of sending to India as governor-general one of his own countrymen, he actually ' appointed the fittest person he could find, Sir John Shore.' And into such matters did this spirit descend, that even early in the present century the Scotch farmers rejected ' as an old English practise ' that plan of folding sheep on the land which they now generally adopt.[1]

The intercourse between the two nations, it may easily be supposed, was neither cordial nor frequent. The Scotch, indeed, flocked to London, because it was a wealthy city, and because they hoped to participate in the riches of its inhabitants, whom they considered to be more remarkable for their money than for their wit. But the Londoners themselves did not care to return the attention. Pennant, the well-known antiquary, visited the

[1] Laing's Denmark, p. 134.

southern part of Scotland in the middle of the eighteenth century. He was very proud of having accomplished what he considered so hazardous a feat ; and in his minute account of Edinburgh he tells us that he was the first Englishman whom motives of curiosity had ever carried to that city. Indeed, several years later, when the facilities of travelling were so much greater, there were few Englishmen who ventured to imitate so bold an example ; and Captain Topham, who, in 1774, passed some months in Edinburgh, says that the Scotch were greatly surprised when they learnt that this Englishman intended to spend the winter in their capital.

Although the Scotch universities were in the middle of the eighteenth century infinitely superior to those of England, and were possessed of men whom European reputation placed far above the professors at Oxford and Cambridge, there was hardly to be found a single Englishman who would send his sons to be educated in so hated a country.

The existence of such feelings as these tended to prevent that fusion of the two literatures by which both countries would have been greatly benefited. But this was not all. In addition to these national prejudices, the almost exclusively inductive, and, if I may so say, mechanical character of the English still further indisposed them to welcome the large and philosophical investigations of their northern neighbours. The consequence was that the few productions of Scotch literature which in our own country met with much attention were of a less elevated character than those which were treated with comparative contempt. The profound investigations of Adam Smith, which he published at an early period of his life, excited in England but little curiosity, although they were set off with every charm that language and fancy can afford. Even the masterpiece of his intellect, the Wealth of Nations, was not only neglected, but was treated with contempt by such men as Johnson and Warburton.

In the same way the History of England, by Hume, for some time scarcely found a single purchaser ; and yet the History of Scotland, by Robertson, which is infinitely its inferior, was received with transports of applause, and was considered superior not only in learning but also in style. Indeed, the long prevalence of mere practical pursuits had perverted our national taste to an almost incredible extent. One of the most popular books of the age was Smollett's History of England, a work which at the present day scarcely any one would begin to read, and which, I suppose, no one who made the attempt would ever live to finish. The discouragement thus given to the greatest efforts of Scotch genius must in the ordinary course of affairs have produced injurious results, and have tended to degrade the national literature.

The Heritable Jurisdiction Bill, in 1747, was violently opposed by the Scotch. Three years after the battle of Culloden the Scotch pride was still further wounded by a law forbidding the Highlanders to wear their national garb. Ridicule was thrown on the speech of George III. that he was 'born a Briton.' During the Wilkes riots in 1768 the inhabitants of London were particularly indignant that a 'Scotch regiment' should be called to quell the disturbances.

Wedderburn, afterwards celebrated as Lord Loughborough, was the first educated man in Scotland who ventured to practise at the English bar ; and this was considered so hazardous an enterprise that, nearly twenty years after his first arrival in London, we find Lord Chatham expressing a fear that his country would prevent his promotion. And when Lord Bute first received his appointment, the Spanish ambassador, then residing in London, foretold the speedy demolition of his administration ' on account of the circumstance of his country.'

Indeed, to say *a man acted like a Scotchman* became a proverbial expression for a base action.

   .   .   .   .   .   .

' Learning and philosophy ' made ' atheists,' said in her ' last words ' Lady Coltness, the idol of the faithful.[1] In 1648, Baillie, the most learned and one of the most moderate of the clergy, wonders what any one can see in Descartes, ' a very ignorant atheist.' The Rev. J. Scrimzeor 'often wished that most part of books were burned, except the Bible and some short notes thereon.'[2] Wodrow calls Locke one of the main props of the Socinians and Deists. For men to be conscious of their own abilities was blasphemous. An eclipse sent to prevent men knowing too much. If a youth got on too fast in his studies the Lord sent him a fever. Tutors at the universities should not read classics, for the fathers were better; and ' philosophy is more prejudicial to piety than handiwork or manufacture.' An eclipse of the sun was sent sometimes to prevent men studying astronomy. From the passing of the Perth Articles (which caused a deluge) there were twenty years of barrenness, when the ground refused to yield until the Covenant restored its fertility. We laugh at this, but look at our queen and ministers offering up prayers for cholera and for war ! ! ! In 1621 there was an inundation at Perth 'on account of the five Episcopalian articles passed there by the General Assembly three years before.' 'There is nothing by which a man will be more readily puffed up than the inward gifts of the mind, if they be not sanctified, such as wit, knowledge, eloquence, memory,' &c.[1] History was only studied with a theological view, to know all about Antichrist. The clergy wished to stop people from reading *unknown* books. Abernethy[2] says that for the study and solace of the heart, 'in old times philosophers did supply this place ; but now amongst Christians the fittest man is a true theologue.' The clergy hated statistics ; and Abernethy[3] says Satan 'caused David to number his people.' The grass refused to grow not on account of soil or chemical laws, but because incest was committed there. They insisted on humility, for that secured their own power ; but they had none of it themselves. All geological speculations as to the origin of the world before man existed were criminal.[4] Nothing known in arts and trades since Jubal and Tubalcain.[5] Until man fell he had great reason ; but now nothing is left save 'some little spunk or sparkle.'[6] 'We have some remnant of reason in us that hath some petty and poor ability for matters of little moment, as the things of this life.' 'Believing ignorance is much better than rash and presumptuous knowledge.' To be even *silently* conscious of superior abilities is 'a loud blasphemy in God's ear.'[7] 'Whatever wanton and lascivious reason can object against absolute reprobation.'[8] On the winnowing machine see Burton's History, vol. ii. p. 396 ; Penny's Traditions of Perth, p. 147. It is very foolish for men to try 'to be accounted wise and learned,' 'seeing that our days are so few, and that we are of so short continuance in the world.'[9] Cockburn says [10] men are foolishly occupied 'in curious inquiries about the motions and transactions of some remote prince which little concerns them.' The

[1] Fergusson on the Epistles, p. 354.
[2] Ibid. p. 190.
[3] Cowper's Heaven opened, p. 301.
[7] Ibid. vol. i. pp. 30, 143 : vol. ii. p. 427.
[8] Rutherford's Christ Dying, p. 416.
[9] Cockburn's Jacob's Vow, p. 131.

[5] Physicke for the Soul, p. 16.
[4] Binning, vol. i. p. 194.
[6] Binning, vol. i. p. 29.

[10] Ibid. p. 305.

Scotch clergy bemoaned the 'general ignorance;' and to relieve it, they recommended the most trumpery theological books.[1]

CHARACTER ETC. OF THE RUSSIANS.

AFTER forty the lower class of the Russians look old. This is caused by the vapour bath.[2] The Russians are the greatest dissimulators and negotiators in Europe.[3] The Russians show their improvidence by the rapidity and want of durability with which they build their palaces.[4] Kohl says[5] of St. Petersburg, 'There is no other European capital where the inhabitants are content to make use of goods of such inferior quality, or where, consequently, they have such frequent occasion to buy new articles, or to have the old ones repaired. . . . . A Russian seldom buys anything till just he wants to use it ; and, as he cannot then wait, he must have it ready to his hand.'

The 'fickleness' of the Russians in their purchases is extraordinary.[6] Kohl says,[7] 'The Russian is by nature a light-hearted creature, and by no means given to reflection.' Even the population of St. Petersburg is constantly changing, so fluctuating and uncertain are Russian movements.[8] A great passion for reading has lately sprung up among the lower orders ;[9] and Russian authors are highly paid.[10] Extraordinary superstition of the Russians.[11] But the Greek church is, however, tolerant.[12] Kohl[13] says, 'Nearly all the charitable institutions in Russia are presided over by Russians.' The merchants are German or English ; for 'no Russian either in St. Petersburg or any other part of the empire engages in maritime trade ; he has neither the knowledge nor the connection necessary thereto, still less the true commercial spirit of enterprise.'[14] Kohl[15] says, 'The Russians know so little of those prejudices against illegitimate births which have

---

[1] See A Cloud of Witnesses, p. 56.
[2] See Mayo's Philosophy of Living, 2nd edit. 8vo. 1836. p. 176.
[3] Alison's History of Europe, vol. vi. p. 594 ; xi. 119 ; xiii. 220.
[4] See Kohl's Russia, 8vo, 1844, p. 9.   [5] Ibid. p. 49.
[6] Ibid. p. 227.   [7] Ibid. p. 51.
[8] Ibid. pp. 51, 52.
[9] Ibid. pp. 88, 223, 393.   [10] Ibid. pp. 132, 133.
[11] Ibid. pp. 53, 56, 61, 131, 132, 136, 160, 229, 250 et seq. 262, 269, 354.
[12] Ibid. pp. 267, 396, 397.   [13] Ibid. p. 111.   [14] Ibid. pp. 117, 118.
[15] Ibid. p. 113.

descended to us from the middle ages, that there is scarcely a
word in their language to express the idea.' Kohl[1] mentions
the 'extraordinary uniformity of dialect through the empire.'
The Russians *like* being commanded.[2] Eccentric persons are
found most commonly in England ; hardly ever in Russia.[3]
Extraordinary loyalty.[4] The ablest governors, merchants, &c.,
in Russia are from the Baltic provinces.[5] Walk is between Riga and Dorpat ; and 'in Walk the Lettish dialect is
still spoken, but just beyond it begins the territory of the
Esthonians. The Lettes and Esthonians are two very different
races, and they hate one another with all the bitter animosity of
contiguous nations.'[6] Kohl says,[7] 'The peninsula of Courland
and the country round the mouth of the Dwina, and that bordering on the Aa, are the districts inhabited by the Lettes. A line
drawn through Livonia from the south point of the Peipus lake,
through Verro and Walk to the Gulf of Riga, would be about the
boundary between the two races. The Esthonians occupy the
whole of Esthonia, the Œsel Archipelago, and the northern parts
of Livonia.' And,[8] 'The country bordering on the Niemen, and
on its various tributary rivers, is inhabited by Lithuanians. The
country around the mouth of the Dwina, the whole of Courland,
and the southern half of Livonia, is inhabited by Lettes.' This
was in 1840. At p. 397 Kohl has a striking passage on the
eminently religious character of the Russians.

CHARACTER ETC. OF THE GERMANS.

IN 1669 it was supposed that, on account of taking opium, 'the
Germans are, of all nations, most continent and least addicted to
women.'[9] In Germany the fine arts, music, and painting are the
only points of contact between the higher and lower intellects ;
hence they flourish, as they did in Greece. Kohl[10] says, 'The
Germans are the most loyal people in the world. They cling to
the present ; and, whatever may be the origin or nature of the
governing authority for the time being, they always show them-

[1] Kohl's Russia, p. 283.
[2] Ibid. p. 279.
[3] Ibid. pp. 286, 287.
[4] Ibid. pp. 289, 290.
[5] Ibid. pp. 344, 345.
[6] Ibid. p. 342.
[7] Ibid. p. 366.
[8] Ibid. p. 372.
[9] Ray's Correspondence, by Dr. Lankester, 8vo, 1848, p. 52.
[10] Russia, 8vo, 1844, pp. 395, 396.

selves faithful to it.' Neander[1] says that, about the thirteenth
century, the German bishops became *political* and too secular.
Bancroft[2] says that, in 1756, the question was whether Prussia, 'a
Protestant revolutionary kingdom,' should be allowed to exist in the
Europe of the middle ages; and that it was to settle this question
that 'France and Austria put aside their ancient rivalry, and
joined to defend the Europe of the middle ages,' with its traditions
and ecclesiastical influence, against Frederick the Great. In 1758,
Washington took great interest in the fortunes of Frederick.[3] In
1762 the reactionary character of our George III. showed itself in
attempting to weaken Prussia.[4] At vol. ii. p. 1, Bancroft says, 'The
successes of the Seven Years' War was the triumph of Protestantism.'

AMERICA.

THE fault of the Americans is the opposite of the French. With
them liberty has outstripped scepticism. Read the long account
of America in vol. xiii. of Alison's History of Europe; and for
proof of the great influence of the clergy see p. 317. Hence we
find that their only original works have been on jurisprudence.[5]
On the intellectual independence natural to the democratic mind
see Wahrheit und Dichtung in Göthe's Werke, Band ii. Theil ii.
p. 192.

In 1775 Congress undertook an expedition against Canada,
and Colonel Arnold summoned De la Place to surrender 'in the
name of the great Jehovah and the Continental Congress.'[6] In
1774, General Lee writes that, latterly, even the manners and
appearance of New Englanders had been changed, their slouching
appearance having become erect and firm.[7] In 1778 it was said
that not one in one hundred of the American merchants knew
anything of French.[8] In 1838 the Americans were greatly impressed with the importance of spreading education.[9] See[10] a
classification of the works published on the United States in 1835.

[1] History of the Church, vol. vii. p. 296.
[2] History of American Revolution, vol. i. pp. 315-317.
[3] Bancroft, vol. i. p. 359.   [4] Ibid. p. 495.
[5] Alison's History of Europe, vol. xiii. p. 345.
[6] Adolphus's History of George III. vol. ii. p. 233.
[7] Burke's Correspondence, vol. i. p. 518.
[8] See Parliamentary History, vol. xix. p. 940.
[9] Journal of the Statistical Society, vol. i. p. 383.   [10] Ibid. vol. iii. p. 382.

The Americans have more newspapers than all Europe put together, but the style is wretched.[1] The United States are unhealthy ; and, little attention being paid to improving their towns, the Americans are short-lived ; hence the prevalence of *young* men with violent passions, &c.[2]

The Americans have done much for establishing public libraries.[3] On the extraordinary increase of the United States between 1840 and 1850 see Statistical Society, vol. xv. pp. 65, 66. The white population is increasing more rapidly than the black.[4] The Americans, in 1851, had 10,289 miles of railroad, while in Great Britain and Scotland there were only 7,000.[5] Comte[6] well says that the reason why slave States, as Virginia, have produced great politicians, is because ability, being never turned into manufactures, trade, &c., has no vent but in politics. Ségur, who was in America in 1782, speaks very highly of the elegance of American women.[7]

Bancroft[8] says that, in 1754, Washington, by ' repelling France from the basin of the Ohio,' began the revolution by beginning the movement which freed America from France and the ' institutions of the middle ages.' [9] On the *proportions* of American population in 1754, see Bancroft, vol. i. pp. 144, 145. In 1754 the English clergy sent out to America to hold livings were ' too often ill-educated and licentious men.' [10] The English forbade the Americans to print a Bible ; and ' no trace of an American edition of the Bible, surreptitious or otherwise, previous to the Declaration of Independence, has been found.' [11] In 1765, John Adam says, ' A native American who cannot read and write is as rare an appearance as a comet or an earthquake.' [12] Bancroft [13] says, ' The exceedingly valuable history of the American Revolution, by Gordon.' An able American writer, who is unfavourable to slavery, says that a belief in the inferiority of *race* is ' an opinion which the most philosophical of the citizens of the South con-

[1] Journal of the Statistical Society, vol. iv. pp. 120, 121.
[2] Ibid. vol. vii. pp. 26, 27 ; but compare p. 48.   [3] Ibid. vol. xi. p. 274.
[4] Ibid. p. 67.   [5] Ibid. p. 111.
[6] Traité de Législation, vol. iv. p. 243.
[7] See Mémoires de Ségur, tome i. p. 387.
[8] History of the American Revolution, 8vo, 1852, vol. i. p. 133.
[9] Ibid. pp. 524, 525.
[10] Vol. i. p. 151 ; see also p. 156.   [11] Ibid. vol. ii. pp. 302, 303.
[12] Bancroft, vol. ii. p. 368.   [13] Ibid. vol. i. p. 430.

scientiously maintain.'[1] The greatest astonishment was felt at an African girl being able to read in eighteen months.[2] Lord Brougham[3] says, 'The never-ceasing state of party agitation, there being no office from the highest to the lowest, from president to penny postman, which may not be changed at each renewal of that high functionary's term.' This must *educate* the people in the art of organisation, &c. Lord Shaftesbury says, 'All the powers of government are consigned to the younger persons;'[4] and he mentions a letter from a friend of his, who writes, 'I have travelled over a considerable part of the Union, and I do not hesitate to say that during the last two months I have not met with a single old man who was in a hale condition.'[5] On the energy shown by the Americans in codifying their laws, see pp. 195-197. On persecution of Quakers in America about 1660, see Fox's Journal, vol. i. pp. 498, 499. This was *hearsay*; and Fox, who was in America in 1672, and gives an account of his visit (which ends at vol. ii. p. 167), does not mention any persecution.

GENERAL REMARKS ON NATIONAL CHARACTER.

HARE[6] observes that Thirlwall and Schlegel notice the importance of the great extent of coast possessed by Greece, as compared with the entire surface of the country. Hare adds[7] that the same advantage is possessed by Italy and England. Malcolm says of Kurdistan,[8] 'I travelled through the entire country in 1810, and should judge from what I have read and seen of its inhabitants that they have remained unchanged in their appearance and character for more than twenty centuries.' See some ingenious remarks in Laing's Denmark, pp. 204-207. He says the Irish, French, and Scotch have a national character very strongly marked in each individual, but have 'very little individuality of character among them.' The English, Americans, Danes, Norwegians, and Dutch have both national character and individuality; while the Austrians, Prussians, &c., have neither individuality nor nationality.

[1] Tucker's Life of Jefferson, vol. i. p. 122.
[2] Abdy's United States, vol. i. p. 166; and see vol. iii. p. 237.
[3] Transactions of Social Science Association, 1859. p. 41.
[4] Ibid. p. 90.
[5] Guesses at Truth, first series, p. 100.
[6] History of Persia, 8vo, 1829, vol. i. p. 82.
[7] Ibid. p. 101.

Laing says 'nationality of character' depends on the same people being knit together by common interests, &c., while 'individuality of character' proceeds 'from a higher source,' and depends on men being *let alone* by government. Therefore in the French and German drama we find no individuality, but always the type of some class, and the same thing in painting.[1] And in his second series of Notes[2] he says that from Tacitus to the present time the Germans have had no nationality, for 'the social cement which binds populations together into one nation is their mutual material interests. . . . . What common interest, for instance, have the people of Bavaria, on the Danube, or on the shores of the Lake of Constance, with the people on the Vistula, or on the shores of the Baltic? They have nothing to exchange with each other.'[3] See also Notes of a Traveller, first series, pp. 477–481, where Laing says this is the reason the Italians have no nationality; their soil and climate are too good.

INCREASE OF HUMANITY AND VIRTUE.

BECAUSE Sir Matthew Hale would not receive a present of game from a gentleman whose cause he had to try, his refusal 'was somewhat censured as an affectation of an unreasonable strictness.'[4] And Burnet[5] mentions it as a 'remarkable instance of his justness and goodness,' that when he had received bad money he abstained from passing it to other people.

The real difference between this and any other age is the education of the people. This is the only guarantee against a return to barbarism. Not only is the light of civilisation more brilliant than ever, but its basis is larger and more secure.

Evelyn, one of the most humane men of his time, went in 1650 to see a child cut for the stone;[6] and, a few months later, he, actuated by mere curiosity, went to see the most horrid tortures inflicted on a criminal.[7]

In 1650 the Marquis of Montrose was executed, and the Marchioness of Argyle was present with her family to see him die; but, before the last moment, 'the marchioness expressed her

[1] See also Laing's Notes of a Traveller, first series, p. 368.
[2] 8vo, 1850, pp. 518–522.   [3] Ibid. pp. 520–521.
[4] Life of Hale in Burnet's Lives, edit. Jebb, 8vo, p. 48.   [5] Ibid. p. 58.
[6] Diary, 8vo, 1827, vol. ii. p. 17.   [7] Ibid. pp. 29, 32.

spite at the fallen hero by spitting at him.'[1] Montaigne[2] says that he never opens letters addressed to other people. De Foe says, 'When you would speak well of a man you say he is an honest, drunken fellow, as if his drunkenness was a recommendation of his honesty.'[3] The Duke de la Rochefoucault, 'un des plus nobles caractères d'un beau siècle,' wished to assassinate Retz.[4] Charles Comte[5] observes that the progress of morals has been aided by *analytic* studies.[6] The breed of cultivated plants and of domestic animals has been improved by 'constant elimination of imperfect types, and the selection of the finest individuals.' This applies in some degree to man : for neither idiots, cretins, nor great criminals often marry ; but the beautiful, the healthy, and the good are attractive and *do*. Hence, perhaps, the race is improving.[7] Even to the beginning of the eighteenth century, 'hitherto the utility of hospitals as curative institutions had been exceedingly equivocal. We had actually diseases in hospitals which exist nowhere else, diseases named after hospitals, hospital gangrene, hospital erysipelas, hospital pyæmia, hospital fever.'[8]

DIMINISHED SUPERSTITION.

BURNET, in his Life of Hale, says, 'In the year 1666 an opinion did run through the nation that the end of the world would come that year.'[9] In 1652 an eclipse of the sun 'so exceedingly alarmed the whole nation that hardly any one would work nor stir out of their houses.'[10] The Duke of Monmouth was executed in 1685. In his pockets were found charms and spells in his own handwriting.[11] In 1687, Bishop Cartwright, one of the most corrupt of men, writes,[12] 'Being my birthday, I made my last will and testament.'

[1] Chambers's Traditions of Edinburgh, 8vo, 1847, p. 285.
[2] Essais, Paris, 8vo, 1843, livre ii. chap. iv. p. 224.
[3] Wilson's Life of De Foe, 8vo, 1830, vol. i. p. 37.
[4] Saint-Aulaire, Histoire de la Fronde, tome ii. p. 141.
[5] Traité de Législation, vol. i. pp. 56, 60.   [6] See also p. 114.
[7] See interesting remarks by Dr. Farr in Transac. of Association for Social Science, 1859, pp. 508, 509.   [8] Ibid. p. 536.
[9] Lives, &c., edit. Jebb, 8vo, 1833, p. 108.
[10] Evelyn's Diary, 8vo, 1827, vol. ii. p. 52.
[11] Reresby's Memoirs, 8vo, 1831, 3rd edit. p. 312.
[12] Diary, Camden Society, 1843, p. 76.

DECLINE OF IGNORANCE.

In the reign of James II., Lord Conway, one of the ministers, on hearing of 'the circles of the empire,' wondered 'what circles should have to do with politics.'[1]

MAHOMETANISM.

THE Mahometan missionaries are very judicious.[2]   Ranke[3] thinks that but for the Carlovingian kings France would have been conquered by the Mahometans.

INSANITY.

THERE are four kinds—Moral Insanity, Monomania, Mania, and Incoherence.[4]

According to Heinroth, all insanity is referrible to the feelings, the understanding, or the will.[5]   Prichard says,[6] 'MORAL INSANITY consists in a morbid perversion of the feelings, affections, and active powers, without any illusion or erroneous conviction impressed upon the understanding; it sometimes co-exists with an apparently unimpaired state of the intellectual faculties.' Prichard says,[7] 'The existence of moral insanity as a distinct form of derangement has been recognised by Pinel, Traité sur l'Alienation, p. 156,' and is now generally admitted.[8]   And yet in another work Prichard[9] claims for himself the first recognition of moral insanity, though he allows [10] that Georgel recognised its existence.   He says,[11] 'The prognosis in cases of moral insanity is often more unfavourable than in other forms of mental derangement.'

MONOMANIA is often preceded by moral insanity.[12]

MANIA or RAVING MADNESS is distinguished from Monomania, first by its violence, and secondly, by the fact that 'the derangement of the intellect is not partial.'[13]   In this condition the

---

[1] Mackintosh's Revolution of 1688, 4to, 1834, p. 6.
[2] See Crawford's History of the Indian Archipelago, Edinb. 8vo, 1820, vol. ii. p. 307.
[3] Civil Wars and Monarchy in France, 1852, 8vo, vol. i. p. 16.
[4] Prichard on Insanity, 8vo, 1835, p. 6.   [5] Ibid. p. 8.
[6] Ibid. p. 12.   [7] Ibid. p. 14.   [8] Ibid. see pp. 21, 47, 50.
[9] Insanity in relation to Jurisprudence, p. 36.   [10] Ibid. p. 99.
[11] Treatise on Insanity, p. 25.   [12] Prichard, p. 28.   [13] Ibid. pp. 71, 72.

muscular strength is great, the memory remains unimpaired, and the patient escapes contagious and epidemical diseases.[1]

INCOHERENCE or DEMENTIA.—The 'ultimate tendency of insanity is to pass' into this state.[2] The mind is occupied by unconnected thoughts, sometimes 'without any symptoms of other insanity.'[3]

'Insanity does not consist in disease of the sensitive or perceptive powers,'[4] but 'in disturbance of the understanding;'[5] though, says Prichard,[6] 'perhaps we may observe in general that the power of judging and of reasoning does not appear to be so much impaired in madness as the disposition to exercise it on certain subjects.' There seems reason to think 'that the primary seat of mental alienation is generally in the region of the stomach and intestines.'[7] If we except congenital predisposition, the moral causes of insanity are more frequent than the physical ones.[8] Insanity is often connected with disorders of the heart,[9] but not with the liver.[10] Madness is not a disease of the mind,[11] and Prichard thinks[12] that even 'moral insanity depends in some instances at least on disease of the brain.' Insanity not dangerous to life.[13] Often hereditary,[14] and aided probably by the marriage of persons near akin.[15] It is rare before puberty,[16] and the longer men live the more likely they are to be subject to it.[17] In insanity the skull is generally natural, and the brain without disease.[18] Insanity is, on the whole, more common among women,[19] but male lunatics are most numerous in the south of France, and in Italy (particularly in Naples) and in Great Britain ; and it is said that the excess of male lunatics is greater in the higher than in the lower classes,[20] while it seems to be greatest of all in the United States.[21] Winter is most fatal to the insane.[22] Sir A. Halliday, who paid the greatest attention to the subject, said that in 1826 there were more than 8,000 lunatics in England and Wales ;[23] in Scotland, 3,700 ; in Ireland, 3,000.[24] But in 1829

[1] Prichard, Treatise on Insanity, pp. 77, 78.
[2] Ibid. pp. 83, 85.
[3] Ibid. p. 120.
[4] Ibid. p. 116.
[5] Ibid. p. 116.
[6] Ibid. pp. 228, 229.
[7] Ibid. p. 122.
[8] Ibid. pp. 173, 174, 177.
[9] Ibid. p. 247.
[10] Ibid. p. 232.
[11] Ibid. p. 235.
[12] Ibid. pp. 160, 161.
[13] Ibid. p. 146.
[14] Ibid. p. 158.
[15] Ibid. pp. 210, 211, 213.
[16] Ibid. p. 165.
[17] Ibid. p. 168.
[18] Ibid. pp. 163, 164.
[19] Ibid. pp. 162, 163, 164.
[20] Ibid. pp. 163, 164.
[21] Ibid. p. 164.
[22] Ibid. p. 152.
[23] Ibid. p. 331.
[24] Ibid. p. 332.

Halliday says 14,000 in England, and 2,500 in Wales.[1] In France the insane are one in 1,000, 'a proportion less than that believed to exist in Great Britain and some other countries.'[2] Among savages mental diseases are hardly known.[3] As to recovery, the most unfavourable form of insanity is complication with general paralysis.[4] Most recoveries are in summer.[5] In *recent* cases, at least seven out of eight recover,[6] but there is a case of a lady recovering after being mad twenty-five years.[7] 'Esquirol observes that the most favourable age for recovery is between the twentieth and thirtieth year, and that few are cured after the fiftieth:[8] 'insanity is, generally speaking, more curable in women than in men.'[9] Perhaps in *all* cases one-third recover.[10] There is a great difference of opinion respecting the propriety of bleeding in insanity,[11] but Prichard is in favour of it.[12] Purgatives are very useful,[13] and digitalis and other narcotics,[14] and rotatory motion to cause nausea and diminish the nervous power.[15] Pinel[16] has suggested that perhaps in women reason, as well as the aberration of reason, is sooner developed than among men. Georgel[17] says that at least ninety-five per cent. of the insane cases result from moral causes. Georgel[18] agrees with Esquirol that the moon has no connection with it any more than that the patients are frightened by its clearness. Even Patin never mentions insanity as nervous disease.[19] We find from the Commission in Lunacy that among paupers the female insane exceed the male by one-third ; but among 'private patients' the number of females 'falls short of that of the males by nearly a ninth.'[20]

Among both paupers and private patients, more males die than females.[21] At vol. iv. p. 18 of Journal of the Statistical Society, it is said, 'At the Middlesex Asylum, no strait waistcoats, straps, or other instruments of personal coercion have been used since

[1] Prichard, Treatise on Insanity, p. 333.

[2] Ibid. p. 343, where, however, there seems to be a misprint.

[3] Ibid. pp. 174, 175, 349.   [4] Ibid. p. 127.   [5] Ibid. pp. 136, 152.

[6] Ibid. p. 129.   [7] Ibid. p. 134.   [8] Ibid. p. 135.

[9] Ibid. p. 135.   [10] Ibid. p. 138.   [11] Ibid. pp. 252-257.

[12] Ibid. p. 258.   [13] Ibid. p. 265.   [14] Ibid. p. 268.

[15] Ibid. pp. 273, 274.

[16] Aliénation Mentale, p. 415.   [17] De la Folie, p. 160.   [18] Ibid. p. 440.

[19] See Lettres de Gui Patin, tome i. p. xvi.

[20] Journal of Statistical Society, vol. iii. p. 148.

[21] Ibid. pp. 148, 149, and vol. vii. p. 311 ; see also on the mortality, vol. iv. pp. 20, 24.

September 21, 1839.[1] It is said that out of 500 English one is insane.[2] Insanity is more common among men than among women ; and Esquirol and other writers who follow him in asserting insanity to be more frequent among women, have erroneously conducted their statistical analysis, having, in the first place, neglected to consider that adult females are more numerous than adult males ; and, in the second place, having estimated not the *occurring* cases, but the *existing* cases.[2] In Scotland, one in every 1,139 is mad ;[3] in England and Wales, one in 1,120.[4] At pp. 59–60 it is wrongly said that women are more prone to insanity than men. At p. 61, Dr. Stark ascribes the frequency of insanity in Scotland to intermarriage ; hence less insanity in Catholic countries,[5] and in Ireland.[6]

Marsden[7] says of the Sumatrans, ' When a man is by sickness or otherwise deprived of his reason, or when subject to convulsions or fits, they imagine him possessed by an evil spirit.' In Western India (about the Rajpoot country), Bishop Heber[8] saw a mad woman, and 'all the people called her a Moonee or inspired person, and treated her if not with respect, at least with forbearance.'[9] The phenomena of insanity were formerly surveyed with a theological eye,[10] and fanaticism ascribed them to possession by demons.[11] Even within fifty years madmen were shown as a curiosity.[12] Among barbarous people the insane are respected as inspired. Then comes the second stage, when they are believed to be possessed by demons. Hence formerly the keeper of the insane became hardened into cruelty.[13] Pinel says[14] that prejudice and ignorance made men believe insanity incurable.[15]

SLAVERY.

TOCQUEVILLE[16] says that even the negroes themselves often believe the inferiority of their own race. In the Northern States

[1] Journal of Statistical Society, vol. iv. p. 278.
[2] See the interesting essay, On the relative Liabilities of the Two Sexes to Insanity, in Journal of Statistical Society, vol. vii. pp. 310–316, and in particular, pp. 310, 311, 312, 314. [3] Journal of Statistical Society, chap. xiv. p. 52.
[4] Ibid. p. 53. [5] Ibid. p. 62. [6] Ibid. pp. 53, 54.
[7] History of Sumatra, p. 156.
[8] Journey through India, vol. ii. p. 471. [9] Ibid. p. 477.
[10] Quote Georgel, De la Folie, p. 10. [11] Ibid. p. 68. [12] Ibid. p. 294.
[13] Pinel, Aliénation Mentale, p. 360. [14] Ibid. pp. 404, 405.
[15] See also pp. 445, 476, and pp. 263, 264, 312.
[16] Démocratie en Amérique, vol. iii. p. 110.

slavery has been abolished because the masters saw it was their interest to do so ; while Christianity merely attacked slavery on the ground that it was contrary to the rights of the slave.[1] I believe that slavery was necessarily abolished as soon as labour ceased to be disgraceful, for then it was found contrary to the interest of the master ; and as we approach the South we find idleness held in honour.[2] Tocqueville[3] has confirmed from experience the theoretical conclusion of Adam Smith that slavery is more costly than free labour.   In France the diminution of slavery was slower in the domains of the church than anywhere.[4] On the history and different kinds of slavery, see Comte, Traité de Législation, tome iii. pp. 469–535, and the whole of tome iv. Mr. John Stanley in 1791 spoke against abolishing slavery on the ground that St. Paul and 'several other saints' had not opposed it.[5] Slavery is allowed by the French Protestants in 1637.[6] In 1799 it was attempted to show that Christianity *did* forbid slavery.[7] Comte[8] says that neither Macchiavelli nor Montesquieu nor Rousseau says anything against slavery.   In 1790 the celebrated Hugh Blair writes to Bruce from Restalrig, 'I am in the same sentiments with you about what you call the paroxysm of modern philanthropy respecting the slave trade ; but I do not see that you had much occasion to enter into that controversy.'[9]

[1] Tocqueville, vol. iii. pp. 156, 164.   [2] Ibid. pp. 166, 173.   [3] Ibid. p. 161.
[4] See note in Monteil, Hist. des Français des Divers États, tome vi. p. 101.
[5] Parliamentary History, vol. xxix. p. 315.
[6] See Quick's Synodicon In Gallia, 1692, vol. ii. p. 348.
[7] Parliamentary History, vol. xxxiv. 1136, 1137.
[8] Traité de Législation, vol. iii. p. 515.
[9] Murray's Life of Bruce, p. 279.

COMMON PLACE BOOK.

—◆—

ANTIQUITY OF CUSTOM OF SALUTING ON OCCASION OF SNEEZING.

'On date communément du siècle de Brunchaut et du ponti-
ficat de saint Grégoire le Grand l'usage si familier aujourd'hui de
faire des souhaits en faveur de ceux qui éternuent. On prétend
que du temps de ce saint prélat, il régna dans l'air une malignité
si contagieuse que ceux qui avaient le malheur d'éternuer expi-
raient sur le champ, ce qui donna occasion au religieux pontife
d'ordonner aux fidèles certaines prières, accompagnées de vœux,
pour détourner de dessus eux les effets dangereux de la corruption
de l'air. C'est une fable imaginée contre toutes les règles de la
vraisemblance, puisqu'il est constant que cette coutume existait de
toute antiquité dans toutes les parties du monde connu ' (*Velly,
Histoire de France*, 4to, Paris, 1770, tome i. p. 110).

The custom of blessing people when they sneeze is mentioned by *Montaigne, Essais*, Paris, 8vo, 1843, livre iii. chap. vi.
p. 570.

Davis, Examination of the 15th and 16th Chapters of Gibbon,
8vo, 1778, pp. 25-28. D'Israeli's Curiosities of Literature, 8vo,
1841, p. 45. Brand's Popular Antiquities, Ellis's edit. 8vo, 1841,
vol. iii. pp. 65-67. See Le Clerc, Bibliothèque universelle, tome
xxv. p. 523, Amsterdam, 1700. Fosbroke's British Monachism,
3rd edit. 1843, p. 159. Blunt's Vestiges of Ancient Manners in
Italy and Sicily, 8vo, 1823, pp. 174, 175. 'If the king of
Fundah sneezes, every one present must say Salam Aleikum !'
(*Laird and Oldfield's Expedition up the Niger*, 8vo, 1837, vol. i.

p. 225). Bowdich (*Mission to Ashantee*, 4to, 1819, p. 294) says, ' When the king of Ashantee sneezes, every person present touches or lays the two first fingers across the forehead and breast.' Clapperton (*Second Expedition*, 1829, 4to, p. 16) says the custom of clapping hands and snapping fingers when a great man sneezes ' is common to Benin, Lagos, and Dahomey, and similar to our exclamation of "God bless us," on the same occasion.' In 1800, Southey writes from Lisbon, ' The Portuguese despise the negroes, and by way of insult, sneeze at them as they pass : this is their strongest mark of contempt' (*Life and Correspondence of Robert Southey*, 8vo, 1849, 1850, vol. ii. p. 69). When the Thugs are engaged in one of their murderous expeditions, they consider a sneeze as the worst omen that can happen to them. ' Sneezing entitles all the travellers within the gripe of assassins to the privilege of an escape ; and no one dare to put them to death' (*Illustrations of the History and Practices of the Thugs*, 8vo, 1851, p. 80). Boswell's Life of Johnson, 8vo, 1829, p. 163. The islands of Samoa are in the Pacific, lat. 14° S. The inhabitants considered sneezing so ' unlucky' that ' when any one of a party sneezed on a journey, their future progress was postponed' (*Prichard, Physical History of Mankind*, vol. v. p. 154). Charron (*De la Sagesse*, Amsterdam, 8vo, 1782, tome i. p. 28) says that in illness sneezing is a sign of recovery. Mariner's Tonga Islands, 8vo, 1818, vol. i. p. 440 ; vol. ii. p. 146. Sir Thomas Browne's Works, vol. iii. pp. 33–36. See my Eighteenth Century, No. 1713.

GREAT PRICE PAID FOR PAINTINGS IN ENGLAND IN THE SEVENTEENTH CENTURY.

' Painting is in that esteem with the ingenious of this age, that it may seem superfluous to trouble the reader with arguments to increase it by setting before them the value the ancients put upon performances of this nature. . . . . Indeed, the relations we find in Pliny would seem almost incredible, if it were not that we every day see those of our modern masters in that art sold for 1,000 or 1,500 pounds apiece ' (*The Young Student's Library, containing Extracts and Abridgments of the most valuable Books printed in England and in the Foreign Journals, from the year Sixty Five to this Time, by the Athenian Society*, Lond. printed for John Dunton, folio, 1692, p. xiii).

It appears from Pepys's Diary that pictures fetched high prices. See some pertinent remarks in *Lord Jeffrey's Essays*, 8vo, 1844, i. 494. At the end of the sixteenth century the more valuable ones formed a chief ornament in rooms, and were protected by curtains (*Drake's Shakespeare and his Times*, 1817, 4to, ii.·119). M. Storch seems to deny the influence of superstition or religion on painting and statuary (see his ingenious, but I think unsound, remarks in *Economie politique*, St. Petersburg, 8vo, 1815, tome v. pp. 148, 149). Even Chevenix, whose enthusiasm for his own country too often weakens his judgment, allows that the English genius is ill adapted for painting (*Essays on National Character*, 8vo, 1832, i. 477, 478). A century ago, Dr. Shebbeare, who, though a reckless and unprincipled politician, was an acute observer, noticed the indisposition of the English to admire paintings. He says they cared for nothing but portraits (see his curious remarks in *Letters on the English Nation, by B. Angeloni*, 8vo, 1755, vol. i. pp. 94, 95). He speaks of *one* painter who received 'five-and-twenty guineas for a three-quarters length,' which he evidently considers an enormous sum (vol. ii. p. 44). He says England has never produced a good painter (ii. 51, 107).

REMARKABLE FECUNDITY WHICH FOLLOWED THE BLACK PLAGUE.

'After the cessation of the Black Plague a greater fecundity in women was everywhere remarkable—a grand phenomenon, which, from its occurrence after every destructive pestilence, proves to conviction, if any occurrence can do so, the prevalence of a higher power in the direction of general organic life. Marriages were almost without exception prolific ; and double and treble births were more frequent than at other times' (*Hecker, On the Black Death*, p. 31, published by the Sydenham Society, 8vo, 1844).

Hecker, generally profuse in his notes, has, strange to say, cited no authority for this assertion.

Malthus (*Essay on Population*, 6th edit. 1826, vol. i. pp. 505, 506) follows Dr. Short in asserting that even the *mortality* diminishes after a plague. If this is true, I suppose it would be accounted for by the plague having taken off the old and the sickly. Storch has brought forward some evidence to show that marriages are more prolific after a plague (*Economie politique*, St. Petersburg, 8vo, 1815, tome v. p. 131). Quetelet, Sur l'Homme, Paris, 8vo, 1835, tome i. pp. 93-95.

SOME PARTICULARS RESPECTING DANCING.

Du Bos (*Réflexions critiques sur la Poésie et sur la Peinture*, Paris, 12mo, 1770) says (part iii. pp. 230, 231) that there were two sorts of dances among the ancients, and he adds (p. 233) that the word 'saltatio' does not always mean 'dance' (see also p. 236). Cahusac (*Traité historique de la Danse*, La Haye, 12mo, 1754) has undertaken to refute this hypothesis of Du Bos. He treats this subject *con amore*, and (tome i. p. vi) is very angry with Du Bos, whom he accuses of unjustly depreciating the Greeks and Romans ; and adds, ' Il prétend que leur chant n'était point un chant et que leur danse n'était point une danse' (see also pp. xii, xiii). It is stated (tome i. p. 25) that dances are alluded to in the Psalms. Respecting the dances of the early Christians see tome i. pp. 41, 51, and 54. In tome ii. pp. 57, 66, he occupies himself with establishing the 'perfection réelle de la danse ancienne.' In tome ii. pp. 71-79 he treats of the origin of Ballets (and see p. 103). He ascribes to the tragical death of Henry II. in 1559 the discouragement of tournaments and the consequent increase of dancing (tome ii. pp. 126, 127). He has given (pp. 128-140) an account of the court entertainments in the reign of Henry III., and has expatiated with delight on Henry IV.'s passion for dancing (pp. 141-145), and with disdain (tome iii. p. 3) on the ballet in the court of Louis XIII. ; and see (p. 10) what he says of Richelieu. Jackson says that dancing is a cause of the superiority of the French in war (see *Jackson, On the Formation of Armies*, 8vo, 1845, pp. 141, 249, 355).

In an illuminated MS. of the thirteenth century Herodias is represented in the presence of Herod not as *dancing*, but as *tumbling*, a proof that formerly they little differed (see *Strutt's Habits and Dresses*, edit. Planché, 1842, ii. 193).

1. In the thirteenth century Lorraine was famous for its dancers (see *Le Roux de Lincy, Livre des Proverbes*, 1842, tome i. p. 234).

2. Huber, a learned civilian, wrote strenuously in favour of dancing (see *Le Clerc, Bibliothèque universelle*, tome vi. pp. 372,

435). 3. Heylin says, 'Dancing, an exercise much used by the French, who do naturally affect it' (*Retrospective Review*, vol. iii. p. 29). He travelled in France in 1625 (*ibid.* p. 24). 4. Michaelis has shown that among the Hebrews dancing was always considered lawful (*Commentaries on the Laws of Moses*, 8vo, 1814, vol. iii. pp. 189-192). 5. The Africans are fond of it, and 'pass their nights at new and full moon in this amusement' (*Laird and Oldfield's Expedition up the Niger*, 8vo, 1837, vol. ii. p. 91 ; and for a description of their dance, pp. 95, 96). 6. Dobell (*Travels in Kamtchatka and Siberia*, Lond. 8vo, 1830, vol. i. pp. 77, 78) has given a description of the Kamtchatdale national dance, which is more lively than decent (see also *Lesseps's Kamtchatka*, vol. i. p. 89, and *Cook's Travels*, 8vo, 1821, vol. vii. pp. 199-281). 7. Moorcroft, who was some time in Tibet, says, 'Dancing is a favourite amusement of the Ladakhis with both men and women, but the performances are in separate bodies' (*Moorcroft and Trebeck's Travels in the Himalayan Provinces of Hindustan*, &c., edited by H. H. Wilson, 8vo, 1841, vol. i. p. 345). 8. Rarely practised by the Kaffirs (see *Barrow's Southern Africa*, 4to, 1806, 2nd edit. vol i. p. 169). 9. For an account of the Mandingo dance see Park's Travels in Africa, 8vo, 1817, vol. i. p. 62. The king of Dahomey is fond of dancing (see *Duncan's Western Africa*, 8vo, 1847, vol. i. pp. 247-255 ; see also p. 292). Henderson (*Biblical Researches, &c., in Russia*, 8vo, 1826, p. 486) says that the Ingush, south-east of Georghviesk, 'are fond of dancing, but it is an established custom among them that the sexes never dance together.' In *Wright's Elizabeth* (8vo, 1838, vol. i. p. 498) there is a letter from Sir. H. Killigrew, dated Edinburgh, June 1574. In it he gives an account of the young James VI., and says, 'They did also make his Highness dance before me, which he likewise did with a very good grace.' The year after Wesley's death the Methodist preachers ordered that any parents who allowed their children to learn dancing should be expelled from the Methodist society, and this monstrous absurdity was defended in a formal dissertation by Dr. Adam Clarke (see *Southey's Doctor*, edit. Warter, 8vo, 1848, p. 501). Little facts like this should be preserved ; they show what priests would do if they had power.

POPULATION OF ENGLAND IN THE FOURTEENTH AND SIXTEENTH CENTURIES.

'The population of this island does not appear to me to bear any proportion to her fertility and riches. I rode, as your magnificence knows, from Dover to London, and from London to Oxford, a distance of more than two hundred Italian miles, and it seemed to me to be very thinly inhabited. . . . The same thing is asserted by those who wrote the history of King Richard the Second, for they state that England being threatened with an invasion by the French about the year of grace 1390, the number of men capable of bearing arms was computed, and found to be 200,000 archers. And the bow being as decidedly the weapon of the English as the pike is that of the Germans, I apprehend that there were not many more soldiers in England at that time' (*Relation of England about the Year* 1500, p. 31, Camden Society, 1847; see also Miss Sneyd's note at end, p. 85).

1. Malthus (*Essay on Population*, 6th edit. 1826, vol. ii. p. 214) loosely says, 'The population of England in the reign of Elizabeth appears to have been nearly five millions.' 2. Camden says (*Annals of Elizabeth* in *Kennett*, vol. ii. p. 393) that, in 1563, the plague was so fatal that 'there were carried out of the city of London alone, which consists of 121 parishes, 21,530 corpses;' he says (p. 574) that, in 1593, 'the sickness raged violently in London, insomuch that when the year came about, there died of the sickness and other diseases in the city and suburbs 17,890 persons.' He adds (p. 476) that in 1580 London was rapidly increasing, 'whilst the rest of the cities and towns of England ran to decay.' 3. In a contemporary pamphlet it is said that, at the time of the Armada in 1588, some of the counties could supply 'forty thousand able men' (*Harleian Miscellany*, 1808, 4to, vol. i. p. 145). In a petition to Henry VIII. in 1538 it is stated that 'there are within your realm of England 52,000 parish churches, and this notwithstanding that there be but ten households in every parish, yet are there 520,000 households, and of every of these households hath every of the five orders of friars a penny a quarter for every order' (*Harleian Miscellany*, ii. 539). In 1548, Warwickshire is spoken of as a very populous county (see *Haynes, State Papers*, p. 77). Mr. Alison, on the authority of Hume, and

Porter's Progress of the Nation, says, 'So late as the time of Elizabeth the population of England amounted only to about 3,000,000 souls' (*Alison's Principles of Population*, 8vo, 1840, vol. i. p. 24).

PHLEGMATIC TEMPERAMENT FAVOURABLE TO POETRY.

'Bien qu'il semble que le tempérament de feu soit plus propre à la poésie que le tempérament flegmatique, néanmoins l'expérience fait voir que les poètes abondent plus dans les pays où le flegme règne que dans les pays où le feu brille davantage. Cela se remarque principalement en Italie, où, le flegme étant, pour ainsi dire, dans son élément, il se trouve une infinité de poètes. En Normandie, qui est une province toute flegmatique, les poètes y naissent plus facilement que dans les autres provinces de France. Clément Marot était originaire de Normandie, fils de Jean Marot de Caen, *poète de la magnifique reine Anne de Bretagne* ; c'est la qualité qu'il prenait à la tête de ses ouvrages. M. de Malherbe était de Caen, Messieurs Patrés et Sarrazin en étaient aussi ; et M. de Segrais en est encore. M. de Scudéry et sa sœur sont nés au Havre de Grâce. Saint-Armand, les deux Corneille, et M. de Brebœuf étaient de Rouen. M. de Fontenelle est de la même ville. M. de Benserade était de Lions, proche de Rouen. M. le Cardinal du Perron était de la Basse-Normandie' (*Mélanges d'Histoire et de Littérature, par V. Marville*, Paris, 1725, tome i. pp. 214, 215).

Sir Humphrey Davy, himself no mean poet, writes in 1824, 'I have lately seen some magnificent country in the Scandinavian peninsula, where Nature if not a kind is at least a beautiful mother. I wonder there have not been more poets in the north' (*Paris, Life of Sir H. Davy*, 8vo, 1831, vol. ii. p. 284). In 1592, Greene writes of one 'whome by his carelesse slovenlie gate at first sight I imagined to be a poet' (*Quip for an Upstart Courtier*, in *Harleian Miscellany*, vol. v. p. 420).

NOTE ON ALCHEMY.

'Of alchemy and its royal bubbles there is a good account in a tract by J. F. Buddeus, "An Alchemistæ sint in republica tolerandi," Halæ Saxonum, 1712, 12mo. This tract contains a curious anecdote which appears to have a circulation in Germany, § 3. Martin Delrio, Disq. Mag. lib. i. c. lix. 4, says that "there was formerly a law in England against any person exercising the practice of alchemy without a licence of the king, under pain of death. But Henry IV. of the same kingdom proposed a contrary law, enacting by *four edicts* that all and singular his subjects should bestow their utmost attention in preparing the philosopher's stone to relieve the commonwealth of debt." And a pleasant reason is given for inducing the clergy to devote themselves to the study of the transmutation of metals, viz. "that as they were able to change bread and wine into the body and blood of Christ, they would easily convert the baser metals into gold." Jo. Peltus, an Englishman, mentions these edicts in his Fodinis Mineralibus, or the history, laws, and places of the chief mines and mineral works in England, p. i. c. 27, from whom George Paschius relates them in his book De Inventis nov. antiquis, c. vi. p. 332, who also brings the testimony of Morrhosius to the same purpose, De transmutatione Metallorum, § 12, p. 287, who, inquiring into the above act, was told by the keeper of the public records that the original document was still extant in the archives. The four Acts of Parliament, Henry IV., recommending the study of alchemy in order to pay the national debt, would be a curious accession to the Statute Book' (*Note signed H.* [I suppose Lord Hailes] in *Sibbald's Chronicle of Scottish Poetry*, vol. i. p. 311, Edinburgh, 1802, 8vo).

In 1721 there were many alchemists in Paris (see *Lettres Persanes*, Nos. xlv. and lviii., *Œuvres de Montesquieu*, Paris, 1835, pp. 29, 39).

1. Pettigrew, On Superstition connected with Medicine and Surgery, 8vo, 1844, p. 9. 2. Nicolas, Testamenta Vetusta, 8vo, 1826, vol. i. p. 411. 3. Lylie's Euphues and his England, 1605, 4to, signature p and p 2. 4. Roger Bacon believed in it (see *Histoire littéraire de la France*, xx. 237, and Kippis's edition of *Biographia Britannica*, vol. i. p. 422). 5. Niebuhr met in Arabia an alchemist (see the account of him in *Niebuhr, Description de l'Arabie*, 1774, 4to, pp. 123, 124). 6. In 1784, Dr. James Price, F.R.S., attempted in London to revive alchemy, and in a series of public experiments pretended to convert mercury into the precious metals (see *Parke's Chemical Essays*, 3rd edit. 8vo, 1830, p. 572). 7. M. Jacob (*Historical Inquiry into the Precious Metals*, 8vo, 1831, vol. i. p. 366) says that a belief in alchemy ' may be

traced in the statutes and other public documents, almost to the first year of William and Mary, when the Act of 5 Hen. IV. was repealed, which had been enacted to prevent the "craft of the multiplication of gold."[1] But I know of no instances so late. 8. Phillips, without quoting any authority, says, 'In 1552 all books on geography and astronomy in England were ordered to be destroyed, as being, it was supposed, infected with magic. It is very probable that works on the virtues of herbs underwent the same fate, as witchcraft was thought to be assisted by various plants ' (*History of Cultivated Vegetables*, 8vo, 1822, vol. i. p. 10). Ben Jonson ridiculed it in the Alchemist, which was acted in 1610. Gifford (*Works of Ben Jonson*, iv. 191) greatly exaggerates the effect of this able satire ; indeed, the visions of Sir Epicure are so magnificent that I should think they would have rather inflamed the popular credulity. In the Fox, which was brought out in 1605, however, a very effective spirit of banter is directed against quacks and their nostrums (*Works of Jonson*, vol. iii. pp. 210–220). The first of the celebrated Bakerian Lectures was delivered in 1775 by ' Peter Woulfe, the last of the alchemists ' (*Paris, Life of Sir Humphrey Davy*, 8vo, 1831, vol. i. p. 219). On the influence of the Royal Society in discouraging witchcraft and divination, see Paris's Life of Davy, ii. 178. Dr. Paris observes that it was with this intent that its charter states it to be established for the improvement of *natural* science, in contradiction to *supernatural*. In Middleton's Works, iv. 431, we have ' this fruitless, if I may not say this idle, study of alchemy.' In a tract published in 1660 the study of alchemy is put on a level in point of absurdity with other extravagances, such as keeping ' wenches or hangers on ' (*Harleian Miscellany*, edit. Park, vol. i. p. 17). ' Like other kinds of mysticism, alchemy seems to have grown out of the notions of moral, personal, and mythological qualities, which were associated with terms of which the primary application was to physical properties ' (*Whewell's History of the Inductive Sciences*, 8vo, 1847, vol. i. p. 320). Menzel says (*German Literature*, vol. iii. p. 40), ' Jugel in Berlin was, about 1785, the last who believed in this ancient art.' Comte (*Philosophie positive*, vi. 249) observes that while astrology was useful in raising the idea of our sagacity, alchemy was useful in increasing the idea of human power which theology had degraded.

SCOTCH FARTHINGALES FASHIONABLE.

'Sic farthingallis on flaggis als fall as quhaillis.'

A satire by Dunbar, or by Inglis, written in reign of James IV. of Scotland, upon which Sibbald notes (*Chronicles of Scottish Poetry*, vol. i. p. 382, Edinburgh, 1802), '"Sic farthingallis" from the French *verdugalle*, a corruption of *vertu-garde*, a hoop petticoat. It will be scarcely believed in this age, that in the last, the city ladies reformed their hereditary farthingales after the Scottish fashion. In a comedy called Eastward Hoe (act i. Dodsley's Collection of Old Plays, vol. iv. pp. 155-157), "Enter Poldavy, a French tailor, with a Scottish farthingale and a French fall in his arms." Mildred says, "Tailor Poldavy, prithee fit, fit it. Is this a right Scot? does it clip close and bear up round?"'

See p. 8 of Barnsley's Treatise, showing and declaring the Pryde and Abuse of Women, reprinted for Percy Society, but suppressed. Utterson's Early Popular Poetry, 8vo, 1817, vol. ii. pp. 131-133, and at p. 135 a description. *Harrington's Metamorphoses of Ajax*, p. 52. Sonnet de Courval says, 'Vertugadins, autrement ditz cachebastards.' (See his Response, &c., in p. 176 of his *Satyre Ménippée*, Lyon, 1623, 8vo.) Miss Strickland's Life of Mary, p. 402, Queens of England, vol. v. Strutt's Dresses, edit. Planché, 1842, 4to, vol. ii. p. 144. The author of a curious contemporary history of James I. says that during his reign the use of the farthingale greatly increased (see *Autobiography of Sir Simon d'Ewes*, edit. Halliwell, 8vo, 1845, vol. ii. p. 354).

BELIEF IN THE ELEVENTH CENTURY THAT THE WORLD WAS DRAWING TO AN END.

'From the chronological misinterpretation, it was in the year 1000, and for more than a century afterwards, universally expected that the world was drawing near to its termination. For St. John's thousand years were reckoned from the Christian era; whence the result was, that Satan having been bound during that millennium, was loosened in the year 1000; while from that result, by the persons who lived through the eleventh century, it was additionally concluded, that after Satan should have prevailed over the saints during his short permitted period of freedom, through his special minister Antichrist, the world would be destroyed. There is much on this curious subject in Usser, De Eccles. Success. capp. i.-vi. Perhaps I may be allowed to add the following to the authorities collected by the archbishop' (*Faber's Inquiry into the History and Theology of the Ancient Vallenses and Albigenses*, 8vo, 1838, p. 389 ; at pp. 390, 391, Faber gives the additional authorities to which he refers).

Guizot accounts for this belief in another way (see his *Civilisation en Europe*, Paris, 1846, 8vo, p. 95). Beaven's Account of Irenæus, 8vo, 1841, pp. 250 256. The Benedictines suppose that the disorders of the times produced this belief (*Histoire littéraire de la France*, vii. 6). In the twelfth century, Otho of Friesland thought that the end of the world was drawing near (*Histoire littéraire de la France*, xiii. 273). In the tenth century it was announced from the pulpits (*Hist. lit. de la France*, vi. 11). Near Tiflis, the capital of Georgia, is a colony of German Millenarians (see an account of these absurd people in *Henderson's Biblical Researches, &c., in Russia*, 8vo, 1826, pp. 524-529 ; see also *Pinkerton's Russia*, 8vo, 1833, pp. 143-151).

GREAT MEN WHO HAVE DISLIKED MATHEMATICS.

'Bossuet n'a laissé apercevoir dans aucun temps de sa vie du goût pour l'étude des mathématiques' (*Bausset, Histoire de Bossuet*, tome i. p. 16, Paris, 8vo, 1814). In tome i. p. 367, speaking of the education of the dauphin, Bausset says, 'De toutes les sciences, celle des mathématiques fut la seule dont Bossuet ne donna pas lui-même des leçons à son élève ;' and for the truth of this assertion Bausset quotes the MSS. of Le Dieu, who, he says (tome i. p. 76), lived with Bossuet for twenty years.

Cooke (*History of Party*, vol. iii. p. 214) says of Fox, 'For the mathematics he had little taste.' Wakefield says that in his time it was a common observation, that the inhabitants of the northern counties of England 'are usually the profoundest proficients in mathematics and philosophy.' This he accounts for by the little attention paid in the north to classics (see *Life of Gilbert Wakefield, by Himself*, 8vo, 1804, vol. i. pp. 83, 84). M. Cousin says that Kant and Dugald Stewart have proved that mathematics are *not* a series of identical propositions (*Histoire de la Philosophie*, part i. tome iii. p. 137). 'Plus les sciences physiques ont fait de progrès, plus elles ont tendu à rentrer dans le domaine des mathématiques'

(*Quetelet, Sur l'Homme*, Paris, 8vo, 1835, tome i. p. 276). Whewell (*Philosophy of the Inductive Sciences*, 8vo, 1847, vol. ii. pp. 369, 370) notices the evil effects of mathematics, and suggests as a counterpoise the study of natural history. He denies the opinion of Dugald Stewart, that its reasonings depend upon definitions (ii. 598). Mr. Green controverts the opinion of Locke 'that mathematics may be substituted for logic' (*Mental Dynamics*, 8vo, 1847, p. 27). For a singular instance of a young girl, 'a prodigy in mathematical and musical skill,' see *Clarendon Correspondence*, 1828, 4to, vol. ii. p. 149.

SOME PARTICULARS RESPECTING TOBACCO.

'Tobacco is an annual plant, a native of America, from whence it was imported into Europe. We learn from Humboldt that it has been cultivated from time immemorial by the native people of the Oroonoko, and was smoked all over America at the time of the Spanish conquest. Hernandez de Toledo sent it unto Spain and Portugal in 1559, when Jean *Nicot* was ambassador at the court of Lisbon from Francis II. ; and he transmitted or carried either the seed or the plant to Catherine de Medicis, as one of the wonders of the New World, and which, it was supposed, possessed values of a very extraordinary nature. This seems to be the *first* authentic record of the introduction of the plant into Europe. From this person (Jean Nicot) the plant received its generic name *Nicotiana*, the specific appellation being taken from *tabac*, the name of an instrument used by the natives of America in smoking the herb. In 1589 the Cardinal Sante Croce, returning from his nunciature in Spain and Portugal to Italy, carried with him thither tobacco ; and we may form some notion of the enthusiasm with which its introduction was hailed from a perusal of the poetry which the subject inspired. It is said that the smoking tobacco was first introduced by Sir Walter Raleigh, on his return from America ; and the avidity with which the custom was immediately adopted is shown by the philippic written by King James against it, entitled the "Counterblaste to Tobacco." . . . . In 1624, Pope Urban VIII. published a decree of excommunication against all who took *snuff* in the church. Ten years after this smoking tobacco was forbidden in Russia, under the pain of having the nose cut off. In 1653 the Council of the Canton of

Appenzel cited smokers before them, whom they punished; and they ordered all innkeepers to inform against such as were found smoking in their houses. The police regulations of Berne, made in 1661, were divided according to the Ten Commandments, in which the prohibition of smoking stood immediately beneath the command against adultery. This prohibition was renewed in 1675, and the tribunal instituted to put it into execution, viz. "Chambre au Tabac," continued to the middle of the eighteenth century. Pope Innocent XII. in 1590 excommunicated all those who were found taking *snuff* or using tobacco in any manner in the church of St. Peter's at Rome. Even so late as 1719 the Senate of Strasburg prohibited the cultivation of tobacco, from an apprehension that it would diminish the growth of corn. Amurath IV. published an edict which made the smoking tobacco a capital offence; this was founded on an opinion that it rendered the people infertile' (*Paris and Fonblanque's Medical Jurisprudence*, vol. ii. pp. 414-416, 8vo, 1823. See also vol. i. p. 209).

1. Hallam, Literature of Europe, ii. 241, 2nd edit. 1843. 2. Camden says, in his History of Queen Elizabeth, which was first published in 1615, that tobacco was introduced into England by Sir Francis Drake in 1585. He adds the curious information that 'tobacco shops are now as ordinary in most towns as tap-houses and taverns' (see *Camden*, in *Kennett's Complete History*, vol. ii. pp. 509, 510, Lond. 1719, folio). 3. Dulaure, Histoire de Paris, 12mo, 1825, tome vi. p. 251. Tytler's Life of Raleigh, 5th edit. Edinburgh, 1844, 8vo, pp. 57, 58. It is said that tobacco may be smoked through the ears, or, to speak more properly, that the smoke may be passed through the ears (see *Sprengel, Histoire de la Médecine*, tome iv. p. 289, Paris, 8vo, 1815). At the end of the sixteenth century Englishmen were so fond of it that they used to *drink* it in the middle of dinner (*Phillips, History of Cultivated Vegetables*, 8vo, 1822, vol. ii. p. 336). Phillips supposes (p. 337) that it was first introduced into Europe about 1560; and says (p. 339) that Drake, in 1570, first brought it to England. He is mistaken in saying (p. 340) 'snuff did not come into fashion until after the Restoration.' We learn from Every Man in his Humour that in 1595 it was 'an herb generally received in the courts of princes, the chambers of nobles, the bowers of sweet ladies, the cabins of soldiers' (*Ben Jonson's Works*, 8vo, 1816, vol. i. p. 99; and see vol. ii. p. 122). In 1599 it used to be taken in the best

parts of the theatre (*Jonson's Works*, vol. ii. pp. 69, 110, 224 ; and
vol. iv. p. 512). Even thus early it used to be perfumed (p. 97).
Gifford gives (vol. ii. p. 127) a representation of an old tobacco-
pipe. In 1599 the smoke was sent through the nose ; see Jonson,
vol. ii. p. 140, where a man is described as having 'opened his
nostrils with a poking-stick, to give the smoke a more free delivery '
(compare vol. iv. p. 429). In 1600, gallants used to carry it about
in boxes (vol. ii. p. 233). In 1609 is the expression ' He lies on
his back droning a tobacco-pipe,' which Gifford does not understand (*Ben Jonson's Works*, vol. iii. p. 424). In the Alchemist, in
1610, there is a very curious description of a fashionable tobacco-
nist's shop, which contained very luxurious accommodation for
smoking it. There was a maple block for shredding the leaf,
silver tongs for holding the coals, and a fire of juniper at which the
pipes were lighted (*Ben Jonson's Works*, vol. iv. p. 38, and see
p. 106). It would seem to be commonly sold in 2d. packets (see
vol. iv. p. 153). In Bartholomew Fair, acted in 1614, is mentioned
' the black boy in Bucklersbury, that takes the scurvy roguey
tobacco there' (iv. 389). In The Devil is an Ass, which was
acted in 1616, we are told that even chimney-sweepers took
tobacco (vol. v. p. 15). In 1604 it was smoked at theatres, even
on the very stage (*Middleton's Works*, 1840, vol. v. p. 544), and
we are told (p. 569), ' There is no gallant but hath a pipe to burn
about London.' It was commonly smoked at alehouses (see
Maroccus Extaticus, 1595, p. 11, Percy Society, vol. ix.)

LIBRARY OF THE DUKES OF BURGUNDY IN THE
FIFTEENTH CENTURY.

Notes from ' *Catalogue d'une Partie des Livres composant la
Bibliothèque des Ducs de Bourgogne au XVe Siècle, par G. Peignot*,'
Dijon, 1841. In p. 17, Peignot remarks that Charles the Bold,
who in 1467 succeeded his father, Philip the Good, was very fond
of reading—'Son règne très-agité n'a été que de dix ans, et malgré
cela il s'est occupé de sa bibliothèque. On en voit la preuve dans
le prologue des *Chroniques de Pise*, traduites de l'italien, où le
traducteur assure qu'il a fait cette version pour complaire au Duc
Charles.' In p. 42, among the books in the library of the Dukes
of Burgundy, Peignot mentions ' *La Bible ystoriée*,' respecting which
he says, ' Je présume que c'est une copie de la Bible traduite en

français sous ce titre, par Guyard des Moulins, chanoine, puis
doyen, de Saint Pierre-d'Aire. Elle a été commencée en 1291
(il avait alors 40 ans), et terminée 1294 (Extrait de la Souscription).
Pierre Comestor l'avait traduite avant lui. Ce pourrait bien être
la même traduction corrigée depuis, mais non composée, par
Nicolas Oresme. Il est certain que Nicolas Oresme n'a pas
traduit la Bible en latin ; tous ceux qui lui ont attribué cette
version française se sont trompés. Richard Simon, dans la seconde
partie de son Histoire Critique du Nouv. Testament, chap. 28, a
fait voir qu'il n'y avait alors d'autre Bible française que celle de
Guyard des Moulins, commencée au mois de juin 1291 et finie,
non pas comme il le dit, à la Saint-Remi, 1297, mais au mois de
février 1294. Ce qui a trompé Richard Simon c'est que Guyard
de Moulins, après avoir marqué le mois de février 1294, temps où
il a fini sa traduction, ajoute qu'en 1297, le jour de Saint Remi
(1er octobre) il fut fait doyen de Saint-Pierre d'Aire. Cette Bible
n'est autre chose, comme le traducteur lui-même remarque, qu'une
version de l'Histoire scolastique de Pierre Comestor (V. La Croix
du Maine, tome ii. p. 192).'

In an inventory made in 1405 of the library of the Duke of
Burgundy is ' Le Romaunt du Roy Arthur ' et ' Lancelot du Lac,'
respecting which Peignot remarks (*Catalogue d'une Partie des Livres,
&c.*, Dijon, 1841, p. 65), ' Le P. Labbé dans sa Nova Biblioth.
Manuscriptorum (p. 309) dit que le Roman de Lancelot a été
mis en français par Robert de Borrow, par le commandement
d'Henri roi d'Angleterre. Ce doit être Henri II, mort en 1189.
Je crois qu'il a été traduit du latin de Gautier Mape, quoique
M. de Roquefort dise qu'il a été mis en français par Gautier. Ce
même Gautier avait fait aussi le Roman de "La Mort du roi
Arthur, dernière partie des Romans de la Table Ronde." '

In the inventory made in 1405, Peignot gives (pp. 68, 69) as
one of the items ' Le Livre en papier de Jehan Mandeville,'
respecting which Peignot remarks, ' Il est présumable que c'est
l'ouvrage connu sous le titre suivant : "Ce livre est appelé Mandeville, et fut fait et composé par M. Jehan de Mandeville, chevalier
natif d'Angleterre, de la ville de Saint Alban ; et parle de la terre
de promission, c'est à savoir de Jhérusalem, et de plusieurs autres
isles de mer et les diverses et estranges choses qui sont es dites
isles." A la fin de l'ouvrage on lit : "Cy finist ce très-plaisant livre
nommé Mandeville, parlant moult autentiquement du pays et terre

d'oultre mer."' Peignot (*Critique d'une Partie, &c.*, Dijon, 1841,
p. 128) says that in the 'Catalogue de la Bibliothèque des Domini-
cains de Dijon, rédigé en 1307,' there is mentioned a copy of
the 'De Proprietatibus Rerum,' respecting which he says, 'Cet
ouvrage est de Barthélemi d'Angleterre (Bartholomæus Anglicus),
auquel on donne le surnom de Glanville. Presque tous les auteurs
qui en ont parlé le font vivre vers 1360 ; mais puisque son traité
est inscrit dans ce Catalogue-ci, rédigé en 1307, il n'y a pas de
doute qu'il florissait avant 1360 ; ou bien il faudrait l'opinion du
P. Quetif, qui dans ses Scriptores Ordinis Prædicatorum, tome i.
p. 486, cherche à prouver que le Glanville qui florissait vers la fin du
xiv⁴ siècle ne peut être l'anglais Barthélemi qui a écrit le "De
Proprietatibus Rerum," avant la fin du xiii⁴ siècle. Antoine
Ponevin, dans son "Apparatus sacer," donne à Barthélemi le
surnom de Grannuyse ; on ignore où il a puisé ce surnom employé
par lui seul.'

Le Clerc, Bibliothèque universelle, tome xxiii. p. 494. Irving
(*History of Columbus*, 8vo, 1828, vol. iv. p. 411), speaking of the
strange ideas of Columbus respecting the situation of the terrestrial
paradise, says, ' Many of these opinions are cited by Glanville,
usually called Bartholomeus Anglicus, in his work " De Proprietatibus Rerum," a work with which Columbus was evidently
acquainted.' But of this ' evident acquaintance ' Irving gives no
proof, and merely says ' it was a species of encyclopædia of the
general knowledge current at the time, and *likely* to recommend
itself to a curious and inquiring voyager.'

STUDY FAVOURABLE TO HEALTH.

'C est une grande erreur de croire que l'étude soit contraire à
la santé. On voit autant vieillir de gens de lettres, que de toute
autre profession. L'histoire en fournit une infinité d'exemples.
En effet cette vie réglée, uniforme, paisible, n'entretient-elle pas
la bonne constitution et n'éloigne-t-elle pas toutes les causes qui
la peuvent altérer ? Pourvu que la chaleur naturelle soit d'ailleurs excitée par un exercice modéré et ne soit pas étouffée sous
une quantité d'aliments disproportionnée aux besoins de la vie
sédentaire' (*Huetiana*, No. 3, p. 5, edit. Amsterdam, 1723, 12mo).

See Giles's Life of Bede, p. xviii, prefixed to Bede's Ecclesiastical History, edit. Bohn, 8vo, 1847. Kant died aged eighty. Stow

was eighty when he died. Strype, ninety-four. The famous Thomas
Hobbes of Malmesbury was ninety-one. Sir Richard Maitland was
ninety (see *Irving's Scottish Poets*, 2nd edit. 1810, 8vo, 11, 149).
Etienne Pasquier was eighty-six. Lardner, the learned author of
the 'Credibility' &c., was eighty-four. Lanfranc, Archbishop of
Canterbury, died in 1089, aged eighty-three (*Hist. lit. de la
France*, viii. 275). Berenger died in 1088, almost ninety (*Hist.
lit. de la France*, viii. 214). The learned Allalius died in 1669,
aged eighty-three (*Biog. univ.* i. 583). Montfaucon died in 1741,
aged eighty-seven (*Biog. univ.* xxix. 537). The celebrated Jacques
Sismond, 'l'un des plus savants hommes dont s'honore la France,'
died in 1651, aged ninety-two (*Biog. univ.* xlii. 427, 428). Antoine Magliabecchi, the great bibliographer, died in 1714, aged
eighty-one (*Biog. univ.* xxvi. 131). The celebrated traveller,
Carsten Niebuhr, died in 1815, aged eighty-two (*Biog. univ.* xxxi.
271). The longevity of men of letters in France in the eighteenth
century was something remarkable (see *Lord Jeffrey's Essays*, 8vo,
1844, vol. i. p. 364). Cumberland, the learned Bishop of Peter-
borough, lived to be eighty-six (see *Cumberland's Autobiography*,
8vo, 1807, vol. i. p. 5). Sir Isaac Newton was eighty-four. Reed,
the metaphysician, was eighty-six. Voltaire was eighty-four. Fontenelle was nearly one hundred. Simson, the celebrated restorer of
the Greek geometry, was turned eighty (*Brougham's Men of Letters
and Sciences*, 1845, vol. i. p. 513). Watt died in 1819, aged
eighty-three (see p. 385). Lord Kames died in 1792, aged
eighty-six (*Tytler's Life of Kames*, Edinburgh, 1814, vol. ii.
p. 328). Blair was eighty-two (*Bower's History of the University
of Edinburgh*, iii. 17).

PARTICULARS RESPECTING MARRIAGE LAWS.

The following I extract from a very curious work, the materials
of which are principally manuscript sources. It is entitled
'The Fleet Registers, comprising the History of Fleet Marriages,
and some account of the Parsons and Marriage-House Keepers.
With extracts from the Registers. To which are added Notices
of the May Fair, Mint, and Savoy Chapels, and an Appendix
relating to Parochial Registration. By John Southerden Burn,
author of the History of Parish Registers,' Lond. 8vo, 1833.

Burn says (p. 1), 'It was not until the *Council of Trent*

(1439)[1] that the intervention of a priest or other ecclesiastical functionary was deemed in Europe indispensable to a marriage. It was then ascertained that the existence of the marriage contract as a mere civil engagement, unhallowed by any spiritual sanction, tended much to the formation of clandestine connections and their concomitant evils.   The celebrated decree passed in that session interdicted any marriage otherwise than in the presence of a priest and at least two witnesses. But in England, previous to 1754, the Common Law continued to regulate the law of marriage, the authority of the Council of Trent not having been acknowledged in this country ; and while, in virtue of domestic institutions, a form was enjoined for the more solemn celebration of matrimony, and persons departing from these regulations were liable to ecclesiastical censure, still other and more private modes of contracting a marriage were tolerated and acknowledged by law.   Hence a contract *per verba de præsenti*, that is to say, between persons entering into a present engagement to become man and wife, or a promise *per verba de futuro* which was an agreement to become husband and wife at some future time, if the promise were followed by consummation, constituted marriage without the intervention of a priest.'

At p. 2, Burn says, ' The author has many curious particulars relative to espousals, which was the contract *per verba de futuro*. It must suffice, however, merely to give an entry of espousals in the parish register of Boughton Monchelsea, Kent, the only one he has ever met with : 'Michaelis 1630 : Sponsalia inter Gulielm' Maddox et Elizabeth Grimestone in debitâ juris formâ transacta 10 die Januarii.   Michaelis 1633 : Nuptiæ inter Gulielm' Maddox et Elizabetha Grimestone ultimo Octobris'—' By the Civil Law, whatsoever was given *ex sponsalitia largitate* betwixt them that are promised, have a condition (for the most part silent) that it may be had again if marriage ensue not.—Si sponsus dederit aliquid et aliquo casu impediantur nuptiæ, donatio penitus rescinditur nisi osculum intervenit ; but if he had a kiss for his money, he loseth one-half of that which he gave. But with the woman it is otherwise ; for kissing or not kissing, whatsoever she gave, she

---

[1] What council was this ? Madan (Thelyphthora, and edit. vol. ii. p. 143. 8vo, 1781) says, though without giving any authority, that 'Soter, fifteenth Bishop of Rome, at the end of the second century, ordained that no woman should be deemed a lawful wife unless formally married by the priest.'

may ask and have it again.   This is but for gloves, rings, brace-
lets, and other small wares, and in releaving a woman hath greter
favour in greater guifts than a man hath " (*Spon.* crud. 9, fo. 13).'

1. See Reeve's History of the English Law, vol. iv. pp. 52, 55,
8vo, 1787, 2nd edit.   2. Kissing was the common form of salutation
among the Romans (see *Suetonius* in *Tiberius Nero*, cap. xi. and
note of Pitescus in *Opera Suetonii*, i. 408, Lœwardiæ, 1714, 4to).
Troth-plighting or affiancing was very common in the sixteenth
century, and though not a legal marriage was often followed by
cohabitation (see *Drake's Shakespeare and his Times*, 1817, 4to,
vol. i. pp. 222, 223).

At p. 3, Burn says, ' Banns were first directed to be published
by Canon Hubert Walter, No. 22 (1200) ; and the constitution
of William la Zouch, No. 7 (1347), notices the performance of
clandestine marriages, and that "some contriving unlawful marriages and affecting the dark lest their deeds should be reproved,
procure every day in a damnable manner marriages to be celebrated without publication of banns duly and lawfully made, by
means of chaplains that have no regard to the fear of God and
the prohibition of the laws." '

1. Although banns be comparatively modern, yet there was
something analogous in the early churches ; for the passages cited
by Bingham (*Antiq.* xxii. 2, 11 ; *Works*, vii. 285, 286) show that
'all Christians were obliged to acquaint the church with their designs
of marriage before they completed it.'   2. Lylie's Euphues, edit.
1631, 4to, sig. D 5.   Wycherley's Gentleman Dancing-Master, act i.
sc. ii. p. 40A.

'The marriage at the Fleet (says Burn, p. 15) of the Hon.
Henry Fox (afterwards Baron Holland) with Georgiana Caroline,
eldest daughter of Charles second Duke of Richmond, was in
1744 a subject of general conversation ; but it was not until 1753
that the law of marriage was taken up with effect, when Lord
Hardwicke brought in a bill (26 George II. c. 33) enacting that
every person solemnising matrimony in any other than a church
or public chapel without banns or licence should on conviction be
adjudged *guilty of felony*, and be transported for fourteen years,
and that all such marriages *should be void*.   Such an impediment
to matrimony, which thitherto had been validly contracted without even the presence of a clergyman—such "an *innovation*" (to
use the words of Blackstone) "*upon our ancient Laws and Consti-*

tution"—could not be expected to pass into law without a violent opposition.' At pp. 16, 17, Burn mentions that the chief opposition came from the lower orders. The bill, however, was passed, though mutilated and much shorn of its original proportions.

At pp. 13, 15, Burn has given a very curious extract from the Grub Street Journal, January 1734-1735, illustrating the great disorders openly practised in the principal London streets by men whose object it was to effect *compulsory* marriages. At pp. 25, 26, Burn has given a curious account of a clergyman, Dr. Gaynam, who performed marriages at the Fleet from about 1709 to 1740. At pp. 51-57, Burn has given some extraordinary extracts from the books kept by the Fleet clergymen. It seems that when these exemplary gentlemen had an entry to make more than usually scandalous, they used to write it in 'Greek characters,' of which a comical instance is given at p. 52.

For an instance of coarse manners see ART. 2212.

NOTES ON THE PROGRESS ETC. OF THE PAPAL POWER.

The eighteenth chapter of the third book of Pasquier's Recherches (*Œuvres de Pasquier*, Amsterdam, 1723, tome i. folio, 230-239) is headed 'Que nos rois sont francs et exempts des censures de la cour de Rome.'

Ammianus Marcellinus, A.D. 380, speaks of 'the authority of that superior power which belongs to the bishops of the eternal city' (*Lardner's Heathen Testimonies*, chap. 51 ; *Works*, viii. 49) ; and for their splendid manner of living see p. 57. In the Council of Vaison, A.D. 529, it was ordered 'que le nom du Pape soit récité dans nos églises' (*Guizot, Histoire de la Civilisation en France*, Paris, 1846, tome iii. p. 111) ; and respecting the early influence of the Popes, see tome i. pp. 78, 79. Even Southey (*Book of the Church*, 8vo, 1824, vol. i. p. 284) confesses that 'with all its errors, its corruptions, and its crimes, the Papacy was morally and intellectually the conservative power of Christendom.' Townshend (*Accusations of History against the Church of Rome*, 8vo, 1825, p. 112) says that 'Victor, Bishop of Rome, excommunicated all the churches of Asia, and was indignantly reproved for so doing by Irenæus, the Metropolitan of France.' 'Metropolitan of France'!!! Le Clerc (*Bibliothèque choisie*, xxv. 276) says, 'Il n'y avait en ce temps-là, autant qu'on peut le recueillir du silence des anciens, aucun évêque en France ; ' so that the 'Metropolitan of France' resolves himself into the only bishop in France ! Beaven indeed (*Account of Irenæus*, 8vo, 1841, p. 18) says ' there is nothing but the *presumption* that there was no other bishop in Gaul but the Bishop of Lyons. And if there were, *as is not improbable*, Bishops of Autun, of Arles, and of Vienne at the time——' But a little consideration would have taught the reverend author that in the absence of positive testimony the silence of contemporaries is a weighty argument ; and that, in fact, the ' presumption ' is on his side for venturing to assert the ' probability ' of existing bishoprics in Gaul.

There are some particulars relative to the opinions of the Christians in the end of the second century respecting Rome in Deaven's Account of Irenæus, 8vo, 1841. Beaven mentions (p. 11) that in A.D. 177 he [Irenæus] was ' chosen by the martyrs of Lyons, then in prison, as a fit person to send to Eleutherus, Bishop of Rome, with their testimony against the Montanists.' See also what he adds (pp. 15, 16) respecting the journey to Rome. Beaven (p. 23), though so violently opposed to the Romish supremacy, confesses that ' the Christians of that age looked with peculiar anxiety to Rome as the church where, from the constant meeting together of Christians from the provinces, the traditions of the Catholic Church were most accurately preserved ' (see also pp. 51, 82). Another remarkable fact is mentioned by Beaven (p. 33), viz. that Irenæus in the beginning of his third book against Gnosticism gives ' a list of the Bishops of Rome ' (see the list at p. 59). Why should he do that if he did not think them more important than other bishops? Respecting the threat of Victor, Bishop of Rome, to excommunicate the churches of Asia Minor, a threat which Irenæus protested against, see pp. 51–52. Beaven mentions (p. 58) that Irenæus ' particularly specifies that the Church of Rome was founded by St. Peter and St. Paul, who appointed its first bishop, Linus.' Beaven says (p. 63), ' Irenæus speaks of the Church of Rome not only as having been founded and settled under its first bishop by St. Peter and St. Paul, but as being one of the greatest and most ancient, well known to all men, preserving the true doctrine by the resort of persons from all quarters, and possessing from this circumstance a more powerful pre-eminence, and states that all churches must on that account resort to it.' This powerful passage Beaven has attempted to get

T 2

rid of by examining word for word. His quibbles are like the logic of the too famous Peter, who in the Tale of a Tub attempts, by similar quibbles, to induce his brethren to reject their father's will. On this important passage see Le Clerc, Bibliothèque choisie, tome xxv. pp. 295, 296. Le Clerc (*Bibliothèque choisie*, xxv. 279) says that Irenæus 'écrivit à Victor une lettre *assez forte*.'

The celebrated Dominican, Vincent de Beauvais, speaks in the highest terms of the papal power (*Histoire littéraire de la France*, xviii. 496). But St. Bernard, in 1126, denied the right of the Pope to authorise a monk to quit one monastery and go into another (see *Fleury, Histoire ecclésiastique*, livre lxvii. sect. 48, tome xiv. p. 348, 12mo, 1757, Paris). See also Histoire littéraire de la France, xiii. 149, 150. We find him also (p. 155 ; see also *Hist. littéraire*, xiii. pp. 205–210) censuring the conduct of the Pope in the most open manner ; and yet on another occasion asserting (p. 160) ' que le Pape peut évoquer des confins du monde et citer à son tribunal les personnages du rang le plus sublime,' &c.; and again, declaring the duties of the Pope to be 'ad præsidendum regibus, ad regna et imperia disponenda !' In 1025 a council of Anse, near Lyons, declared that the Pope had had no power to grant to a monastery exemption from episcopal jurisdiction (*Fleury, Histoire ecclésiastique*, livre lix. No. 7, tome xii. pp. 450, 451). However, in 1049, Leo IX. *confirmed* the exemption (xii. 546), and the council of Chalons, in 1063, sentenced the Bishop of Mâcon to a penitence for violating it (xiii. 131). In the twelfth century, Otho of Friesland does not place their *rightful* power very high (see *Histoire littéraire de la France*, xiii. 272–275). Theodosius the Great ordered that all nations should adopt the opinions of the Pope, and Valentinian III. forbade the bishops to make any alterations without his consent (*Ranke, Die Römischen Päpste*, Berlin, 1838, band i. pp. 12, 13).

IN THE TIMES OF CHIVALRY WOMEN WERE BADLY TREATED.

For the fourteenth century see some evidence in the second series of the Retrospective Review, vol. i. pp. 189, 190. Dunlop has observed (*History of Fiction*, 2nd edit. Edinburgh, 8vo, 1816, vol. i. p. 365) that ' in the romances the knight is always more interesting than the heroine, which must appear strange when we reflect that these romances were composed in an age when devotion to the ladies formed the essence of chivalry.' The difference between the *real* and *imaginary* condition of women is a problem well worth considering, and which Dunlop has not attempted to solve. The late M. Fauriel, in his valuable posthumous work, has some curious remarks on this subject (see his *Histoire de la Poésie Provençale*, Paris, 1846, 8vo, tome i. pp. 478-515). He has shown, by extracts from the Provençal literature, that it was only *after* marriage that women were treated so contemptuously, which arose from the universal opinion that love and marriage were incompatible. 'Il était tellement convenu en principe,' says Fauriel (tome i. p. 506), 'que l'amour ne pouvait exister dans le mariage, que l'on ne croyait pas qu'il pût durer, *même entre les époux qui auraient été amants avant d'être mariés*.' It is, then, the operation of this principle (which Fauriel terms 'un point anti-conjugal de morale chevaleresque') which must be principally considered ; and we shall find that there was no *real* difference between the state of women in society and in romance ; but that the *apparent* difference has arisen from their being made more prominent in romance *before* marriage and in society *after* marriage. That is to say, in the romance we find woman described in what was in those times her most favourable and important condition ; and in history we meet with her in her most unfavourable condition. The codes of the old Courts of Love consisted of thirty-one articles, one of which was 'Le mariage n'est pas une excuse légitime contre l'amour' (see *Raymond, Choix des Poésies des Troubadours*, tome ii. p. cv). In pp. cvii and cviii we have this decision of the Countess of Champagne in one of the Courts of Love : 'Nous disons que l'amour ne peut étendre ses droits sur deux personnes mariées.'

1. See the interesting remarks of Guizot (*Histoire de la Civilisation en France*, Paris, 1846, tome iii. pp. 331-334). He says (pp. 333-334), 'Cette élévation de la condition des femmes s'accomplit entre le ix* et xii* siècles. . . Au xi* siècle elle fut à peu près consommée.' In the feudal times, although by the common law of England a woman could claim one-third of her husband's lands as dower, yet if he endowed her at the door of the church with *less* than one-third, she could not take what the common law gave her. On the other hand, if he had endowed her with more than one-third, she was referred to the same common law, and obliged to content herself with the third. But Littleton, in the

reign of Edward IV., first lays down that if a woman is endowed *ad ostium ecclesiæ* with more than one-third, she may after her husband's death choose whether she will accept it or betake herself to her dower at common law (*Blackstone's Comment.* 8vo, 1809, ii. 133-136).

NOTES ON THE OPINIONS HELD RESPECTING THE SOUL.

For the sentiments of Hincmar in the ninth century, see *Histoire littéraire de la France*, tome v. p. 559. See the word 'Âme,' in index to Le Clerc, Bibliothèque choisie. In the Mahometan Legends it is said that the soul of Adam was created a thousand years before him (see *The Bible, the Koran, and the Talmud, by G. Weil*, 8vo, 1846, Lond. p. 2), and as to the mode in which it might leave the body see ibid. p. 143. See p. 298 of The Creed and Ethics of the Jews, exhibited in Selections from Maimonides, by H. H. Bernard, Cambridge, 1832. See Guizot, Civilisation en France, 1846, tome i. pp. 162-176. He observes that from the first century most of the fathers believed in the materiality of the soul, which was (p. 163) an opinion 'non seulement admise mais dominante,' and this doctrine they maintained against the pagan writers (p. 164) ; but at the fourth century the doctrine of its immateriality began to make way through the influence of Augustine, of Nemesius, and of Mamert Claudien (p. 165). Of the treatise of the last, Guizot (pp. 165-175) has given an interesting account ; and he observes (p. 176) that the arguments by which these Christian writers demonstrated the spirituality of the soul were pagan. Irenæus believed ' that the soul in a state of separation from the body retains its individuality, so that disembodied souls may know each other' (*Beaven's Account of Irenæus*, 8vo, 1841, p. 234 *et seq.*) St. Bernard of Clairvaux said that the happiness after death would not be complete, nor would the face of God be seen, until *after* the resurrection of the body (xiii. 184). But he elsewhere expresses a contrary opinion (ibid.) The celebrated Bishop Caius, in the third century, is said by Photius to have written a treatise on the soul, in which ' il attribuait à l'âme la figure du corps humain ' (*Histoire lit. de la France*, tome i. part i. p. 360). But it does not seem quite certain (p. 359) whether or no this treatise, called the Labyrinth, *is* by Caius. In the fourth century Lactantius maintained that the soul was immortal and in-corporeal (see *Hist. lit. de la France*, tome i. part ii. p. 69). St. Hilary, Bishop of Poitiers, 'ayant occasion de parler de l'origine de l'âme, enseigne qu'elle ne vient point par transfusion, mais qu'elle est immédiatement créée de Dieu' (*Hist. lit. de la France*, tome i. part ii. p. 162). He also maintains (p. 189) 'sa nature spirituelle et différente de celle du corps.' But St. Phebade, Bishop of Agen, who lived till the very end of the fourth century, calls *every-thing* that exists *body*. This *may be* merely a mode of expression (*Hist. lit. de la France*, tome i. part ii. p. 271). St. Ambrose, Bishop of Milan, says that the perfect soul has *its* body in aversion (*Hist. lit. de la France*, tome i. part ii. pp. 358, 359). He asserts the immortality of the soul (p. 359). The materiality of the soul is distinctly affirmed by Tertullian (*Ceillier*, ii. 438, 445, 446, 453, and *My Life*).

NOTE ON MANNER ETC. OF KEEPING SUNDAY.

Bingham, Antiq. xvi. 8, iii. (*Works*, 1844, vol. vi. p. 188), has shown that it was considered a day of rejoicing ; and St. Augustine says that the ' impious Manichees' had chosen that day to fast in ' opposition to the Church ' (see also vol. vii. p. 38). Hence it was (p. 189) that many canons excommunicated those who fasted on Sunday. Bingham says (sect. iv. p. 190) that 'the imperial laws forbade all public games and shows on Sunday,' but the earliest law he has quoted is one of Theodosius the Great. (See also vol. vii. p. 31.) There were several canons (p. 191) ex-communicating those who went to shows. See also Bingham, book xx. chap. ii., *Works*, vii. 13 *et seq.* The passage he cites from Pliny (p. 14) is not decisive as to the difference between Sunday and the Sabbath ; but he quotes (p. 15) one of the epistles of Ignatius, in which that father 'bids the Magnesians not to sabbatise with the Jews, but to lead a life agreeable to the Lord's day.' Constantine forbade all lawsuits on Sundays (p. 16), 'with the exception of such actions as the law calls *votiva*, " good offices "' (p. 19). Constantine also obliged his army to rest from all military exercise (p. 21). However, he allowed 'countrymen to follow their works of husbandry,' but by other and later laws that liberty was in a great measure restrained (p. 24), and even the earlier fathers, such as Irenæus and Tertullian, were opposed

to any such liberty (see pp. 24, 25), and many canons up to the
time of Charlemagne show that the church did not approve the
liberty granted by Charlemagne (pp. 26, 27). It appears that all
fasting was prohibited on Sunday, even during the time of Lent
(pp. 37–39, 40). Bingham says (vii. 41, 42), 'Another custom as
generally prevailing was, always to pray standing, and never
kneeling, on the Lord's day. . . . This custom was not only general, but of long continuance in the church ; and when or how it
came to be altered or laid aside, I think, is not very easy to determine. . . . This custom may be traced as high as Irenæus'
(iv. 326, Antiq. xiii. viii. iii.) Bingham (iv. 326–330) has given a
string of testimonies showing that from Irenæus to the third
Council of Tours, in the time of Charlemagne, the custom of not
kneeling on Sundays was general. Beaven's Account of Irenæus,
8vo, 1841, p. 202.

Lord Howard of Effingham, in an account of the negotiations
for peace at Château-Cambresis, writes to Elizabeth, in 1559,
'And for because we had no good time to talk thereof there, we
appointed to meet the next day, being Sundaye, in the church,
and there to talk at better leisure of it ; and as we had agreed, so
we did' (Forbes's Elizabeth, i. 48 ; see also p. 52). In the same
year Sir Nicholas Throckmorton writes to the Lords of the
Council, that at Nôtre Dame in Paris, 'I took occasion in the
church to remove from my place to talk with De l'Aubespine the
secretary' (Forbes, i. 144). The oath was taken on Sunday
(p. 106). In 1821, Southey writes that a son of Mr. Raikes 'introduced Sunday schools into the kingdom ;' and he or his son,
the editor of his correspondence, adds in a note, 'I know not
where or when they were first instituted, but they are noticed in
an ordinance of Albert and Isabel, in the year 1608, as then
existing in the Catholic Netherlands, the magistrates being enjoined to see to their establishment and support in all places where
they were not set on foot' (Life and Correspondence of Robert
Southey, edited by his son, the Rev. C. C. Southey, 8vo, 1849–
1850, vol. i. p. 37). In the reigns of Edward VI. and Mary,
audiences on state affairs were generally given on Sunday (see
Ambassades de Noailles, Leyde, 1763, tome ii. pp. 40, 52, 122,
123, 141, 265, 267, 282, 334 ; tome iii. pp. 132, 250 ; tome iv.
pp. 93, 149, 157, 175 ; tome v. pp. 27, 311 ; and Haynes's State
Papers, p. 236). In 1571 we find the Bishop of Ross writing a

state letter on Sunday (see *Murdin's State Papers*, p. 6) ; and in 1572 the queen gave a grand banquet on Sunday (p. 219). See Correspondance diplomatique de la Mothe-Fénelon, Paris, 8vo, 1840, tome i. p. 181 ; tome iii. pp. 130, 379 ; tome iv. p. 321 ; tome v. pp. 16, 160, 346 ; tome vi. p. 445. The Bishop of Winchester justifies bishops in playing at bowls on Sunday (see *Cooper's Admonitions*, 1589, pp. 43, 44, 8vo, 1847). In 1585 and 1586 we find Elizabeth's ministers writing their despatches on Sunday (see *Leycester Correspondence*, edit. Camden Society, pp. 44, 113). In 1559 the queen went on Sunday to a great banquet at Lord Arundel's (*Machyn's Diary*, p. 206, Camden Society, vol. xlii.) However, in 1562 we find the Ironmongers' Company ordering that the day on which they yearly gave a great dinner should be altered from Sunday to Monday (*Nichols's Note to Machyn's Diary*, p. 390). In the Chronicle of London, written in the fifteenth century, a curious anecdote is related to the effect that in A.D. 1258-1260 a Jew on Saturday fell into a 'privy' at Tewkesbury, but out of reverence for *his* Sabbath would not allow himself to be drawn out. The next day being Sunday, the Earl of Gloucester would not let any one draw him out ; 'and so,' says the Chronicler, 'the Jew died in the privy' (*A Chronicle of London from* 1089 *to* 1483, London, 1827, 4to, p. 20).

THE JEWISH SABBATH KEPT BY THE EARLY CHRISTIANS.

There is some interesting information on this point in Bingham's Antiquities of the Christian Church, book xx. ch. iii. Works, vii. 51 *et seq.* : 'The ancient Christians unanimously agreed in keeping Saturday, or the seventh day, as a more solemn day of religious worship and adoration (p. 51). It appears from Socrates, St. Basil, &c., that they not only had the Scriptures read and sermons preached, but the eucharist administered (p. 54). Still Sunday was thought superior : for, first, there was no ecclesiastical law obliging men to *pray standing* ; secondly, there were no imperial laws forbidding lawsuits, &c., on that day ; thirdly, there were no laws forbidding public shows, &c. ; fourthly, there were none obliging men to abstain from bodily labour—on the contrary, there were canons *forbidding* the Christians to 'Judaise or rest on the Sabbath ' (p. 55).

The *cause* of this compliance of the Christians with the Jewish superstition respecting the Sabbath is fairly stated by Bingham, p. 57. In the Western Church it was kept as a fast—in the Eastern Church as a feast ; which, amid many other testimonies, we learn from Augustine (p. 52). Bingham attempts (sect. v. pp. 58-60) to account for the difference in respect to the observance of the Sabbath between the Eastern and the Western Churches, but his reasoning seems unsatisfactory. He has, however, shown (sect. vi. pp. 60-65) that originally the Sabbath was kept as a festival in the Western Church, for which he cites Tertullian. The change from a festival to a fast seems to have taken place very shortly after (p. 61) the time of Tertullian.

See also Antiq. xiii. 9, iii. and iv. ; Bingham's Works, iv. 357-366. Bingham has probably generalised too much. The Bishop of Lincoln says that ' the custom of observing every Saturday as a fast, which became general throughout the Western Church, does *not* appear to have existed in Tertullian's time' (see p. 389 of his *Tertullian*, 1845, 3rd edit.) I have since observed that Bingham also mentions this (*Antiq.* xx. 3, vi. ; *Works*, vii. 60-65). The learned Böhmer thought that the 'status dies' of Pliny referred to the Sabbath (see *Le Clerc, Bibliothèque choisie*, xxiv. 443). See what Julian 'the Apostate' says (*Lardner, Works*, 8vo, 1838, vol. vii. p. 624). Lardner has no doubt but that Pliny meant to refer to Sunday (*Heathen Testimonies, Works*, vii. 38, 74). Tertullian (*adv. Judaeos*, cap. iv. *et seq.*) says that the observance of the Sabbath was only for a time ; seeming thus to intimate that it had passed away (see *Ceillier*, ii. 436). I think it likely that the custom of making Saturday a holiday is a remnant of the Jewish superstition. Southey says, ' In the north of England, Saturday as well as Sunday is a Sabbath to the schoolmaster' (*The Doctor*, edit. Warter, 8vo, 1848, p. 23).

REASONS WHY FASTING HAS BEEN SO OFTEN THOUGHT A RELIGIOUS ESSENTIAL.

For some interesting remarks on this see p. 326 of Salverte, Des Sciences occultes, Paris, 8vo, 1843, 2nd edit. He has observed that fasting produces a singular effect on the imagination ; and thus predisposing it to *see* miracles, becomes an important implement in the hands of an artful priesthood. The famous vision of Peter, which effected such an important change in Christianity, took place when 'he became very hungry, and would have eaten ' (Acts x. 10).

1. Tertullian and Clemens Alexandrinus testify to the Christians fasting every Wednesday and Friday (see pp. 131, 132 of part ii. of *King's Inquiry into Constitution, &c. of Primitive Church*, 8vo, 1713). 2. The Koriacs of Kamtschatka fast all day on the eve of their religious ceremonies (see *Lesser's Travels in Kamtschatka*, 8vo, 1790, vol. ii. p. 104). For proof of the rigour with which the Puritans in the middle of the seventeenth century kept their fasts, see a curious passage in The Autobiography of Joseph Lister of Bradford, edited by Thomas Wright, Lond. 8vo, 1842, p. 6. See my Life of Tertullian. The Mahommedans fast until they produce a sort of trance, in which they see God (see *Niebuhr, Description de l'Arabie*, 4to, 1774, p. 108).

NOTE ON JEWISH CUSTOM OF TRANSFERRING PROPERTY BY TAKING OFF THE SHOE.

' From Ruth iv. 7 we have another singular usage on occasion of purchase, cession, and exchange, viz., that the transference of alienable property had in earlier times been confirmed by the proprietor plucking off his shoe, and handing it over to the new owner. We see at the same time that in the age of David this usage had become antiquated; for the writer introduces it as an unknown custom of former times, in the days of David's great-grandfather. I have not been able to find any further trace of it in the East, nor yet has the Danish travelling mission to Arabia, as Captain Niebuhr himself informs me. Bynæus, in his book De Calceis Hebræorum, i. 6, 7, treats of it at great length; but excepting the mere conjectures of modern literati, he gives no account of the origin of this strange symbol of the transfer of property. In the time of Moses it was so familiar, that *barefooted* was a term of reproach, and probably signified a man that had sold everything, a spendthrift, and a bankrupt; and we see from Deut. xxv. 9, 10, that Moses allowed it to be applied to the person who would not marry his brother's widow. Could it have been an Egyptian custom, as we do not find it again in the East? The

Egyptians, when they adored the Deity, had no shoes on ; and of this the Pythagoreans gave the following explanation : " The philosopher who comes naked from his mother's womb should appear naked before his Creator ; for God hears those who are not burdened with anything extrinsic." See Demophili Sententiæ Pythagoreæ. Among the Egyptians, too, *barefooted* was equivalent to *naked*, and naked synonymous with *having no property but oneself* (*Michaelis, Commentaries on the Laws of Moses*, 8vo, 1814, vol. i. pp. 434, 435). And see Prichard's Egyptian Mythology, 8vo, 1838, p. 393.

1. When Park paid his respects to the Pagan king of Bondore, his 'guide and interpreter, according to custom, took off their sandals ' (*Park's Travels*, 8vo, 1817, vol. i. p. 79). 2. Bruce (*Travels*, Edinburgh, 4to, 1790, vol. iii. pp. 120, 121) says, 'In Abyssinia it is not good breeding to show or speak of your feet, especially if anything ails them ; and at all times they are covered.' And yet in another place (vol. iii. pp. 314, 315) he says, 'You are barefooted whenever you enter the church.' 3. It is remarkable that walking with naked feet is forbidden by Zoroaster (see *Zendavesta*, édit. du Perron, tome ii. p. 33). 4. The Druids gathered ' the Selago, a kind of hedge hyssop,' and the gatherer was to have 'his feet naked ' (*Borlase, Antiquities of Cornwall*, Lond. 1769, p. 95). 5. Michaelis, Recueil de Questions, Amsterdam, 1774, 4to, p. 117, No. lix. Denham and Clapperton's Africa, 1826, 4to, p. 67. Many of the early Christians used to put off their shoes before entering church, and the Abyssinian Christians practised it as late as the eighteenth century. (See the evidence in *Bingham's Christian Antiquities*, Book viii. ch. 10, sect. vi., *Works*, vol. ii. pp. 555-556, 8vo, 1843.) According to the statutes of Cluni, as collected by Ulric in A.D. 1091, the monks on Good Friday were to assemble in the cloister with *naked feet* (*Fleury, Histoire ecclésiastique*, livre lxiii. No. 60, tome xiii. p. 501). In A.D. 1126 the associates of Pons, before receiving absolution from Honorius II., 'entrèrent au palais *nuds pieds*' (*Fleury*, livre lxvii. No. 46, tome xiv. p. 344). The Japanese consider it a mark of respect to take off their shoes (see *Golownin's Captivity in Japan*, 8vo, 1824, vol. ii. p. 333, and vol. iii. p. 129). And so do the Persians. See *Morier's First Journey through Persia*, Lond. 4to, 1812, pp. 39, 189, 214, 218 ; and his *Second Journey through Persia*, 4to, 1818, pp. 95, 171, 173 ; and in particular p. 241, where Morier says, 'The Persians

look upon the omission of taking off shoes as the greatest in-
dignity that could be offered to them ' (see also p. 403).

OF THE LEVIRATE MARRIAGE—OR MARRIAGE OF
A CHILDLESS BROTHER'S WIDOW.

There are some interesting details respecting this in Art. 98 of
Michaelis's Commentaries on the Laws of Moses, 8vo, 1814, vol. ii.
pp. 21-33. He observes that before the time of Moses such
marriage was compulsory, as appears from the story of Judah and
his daughter-in-law Tamar, related in Gen. xxxviii. (*Michaelis*,
p. 23). See also pp. 29-33, where he has instanced those points
in which Moses softened the operation of the law : first, forbidding the marriage if there were children by the first husband
alive ; and secondly, allowing the brother either to marry her, or
to declare in court that he would not marry her ; upon which she
was allowed to revile him and give him the name of *Barexole*,
which anybody might apply to him—no very severe punishment
when we think that *Barexole* merely means ' a man who has given
a woman the refusal.' As to the origin of this law he says (p. 24)
that ' very lately Euler learnt it from the Russian generals, and
Süsmilch, from Euler's communication, declared the mystery to
the world in his work entitled "Göttliche Ordnung," &c. . . . It
had been commonly believed that its only foundation was the
peculiar notion of the Israelites on the subject of having descendants.' But the Mongols, ' who give themselves very little concern
about their genealogies and descendants, have a law which in like
manner enjoins the marriage of a brother's widow.' Nor can we
possibly account for this by supposing the Mongols to be descendants of the Jews. But it has been thus brought about. Among
the Mongols, whose daughters are—from the practice of polygamy
—bought by their richer neighbours, young women are so scarce
that every man cannot have a wife, and hence has arisen the
custom of all the brothers in a family being satisfied with one
and the same wife, whom they purchase in common with the
agreement that her first child is to be considered the son of the
eldest brother, the second child of the second brother, and so on.
This was communicated to Euler by the Russian generals, who
well knew the country. And we have only to suppose a small
degree of refinement, and conceive a dislike to such a community

of property, and the result would be this. As young women are scarce and dear, only one of the brothers would marry, and when he dies the widow with the inheritance will devolve to the next brother, whether she have children or not. Another step, and the widow, if she *have* children, will not go to the next brother, 'her children having in a manner repaid the price which she cost;' but if she have no children, the marriage must take place. Thus it was among the Jews; and Judah, when he heard of Tamar's pregnancy, wished her to be burnt as an adulteress. *Levirate* (p. 21) comes 'from the word *Levir*, which, though it appears not in the ancient classic authors, but only in the Vulgate and the Pandects, is nevertheless really an old Latin word, and is explained by Festus to signify "*a husband's brother*."'

Luther's mode of accounting for Levirate laws is unsatisfactory enough (see *Propos de Table de M. Luther*, édit. Brunet, Paris, 1844, pp. 74, 75). Michaelis, Recueil de Questions, Amsterdam, 1774, 4to, p. 118, No. lx. Niebuhr (*Description de l'Arabie*, Amsterdam, 1774, 4to, pp. 61-62) throws doubts on the theory of Michaelis. Malthus was evidently ignorant of Michaelis's explanation. He accounts for these marriages by supposing they originated in the fear of a redundant population (*Essay on Population*, 1826, 6th edit. vol. i. pp. 200-204). Southey says (*The Doctor*, 8vo, 1848, p. 8) that the law prohibiting a man to marry his brother's widow 'is not sanctioned by reason, and that instead of being in conformity with Scripture, is in direct opposition to it, being in fact the mere device of a corrupt and greedy church.' In some parts of Italy it is still the custom for only one of the sons to marry (see *Mill's Political Economy*, 1849, i. 433). In Madagascar a man often takes the wife of his deceased brother (see *Drury's Madagascar*, 8vo, 1743, p. 242); and see for it in India, Transactions of Literary Society of Bombay, vol. ii. p. 227, 4to, 1820.

NOTES ON THE WORSHIP AND RITES CONNECTED WITH THE VIRGIN MARY.

'Divers historiens ont déjà remarqué que ce fut Saint Bona-venture qui introduisit le pieux usage d'adresser à la Sainte Vierge une prière après complies, et de sonner une cloche pour en rappeler le souvenir aux fidèles. Il était persuadé que c'est dans cette heure du jour que s'accomplit le grand mystère de l'Incarnation, et voilà l'objet qu'il se proposa dans cette institution' (*Colonia, Histoire littéraire de la Ville de Lyon,* tome ii. pp. 315, 316, Lyon, 1730, 410).

The same thing is asserted by Petit Radel (*Histoire littéraire de la France,* xix. 270), who adds, 'C'est un des *premiers vestiges* de la coutume introduite dans l'église de *sonner* l'Angélus.' But neither Colonia nor Petit Radel quotes any authority for their statement. Petit Radel adds that he also ordered that on each Saturday the Franciscans should celebrate a solemn mass in honour of the Virgin ; 'usage qui a aussi passé dans l'église, où le samedi est devenu un jour consacré à la Vierge Marie ' (*ibid.* p. 270). But the custom is much older. Suger, the famous minister to Louis VI. and Louis VII., enacted by a charter that every Thursday and Saturday 'on fera mémoire de la Sainte Vierge ' (*Histoire littéraire de la France,* tome xii. p. 400). It is also mentioned by Peter Damien in the middle of the eleventh century (see *Fleury, Histoire ecclésiastique,* livre lx. No. 54, tome xiii. pp. 104, 105), who says that the reason was because God rested on Saturday (see also *Ceillier, Auteurs ecclésiastiques,* xx. 556). Bernier, monk of St. Remi, at Rheims, flourished in the middle of the tenth century. Among his works, still MS., 'il se trouve un traité où l'on rend raison pourquoi l'on fait chaque samedi mémoire de la mère de Dieu ' (*Ceillier,* xix. 665).

Petit Radel says (p. 282) that Bonaventure's ' Meditationes Vitæ Christi' contain everything he has written on the Virgin Mary ; and he adds that though this work has been deservedly blamed, the best critics 'ne mettent pas en doute son authenticité ; ils l'imputent à Saint Bonaventure.' Saint Bernard of Clairvaux wrote four homilies on her (*Histoire littéraire de la France,* tome xiii. p. 153), but *denied* that she was free from original sin (p. 232). And Saint Anselm *appears* to have held the same opinion, if one may judge from his not contradicting the assertion of Bosou, afterwards abbot of Bec (see *Fleury, Histoire ecclés.* lxiv. No. 52, tome xiii. p. 614). The Works of Albert the Great, who died in A.D. 1280, are published at Lyons in twenty-one volumes folio, 1651 ; and the twentieth volume contains treatises on the Virgin Mary (*Histoire littéraire de la France,* xix. 366). See also what Peter the Venerable (de Cluni) in the twelfth century says (*Histoire littéraire de la France,* xiii. 257). Abelard tells us that in his time there was a sect 'qui a la témérité d'enseigner qu'avant l'incarnation la foi au Messie n'était point nécessaire au salut ; que le corps de Jésus-Christ a été formé dans les entrailles de la Vierge à la manière ordinaire, excepté que l'homme n'y a point concouru' (*Histoire littéraire de la France*, xii. 121 ; see also pp. 133, 150). The preface to the mass in honour of the Virgin has been ascribed to St. Bruno, the famous founder of the Carthusians ; but the Benedictines peremptorily reject this assertion, though they confess that its real author is unknown (*Histoire littéraire de la France*, viii. 533; ix. 251). In the eleventh century Jean de Garlande made a collection of her miracles (*Hist. lit. de la France*, viii. 87), and a certain William wrote a panegyric on her in the same century (*Hist. lit. de la France*, viii. 679, 680). In the eleventh century the church of Chartres possessed the Virgin's shift (*ibid.* viii. 351). The establishment of 'le petit office de la Sainte Vierge' has been ascribed to Urban II., who died in 1090 ; but it is older than he (*Histoire littéraire de la France*, viii. 532). It is recommended by Peter Damian in the middle of the eleventh century, who illustrates its use by a pleasant anecdote ; and it was practised in the preceding century (*Fleury*, livre lx. No. 54, tome xiii. pp. 104, 105). But he introduced it among the *monks* (p. 580).

Gregory of Tours died in 595. He wrote on the Virgin, but took his account from 'le faux Meliton de Sardes, que le Pape Saint Gélase avec le concile de Rome avait mis au rang des livres apocryphes' (*Hist. lit. de la France*, iii. 383). The Benedictines add that Gregory 'est au reste le premier des anciens qui ait parlé clairement de l'assomption ou résurrection de la mère de Dieu.' But Hampson (*Medii Ævi Kalendarium*, 8vo, 1841, vol. ii. p. 23) says that the festival of her assumption was instituted by Damasus about 364. See also pp. 166, 167, where Hampson connects it with the rape of Proserpine, which occurred in February. Ceillier (*Histoire générale des Auteurs sacrés*, tome xvii. p. 16) says, 'Saint Grégoire, évêque de Tours, est le premier des anciens qui ait dit que la Sainte Vierge fût après sa mort enlevée en corps et en âme dans le ciel.' See also p. 44, where Ceillier gives the passages from Greg. Lib. de Gloria Martyr., capp. 4 and 9.

Some hymns on the Virgin Mary have been ascribed to Anselm, Archbishop of Canterbury, but it is doubtful if he wrote them

(*Histoire littéraire de la France*, ix. 435). Ceillier seems inclined to think he wrote the hymns but not the psalter (see *Histoire générale des Auteurs sacrés*, xxi. 312). Another work on her is attributed to him, which the Benedictines (ix. 444) also reject, because it makes mention of the 'Fête de la Conception. Or il est constant qu'on ne commença à parler de cette fête que du temps de St. Bernard.' Hampson says, 'Anselm, who died in 1109, invented this festival' (*Medii Ævi Kalendarium*, 8vo, 1841, vol. ii. p. 147).

Frodoard, canon of Rheims, died in A.D. 966. He wrote an account of the miracles effected in the cathedral of Rheims by the intercession of the Virgin Mary ; but it is lost (tome vi. p. 329).

Nolker the Stammerer died in A.D. 912. He made a collection of Sequences, among which are some for the Feast of the Assumption of the Virgin, and her nativity (*Hist. lit.* vi. 138, 139). Mabillon supposes he invented Sequences, but that is a mistake (p. 138). Innocent IV., in the third session of the Council of Lyons (A.D. 1245), ordered the celebration of the octave of the nativity of the Virgin (*Fleury, Histoire ecclésiastique*, livre lxxxii. No. 27, tome xvii. p. 369). Saint Ennodius, Bishop of Pavia, died in A.D. 521. He wrote poetry in honour of Mary (*Ceillier*, xv. 431). Theophanes, Archbishop of Nicea, flourished in the middle of the ninth century (*Ceillier, Auteurs sacrés*, xviii. 701). He wrote a hymn in honour of the Virgin (p. 702). Joseph, deacon of the church of Constantinople, died in A.D. 883. 'Il composa des hymnes pour toutes les fêtes de la Sainte Vierge' (*Ceillier*, xix. 498). Saint Fulbert, Bishop of Chartres, who died in 1028, wrote poems in honour of Mary (*Ceillier*, xx. 148, 149). Jean Macropus, metropolitan of Euchania, in Asia Minor, died at the end of the eleventh century. He wrote a hymn on the Virgin (see *Ceillier*, xx. 395). He also addressed to her seventy-seven canticles (p. 369). Jean de Garlande, an Englishman, in the middle of the eleventh century wrote an epithalamium in her honour (*Ceillier*, xx. 397). John the Geometer, in the eleventh century, composed four hymns in honour of the Virgin (*Ceillier*, xx. 399). John Zonaras, in the twelfth century, wrote a hymn on her (*Ceillier*, xxi. 548), and so did Geoffroi early in the twelfth century (xxi. 569). The venerable Peter de Cluni, who died in 1156, wrote poems in her honour (xxii. 512). Symeon Metaphraste, master of offices and great chancellor at Constantinople,

flourished in the middle of the tenth century. He is the author
of a prayer to the Virgin Mary (*Ceillier, Auteurs sacrés,* xix.
598). Rosvithe, or Hroswitha, a nun in the convent of Ganders-
heim, in Lower Saxony, flourished about the middle of the
tenth century. She wrote a history of the birth and life of Mary
in hexameters (*Ceillier,* xix. 686). Abelard died in 1142. Of
him Ceillier (*Auteurs sacrés,* xxii. 180) says, 'Ce qu'il dit de la
rencontre de tous les apôtres au moment du trépas de la Sainte
Vierge est tiré de Saint Grégoire de Tours.' The original source
of this story seems to have been a work attributed to St. Meliton,
Bishop of Sardes, in the reign of Marcus Aurelius (see *Ceillier,*
ii. 79). Innocent III. was Pope from 1198 to 1216. The sixth
book of his Mysteries of the Evangelical Law contains a eulogy
of the Virgin (*Ceillier, Histoire générale des Auteurs sacrés,* xiii. 457).
Hildebert, Bishop of Mans, died in 1133 or 1134. In his fifty-
eighth sermon 'il dit que de son tems on avait coutume de prier
la Sainte Vierge avec plus d'affection que les autres saints, et que
lorsque l'on prononçait son nom on fléchissait les genoux' (*Ceillier,*
xxii. 30).

STATE OF LEARNING AND LITERATURE IN GAUL IN THE TWELFTH CENTURY.

See Dissertation sur l'État des Lettres en France—douzième
siècle, in Benedictine Histoire littéraire de la France, tome ix.
pp. 1-225. This was superior to every century since the reign of
Charlemagne (p. 1), and so notorious was the height to which it
reached that an Italian writer at the end of the century calls
France the mother of all philosophy and the inventor of all
sciences (p. 3).

Much of this advancement the Benedictines attribute to the
personal characters of Louis VI., Louis VII., and Philip II.
(Augustus), whose united reigns lasted from A.D. 1108 to A.D.
1222 (see p. 5). But see also the severe remarks of Guizot upon
Louis the Young (VII.) in Histoire de la Civilisation en France,
8vo, 1846, vol. iv. p. 108. Louis VII. and Philip Augustus
granted privileges to the students at Paris, though we do not precisely know what these privileges were (p. 9).

Another reason for the increase of learning was (p. 11) 'la
multiplication prodigieuse des maisons religieuses, dont l'entrée

exigeait ordinairement que ceux qui y aspiraient eussent quelque
teinture des lettres.' But the increase of learning met with many
serious obstacles ; among which (p. 12) must be noted the practice of paying no regard to merit in ecclesiastical promotions,
which was carried to such a height that often the highest dignities
of the church were conferred on children. The consequence was,
there were to be found priests ignorant of the common rudiments
of Latin (see p. 28). Another blow was sustained when Philip II.
in 1182 banished the Jews (p. 13), and indeed the effects were so
obvious that in 1198 he recalled them. Other obstacles were the
disputes between the regular canons and the monks, and between
the Clunists and the Cistercians, though indeed the very collision
may have given an impetus to literature (p. 14). The Benedictines are compelled to allow (p. 16) that in this latter controversy Peter de Cluni displayed great moderation, while the observations in which Bernard indulged ' peuvent être regardés
comme une invective.'

    The crusades were prejudicial, ' au moins indirectement, à la
culture des lettres ' (p. 16). They add that, owing to the indulgences granted to those who were connected with the crusades,
the canonical penances became abandoned to the discretion of
confessors, and this produced a decline of the study of that part
of the canon law. They also plausibly observe (p. 17) ' que les
croisades ayant en ce siècle donné naissance aux premiers ordres
de chevalerie, ceux qui s'y engageaient n'étant point obligés
d'être lettrés, plusieurs pères de famille négligèrent de faire
étudier leurs enfants, dans l'espérance qu'ils pourraient prendre
parti dans ces ordres sans sçavoir les lettres.' They think (p. 19)
that tournaments were ' plus préjudiciables qu'utiles à la culture
des lettres.' They observe that in this century the church condemned them severely, that St. Bernard calls them *figmenta
diabolica*, &c., and that the Council of Rheims before him had
employed similar expressions. To this I may add that the Council
of Rheims in 1131 decreed that those who were killed at tournaments should be refused ecclesiastical burial (*Fleury, Histoire
ecclésiastique*, xiv. 403) ; that in 1179 the Council of Lateran
renewed the prohibition of them (*Fleury*, xv. 412), but without
attaching any penalty. Indeed, it would appear that they were
gaining ground, for in 1254 the Council of Albi contented itself
with forbidding *clerks* to attend tournaments (*Fleury*, xviii. 536).

However, in 1279 we find Pope Nicholas writing a very angry letter to Philip the Bold (*Fleury*, xviii. 269, 270), and blaming him for *re-establishing* tournaments. The Benedictines nevertheless confess (p. 19) that tournaments were favourable to the cultivation of the vernacular poetry and romances, but they add, with their monastic littleness, that such literature had better never have existed ! ! ! and they particularly indulge (p. 20) in a tirade against romances.

Another circumstance unfavourable to learning was the custom in the public schools of receiving money for lessons (pp. 25, 26). Abelard confesses that he opened in the first instance a school with the view of gaining wealth. Other contemporaries attest the same practice, and it was even usual, on leaving a school, to sell to others what we should call the '*goodwill.*' The Council of London, in 1138, indeed forbade the practice, but in France it spread rapidly. ' Le chapitre de Châlons-sur-Marne fut un des premiers qui le mirent en pratique, et bientôt ce prétendu droit d'exaction trouva entrée dans les autres églises de France, où les *scolastiques en particulier* avaient grand soin de le faire valoir à la rigueur.' Alexander III., hearing of this, issued two letters forbidding that learning should be *paid for*, and ordering that *all* clerks capable of giving lessons should be allowed to open schools. See also Histoire littéraire de la France, xii. 92. It is, however, well worthy of remark, that in the twelfth century the Jews at Lunel not only taught gratuitously, but supplied their pupils with the necessaries of life (*Histoire littéraire de la France*, ix. 133). The same thing is observable of the school at Beaucaire.

The adversaries of Abelard, in advancing reasons for the condemnation of his treatise upon the Trinity, which the Council of Soissons burned in 1121, said that to incur this penalty it was sufficient that he had circulated copies of a book which neither Pope nor church had approved. In this, say the Benedictines, 'il nous semble apercevoir dès ce siècle-ci les premiers vestiges de ces approbations qu'on jugea nécessaires dans la suite, surtout pour les écrits qui traitaient des matières de religion.' But what the Benedictines call 'les adversaires d'Abélard' (p. 28) seem to consist only of St. Bernard (at least they cite no other authority but his letters), and he was a likely man enough—under pretence of tradition—to innovate on the side of tyranny. Besides this, they confess (p. 29) that, 'au reste, quelque bien marquée que

soit ici cette source d'approbations, nous ne trouvons point dans
le cours de ce siècle qu'on en ait demandé ou accordé pour les
écrits qu'on publiait.'

They say that before the end of the twelfth century learning
declined (p. 29); 'décadence dont presque toutes les facultés de
la littérature se ressentirent ; mais la philosophie, la théologie et
les belles-lettres plus que les autres.' But they add (p. 30) that
before this decline letters were cultivated in the twelfth century
'avec plus de zèle et d'ardeur qu'elles n'avaient encore été depuis
plusieurs siècles' (and see p. 24). One great cause of this decline
was (p. 21) 'la mauvaise dialectique et la scolastique encore plus
mauvaise qu'on enseignait.' Hence, add they, the mischievous
custom (p. 11) of neglecting tradition, and 'il ne doit donc pas
paraître étonnant qu'il se trouve tant de doutes, tant d'opinions,
tant de probabilités et si peu de démonstrations dans les écrivains
de ce temps-là.' This strikes me as very high praise, though the
Benedictines mean it for censure. They, however, allow (p. 22)
that the scholastic theology *has* its advantages, and that it frequently served for defence of the doctrines of the church. According to the Benedictines, the good writers of the eleventh century had foreseen this 'alliance de la mauvaise dialectique avec la
théologie ;' and Fulbert de Chartres, Lanfranc, Anselm, and others
'avaient montré que dans les choses de la foi la raison humaine
est un guide trompeur et infidèle, qui livre à l'erreur et à l'illusion
ceux qui le suivent sans le secours de la révélation et de la tradition ;' *and in the early part of the twelfth century* (p. 23)
Guibert, abbé de Nogent, and Guillaume de Thierry attacked the
scholastics ; while even Abelard himself, 'revenu de ses égare-
ments, reconnaît lui-même que la manière dont la plupart traitaient alors la théologie avait donné lieu à quantité d'erreurs, dont
il fait une assez longue liste. C'est à quoi il emploie une partie du
troisième et du quatrième livre de sa Théologie Chrétienne.' Besides these writers, Pierre le Chantre, Pierre de Celle, and Jean
de Cornouaille opposed this new philosophy (p. 23), as also did
Gautier, prior of St. Victor, in a work which, though only published
in part, became very famous (p. 24, and see pp. 211-212). They
say (p. 183), 'Ce siècle-ci ne reconnaissait que trois parties dans
la philosophie—la logique ou dialectique, la morale et la physique.'
Of these, dialectic was almost the only one cultivated ; 'et cette
dialectique n'était autre pour le fonds que celle d'Aristote'

(p. 183); and then the good Benedictines launch out (p. 184) into an abuse of the obscurity of Aristotle. Peter de Celle (see p. 23), an able opponent of the scholastics, says, 'Il faut bien se donner de garde de planter la forêt d'Aristote auprès de l'autel du Seigneur.' But, on the other hand (see p. 57), we learn from John of Salisbury that 'Bernard le scolastique se mit à professer la dialectique, et quoique parfait Platonicien, *il tenta de concilier Platon avec Aristote. Mais il vint trop tard pour y réussir'* (see also p. 184). It may perhaps be doubted if Aristotle had such a very great share in forming the scholastic philosophy, for we are told (p. 184) that the great geniuses of the age '*tous* l'embrassèrent comme les autres,' and 'il n'y a guères qu'Helmand entre les philosophes qui conçût du mépris pour Aristote jusqu'à le mettre au rang des monstres de la nature.' However, Abelard (p. 184) thought Aristotle not sufficient to form a dialectician, but that a perusal of other writers was also necessary.' Others, and among them John of Salisbury, wished to join Porphyry to Aristotle ; others wished for Plato ; and (p. 185) 'la plupart enfin joignoit à celui-ci Averroes, Avicenne, et dans la suite, avant la fin du siècle, beaucoup d'autres subtilités philosophiques d'auteurs arabes, qui jettèrent encore une nouvelle obscurité dans la dialectique.' Among other writers, William de Conches (p. 185) 'donna un corps entier de philosophie, où il semble que les philosophes de ce siècle puisaient, comme les canonistes dans le Décret de Gratien, et les théologiens dans le Recueil de Pierre Lombard ' (see also pp. 211 –213). Such, they say, was the state of dialectic early in the twelfth century ; and (p. 186), 'bien loin de devenir plus heureux dans la suite, il alla toujours empirant.' The disputes respecting Nominalism and Realism occupied much attention, or, as the Benedictines say, 'on perdit beaucoup de temps à ces questions et disputes inutiles ' ! ! (p. 187). At p. 207 they again complain 'que le goût dominant pour les subtilités, les questions curieuses, les vains raisonnements, fit négliger les écrits des SS. Pères et des autres anciens auteurs.' The consequence was (pp. 207, 208) that in the twelfth century there were formed two different classes of theologians : 'les uns traitaient les matières de religion par

---

[1] Mr. Morell, who is anything but a sceptical writer, says 'without Plato the early Christian philosophy would not have seen light ; and without Aristotle the scholastic philosophy could not possibly have arisen' (*Morell's Historical and Critical View of the Speculative Philosophy of Europe*, 8vo, 1846, vol. I. p. 16).

l'autorité de l'Écriture, des Conciles et des Pères de l'Église, en y joignant quelquefois des propositions démontrées par la lumière naturelle. Les autres n'y employaient que de purs raisonnements et l'art de la dialectique ; ou s'ils citaient l'Écriture, c'était en des sens allégoriques et arbitraires' (p. 208). The first was called positive, the second scholastic theology. This scholastic method excited the alarm of Pope Alexander III., who in 1164 prohibited it, or rather, as it appears, prohibited that extreme abuse of it which went ' jusqu'à mettre en problème les dogmes les plus incontestables de la foi' (p. 209).[1] It is generally supposed that Roscelin of Compiègne was the first author of this 'mélange de la dialectique avec la théologie' (p. 209). ' Mais Abélard s'avoue ouvertement le père de cette méthode.' Peter Lombard (p. 210), in his Book of the Sentences, ' ne suivit pas la méthode qui fit tomber Roscelin, Abélard et d'autres dans des erreurs. Il prit une tout autre route, et sans citer Aristote, ni s'abandonner au raisonnement humain, il s'appliqua à rapporter les sentiments des SS. Pères.' They say (p. 210), 'C'est à Abélard qu'est due l'invention de traiter problématiquement les matières théologiques. Il est effectivement le premier qui ait employé cette méthode dans son ouvrage encore manuscrit, mais indigne de paraître au grand jour, intitulé Sic et Non, le pour et le contre.'

We now come to the schools, and first of the episcopal ones (p. 30); they were both schools and seminaries. There was always a master to watch over the education of the young ; but those more advanced were generally taught by the bishop, ' qui se chargeait lui-même d'instruire ceux qui étaient plus avancés.' This at least was frequently the case, but in other instances the bishops allowed masters to teach in their place (p. 31). These masters were at first removable ; but before the end of the twelfth century they 'devinrent fixes et permanents, en devenant attachés par des bénéfices aux églises où ils enseignaient' (p. 31). There is proof of this in the year 1077 ; and after the middle of the twelfth century this establishment became common in the cathedrals, 'en conséquence du canon du concile de Latran, en 1179, qui le prescrit expressément' (p. 31) ; and in 1215 another council of the Lateran repeated the order (p. 32). Among these episcopal

[1] When did the positive theology arise ? Gregory of Tours, who died in 595, speaks of the authority of the Fathers and the Bible as forming the grounds for belief. (See Hist. litt. de la France, vol. III. p. 393.)

schools, that of Rheims was eminent in the tenth and eleventh centuries (p. 32), and in the twelfth century sustained its reputation (pp. 32-34). The episcopal school of Laon (pp. 35, 36), which in the eleventh century had been so celebrated, preserved its reputation in the twelfth century. For an account of the other episcopal schools see pp. 37-60, and in particular pp. 40-41 for an account of that of Liège.

We now come to the schools of Paris (p. 61). They were opened at the latest at the end of the tenth century, and were distinguished from the schools of the cathedral, a distinction many writers have not attended to, though indeed ' il faut au reste avouer qu'il est fort difficile de discerner les docteurs qui ont enseigné à l'école épiscopale d'avec ceux qui ont exercé les mêmes fonctions dans les autres écoles de la ville.' It will be well to begin with the episcopal school, and then pass to the other schools of Paris. The episcopal school of Paris was originally held in the house of the bishop (p. 61), or in the cloister of the cathedral, but at the end of the twelfth century it was transported to the parvis between the episcopal palace and the Hôtel-Dieu. But early in the twelfth century the number of students became so great that the bishop, in concert with the canons, forbade any to remain ' qui n'étaient pas du corps de la cathédrale ' (p. 61), and thus ' l'école épiscopale se trouva donc alors réduite aux jeunes clercs de la cathédrale et aux enfants de naissance qu'on élevait avec eux.' Still, this school produced a great number of eminent men (for a list of whom see pp. 62-63), and it is in particular to the reputation with which Guillaume de Champeaux taught in the school that the immense rush of students from every part is to be attributed. He, however, in 1108 retired to St. Victor, nor do we know who succeeded him (p. 63). Whoever it was, the episcopal school sustained its reputation ; and it is said, though on doubtful authority, that Peter de Lombard was one of the professors of theology there (p. 64). The Benedictines say (p. 64) that it is certain ' que *l'école épiscopale de Paris fut l'origine de toutes les autres écoles,* qui se multiplièrent prodigieusement, tant dans la ville qu'aux environs ;' and from hence arose the subordination of those schools to the bishop and to the church ; so that after the establishment of academic degrees they were taken in the bishop's house (p. 64 ; and for proofs of the jurisdiction of the Bishop of Paris see p. 65).

We now come to the public schools of Paris and its neighbourhood (p. 65). That of St. Victor was the first and most persevering. This was the most celebrated of the schools of the canons regular (p. 113), to which Guillaume de Champeaux in 1108 transferred the school 'qui tenait au cloître Notre-Dame.' 'En peu de temps Saint-Victor devint par là une des plus brillantes académies de l'Europe ' (p. 114). In 1113, Guillaume de Champeaux was made bishop at Châlons-sur-Marne, but nevertheless the school kept up its reputation. 'On a des indices que cette école se maintint avec avantage tout le reste de ce siècle' (p. 114), and in the twelfth century this single abbey gave to the church no less than seven cardinals (p. 115). In 1148 the Institute of the Canons Regular passed from St. Victor to the abbey of Sainte Geneviève, where it is probable letters were already cultivated. At all events, they *had* been at the end of the tenth century (p. 116) ; and at least *after* this period the school of Ste. Geneviève flourished exceedingly (see pp. 117, 118). A little *prior* to this Abelard himself had taught there (p. 65), and had for his pupil the famous John of Salisbury (as he himself relates), and this *must* have taken place *about* 1118, since in 1120 Abelard became monk at St. Denis (p. 66). Besides this there was (p. 67), contemporary with Abelard, *another* school, held on the Mont Sainte-Geneviève, by Jocelyn, afterwards Bishop of Soissons ; and there were also *two other* schools then (p. 67). There were in Paris two other schools, but we know not where they were held (p. 68), and for an account of the other schools in Paris see pp. 69-81. These schools were crowded, and in particular by the English (pp. 73 and 76). Towards the end of the twelfth century (p. 74) 'les professeurs publics s'y multiplièrent prodigieusement ; ' that is, there were ten or twelve of them at the same time, and in fact (p. 78) Paris became a second Athens. Still the *name* of University was not given until the thirteenth century (p. 81), and in the twelfth century we merely find the name of *Academy*. It must, however, under the latter name, have reached a considerable organisation, since it was appealed to by Henry II. and Thomas Becket, Archbishop of Canterbury. It has hence been supposed that under the reign of Louis the Young, 'vers le milieu de ce siècle elle commença à se former en corps d'université, et qu'elle en est redevable à Pierre Lombard. Mais si l'on veut bien y regarder de plus près, on conviendra que ses premiers commencements, non sous la dénomination d'Université, qui ne fut en usage qu'au siècle suivant, mais sous le titre d'Aca-

démie ou d'École publique, remontent plus d'un siècle plus haut'
(p. 80). Indeed, there were all the elements of a university but its
name. Before the end of the twelfth century there were several
colleges, and during the reign of Philip Augustus some English
clerks, finding themselves overtaxed by Richard I., settled in Paris
and were formed into a college (p. 81). Nor were academical
degrees wanting. It is supposed that towards the middle of the
twelfth century the title of Doctor was created, in order to succeed to that of Master; and that this was effected by Peter Lombard and Gilbert de la Poirée. But this is opposed by history
(p. 81). Although the titles of Doctor and Master *were* synonymous, still the former was in usage long before. 'Il y en a mille
exemples, mais il suffit pour en convaincre de produire celle de
Thomas d'Estampes, qui écrivait dès la fin du xi⁰ siècle, et qui
prend indifféremment dans l'inscription de ses lettres le titre de
Docteur et celui de Maître.' They add (p. 82) that the title
of Master was more common after the middle of the twelfth
century than before it, although subsequently the title of Doctor
was preferred to that of Master. It appears from the Council of
Rouen, in 1074, 'que le premier degré académique très connu est
celui de *Licence*. . . . Ce degré, quoique le premier institué et
l'unique en usage à la fin du xi⁰ siècle et pendant plus de cin-
quante ans du siècle suivant, fut néanmoins précédé depuis du degré
de Baccalauréat, et suivi du degré de Doctorat.' As to the title of
Doctor, it appears probable (p. 82) that it was first erected into a
title of honour given to those who read publicly the sentences of
Peter Lombard, from whence it soon extended itself to those who
professed theology, medicine, and law. As to that of *Bachelor*,
which was originally confounded with that of Doctor, it is derived
from the rod they put into the hands of those doctors before they
began their public lessons. This rod or stick was called *bacillus*,
hence *bachelor* (p. 83). At the same time the word *bacalarius* is as
ancient as the early part of the eleventh century (p. 83). But
of all the different titles of the twelfth century, none was more
common than that of Master (p. 83).

It is evident, from an expression of Peter de Blois, 'qu'il y
avait dès ce siècle-ci des libraires à Paris' (p. 84; see also p. 142).

As to other schools out of Paris and not episcopal, see
pp. 84-91. In particular are observable those of St. Denys, of
Provins, of Montpellier, of Gueldre, and a great variety of Nor-

mandy. 'Les écoles de l'Armorique ne formèrent guère moins d'illustres élèves en ce siècle' (p. 90). The monastic schools (pp. 92-110) of the original order of St. Benedict were very numerous. Among the most celebrated may be mentioned that of Marmoutier, of St. Denys, so long presided over by Suger, and a variety of others. The only one of them I find mentioned as falling off is that of Bec (p. 108), but then it was scarcely possible for any merit to secure the reputation of such men as Lanfranc and Anselm, who in the eleventh century had taught there. The Order of Cluni had declined under the abbot Pons. 'Cependant St. Pierre-Maurice, surnommé le Vénérable, qui en fut abbé plus de trente ans, trouva moyen de remédier à toutes choses. De sorte que sous son gouvernement Cluni recouvra sa première splendeur, et devint de nouveau un aigle de la science et de la vertu' (p. 111). Indeed, they were reproached with studying Pagan authors at those times when, by the rule of St. Benedict, they should have been engaged in exercises of piety. Under the guidance of Peter de Cluni were formed so many illustrious men 'qu'il ne serait pas aisé d'en faire l'énumération' (p. 112, where is given a list of *some* of them). But at the end of this century Cluni declined, which the Benedictines (p. 113) ascribe to the remissness of their copyists, the multiplication of prayers, and the increase of wealth (see ART. 1349). Another reproach directed against the Clunists was that they ventured by miniatures and otherwise to *adorn* their MSS. (p. 142).

The canons regular 'se distinguèrent en ce siècle par leur application à la culture des lettres' (p. 113). That of St. Victor of Paris was the most celebrated, and in 1108 it received an immense accession of fame from William de Champeaux, who transferred the school there (p. 113). This of St. Victor was the greatest of those belonging to the canons regular (pp. 113-116), and when in 1148 their rule became transferred to Sainte-Geneviève de Paris, that also became very celebrated (pp. 116-118).

The Carthusians had no public schools like the canons regular, and the monks of the old order of St. Benedict (p. 119). 'Il ne paraît pas même qu'ils eussent d'études réglées dans leurs maisons, non plus qu'ils n'en ont point aujourd'hui.' Still, from the taste which their founder Bruno gave to his followers, they cultivated letters with success, and were particularly useful in copying books (p. 119). Their fifth prior, indeed, ordered this in one of his statutes : 'C'est pourquoi l'on ne recevait presque personne dans l'ordre qui ne sçût au moins écrire.' Nor were they mere servile copyists : 'On en a un exemple célèbre en la personne du vénérable Suigues, qui, occupé à transcrire les ouvrages de St. Jérome, en fit une réunion dont les meilleurs critiques des temps postérieurs ont sçu profiter.' We need not therefore be surprised to find that their order produced several men of considerable eminence (see pp. 120, 121). Histoire littéraire de la France, vol. vii. p. 12.

The Cistercians (though so beneficial to learning), like the Carthusians, had no public schools, nor any regulations for study (pp. 121, 122), though it appears that in 1128 there was at one of their abbeys at least a school 'ad docendum pueros' (note at p. 122). They produced, as is well known, a number of great men (pp. 122, 123), and like the Carthusians they were much employed in copying MSS. (p. 123). 'L'ordre de Prémontré, qui n'est proprement qu'une congrégation particulière de celui des chanoines réguliers, commença au diocèse de Laon en 1121, et s'étendit avant la fin du siècle dans toute l'Europe et jusqu'en Orient' (p. 126). It was founded by St. Norbert, and in this century became so celebrated that the Benedictines think (p. 125) it may be considered equal to the Cistercians in its attention to learning. It does not, however, appear that the Prémontrés had in the beginning any regulated studies (p. 126). The words of the Benedictines are 'en ces premiers temps,' which is loose enough, and they have omitted to tell us *when* they began to have fixed studies. I suppose we may infer that they had no public schools. At all events, they produced many illustrious men (pp. 126, 127).

Great attention was paid to the education of nuns (p. 127). For some time the Latin had ceased to be vernacular, but they were obliged to learn Latin, 'sans la connaissance duquel on n'admettait point de filles à la profession religieuse' (p. 127), a positive assertion for which the Benedictines have brought *no proof*, although they *have* shown (pp. 129, 130) that the nuns were generally acquainted with Latin. They had schools in which, besides the works of the fathers, they studied medicine and surgery (p. 128). But during this century there were many women not nuns who cultivated letters (pp. 131, 132).

This century was also remarkable in reference to the Jews, 'qui depuis le ve siècle avaient fort négligé les études' (p. 132).

But 'elles s'y renouvelèrent alors sans doute à l'émulation de ce qui se pratiquait chez les chrétiens.' This appears probable if the Benedictines are accurate in adding that the French Jews were superior to those of other nations. They had an academy at Narbonne, where there were about three hundred Jews. 'On peut regarder Narbonne comme le centre d'où la doctrine de la loi se communiquait à tous les pays où il y avait des juifs' (p. 132). They had also an academy at Beziers and at Montpellier. One which they had at Lunel, consisting of three hundred Jews, showed 'beaucoup de générosité. Non-seulement ils enseignaient gratuitement ceux qui venaient d'ailleurs s'instruire à leur école, mais ils fournissaient aussi tout ce qui leur était nécessaire pour la vie.' There was also an academy at Beaucaire, which was celebrated, though only consisting of about forty Jews. At Arles there was an academy directed by six rabbins (p. 134), and at Marseilles there were nearly three hundred Jews, who had two colleges. The Jews at Paris had also their academy ; and indeed 'Benjamin nous donne à juger qu'il n'y avait point de ville en France où il se trouvait des juifs qui n'eût son collège ou académie à l'usage de cette nation.' Nor did they merely study their own religion. That which they most cultivated, after their sacred books, was medicine ; 'à raison du lucre qui en revient,' is the charitable commentary of the Benedictines (p. 134). They allow (p. 135) that the Jews were much aided in this study by their knowledge of Arabic ; and why may not this facility have been the *cause* of their study of medicine ? I may add here what the Benedictines have collected respecting the study of medicine in the twelfth century. They say (p. 10) that the three most lucrative sciences were medicine, the canon law, and the civil law. The same thing is said at p. 30, where it is added that in this century medicine was much studied (see p. 191). The University of Paris did not permit any of their professors to marry (p. 65), 'coutume qui fut exactement observée jusqu'au Cardinal d'Estouteville, qui permit aux docteurs de médecine de se marier.' The academy of Montpellier in the twelfth century was particularly famous for medicine and canon law, and indeed *some writers* pretend that *medicine* was studied there *as early as the tenth century* (p. 86). This the Benedictines seem inclined to discredit, but they have quoted a letter of St. Bernard in 1153, showing that Montpellier was then celebrated for medicine ; and from a passage in John of Salisbury, it was so celebrated at the beginning of the twelfth century (p. 86, and see p. 87). But may not these be references to the Jewish academy there? The monks of St. Denys, both in the eleventh and twelfth centuries, were acquainted with medicine (p. 94). At the Paraclete, of which Heloise was abbess, the nuns studied both medicine and surgery (p. 128, and see pp. 191, 192). The French in this century were not content with studying medicine at Paris and Montpellier, but they went for that purpose to Salerno (p. 191). Still medicine made little progress (p. 192), for the students of it neglected anatomy and botany. They read indeed the works of Galen and Hippocrates, and in 1101 was brought into France 'L'École de Salerne,' which had been composed in the eleventh century, and was a collection of recipes and secrets to cure disease and preserve the health (p. 192) ; and this gave rise to similar collections (p. 193) published in France during the twelfth century. There was also a famous treatise by Giles de Corbeil, called ' *De Judiciis Urinarum*,' from which it appears that there were then physicians who judged diseases by the urine (p. 193). For a list of those physicians who became famous see pp. 193, 194. However, in 1131 Innocent III. forbade to monks and regular canons the study and exercise of medicine (p. 194). The same prohibition was repeated in the Council of Lateran in 1139, and in that of Tours in 1163 (p. 195). But, add the Benedictines, it appears from the language of these councils that the prohibitions were directed against the spirit of avarice with which medicine was pursued, ' de sorte que les moines et les chanoines réguliers pouvaient légitimement étudier et exercer la médecine comme ils continuèrent en effet de le faire, pourvu qu'ils évitassent ces inconvénients.' As to the secular clerks, they were always allowed to exercise it, on account of the ignorance of the laity (p. 195). It seems probable that during this century medicine and surgery were united, though Pasquier is of opinion that before the end of the twelfth century they had become distinct professions. The business of the apothecary was, as might be expected, united with the profession of medicine (p. 196), but by the end of the twelfth century a distinction began to be drawn between apothecaries and physicians. The proof is that Henry II. of England, besides his physician, had an apothecary named Richard, who died Bishop of London in 1198. But an *apothecary*, according to our acceptation of the word, was not likely to be made a bishop ; and may it not be that *apothecary* and physician were synonymous, and that Henry II. had two physicians ? It is observable that this is the only instance the Benedictines quote. Treacle is first mentioned by Foucher de Chartres, who wrote about 1124, and who acquired a knowledge of it in the East during the first crusade (p. 196). Hugues Metel, in 1134, enters more into detail. It was then the opinion that treacle would produce death unless it found in the body some poison to expel. The art of composing it was not then known in France, at least it would appear so, since that which they used was brought from Antioch. From France the use of it passed into Denmark about 1182. In 1561, Tusser mentions it as a common medicine (*The Points of Housewifery*, edit. Mavor, 1812, p. 274). Greene, in his Quip for an Upstart Courtier, 1592, speaks of ' a little treacle to drive out the measels,' and it is evident from the context that apothecaries sold it (*Harleian Miscellany*, edit. Park, vol. v. p. 406) ; and in 1599, Nashe says that it was prescribed by physicians (*Harleian Miscellany*, vi. 158). Evelyn was at Venice in 1646, and made a point of seeing the manufacture of treacle, some of which he brought away with him (*Diary*, 8vo, 1827, vol. i. p. 346). In 1690, Lord Clarendon being seized with colic, was ordered to take some ' Venice treacle ' (*Clarendon Correspondence*, 4to, 1828, vol. ii. pp. 302-310). In 1757, Wesley (*Journals*, 8vo, 1851, p. 410) says, ' My toothache was cured by rubbing treacle upon my cheek ' (see also p. 701).

For the study of Greek I do not perceive much can be said. Of John of Salisbury it is said (p. 58), ' Il possédait à fond les deux langues, la grecque et la latine.' ' Guillaume de Gap, abbé de S. Denys, sçavait le grec et la médecine ' (p. 94). ' Jean Sarrasin, qui fut ensuite abbé à Verceil, possédait la langue grecque' A monk at St. Martin de Tournai copied, in 1105, a Psalter in four columns ; and 'comme il y avait le texte hébreu sur une de ces colonnes et le texte grec sur une autre, il est à présumer que le copiste entendait les deux langues ' (p. 101). The Benedictines think (p. 124) that Thierri, abbot of Orval, knew Greek or the Oriental languages, because ' il amassa avec grands frais une riche bibliothèque, composée de livres en toutes sortes de langues.' However, they seem to have reason for saying (p. 151), ' A l'égard du grec, de l'hébreu, et des autres langues orientales, on doit compter pour presque rien le progrès que firent les Français en ce siècle.' They give the names of some 'qui donnèrent une certaine application au grec.' They are Théofride, abbé d'Epternac, Otton de Frisingue, and Rupert, abbé de Trey. 'Abélard, Héloïse, St. Pierre Maurice, Jean de Salisbury, Helimand de Froimond, et *divers autres*, en avaient aussi quelque connaissance.' . . . . 'Mais *le plus habile* de tous nos Français en cette langue fut Macaire, abbé de Fleury. On lui attribue effectivement un Lexicon ou Dictionnaire Grec' (p. 151). St. Bernard and others, who were ignorant of Greek, nevertheless quote the Greek fathers, which shows they must have been already translated into Latin. A glorious enterprise was originated by Eugenius III. (who succeeded Lucius II. in 1145), and under his directions executed by Bourgoudion, the first magistrate of Pisa. This was the translation from the Greek of the works of Chrysostom, of St. Gregory of Nyssa, and of Jean de Damas (pp. 151, 152). The French, however, had nothing to do with this, except (p. 151) 'le fruit qu'ils en tirèrent en lisant en latin ce qu'ils n'auraient pu lire en grec.' Daunou says that Otho of Friesland knew Greek (*Histoire littéraire de la France*, xiii. 284). Bruno, founder of the Carthusians, died in 1101. He knew Greek (*Hist. lit. de la France*, ix. 247).

Hebrew seems to have been even less known than Greek. The Benedictines assign indeed to an anonymous monk a knowledge of it (p. 101), but their only reason for doing so is that he copied a Psalter, one column of which was Hebrew, which seems to me no reason at all. They pretend, indeed (pp. 123, 124), that the revision of the Bible made by Estienne, abbé de Cisteaux, in 1109, displays knowledge of Hebrew, and yet (at p. 152) they quote Martene to show that this very *Cistercian order* 'fit une *défense expresse* à ses moines de *s'adresser* aux *juifs pour apprendre les langues orientales*, et mit en pénitence un moine de Poblet, en Catalogne, qui se trouvait dans ce cas.' They quote Abelard (p. 152), who says that Heloise knew Hebrew as well as Latin (and see p. 128). They say (p. 152) 'Hugues d'Amiens, Archevêque de Rouen, et l'anonyme qui a écrit contre les juifs, *paraissent* par leurs ouvrages en avoir eu une connaissance plus que médiocre. Il faut porter le même jugement de Segebert, de Gemblon, de Théofride, abbé d'Epternac, des moines de Citeaux que St. Etienne, leur abbé, employa à la révision de la Bible, et peut-être d'Odon, abbé de St. Martin de Tournai.' 'Abélard l'avait étudié' (p. 152) ; for this they give no authority. They had before told us (vii. 116), 'On sçait qu'Abélard avait acquis une assez grande connaissance de l'hébreu,' and then also they quote no evidence for the fact. And these same Benedictines in the same work tell us (tome xii. p. 148), in their laboured account of Abelard, 'qu'il entendait à peine le grec, encore moins l'hébreu.' Many writers in this century refuted the Jewish dogmas, without thinking it necessary to learn Hebrew (p. 135). Bruno, founder of the Carthusians, died in 1101. He knew Hebrew (*Hist. litt. de la France*, vol. ix. pp. 245, 247).

The only notice I find of the study of Arabic is at p. 153, where they say that it is surprising, considering the facilities afforded by the crusades, so few should have availed themselves of them to study Arabic. 'Nous ne connaissons que trois personnes de lettres qui sçurent profiter de leur séjour en Orient pour se mettre au fait de la langue grecque, de l'arabe et des autres sciences des orientaux.' The first of these was William, Archbishop of Tyre, who was so well acquainted with Arabic that he wrote a history in that language. The second was Philip Clerc de Gui de Valence, Bishop of Tripoli, who by order of the Archbishop of Tyre translated from Arabic into Latin a letter of Aristotle to Alexander, called '*Secretum Secretorum Aristotelis.*' The third person was an Englishman, Adelard of Bath, who translated from Arabic into Latin the elements of Euclid. They add, however, a fourth, Rodolph of Bruges, who translated the Planisphere of Ptolemy from Arabic into Latin. But the best proof of the little knowledge of Arabic is that Peter the Venerable, wishing to have the Koran translated into Latin, was obliged to go into Spain in order to carry out his plan (p. 153). The Jews for the most part knew Arabic (see p. 135).

The twelfth century was remarkable for an increased ardour in copying manuscripts (p. 139). The library of Foulfroide, in the diocese of Narbonne, must, for instance, have been extensive, since on one single occasion sixty volumes were taken from it (p. 142). The general desire for multiplying manuscripts naturally led to the idea of forming rules for that purpose. The first rule of this nature (p. 140) was made by Udon, abbot of S. Père-en-Vallée, at Chartres, by which a certain yearly tax was to be paid to the librarian for the purchase of manuscripts.

The learned in the middle ages only recognised seven divisions of literature—the Trivium and Quadrivium. The first, com-

prising grammar, rhetoric, and dialectic, sufficed for those who
only aimed at a moderate knowledge (p. 143). But those who
aspired higher added the Quadrivium—that is, arithmetic, music,
geometry, and astronomy. The eleventh century added to these
medicine, scholastic theology, canon law, civil law, and study of
languages. In the twelfth century grammar was considered the
most important of the seven liberal arts (p. 144), but towards the
close of the century the study of it considerably relaxed, and this
was probably owing to the efforts of a would-be scholar whose
name is unknown to us, but who condemned the study of eloquence, dialectic, and grammar. He found partisans, and formed
the sect of Cornificiens ; at least, so they are named by John of
Salisbury, who, writing against the founder, conceals his real
name, and calls him Cornificius, apparently alluding to the famous
poet of that name who criticised Virgil. Still, the energy with
which grammar was studied in the early part of the century produced its effects (pp. 145, 146). 'Nous en avons une preuve
sensible dans la manière d'écrire de plusieurs de nos auteurs du
même siècle, dont le latin est beaucoup meilleur qu'il n'était
communément aux siècles précédents.' They instance Abelard,
Heloise, Bernard, Peter the Venerable, and John of Salisbury,
though they allow that their style is too affected. It is singular
(p. 146) that some writers of this century thought to express their
respect when writing to people of rank by putting *vos* instead of
tu, but conducted the compliment so clumsily that they put a
singular adjective with the plural pronoun.

The vernacular language of France was cultivated in the twelfth
century (p. 147), though the orthography and construction were
entirely neglected. It was frequently employed in sermons
(p. 148). 'St. Vital, fondateur et premier abbé de Savigni, un
des plus grands prédicateurs de son temps, ne prêchait qu'en
romance,' and many others preached indifferently in Latin or
Romance (and see p. 180). Respecting works written in Romance
see pp 148, 149. Books on history, physics, and medicine were
translated into it, and even part of the Code of Justinian (p. 150).
It also produced original poets (p. 172), and Abelard was one of
the first who laboured to embellish the vernacular poetry ; and
many of his verses, addressed to Heloise, were long after sung in
different countries (p. 173). The Provençal poetry was even still
more cultivated (see the account given in pp. 174-177).

The twelfth century seems to have been very ignorant in matters of geography. See the instances from St. Bernard at p. 154. See also a trait from Otho of Friesland in Hist. littéraire, vol. xiii. p. 271. It is, however, singular (p. 155) that some visionary in this century had an idea that the earth was round like a globe. Indeed, it would appear that four hundred years before this, St. Virgil, Bishop of Saltzbourg, 'découvrit effectivement les antipodes,' though this *discovery* seems to have been merely an *assertion.* They say (pp. 155-156) that Otto de Frisingue was the best geographer of the age. Indeed, the Benedictines (p. 156) speak of his accuracy in the highest terms.

A remarkable evidence of the activity of this century is to be found in the increase of letters 'qu'enfanta le siècle qui nous occupe ; jamais il n'en parut un si grand nombre, et qui contiennent plus de faits.' See p. 159, where there is a list of the great letter-writers of the twelfth century.

From what they say (pp. 160, 161) of the History of Othon de Frisingue, it would appear to be the first critical history the middle ages had produced. Of some of the historical fables universally received he speaks with evident doubt, others he flatly denies. 'Guibert, abbé de Nogent, fut un des meilleurs critiques de son temps' (p. 162). Thus we find him showing against Eusebius of Cæsarea that the letter of Christ to Abgarus, king of Edessa, was not genuine. He also exposed the fables respecting Denys the Areopagite, and refuted what Bede had advanced upon this head. Thus, too, we find (p. 163) John of Salisbury and Peter of Blois rejecting the pretended prophecies of Merlin (see also p. 164). The same spirit of criticism was displayed in copying manuscripts. The venerable Guigues is an instance (p. 120), 'qui, occupé à transcrire les ouvrages de St. Jérôme, en fit une révision dont les meilleurs critiques des temps postérieurs ont sçu profiter.' And (at pp. 123, 124), 'On ne se bornait pas à copier seulement les bons livres ; on poussait encore le travail jusqu'à en faire une critique grammaticale afin d'en avoir le texte pur et correct.' The revision of the Bible, undertaken in 1109 by Étienne de Cisteaux, was an evidence of this.

In the twelfth century 'la poésie latine fut extrêmement cultivée' (p. 167). . . . 'Tous nos hommes de lettres du xiie siècle, si l'on en excepte St. Bernard, Pierre de Celle, et fort peu d'autres, se mêlèrent de versifier.' Medicine, history, and legends

X 2

were poetised (pp. 167-172).   But it is a mistake to ascribe the
invention of Leonine verses to the poet Leonius, who died in
1195, since they were known long before (p. 172).

Rhetoric was much studied (p. 178), but few good orators were
produced, which arose from the bad taste of the age.   Still there
were able orators, and towards the end of the eleventh century
there was revived the custom of funeral orations (p. 179).
' Depuis *l'oraison funèbre* de St. Honorat, évêque d'Arles, par
St. Hilaire, son successeur, vers 413, il ne s'en était point fait en
France, que l'on sache, jusqu'à celle de Guillaume le Conquérant
en 1087, par Gilbert, non de Lisieux, mais d'Evreux.'   In the
twelfth century these orations greatly increased, and from France
passed into Germany, as appears from that which Imbricon, Bishop
of Wirtzbourg, made at the funeral of St. Othon, Bishop of
Bamberg, who died in 1139.   Respecting the most celebrated orators
see pp. 180, 181.   At p. 182 they mention that Helinand *quoted*
continually in his *sermons* Virgil, Horace, Terence, Cicero, Juvenal,
&c.   (See also *Histoire littéraire de la France*, vol. vii. p. 123 ;
Fleury, Histoire ecclésiastique, livre lxiii. No. 38, tome xiii. p. 462.)

Metaphysics seem to have been neglected (p. 183).   The
twelfth century only recognised three parts of philosophy—logic or
dialectic, morals, and physics.   The author of the Life of St. Eber-
hard only speaks of these three parts, and does not make the
least mention of metaphysics, nor does John of Salisbury (p. 183).
Of these three parts, dialectic was the most studied, and this was
essentially the Logic of Aristotle.   It was in the eleventh century
that Aristotle began to be known, and soon upset that logic which
had been generally taught and was attributed to Augustin (p. 184).
They draw a melancholy picture (pp. 184 186) of the state of
logic before the middle of the twelfth century, and after that
time instead of advancing it went on degenerating (p. 186).   This
they ascribe (p. 187) to the ' questions et disputes inutiles ' which
occupied men's minds, such as the wars of the Nominalists and
Realists, &c.   It is surprising (p. 190) that, Anselm having revived
metaphysics, the philosophers who succeeded him should have so
despised or forgotten it as not even to allow it to be a part of
philosophy. ' Il est *certain* d'ailleurs, *qu'ils n'en firent point de leçons
publiques dans tout le cours de ce siècle*,' though the Benedictines
think it must have been studied in private ; and they particularly
praise (p. 190) Isaac de l'Estoile and Peter de Celle, the former

of whom wrote a treatise on the soul 'dans lequel il raisonne en bon métaphysicien. . . . La définition qu'il y donne de l'esprit humain est la même qu'en apportent les meilleurs philosophes modernes.' There were also other metaphysical writers (pp. 190, 191).

Physics seem to have been entirely neglected (pp. 189, 190), in proof of which the Benedictines instance Peter Lombard, 'qui passait pour un des plus sçavants hommes de son siècle. Cependant il supposait le firmament solide, et les petits insectes produits de corruption.' 'Othon de Frisingue passait pour le plus habile naturaliste ou physicien de son temps, et nous a laissé des preuves qu'il croyait la matière divisible à l'infini' (p. 190). At all events, it may be observed (p. 183) that physics *were* recognised as part of philosophy, an honour which was not paid to metaphysics.

Mathematics also fared very badly. ' De toutes les facultés de la littérature alors en usage, il n'y en a point qui fussent plus négligées que les mathématiques ' (pp. 196, 197). Arithmetic was included in the Quadrivium, but the Quadrivium was only studied by the more ambitious class of scholars (p. 143) ; and the Benedictines assure us (p. 197) that almost the only persons who were acquainted with arithmetic were those whose business it was to find out Easter, and to regulate those fasts which depended on it during the year. ' Il ne paraît point que les professeurs publics en donnassent des leçons particulières comme ils faisaient de la grammaire, de la rhétorique, de la dialectique, et des autres sciences qui avaient le plus de vogue' (p. 197). However, there *were* a few works published on arithmetic in the course of the century (p. 197).

There was more *attention* paid to astronomy, but the progress in it was not greater than in arithmetic, that is, none at all (p. 197). Works were published, indeed, to facilitate its study by Adelard of Bath, and Rodulph of Bruges. Still, 'l'astronomie de ce siècle dégénéra encore, comme auparavant, en pure astrologie' (p. 197). They add (p. 198) that the greatest men of the age 'n'étaient attentifs aux phénomènes célestes que pour en tirer des présages de l'avenir ;' and it was with this view that *almanacks were originated* (p. 198). John of Salisbury, who mentions them, laughs at their predictions, but himself was in some degree inclined to believe them. Whewell says that the first view entertained of astronomy as a science was to conceive some mechanism by which the motions of the planets might be produced (*Philosophy of the Inductive Sciences*, 8vo, 1847, i. 152). He adds (p. 155) that Plato rather looked on mathematics 'as the essence of the science of astronomy than as its instrument.' He says (p. 158) that in England physical astronomy languished because men would employ the synthetical method of Newton, which none but minds as powerful as his can wield with effect. 'Musty sheets of an old almanack' occurs in Dekker's Gull's Horn Book, p. 13, 1609, edit. Bristol, 1812, 4to. Otho of Friesland connects the appearance of a comet with William's conquest of England (*Histoire littéraire de la France*, xiii. 275). Yves, Bishop of Chartres, died in 1115. In a sermon on the Epiphany, 'il croit que les Mages étaient des philosophes qui avaient appris, par des expériences, à connaître par les astres les événements' (*Ceillier, Histoire des Auteurs sacrés*, tome xxi. p. 483). Almanack is connected with the Hebrew *manah*, to measure (*Whewell's History of the Inductive Sciences*, 8vo, 1847, vol. i. p. 136).

In navigation they have more to boast of. 'Le xiie siècle eut la gloire à perfectionner considérablement la navigation' (p. 199). The invention of the *compass* in the twelfth century gave a great spur to everything connected with navigation. It is evident that it was known before A.D. 1200, and the Benedictines add that from the north being indicated by the fleur-de-lis, it is evident that it is a French invention (p. 199) ; but this is a miserable argument, and has been also employed to show that cards were a French invention. But Singer has well remarked that the fleurs-de-lis were common to many other nations besides the French (*Singer, On Playing Cards*, 1816, 4to). That writer, indeed (p. 131), ascribes the invention to the French, but merely on the authorities of Brunetto Latini and Guyot de Provins. M'Culloch (*Dictionary of Commerce*, 8vo, 1849, p. 390) supposes that Company (*Questiones criticas*, p. 73) has pointed out the first mention of it [the compass], namely, a passage in Raymond Lully's De Contemplatione, published in 1272. It is mentioned as being by no means a new thing in the laws of Alonso the Wise, of Spain, which were published in 1258 (see the quotation in *The Life and Correspondence of Robert Southey, edited by the Rev. C. C. Southey*, 8vo, 1849, 1850, vol. ii. p. 317). On the *fleur-de-lis* see the extravagant claims in Audigier, L'Origine des Français, Paris, 1676, tome ii. pp. 471, 473, 521.

Respecting music see pp. 200-202. This was part of the

Quadrivium which, as we have seen (p. 143), was only studied by the more aspiring students ; and yet the Benedictines say (p. 200), in contradiction to their own statement, ' La musique fut assez généralement cultivée. Presque tous les gens de lettres l'étudiaient.' And in the twelfth century the cathedrals—at all events some of them (p. 200)—had masters of music. ' Le *plus grand service* que reçut alors le chant ecclésiastique *lui vint de l'ordre de Cîteaux* ' (p. 201) ; while, on the other hand, the Clunists were accused of allowing the church music to degenerate into ' un chant efféminé,' and St. Bernard charges them with using certain juices to soften the voice.

The study of theology (*not* scholastic) made great progress in this century (p. 203). ' Une autre preuve non équivoque de l'application qu'on donna alors à cette sorte d'étude est le nombre prodigieux de *commentaires* qu'on publia sur tous les livres sacrés. *Jamais siècle jusqu'ici n'en vit tant éclore* ' (p. 204).

The zeal with which dialectics were studied introduced the custom of refining upon every point. ' Accoutumés à traiter scolastiquement la théologie, ils voulurent aussi étudier scolastiquement l'Écriture.' This was partly cause and partly effect of the mystic theology, ' dont l'origine se rapporte à ce siècle ' (p. 205). ' Sainte Hildegarde et Sainte Elizabeth de Senange, les deux premiers saints que l'on sache s'être attachés au sens mystique, étaient voisines de la France et y avaient des relations,' and it was owing to them that this mystic theology was so spread in France. But their mode of interpretation was opposed by all those ' que le mauvais usage de la dialectique n'avait pas gâtés ' (p. 206). It was apparently owing to this that the study of the Fathers was so much neglected during this century (see pp. 206, 207).

Whewell mentions Picus, Reuchlin, Helmont, Dœhmen, and adds, ' Thus we have a series of mystical writers, continued into modern times, who may be considered as the successors of the Platonic school ' (*Whewell's Philosophy of the Inductive Sciences*, 8vo, 1847, vol. ii. p. 185). For an account of the mysticism of the Mahommedans, or Sufism, see Transactions of the Literary Society of Bombay, vol. i. pp. 89, 119, London, 4to, 1819.

We now come to the canon law. This was one of the most lucrative sciences in the twelfth century (p. 10). But they say (p. 214), ' Il ne paraît pas qu'avant le milieu de ce siècle on enseignât publiquement en France le droit canonique.' Those for whom it was necessary, such as the bishops and the ecclesiastics of the second order, studied it in private. There had been already made several collections of canons (see them enumerated at p. 214), and by the help of these, and reading the Fathers, many writers at the beginning of the twelfth century, 'ne réussirent pas mal à traiter divers points de la discipline ecclésiastique.' Thus stood the canon law in France when, in 1151, Gratian, monk of St. Felix, at Bologna in Italy, published his famous Decretals.[1] Eugenius III. immediately ordered that it should be the rule of ecclesiastical tribunals, and be read in the public schools (p. 215). Other collections appeared, and there arose 'une nouvelle ardeur pour l'étude du droit canonique' (p. 216). And even separate schools were opened for it. Orleans in particular was celebrated for the study of it, as Bologna was for civil law, and Salerno for medicine. But the most celebrated was at Paris, where Gerard le Pucelle taught it from 1160 to 1177, and many Frenchmen crossed the sea and went to Oxford to study it, where there was a school celebrated for it (p. 216). The consequence was that there arose in France during the latter half of the twelfth century many skilful canonists (p. 217).

The civil law was, like the canon law, very lucrative (p. 10), and it had the advantage of being publicly taught long before (p. 217). For at the commencement of the eleventh century it was taught in the school of Toul, and even in the *tenth century in that of Angers*; which arose from the fact that the Counts of Anjou were the first judges in the kingdom. But as to its being taught in the tenth century see ART. 1375, and Histoire littéraire, vii. 24. Ledwich imagines that its study was owing to its 'discovery' at Amalfi in 1127 (*Antiquities of Ireland*, Dublin, 1804, 4to, p. 320). In the twelfth century there were public chairs of the civil law at Paris and Montpellier (p. 217). Indeed, at Paris nearly all who taught canon law also taught civil law (p. 218). In monastic schools the civil law was not taught, but each one studied it in private. In this century there were formed among the clergy and in the cloister a number of skilful jurisconsults, who took the name of *Causidicus*. But in 1131 the Council of Rheims, under Innocent III., forbade monks and canons regular to study

---

[1] Hallam says the Decretum of Gratian appeared about 1140 (*Europe during the Middle Ages*, vol. ii. p. 2, 8vo, 1846).

the civil law and act as advocates 'par un motif d'avarice.' In 1139 the second Council of Lateran, and in 1163 that of Tours, issued the same prohibition—secular clerks are not mentioned. It would appear from the Benedictines (pp. 218, 219) that these prohibitions were directed not against the monks and canons regular for *practising* the law, but because they practised it with *avaricious* views. However, the prohibition seems to have been little attended to; at all events, during the time of Peter the Venerable the monks of Cluni were reproached with performing the functions of *advocates* (p. 219).

At pp. 220–225 the Benedictines give a short and very superficial view of the state of the fine arts, &c., in the twelfth century. They say (p. 224), 'Il était extrêmement rare de voir alors en Europe des manufactures d'étoffes de soie; peut-être n'y étaient-elles pas même connues, au moins dans la pratique. Mais il s'y en établit en ce siècle, et la France ne fut pas la dernière qui en eut.' They go on to say that Roger, king of Sicily, in 1145 introduced into his kingdom some silk manufacturers, whom he placed at Palermo, and who explained to his subjects the art of making silk. From them the art communicated itself to the other parts of Italy, and to all the West. But as to the French 'not being the last people' to receive this art, this is an assertion which the Benedictines have not proved. They say, indeed, '*Il n'y a pas lieu de douter* que les Français n'apprissent bientôt cet art aussi curieux que lucratif,' but they mention no date; and M'Culloch says (*Commercial Dictionary*, 1849, p. 1182) it was first introduced into France in 1480.

Strutt (*Habits and Dresses*, edit. Planché, 1842, vol. ii. p. 89) cannot find any mention of the silk manufacture in England before the middle of the fifteenth century; and Mr. M'Culloch (*Commercial Dictionary*, 8vo, 1849, p. 1182) says 'the manufacture seems to have been introduced into England in the fifteenth century.' Chevenix (*Essay on National Character*, 8vo, 1832, vol. iii. p. 93) says, 'It was under Francis I. that the manufacture of silk, which the French had learned at Milan, was introduced into France.'

The Benedictines say (p. 225), 'Entre les autres manufactures établies alors dans le roiaume, on faisait beaucoup de cas de celles des draps de Flandres.' And in order to encourage them the Count Philip obtained from the Emperor Frederick permission for the merchants to sell them at Aix-la-Chapelle and other towns of Germany. M'Culloch says, but without quoting any authority, 'Manufactures of wool and flax had been established in the Netherlands as early as the reign of Charlemagne' (*Dictionary of Commerce*, 1849, p. 657). It is said that in the 28th Edward III. the estimate of our yearly export of wool was more than 100,000 sacks (*Stow's London*, edit. Thoms, 8vo, 1842, p. 169). Chevenix says, 'About the middle of the tenth century Flanders began this branch of manufacture' (*Essay on National Character*, 8vo, 1832, vol. i, p. 70). In 1808, Southey writes, 'The last odd thing that has turned up in my reading is that the Merino sheep were originally English, and transported from hence into Spain' (*Life and Correspondence of Robert Southey*, 8vo, 1849, 1850, vol. iii. p. 170). In 1549, Thomas Woodhouse complains, 'I am spoiled of two thousand sheep' (*Tytler's Edward VI. and Mary I.* 196, 8vo, 1839).

HISTORY OF THE WORSHIP OF THE VIRGIN MARY.

St. Epiphanius lived from A.D. 310 to 403. He heard that in Arabia there had arisen a sect called Antidicomarianites, who said that Mary did not remain a virgin, and that after the birth of Jesus Christ she had children by Joseph. This opinion Epiphanius refuted, as he also did the opinion of an opposite sect called Collyridiens (so called because they offered to the Virgin cakes named in Greek collyrides), who looked on the Virgin as a sort of divinity. This superstition had come from Thrace and Upper Scythia into Arabia, and St. Epiphanius attacked it, 'puisqu'il n'a pour objet que Marie, qui, toute parfaite qu'elle est, n'est qu'une créature simple.' The saint concludes by mentioning some traditions respecting the family, &c., of the Virgin (*Fleury*, *Histoire ecclésiastique*, livre xvii. No. 26, tome iv. pp. 329, 330). For the opinions of Epiphanius see also Ceillier, Histoire générale des Auteurs ecclésiastiques, tome viii. pp. 735, 736. St. Jerome refuted the Antidicomarianites (*Ceillier*, vol. x. p. 387).

The Nestorian heresy broke out in A.D. 428, the year in which Nestorius was made patriarch of Constantinople; and in that year his confidant and one of his priests, Anastasius, maintained in a sermon that Mary was not the mother of God, for that she was a woman. This scandalised every one, but was supported by Nestorius himself, who held that she was the mother of Christ and not of God (*Fleury*, livre xxv. No. 1, tome vi. pp. 1, 2). However, through the influence of Cyril of Alexandria the doctrines of Nestorius were condemned, and he himself deposed in A.D. 431, by the third General Council at Ephesus (*Mosheim's Ecclesiastical History*, vol. i. p. 134).

In A.D. 450 the Emperor Theodosius died ; and his widow Eudoxia sent to Pulcheria the image of the Virgin which was made by St. Luke ! (*Fleury*, livre xxvii. No. 47, tome vi. p. 344). Pulcheria, who built three churches in honour of the Virgin, put this image in one of them (*Fleury*, xxviii. No. 42, tome vi. p. 453). In A.D. 656, the tenth Council of Toledo fixed the celebration of the Annunciation of the Virgin on the 18th of December (*Fleury*, xxxix. No. 21, tome viii. p. 474). In A.D. 698, Pope Sergius instituted processions for the Annunciation of the Virgin, for her *nativity*, for her *dormition* or death, and for her purification (*Fleury*, xli. No. 5, tome ix. p. 130). Early in the eleventh century an attempt was made in a council in France (Fleury does not say which ; see *Histoire ecclésiastique*, livre lviii. No. 14, tome xii. p. 356) to imitate Spain, and remove the feast of the Annunciation from the 25th of March to the 18th of December, in order that it might be celebrated out of Lent. But the advocates of the old custom conquered, and the 25th of March remained the day. Butler (*Lives of the Saints*, Dublin, 8vo, i. 395) says, 'This festival is mentioned by Pope Gelasius I. in 492.' But if Fleury is right, he is mistaken in affirming that 'both Eastern and Western churches celebrate it on the 25th of March, and have done so ever since the fifth century ; ' for in Spain it was kept on the 18th of December and the Council of Toledo, which fixed it on the 18th of December, is mentioned by Ceillier (*Histoire générale des Auteurs sacrés*, xviii. 827).

In A.D. 542 they *began* at Constantinople on the 2nd of February to celebrate the Feast of the Purification (*Fleury*, livre xxxiii. No. 7, tome vii. p. 378), and in A.D. 698 Pope Sergius instituted processions for it (xli. No. 5, tome ix. p. 130). Processions ordered in 824 (*Fleury*, xlvi. 55, tome x. p. 230) and in 813 (tome x. p. 132).

Adamnan, an Irish saint, wrote early in the eighth century. He is the author of a description of Palestine, in which he says that the sepulchre of the Virgin was in the valley of Josaphat ; ' Mais, ajoute-t-il, on ne sçait en quel temps, par qui, ni comment

son corps en a été ôté, ni en quel lieu il attend la résurrection.
On croyait donc dès lors que la Sainte Vierge *était morte à
Jérusalem*, comme il le marque ensuite expressément, mais on ne
croyait point encore qu'elle fut ressuscitée ' (*Fleury*, livre xli. No.
10, tome ix. pp. 139, 140).   Pope Pascal died in A.D. 824.   He
repaired and endowed many churches in Rome.   ' Entre les
ornemens des églises, il est fait mention de deux, où était repré-
sentée l'Assomption de la Sainte Vierge en son corps, ce qui
montre qu'on la croyait dès lors à Rome ' (*Fleury*, livre xlvi. No. 52,
tome x. pp. 223, 224).   The observance of the Assumption is
ordered by the Council of Mayence in A.D. 813 (see *Fleury*, xlvi.
No. 4, tome x. p. 132).   It is also ordered before A.D. 824 by the
capitulary of Hecton, or Acton, Bishop of Basle (see *Fleury*, livre
xlvi. No. 55, tome x. p. 230).   Leo IV., who died in A.D. 855,
' institua l'Octave de l'Assomption de la Sainte Vierge, qui ne se
célébrait point encore à Rome ' (*Fleury*, livre xlix. No. 25, tome x.
p. 502).   It is remarkable that the celebrated Guibert, abbé de
Nogent, who early in the twelfth century composed a treatise on
relics, says that the church had not ventured to assert that the
Virgin had been resuscitated (livre lxvii. No. 36, tome xiv. p. 321).
And Arnaud, abbot of Bonneval, the friend and correspondent of
St. Bernard, who died after the middle of the twelfth century
(see *Ceillier*, *Auteurs sacrés*, xxiii. 128), is the author of a sermon
in praise of Mary.   Respecting this sermon Ceillier says (xxiii. 133),
' Parce que l'Écriture ne nous apprend pas de quelle manière la
Sainte Vierge est montée au ciel, si c'est en âme seule, ou avec
son corps, Arnaud ne veut rien décider là-dessus ; il croit seulement que son séjour sur la terre depuis la mort de son fils ne fut
pas long.'   On the other hand, Amadeus, Bishop of Constance,
has left us eight sermons, all of which are upon the Virgin.   ' Dans
les deux derniers,' says Ceillier (xxiii. 142, 143), 'il célèbre le
triomphe de son assomption dans le ciel, ne doutant point qu'elle
n'y eût été élevée en corps et en âme, sans avoir depuis sa mort
essuyé aucune corruption.'   In the fourth Council of Lateran,
holden in A.D. 1215, Rodrigue Chimenez, Archbishop of Toledo,
mentions ' le corps de la Sainte Vierge, que nous croyons ferme-
ment être dans le ciel.'   See Fleury (*Histoire ecclésiastique*, livre
lxxvii. No. 41, tome xvi. p. 356), who adds, ' Nous voyons ici le
progrès qu'avait fait depuis un siècle l'opinion de l'assomption
corporelle de la Sainte Vierge ; puisque Guibert de Nogent

témoigne, que l'église n'osait l'assurer de son temps, et permettait seulement de le penser ; au lieu que Rodrigue, en plein Concile général, le soutient comme une créance reçue.'

Some time *before* A.D. 844, Pascase Ralbert wrote a treatise ' de l'enfantement de la Vierge,' which was produced under these circumstances : Ratram, a monk of the abbey of Corbie (of which Ralbert was afterwards abbot), having heard that in Germany they maintained that Christ did not proceed from the womb of His mother in an ordinary, but rather in a miraculous, manner, bitterly attacked this opinion, and pronounced it a heresy. At the same time he allowed that, according to the Catholic faith, Mary remained a virgin *after* as well as *before* her delivery. It was this work of Ratram which Pascase Ralbert opposed. This latter affirmed that Jesus Christ was born miraculously and without pain to His mother (*Fleury*, livre xlviii. No. 34, tome x. pp. 398, 399). The Benedictines have given a short and hurried account of this amusing dispute (see *Histoire littéraire de la France*, tome iv. p. 358, and tome v. pp. 307-309). It is observable that Fleury (x. 398) says that Ralbert wrote this treatise *before* he was abbot, that is before A.D. 844, and the Benedictines, without taking any notice of Fleury's assertion, maintain (tome v. p. 308) that it was written ' vers 855,' but their only reason is that Ralbert says in it of himself ' multo jam senio confectus.' But this argument can have no weight, because these same Benedictines confess (v. 287) that the time of his birth is unknown, and they loosely place it 'sur la fin du viii⁰ siècle.' But Ceillier (*Histoire générale des Auteurs sacrés*, tome xix. pp. 118-121) has given a longer account of these works of Ralbert's, and he thinks that both his treatises on the Virgin were written before A.D. 845. For an account of the work of Ratram, see Histoire littéraire de la France, v. pp. 344, 345. His defence is lost (p. 351 ; see also *Ceillier, Histoire générale des Auteurs sacrés*, xix. 148-150). Tertullian died ' vers l'an 245 ' (*Ceillier, Histoire générale des Auteurs sacrés*, ii. 377). He says (*Lib. de Carne Christi*, cap. 23) that Mary was a virgin, inasmuch as she knew not man ; but was not a virgin in reference to her delivery; since that took place according to the manner of other women. He also says (*Lib. de Monog.* cap. viii.) that she was married after the birth of Christ ; a disagreeable assertion, which Ceillier attempts to explain away (see his *Histoire générale*, tome ii. pp. 520, 521).

But the Bishop of Lincoln (*Ecclesiastical History of the Second and Third Centuries illustrated from the Writings of Tertullian*, 8vo, 1845, p. 58) says that *both* these works, ' De Carne Christi ' and ' De Monogamia,' were certainly written after he became a Montanist. Neander is of the same opinion respecting De Carne Christi' and 'De Monogamia' (*ibid.* pp. xvii, xviii). Origen died in A.D. 253 (*Ceillier*, ii. 597). He says that Mary was delivered like other women, but in a much purer manner (*Ceillier*, ii. 725). Saint Nil, priest and solitary of Sinai, died *after* A.D. 430 (*Ceillier*, xiii. 150). He says that Mary was delivered in a miraculous manner, and that Christ proceeded from her womb ' without breaking the seal of her virginity' (xiii. 185). Hugues, canon regular of St. Victor, died in 1142. In a treatise on the Virgin he lays down four dogmas, of which the third is ' qu'elle enfanta sans douleur et sans blesser sa virginité' (*Ceillier*, xxii. 213).

It would appear that Anselm, Archbishop of Canterbury, did not believe in the Immaculate Conception (*Fleury*, lxiv. No. 52, tome xiii. p. 614). About the year 1140, St. Bernard wrote a letter to the Canons of Lyons ' touchant la fête de la Conception de la Sainte Vierge, nouvellement introduite chez eux,' in which he blames them for introducing this new festival unknown to the church (see the analysis of his letter in *Fleury*, livre lxviii. No. 70, tome xiv. pp. 527–530). See also Colonia (*Histoire littéraire de la Ville de Lyon*, tome ii. pp. 233–242). This learned Jesuit, in attempting to reconcile the discordant opinions of St. Bernard and the church of Lyons, has indulged in some eccentric quibbles (pp. 237, 238) on the different meanings of the word *Conception*. Colonia says (p. 234) that forty years before this, Saint Anselm had introduced into England, Normandy, Burgundy, the Lyonnese and other provinces, ' la dévotion envers l'Immaculée Conception de la Vierge.' But for this he gives no authority except (p. 237) the declaration of a Council of London in 1328, in which it is said that St. Anselm established the festival of the Conception in England (and see *Fleury*, tome xx. p. 184). According to the ' exacte supputation du père Mabillon' (says Colonia, p. 234), the church of Lyons did not celebrate this festival until A.D. 1140, on which occasion the above letter of St. Bernard was written, and this was done without asking the consent of the Pope. And yet, according to Mabillon (*Colonia*, p. 237), this festival was established in Spain 'du moins dans le dixième siècle,' and it is even *said* in the seventh century. But it was not authorised by the Romish See (p. 238) until the pontificate of Sixtus IV. in 1476. However, some have supposed (p. 239) that it was authorised by Innocent III., and Colonia has ingeniously advanced three arguments to show the probability of this (see them in pp. 239–242). Colonia (p. 242) has quoted the testimony of Thomas Aquinas, who very positively affirms that the Virgin was free from original sin. Ceillier has also given an account of this letter (see *Histoire générale des Auteurs sacrés*, tome xxii. pp. 355–357). But what is very remarkable, I cannot find, nor do I remember having read any account of this letter in the elaborate Life of St. Bernard in Histoire littéraire de la France, xiii. pp. 129–235, as although Daunou mentions (p. 231) that St. Bernard maintained the original sin of the Virgin, yet he does not tell us in what part of his works that sentiment is to be found.

Southey seems to suppose that the Immaculate Conception of the Virgin originated with the Franciscans (see p. 517 of *Vindiciæ Ecclesiæ Anglicanæ*, Lond. 8vo, 1826). In A.D. 1166 we find the Greeks celebrating the Conception, but not the *Immaculate* Conception of the Virgin (see *Fleury, Histoire ecclésiastique*, livre lxxi. No. 36, tome xv. p. 214). And the same thing is observable in Armenia in 1228 (*Fleury*, livre lxxix. No. 46, tome xvi. p. 612). It is supposed that the office of the Conception of the Virgin was first established in Paris by Renoul de Homblières, Bishop of Paris, who died in A.D. 1288 (see *Fleury, Histoire ecclésiastique*, livre lxxxix. No. 11, tome xviii. p. 452). John Duns Scotus died in A.D. 1308. In 1305 he was made doctor by the University of Paris, and maintained then the Immaculate Conception of the Virgin. At the same time he does not speak dogmatically, but merely says it is an opinion 'qui semble convenable,' and confesses 'qu'on dit communément qu'elle a été conçue en péché originel' (*Fleury, Histoire ecclésiastique*, livre xci. No. 29, tome xix. p. 150).

In 1387, Jean de Montson, a Dominican, a doctor of theology, advanced certain propositions, among which was one declaring that the doctrine of the Virgin being free from original sin was opposed to the faith. These propositions were condemned by Peter d'Orgemont, Bishop of Paris, but Jean de Montson appealed from his decision to Clement VII., and repaired to Avignon to support his appeal. On the other hand, the University of Paris sent delegates to justify the sentence they and the bishops had passed. Clement VII. was so evidently opposed to him, that De Montson, without waiting for his sentence, left Avignon, went into Arragon, and recognised the Anti-Pope Urban VI., and in 1389 he was, by order of Clement, excommunicated. In consequence the University of Paris issued a decree ordering all her members to take an oath condemning the opinions of Montson, and declaring that none should receive degrees who refused to do so. This the Dominicans refused to do, and in consequence were shut out from the university, and incurred general odium, and finally they were obliged to celebrate in France the Festival of the Conception, and preserve silence respecting the original sin of the Virgin. Nor was it until 1401 that they were readmitted into the University of Paris. Finally, in 1496, the university formally decreed that all those who were admitted into her body should sign an opinion in favour of the Immaculate Conception (*Continuation de l'Histoire ecclésiastique de Fleury*, Introduction à l'Histoire du xv⁴ Siècle, Nos. 18-22, tome xxi. pp. xxdii-xxviii ; and see *Fleury*, livre xcviii. Nos. 38 and 45, tome xx. pp. 364, 365, and pp. 372-374). In A.D. 1416 the famous Gerson preached a sermon before the Council of Constance, in which he speaks doubtfully of the Immaculate Conception, but states his opinion 'que le concile doit décider si cette question est de foi ou non ' (*Continuation de Fleury*, livre ciii. No. 206, tome xxi. pp. 424, 425). In 1439 the Council of Basle pronounced in favour of the Immaculate Conception, and ordered that the festival should be kept in every church on December 8 (see *Continuation de Fleury*, cviii. No. 85, tome xxii. p. 290). The continuator of Fleury thinks proper to assert that this council did not establish it 'comme un article de foi,' but 'comme une opinion picuse,' and yet any person was forbidden either to teach or preach the contrary !! In A.D. 1457 a council was held at Avignon, the principal object of which was to confirm the above decree of the Council of Basle touching the conception of the Virgin. They not only confirmed it, but excommunicated any one who should preach or publicly assert the contrary (*Continuation de Fleury*, livre cxi. No. 42, tome xxiii. p. 30). In A.D. 1475, Sixtus IV. issued a bull granting indulgences to those who celebrated the festival of the Conception of the Virgin, whom he calls

immaculate. The continuator of Fleury asserts (livre cxiv. Nos.
83, 84, tome xxiii. pp. 417, 418) that 'cette fête, jusqu'à la bulle
de Sixte IV, avait été d'observation libre et arbitraire sans aucun
décret qui en rendît la solennité publique, tant à Rome et en
Italie qu'en France, lorsqu'en 1439 le Concile de Basle fit une
constitution pour la prescrire par toute l'Église. Mais comme on
avait rejeté ce décret à Rome, où le Pape Eugène IV regardait
l'assemblée de Basle comme schismatique et illégitime, on reçut
avec plaisir cette constitution de Sixte IV ; ce fut donc le
premier décret qui parut de l'église romaine touchant la fête de
la Conception.' But there is a decree attributed to Innocent III.
authorising this festival. Its authenticity, indeed, is suspected
by Mabillon, but Colonia is inclined to give credit to it. See the
three arguments he has advanced in Histoire littéraire de la Ville
de Lyon, tome ii. pp. 239-242, Lyon, 1730, 4to. In 1483, Sixtus IV.
issued another bull in favour of the Conception, the object of
which was to put an end to the audacity of certain men who
ventured to affirm that the Virgin Mary was conceived in sin
(*Continuation de Fleury*, livre cxv. Nos. 101, 102, tome xxiii.
pp. 563-565). In A.D. 1484, Innocent VIII. confirmed the order of
the Nuns of the Conception, which Beatrix de Sylva, a lady of
noble Portuguese family, had founded at Toledo. The Pope
appointed for them the Cistercian rule, but in 1511 Julius II.
submitted them to the Franciscan (*Continuation de Fleury*, livre
cxv. No. 149, tome xxiii. pp. 601, 602). In A.D. 1494, John
Trithemius (author of 'Catalogue of Ecclesiastical Authors') wrote
a treatise on St. Anne, in the seventh chapter of which he
speaks of the Immaculate Conception. His sentiments on this
head were attacked by Vigand, a Dominican of Frankfort, and a
controversy ensued which lasted nearly two years. Finally Trithemius triumphed, and 'Vigand rétracta ce qu'il avait dit au sujet
de la Conception, condamna son opinion comme contraire à la
pureté de Marie, et fit ses excuses à Trithème des injures qu'il lui
avait dites ' (*Continuation de Fleury*, livre cxvii. No. 136, tome xxiv.
pp. 224, 225). In 1497 the theological faculty of Paris compelled a
Dominican to retract what he had said in a sermon, not because
he had asserted that the Virgin was not free from sin, but because
he had injudiciously stated some arguments in support of her not
being free. In the same year the university formally separated
from her body those who ventured to deny the Immaculate

Conception, and compelled another Dominican to retract what he
had said against the Virgin (*Continuation de Fleury*, livre cxviii.
No. 132, tome xxiv. pp. 329-332). In A.D. 1521 the faculty of theology
of Paris formally censured the doctrines of Luther, and condemned
a proposition in which he had merely mentioned the Conception,
and had not rejected the assertion that she was born in original
sin (*Continuation de Fleury*, livre cxxvii. No. 20, tome xxvi. p. 26).
In 1546 this question was discussed by the Council of Trent, the
Dominicans maintaining that the sin of Adam had descended
to *all*, thus including the Virgin. But what is remarkable, the
Franciscans did not speak so positively as before, though they
required that the council should except the Virgin. However, the
fathers decided on leaving the question alone, and giving no opinion
between the two parties (*Continuation de Fleury*, livre cxlii.
Nos. 133, 134, tome xxix. pp. 159, 160). However, we find the council
breaking this prudent rule. In the same year, after fulminating a
variety of anathemas against those who denied the universality of
original sin, it adds that in this decree the 'holy and immaculate
Virgin' is not included, but that on this subject it agrees with and
renews the constitutions of Pope Sixtus IV. (see *Continuation de
Fleury*, livre cxlii. No. 138, tome xxix. p. 166). Still the fathers of
Trent were not satisfied, and in the same year this question was again
opened (A.D. 1546), some urging that a positive opinion should be
given that the Virgin was conceived without sin. But the more
moderate party prevailed, and it was decided that the former decree
should not be changed (*Continuation de Fleury*, cxlii. No. 140,
tome xxix. pp. 173-175). But it appears to me that this dispute
was about nothing, for the council, by recognising the constitutions of Sixtus IV., had already pronounced in favour of the
Immaculate Conception. The celebrated Ambroise Catharin died
in 1552. He wrote much in favour of the Immaculate Conception, and to justify his view cites a variety of authorities, among
which is St. Augustine (*Continuation de Fleury*, livre cxlviii.
Nos. 151, 152, tome xxx. p. 447). Jean Maldonat, a learned
Jesuit, head professor of theology at Paris, in the College of
Clermont, taught in A.D. 1575 that the Immaculate Conception
was a problematical opinion. A complaint was made against him
on this account by the faculty of theology in Paris, but Peter de
Gondy, Bishop of Paris, learning that he had not *denied* the
doctrine of the Immaculate Conception, but had merely asserted

that it was not a dogma of faith, absolved him from the charge. Upon this a meeting of the Sorbonne was held, and complaints made against Maldonat ; but the bishop forbade the rectors and doctors of theology to proceed, and threatened them with excommunication. The university now appealed to the parliament ; which, after hearing the cause with closed doors, decided in favour of the former. The decree of the bishop was then rescinded, and Maldonat was obliged, or deemed it prudent, to abstain from preaching (*Continuation de Fleury*, livre clxxiv. Nos. 48 51, tome xxxv. pp. 298–301). The Immaculate Conception is denied by Rupert, abbot of Tuy or Duits, who died in 1135 (*Histoire littéraire de la France*, tome xi. p. 495). But the 'venerable' Hildebert, Archbishop of Tours, who died in 1133 or 1134, *seems* to maintain it (see Ceillier, Bibliothèque des Auteurs sacrés, tome xxii. p. 29). The title of 'venerable' was given to Hildebert by no less a man than St. Bernard of Clairvaux (see *Histoire littéraire de la France*, tome xi. p. 277), and the Benedictines (p. 411) do not hesitate to call him 'un des plus grands prélats de son siècle, tant pour sa science que pour sa piété et toutes ses grandes qualités.' But St. Ambrose, Archbishop of Milan, who died in A.D. 397, seems to make a great step towards believing in the Immaculate Conception. He does not, indeed, deny the original sin of the Virgin ; but he says that when disputing on sin we ought not to include her, because we must believe that she would have received grace not to *commit* any (see *Ceillier, Histoire générale des Auteurs sacrés*, tome vii. p. 622) ; at the same time, 'parlant en général de la contagion du péché, il n'en excepte que Jésus-Christ.' But see Ceillier's explanation of this (pp. 622, 623). Saint Ephrem, deacon of Edessa, died *after* A.D. 379 (*Ceillier*, viii. 8). He says that she *was* sullied with sin before the birth of Christ ; and yet he compares her with Eve in a state of innocence (*Ceillier*, viii. 93). Saint Gregory of Nyssa, who died quite at the end of the fourth century, seems to ascribe sin to her, for he likens her to a thicket of briars (*Ceillier*, viii. 407). Saint Chrysostom, Archbishop of Constantinople, who died in A.D. 407, goes so far as to think that when wine was wanting at Cana during the nuptial feast, Mary 'souffrit quelque chose de la fragilité humaine ;' and that it was for that Jesus rebuked her, saying, 'Quid mihi tibi est, mulier?' (*Ceillier*, tome ix. p. 691). Saint Augustine, Bishop of Hippo, speaking of sin, says, '" Excepta itaque Sancta Virgine Maria, de qua propter honorem Domini nullam prorsus cum de peccatis agitur haberi volo questionem." Lib. de Nat. et Grat. cap. 36, n. 42' (*Ceillier*, xii. 552). 'Saint Fulgentius, Bishop of Ruspa, died in A.D. 533 (*Ceillier*, xvi. 16). He distinctly states the original sin of Mary. "Caro Mariæ quæ in iniquitatibus humana solemnitate pura concepta, caro fuit utique peccati, quæ Filium genuit in similitudinem carnis peccati." Fulgent. Epist. 17' (*Ceillier*, xvi. 83 ; see also p. 103). Saint Césaire, Bishop of Arles, died in 542 (*Ceillier*, xvi. 232). He says Mary was free from sin, but I do not know if this means original sin. ' " Mariâ Virgine, quæ Virgo ante partum et Virgo post partum semper fuit, et ubique contagione vel macula peccati perducavit." Cæsar, Hom. 54' (*Ceillier*, xvi. 246).

Colonia (*Histoire littéraire de la Ville de Lyon*, ii. 237) says that Julian of Toledo, in his Life of Ildephonse, Archbishop of Toledo, asserts that that saint established the festival of the Immaculate Conception, and adds, 'Ils vivaient tous deux dans le septième siècle.' It is remarkable that Ceillier, in his account of Ildephonse (*Histoire générale des Auteurs sacrés*, xvii. 712-719), says nothing about this assertion. Georges, Archbishop of Nicomedia, flourished towards the end of the ninth century. He wrote a homily on the conception of the Virgin ; and Ceillier says (*Auteurs sacrés*, xix. 454), 'Il est le plus ancien qui ait parlé de la fête que l'église grecque célébrait à cette occasion ; elle n'eut lieu dans l'église latine que longtemps après.'

The early fathers availed themselves of some current fables respecting a bird called Rachamah, and attempted from it to *rationalise* the account of the birth of Christ without the intervention of a male. See some curious remarks in Bruce's Travels, Edinburgh, 1790, vol. v. pp. 164, 166.

St. Bernard in his famous letter to the church of Lyons, written in A.D. 1140, speaks in a way which clearly intimates that there was no festival kept in honour of the Virgin's father and mother. See Fleury (livre lxviii. No. 70, tome xiv. p. 529), who adds, 'C'est que les fêtes de Saint Joachim and de Sainte Anne n'ont été instituées que plus de quatre cents ans après.' Fleury probably alludes to the bull of Gregory XIII. in A.D. 1584, ordering the feast of St. Anne to be celebrated (see *Continuation de Fleury*, livre clxxvi. No. 114, tome xxxv. p. 603). Anne and Joachim are mentioned by Epiphanius, who says that the Virgin was born of them in the ordinary course of nature (*Fleury*, livre xvii. No. 26, tome iv. p. 330). At all events, in the middle of the eighth century we find a church dedicated to St. Anne at Proconese (*Fleury*, livre xliii. No. 36, tome ix. p. 384).

In A.D. 1389, Pope Urban VI. instituted the festival of the Visitation of the Virgin, which he fixed on the 2nd of July (*Fleury*, *Histoire ecclésiastique*, livre xcviii. No. 46, tome xx. p. 375). The Council of Basle, in A.D. 1441 (on its own authority, without making mention of the Pope), ordered the festival of the Visitation of the Virgin to be celebrated in every church on the 2nd of July. See the *Continuation de Fleury* (livre cviii. Nos. 176, 177, tome xxii. pp. 358, 359), where it is said that this festival was established by Boniface IX., although Fleury (tome xx. p. 375) said that his predecessor, Urban VI., was the author.

In A.D. 1373, Philip de Maisières informed Charles V. that the festival of the Presentation of the Virgin, though unknown to the West, was celebrated in the East. He added that he had persuaded the Pope to allow it to be celebrated at Avignon. On hearing this, Charles V. on the 21st of November, 1373, caused it to be celebrated in his chapel by the papal nuncio, and wrote to the college of Navarre, exhorting them likewise to keep it (*Fleury*, livre lxxxvii. No. 30, tome xx. p. 245). In A.D. 1585 a bull of Pope Sixtus V. ordered the celebration of the Presentation of the Virgin on the 21st of November; 'et depuis ce temps-là,' says the continuator of Fleury (livre clxxvii. No. 38, tome xxxvi. p. 39), 'elle n'a point cessé d'être de précepte à Rome, ayant été insérée dans le nouveau . martyrologe romain, aussitôt après la publication de la bulle.'

In 1424 the Council of Cologne ordered that the Festival of Pains, or of the Compassion of the Virgin, should be celebrated yearly in Lent, the Friday after Jubilate Sunday; but if that day happened to be a festival, it should be kept on the succeeding Friday (*Continuation de Fleury*, livre civ. No. 133, tome xxi. p. 593).

About 1480 a dispute broke out between the inhabitants of the towns of Perouse and Cluse respecting the ring with which Joseph had married the Virgin. The people of Perouse declared that they had received it in a miraculous way, that the inhabitants of Cluse had stolen it from them, and that they were determined to risk their property and their lives to recover it. The matter was finally arranged by Innocent VIII., who determined in favour of

Perouse. In 1622 a history was published at Rome of this dispute by Jean Baptiste Laure, a native of Perouse (*Continuation de Fleury*, livre cxv. No. 52, tome xxiii. p. 527).

Some propositions in the works of Erasmus were censured by the faculty of theology at Paris (see *Continuation de Fleury*, livre cxxxi. No. 74, tome xxvi. p. 533).

Gregory of Tours, who died A.D. 595, mentions the custom of placing in churches the image of the Virgin (see *Ceillier, Histoire générale des Auteurs sacrés*, tome xvii. p. 44). In the church of the monastery of St. Dol there was a miraculous image of the Virgin, and Hervé, a monk in the middle of the twelfth century, recorded all the miracles performed by its intervention. See Ceillier (xxii. 297), who duly adds, 'Son recueil faisait un livre assez gros.' In A.D. 1559 images of the Virgin were placed in the streets of Paris, in order to serve as a test for heretics, and those who passed by without saluting them, or refused to contribute money to pay for the wax tapers, were fallen on by the people as Huguenots (see *Continuation de Fleury*, livre cliii. No. 143, tome xxxi. p. 377). In A.D. 1566, 'on établit une dévotion de la Sainte Vierge en Flandre,' and struck medals in her honour (*Continuation de Fleury*, livre clxix. No. 101, tome xxxiv. pp. 326, 327).

In 1571, Don John of Austria defeated the Turks in the great battle of Lepanto, and in consequence Pius V. by a bull instituted a festival on the 7th of October, in honour of the Virgin Mary, under the name of 'Notre Dame de la Victoire' (*Continuation de Fleury*, livre clxxii. No. 62, tome xxxv. p. 75).

In A.D. 1594, Pope Clement VIII. by a bull 'approuva la congrégation dite de la Bienheureuse Vierge Marie du Suffrage, déjà établie à Rome pour la délivrance des âmes du purgatoire' (*Continuation de Fleury*, livre clxxxi. No. 19, tome xxxvi. p. 513).

NOTE ON THE SACREDNESS OF SALIVA, AND ITS CONNECTION WITH BAPTISM.

Blunt (*Vestiges of Ancient Customs and Manners*, 8vo, 1823, pp. 164–168) has some curious remarks on saliva. Pliny mentions that it was used as a charm, and quotes authorities to show that serpents, &c., may be rendered harmless by spitting into their mouths. At the present day there exists in Sicily a set of men who profess to heal the wounds of venomous animals by spittle. 'It is remarkable,' adds Blunt (p. 167), 'that in administering the rite of baptism, the priest, among other ceremonies, moistens a napkin with human saliva, and then touches with it the eyes and nose of the child, accompanying the action by the word " Ephphatha." It was with a similar rite that Roman infants received their names on the " Dies Lustricus."

> " Ecce avia aut metuens Divum matertera, cunis
> Exemit puerum ; frontemque atque uda labella
> Infami digito et *lustralibus ante salivis*
> *Expiat*," Persius, Sat. ii. 31.'

See also, at pp. 168, 169, Blunt's remarks on the miracle performed by Jesus, when by the aid of saliva He restored sight to the blind and hearing to the deaf.

See Michaelis, Recueil de Questions, Amsterdam, 1774, 4to, No. 58, pp. 116, 117 ; and Niebuhr, Description de l'Arabie, Amsterdam, 1774, pp. 26–53. 'Fasting spittle' was an ingredient in charms (see *Ben Jonson's Works*, 8vo, 1816, iii. 226).

1. See what Ledwich (*Irish Antiquities*, Dublin, 1804, 4to, p. 123) has said respecting the pagan origin of the custom of giving milk and honey after baptism to infants. 2. Bingham has pointed out passages from Tertullian, Clemens Alexandrinus, and Jerome, which prove how general the practice was of giving what he delicately calls 'a little taste of honey and milk to the newly baptised' (*Antiquities of the Christian Church*, book xii. chap. vi. sect. 6 ; *Works*, vol. iv. pp. 50–52, 8vo, 1844 ; see also xv. 2, 3, vol. v. p. 35). 3. The Japanese have an idea of its curative qualities (see *Golownin's Captivity in Japan*, 8vo, 1824, vol. ii. p. 69). 4. Bowdich (*Mission to Ashantee*, 4to, 1819, p. 224) says, 'When the king of Ashantee spits, the boys with the elephants' tails sedulously wipe it up or cover it with sand.' 5. Mungo Park passed through the wilderness which separates the kingdom of Woolli and Boudon at about 12° W. long., and 15° N. lat. He says (*Travels*, 8vo, 1817, vol. i. pp. 63, 64), 'We had not travelled more than a mile before my attendants insisted on stopping that they might prepare a *saphie*, or charm, to insure us a safe journey. This was done by muttering a few sentences, and spitting upon a stone which was thrown before us on the road. The same ceremony was repeated three times.' See also (at pp. 409, 410) a curious case of baptism by saliva. Park also says (p. 413) that, on the

appearance of the new moon, both Pagans and Mahometans, after praying, 'spit upon their hands and rub them over their faces.' 6. Among the ancients, 'a common mode of averting fascination was by spitting into the folds of one's own dress' (*Smith's Dictionary of Greek and Roman Antiquities*, 8vo, 1842, p. 410). 7. See Deuteronomy xxv. 9 ; and Michaelis, Commentary on the Laws of Moses, vol. ii. p. 30, Lond. 8vo, 1814. 8. Henderson (*Biblical Researches, &c. in Russia*, 8vo, 1826, p. 231) says that the Rabbis so hate the name of Jesus that they will never pronounce it without spitting three times on the ground. 9. Pinkerton (*Account of Russia*, 8vo, 1833, p. 155) says that if you inquire into the sex of a Russian infant, the mother or nurse suspects a magical intention, and 'spits several times on the ground, repeating at the same time prayers against the effect of the evil eye and all Satanic influences.'

DIVISION OF THE ANCIENT EGYPTIANS INTO CASTES.

See Heeren's African Nations, Oxford, 1838, vol. ii. He says (pp. 119-120) that the most brilliant period of Egypt was from B.C. 1500 to B.C. 800, during which time the division into castes was finally consummated (p. 121). The priests were of course the highest caste ; and it was probably (p. 125) a daughter of the high priest whom Joseph married. Respecting the priest caste see pp. 125-130. For the warrior caste see pp. 131-136, and for the trading caste, 136-140. There was also a caste composed of navigators of the Nile (pp. 140, 141), one of interpreters (pp. 141, 142), and one of herdsmen (pp. 143-148). The kings of Egypt did not generally belong to the priest caste, but probably to the warrior caste (p. 150). So completely were the Egyptians imbued with this spirit of caste that we find (p. 162) not only a caste of physicians, but physicians for particular members of the body, and for the disease to which they were subject ; and the very prostitutes formed a separate caste (p. 339).

M'Culloch says that the strictness with which the Indians observe caste is greatly exaggerated (*Dictionary of Commerce*, 1849, pp. 554-556). In one part of Madagascar scarcely any one will eat beef 'unless it is killed by one descended from a race of kings' (*Drury's Madagascar*, 8vo, 1743, p. 154). 1. Heeren says (p. 130) that everything relating to the Egyptian priests has been

collected by De Schmidt in his De Sacrificiis et Sacerdotibus
Ægyptorum, Tubingæ, 1768, 8vo. 2. The Ceylonese are divided
into castes (see *Percival's Ceylon*, 4to, 1805, 2nd edit. pp. 258 260,
269). 3. The Malagasy have a sort of caste, for Ellis (*History of
Madagascar*, vol. i. p. 164) says, 'Certain ranks are not permitted
under any circumstance to intermarry;' and see further on the three
limitations as to caste. However, the civil and military professions
'are not hereditary' (p. 293). 4. Harvard (*Mission to Ceylon
and India*, 8vo, 1823, p. xliii) says, 'The distinction of caste
which prevails among the natives of continental India is found
also among the Singalese, though not in so rigid a degree as on
the continent. In Ceylon it is of a more political character than
among the Hindoos.' But, from the anecdote Harvard (p. xlii)
himself relates, it is evident that the division into caste is social
as well as political. 5. A. W. Schlegel has defended the institution
of castes (see pp. xxxix, xl, of his *Preface* to *Prichard's Egyptian
Mythology*, 8vo, 1838). Prichard himself has some good remarks
on the Egyptian castes (see pp. 373-378, and 397-404). He
is inclined to think (p. 375) that the opinion that the Hindoo
castes were originally different nations may be true, but that
that cannot be the case with ancient Egypt. 6. Malthus (*Essay
on Population*, 8vo, 1826, vol. i. p. 193) has well pointed out the
effect of the institution of caste in keeping down population. The
effect of caste, as Storch observes, is to prevent there being any
current and average rate of wages and profits (*Économie politique*,
St. Petersburg, 8vo, 1815, tome ii. p. 184). M. Cousin takes an
unusually superficial view of the establishment of castes, in which
he can only see 'une institution bizarre et vivace' (*Histoire de la Philosophie*, Paris, 1846, part i. tome iii. p. 320). Frederick Schlegel
makes a whimsical attempt to trace the origin of caste to the Hebrew
nation (*Philosophy of History*, London, 8vo, 1846, pp. 100, 149-152).
He says (p. 142) that it has a republican tendency. Lord Brougham
says (*Political Philosophy*, 2nd edit. 8vo, 1849, vol. i. p. 130),
'Castes are wholly unknown to the nations beyond the Ganges.'

OPINION OF THE EGYPTIANS RESPECTING THE IMMORTALITY OF THE SOUL

Heeren (*African Nations*, ii. 188) quotes Herodotus, who says,
'The Egyptians are the first who have asserted that the soul of

man is immortal ; for when the body perishes it enters the body of
a newly born animal ; but when it has passed through all the land
animals, sea animals, and fowls, it again returns to a human body.
This transmigration is completely performed in three thousand
years.' But, asks Heeren, how is this doctrine to be reconciled
with the attention paid to dead bodies? Zoega, indeed, supposes
that Herodotus meant to say that the soul descends with the body
into the lower world, and first commences its wanderings when the
latter is decayed. To this Heeren replies, ' But we very naturally
demand, how could this opinion prevail among a people who so
embalmed the corpses that they *never decayed at all*?' The only
way, says Heeren, to get over this difficulty is to believe that there
was a difference between the religion of the vulgar and that of the
priests. The doctrine of transmigration of souls is too refined
for popular belief, and ' bears about it too clearly the marks of
having been formed according to a scientific system.' Heeren
alludes to the three thousand years, ' which was without doubt
determined upon from astronomical and astrological observation,'
and he refers on this head to a treatise of Selterer. This opinion,
that the belief in the transmigration of souls was confined to the
priests, is supported (p. 190) by what is said by Diodorus Siculus,
who informs us that the Egyptians considered a quiet repose after
death as much more important than the present life. Diodorus
does not say what this idea of *continuance* after death was; but ' if
we consider their whole proceedings with regard to their dead, a
doubt can scarcely remain upon the subject. It was closely connected by them with the *continuance* of the body, and was therefore for the most part a coarse, sensual kind of notion' (see also
pp. 195, 196).

See Pettigrew's History of Egyptian Mummies, Lond. 4to, 1834,
pp. 14, 15. He seems to have given a better explanation than
Heeren, and observes that 'those who held the doctrine of transmigration of souls would take extraordinary pains to preserve the
body from putrefaction, in the hope of the soul again joining the
body it had quitted;' and he has quoted Servius, who in his
Commentary on Virgil says that the Egyptians embalm their
dead 'ut anima corpori sit obnoxia, ne cito ad aliud transeat.'
This is all very pertinent, but I cannot understand why he has
followed Larcher in thinking that Herodotus says, *not* that the
Egyptians were the first who held the immortality of the soul,

but they were the first *who, believing it,* superadded the doctrine of transmigration. Of course the explanation of Pettigrew will not hold if Herodotus means to say that the soul transmigrated, not on the death, but on the *dissolution* of the body. For, as Heeren says, this never could have been believed by a people who embalmed their corpses so as to *prevent* dissolution. This absurdity must have been as obvious to Herodotus as it is to us, therefore I am inclined to think he meant that the transmigration began after *death.*

1. Schlegel (*Preface to Prichard's Egyptian Mythology,* 8vo, 1838, p. xxxii) says, 'Immortality in the form of transmigration of the soul is an entirely peculiar doctrine, which we only find clearly expressed among all the nations of antiquity by the Indians and Egyptians; Greek philosophers borrowed it from the latter.' 2. The Benedictines gravely suggest that the Gaulish Druids received their knowledge of the immortality of the soul from Japhet (*Histoire littéraire de la France,* tome i. part i. p. 9). 3. In the third century St. Hippolyte wrote against the metempsychosis (*Hist. lit. de la France,* tome i. part i. pp. 389, 398). 4. The Bedouin believes that men are sometimes transformed into goats, and on purchasing a goat searches for certain marks by which he can recognise such unfortunates (*Wellsted's Travels in Arabia,* 8vo, 1838, vol. i. p. 161). Kant, even to the very last year of his long life, believed in metempsychosis (see *Cousin's Littérature,* 8vo, 1849, tome iii. p. 341). Frederick Schlegel had a strange notion that it was a corruption of the doctrine of purgatory (*Philosophy of History,* 8vo, 1846, pp. 157-160). Among the negroes of Western Africa metempsychosis is a very common doctrine (see *Prichard's Physical History of Mankind,* vol. i. pp. 210, 211, 8vo, 1841), and it is held by some of the Australians (*Prichard,* vol. v. p. 264) and by the ancient Mexicans (vol. v. p. 366). In the Friendly Islands it is believed that only the chiefs live hereafter, but that the common people have only mortal souls (see *Mariner's Tonga Islands,* 8vo, 1838, vol. i. p. 419 ; vol. ii. p. 128). Wesley was inclined to think that brutes had immaterial souls (see *Southey's Life of Wesley,* 8vo, 1846, vol. ii. p. 93). Beechey's Voyage to the Pacific, 8vo, 1831, vol. i. p. 244.

WOMEN OF KAMTSCHATKA SOMETIMES DO NOT WEAN THEIR CHILDREN FOR FOUR OR FIVE YEARS.

'They have no limited time for suckling their children, and I have seen instances of its continuing for four or five years' (*Travels in Kamtschatka during the years 1787 and 1788, by M. de Lesseps*, London, 1790, 8vo, vol. i. p. 134).

At Wawa, a woman is flogged and sold as a slave 'if, when she has a child at the breast, she is known to go with a man' (*Clapperton's Second Expedition*, 1829, 4to, p. 95).

Queen Elizabeth was weaned at thirteen months (*Miss Strickland's Queens of England*, vol. vi. p. 7, 8vo, 1843).

1. The Persian mothers nurse their children from between two to three years (see *Morier's Second Journey through Persia*, 1818, 4to, p. 107). 2. The women on the Gold Coast of Africa 'suckle their children until they are able to walk about' (*Meredith, On the Gold Coast*, 8vo, 1812, p. 109), and up the Niger women 'are publicly flogged if they are known to associate with the other sex before the expiration of three years after the birth of an infant; that being the period mothers are obliged to suckle their offspring' (*Laird and Oldfield's Expedition up the Niger*, 8vo, 1837, vol. ii. p. 97). 3. 'The mothers in Madagascar often suckle their children for several years' (*Ellis's History of Madagascar*, 8vo, 1838, vol. i. p. 160). 4. Park's Travels, 8vo, 1817, vol. i. pp. 402, 403.

NOTE ON HUMAN SACRIFICES.

I have not seen any proof of their being practised by the Malagasy, although from the anecdote related by Ellis (*History of Madagascar*, 8vo, 1838, vol. i. p. 345) it would appear that they were not quite unknown; and it seems that in one province (Vangardrano) 'human sacrifices were formerly offered' (i. 422). In the South Sea Islands they are 'comparatively of modern institution' (*Ellis, Polynesian Researches*, 8vo, 1831, vol. i. p. 106; see also vol. iv. p. 150). They are practised in the Friendly Islands (see *Mariner's Account of the Tonga Islands*, 2nd edit. 8vo, 1818, vol. i. pp. 217, 366).

Moffat (*Missionary Labours in Southern Africa*, 8vo, 1832, p. 243), who resided many years among the Bechuanas, says that human sacrifices are not practised by them ; indeed, he says (pp. 276, 279) that they have no idea of any sacrifices. Mungo Park, as far as I can remember, makes no mention of human sacrifices, but Isaaco says that at Sego the custom is, when a male child of the king's wives is born on a Friday, that his throat should be cut, which is done immediately' (see *Isaaco's Journal* in *Park's Travels*, 8vo, 1817, vol. ii. p. 283). We know with certainty, both from ancient writers and from extant monuments, that the ancient Egyptians practised human sacrifices (see *Prichard's Egyptian Mythology*, 8vo, 1838, pp. 361-363).

See the two notes at Milman's History of Christianity, 8vo, 1840, vol. i. pp. 27, 28. He observes that they were certainly practised by the Greeks and Romans, but he thinks that in regard to the latter we merely see 'the sanguinary spirit of the age of proscriptions taking for once a more solemn and religious form.' However, he adds, 'Human sacrifices are said to have taken place under Aurelian (Aug. Hist. Vit. Aurel.), and even under Maxentius.'

Human sacrifices were practised by the ancient Slavonians, and we find an instance as late as A.D. 983 (*Pinkerton's Russia*, 8vo, 1833, pp. 197, 200).

The Otaheitans offer human sacrifices, but *perhaps* only criminals or enemies. See Cook's Voyages, 8vo, 1821, vol. iii. p. 194, and compare vol. vi. pp. 30-34, 37, 38, 39, 40, 51. They look on them as food for their gods (vi. 41). The Sandwich Islanders offer human sacrifices (*Cook*, vi. 188), and appear to have appropriated Cook's body to some such purpose (vii. 65, and see p. 75). King says (*Cook*, vii. 149), 'Human sacrifices are more frequent here, according to the account of the natives themselves, than in any other islands we visited.' The inhabitants of the Friendly Islands offer human sacrifices, according to Cook (*Voyages*, 1821, vol. v. pp. 407, 457), who, however, does not say he *saw* them. The New Zealanders generally offer some on the death of a chief, with circumstances of peculiar cruelty (see *Earle's New Zealand*, 8vo, 1832, pp. 78-124).

Chevenix considers human sacrifices as the result of cruelty acting upon ignorance in fertile countries, where labour is of little value (*Essay on National Character*, 8vo, 1832, vol. i. pp. 181-187). The remark is acute; and I do not remember any instance of human sacrifices being extensively offered by nations inhabiting a country where the soil is barren and the climate cold.

But they are known to the North American Indians (see *Catlin's North American Indians*, 8vo, 1841, vol. i. p. 133). Mackay's Progress of the Intellect, vol. ii. pp. 406-413.

RACES OF MANKIND BY INTERMIXTURE INCREASE IN FERTILITY.

'Those Hottentots who do marry have seldom more than two or three children, and many of the women are barren. This, however, is not the case when a Hottentot woman is connected with a white man. The fruit of such an alliance are not only in general numerous, but are beings of a very different nature from the Hottentot men, of six feet high, and stout in proportion, and women well made, not ill-featured, smart and active' (*Travels into the Interior of Southern Africa, by John Barrow*, 2nd edit. 4to, 1816, vol. i. p. 97).

Lindley's Introduction to Botany, 8vo, 1848, ii. p. 250. Dalfour's Botany, 8vo, 1849, p. 249.

Bruce (*Travels*, 4to, 1790, vol. iv. p. 468) says that a white Arab marrying a black woman has white children. Paris and Fonblanque (*Medical Jurisprudence*, 8vo, 1823, vol. i. pp. 168, 169) assert very positively that intermarriages long continued in the same family produce mental and bodily deficiencies. But these able writers have not produced the least evidence for this ; unless, indeed, the argument from the analogy of brutes may be considered evidence. Dr. Seybert says, 'A mixture of races most conduces to increase' (*Sadler on Population*, 1830, vol. i. p. 638). Combe takes it for granted as a '*law*,' that 'marriages between blood relations tend to the deterioration of the physical and mental qualities of the offspring' (*The Constitution of Man*, Edinburgh, 8vo, 1847, p. 226). See *Prichard's Physical History of Mankind*, 8vo, 1841, vol. i. pp. 138-150. He allows (p. 138) that Rudolphi has shown that all hybrid productions are not sterile. Still, he says (p. 146) that generally 'the energy of propagation is very defective in the union of different species,' but 'the undoubted fact is that all mixed races of men are remarkable for their tendency to multiplication' (p. 147). Combe (*Lectures on Moral*

Philosophy, 8vo, 1840, pp. 116, 117) takes for granted that in men, as in the lower animals, the intermarriage of near relations causes deterioration.

NOTE ON THE WORSHIP ETC. OF THE MOON.

'The only chronology of the Kaffirs is kept by the moon, and is registered by notches in pieces of wood' (*Barrow's Travels in Southern Africa*, 2nd edit. 4to, 1806, vol. i. p. 171).

The Namaguas say ' that the moon had told to mankind that we must die, and not become alive again ; that is the reason that when the moon is dark we sometimes become ill ' (*Missionary Labours in Southern Africa, by Robert Moffat*, London, 8vo, 1842, p. 12) ; and see at p. 260 Moffat's remarks on the refreshing beauty of an African moon. He adds (p. 337) that among the Bechuanas 'the vague though universal notion prevails, when the moon is eclipsed, that a great chief has died.' Mungo Park (*Travels*, 8vo, 1817, vol. i. pp. 412, 413) says that he 'frequently put questions to the Africans respecting what became of the sun during the night, &c., but found they considered the *question as very childish.* . . . The moon, by varying her form, has *more attracted their attention.* On the first appearance of the new moon, which they look upon as being newly created, the Pagan natives, as well as Mahomedans, say a short prayer ; and this seems to be the only visible adoration which the Kaffirs offer up to the Supreme Being. . . . At the conclusion they spit upon their hands and rub them on their faces. This seems nearly the same ceremony which prevailed among the heathens in the days of Job (chap. xxxi. verses 26-28).' Bruce (*Travels*, Edinburgh, 4to, 1790, vol. iv. pp. 420, 421) found near Sennaar some Pagan Nuba, who 'pay adoration to the moon. . . . They testify great joy by motions of their feet and hands at the first appearance of the new moon. I never saw them pay any attention to the sun, either rising or setting.' Duncan (*Travels in Western Africa*, 8vo, 1847, vol. i. p. 219) says that, in Abomey, 'all reckoning is by the moon.' Clapperton (*Second Expedition*, 1829, 4to, p. 130) says that at Koolfu, 'This night the new moon was seen, and Mahommedans joined in the cry of joy.' Borlase (*Antiquities of Cornwall*, London, 1769, p. 61) supposes that the worship of the moon being performed in the night, ' introduced every kind of pollution, which the day in some measure would have shamed.' Prichard (*Analysis of Egyptian Mythology*, 8vo, 1838, pp. 136-138) has collected some proofs of the general superstition that things prospered more at the full moon than when the moon was waning ; and he supposes that Boubastis, or the Egyptian Diana, signified the beneficent influence exercised by the moon over pregnant women. See also p. 156 for the opinions of the Greenlanders (see also pp. 371, 372). There is a widely spread belief that the moon and tides influence disease. To this Mrs. Quickly alludes in her account of Falstaff's death in Henry V. On this subject there are some curious remarks in Southey's Doctor, edit. Warter, 8vo, 1848, pp. 207-209 ; and the danger of a flowing tide to the sick is mentioned by Tusser (*Five Hundred Points of Husbandry*, edit. Mavor, 1812, p. xl). 'The Otaheitans, in speaking of time either past or to come, never used any term but Malama, which signifies moon,' but they are acquainted with the solar year (*Cook's Voyages*, 8vo, 1821, vol. i. p. 225). 'The Arabs alone, who practise neither agriculture nor navigation, have a year depending upon the moon only, and borrow the word from other languages when they speak of the solar year' (*Whewell's History of the Inductive Sciences*, 8vo, 1847, vol. i. p. 125).

NOTE ON THE BELIEF ETC. IN THE RESURRECTION.

Moffat (*Missionary Labours in the South of Africa*, 8vo, 1842, pp. 404, 405) details a conversation he had with Makaba, which shows how much this dogma offended the untutored intellect of the Africans (see also p. 245). Mungo Park (*Travels in Africa*, 8vo, 1817, vol. i. p. 415), speaking of the negroes, says, 'I have conversed with all ranks and conditions upon the subject of their faith, and can pronounce without the smallest shadow of doubt, that the belief of one God, and of a future state of reward and punishment, is entire and universal among them.' The Fantees often bury ornaments belonging to the dead with them (*Duncan's Western Africa*, 8vo, 1847, vol. i. p. 27); and the Dahomans believe in the separate existence of the soul (i. 125, 126), and in 'the great Fetish' (ii. 246).

Milman (*History of Christianity*, 8vo, 1840, vol. i. pp. 75, 76) observes that there is much difficulty in deciding on the opinion of the earlier Jews on this point; but that it is clear, from various passages in Daniel and Ezekiel, that the later Jews believed 'in a final resurrection.' He adds, what is well worthy of remark, 'This belief appears, however, in its more perfect development soon after the return from the Captivity' (i.e. after the Jews had become acquainted with Eastern philosophy). We find in 2 Maccabees (xii. 44) 'a solemn ceremony performed for the dead,' and from henceforth the doctrine of the resurrection becomes the great point of contention between the Sadducees and Pharisees, and even Tacitus (Hist. v. 5) was 'struck with the effect of this opinion on the Jews.' Milman proceeds to remark, on the authority of Hyde, Beausobre, Klenker, and Gesenius, that 'in the Zoroastrian religions a resurrection holds a place no less prominent than in the later Jewish belief.' See ART. 1814. Tertullian (Ad Uxorem, cap. i.) says that in the future world there will be no distinction of sexes; and yet he says (Ad Gent. lib. i. capp. xviii. xix.) that the resurrection will be effected by uniting the soul with the *same* body. In Apol. cap. 48, he again affirms the general resurrection of the body. See also in De Resur. Carnis, where he, however, adds that our body, though it will still be by nature passible, will receive the gift of impassibility (see *Ceillier*, tome ii. pp. 391, 411, 426, 452, 455).

St. Hippolyte, in the third century, wrote on the resurrection of the body. A fragment of his work remains (see *Hist. Lit. de la France*, tome i. part i. p. 381, and pp. 389. 398); and the resurrection of the body is asserted by Irenæus (*Hist. Lit.* tome i. pt. i. p. 333).

HISTORICAL NOTES ON THE OBSERVANCE OF SUNDAY.

Stukeley, in p. 2 of the dedication prefixed to his Stonehenge (Lond. fol. 1740), complains of 'that too fashionable custom of travelling on Sundays.' Stukeley (*Abury described*, Lond. 1743, p. 35) thinks that 'we cannot doubt of the Druids' observance of the sabbath'! Stukeley (*Abury described*, p. 68) thinks that the observance of the sabbath was 'a custom older than Judaism.' See his quotations from the Scholiast of Pindar, from Gale, from Usher, from Hesiod, and from Porphyry, as cited by Eusebius.

Henderson (*Biblical Researches in Russia*, 8vo, 1826, pp. 146, 147) was during Sunday at Tala, south of Moscow, where he found that the inhabitants held a regular fair on that day. In England fairs used to be held in churchyards (*M'Culloch's Dictionary of Commerce*, 8vo, 1849, p. 593).

In Finland, the acts of the Legislature, decrees of magistrates, &c., are read on Sunday in the churches, after the service has begun and before it is ended; and the same custom 'prevails in every part of Sweden.' See Pinkerton's Russia (8vo, 1833, pp. 397, 398), who relates what he *saw*.

St. Hilary, Bishop of Poitiers, died in A.D. 368 (*Hist. lit. de la France*, tome i. part ii. p. 145). The Benedictines say (p. 176), 'Il fait mention de la coutume qu'observaient les fidèles, de ne point jeûner ni de se prosterner dans la prière les jours de dimanche.' This was probably borrowed from the Montanists. See my Life of Tertullian, xx. Tertullian, Apolog. cap. xvi. (*Ceillier*, p. 417), says that it was usual to celebrate Sunday—the day of the sun—by feasting and pleasure. He also says, De Idol. capp. xiii. xiv. (*Ceillier*, p. 443), that the Pagans would not keep any of the Christian holidays, not even Sunday or Pentecost. He, when a Montanist (*Ceillier*, ii. 486, 487), says (De Coron. capp. iii. iv.), 'Die Dominico jejunium *nefas* ducimus, vel de geniculis adorare.'

Cecil says, in a letter written in 1564, 'Yesterday, being Sonday, the Spanish ambassador presented to her majesty a writing,' &c. (*Wright's Elizabeth*, 8vo, 1838, vol. i. p. 181). A good deal of the diplomatic correspondence in the sixteenth century in England is dated Sunday. See, for instances, Wright's Elizabeth, 8vo, 1838, vol. i. p. 181; vol. ii. pp. 72, 174; and, for Sunday travelling, see vol. ii. p. 207. The miserable absurdity of calling Sunday the *Sabbath* occurs in a letter from Fletewood in 1583 (*Wright*, ii. 186). Alehouses were open on Sundays (see *Rich's Honestie of this Age*, 1614, p. 54, Percy Society, vol. xi.)

Irving says (*History of Columbus*, 8vo, 1828, vol. ii. p. 317), 'It was contrary to the custom of Columbus to weigh anchor on Sunday when in port, but the people murmured, and observed that when in quest of food it was no time to stand on scruples as to holidays (Hist. del Almirante, cap. 62).'

Sir Simon D'Ewes, speaking of the fire in the Six Clerks' Office in 1621, says that it was a judgment of God for the sins of

the six clerks. One of their sins was 'their atheistical profanation of God's own holy day, sitting (excepting one Mr. Henley,
come in but a few years before, that had some religion) in their
studies most part of the Sunday in the afternoon, to take their
fees and do their office business, many of their underclerks following their profane example' (*D'Ewes, Autobiography*, edit.
Halliwell, 8vo, 1845, vol. i. p. 210). At vol. ii. p. 196 there is a
letter of D'Ewes, dated May 5, 1628, giving an account of 'the
horrible profanation of Sunday' at the court of Charles I. In
the same year, 'last Lord's day were four new privy counsellors
sworn' (vol. ii. p. 202).

On 31st May, 1798, Hannah More, in a letter to her sister,
gives an account of the duel fought by Pitt. She says, 'To complete the horror, too, they chose a Sunday!' (*Robert's Memoirs
of Mrs. Hannah More*, 2nd edit. 8vo, 1834, vol. iii. p. 31). See
also Cumberland's Memoirs, by Himself, 8vo, 1807, vol. ii. p. 428.
Hannah More, in her 'Thoughts on the Manners of the Great'
(the preface to which is dated 1809), mentions 'Sunday concerts'
at which sacred music was played as being then very fashionable,
and an 'evil newly crept into polished society' (*Works of H. More*,
Lond. 8vo, 1830, vol. xi. p. 26).

In 1585 a clergyman named Smith ventured, in a sermon
before the University of Cambridge, to maintain that plays and
sports were unlawful on Sundays. This was considered so monstrous a doctrine that he was immediately summoned before the
vice-chancellor (see *Neal's History of the Puritans*, 8vo, 1822,
vol. i. p. 371). Aylmer, Bishop of London, 'usually played at
bowls on Sundays in the afternoons' (*Neal*, i. 450). Towards the
end of Elizabeth's reign, Dr. Bound published a treatise in which
he maintained that the observance of Sunday was absolutely obli-
gatory. The doctrine was declared by Whitgift to be opposed to
the law of the church, and by the Lord Chief Justice to be
opposed to the law of the land, and the work was ordered to be
called in (*Neal*, i. 451, 452). Collier accuses the Puritans of
'magnifying the Sabbath day as they call Sunday' (*Ecclesiastical
History*, 8vo, 1840, vol. vii. p. 182). In the injunctions issued by
Edward VI. 'the curates are obliged to instruct their parishioners
that in harvest-time it is lawful for them to work on holidays;'
and the king directed that the Lords of the Council 'should
upon Sunday attend the public affairs of the realm, ... and

z 2

that on every Sunday night the king's secretary should deliver
him a memorial of such things as are to be debated by the Privy
Council in the week ensuing' (*Collier's Ecclesiastical History*,
vol. v. pp. 201, 202). Mr. Soames ignorantly says that keeping
holy the Sunday 'is one of the many substantial benefits for
which we have to thank the Reformation' (*Soames, History of
the Reformation of the Church of England*, vol. ii. p. 692, 8vo,
1827). The Bishop of Asaph says, that as to 'the change in the
day of the week, the alteration has been admitted since the time
of the Apostles' (*Short's History of the Church of England*, 8vo,
1847, p. 153). In 1599 there was held in London on Sunday a
great tilting-match between several persons of rank (see *Sydney
Letters*, edit. Collins, fol. 1746, vol. ii. p. 142).

INFANTICIDE.

Prichard (*Egyptian Mythology*, 8vo, 1838, p. 413), speaking of
the ancient Egyptians, says, 'Infanticide was punished by obliging
the parents to hug their dead children in their arms for three
successive days and nights. This, if true, gives countenance to
the idea suggested by Warburton, that infanticide was commonly
practised in Egypt in the time of Moses. The account of the
Egyptian midwives in Exodus indicates, as the bishop observes,
that the office they were employed in was not altogether foreign
to the national customs. So strange a punishment as that above
mentioned would have been scarcely appointed if the crime had
not been frequently practised and tolerated in the preceding
times.'

If the above remarks are true, and if we may rely on what
Prichard has said before, then it follows that the doctrine of
emanation in Egypt, or at all events the consequences of that
doctrine, was not so old as the time of Moses. For it seems
clear that if the belief of the divine spirit permeating all living
things was sufficient to prevent them killing animals, and even
to induce them to worship them; it must, *à fortiori*, have been
strong enough to prevent them habitually killing their own
children.

1. The Otaheitans believe that all things, even trees and stones,
have souls which are absorbed by the Deity (see *Cook's Voyages*,

8vo, 1821, vol. vi. p. 154). And yet their very laws allow infanticide (vi. 161), and that independently of their arreoys, where infanticide is avowedly and universally practised (vol. i. pp. 206, 207 ; and for a description of the *mode*, vol. vi. p. 147). 2. The New Zealanders used to destroy most of their female children (see *Earle's New Zealand*, 8vo, 1832, p. 243). 3. Malthus (*Essay on Population*, 8vo, 1826, 6th edit. vol. i. p. 75) follows Hume in thinking that the practice of infanticide is favourable to an increase of population (see also pp. 213, 214, 234). 4. Sadler (*Laws of Population*, 1830, vol. i. pp. 616, 617) has brought forward some evidence to show that infanticide is not so general in China as is usually supposed. 5. Mr. M'Culloch (*Principles of Political Economy*, Edinburgh, 8vo, 1843, p. 238) says, but without quoting any authority, that infanticide was not prohibited at Rome till A.D. 374, and that the exposition of children continued long afterwards, the unfortunate infants being legally slaves until A.D. 530. 6. Thornton (*Over Population*, 8vo, 1846, p. 118) speaks of infanticide as a check to population, but it is only a check when opposed by popular opinion. Storch (*Économie politique*, St. Petersburg, 8vo, 1815, vol. ii. p. 13) says, 'Le mariage n'est pas encouragé à la Chine par le profit qu'on retire des enfants, mais par la permission de les détruire.' Chevenix (*Essay on National Character*, 8vo, 1832, vol. i. p. 183) says, 'Infanticide is the most common check which savage societies have devised to remove the evils of redundant population.' Eyre says that among the aborigines of Australia 'infanticide is very common, and appears to be practised solely to get rid of the trouble of rearing children, and to enable the woman to follow her husband about in his wanderings, which she frequently could not do if encumbered with a child. The first three or four are often killed' (*Eyre's Central Australia*, Lond. 8vo, 1845, ii. 324).

REMARKS ON THE PROGRESSION OF HINDOO AND EGYPTIAN MYTHOLOGY.

For an account of Frederick Schlegel's view of the History of Hindoo Mythology see Prichard's Egyptian Mythology, 8vo, 1838, p. 224 *et seq.* Schlegel divides the Hindoo mythology into four principal eras, which follow each other in chronological succession :

1st. Emanation and transmigration of souls ; 2nd. The worship of nature, of stars, &c. ; 3rd. Dualism—the belief in two principles, and the struggle between light and darkness ; 4th. Pantheism, a more metaphysical doctrine, approximating to the European philosophy (pp. 224, 225).

1st. Emanation and transmigration are found in the code of Menu, 'a relic some thousand years old' (p. 227) ; and we must be careful, with our European ideas, not to confuse the *declining* dogma of emanation with pantheism (p. 228), which we should do if we were to take Eastern hyperboles literally. The *difference is essential*, for in the Hindoo doctrine of emanation individual exist-ence is not denied, and the reunion of the spirit with the divinity is only *possible*, not *necessary* (p. 228). Again (p. 229), pantheism teaches that as every being is part of the one great soul, so actions are performed by his immediate agency, and every appearance of evil is a mere deception. Hence the practical mischiefs of pan-theism. With believers in emanation, on the other hand, the human race has deteriorated *since* the spirit emanated from the Supreme Being. Hence the dogma of four ages, each of which is worse than the preceding one (pp. 230, 231). Hence, too, the emanations themselves progressively deteriorate. It is clear (p. 232) that the Hindoo sages believed in *one God* true and great, and it must be allowed (p. 233) that the imagination could not fill up the void between supreme beatitude and the imperfections of the created world in a more natural way than by supposing the dogma of emanations.[1]

From their ideas respecting gradation, and the degrees to which souls approximated to or diverged from the great source, *arose* the doctrine of transmigration.

2nd. From the doctrine of emanation naturally sprung fatalism or *predestination* (p. 235), and from that arose (p. 236) *astrology*[2] as a means of divination. Indeed, materialism seems to be the immediate step subsequent to emanation (p. 237), and we find in

---

[1] The Malagasy worship the 'only one supreme God' (see *Drury's Madagascar*, 8vo, 1743. p. 226).

[2] Dr. Whewell thinks that astrology preceded astronomy (*Whewell's History of the Inductive Sciences*, 8vo, 1847, vol. i. pp. 149, 297, 309–320). The Malagasy are confirmed fatalists, and believe in a 'stern, unbending, fixed, immutable destiny (see *Ellis, History of Madagascar*, 8vo, 1838, vol. i. pp. 388, 389). Coleridge (*Literary Remains*, iii. 357) says 'astrology was prior to astronomy.'

Menu traces of it. From this naturally arose the *worship* of *animals*, as well as of the planets (pp. 239, 240).

3rd. Dualism seems always to have been set up as a restoration of the ancient doctrine (p. 241). It is very similar to the idealistic philosophy of the West (p. 242); and it maintains that energy and life are the only operative principles, absolute inertia being only *negative*, or the principle of death, while *pantheism* destroys the distinction between good and evil (p. 242), and the doctrine of emanation depresses the freedom of the will by the idea of an infinite degree of innate guilt (p. 243). A middle place between these two extremes is held by dualism. The worship of Vishnu belongs to this period (p. 244), the incarnation of whom shows the philosophical improvement of the Hindoos (p. 245).

4th. We find pantheism in the doctrines professed by the Buddhists of India and of China (p. 249); at least, the doctrine that the universe is substantially nothing is assigned as an esoteric doctrine of Fo.[1] It is clear (pp. 249, 250) that the belief in a Supreme and Omnipotent Being must have been much weakened before it could resolve itself into one sole Being, who can scarcely be distinguished from non-existence. Another proof (p. 250) of the more modern date of pantheism is, that while other doctrines of the Orientals are founded on *miracles* and an appeal to revelation, this has originated entirely in metaphysical refinements (p. 250). The Sanchya school is complete pantheism, as appears from the Bhagvat Gita (p. 251).

Thus far Schlegel.—But Prichard (p. 253 *et seq.*) observes that in the above sketch too strong a distinction is drawn between emanation and pantheism; and he has given (pp. 254-257) some extracts from the Vedas to show that 'the departments and elements of nature are identified with, or rather included in, the description of the divinity.' At the same time I may observe that Prichard has, perhaps, taken too literal a view of the inflated language of the Hindoos, and, if I mistake not, passages almost as pantheistic as those in the Vedas might be found in the Hebrew

---

[1] See the remarks of Hallam. He says (*Literature of Europe*, III. 355, 8vo, 1843). 'All pantheism must have originated in overstraining the infinity of the Divine attributes till the moral part of religion was annihilated in its metaphysics. . . . It could not have arisen except among those who had elevated their conceptions above the vulgar polytheism that surrounded them to a sense of the unity of the Divine nature.'

Scriptures. Indeed, Prichard (p. 257) cannot avoid expressing his surprise that pantheism should be 'found combined or rather confounded with a dogma so distinct from it, and which seems so opposite in its nature, as the system of emanation.' He allows (pp. 257, 258) that pantheism was a corruption of the dogma of emanation, and he looks on it as the *second* stage of the Hindoo philosophy—Schlegel having made it the *fourth*. The third stage he considers to have been 'materialism, or the worship of the visible elements and departments of the universe.' This, as he says (p. 258), seems a natural result of pantheism. At p. 265 *et seq.*, Prichard has an ingenious inquiry into the *succession* of Egyptian creeds as illustrative of the history of Hindoo philosophy. He thinks (pp. 265, 266) that the whole of the Egyptian doctrines 'may be referred to the transition from the more ancient to the later system.' But the passages which he has cited (pp. 266-268) do not seem to me absolutely pantheistic. In confirmation of his view he notices (p. 269) that where in India abstract ideas of emanation declined, splendid and indecent ceremonies grew up, and this we find in Egypt. Such were Siva and Durga, and such were Osiris and Isis. We even find (p. 270) in the Egyptian Trinity the personification of the theory of generative, destructive, and renovative powers.[1] See also pp. 271-282 for similarities between the Hindoo and Egyptian Trinity. But Prichard (pp. 287-292) allows that the esoteric doctrines of the Egyptians were similar to those of the Hindoos at the earliest period. We find in these esoteric opinions of the Egyptians the doctrines of emanation, though, says Prichard, 'they could not resist the propensity to material and sensual analogies' (p. 289).

But here an important consideration suggests itself, which Prichard seems to have lost sight of. We judge of the theology of the Hindoos from *their own works*, great numbers of which have come down to us. But of the ancient Egyptian Scriptures nothing is preserved, and we are compelled to rely on the imperfect accounts of the Greek writers. Setting aside the ignorance of the Greeks, we must remember that, according to Prichard's own view, a religion in its progress materialises, and the only accounts left to us of Egypt are quite modern compared with the Vedas, and even to the code of Menu.

[1] Mr. Green supposes that the Trinity can be proved à *priori*!!! (see *Green's Mental Dynamics*, 8vo, 1847, p. 61).

Storch thinks that polytheism is the earliest form of religion, and that it originated in personations of the powers of nature (*Économie politique*, St. Petersburg, 8vo, 1815, tome v. pp. 185–189).

ETYMOLOGY OF SLAVONIANS, AND FIRST MENTION OF THEM.

'The first mention we have of the Slavonians under this identical name is in Jordanus (De Gothorum Origine, cap. xxiii.), who describes them as existing in the year of our Lord 376. . . . With respect to the origin of the name given to this people, a great difference of opinion has existed among the learned. That it is not to be written *Sclavonian* is agreed on all hands; for although the Greeks wrote Σκλάβοναι, it arose from necessity, there not being any such combination as σλ in their language; and it is evidently from them the Latins adopted their Sclavi and the Arabic geographers their اصلاب. The attention of native etymologists has been principally directed to two words in their language; *slovo*, "word, speech," and *slava*, "glory, renown." In favour of the former it has been alleged that the Slavonians appropriated the name to themselves in contradistinction from foreigners, to whom they gave the name of *Němtsi*, or "the speechless," because their language was unintelligible to them; and this is the epithet by which they still distinguish the Germans in the present day. The partial use of the *o* in the names of certain tribes of this people, such as the Slovaks, Sloveas, &c., would seem to confirm this derivation; but, on the other hand, the frequent occurrence of the syllable *Slav* in proper names, at a very ancient period of Slavonic history, and the authority of the earliest foreign writers who have occasion to mention them, seem to decide the question in favour of *slava*, which with a certain modification is adopted by Dobroosky in an interesting dissertation on this subject in the sixth volume of the transactions of a private society of Bohemia. This profound Slavonic scholar considers the word, when occurring as part of a compound in proper names, to be equivalent to the Greek termination -ωνυμος, so that the Svatoslav Blagoslav are merely etymological translations of ἱερώνυμος and εὐώνυμος. The reason he conceives why the Slavonians assumed this name as a people was their being

accustomed to give names to the places of which they possessed
themselves, agreeably to the received usage of words in their own
language. All foreigners and foreign places they regarded as anonymous, on account of the insignificancy of their names to people of
Slavonic origin ' (*Henderson's Biblical Researches, &c. in Russia,*
1826, pp. 61, 62).

On slavery see Kemble's Saxons in England, vol. i. pp. 186
–199.

Slav forms at least a very common element in the names of
Russian princes (see *Pinkerton's Russia,* 8vo, 1833, p. 160). In
1787, Hannah More writes from Cowslip Green to Mrs. Carter,
' The great object I have so much at heart—the project to abolish
the slave trade in Africa. This most important cause has very
much occupied my thoughts this summer ; the young gentleman
(Mr. Wilberforce) who has embarked in it with the zeal of an
apostle has been much with me, and engaged all my little interest
and all my affections in it ' (*Roberts's Memoirs of Mrs. Hannah
More,* 2nd edit. 8vo, 1834, vol. ii. pp. 70, 71). In July 1790 she
writes from Cowslip Green to Horace Walpole (*Memoirs,* 8vo,
1834, vol. ii. p. 235), ' I cannot forbear telling you that at my city
of Bristol, during church-time, the congregations were surprised
last Sunday with the bell of the public crier in the streets. It was
so unusual a sound on that day, that the people were alarmed in
the churches. They found that the bellman was crying the reward
of a guinea to anybody who would produce a poor negro girl who
had run away, because she would not return to one of those
trafficking islands whither her master was resolved to send her. To
my great grief and indignation, the poor trembling wretch was
dragged out from a hole in the top of a house, where she had
hid herself, and forced on board ship' (vol. ii. p. 235). Storch
observes that one of its worst effects is that it prevents the division
of labour (*Économie politique,* St. Petersburg, 8vo, 1815, vol. i.
p. 207). When a nation entirely consists of hunters and fishers,
prisoners are troublesome and costly, therefore they are slain ; but
in the pastoral state of man their labour is useful, and here is the
beginning of slavery. The desire of procuring slaves is at the
same time a fresh cause of wars (*Storch,* iv. 220, 221). Among an
agricultural people the lot of slaves is at first more severe than
among a pastoral people ; but the increasing difficulty of procuring
them raises their value and ameliorates their condition, thus pre-

paring the way for their final emancipation (*Storch*, iv. 255-261).
I may add that this last step is in the natural course of things a
triumph reserved for commerce and manufactures, but in Europe
has been greatly hastened by the influence of Christianity. See
further respecting slavery, Storch, tome v. 265-298, 296, 315.
Alison observes that slavery was at first beneficial, by compelling
indolent savages to work, and by giving the labouring classes *pro-
tectors* it prevented them from being exterminated (*Alison's Prin
ciples of Population*, 8vo, 1840, vol. ii. pp. 170-172). Hence,
when slavery is done away with, poor laws begin (pp. 174, 175).
Slavi is derived, *not* from *slava*, glory, but from *slovo*, speech (see
Talvi's Languages and Literature of the Slavic Nations, New York,
8vo, 1850, pp. 2, 3).

ON THE STATE ETC. OF WOMEN.

Henderson (*Biblical Researches, &c. in Russia*, 8vo, 1826,
p. 225) says that among the Jews 'it forms part of their daily
prayer, "Lord of the world, I thank Thee that Thou hast not made
me a woman."' This contempt of woman is at once the cause and
the effect of the barbarism of this stupid and brutal nation.

The Otaheitans dislike eating in company, and will never eat
with women (see *Cook's Voyages*, 8vo, 1821, vol. i. p. 202;
vol. vi. p. 145). In the Sandwich Islands the men and women
do not eat together (see *Cook*, vi. 202, 217; vii. 131). But in the
Friendly Islands they do (*Cook*, v. 299, 451).

Lord Jeffrey says (*Essays*, 8vo, 1844, vol. i. p. 115), 'Women
were from the beginning of more account in the estimation of
the Romans than of the Greeks.' An evidence, I think, of the
little influence of women among the Romans many be found in
the Civil Law, which inflicts the same penalty on the seducer of a
woman whether she consented or not. Cod. 9, tit. 13, quoted in
Blackstone's Commentaries, 1809, vol. iv. p. 210.

For all treasons women were burnt alive until the 30th Geo. III.
c. 48. Blackstone (*Commentaries*, 1809, vol. iv. p. 93, and pp.
204, 376) explains this barbarism by saying that it would have
been too indecent to inflict the embowelling and exposing their
bodies. One cannot avoid a smile at that sense of decency
which burns a woman alive in order to avoid stripping her naked.

Mr. Hallam (*Const. Hist.* 8vo, 1842, i. 32) says that for high treason 'women till 1791 were condemned to be burned,' but I believe they were for *any* treason.

Frederick Schlegel has remarked it as a singular circumstance that among the Brahmins, where they could not be priestesses, they were highly respected (*Philosophy of History*, 8vo, 1846, p. 145). He might have added that among the Greeks and Romans they were despised, and yet were priestesses.

INFLUENCE OF THE ARABS ON EUROPEAN CIVILISATION.

See on this subject *Humboldt's Cosmos*, edit. Otté, 1848, vol. ii. pp. 571 600. He ascribes (p. 572) their great achievements in arms and literature to 'the tribe of the Hedschaz, a noble and valiant race—unlearned, but not wholly rude—*imaginative*,' &c. ; and see p. 615 respecting their love of Aristotle.

He says (p. 579), 'The Arabs, I would again remark, are to be regarded as the actual founders of physical science, considered in the sense which we now apply to the words ;' and he adds (p. 580) that it was reserved for them first to reach the third and highest stage of physical knowledge, 'which embraces an investigation into natural forces, and the powers by which these forces are enabled to act, in order to be able to bring the substances liberated into new combinations.'

At p. 581, 'The science of medicine which was founded by Dioscorides, in the school of Alexandria, when considered with reference to its science development, is essentially a creation of the Arabs, to whom the oldest, and at the same time one of the richest sources of knowledge, that of the Indian physicians, had been early opened.' On the knowledge which the Arabs derived from the Hindoos regarding Materia Medica, see Wilson's important investigations in the Oriental Magazine of Calcutta, 1823, February and March, and those of Royle, in his Essays on the Antiquity of Hindoo Medicine, 1837, pp. 56-59, 64 66, 73, and 92. Compare an account of Arabic pharmaceutical writings, translated from Hindostanee, in Ainslie (Madras edition), p. 289. Respecting the translations of medical works made from the Sanscrit into Arabic under the Caliphate, see p. 588, where it is said,

'Avicenna is acquainted, as the learned Royle observes, with the true Sanscrit name of the Deodwar of the Himalayan Alps.' He says (p. 589), 'The most powerful influence exercised by the Arabs on general natural physics was that directed to the advance of chemistry, a science for which this race created a new era.'

Humboldt says (p. 584), 'According to the testimony of Frähu, Ptolemy's geography was translated into Arabic by order of the Caliph Mamum, between the years 813 and 833; and it is not improbable that several fragments of Maximus Tyrius, which have not come down to us, were employed in this translation. . . . Geography never acquired a greater acquisition of facts, even from the discoveries of the Portuguese and Spaniards. . . . The "Oriental Geography of Ebn Haukal," which Sir William Ouseley published in London in 1800, is that of Abu-Ishak el-Istáchri, and, as Frähu has shown, is half a century older than Ebn Haukal.'

Humboldt says (pp. 628, 629) that Vincent de Beauvais, in his Mirror of Nature, uses 'the Arabic designation Zohron and Aphon (*north* and *south*).' See at p. 668 what he says of Dante's 'quattro stelle.' Washington Irving (*History of the Life and Voyages of Christopher Columbus*, 8vo, 1828, vol. i. p. 3) says, 'Xerif al Edrizi, surnamed the Nubian, an eminent Arabian writer, whose country-men were the boldest navigators of the middle ages, and possessed all that was then known of geography.' See also vol. i. pp. 11, 12.

Humboldt says (p. 596), 'The process of establishing a conclusion by a progressive advance from one proposition to another, which seems to have been unknown to the ancient Indian alge-braists, was acquired by the Arabs from the *Alexandrian School*. This noble inheritance, enriched by their additions, passed in the twelfth century, through Johannes Hispalensis and Gerhard of Cremona, into the European literature of the middle ages,' &c. &c. And see at pp. 597–599 the very interesting remarks of Humboldt on the numerals which the Arabs procured from India and Persia. He thinks 'it is more than probable that the Christians in the west were familiar with Indian numerals even earlier than the Arabs,' &c.; 'and that they were acquainted with the use of nine figures or characters, according to their position value, under the name of the system of *Abacus*.'

He observes (p. 620), 'As Roger Bacon, like the Arabs, always calls Hipparchus Abraxis, we may conclude that he also made use of only a Latin translation from the Arabic.'

Frederick Schlegel has some remarks on the great religion of Mahomet, which are absurdly illiberal (*Philosophy of History*, Lond. 8vo, 1846, pp. 318, 320-331). He actually taunts Mahomet with not having performed miracles (p. 328). Dr. Whewell, on the whole, does not rate their literature highly—at least in a scientific point of view (*Whewell's History of the Inductive Sciences*, 8vo, 1847, vol. i. pp. 225, 236, 244, 265, 292, 355-360, and *Whewell's Philosophy of the Inductive Sciences*, 8vo, 1847, vol. i. p. 157). The celebrated Athelard of Bath, who was born at the end of the eleventh century, studied among the Arabs, whose knowledge he introduced into Normandy. It is evident from what he says that such knowledge was then quite new, so that William of Malmesbury is mistaken in supposing that it had been introduced into the West by Gerbert (*Wright's Biographia Literaria*, vol. ii. pp. 94-97, 8vo, 1842). Mr. Wright (p. 96) quotes a passage in which he says, 'Athelard describes briefly the principle of the school of natural philosophy which he was founding, and which was more perfectly developed at a later period by the great Lord Bacon.' Wright says (ii. 116), 'The first Englishman after Athelard, so far as we can discover, who travelled among the Arabs to indulge his ardour in the pursuit of science, was Robert de Retines,' who flourished in A.D. 1143. Roger of Hereford, who flourished in 1170, 'appears to have been a follower of the Arabian sciences' (*Biog. Brit. Lit.* ii. 219). Daniel de Merlai was a native of Norwich, and flourished in 1175. He, disgusted with the mode of study at Paris, 'went thence to Toledo, then the chief seat of learning among the Spanish Arabs' (*Biog. Brit. Lit.* ii. 227). A very fair judger of such matters says, 'The Arabs, however, appear at no period of their history to have been a people addicted to fanciful invention. Their minds are acute and logical, and their poetry is that of the heart rather than of the fancy' (*Keightley's Fairy Mythology*, Lond. 1850, p. 24). Ranke says that the Arabs collected ancient literature with a zeal hardly inferior to that of the Italians in the sixteenth century; though he adds that they often destroyed the originals (*Die Römischen Päpste*, Berlin, 1838, band i. p. 63).

MARRIAGE CEREMONIES IN ENGLAND IN THE SIXTEENTH CENTURY.

In Wright's Elizabeth (8vo, 1838, vol. i. pp. 199-204) there is a letter from Randolph to the Earl of Leicester in 1565, giving an account of the marriage of Mary of Scotland. He says (p. 202), 'The rings, which were three, the middle a rich diamonde, were put upon her finger.' He adds (p. 203) that after the marriage, 'she suffered them that stood bye, every man that could approach, to take out a pin, and so being committed unto her ladies, changed her garments.'

It is said that about 1589 early marriages became much more usual among the lower orders than they had been (see *Wright's Elizabeth*, vol. ii. p. 406). In Porter's Angrie Women of Abington (1599, p. 32, Percy Society, vol. v.) it is said that fifteen was the ordinary age at which girls married. In Johnson's Crowne Garland of Goulden Roses, 1612, p. 58, Percy Society, vol. vi., a young lady having reached the age of twenty in a single state despairs of being married, and uses the same sort of complaint that our poets now would hardly put into the mouth of a woman under thirty. These ballads, though printed in 1612, were written in the reign of Elizabeth (see Mr. Chappell's Preface, p. v). M. Villers actually supposes that the stimulus given to population by discouraging celibacy was a great service the Reformation rendered to humanity (*Essai sur la Réformation*, Paris, 1820, p. 132).

In 1599, Nashe writes, 'as white as a ladie's marrying smocke' (*Harleian Miscellany*, vi. 172). In 1559, Elizabeth ordered that no clergyman should marry without consent of his bishop, of two justices of the peace, and of the parents of the woman. She also ordered that no bishops should marry without the consent of their metropolitan and of the royal commissioners (see *Neal's History of the Puritans*, edit. Toulmin, 8vo, 1832, vol. i. p. 128). Did the Puritans encourage marriage? Among the opinions of Cartwright, in 1570, one was, 'It is papistical to forbid marriages at certain times of the year; and to give licences in those times is intolerable' (*Neal's History of the Puritans*, 8vo, 1822, vol. i. p. 213). In 1584 the Puritans brought in a bill 'to marry at all times of the year' (*Neal*, i. 364), which, to the great indigna-

tion of Whitgift, passed the Commons (p. 365). In 1575–6 it
was ordered by Convocation 'that marriage may be solemnised
at all times of the year, provided the banns are published in the
church three Sundays or holidays, and no impediment objected,'
but this article was not published because Elizabeth refused her
consent (*Collier's Ecclesiastical History*, 1840, vi. 561). In 1584
Archbishop Whitgift complained to the queen that the House of
Commons had 'passed a bill giving liberty to marry at all times
of the year without restraint, contrary to old canons continually
observed amongst us' (*Collier's Eccles. Hist.* vii. 40).

OBSERVATIONS FOR THE HISTORY OF THE ENGLISH LANGUAGE.

In a letter written in 1569, in which White gives an account
of Mary at Tutbury, he says, 'Her grace fell in talke with me
of sundry matters from six to seven of the clocke, beginning
first to excuse her ill Englishe, declaring herself more willing
than apt to learn that language ; how she used translations as a
meane to atteyne it,' &c. (*Wright's Elizabeth*, 8vo, 1838, vol. i.
p. 308).

Axed for *asked* occurs in a letter from Sir Thomas Smith to
Burleigh, dated Windsor, 1572 (*Wright's Elizabeth*, 8vo, 1838,
i. 444, and see p. 452). 'Will they nill they,' in letter from
Fletewood in 1583 (*Wright's Elizabeth*, ii. 206). For some
curious information respecting the cant words of thieves in the
middle of Queen Elizabeth's reign, see Wright's Elizabeth, 8vo,
1838, vol. ii. pp. 246–251.

Camden (*Annals of Elizabeth* in *Kennett*, ii. 619) says of
Hooker, 'His Books of Ecclesiastical Polity were written in
English, but do very well deserve a translation into a more
universal language.'

The earliest English letter known to be written by a lady is
dated 1441. It is from Lady Husee to Henry VI., and is printed
by Miss Wood, who says that towards the end of the reign of
Henry VI. there are yet extant several letters from women
written in English (*Letters of Royal and Illustrious Ladies*, 8vo,
1846, vol. i. p. 92).

'Perséver' is in Ben Jonson's Works, 8vo, 1816, vol. iii.

p. 275. In 1609, Sir Robert Shirley sent to England a *chiaus*, or messenger, from the Grand Signior. He cheated some merchants—hence our word *chouse*, to *cheat*. 'A chiaus' occurs in the Alchemist, which was acted in 1610 (see *Ben Jonson's Works*, 8vo, 1816, vol. iv. pp. 27, 28). 'Defend,' commonly used for *forbid* (*Ben Jonson's Works*, 8vo, 1816, vol. v. p. 26). 'Emissaries? Stay, there's a fine new word, Tom' (*The Staple of News*, acted in 1625, *Jonson's Works*, v. 175). 'Furlough' comes from the Dutch 'Vorloffe,' and is first used by Ben Jonson (*Works*, 8vo, 1816, vol. v. pp. 292, 293).

In 'A Tale of a Tub' we have a country dialect just like that in Gammer Gurton's Needle, 'Ich' and 'cham,' &c., &c. (*Ben Jonson's Works*, 8vo, 1816, vol. vi. pp. 136, 137). Gifford thinks (p. 174) that this, which was the western dialect, was 'once more general than is commonly supposed.' In the Sad Shepherd we have a specimen of the Lowland Scottish dialect (*Ben Jonson*, vi. 174, 279). Ben Jonson says in his Discoveries, written about 1630, 'You are not to cast a ring for the perfumed terms of the time, as *accommodation, compliment, spirit*, &c., but use them properly in their places as others' (*Jonson's Works*, vol. ix. p. 232). In 1600, Ben Jonson notices and ridicules the rage for introducing new words (*Works*, edit. Gifford, 8vo, 1816, vol. ii. p. 269). The expression of 'showing the lions' for seeing anything remarkable is as old as 1610 (see *Ben Jonson's Works*, 8vo, 1816, vol. iv. p. 134). Ben Jonson in his Grammar gives 'the English language now spoken and in use' (*Works*, ix. 253). Among his instances are 'worse—worser' (p. 300). 'Most basest,' &c., which he calls 'English Atticism, or eloquent phrase of speech' (pp. 330, 331). He finds great fault with 'the prince, his house,' instead of 'the prince's house,' and speaks of it as a comparative novelty (p. 301). Until the time of Henry VIII. the plural of verbs was formed by *en*, as *loven, sayen*, and Jonson rejects the alteration (p. 305). He truly observes (p. 318) that all precepts of grammar should be founded on common speech. In *art*, the *a* was pronounced as in *act, apple, ancient*, i.e. 'less than in the French *a*' (p. 261). *Folly* was pronounced with the *o* 'sharp and high' as in *chosen, open* (p. 267). *Prove* was pronounced 'more flat,' as in 'cosen, mother, brother' (p. 267). In *host, honest, humble*, the *h* was *not* pronounced (p. 285). The accents seem to have been pretty much the same as at present (see pp. 292-294).

In 1599 we have a 'horse-trick' (*Middleton's Works*, 8vo, 1840, voL i. p. 63). In 1602 an affected pronunciation of *chithy* for *city*, *chick* and *chickness*, for *sick* and *sickness* (*Middleton's Works*, 8vo, 1840, vol. i. pp. 236, 276, 277, 279, 280). Early in the seventeenth century women who pretended to fashion used to pronounce *o* like *a*. Thus we have 'pax on it' for 'pox on it' (see *Middleton's Works*, 8vo, 1840, vol. ii. pp. 24, 76, 78, 235, 250, 269). In Middleton's Works, 8vo, 1840, vol. ii. pp. 538-542, there is a very curious list of the cant words used by thieves in 1611. Many of them are nearly the same as those in 'Oliver Twist.' 'I smell a rat' (*Middleton's Works*, i. 284). 'Enough to sow your wild oats' (*Middleton's Works*, iii. 12). 'Hare mad' (*Middleton's Works*, iv. 54).

For some English prose of the fourteenth century see Harleian Miscellany, 4to, 1808, vol. vi. pp. 94-117. In vol. xix. of Percy Society, Mr. Black has published the Life of Thomas Becket from a MS. A.D. 1300. In vol. xiv. of Percy Society, Audelay's poems afford a curious 'specimen of the Shropshire dialect in the fifteenth century.' In Wright's Political Ballads (Percy Society, vol. iii. pp. 1-8) there is a curious specimen of the dialect of the west of England in 1647. In vol. iv. of Percy Society Mr. Wright has published some lyric poetry in the reign of Edward I., and Mr. Halliwell has published 'The Boke of Curtasye, an English poem of the fourteenth century.' At the beginning of vol. xi. of Percy Society, Mr. Wright has published some English poetry of the thirteenth century.

In 1800 Southey writes from Lisbon, 'The *gift of the gab* must also be of Portuguese extraction; *gaban* is to praise, to coax' (*The Life and Correspondence of R. Southey, by the Rev. C. C. Southey*, 8vo, 1849, 1850, vol. ii. p. 70). In 1806 Southey writes (*Life and Correspondence*, 1849, 1850, vol. iii. p. 9), 'I do not recollect any coinage in Madoc, except the word *deicide*; and that such a word exists, I have no doubt, though I cannot lay my finger upon any authority, for depend upon it the Jews have been called so a thousand times.'

According to Christian (Note in *Blackstone's Commentaries*, i. 137), 'the first statute in which the word *transportation* is used is the 18 Car. II. 3.'

In 1818 the word *influential* seems to have been little or not at all used in England, for Canning expressed an opinion that 'there was no such word as *influential* except in America' (*Rush's Residence at the Court of London*, 8vo, 1833, p. 233). The same thing may be said of the word *lengthy*, which Lord Harrowby spoke of as being peculiar to America (*Rush's Residence*, p. 266).

Our records are always in Latin until the time of Cromwell, who had them made in English. But at the Restoration the Latin was adopted as before, until in 1730 it was ordered by statute 4 Geo. II. c. 26, that 'the proceedings at law should be done into English' (*Blackstone's Commentaries*, edit. Christian, 1809, vol. iii. p. 322). The expressions, 'I will take the sacrament upon it,' 'may this morsel be my last,' allude to the ordeal by eating a piece of consecrated bread called *corsned* (see *Blackstone*, 8vo, 1809, vol. iv. p. 345).

The *tartar* of the teeth is a name given by Paracelsus—' *Tartarus*, because it burns like the fire of hell.' (*Whewell, Philosophy of the Inductive Sciences*, 8vo, 1847, vol. i. p. 552. He quotes Sprengel ; and see *Herschel's Discourse on Natural Philosophy*, p. 112, 8vo, 1831.)

Reid, in his Inquiry into the Human Mind on the Principle of Common Sense, nearly always uses 'hath' instead of 'has.'

Schlegel says we have the word *pander* from Shakespeare's Pandarus (*Lectures on Dramatic Art*, Lond. 1840, ii. 223, 224).

'Mystification' seems to have been introduced into English in this century (see Note in *Schlegel's Dramatic Art*, Lond. 1840, ii. 238).

'Still less is he able to *secern* the truth from the falsehood' ·(*Dawson Turner's Tour in Normandy*, Lond. 8vo, 1820, p. 94).

For origin of the expression 'a good shot' see Mr. Bruce's note at p. 52 of Hayward's Annals of Elizabeth, Camden Society, 1840.

Cocket is 'a certificate that goods had paid duty, and is thought to be a corruption of *quo quietus*' (*Leycester, Correspondence*, p. 56).

Lord Ellenborough, Perceval, and Fox always said 'Lunnun and Brumagem' (*Brougham's Sketches of Statesmen*, vol. vi. p. 11, 1845).

In 1753 Hume writes to know if the English pronounce the plural of enough, *enow* (*Burton's Life of Hume*, 1846, i. 384).

Honor instead of *honour* was used by Bolingbroke, Middleton, Pope, and at first by Hume (*Burton's Life of Hume*, 1846, ii. 43). In 1768 Hume writes to Robertson that 'maltreat ' ' is a Scotticism,' and that 'hath' is incorrect (*Burton's Life of Hume*, ii. 413)

In 1774 'amœnity' was a new word (see *Topham's Letters from Edinburgh*, Lond. 8vo, 1776, p. 55). In 1766 the Earl of March writes to Selwyn about being *doved* at Almack's, i.e. losing money at play (*Jesse's Selwyn and his Contemporaries*, 1843, vol. ii. p. 45). In 1766 the Earl of March, in a letter to Selwyn, expresses his fear lest he should be *a lame duck*, i.e. not able to pay some debts (*Jesse's Selwyn*, 1843, vol. ii. p. 47). In 1776 the word *bore*, as said of a disagreeable thing, was considered vulgar, and seems to have been rather a new expression (see *Jesse's Selwyn*, vol. iii. pp. 162, 163). In 1779 the Rev. Dr. Warner writes that 'the boys at Eton' used to call port wine *black-strap* (*Jesse's Selwyn and his Contemporaries*, iv. 131, 132). The word Troubadour was first naturalised in English in 1765, and in French in 1774 (see *Pinkerton's Correspondence*, 1830, i. 357).

Was the word *Don* first used contemptuously of the Spaniards who came over in the reign of Charles II.? At all events it is used in 1681 (see *Thoresby's Diary*, 8vo, 1830, vol. i. p. 109). In 1688, to bring a question 'on the tapis' (*Clarendon Correspondence*, 4to, 1828, vol. i. p. 565 ; vol. ii. p. 312). In the middle of the seventeenth century *muffes* for *stupid fellows* appears to have been a new word (see *Sir John Reresby's Travels*, 8vo, 1831, p. 157). 'A priest-codding, or catching' (*Reresby's Memoirs*, 1831, p. 374). *Selfish* was a new word in the reign of James I. (see *Coleridge, Literary Remains*, ii. 199). In 1741 'we took French leave' (*Nichols, Literary Illustrations of the Eighteenth Century*, vol. i. p. 89). In 1729, *nicety* is called a 'quaint word' (*Nichols, Literary Illustrations*, vol. ii. p. 217). In 1813 *capability* instead of *capacity* was considered affected (*Nichols, Literary Illustrations*, vol. iii. p. 822). Origin of Methodists being called Swaddlers (*Wesley's Journal*, 8vo, 1851, p. 309). In 1764 'mahogany' chairs (*Wesley's Journal*, p. 538). 'A Scotch mist' (*Wesley's Journal*, p. 632). Carlyle (*Critical Essays*, 3rd edit. 8vo, 1847, vol. i. pp. 9, 10) says that *æsthetics* is a word invented by Baumgarten, some eighty years ago, 'to express generally the science of the fine arts. Perhaps we also might as well adopt it, at least if any such *science* should ever arise among us.' (This remark was written by Carlyle in 1827.)

Burt, between 1726 and 1730 (*Letters from the North of Scotland*, 8vo, 1815, vol. i. p. 134), says the word *police* was French, and not known in London, or used in the English language. In 1753, *leer, ogle,* and *stare* were vulgar (see *Richardson's Correspondence*, 8vo, 1804, vol. iv. p. 82). At pp. 277, 316, 364, we have a *white fib.* Lord Campbell (*Lives of Chancellors,* iii. 128) says 'a change from mercenary motives is conveyed by the modern word *ratting.*' At p. 495 he observes that *roiled* is an old English word still used in America. Lord Campbell (vol. v. p. 318) only knows 'two instances of the word *unwhig.*' Was *succumb* a new word in 1800? (see *Life of Wilberforce, by His Sons,* ii. 371). In 1803 *grippe* was a new word for influenza (*Life of Wilberforce,* iii. 87). Did Sir W. Temple (*Works,* iii. p. 111) introduce the word *truant?* *Amission,* for loss, in Sir T. Browne's Works, vol. i. p. 338. On the 'improper use' of English words in America, see a letter in 1789 in Franklin's Correspondence, 2nd edit. 8vo, 1817, vol. i. pp. 269, 270.

In 1762 *forsooth* a vulgar word (*Harris, Life of Lord Hardwicke,* vol. iii. p. 281). 'The country people see him *rule the roast,* as they say' (*Lives of the Norths, by Roger North,* 8vo, 1826, vol. i. p. 75).

After 1688 '*Priestcraft* grew to be another word in fashion' (*Burnett's Own Time,* Oxford, 8vo, 1823, iv. 378). *Turban,* or *turbent,* a new word (*Coryat's Crudities,* edit. 8vo, 1776, vol. i. pp. 90, 296). In 1700 'the cat's foot' for 'cat's paw' (*Vernon Correspondence, by James,* ii. 446). In 1776 'office letter' instead of 'official letter' (*Chatham Correspondence,* iii. 29). In 1767 George III. uses 'whittled' for 'cut down' (*Chatham Correspondence,* iii. 170). Dr. Bell often used the expression 'dined with Duke Humphrey' (*Southey's Life of Bell,* vol. ii. p. 114).

COLLECTION OF LATINISMS IN ENGLISH WRITERS.

Stukeley, speaking of Druidical circles, says, 'They add much to the solemnity of the place by the *crebrity* and variety of their intervals' (*Stukeley's Stonehenge,* p. 20). Stukeley (*Stonehenge,* p. 24) uses the verb 'to adumbrate.' Stukeley (*Abury,* Lond.

1743, pp. 47, 48) uses 'posited' instead of placed or posted.
Stukeley (*Abury*, p. 49) says 'the great coveting stone is luxated.'

'Oblectate the heart' (*Venner's Via Recta ad Vitam Longam*,
4to, 1650, p. 7, and pp. 108, 137, 141). 'Oppilate' (Idem,
pp. 27, 116; also *Ben Jonson's Works*, vi. 67). 'Impinguateth'
(*Venner's Via Recta*, pp. 49, 117, 162). 'Abstersive' (pp. 123,
138). 'Siccity' (p. 150). 'Obtund and weaken' (p. 226). 'Cali-
ginousnesse of the eyes' (p. 241). 'Alliciated' (p. 241). 'Par-
city' (p. 256). 'The strong bodies of agrestic men' (pp. 260,
263, 314). 'Circumligated' (p. 311). 'The stomach must not
be perfricated' (p. 320). 'Thorow the nose by exsufflation'
(p. 323). 'Sternutation' (p. 323). 'Lenifie the skin' (p. 325).
'Fuliginous' (pp. 325, 409, 410). 'Megerean kind of fury'
(p. 329). 'The vapours are not so grosse and adusted' (p. 356).
'Be cautelous' (p. 366). 'Some lubrifying cleansing extract'
(p. 392).

'The tyme passing almost irrecuperable' (*Letter from Sir T.
Smith*, dated 1574, in *Wright's Elizabeth*, 8vo, 1838, vol. ii. p. 1).
'Nefandous,' for shameful (*Life of Thomas Gent, by Himself*,
written in 1746, 8vo, 1832, pp. 98, 169). 'Impetration,' obtaining.
Letter from Margaret of Scotland to Wolsey in 1516 (*Miss Wood's
Letters of Royal Ladies*, 8vo, 1846, ii. 9).

'Declining their way,' i.e. turning out of the way (*Ben Jonson's
Works*, 8vo, 1816, iii. 116). It 'arrides me,' i.e. pleases me (ii. 52,
288). 'Suculent lady' (vol. ii. p. 62). 'Pulchritude' (vol. ii. p.
62). 'Copy of wit,' i.e. abundance, from *copia* (vol. ii. pp. 63, 102,
327). 'Concluded' for 'included or confined' (vol. ii. p. 493).
'Quotidian,' daily (ii. 512). 'To provide,' to foresee (iii. 144, 164).
'They hear so ill,' i.e. are so ill spoken of, *tam male audiunt* (iii.
161, iv. 469). 'Delate,' accuse, complain of (iii. 227). 'Faci-
norous acts,' wicked (iii. 368). 'Instructed me to this fate,' i.e.
designed, appointed me (vol. iii. p. 438). 'Salts,' i.e. leapings or
boundings (vol. v. p. 67). 'Costs of a ship,' i.e. its ribs (vol. v.
p. 239). 'Rapt from the flames,' i.e. snatched, saved (v. 347).
'Statuminate,' to support. Pliny has 'Statuminibus firmare' (vol.
v. p. 368). 'Comminatory,' threatening (vol. vi. p. 14). 'Nocent,'
injurious (vol. vi. p. 296). 'Proclive and hasty' (vi. 340). 'Re-
percussive sound' (vi. 343). 'Regression,' return (vi. 375).
'Wealthy witness,' i.e. full, sufficient, 'testis locuples' (viii. 195).
'Indagations,' wanderings? (ix. 181). 'Excogitate,' to think

over (ix. 212). 'Scabrous and rough' (ix. 220). 'Prolation' (ix. 281). Gifford (vol. iii. p. 475) says that Ben Jonson has not more Latinisms than his contemporaries.

'*Questuary*,' profitable, ex. gr. 'Questuary and gainful arts' (*Middleton's Works*, 8vo, 1840, vol. ii. p. 188).

ON THE COAL TRADE.

Surtees (*History of Durham*, vol. i. p. 256) says, 'It was probably about the latter end of the reign of Elizabeth, or in that of James, that the coal trade began to find its way into the port of Sunderland, which, in consequence, gradually rose into importance; whilst Hartlepool, the ancient port of the palatinate, was dwindling in an inverse proportion into a fishing town.'

Surtees says (*History of Durham*, vol. iii. p. 135, Lond. 1823, folio), 'Two grants of corrodies, which occur on Hatfield's Rolls, may serve to explain the sort of subsistence which was provided for the poor brethren [i.e. the forty poor brethren of the Hospital of Greatham]. . . . In 1352, William Donant releases his corrody, viz. every day a loaf of second bread, half a pitcher of second ale, a rackfull of hay, a peck of oats, a candle, and a peck of *coals* in winter,' &c. (The original of the above surrender of a corrody in 1352 is printed in the Appendix to *Surtees' History of Durham*, vol. iii. p. 391; in the Latin it is 'uno peck carbonum annuatim in hieme.')

Sir John Herschel says (*Discourse on Natural Philosophy*, 8vo, 1831, p. 60), 'The annual consumption of coal in London is estimated at 1,500,000 chaldrons.'

1. There are some remarks on the history of the coal trade in Wright's Elizabeth, 8vo, 1838, vol. i. p. 222, note. 2. In December, 1562, the Earl of Warwick writes to the English council from Newhaven, where he was governor, complaining of a deficiency of the means of defence, &c.; he adds, 'Here is no provision either of wood or cole' (*Forbes, Elizabeth*, ii. 214), and two months later he again writes (p. 337), 'We do not a little marvel that we hear nothing of the Newcastle coles, for the which we have so often written.' In 1430 an institution was founded in London, 'for poor impotent priests,' who were to receive 'a certain allowance of bread, drink, and coal' (*Stow's London*, edit.

Thoms, 8vo, 1842, p. 55), and in 1521 some almshouses were
built near the Tower, and their charitable founders directed that
in two parishes the poor should receive 'every year one load of
chare coal, of thirty sacks in the load' (p. 56). Some notices of
the use of coals before the accession of Elizabeth may be found in
Tusser, but I have mislaid my references to them, and I am not
inclined again to read his jingling rhymes. In 1574 coals were
eighteenpence a sack ; in 1576 they were eightpence ; in 1578
also eightpence ; in 1580 they had risen to tenpence-halfpenny,
and in 1581 they were a shilling (see the *Accounts of the Revels at
Court*, edited by Mr. Cunningham, 8vo, 1842, pp. 87, 119, 124,
164, 166, 174). In 1573 they were twenty-two shillings, in 1580
twenty-six shillings a load (see pp. 63, 70, 157, 158, 171), but it is
remarkable that in 1581 they fell to eighteen shillings (pp. 180,
181). In 1553 the French ambassador mentions 'charbon de
terre' and 'plomb' as two very old exports from England to
France (*Ambassades de Noailles*, Leyde, 1763, tome ii. p. 332).
In 1548 the queen-dowager Catharine used to burn coals ; for
we read, 'a cole basket comyng out of the chambre' (*Haynes,
State Papers*, p. 96). In 1560 'the coel myners at Newcastle'
were numerous enough for Lord Grey to suggest that they should
be employed to spring a mine under Leith (*Haynes*, 295). In
1563 Cecil drew up a 'memorial,' one article in which is, 'To
prohibit the carrying of Newcastle coals to the French' (*Haynes*,
404). In 1557 we exported coals (see Reports of Michele, the
Venetian ambassador, in *Ellis's Original Letters*, 2nd series, vol. ii.
p. 219).

In 1555 Bonner caused Philpot, archdeacon of Winchester,
to be burnt, having, as Collier tells us, already 'treated him very
coarsely, lodged him in his coal-house, and set him in the stocks'
(*Ecclesiastical History*, vi. 135).

NOTE ON THE OPINIONS OF THE EGYPTIANS
RESPECTING THE SOUL

On this subject see Prichard's Analysis of the Egyptian Mythology, Lond., royal 8vo, 1838, pp. 195-217.   Gouget, on the
authority of Servius, supposed that they *embalmed* the bodies of
their dead in order to prevent the soul from *transmigrating*

(p. 196), and it has been imagined by Harmer that Ecclesiastes, chap. xii., confirms this view; but Prichard thinks that this is very doubtful (p. 197); and he adds (p. 198) that there is not the least proof that the Egyptians believed in the *resurrection* of the *body*—indeed it seems probable (p. 199) that they did *not*. Prichard thinks (p. 200) that the Egyptians, like the Greeks and Romans, believed that funeral solemnities 'expedited the journey of the soul to its appointed region,' and that this was the reason why they *embalmed*. This opinion is confirmed by a passage in Porphyrus (p. 201, and see pp. 202-204). The Hindoos (p. 216) have the same opinion of the efficacy of funeral rites.

It seems highly probable (p. 205) that the Egyptians 'set a limit to the *metempsychosis*,' and looked on transmigration 'as a sort of purgatorial chastisement inflicted on the soul as the consequence of previous delinquencies.' Indeed, it would appear (pp. 206, 207) that the ancients before Cicero did not believe in the *immortality* of the soul 'in its *individual* character,' while we know (pp. 208-210) that the Ionic school maintained the emanation and refusion of the soul, and this in Prichard's opinion (p. 211) was an Egyptian dogma. But see what Prichard says (at pp. 294, 295), which, however, he perhaps does not apply to the *individual* soul.

The Rabbis held that souls sometimes passed into *stones*, as well as into animals, and they evidently looked on the transmigration as a *punishment*. (See the curious passage in the note to *Prichard's Egyptian Mythology*, at pp. 344, 345.) I may observe that the belief of the transmigration into *stones* perhaps affords some key to their *worship*.

According to Anderson, who when in Otaheite paid particular attention to the subject, the Otaheitans 'maintain that not only all other animals, but trees, fruits, and even stones, have souls, which at death, or upon being consumed or broken, ascend to the divinity, with whom they first mix, and afterwards pass into the mansion allotted to each' (*Cook's Voyages*, Lond. 8vo, 1821, vol. vi. 154). When Columbus discovered the island of Hayti, he found a curious myth among the natives. They held that the first men inhabited a certain cavern in their island, and 'dared only venture forth at night, for the sight of the sun was fatal to them, turning them into trees and stones' (*Irving's History of Columbus*, 8vo, 1828, vol. ii. p. 118).

OBSERVATIONS ON THE PROBABLE SOURCES OF MYTHOLOGY.

See Prichard's Analysis of the Egyptian Mythology, 8vo, Lond. 1838. He thinks (pp. 24–27) that the objects of worship among the Greeks and Romans were either personifications of the elements or allegorical beings. See also (pp. 48–51) where Prichard observes that Warburton, in his Divine Legation of Moses, maintains the opposite opinion, viz. that the gods of the Pagans, and particularly of the ancient Egyptians, were deified mortals. From two passages of Cicero, Warburton with plausibility infers that such was the case regarding the Greek and Roman gods, and he particularly insists on the testimony of Herodotus, who 'plainly asserts that the names and offices of nearly all the Grecian gods were of Egyptian origin' (p. 48). Besides this Warburton quotes a letter, mentioned by Augustine and Cyprian, which is supposed to have been written by Alexander the Great, from Egypt to his mother Olympias. In this letter Alexander is made to say that he was informed by a Greek hierophant that all the gods were in reality only mortal men. But this letter, says Prichard (p. 51), is 'spurious,' and 'a palpable forgery'; although Warburton quoted it to serve his turn.

There only then remain the testimonies of Cicero and Herodotus. Upon these, Prichard well observes (p. 49) that the attributes, names, &c., of the Grecian gods 'may have been originally derived from a mythology founded on very different principles from the deification of men; yet they may have become subsequently associated with the memory of celebrated warriors or the worship of heroes.' As a proof of this, he instances the case of Odin, who was an ancient god of the Gothic tribes before they emigrated from Scythia, and yet his name, &c., is given to a chieftain who lived at a much later period. (But this seems to me rather doubtful, and Prichard has not advanced the slightest evidence to connect Odin with Buddha and Fo.) In 1805 Southey writes, 'I think I have discovered that one of the great oriental mythologies was borrowed from Christianity, that of Budda, the Fo of the Chinese; if so, what becomes of their chronology?' (*Life and Correspondence of Robert Southey*, 8vo, 1849 1850, vol. ii. p. 342). Frederick Schlegel says, 'The name.

of Duddha, which the Chinese have changed or shortened into that of Fo, is rather an honorary appellation,' &c. (*Philosophy of History*, Lond. 8vo, 1846, p. 139.) See also his Lectures on the History of Literature, vol. i. pp. 258, 259, where he defends the reality of Odin.

At p. 128 Prichard says, 'The gods of the Egyptians had in general their origin in some physical idea rather than in any metaphysical or abstract conception;' and see at pp. 348, 349 the illustration of a passage in Diodorus on this subject. But see the observations of Milman (*History of Christianity*, 8vo, 1840, vol. i. pp. 17-21). He discriminates (p. 20) between Greek and Roman polytheism by observing that the former looked on their gods as avengers and heroes; the latter ' with a stronger moral element ' even deified their own virtues.

NOTE ON THE LAWS REGULATING POPULATION ETC.

See Turner's Sacred History of the World, vol. iii. p. 41, Lond. 8vo, 1837. He says that in the beginning of this century Malthus defended this idea (which had before been advocated by others p. 41, note), that in animal life there was a constant tendency to increase beyond the nourishment provided for it. He affirmed that the population doubled itself every twenty-five years; and whilst the means of sustenance *could* not do more than increase in an arithmetical ratio, population would increase in a geometrical one. He proceeded to say that mankind never could exist unless continued destructive checks were extirpating it. The ablest of Malthus's opponents was Sadler, who at once denied the principle (p. 46), and said that population does *not* increase in a geometrical ratio. He asserted (p. 47) that the prolificness of human beings varied *inversely to their number*.

On these conflicting opinions Turner proceeds to offer his own remarks. He says (p. 56) that the mistake made by Malthus, in taking the population of North America as a standard, was that he did not make a sufficient allowance for emigration. Turner (pp. 65, 66) has made it appear that in North America life is shorter than in Europe, while marriages are *not* more prolific. It appears (note at p. 65) from the North American census of 1800, that nearly one-third of the whole population was under ten years of age, more than half were under sixteen, and (p. 66) that only one-eighth had reached the age of forty-five. In 1810, in 1820, and in 1830, the results were nearly the same (pp. 66, 67) ; and this holds good of women as well as of men (p. 68). So that (pp. 69, 70) in order to replace the existing population, every woman must have five children ; and Turner seems to have reason in supposing (p. 71) that 'if there had been no immigrants to them, the United States would not have done more in the thirty years we have been surveying than have kept up their own population, or but very gradually have increased it.'

Turner now proceeds to consider our own country. At the time of the Norman conquest the population was about 2,000,000 (p. 78), and in A.D. 1377 there were not more than 2,100,000 (p. 78). (These remarks apply to England alone.) In 1791 the population of England was estimated at 8,175,000 (p. 79) ; so that in upwards of 700 years we only twice doubled our population. Again (p. 80), from 1700 to 1760 the population of England increased only one-fourth, though that was a period of great peace and prosperity. But (p. 80) from 1760 to 1830 we find a greatly increasing ratio, for in these seventy years the population has more than doubled itself. In 1760, it was 6,479,730 ; in 1830 it was 13,840,751. Since 1801, according to Rickman (*Turner*, p. 81), 'the increase of population in Great Britain has not been materially accelerated or retarded, having been always one and a half per cent. per annum' (Pop. Abst. vol. i. p. ix.)

In Scotland, the population only doubled once in a hundred and twenty years (p. 82), for in A.D. 1700 it was 1,050,000. In 1820 it was 2,135,000.

In Ireland it has taken seventy-nine years to double the population (p. 82), for in A.D. 1712 it was 2,099,094, and in 1791 it was 4,206,612.

In France in thirty years the population increased little more than one-seventh (p. 83), for in A.D. 1801 it was 28,216,254, and in 1831 it had only reached to 32,560,934. Turner says (p. 84, note), 'In the Revue Encyclopédique for 1828, the average increase in all France during 1827 was stated to be 6·36 in 1,000, or about one in 150. This would require a century and a half before the whole French population would be doubled.' In the Netherlands, from 1819 to 1825, the population increased every year at the rate of one seventy-fifth. This would take seventy-five years to double the population (p. 84).

Our own population, says Turner (p. 89), has for the last thirty years multiplied about one-tenth every ten years ; and 'to do this the births must on the whole be one-half more than the deaths ;' and this will double the population in about seventy-four years.

In Russia (p. 91), 'from 1811 to 1822 inclusive, the births exceeded the deaths by about one-third.' In Russia, in 1833 (p. 92), the deaths were 1,485,291, the births 1,845,045 ; an increase of much less than one-third ; but in 1834, the deaths were 1,292,998, and the births 1,968,678, i.e. an excess of nearly one-half. In Prussia and Lithuania, from 1693 to 1756 inclusive, 'the births exceeded the deaths by only a little more than one-fifth part of their own number' (p. 93).

In England and Wales, from 1826 to 1830 inclusive, there was annually one marriage for every 128 persons (p. 108). In France, in 1827, the annual marriages were one in 138 (p. 110) ; and on an average of seventeen years the marriages in France were one in 131 (p. 110). Of the proportion of marriages to the population, in different countries, the extreme annual limits are one in 90, and one in 175 (p. 111). Taking therefore one in 128 as the average of marriages, and giving to every marriage its fair average of four births, it would evidently require thirty-two years to replace the existing population. And if we allow a generation to last for thirty-three years, the addition to the population would be but $1\frac{1}{8}$ (p. 111). We may take as an average of child-bearing in women thirty years, i.e. from fifteen to forty-five (p. 112). Now we find (p. 113 et seq.) that on an average three-eighths of the females are between fifteen and forty-five, so that to replace the existing population each woman must have $4\frac{1}{2}$ children. Again, on an average, one-third of the population is actually married (pp. 116, 117), so that every wife must average six children to replace the existing population (p. 118). (Turner forgets illegitimate children.) On a series of observations, the average births in England have been not quite $4\frac{1}{2}$ to each marriage (p. 124). In Prussia and Lithuania about the same (p. 124). In France, each marriage has averaged less than four children (p. 125). In other European countries a marriage has produced on an average from four to five children

(pp. 126, 127) ; and in no country has there been continuously
so many as six or few as three to each average marriage (p. 129).

In England and Wales, since 1820, the annual proportion of
births to population has been as one to twenty-eight (p. 133),
and in all countries from which we have returns the highest
annual proportion of births to the population is as one to twenty,
the lowest as one to fifty (p. 134). Sadler and others have drawn
attention to the curious fact (pp. 135, 136) that a greater *relative*
number of births occur when the population is smaller ; and that
in dense masses the percentage of births on the population is considerably diminished. In England 'the average of the deaths between 1796 and 1806 was one in forty-eight ; between 1806 and
1810 one in forty-nine ; between 1816 and 1820, one in fifty-five ;
and between 1826 and 1830 one in fifty-one' (p. 142). From
1801 to 1830 there were born in England 8,335,866 males and
7,987,710 females ; while the deaths were 5,819,923 males and
5,769,015 females (p. 143), and in 'other countries these differences are nearly similar ;' that is to say, though more males
than females are born, there are also more males who die in the
same year (p. 143). In North America, according to the census
of 1830, women lived a little longer than men, or as Turner
(*Sacred History*, iii. 71) has it, 'their vital duration was a little
longer than that of the male sex.'

Turner says (pp. 145, 146), 'For the ten years between 1820
and 1830, the relation between marriages, baptisms, and burials
in England and Wales stood as nearly as can be calculated in this
proportion, on a summary of each, namely 3¾ births to a marriage and 2½ of deaths. . . . This would make about 7½ births
to 5 deaths. . . . In Denmark, in 1830, the same relations were
4 births and nearly 3 deaths to a marriage. . . . In France, in
1831, the relation was 4 deaths and 3¼ births to a marriage. . . .
Sir William considered that in his time, 1682, there were in
England twenty-four births for twenty-three burials' (p. 147),
though contemporary computations reckoned five births to four
burials. He also said (p. 147) 'that in the country' the proportion of annual deaths to the population was one in thirty or thirty-
two ; but this would appear rather an exception, for in another
place he says (*Turner*, p. 148), 'we have good experience that in
the country but one in fifty die per annum.'

In 1827 the deaths in all France were nearly one in forty

(p. 149). In Denmark, in 1830, the ratio was one birth in twenty-eight, and one death in thirty-nine (p. 150). . . . In the Prussian provinces on the Rhine the ratio was nearly the favourable quantity of eight born to five that died (p. 150).

Turner says (p. 157) that out of nearly 4,000,000 persons who were buried in England and Wales between 1813 and 1830 inclusive, nearly four-ninths of the males died under sixteen, and more than half of them under the age of twenty-four. From instances in other nations (pp. 157–163) Turner supposes (p. 163) that the business of increasing the population is only entrusted to from one-third to half of those actually born. 'It is most frequently nearer the one-third, but from these must be deducted those who become too old to be parents ; and for this deduction from a quarter to one-fifth may reasonably be allowed.'

Turner says (p. 165) that 'there is a mysterious connection between the number of births and deaths with respect to each other,' i.e. the more the deaths, the more the births, and the more births the more deaths. This has been pointed out by the French economists, and by Mr. Sadler, and has been observed in several places (pp. 166, 167).

In England, in 1821, as near as possible, half the living males were under twenty years of age (p. 212), and this holds nearly good of Scotland and of Ireland taken separately (p. 213). But in America one-half of the inhabitants are under sixteen (p. 214). In Russia, half die under fifteen, while in Saxony half the population are almost twenty-three (p. 214).

Storch says (*Économie politique*, St. Petersburg, 8vo, 1815, tome v. p. 131), 'On s'est beaucoup plaint du tort que les couvents font à la population, et l'on a eu raison ; mais on s'est mépris sur les causes. Ce n'est pas à cause du célibat des religieux ; c'est à cause de leur oisiveté.' This is very good ; but Storch, through the whole of his work, falls into the error of supposing that a rise in wages will be necessarily followed by an increase of population (*Économie politique*, tome ii. pp. 5, 14, 25, 211 ; tome v. p. 113). To suppose that temporary wars, pestilence, or famine can check population for more than one generation is absurd. The chasm is immediately filled up by an increase of births. This is well put by Mr. Rae (*New Principles of Political Economy*, Boston, 8vo, 1834, pp. 30, 31).

PREVALENCE OF FRENCH CUSTOMS ETC. IN ENGLAND IN THE SEVENTEETH CENTURY.

In Wycherley's ' Love in a Wood ' there is frequent mention made of the ' French House,' which seems to have been a sort of tavern where persons of fashion assembled. It is also a great place of rendezvous in Wycherley's ' Gentleman Dancing Master,' said to have been written in 1661, but which did not *appear* until 1673. One of the chief characters in the ' Gentleman Dancing Master ' is ' Mr. Paris, a vain coxcomb and city heir, newly returned from France, and mightily affected with the French language and fashions.' He (act i. scene 1, p. 37 B) even translates proper names, and speaking of Mr. Taylor and Mr. Smith, calls them ' Monsieur Taileur, Monsieur Esmit.' He adds as the height of degradation of a certain Englishman (p. 37 B), ' His tailor lives within Ludgate, his valet de chambre is no Frenchman, and he has been seen at noon-day to go into an English eating-house.' The use of French footmen in England is mentioned both by him and Gerard (act i. scene 2, p. 40 B). At ' The French House ' there is an English waiter and a ' French scullion ' (act i. scene 2, p. 42 B). Mr. Paris has acquired all these French airs during a residence of ' three months at Paris, in a dame Englis pension ' (act i. scene 2, p. 40 A). His peculiarity is not so much the frequent use of French words, but speaking *broken English*—thus affecting to have forgotten the true pronunciation. Indeed we find, I think, in the earlier plays of the *post-Restoration* period, comparatively few instances of French quotations. In ' Love in a Wood ' (act ii. scene 1, p. 11 B) Sir Simon says of an unattractive heiress, ' She has no more teeth left than such as give a *haut goût* to her breath.' ' A little squab *French page*, who speaks no English ' (*Wycherley's Country Wife*, act iv. scene 3, p. 89 B) ; and in 1604, ' French page ' (*Middleton's Works*, 8vo, 1840, vol v. p. 564). Novel, in Wycherley's ' Plain Dealer ' (act iv. scene 2, p. 129 B), says, ' 'Tis time to come to an *éclaircissement* with you.' In Congreve's ' Way of the World,' the fashionable Mirabel says to Mrs. Millament (act ii. scene 5, p. 267 B), ' You used to have the *beau monde* throng after you ;' and in act iii. scene 7, p. 271 B, Mrs. Marwood says, ' This wench is the *passe-partout*.' In act iii. scene 15, p. 274 B, we are told that there is ' an academy in town ' for teaching French; and in act iv. scene 4, p. 277 A B, the brilliant and fashionable Mrs. Millamant calls a man '*l'étourdi*,' and afterwards says, 'Ye *douceurs*, ye *sommeils du matin*, adieu.' In Congreve's 'Double Dealer' (act i. scene 2, p. 175 A) the dashing Brisk says, 'O! *mon cœur*;' and in act ii. scene 5, p. 181 A, we find '*faux pas*' from Lady Plymouth; and in act iii. scene 6, p. 185 B, Lady Plymouth says, 'So well dressed, so *bonne mine*.'

In Vanbrugh's 'Relapse' (act i. scene 2, p. 304 B), even Lory, Tom Fashion's servant, talks about '*menus plaisirs*,' and '*de haut en bas*;' while Lord Foppington gives us long scraps, and even entire sentences of French (act i. scene 3, p. 305 A; act iii. scene 1, p. 314 A), and (at p. 324 A, act iv. scene 6) he calls Hoyden's nurse '*Madame la gouvernante*.' (See also the end of act iv. p. 326 A; and the end of act v. p. 334 B.) To all this must be added that Lord Foppington has a French valet '*La Vérole*.' There is a curious mention of the rage among English-men for travelling abroad in Congreve's 'Way of the World' (act i. scene 5, p. 261 B). In the next scene Witwoud says, 'Ah! *le drôle*.' Jorevin de Rochefort, whose Travels in England were published in 1672, and have been reprinted in the Antiquarian Repertory, vol. iv. pp. 549–622, 4to, 1809, gives a good deal of insight into the prevalence of French manners. Of the Duke of York he says (p. 564), 'He was dressed nearly in the French fashion, as the English generally are.' Again (p. 573), 'This nation is tolerably polite, in which they have in a great measure a resemblance to the French, whose modes and fashions they study and imitate.' But it would appear from two or three cur-sory notices that the French *language* was not so much studied as is usually supposed. He mentions (pp. 582, 583) meeting with 'a gentleman' who 'had long commanded in the armies in the Low Countries,' but who, from ignorance of French, was obliged to converse with him in Latin. The principal of Dublin College expressed as much curiosity about 'the city of Paris and the French customs' as we should now feel in conversing with a traveller who had just returned from Pekin or Japan (see p. 588). At Leith he thinks it worth recording (p. 607), 'I lodged in the house of one who spoke French,' though even this seems to have arisen from his having 'served Louis XIII. in the Scots' guards.' After this we need not be surprised at a clergyman who could not speak French (see p. 620). At the end of the sixteenth century women of fashion used to make 'French courtesies so most low that every touch should turn her over backward' (see 'The Case is altered,' in *Ben Jonson's Works*, 8vo, 1816, vol. vi. p. 352). In 1609 men of fashion had French tailors and French cooks (*Ben Jonson*, iii. 426, 436). Indeed, it is, I think, clear that it was more usual to follow French fashions than to learn the French language. See Ben Jonson's 88th Epigram, which ridicules those whose bodies, as he says, speak French, but not themselves (*Jonson's Works*, vol. viii. p. 199). A lady, describing an ideal lover, particularly requires that his 'manners' should be French (*Ben Jonson*, vol. viii. p. 314). In 1693, Evelyn (*Diary*, vol. iii. p. 323) thinks it worth mentioning of his daughter that she 'has the French tongue.' In 1661 Sir Thomas Browne (*Works*, vol. i. pp. 3, 14) desires that his son shall travel in France to get rid of English rustic manners.

NOTE ON THE SALT MANUFACTURES OF SOUTH SHIELDS.

For an account of the salt manufactures of South Shields (in the north of Durham) see Surtees' History of Durham, folio, 1820, vol. ii. pp. 94, 95. The first notice of them given by Surtees is in A.D. 1499; and 'the salt pans are frequently mentioned in the reign of Elizabeth, and seem betwixt that period and the reign of Charles to have attracted several settlers to South Shields. . . . In 1696, when the salt trade had reached its height, the number of pans amounted to one hundred and forty-three. From that period this branch of trade has been gradually decreasing, and at present only five salt pans remain.'

In a paper among Dr. Hunter's manuscripts (printed in *Surtees' History of Durham*, vol. ii. p. 95) it is said that 'the ancient manufacture of white salt at South and North Sheeles, Sunderland, and Blyth, ought to be preserved and encouraged for these reasons. First in respect of the public. That in tyme of hostility with Spayne and France, which was in A.D. 1627, 1628, 1629, 1630, there was such a scarcity of salt in this nation that it was sold at extraordinarie rates, viz. 5, 6, 7, 8, 9, 10s. per bushell, and upwards, and in many places not to be had for money. And when peace was concluded, the king of France

made an edict that no salt should be exported out of his kingdom, on confiscation of goods, ships, and life. Peace being concluded between England and Spayne, divers merchants of England
sent between two and three hundred saile of shippes to Spayne
to fetch salt; and the king of Spayne, taking notice of England's
necessity thereof, did not only a long time embargoe the said
shippes, but did immediately impose upon his salt such a
great imposition that it came to double the value of the salt;
whereby the merchants lost several thousand pounds.' Another
reason mentioned in this paper is that 'if the English manufacture of salt fail, which it needs must if not encouraged, then
may the Scots raise their prices as high as they please.'

In 1562 Sir Thomas Smith writes that the Duke of Savoye
'hath newly grieved his subjects with a tax upon salt' (*Forbes's
State Papers*, ii. 166). 'Salt has been at all times the great
native commodity of Cheshire' (*Ormerod's History of Cheshire*,
1819, vol. i. pp. xlv, xlvi); and it is said in King's Vale Royal,
published in 1656, that 'out of the salt wells which they call
brine pits they make yearly a great quantity of fine white salt;
a singular commodity no doubt, not only to the country, but also
to the whole realm; wherein this shire excelleth not only all other
shires in England, but also all other countries beyond the seas. For
in no countries where I have been have they any more than one
well in a country. Neither at Durtwich, in Worcestershire, is any
more than one, whereas in this country are four, and all within
ten miles together' (*Ormerod's Cheshire*, i. 103; see also vol. ii.
p. 47). In 1569 we procured 'sel blanc' from the Low Countries (*Correspondance diplomatique de Fénelon*, Paris, 1840,
tome i. p. 201; and see p. 226, and tome ii. p. 250). Dawson
Turner says that on the coast near Caen salt-works were formerly
very numerous; and that 'ancient charters recorded in the
Neustria Pia trace these works on the coasts of Dieppe, and at
Bonteilles on the right of the valley of Arques, to as remote a
period as 1027, and they at the same time prove the existence of
a canal between Dieppe and Bonteilles, by which in 1390 vessels
loaded with salt were wont to pass' (*Turner's Tour in Normandy*, 8vo, 1820, vol. i. p. 21).

Mr. M'Culloch says that the first duties on salt in England
were imposed by William III. (*Dictionary of Commerce*, 8vo,
1849, p. 1130). Stafford, in 1581, says that we imported salt

(*Brief Conceipt of English Policy*, in *Harleian Miscellany*, vol. ix. pp. 158–168). Indeed, he says (p. 165), 'Of iron and salt, though we have competently thereof, yet we have not the third part to suffice the realm.'

SUNDAY FAIRS AND MARKETS IN ENGLAND.

'Nothing can be a clearer proof of the impiety of our monks than the existence of Sunday fairs and markets held by their authority and under their very eye for several ages. It appears from the charter of Henry VI., granted in 1445, "that the abbot and convent had been used from time immemorial to hold a market at Whitby every Lord's day throughout the year;" and though the market was by that charter transferred to Saturday, and an Act of Parliament was passed three years after to enforce a similar improvement over all the kingdom, still the Act allowed the sale of "necessary victual" on the Lord's day, and suffered the Sunday markets to continue in harvest; so that this reformation was very partial. Statutes at large, i. pp. 618, 619; Charlton, p. 371. Charlton, not aware that the word *Sabbatum* in old records means *Saturday*, has mistranslated Henry's charter representing him as continuing the weekly market on the Lord's day with a view to *sanctify* it; whereas the charter states that the king, willing to sanctify the Lord's day, allowed the market to be thenceforth held on *Saturday*. . . . As the markets at Whitby were under the control of the abbot and convent, their sanctioning so shocking a violation of God's sacred day demonstrates too forcibly a lamentable want of true religion. It was not so in the days of St. Hilda and St. Cuthbert, when even the queen of Northumberland was not permitted to mount her chariot or perform a journey on the Lord's day. (Bed. Vita S. Cudb. c. 27.) Nor did such a contempt of divine institutions appear even in the close of the Saxon period (Wilk. Concil. i. pp. 203, 207, 220, 273); but after the Conquest this impiety grew apace, till in spite of some laudable attempts to stop its progress (ibid. pp. 508, 510, 511, 624, 707; iii. pp. 42, 43) it overspread the whole land like a deluge. Heylin, in his History of the Reformation (p. 38), speaks of the strict observance of the Lord's day as an *innovation*, but it was only a return to the piety of former times; though it must be owned that the profanation of the Christian Sabbath had long been sanctioned by ecclesiastical authority. The synod of Exeter, in 1287, permitted the sale of victuals on Sunday after mass. Wilk. Concil. ii. p. 145. In a mandate of the Archbishop of Canterbury on this subject, issued in 1359, it is stated as a mournful fact, that while the Lord's day was violated by markets and fairs, it was also profaned by feasting, drunkenness, debauchery, meetings of clubs, quarrels, fightings, and even murders. In some places the whole population flocked to these impious fairs, and the churches were totally deserted. Wilk. Concil. iii. p. 43 ' (*Young's History of Whitby*, 8vo, Whitby, 1817, vol. i. pp. 411, 412).

In 1783 Adam Clarke was appointed to preach at the ' Norfolk Circuit.' He says that in Norfolk, 'except among a very few religious people, the Sabbath day was universally disregarded. Buying and selling were considered neither unseemly nor sinful ; and on that day the sports of the field, particularly fowling, were general. Multitudes even of those called religious people bought and sold without any remorse. To find a man saved from this sin was a very rare thing indeed ' (*Life of Adam Clarke*, edited by Rev. J. B. B. Clarke, Lond. 1833, 8vo, vol. i. p. 208). In 1554, on 29th of June, 'was a fayre at Westminster Abbay ' (*Machyn's Diary*, p. 66, Camden Soc.) On a Sunday in 1688 the judges were ' introduced to the king by the Lord Chancellor' (*The Ellis Correspondence*, 8vo, 1829, vol. ii. p. 55). In 1800 Bishop Watson (*Life of Himself*, 2nd edit. 8vo, 1818, vol. ii. p. 113) mentions ' an evil which has increased very much, if it has not entirely sprung up in many places within the last thirty years, the travelling of waggons and stage-coaches on Sundays.' In 1592 Pickering was knighted, made a privy councillor, and entrusted with the great seal on Sunday (*Campbell's Lives of the Chancellors*, vol. ii. p. 188).

OBSERVATIONS ON CANNIBALISM.

The New Zealanders are cannibals (see *Cook's Voyages*, 8vo, 1821, vol. i. pp. 378, 379, 381, and vol. iii. pp. 246, 247, 248, 249), and this does not arise from a deficiency of food (p. 250 ; see also iv. 227, 235 ; and v. 236). They say that they only eat their enemies (v. 215). Cannibalism seems to be part of their religion, for they think that if a man is eaten by the enemy his soul goes to 'a perpetual fire,' but ascends to the gods if his body is rescued (vol. v. pp. 215, 216).

The Feejees are cannibals, and a very ingenious people (v. 428, 429).

See in Cook's Voyages (8vo, 1821, vol. vi. pp. 41, 42, 165, 157) some reasons, though not convincing ones, for thinking that the Otaheitans were formerly cannibals. The inhabitants of Tanna, one of the New Hebrides, are cannibals, and avow it, although they have plenty of food (*Cook*, iv. 55, 56). Cook (vi. 198), speaking of Oneehow, one of the Sandwich Islands, says it is 'certain that the horrid banquet of human flesh is as much relished here amid plenty as it is in New Zealand.' And at Otooi, another of the Sandwich Islands, it was openly avowed (pp. 193–195). But the natives of Owhyhee positively informed Captain King that they were not cannibals (*Cook*, vii. 65), and King thinks (vii. 122, 123) that *none* of the Sandwich Islanders are cannibals.

It seems probable that the inhabitants of Nootka Sound are cannibals (see *Cook's Voyages*, vi. 249, 283). 'From the character and disposition of the native Africans, it may fairly be doubted whether throughout the whole of this great continent a negro cannibal has any existence' (*Tuckey's Expedition to the Zaire*, 1818, 4to, p. 351). During the French Revolution the people were cannibal from revenge (see *Alison's History of Europe*, vol. i. p. 582 ; vol. ii. pp. 164, 222 ; vol. iii. p. 311).

At Mangea, which is about 10° S.W. of the Society Islands, the inhabitants are *not* cannibals (*Cook's Voyages*, v. 224) ; nor are the natives of Valeeso, about 3° N. of Mangea (vol. v. p. 261). See Earle's New Zealand (8vo, 1832, pp. 13, 14, 33, 47, 72, 115, 117, 149, 184, 197), and for an account of one of their cannibal feasts, preparations for which he *saw*, see pp. 112–120. A chronicler who wrote in the fifteenth century says that in England, from A.D. 1315 to 1317, there was a great dearth, 'and the poure people stal children and eten them' (*A Chronicle of London from 1089 to 1483*, Lond. 4to, 1827, pp. 45, 46). The inhabitants of New Guinea are cannibals without being cruel (*Prichard's Physical History of Mankind*, vol. v. p. 225). Mr. Eyre says that among the aborigines of Australia 'cannibalism is not common, though there is reason to believe that it is occasionally practised by some tribes, but under what circumstances it is difficult to say. Native sorcerers are said to acquire their magic influence by eating human flesh, but this is only done once in a lifetime' (*Eyre's Expedition of Discovery into Central Australia*, Lond. 8vo, 1845, vol. ii. p. 255). Cannibalism was formerly practised in nearly all the South Sea Islands (see *Ellis's Polynesian Researches*, 8vo, 1831, vol. i. pp. 357-361).

OBSERVATIONS UPON SUPERSTITIONS CONNECTED WITH DREAMS.

Among the inhabitants of Java, 'if any one is restless, and dreams for two or three nights successively, he concludes that Satan has taken that method of laying his commands upon him' (*Cook's Voyages*, 8vo, 1821, vol. i. p. 328, &c.)

Anderson, who paid so much attention to the religion of the Otaheitans, says of them, 'They have an equal confidence in dreams, which they suppose to be communications either from their god, or from the spirits of their departed friends, enabling those favoured with them to foretell future events' (*Cook's Voyages*, 8vo, 1821, vol. vi. p. 154).

In Congreve's 'Love for Love' (act iv. scene 21, p. 229 n), Valentine says to Jeremy, 'Dreams and Dutch almanacks are to be understood by contraries;' and in act v. scene 4, p. 231 B, Tattle says to Miss Prue, 'Your father will tell you that dreams come by contraries.'

Dr. Arnold was very much affected by the loss of his brother in 1820; and soon afterwards he writes to a friend, 'It is very extraordinary how often I dream he is alive, and always with the consciousness that he is alive after having been supposed dead; and this sometimes has gone so far that I have in my dream questioned the reality of his being alive, and doubted whether it were not a dream, and have been convinced that it was not so strongly, that I could scarcely shake off the impression on waking' (*Stanley's Life of Arnold*, 5th edit. 8vo, 1845, vol. i. p. 68).

Dr. Combe quotes from the Annals of Phrenology (No. 1, p. 37, Boston, 1833) a case mentioned by Dr. Caldwell, of a woman aged twenty-six, who 'had lost a large portion of her scalp, skull-bone, and dura mater, in a neglected attack of lues venerea. A corresponding portion of her brain was consequently bare and subject to inspection. When she was in a *dreamless sleep* her brain was *motionless*, and *lay within* the cranium. When her sleep was imperfect and she was agitated by dreams her brain *moved* and *protruded without* the cranium, forming *cerebral hernia.*' In vivid dreams the protrusion was greater, and when she was awake it was still more remarkable (*Physiology applied to Health*, 3rd edit. Edinb. 8vo, 1835, p. 288).

Gent tells a singular story of a dream which he had, and which turned out to be true (see *Life of Thomas Gent, by Himself*, 8vo, 1832, pp. 120-125). For an instance of a prophetic dream, but not well attested, see Life of Dr. Jackson (p. cvi, prefixed to *Jackson's Formation, Discipline, and Economy of Armies*, 8vo, 1845). Beattie (*Elements of Moral Science*, Edinburgh, 1817, 8vo, vol. i. pp. 90, 91) says, 'It is found in fact, that those people are most apt to dream that are most addicted to intense thinking.' The people in every part of Madagascar believe that God foretells them in dreams what is to happen (see *Drury's Madagascar*, Lond. 8vo, 1743, pp. 173, 174). Dr. Herbert Mayo thinks 'that in sleep all persons always dream, but that all do not remember their dreams' (*Mayo, On the Truths contained in Popular Superstitions*, 8vo, 1851, pp. 78, 79). He adds (p. 85), 'Sir George Back told me, that in the privations he encountered in Sir John Franklin's first expedition, when, in fact, he was starving, he uniformly dreamed of plentiful repasts.' Coleridge relates that his father, the night before his sudden death, dreamed that death had appeared to him (see *Coleridge's Biographia Literaria*, 8vo, 1847, vol. ii. p. 325). There are several cases on record in which the brain, in consequence of injury of the skull, has been seen motionless in dreamless sleep, but agitated during dreams (see *Combe's Constitution of Man in Relation to External Objects*, Edinb. 8vo, 1847, p. 149). Niebuhr, after the death of his first wife, writes respecting her, 'I saw her a few days ago in a dream. She seemed as if returning to me after a long separation. I felt uncertain, as one so often does in dreams, whether she was still living on this earth, or only appeared on it for a transient visit; she greeted me as if after a long absence, asked hastily after the child, and took it in her arms' (*Life and Letters of B. G. Niebuhr*, Lond. 8vo, 1852, vol. ii. p. 103). According to the Persians, 'it is only the dreams of women that go by contraries' (*Malcolm's History of Persia*, 8vo. 1829, vol. i.

p. 29). See Herbert Mayo's ' Philosophy of Living,' 2nd edit.
8vo, 1838, pp. 138-160, 166.

RESPECT PAID TO PERSONS DISORDERED IN THEIR MINDS.

Captain King, in his account of the Sandwich Islands (*Cook's Voyages*, 8vo, 1821, vol. vii. p. 121), says, ' We met with two instances of persons disordered in their minds, the one a man at Owhyee, the other a woman at Oneehcow. It appeared, from the particular attention and respect paid to them, that the opinion of their being inspired by the divinity, which obtains among most of the nations of the East, is also received here.'

1. M. Souvestre says that the peasants of Brittany are anxious to have the prayers of idiots, which they consider particularly acceptable to God (*Les Derniers Bretons*, Paris, 1843, p. 340). 2. Southey, speaking of an idiot, says, ' Natural feeling, when natural feeling is not corrupted, leads men to regard persons in his condition with a compassion not unmixed with awe' (*The Doctor*, edit. Warter, 8vo, 1848, p. 28). 3. In 1614 we have, ' They say a fool's handsel is lucky' (*Ben Jonson's Works*, 8vo, 1816, vol. iv. p. 410). It is said that the commonest age for going mad is between twenty and thirty, and that as civilisation advances madness, ' la folie,' becomes more frequent (see *Tissot, De la Manie du Suicide*, Paris, 8vo, 1840, pp. 60-62). ' Idiots, who in Barbary are revered as saints, are likewise so in India' (*Transactions of Literary Society of Bombay*, 4to, 1819, vol. i. p. 102).

OBSERVATIONS ON QUAKERS.

In Congreve's ' Way of the World' (act i. scene 9, p. 264 A) Witwoud says, ' She hates Mirabel worse than a Quaker hates a parrot.'

See some account of them in the ' Travels of Cosmo through England in 1669,' Lond. 1821, 4to, pp. 447-451. It is there stated (p. 449) that at the Restoration they were estimated ' at upwards of sixty thousand.' As early as 1573, Asplyn, the printer of Cartwright's Works, talks about the spirit moving him (see Letter from the Archbishop of Canterbury in *Wright's Elizabeth*,

i. 493). In 1591 Hacket and some of his friends were brought before the magistrates for prophesying and blaspheming. These people anticipated the Quakers in one of their absurdities, and would not take off their hats to the magistrate (see *Camden's Elizabeth*, in *Kennett*, ii. 564). Lord Jeffrey (*Essays*, 8vo, 1844, vol. iv. p. 244) says, 'The Quakers had the merit of passing a severe censure upon the slave trade as long ago as 1727.' In 1721 the shops in Gracechurch Street were mostly kept by Quakers, and the pretty Quakeresses formed the chief attraction. They are described by a contemporary as gravely but richly dressed, and without hoops (see *The Merry Travellers, a Trip from Moorfields to Bromley* [*by Ned Ward?*], 2nd edit. Lond. 8vo, 1724, part i. p. 9). By the charter of the Bank of England in 1694, every member might be required 'to take the oath of stock, or the declaration of stock in case he be one of the people called Quakers' (see The Charters in *M'Culloch's Dictionary of Commerce*, 8vo, 1849, p. 75).

At Cleves, in 1664, the Quakers were increasing (see *Lord King's Life of Locke*, 8vo, 1830, vol. i. p. 45).

Dr. Shebbeare has given some particulars respecting the Quakers a century ago (*Letters on the English Nation, by B. Angeloni*, 8vo, 1755, vol. i. pp. 128-130). He says 'they never take off their hats, nor will they say grace either before or after meals.' He adds, 'They are almost all in trade, and therefore once in the year they meet in the several towns in England, to know the state of those parts of the country.' In a ballad in 1659, the 'shivering Quakers are mentioned' (*Wright's Political Ballads*, p. 135, Percy Society, vol. iii.) 'Quakers' are also mentioned at p. 243 in a ballad in 1660. In 1573 a sect in the Isle of Ely 'maintained the unlawfulness of taking an oath on any account, or before any person whatsoever' (*Collier's Ecclesiastical History*, vi. 540). It is stated by M. Ferri de Saint-Constant that 'il n'y a presque pas d'exemple de quaker condamné à mort ou à des peines infamantes. En 1791, il y avait plus de vingt ans qu'aucun quaker n'avait été assigné à Old Bailey' (*Villers, Essai sur la Réformation*, Paris, 1820, p. 272). Voltaire says of a Quaker he knew in England, 'Il était vêtu comme tous ceux de sa religion, d'un habit sans pli dans les côtés, et sans boutons sur les poches ni sur les manches, et portait un grand chapeau à bords rabattus, comme nos ecclésiastiques,

&c.' (*Lettre I. sur les Anglais*, in *Œuvres de Voltaire*, Paris, 1821, tome xxvi. p. 8).

In 1774 Captain Topham observes that the Scotch, in conversation, often 'use the word Friend, even to strangers' (*Topham's Letters from Edinburgh*, Lond. 8vo, 1776, p. 49).

The Quakers told Voltaire, 'Nous portons aussi un habit un peu différent des autres hommes, afin que ce soit pour nous un avertissement continuel de ne leur pas ressembler' (*Lettre I. sur les Anglais*, in *Œuvres de Voltaire*, tome xxvi. p. 12, Paris, 8vo, 1821). Voltaire adds (p. 25) that in London the Quakers were rapidly diminishing. See some extraordinary abuse by a Quaker in Southey's 'Life of Wesley' (1846, vol. i. p. 442).

In 1813 Lord Jeffrey, I hardly know whether in jest or in earnest, writes from Liverpool that 'a very intelligent physician' told him that the 'richer' Quakers actually 'die of stupidity : that they rarely live to be fifty, eat too much, take little exercise, and, above all, have no nervous excitement' (*Cockburn's Life and Correspondence of Lord Jeffrey*, Edinb. 8vo, 1852, vol. ii. p. 142). Saltmarsh 'was the first that began to be scrupulous of the hat, and using common language.' This was one year before Fox (see *King's Life of Locke*, 8vo, 1830, vol. i. p. 310). In 1835 there were 22,000 or 23,000 Quakers in England and Scotland (see *Prichard on Insanity*, 8vo, 1835, p. 200).

STATE OF THE CLERGY IN ENGLAND IN THE SIXTEENTH CENTURY.

Lingard (*History of England*, Paris, 1840, vol. v. p. 11) says that in 1560, in consequence of the number of clergy who refused to take the oath of supremacy, and were therefore expelled, 'it became necessary for the moment to establish a class of lay instructors, consisting of mechanics, licensed to read the service to the people in the church, but forbidden to administer the sacraments.' For this he cites Strype, i. 139, 178, 240. See the complaint made by the Bishop of Ely in a pitiful letter, written in 1574, and printed in Wright's Elizabeth, 8vo, 1838, vol. i. p. 497. In 1559 Elizabeth was obliged to order 'that the clergy shall not haunt alehouses or taverns, or spend their time idly at dice, cards, tables, or any other unlawful game ' (*Neal's History of the Puritans*, edit. Toulmin, 8vo, 1822, vol. i. p. 127); but this did little good, for in 1571 the House of Commons addressed the queen, and stated that 'great numbers are admitted ministers that are infamous in their lives and conversation' (*Neal*, i. 219). Neal says (i. 293) that in 1579, 'in the county of Cornwall, there were one hundred and forty clergymen, not one of which was capable of preaching a sermon, and most of them were pluralists and non-residents.' In 1584 some of the inhabitants of Essex presented a petition to the council, in which they complained that their clergy were 'men of occupation, serving men, the basest of all sorts, . . . rioters, dicers, drunkards, and of offensive lives' (*Neal*, i. 329 ; see also p. 349). Nor must this be considered a mere factious mis-representation, for in 1584 the Lords of the Council addressed a letter to the Archbishop of Canterbury, in which they state it to be a notorious fact that 'great numbers of persons that occupy cures are notoriously unfit ; most for lack of learning—many chargeable with great and enormous faults, as drunkenness, filthiness of life, gaming at cards, haunting of alehouses' (*Neal*, i. 341). In 1585 and 1586 there was made a very careful and minute survey of the state of the church in reference to the clergy. From it we learn that there were only 2,000 preachers to nearly 10,000 parishes (*Neal*, i. 382). Fenner, a contemporary writer, says that in 1586 a third of the clergy were suspended (*Neal*, i. 382). From a survey made in 1587, it appears that there were only nineteen 'resident preachers abiding in London' (*Neal*, i. 391).

1. Camden says that in 1559 several mechanics received 'ecclesiastical promotions, and good prebends, and fat benefices' (*Annals of Elizabeth*, in *Kennett*, vol. iii. p. 377). 2. In 1571 even Bishop Grindal was obliged to issue an order that no unmarried clergyman 'should keep any woman in his house under sixty years of age, excepting she was his mother, aunt, sister, or niece' (*Collier's Ecclesiastical History*, 8vo, 1840, vol. vi. p. 501). 3. Blackstone (*Commentaries*, 1809, iii. 54) says that from 1373 all the chancellors were ecclesiastics or statesmen (but never lawyers), until Henry VIII. in 1530 promoted Sir Thomas More. After this the great seal was intrusted to lawyers, courtiers, and churchmen indifferently, until in 1592 Sergeant Pickering was made Lord Keeper, 'from which time to the present the Court of Chancery has always been filled by a lawyer, excepting the interval from 1621 to 1625,' when the seal was intrusted to Williams, Dean of Westminster, afterwards

Bishop of Lincoln. + Under Mary, the clergy who were deprived are said to have been less than one-fifth of the whole (see Tierney's Note in *Dodd's Church History*, vol. ii. p. 182).

OBSERVATIONS ON THE RELATIVE NUMBERS OF CATHOLICS AND PROTESTANTS IN ENGLAND IN THE SIXTEENTH CENTURY.

Lingard (vol. v. p. 264), speaking of affairs in 1587, just before the Armada, says, 'The real number of the English Catholics was unknown (for the severity of the penal laws had taught many to conceal their religion), but it was loosely conjectured that they amounted to at least one-half of the population of the kingdom. Dr. Allen was positive that they amounted to at least two-thirds. Apud Bridgewater, 374. The same was asserted in a paper found upon Creighton. Strype, iii. 415.'

Dr. Venner, who wrote in 1649, says, 'It was a common saying fifty or sixty years since, that all physicians that were learned were Papists' (*Venner's Via Recta ad Vitam Longam*, 4to, 1650, p. 360).

See also Lodge's Illustrations of British History, vol. ii. p. 68, 8vo, 1838. In Wright's Elizabeth, 8vo, 1838, vol. i. p. 485, there is a very remarkable letter from the Earl of Essex to Lord Burghley, dated 20th July, 1573. In this letter Essex gives an account of an interview he had with the queen before going on his expedition to Ireland, in which she particularly charged him 'not to seek too hastily to bring people that had been trayned in another religion, from that which they have been brought up in.' So much for Elizabeth being a persecutor! The Catholics were probably numerous in London. In Wright's Elizabeth (8vo, 1838, vol. ii. pp. 37–41) there is a letter from Fletewood to Lord Burghley in 1572, giving a curious account of the seizure of several 'masse mongers' in the very act of celebrating service in the house of Geraldi the Portuguese ambassador. See also (at pp. 86, 87) another letter from this same Fletewood in 1578, in which he says that several Englishmen were in the habit of going to the French ambassador's to hear mass.

In 1579 Leicester writes to Burghley, 'Since Queen Mary's tyme the Papists never were in that jollity they be at this present in this country' (*Wright's Elizabeth*, vol. ii. p. 102); and in another letter to Lord Burghley, written by Sir Amias Paulet in 1585, respecting Mary, Paulet says, 'This country is so ill affected (a thing not unknowen unto you), as I thinke no man of judgement would willingly take the charge of this queen in any house in this sheere out of this castle ' (i.e. Tutbury) (*Wright*, vol. ii. p. 257). In 1586 B. Bland, who had just returned from Spain, wrote, ' The Spaniards are certainly persuaded by letters out of England that th' one halfe of England will take their part' (*Wright*, vol. ii. p. 303). In 1587 Thomas Tuncker writes to William Watson, ' England in the north parts, where for religion they shall find the fifth man to be given to Papistry ' (*Wright*, vol. ii. p. 351). Camden says that the northern rebellion of 1569 was joined by very few Catholics (*Annals of Elizabeth*, in *Kennett*, ii. 422). In 1574 Mary of Scotland writes that most English Catholics were through fear beginning to obtain permission to travel abroad (*Sharp's Memorials of Rebellion of* 1569, 8vo, 1840, p. 300). In 1569 Sir R. Sadler wrote that in the north of England there were not ten gentlemen who favoured the queen's proceedings. This, which is an evident exaggeration, is twice quoted in Sir C. Sharp's Rebellion of 1559, pp. x, 92. Ormerod says that in the reign of Elizabeth ' considerably more than one-fourth of the entire number of the population of Cheshire were Catholic recusants' (*History of Cheshire*, folio, 1819, vol. i. pp. xxxiii, xxxiv). For proof of this he refers to vol. i. p. 75, but neither there nor in any other part of his work can I find any evidence on this subject.

Mr. Soames says that at the accession of Elizabeth two-thirds were Catholics (*Elizabethan Religious History*, 8vo, 1839, p. 13).

In a letter said to be written in 1588, by Richard Leigh, a seminary priest, to the Spanish ambassador in France, the decline of the English Catholics is strongly put. The writer says that, compared with their number at the accession of Elizabeth, 'there are not as many tens as we accounted hundreds' (*Harleian Miscellany*, 1808, 4to, i. 146). But is this letter genuine ? and if so, where is the original ? We know on the authority of Munday, in 1581, that there were several places in London where mass could be heard (see his *English Romayne Life*, reprinted in *Harleian Miscellany*, edit. Park, vol. vii. p. 144). In 1570 Storey confessed 'that about two years since he did deal by writing with Courterile, shewing unto him that the Catholics in England did daily decay and the schismatics did then daily increase;

and therefore if the king of Spain had any meaning to write to the queen of England, or otherwise to help to restore religion in England, he should do it betime, or else it would be too late' (*Harleian Miscellany*, viii. 612). In Burleigh's advice to Eliza-beth, about 1583, it is said that 'the greatest number of Papists is of very young men ;' and Burleigh goes on to say, 'I account that putting to death does in no way lessen them, since we find by experience that it worketh no such effect ; but like Hydras' heads, upon cutting off one, seven grow up, ... so that for my part I wish no lessening of their numbers but by preaching and by education of the younger under good schoolmasters' (*Harleian Miscellany*, vii. 60). After the visitors appointed by Elizabeth had in 1559 gone through the whole kingdom, they reported that 'not above two hundred and forty-three clergymen had quitted their livings.' Of these, fourteen were bishops (*Neal's History of the Puritans*, edit. Toulmin, 1822, 8vo, vol. i. p. 133). Jewel, who is considered with reason to be one of the great fathers of the English Church, did not hesitate on the accession of Mary to sign a recantation (this disagreeable fact is hurried over by Neal, *History of the Puritans*, i. 224). He withdrew his recantation almost immediately, but not till he had reached Geneva, and was safe from the hand that would assuredly have punished his third (or second ?) apostasy. Neal says (i. 206) that in 1568, 'in Lancashire, the Common Prayer Book was laid aside, churches were shut up, and the mass celebrated openly.' He adds (i. 271), but without quoting any authority, that in 1574 'many of the queen's subjects resorted to the Portugal ambassador's house in Charterhouse Square, where mass was publicly celebrated ; and, because the sheriffs and recorder of London disturbed them, they were committed to the Fleet by the queen's express command.' Neal says (i. 307), but as usual without any authority, that in 1582 the Catholics 'in the northern counties were more numerous than the Protestants.' During the first ten years of Elizabeth's reign great numbers of Catholics frequented the Protestant churches (see *Collier's Ecclesiastical History*, 8vo, 1840, vol. vi. pp. 264, 265). Mr. Hallam, in a long note in Constitutional Hist. 8vo, 1842, i. 173, seems to consider that in 1559 the Pro-testants were two-thirds of the population. He rejects Butler's assertion (*Memoirs of English Catholics*, i. 146) that the Catho-lics had the majority. In 1549 Paget wrote to the Protector that not more than one-twelfth were Protestants. See Lingard (Paris, 1840, iv. 361), who quotes Strype, ii. Rec. 110. See also p. 339, where Lingard quotes from MSS. Barber, 1208, a curious passage in the despatches of the Venetian ambassador, which represents the English as ready to become either Jews or Mahommedans. In 1554 Parliament were almost unanimous in favour of the reconciliation with Rome; in the Commons only two, in the Lords not a single voice was raised against it (*Lingard*, 341; and *Ellis, Orig. Letters*, 2nd series, ii. 239). In 1553 Noailles (*Ambassades*, tome ii. p. 167) writes to his court that Suffolk and Norfolk were particularly discontented with Mary—but was this political or religious? He adds (p. 168) that the greater part of London was 'de la mesme faction.' In 1566 the Catholics were very numerous in Yorkshire; 'great plenty of papysts' (*Haynes's State Papers*, p. 446). In 1584 Charles Paget mentions the mode of flight 'ordinarily used by Catholics, which daily come out of England' (*Murdin's State Papers*, p. 437). In 1592 the Earl of Pembroke writes to Elizabeth that the Welsh are 'in religion generally ill-affected, as may appear by their use of Popish pilgrimages, their harbour of massing priests, their retaining of superstitious ceremonies, and the increase of wilful recusants' (*Murdin's State Papers*, p. 662). In 1569 there were from twelve to fifteen different places in London where mass was performed (*Correspondance diplomatique de Fénelon*, Paris, 1840, tome i. p. 327). Mr. Butler, on the authority of Reshton de Schismate Angliæ, p. 272, says that early in Elizabeth's reign two-thirds of the English were Catholics (*Butler's Memoirs of the Catholics*, 8vo, 1822, vol. i. pp. 271, 272; and see p. 386, vol. ii. p. 12). Father Holtby, in a report which he sent in 1594 to his superior, Garnet, writes that unless some check was given to the conduct of the English Government, 'it is greatly to be feared that in short time the weak and small number of God's servants shall come to ruin, and the little sparkle of Catholic religion as yet reserved amongst us shall be quite extinguished' (*Dodd's Church History*, edit. Tierney, vol. iii. p. 76). Sandys, in a sermon preached early in the reign of Elizabeth, seems to say that most wealthy persons were Catholics (*Sandys' Sermons*, edit. Parker Society, p. 30).

PROGRESS OF THE LAWS ETC. IN ENGLAND RESPECTING THE INTEREST OF MONEY.

In 1559 the market interest seems to have been ten per cent. (see *Ben Jonson's Works*, 8vo, 1816, vol. ii. p. 141). In 1610 the goldsmiths were the great bankers and money-lenders (see Gifford's note in *Ben Jonson*, iv. 38, 39). The 21st Jac. I. reduced interest from ten to eight per cent. This excited great attention, and is mentioned several times in 'The Staple of News,' which was brought on the stage the next year (see *Ben Jonson's Works*, 8vo, 1816, vol. v. pp. 200, 207, 258). One of the characters in 'The Magnetick Lady,' which was brought out in 1632, is 'Sir Moth Interest, an usurer or money bawd' (*Ben Jonson*, vol. vi. pp. 4, 48). It is by such childish abuse of language as this that the prejudices of the ignorant are fostered by poets and dramatists. In 'The Magnetick Lady' we find 'the usual rate of ten in the hundred' (vol. vi. p. 46). And Ben Jonson's fifty-seventh epigram is 'on bawds and usurers' (vol. viii. p. 182); and in 'The Forest' he says, 'No usurer nor his bawds' (viii. 284). In 1608 ten per cent. seems to have been the usual interest (*Middleton's Works*, 8vo, 1840, iii. 155). At the end of the reign of Henry VIII. it seems to have been usual to pay the interest yearly (see *Udall's Roister Doister*, p. 85, edit. Cooper, Shakespeare Society, 1847). Blackstone adopts the absurd idea that interest was considered unlawful, because Moses forbade it and Aristotle considered money to be barren (*Commentaries*, edit. Christian, 1809, vol. ii. p. 454). In 1548 ten per cent. seems to have been the common interest in England (see *Haynes's State Papers*, p. 64), and we find houses bought for sixteen years' purchase (p. 65). In 1595 the usual interest seems to have been ten per cent. (*Murdin's State Papers*, p. 736). The father of the great D'Aguesseau wrote about 1681 to Domat, who was perhaps the most eminent jurist that France has produced, 'Je savois, monsieur, que l'usure était défendue par l'Écriture et par les lois : mais je ne la savois pas contraire au droit naturel : votre écrit m'en a persuadé' (*Cousin's Littérature*, Paris, 1849, tome iii. p. 163). Bucer wished to have an additional homily, 'Of usury' (*Collier's Ecclesiastical History*, vol. v. p. 402, 8vo, 1840). In the system of ecclesiastical laws drawn up by Cranmer in 1552, the privilege of making a will is denied to 'libellers, strumpets, pandars, and usurers' (*Soame's History of the Reformation of the Church of England*, vol. iii. p. 718, 8vo, 1827). Montesquieu supposes that the influx of precious metals in the sixteenth century caused a fall in the interest of money (*Esprit des Lois*, livre xxii. chap. vi. *Œuvres*, Paris, 1835, p. 380). In 1763 Grimm expresses himself strongly against usury laws (see *Correspondance littéraire, par Grimm et Diderot*, tome iii. p. 382).

1. Cecil, in a letter to Sir Thomas Smith, dated February 27, 1562, says, 'Many other good lawes are passed the nether house, as for liberation of usury under ten per cent. (which notwithstanding I durst not allowe') (see the letter in *Wright's Elizabeth*, 8vo, 1838, vol. i. pp. 125-127). 2. Sir Simon D'Ewes was on one occasion in great distress for money; but would not borrow it, because he 'thought it not lawful to give or take use' (*Autobiography of D'Ewes*, edit. Halliwell, 8vo, 1845, vol. ii. p. 96; see also p. 153). 3. The dislike to interest is said by Michaelis to have originated in an erroneous interpretation of the Mosaic law, combined with an opinion of Aristotle. Calvin was one of the first who recognised the propriety of interest (see *M'Culloch's Principles of Political Economy*, Edinburgh, 1843, pp. 520, 521, and *Commercial Dictionary*, p. 761). 4. See J. S. Mill's Principles of Political Economy, 2nd edit. 8vo, 1849, vol. ii. pp. 492-497. He adopts (p. 492) the idea that the usury laws originated in attempts to adapt Judaism to Christianity. There is no doubt that the tendency of usury laws is to aggravate a commercial panic (*Mill*, ii. 185). 5. Henry II. of France borrowed money at sixteen per cent. (see *Forbes's State Papers*, i. 260). 6. In 1675, 'Your usurer, that in the hundred takes twenty' (*The Civic Garland*, p. 58, edit. Fairholt, Percy Society, vol. xix.) Archbishop Sandys is furious against those who take or pay interest (see *Sandys' Sermons*, edit. Cambridge, 1841, 8vo, pp. 50, 136, 182, 203). In the earliest rules drawn up by Wesley it is forbidden (see *Southey's Life of Wesley*, 8vo, 1846, vol. i. p. 364). In 1676, at Montpellier, Locke writes, 'Interest by law here is 6½ per cent., but those that have good credit may borrow at five' (*King's Life of Locke*, 8vo, 1830, vol. i. p. 104).

SUCCESSION DEVOLVING UPON A SISTER'S SON.

Columbus, in his first voyage to America in 1492, found this custom existing among the naked savages of Cuba. Washington Irving (*History of Columbus*, 8vo, 1828, vol. i. p. 334) says, 'In fact, the sovereignty among the people of this island was hereditary, and they had a simple but sagacious mode of maintaining in some degree the verity of descent. On the death of a cacique without children, his authority passed to those of his sisters in preference to those of his brothers, being considered most likely to be of his blood ; for they observed that a brother's reputed children may by accident have no consanguinity with their uncle, but those of his sister must certainly be the children of their mother.' (I copy this sentence *verbatim* ; the grammar, or rather the sense, is somewhat strange.)

Bede relates a similar custom among the Picts : 'Cumque uxores Picti non habentes peterent a Scotis, ea solum conditione dare consueverunt, ut ubi res veniret in dubium, magis de fœminea regum prosapia quam de masculina regem sibi elegerint, quod usque hodie apud Pictos constat esse servatum' (*Bedæ Historia ecclesiastica*, b. i. c. i. *Opera*, edidit Giles, vol. i. p. 34, Londini, 1843, 8vo).

In Australia 'the names are inherited on the female line, the children of either sex taking the family name of the mother, like the children of the Nairs of Malabar' (*Prichard's Physical History of Mankind*, vol. v. p. 268).

COLUMBUS WAS FAVOURABLE TO SLAVERY.

In a long letter to the Spanish sovereign, Columbus proposes to transfer the Caribs to Spain, to be sold as slaves to merchants in return for live stock. By this means, as he sagaciously observes, the colony will be enriched and the souls of the pagan Caribs will be saved ! See his ingenious reasoning in Irving's History of Columbus (8vo, 1828, vol. ii. p. 82). To sell the Americans as slaves was a favourite measure of finance with Columbus (for further proofs see *Irving*, vol. ii. p. 262 ; vol. iii. p. 19). On one occasion his conduct on this subject greatly incensed his munificent patroness, the amiable but high-minded Isabella (vol. iii. pp. 92, 93).

Christian (note in *Blackstone*, i. 425) quotes I. Lord Ray (147), to the effect 'that the Court of Common Pleas, so late as the 5 W. and M., held that a man might have a property in a negro boy, and might have an action of trover for him, because negroes are heathens.'

1. M'Culloch ingeniously remarks that the existence of slavery, by rendering labour disgraceful, prevented the study of political economy (*Principles of Political Economy*, Edinburgh, 1843, p. 10). 2. Mr. Mill says that in a country where wages are high, slave labour is cheaper than free labour in spite of its inferior efficiency (*Principles of Political Economy*, 2nd edit. 8vo, 1849, vol. ii. p. 226). See also vol. i. pp. 304-309, where he observes that the increase of population in Europe, by making labour cheap, hastened the extinction of serfdom. As to the influence of slavery on value, see i. 589. 3. Jacob remarks that slavery originated in a moral improvement, and was a substitute for putting prisoners of war to death (*History of the Precious Metals*, 8vo, 1831, vol. i. p. 136). M'Culloch (*Dictionary of Commerce*, 8vo, 1849, p. 1199) says that the African slave trade was begun by the Portuguese in 1442, but made little progress till the sixteenth century. 'Sir John Hawkins was the first Englishman who engaged in it, and such was the ardour with which our country-men followed his example, that they exported from Africa more than 300,000 slaves between the years 1680 and 1700.' He has some sensible remarks (p. 1251) on the absurdity of supposing that in tropical countries free labour will be as productive as slave labour. Slavery was opposed by Wesley, but defended by White-field (*Southey's Life of Wesley*, 8vo, 1846, ii. p. 308). See Comte's Philosophie Positive (v. 186-195). He observes that at first slavery was an improvement, because it succeeded the immolation of prisoners. He adds (pp. 188, 189) that without it in a bar-barous and military society there will be no labour. Polytheism, he says (p. 193), is the natural epoch for it. Comte (vi. 58-62) eloquently acknowledges the services rendered by the church of Rome in abolishing slavery. In Tartary slavery is very mild (see *Huc's Travels in Tartary and Thibet*, vol. i. pp. 171, 172).

NOTES ON THE HISTORY OF MEDICINE.

Dr. Baron says that in 1778 there were few country surgeons who could undertake hazardous operations ; 'such knowledge, when Jenner was called upon from his native village, was chiefly confined to hospital surgeons' (*Baron's Life of Jenner*, 8vo, 1838, vol. i. p. 53).

Baron says (*Life of Jenner*, vol. i. p. 224), 'Nearly contemporaneous lived Gilbert in the reign of our first Edward. His compendium of medicine is the earliest medical production that England can lay claim to. . . . He was a servile copyist of the Arabic school.' He adds (i. 225), 'Towards the end of the fifteenth century, or early in the following one, appeared Fernelius, who, becoming professor of medicine in Paris, may well take his rank as the restorer of that science.'

Baron says (vol. i. p. 227), 'Mercurialis and Sennectus, in the sixteenth and early part of the seventeenth century, have added but little to the records of small-pox, though they both improved its mode of treatment by recommending a cooler regimen ; and to abstain from opening the pustules, or otherwise meddling with them. . . . Sydenham discarded all theories about small-pox ; he separated this disease from measles, with which it had always been blended by authors, from the revival of medical learning under the Arabian physicians to his own time ; and he gave such an accurate description of symptoms, and adopted such a judicious plan of cure in both diseases, that he left little room for improvement in either till the introduction of inoculation.' 1. In the county of Londonderry, in Ireland, inoculation was scarcely known even in 1766 ; 'and the usual treatment was as follows : the patient was covered up with a load of clothes in a warm bed, the curtains drawn close to keep off every breath of air, and some spirituous liquor carefully given in order to *strike the pocke out*, as it was termed.' Adam Clarke went through this pleasant process when he took the small-pox (see his own account in *Life of Adam Clarke*, edited by Rev. J. B. B. Clarke, Lond. 8vo. 1833, vol. i. p. 25). Indeed, it would appear, from what Cumberland relates of the death of his sister, that in London in the middle of the eighteenth century the cool regimen was not universally adopted for small-pox (see *Cumberland's Memoirs by Himself*, 8vo, 1807, vol. i. p. 88). It is

said that at the beginning of the nineteenth or at the very end of
the eighteenth century there were in some of the eastern counties
'pesthouses at a small distance from the villages, for the reception
of small-pox patients' (*The Life of Rachel Wriothesley Lady Russell*,
3rd edit. Lond. 8vo, 1820, p. 141). In 1572 some English physician, whose name does not transpire, said that he could cure the
marks left by the small-pox, however bad they might be (see
Correspondance de Fénelon, Paris, 1840, tome v. pp. 45, 52, 72).

Smollett tells us (*History of England*, vol. iii. p. 30, 8vo, 1790)
that in 1790 a bill passed for granting a reward to Joanna Stevens,
on her discovering, for the benefit of the public, a nostrum for the
cure of persons afflicted with the stone ; a medicine which has by
no means answered the expectation of the Legislature (see *Lister's
Journey to Paris*, 8vo, Shaftesbury, pp. 206–210).

According to Feyjoo, the 'theory of nervous diseases' was
first put forth by a Spanish lady, Doña Oliva Sabuco Bariera
(*Southey's Doctor*, edit. Warter, 8vo, 1848, p. 582). Her work
was published at Madrid in 1587, and Southey has given (pp. 583–
586) an interesting account of her curious theories.

English surgeons and apothecaries first attended to the cultivation of medicinal herbs in the reign of Henry VIII., but it was
not till 1640 that the first physic-garden in this country was planted
at Oxford (*Phillips, History of Cultivated Vegetables*, 8vo, 1822,
vol. i. pp. 11, 12).

In 1505 one of the maids of honour of Catherine of Arragon,
Princess of Wales, had something the matter with her eyes, and
Catherine was obliged to send her from London to Flanders for
medical advice (see her letter in *Miss Wood's Letters of Royal
Ladies*, 8vo, 1846, vol. i. p. 132). In 1506 the physician of
Henry VIII. was a native of Genoa (*Wood's Letters*, i. 142). In
1539 walnut water was used in England 'to cure sore eyes' (*Wood's
Letters*, 8vo, 1846, vol. iii. p. 130). Pills were given in 1533 to
the Princess Mary (*Miss Wood's Letters*, 8vo, 1846, vol. ii. p. 245).
In 1601, ' Bitter pills gilded over' (*Harleian Miscellany*, i. 378).
In 'The Magnetick Lady,' acted in 1632, Sir Moth Interest being
seized with a fit, Rut, the physician to Lady Loadstone, revives
him by ordering water to be dashed in his face, his nose to be
pulled, the nape of his neck to be pinched, and his ears to be boxed
(*Ben Jonson's Works*, 1816, vi. 64, 65). The patient was to be bled
in particular parts under particular planets. This infantile super-

stition was in full force in the seventeenth century (see *Middleton's Works*, ii. 98). In 1593 we read of 'an orange pill' (*Harleian Miscellany*, edit. Park, ii. 307). In 1581 it was usual to treat an ague by purging (*Harleian Miscellany*, ix. 184).

> 'And as physicians say,
> Poysons with poysons must be forced away.'

(*The Meeting of Gallants at an Ordinarie*, 1604, p. 6, Percy Society, vol. v.) At the accession of Elizabeth the country was troubled with quacks, female as well as male. These women-physicians were grossly ignorant of medicine, and indeed of everything else. An eminent surgeon, named Halle, of the middle of the sixteenth century, has left some singular details respecting them (see *Halle's Historiall Expostulation*, 1565, in Percy Society, vol. ix. pp. 3, 4, 18 ; and Mr. Pettigrew's preface, pp. ix, xiv). Halle, who wrote in the very beginning of the reign of Elizabeth, objects to the division of medical science (see p. xiv of Mr. Pettigrew's preface to his *Historiall Expostulation*, Percy Society, vol. xi. ; see also *Halle's Historiall Expostulation*, pp. 41, 42). In 1808 Southey writes, ' Ague is beginning to reappear, which had scarcely been heard of during the last generation ; this is the case over the whole kingdom, I believe' (*Life and Correspondence of Robert Southey*, 8vo, 1849, 1850, vol. iii. p. 149). In May 1553 the French ambassador writes from London that the physicians did not expect Edward VI. to recover, ' estant en grand doute qu'il ne crache son poulmon ;' and in another letter he says, 'qu'il y aye en ses excremens rien du poumon' (*Ambassades de Noailles*, Leyde, 1763, tome ii. pp. 25-27). Lingard says Edward VI. had a female physician, for which he quotes ' Hayward, 327 ; Heylin, 139 ; Rop. 10.' Mary's physician told her that she should be delivered of a dead child, because she did not eat enough to keep it alive (*Ambassades de Noailles*, 1763, tome iv. p. 227). In 1570, in England, pills were covered with sugar (see *Correspondance de Fénelon*, tome iii. p. 135). In 1572 Elizabeth took ' mitridat ' (*Fénelon*, v. 184). Between 1774 and 1778 Dr. Jackson used cold water affusion in fevers, i.e. ten years before Dr. Wright and twenty years before Currie (see *Life of Jackson*, p. cx, in *Jackson's Formation of Armies*, Lond. 8vo, 1845).

Roger Bacon says life may be prolonged by eating the flesh of a dragon (*Whewell's Philosophy of the Inductive Sciences*, 1847, ii. 170). The first English medical writer is Gilbertus Anglicus, sometimes called Legle. He flourished in A.D. 1210 (*Wright's Biographia Britannica Literaria*, vol. ii. p. 461). In 1580 we find a sort of water cure, so far as the drinking is concerned (see *Wright's Elizabeth*, 8vo, 1838, vol. ii. p. 110). Even in 1581 the English physicians would only administer certain remedies on certain days (see *Loseley Manuscripts* in *Kempe*, pp. 262-265). It is said that bougies, as remedies for diseases of the urethra, were first invented by Daran when in the army of Charles VI. (*Grimm, Correspondance littéraire*, tome xi. p. 59).

In 1786 it appears to have been common in France for women to take asses' milk (*Grimm, Correspondance littéraire*, xiv. 495).

In the reign of Charles II. the Earl of Southampton died from taking from a woman a medicine for dissolving the stone (*Burnet's Own Time*, i. 432, 8vo, 1823, Oxford). In 1663 the queen was 'so ill as to be shaved, and pidgeons put to her feet' (*Pepys's Diary*, 8vo, 1828, vol. ii. p. 105, and see vol. iv. p. 19).

In 1656 Evelyn (*Diary*, 8vo, 1827, vol. ii. p. 118) saw Dr. Joyliffe, 'that famous physician and anatomist, first detector of the lymphatic veins.' In the reign of Charles I., if we may trust a contemporary painting, patients took pills about the size of a walnut (see *Chambers's Traditions of Edinburgh*, 8vo, 1847, pp. 29, 30).

Montaigne (*Essais*, Paris, 8vo, 1843, livre ii. chap. xxxvii. pp. 486, 487) gives a very curious list of the strange remedies used in his time.

Coleridge (*Lit. Remains*, iv. 78) says that the earlier part of Baxter's Life of Himself contains an interesting account of the state of medicine under Charles I. Wesley (*Journal*, 8vo, 1851, pp. 349, 395, 565) had great faith in electricity in cases of disease.

Dr. Lister (*Paris at the Close of the Seventeenth Century*, Shaftesbury, 8vo, pp. 204, 205) says that the river water made dysentery 'one of the most prevailing diseases in Paris.' In the middle of the eighteenth century the pills of Stahl had great reputation at Paris, where, however, they could not be had genuine ; but in Germany their fame was on the decline (see *Œuvres de Voltaire*, li. 226, 228 ; lviii. 559, 560, and lix. 124). The different modes of taking bark early in the eighteenth century are carefully given in a curious letter in Foster's Original Letters of Locke, Sidney, and Shaftesbury, 8vo, 1830, pp. 262-

266. For a list of absurd remedies see Ray's Correspondence, edited by Dr. Lankester, 8vo, 1848, pp. 86, 147, 238, 311, 333.

Southey, in 'The Doctor,' says that in the sixteenth century the French Government used to furnish annually to the physicians of Montpellier a living criminal for dissection. But it would seem from Lewis (*Methods of Observation in Politics*, vol. i. p. 163) that the accuracy of this statement is doubtful. In 1313 Mondini de Leozzi first publicly dissected the bodies of two females (*Sprengel, Hist. de la Médecine*, ii. 432). After this the custom became annual in all the universities (p. 434).

NOTES FROM LOCKHART'S LIFE OF SIR WALTER SCOTT.

Memoirs of the Life of Sir Walter Scott, by J. C. Lockhart, Lond. 1837, 1838 ; 7 volumes, 8vo.

Scott records in his autobiography that during his illness in 1788 'my only refuge was reading and playing at chess' (vol. i. p. 47). At a little later period he says (vol. i. p. 52), 'Wherever I went, I cut a piece of a branch from a tree ; these constituted what I called my log-book, and I intended to have a set of chessmen out of them, each having reference to the place where it was cut, as, the kings from Falkland and Holyrood ; the queens from Queen Mary's yew tree at Crookston ; the bishops from abbeys or episcopal palaces ; the knights from baronial residences ; the rooks from royal fortresses ; and the pawns generally from places worthy of historical note. But this whimsical design I never carried into execution.' Lockhart says (vol. i. p. 128), 'Scott did not pursue the science of chess after his boyhood. He used to say it was a shame to throw away upon mastering a mere game, however ingenious, the time which would suffice for the acquisition of a new language. "Surely," he said, "chess-playing is a sad waste of brains." However, while apprenticed to his father, he used to play chess with his companions in the office, and hide the board as soon as he heard the old gentleman's footsteps ' (vol. i. p. 143). Early in the nineteenth century some of the principal medical men of London formed themselves into a chess club, of which one of the members was Mr. Cooper, afterwards Sir Astley (*Cooper's Life of Sir A. Cooper*, 8vo, 1843, vol. ii. p. 139). He was always very fond of chess, which, in 1802, he played at the Palais Royal in Paris. This he records in his Journal, but does not say if he won or lost (vol. ii. p. 398). For other notices of chess see vol. ii. pp. 270, 424, 451. Lord Holland was told by those who knew Napoleon at Longwood that he 'occasionally played at chess or billiards, at the first with tolerable skill, but intolerable rapidity ; at the latter neither with mace nor cue, but with his hand' (*Lord Holland's Foreign Reminiscences*, 8vo, 1850, p. 305). Gibbon, when at Lausanne, used often to play at chess (see *Gibbon's Miscellaneous Works*, 8vo, 1837, p. 345). Herbert Mayo (*Philosophy of Living*, 8vo, 1838, p. 265) says that Lewis told him 'that the talent for playing chess bears no relation to the general talent of the player. It may therefore be compared to musical and arithmetical genius.'

In 1789 Scott wrote an essay on the feudal system, in which he 'endeavoured to assign it a more general origin, and to prove that it proceeds upon principles common to all nations when placed in a certain situation.' This opinion he always retained ; for Lockhart says (vol. i. pp. 171, 172), 'One of the last historical books he read, before leaving Abbotsford for Malta in 1831, was Colonel Tod's interesting account of Rajasthan ; and I well remember the delight he expressed on finding his views confirmed, as they certainly are in a very striking manner, by the philosophical soldier's detail of the structure of society in that remote region of the East.' 'The feudal family, the last historical form of patriarchal life' (*Mill's Political Economy*, 8vo, 1849, vol. i. p. 271). In the Birman Empire, 'men hold their offices, and even their possessions, by something resembling a feudal tenure' (*Brougham's Political Philosophy*, 8vo, 1849, vol. i. p. 135, and see p. 336). Lord Brougham says (pp. 323, 324), 'The chief benefit conferred by the feudal scheme upon the character of men was one of the greatest value—the habits of fidelity which it formed ;' but an evil consequence has been to make war considered honourable (p. 325).

Scott says that the first interest excited in Scotland on the subject of German literature was owing 'to a paper read before the Royal Society of Edinburgh, on the 21st of April, 1788, by the author of The Man of Feeling.' Sir Walter adds, 'The literary persons of Edinburgh were then first made aware of the existence of works of genius in a language cognate with the

English, and possessed of the same manly force of expression.'
The consequence was, that in 1792 a German class was formed
in Edinburgh, of which Scott was a member. Their studies were
encouraged by A. F. Tytler, afterwards Lord Woodhouselee,
whose 'version of Schiller's Robbers was one of the earliest from
the German theatre' (vol. i. pp. 203-205). 1. Lord Jeffrey, speaking of the changes which took place in English literature at the
close of the eighteenth century, notices the 'new literature of
Germany, evidently the original of our Lake school poetry'
(*Essays*, 8vo, 1844, vol. i. p. 167). 2. Hannah More raised her
little voice against German literature, which, however, she only
knew from translations. The passage is so characteristic that I
must give it entire. In 1808 she writes to Sir William Pepys,
'To own an unfashionable truth, I am not fond of German poetry
or prose. It seems to me more diffuse and less classical than
that of the other modern languages. I ought to observe, however, that I am a very inadequate judge, as I do not understand
the German. I never took a fancy to it' (*Roberts, Memoirs of
Hannah More*, 2nd edit. 8vo, 1834, vol. iii. p. 262). There are
many things about which Mrs. Hannah More knew as little as she
did German, and upon which her opinions were equally positive.
However, her horror of German literature was perfectly ludicrous.
See her strictures on Female Education in Works, 8vo, 1830,
vol. v. pp. 27-32. From her remarks there no one would suspect
that she was ignorant of German ; for that fact only transpires in
her correspondence. In 1792 Monk Lewis, as he was called,
went to Germany to learn German (see the *Life and Correspondence
of M. G. Lewis*, 8vo, 1839, vol. i. p. 69), the study of which, says
his biographer (p. 181), he 'pursued with ardour and enthusiasm.'

Ritson, the antiquary, never would touch animal food (vol. i.
pp. 359 362). His death is said to have been preceded by madness (vol. i. p. 400).

Scott, speaking of Turner's History of the Anglo-Saxons, complains of his 'detestable Gibbonism' (vol. i. p. 358). What would
he have said if he could have read his 'Sacred History of the
World'? It is a remarkable instance of corrupt taste that Cumberland (*Memoirs, by Himself*, 8vo, 1807, vol. ii. p. 325) should call
Turner 'one of the best writers of his time.'

Respecting the origin of surnames in Scotland see vol. i.

pp. 390, 391. Lockhart says that the 'Ragman's Roll,' published by the Bannatyne Club, confirms Scott's views.

Scott was fond of smoking, though not to excess. He laid aside the habit twice, and twice resumed it (see vol. i. p. 339; vol. vi. pp. 105, 130). Niebuhr 'disliked smoking very much, but took snuff to such an excess that he had finally to give it up' (*Lieber's Reminiscences of G. B. Niebuhr*, Lond. 8vo, 1835, p. 45). Burt says (*Letters from the North of Scotland*, 8vo, 1815, vol. i. p. 212), 'It is very rare to see anybody smoke in Scotland.'

In 1804 Scott often saw Mungo Park. That great traveller related several remarkable stories; and when Scott expressed his wonder that he had not published them in his work, replied that whatever facts he considered of importance he had boldly told, leaving to his readers to believe them or not; but that he would not lessen his credit by relating mere personal adventures, which, though true, were of little importance, and being marvellous would not be believed (vol. ii. p. 11).

Scott told Miss Seward that he admired Cary's Dante, but 'confessed his inability to find pleasure in the Divina Commedia. The plan appeared to him unhappy; the personal malignity and the strange mode of revenge presumptuous and uninteresting' (vol. ii. p. 122). And in 1832 Mr. Cheney says, of Dante he knew little, confessing he found him too obscure and difficult (vol. vii. p. 370); but William Schlegel prefers Dante to Virgil (*Lectures on Dramatic Art*, Lond. 1840, vol. i. p. 6).

It is strange that Scott should think that Milton's Paradise Lost was coldly received. The truth is, its reception was brilliant. See, however, his remarks at vol. ii. p. 124. Hannah More supposes that the Paradise Lost was scarcely known before Addison's famous criticisms on it (*Works of H. More*, 8vo, 1830, vol. vi. p. 325). Dr. Shebbeare says, 'Milton's Paradise Lost passed unobserved until Mr. Dryden called the attention of the world upon it' (*Letters of Angeloni on the English Nation*, 8vo, 1755, ii. 23).

A proposal was made to Scott to publish a *decent* edition of Dryden. He characteristically wrote to Ellis, by way of reply, in 1805, 'I will not castrate John Dryden. I would as soon castrate my own father, as I believe Jupiter did of yore' (vol. ii. p. 77). He well adds that it is not ludicrous indecency that corrupts manners; but 'it is the sentimental slang, half lewd, half methodistic, that debauches the understanding, inflames the sleeping passions, and prepares the reader to give way as soon as a tempter appears' (vol. ii. p. 77).

Scott was a great admirer of Johnson's poetry, and said 'that he had more pleasure in reading " *London* " and " *The Vanity of Human Wishes* " than any other poetical composition he could mention' (vol. ii. p. 307). See also (at p. 308) Lockhart's quotation from Lord Byron's Diary to the same effect. Byron calls it 'sublime.' However, in his Sketch of Johnson's Life, Scott only praises 'the deep and pathetic morality.'

In 1814 Scott visited the Shetland Islands, and at Lerwick went to the Picts' Castle. In his Diary he mentions the smallness of the apertures, &c. ; and says, ' At any rate, the size fully justifies the tradition prevalent here as well as in the south of Scotland, that the Picts were a diminutive race' (vol. iii. p. 148 ; see also p. 196).

Lockhart says (vol. iii. p. 163), ' Mr. W. S. Rose informs me that when he was at school at Winchester, the morris-dancers there used to exhibit a sword dance resembling that described at Camacho's wedding in Don Quixote ; and M. Morritt adds that similar dances are even yet performed in the villages about Rokeby every Christmas.'

In 1818 Scott told Lockhart, that as to Goethe's Faust 'he suspected the end of the story had been left *in obscuro* from despair to match the closing scene of our own Marlowe's Dr. Faustus' (vol. iv. p. 193).

Mrs. Keith, daughter of Sir John Swinton, asked Scott to lend her the novels of Mrs. Aphra Behn. He complied, but the old lady promptly returned them, and said to Sir Walter, 'Is it not a very odd thing that I, an old woman of eighty and upwards, sitting alone, feel myself ashamed to read a book which, sixty years ago, I have heard read aloud for the amusement of large circles, consisting of the first and most creditable society in London ?' (vol. v. p. 137). Scott gives no *date* for this anecdote. In 1780 Hannah More, as we learn from her own mouth, quoted some joke from ' Tom Jones,' which drew upon her a sharp rebuke from Johnson, who expressed his indignation at her having read such a book (see Hannah More's Letters in *Roberts's Memoirs of Hannah More*, 2nd edit. 8vo, 1834, vol. i. p. 169).

Scott, mentioning the suicide of Lord Londonderry (Castle-

reagh), makes no doubt of his being mad ; and gives an extraordinary ghost story which in 1815 he heard him relate in Paris at
one of his wife's supper parties (vol. v. pp. 213, 214).

In 1825 he writes to Daniel Terry, 'All who practise the fine
arts in any department are from the very temperament necessary to
success more irritable, jealous, and capricious than other men,
made of heavier elements' (vol. vi. p. 22). Precisely the same
remark has been made by Adam Smith (see his *Theory of Moral
Sentiments*, vol. i. pp. 174, 175).

In 1826 he writes in his Diary, 'I believe the phenomena of
dreaming are in great measure occasioned by the *double touch*
which takes place when one hand is crossed in sleep upon another.
Each gives and receives the impression of touch to and from the
other, and this complicated sensation our sleeping fancy ascribes
to the agency of another being, when it is in fact produced by our
own limbs rolling on each other' (vol. vi. p. 320). On dreams
see Coleridge's Literary Remains, vol. i. pp. 122, 202, 204. Drew
says that while engaged in writing his 'Essay on the Soul' he
met in a dream with a new and very strong argument in favour of
his views. He suddenly woke and retained the whole thread of
the argument, which, on tracing out in his mind, he was delighted
to find perfectly complete. But he again fell asleep, and in the
morning, he says, 'I did not forget the circumstance, but had
entirely lost every vestige of the argument and the manner of
reasoning, nor have I been able from that day to this to recall
any idea of it. I have frequently regretted my not getting up
immediately and making notes of it.' See this singular circumstance in Drew's own words (*Life of Samuel Drew*, by his Eldest
Son, Lond. 8vo, 1834, pp. 447, 448).

In his Diary in 1826 he says of England early in the seventeenth century, 'The audience must have had a much stronger
sense of poetry in those days than in ours, since language was
received and applauded at the Fortune or the Red Bull, which
could not now be understood by any general audience in Great
Britain' (vol. vi. p. 333). Connect this with ART. 2205.

In 1826, in his Diary, 'Women, it is said, go mad much seldomer
than men. I fancy, if this be true, it is in some measure owing
to the little manual works in which they are constantly employed,
which regulate in some degree the current of ideas, as the pen-
dulum regulates the motion of the time-piece' (vol. vi. p. 349).

The prejudices against port wine, which the hardy Scotch look on as effeminate, still linger in the north. Sir Walter Scott was affected by them. He never willingly drank port, and was fond of quoting John Home's epigram :—

> Bold and erect the Caledonian stood,
> Old was his mutton, and his claret good;
> 'Let him drink port !' the English statesman cried ;
> He drank the poison, and his spirit died.

(Vol. iv. p. 162.)

One of the earliest notices I have seen of port is where Cumberland says that Arthur Kinsman, head master of Bury St. Andrews, was on one occasion too full of what he calls 'priestly port' (*Cumberland's Memoirs*, 8vo, 1807, vol. i. pp. 38, 43). It must have been before 1742, for Bentley was present, and judging from the context I should place it before 1740. But even in 1725, Pope writes from Twickenham to Mr. Wanley for 'a douzaine of quartes of goode and wholesome port wine, such as yee drinke at the Genda Armes' (*Nichols, Literary Anecdotes of the Eighteenth Century*, vol. viii. p. 362). Between 1726 and 1730 it was well known in England, but not at all in Scotland (see *Burt's Letters from the North of Scotland*, 8vo, 1815, vol. i. p. 158). In 1765 Grosley (*Tour to London*, vol. i. p. 80) says 'port wine' consisted of the juice of blackberries, turnips, beer, and litharge. Townsend (*Journey through Spain*, vol. i. p. 241) says, during the War of Succession in 1704, the Spaniards forbade their wines to be sold to the Dutch ; hence we went to Portugal for port wine.

Scott, in his Autobiography, says he never could learn painting or drawing. 'After long study and many efforts, I was unable to apply the elements of perspective or of shade to the scene before me, and was obliged to relinquish in despair an art which I was most anxious to practise' (vol. i. p. 51). Lockhart suggests that this failure with the pencil was an advantage to him. He says (vol. i. p. 127), 'He might have contracted the habit of copying from pictures, rather than from nature itself.'

He says in his Autobiography, 'It is only by long practice that I have acquired the power of selecting or distinguishing melodies ; and though now few things delight or affect me more than a

simple tune sung with feeling, yet I am sensible that even this
pitch of musical taste has only been gained by attention and
habit, and, as it were, by my feeling of the words being associated
with the tune' (vol. i. p. 53). But his smell and taste were as
imperfect as his ear. He could not detect over-kept venison, even
'when his noble company betrayed their uneasiness; . . . neither
by the nose nor by the palate could he distinguish corked wine
from sound. He could never tell Madeira from sherry' (iv. 161,
162). Mr. Adolphus, who stayed with him at Abbotsford, noticed
his disregard for music (vol. v. p. 300) ; and Mr. Moore (the poet)
says, 'He confessed that he hardly knew high from low in music'
(vol. vi. p. 94). In 1825 Scott writes in his Diary, 'I do not
know and cannot utter a note of music ; and complicated harmonies seem to me a babble of confused though pleasant sounds'
(vol. iv. p. 128) ; and in 1831 Sir. W. Scott said to Mr. Scott of
Gala, 'I understand little of painting, and nothing of music'
(vii. 314). That able and, considering his education, most extraordinary metaphysician, Samuel Drew, disliked music, and used
to say, 'I can scarcely distinguish one tune from another' (*Life
of Samuel Drew, by his Eldest Son*, Lond. 8vo, 1834, pp. 407,
408). Dr. Combe notices 'the frequency of nervous affections
in musicians' (*Physiology applied to Health*, 3rd edit. Edinburgh,
1836, 8vo, p. 304). The great John Hunter 'had little relish
for poetry or music' (*Adams's Life of Hunter*, 2nd edit. 8vo,
1818, p. 65). The celebrated Watt, who invented the steam
engine, could not distinguish one note from another (see
Brougham's Lives of Men of Letters and Science, 8vo, 1845,
vol. i. p. 363). The great Niebuhr disliked it. In a letter without date he writes, 'Music is in general positively disagreeable to
me, because I cannot unite it in one point, and everything frag-
mentary oppresses my mind' (*Life and Letters of B. G. Niebuhr*,
Lond. 8vo, 1852, vol. i. p. 187). Miss Aikin (*Life of Addison*,
8vo, 1843, vol. i. p. 210), after observing that Addison failed in
writing an English opera, adds, 'As no fact is more notorious
than that a large proportion of our most harmonious poets—
Dryden of the number—have been totally destitute of musical
ear,' &c.

Mr. Cheney, detailing his reminiscences of him in 1832, says,
'He expressed the most unbounded admiration for Cervantes,
and said that the "novelas" of that author had first inspired him

with the ambition of excelling in fiction, and that until disabled
by illness he had been a constant reader of them' (vol. vii.
p. 370).

RATE OF MORTALITY AND INCREASE OF AVERAGE DURATION OF LIFE.

It appears, from a paper in the Bibliothèque Britannique, that
at Geneva in the sixteenth century the probability of life was
4·883 years ; in the seventeenth century, 11·607 years, and in the
eighteenth century it had increased to 27·183 years (see *Malthus
on Population*, 1826, 6th edit. vol. i. p. 341).

It appears (*Malthus*, i. 372) that before the Revolution the
mortality in France was 1 in 30 or 31⅙. According to Price, the
mortality of London was in his time 1 in 20¾ ; of Norwich, 1 in 24 ;
and of Manchester, 1 in 28. Malthus (vol. i. pp. 406, 407) says
that his statement with regard to the mortality of London is exaggerated, but that what he says of the other towns is correct.
But Malthus adds (p. 408) that the estimated mortality of 1 in
31 for London, given in the Observations on the Population Act,
is too small.

Malthus says that from the 'earliest ages' there has been no
increase in the 'natural duration of life.' By this he does not
mean *average* duration, for that he seems to allow has increased
(see vol. ii. pp. 9-11). M'Culloch (*Principles of Political Economy*, Edinburgh, 1843, p. 176) says, 'The mortality in London
during the first half of the last century is supposed to have been
as high as five per cent.'

At the end of the eighteenth century the Lying-in Hospital of
Dublin was ventilated ; and by this simple measure the proportion of deaths among the children was reduced from one in six to
one in twenty (*Combe's Physiology applied to Health*, 3rd edit.
Edinburgh, 8vo, 1835, p. 224). Dr. Combe, on the authority of
Hawkins, adds (p. 363), 'In London, eighty years ago, the annual
mortality was one in twenty ; it is now as one in forty.' For
some interesting details of the increased duration of life see
Quetelet, Sur l'Homme, Paris, 1835, tome i. pp. 240-246.

Wild (*History of the Royal Society*, 8vo, 1848, vol. i. p. 75)
says, 'Sir William Petty informs us that even in his time the
proportion of deaths to cures in the hospitals of St. Bartholomew
and St. Thomas was one to seven ; whilst we know by subsequent

documents that in the latter establishment, during 1741, the mortality had diminished to one in ten ; during 1780, to one in fourteen ; during 1813, to one in sixteen ; and in 1827, out of 12,494 patients under treatment, only 259, or one in forty-eight.' In 1679, Paris, with a population of 500,000, had a mortality of 19,000 or 20,000, which was greater than London with her 450,000 (see *King's Life of Locke*, 8vo, 1830, vol. i. pp. 153, 154).

NOTE ON THE RESURRECTIONISTS.

Mr. Cooper (*Life of Sir Astley Cooper*, 8vo, 1843, vol. i. pp. 339-446) has given a long and interesting account of the resurrectionists, who supplied anatomists with subjects for dissection. When Sir Astley, then Mr. Cooper, first began to lecture, these men had no particular name ; indeed, so few persons studied anatomy that their very existence was scarcely known (p. 344). The watchmen, whose business it was to guard the burial-grounds, ' were all in the habit of receiving a certain allowance or per-centage out of the sums obtained by the resurrectionists ' (p. 346). Indeed, this was so well known that it was common for the friends of the deceased to sit up themselves by the grave (p. 347). Mr. Cooper says (p. 350) that the account given of the resurrectionists in the ' Diary of a Late Physician' is inaccurate. The resurrectionists were so expert that they could exhume a body and make everything straight again in three-quarters of an hour ; and if the grave was very shallow and the earth loose even in a quarter of an hour (p. 352). Mr. Cooper relates (pp. 375, 376) an anecdote remarkably illustrating the hatred of the mob against them. Indeed, in Scotland, and afterwards in Dublin, it was generally believed that children were kidnapped for the purpose of dissection ; and so high was the popular feeling that it was necessary in Dublin to protect the anatomical schools by the police (p. 381). Sir Astley Cooper stated before a Committee of the House of Commons that the law was quite powerless on this subject. He said, ' There is no person, let his station in life be what it may, whom, if I were disposed to dissect, I could not obtain' (p. 407).

This, of course, gave rise to dreadful crimes, and Mr. Cooper says (note at pp. 407, 408), 'I much doubt whether all the murders committed under the system of *burking* came to light.' Another

object of these men was to get the teeth of the bodies, which the
dentists eagerly bought, and in one night a resurrectionist named
Murphy cleared from teeth alone 6*d*. (pp. 399, 400). One of
these wretches followed the English army to Spain, and by drawing
the teeth of those who were wounded, 'earned a clear profit of
three hundred pounds' (p. 402). As might be expected, they took
every opportunity of robbing the killed ; and, indeed, hovered like
vultures over the field of battle (p. 414). The profits of the resurrectionists were immense. It was usual to pay 5*l*. at the beginning
of a session, and 9*l*. 9*s*. for each body (p. 361). They nearly
always insisted on the opening fee (p. 362). In some few instances
as much as 20*l*. were paid for each body (p. 373). The average
seems to have been 12*l*. 12*s*. (pp. 396, 397). Besides this, if the
resurrectionists fell into any trouble, money was given them by the
surgeons ; and Sir Astley Cooper has expended hundreds of
pounds for this purpose (p. 395).

It appears from Mr. Guthrie's evidence before Parliament, that
the Anatomy Act has worked extremely well (see *Report from the
Select Committee on Medical Education*, folio, 1834, part ii. pp. 39–
41). Indeed, Dr. Somerville, being asked, 'Has the practice of
exhumation ceased ?' replied, 'I have reason to know that there
is not one case of a charge for disinterring bodies in the criminal
calendar ; in fact, the practice cannot exist, while there is a sufficient supply under the provisions of the Act. No one would
employ the exhumator' (part ii. p. 207, No. 6756). He added
that the lower orders had no 'repugnance to dissection,' and this
indifference 'I believe with the majority arises out of a feeling of
almost total indifference to what becomes of their bodies after
death' (part ii. p. 208, No. 6770). Dr. Somerville told the
Committee that before the passing of the Anatomy Act there were
from two hundred to three hundred bodies dissected yearly ; but
'the last year being the first of the operation of the new Act, the
number in London amounted to upwards of six hundred, and in
the country to nearly one hundred' (*Report on Medical Education*,
part ii. p. 210, No. 6793). In the Autobiography of Gent, written
in 1746, are some curious notices of exhumation. Gent says that
at Kingston assizes he heard a 'trial of a wretched sexton (who
seems to have been imitated lately by one Burton, a glazier in
York), for stealing dead bodies out of their graves, and selling them,
as is represented in the Beggar's Opera, to those fleaing rascals

the surgeons' (*Life of Thomas Gent, by Himself*, 8vo, 1832, p. 103).
This seems to have been in 1720. In 1725 he gives an account
of the execution of Jonathan Wild, whose body, he says, was stolen
from its grave by the surgeons (p. 162). At p. 189 he says that
'polite doctors are seldom charged with theft, except stealing
people out of their graves.' Early in the seventeenth century it
was necessary to 'beg' the bodies of the criminals from the sheriffs
(see *Middleton's Works*, 1840, iv. 462).

INFLUENCE OF FOOD ON NATIONAL
CHARACTER

Phillips (*History of Cultivated Vegetables*, 8vo, 1822, vol. i. p. 5)
adopts the opinion of Dr. Veitch, who says, 'I am persuaded
that it will be invariably found true that those who are living
on animal food are more impetuous in temper than those who live
on vegetable aliment.' Dr. Jackson, who was a very observing
man, and had travelled on foot through great part of Europe, at
the end of the eighteenth century says, 'The English consume
animal food in a higher proportion than most European nations'
(*Jackson's Formation, Discipline, and Economy of Armies*, 8vo,
1845, p. 329). He adds (p. 339), 'It is a physical fact well ascertained and obvious in its reasons, that a course of high living
increases animal irritability.' Dr. Prout positively asserts the
uniformity of chyle (see *Prout's Bridgewater Treatise*, 8vo, 1845,
pp. 443, 450). Combe says (*The Constitution of Man in Relation
to External Objects*, Edinburgh, 1848, p. 54), 'From one of a series
of interesting letters on the agriculture of France by M. Lullin de
Chateauvieux, published in the Bibliothèque Universelle, it
appears that the consumption of beef in that country relative to
its population is only one-sixth of what it is in England (*Journal of
Agriculture*, No. iii. p. 390). Mr. Lawrence observes (*Lectures on
Man*, 8vo, 1844, pp. 144, 146, 147) that as men advance in civilisation they eat less animal and more vegetable food; but he
denies the current opinion that on this account strength will deteriorate. In 1654, Sir John Reresby (*Travels and Memoirs*, 8vo,
1831, p. 25) mentions that between Blois and Orleans the people
are very fond of garlic, which they mix with their bread. He
says (p. 102) that in Italy little flesh is eaten, but mostly fruits and

salads ; and fowl is seldom purchased but by people of quality.'
At p. 158 he says the Low Dutch 'feed very sparingly, the best
citizens seldom eating warm flesh above twice in a week, and that
boiled.' The North American Indians are very small eaters (see
Catlin's North American Indians, 8vo, 1841, vol. i. pp. 123, 124).
Herbert Mayo (*Philosophy of Living*, 8vo, 1838, p. 37) thinks 'the
ultimate principle of nutriment is always the same, from whatever
source obtained.' He adds (p. 38), 'The Laplanders are a meagre
race, living exclusively on animal food. The Hindoos, a fine race
of men, feed on vegetables alone.' He says (pp. 85, 86), 'Dr.
Beaumont made the singular remark that anger causes the bile to
flow into the stomach ; hence the indigestion of the choleric man.'
Comte (*Philosophie positive*, iv. 465) says civilised nations eat
less than savages. But compare Lewis on Methods of Observation in Politics, ii. 450.

INDEX.

．

THE END

MENTAL AND POLITICAL PHILOSOPHY.

WORKS BY JOHN STUART MILL.

PRINCIPLES of POLITICAL ECONOMY. Library Edition.
2 vols. 8vo. 30s. People's Edition, 1 vol. crown 8vo. 5s.

A SYSTEM of LOGIC, RATIOCINATIVE and INDUCTIVE
Library Edition, 2 vols. 8vo. 25s. People's Edition, Crown 8vo. 5s.

On LIBERTY. Crown 8vo. 1s. 4d.

On REPRESENTATIVE GOVERNMENT. Crown 8vo. 2s.

AUTOBIOGRAPHY. 8vo. 7s. 6d.

ESSAYS on some UNSETTLED QUESTIONS of POLI-
TICAL ECONOMY. 8vo. 6s. 6d.

UTILITARIANISM. 8vo. 5s.

The SUBJECTION of WOMEN. Crown 8vo. 6s.

EXAMINATION of SIR WILLIAM HAMILTON'S PHILO-
SOPHY. 8vo. 16s.

DISSERTATIONS and DISCUSSIONS. 4 vols. 8vo.
£2. 6s. 6d.

NATURE, the UTILITY of RELIGION, and THEISM.
Three Essays. 8vo. 5s.

ANALYSIS of the PHENOMENA of the HUMAN MIND.
By James Mill. With Notes Illustrative and Critical. 2 vols. 8vo. 28s.

THE WORKS OF ARISTOTLE.

The POLITICS, G. Bekker's Greek Text of Books I. III.
IV. (VII.), with an English Translation by W. E. Bolland, M.A.
and Short Introductory Essays by A. Lang, M.A. Crown 8vo. 7s. 6d.

The ETHICS : Greek Text, illustrated with Essays and
Notes. By Sir Alexander Grant, Bart. M.A. LL.D. 2 vols. 8vo. 32s.

The NICOMACHEAN ETHICS, Newly Translated into
English. By Robert Williams, Barrister-at-Law. Crown 8vo. 7s. 6d.

WORKS BY ALEXANDER BAIN, LL.D.

MENTAL and MORAL SCIENCE; a Compendium of
Psychology and Ethics. Crown 8vo. 10s. 6d.

The SENSES and the INTELLECT. 8vo. 15s.

The EMOTIONS and the WILL. 8vo. 15s.

PRACTICAL ESSAYS. Crown 8vo. 4s. 6d.

LOGIC, DEDUCTIVE and INDUCTIVE. Part I. Deduction,
4s. Part II. Induction, 6s. 6d.

London: LONGMANS, GREEN, & CO.

MENTAL AND POLITICAL PHILOSOPHY.

The **PHILOSOPHICAL WORKS of DAVID HUME.** Edited by T. H. Green, M.A. and the Rev. T. H. Grose, M.A. 4 vols. 8vo. 56s. Or separately, Essays, 2 vols. 28s. Treatise of Human Nature. 2 vols. 28s.

The **WORKS of THOMAS HILL GREEN,** late Fellow of Balliol College, and Whyte's Professor of Moral Philosophy in the University of Oxford. Edited by R. L. Nettleship, Fellow of Balliol College, Oxford. In 3 vols. Vol. I.—Philosophical Works. 8vo. 16s.

BACON'S ESSAYS, with Annotations. By R. R. WHATELEY, D.D. 8vo. 10s. 6d.

BACON'S WORKS, Collected and Edited by R. L. ELLIS, M.A. J. SPEDDING, M.A. and D. D. HEATH. 7 vols. 8vo. £3. 13s. 6d.

BACON'S LETTERS and LIFE, including all his Occasional Works. Collected and Edited, with a Commentary by J. SPEDDING. 7 vols. 8vo. £4. 4s.

The **HISTORY of PHILOSOPHY,** from Thales to Comte. By GEORGE HENRY LEWES. 2 vols. 8vo. 32s.

The **ENGLISH VILLAGE COMMUNITY.** Examined in its Relation to the Manorial and Tribal Systems, &c. By FREDERIC SEEBOHM. 13 Maps and Plates. 8vo. 16s.

The **INSTITUTES of JUSTINIAN;** with English Introduction, Translation, and Notes. By T. C. SANDARS, M.A. 8vo. 18s.

WORKS BY DR. E. ZELLER.

HISTORY of ECLECTICISM in GREEK PHILOSOPHY. Translated by SARAH F. ALLEYNE. Crown 8vo. 10s. 6d.

The **STOICS, EPICUREANS, and SCEPTICS.** Translated by the Rev. O. J. REICHEL, M.A. Crown 8vo. 15s.

SOCRATES and the SOCRATIC SCHOOLS. Translated by the Rev. O. J. REICHEL, M.A. Crown 8vo. 10s. 6d.

PLATO and the OLDER ACADEMY. Translated by S. FRANCES ALLEYNE and ALFRED GOODWIN, B.A. Crown 8vo. 18s.

The **PRE-SOCRATIC SCHOOLS;** a History of Greek Philosophy from the Earliest Period to the time of Socrates. Translated by SARAH F. ALLEYNE. 2 vols. crown 8vo. 30s.